The Painter 8 Wow! Book

The Painter 8 Wow! Book

Cher Threinen-Pendarvis

 Peachpit Press

The Painter 8 Wow! Book

Cher Threinen-Pendarvis

Peachpit Press
1249 Eighth Street
Berkeley, CA 94710
(510) 524-2178
(800) 283-9444
(510) 524-2221 (fax)

Find us on the World Wide Web at: http://www.peachpit.com/wow.html

Peachpit Press is a division of Pearson Education.

Series Editor: Linnea Dayton
Peachpit Press Editor: Cary Norsworthy
Peachpit Press Production Editor: Lisa Brazieal
Cover design: Mimi Heft
Cover illustration: Cher Threinen-Pendarvis
Book design: Jill Davis
Art direction and layout: Cher Threinen-Pendarvis
Editors: Linnea Dayton, Carol Benioff and Dave Awl
Proofreader: William Rodarmor
Indexer: Cristen Gillespie
Production and Prepress Manager: Jonathan Parker

This book was set using the Stone Serif and Stone Sans families. It was written and composed in Adobe PageMaker 6.52. Final output was computer to plate at CDS, Medford, Oregon.

ISBN 0-321-20007-1

0 9 8 7 6 5 4 3 2
Printed and bound in the United States of America.

CREDITS

Cher Threinen-Pendarvis is the originator of *The Painter Wow! Books*. In addition to being the author of this book, she is a fine artist, designer and educator. A California native, she lives near the coast with her husband, Steve, who is an innovative surfboard designer. Cher is enthusiastic about Corel Painter 8, and thoroughly enjoyed working on this edition of *The Painter Wow! Book*. When she's not painting with analog paints or doing Painter sketches using a Wacom Intuos2 tablet and pen, Cher enjoys catching waves at a favorite surfing spot, gardening and traveling with Steve. Cher is extremely grateful to her *Wow!* team members for helping to make this version of the book possible.

Carol Benioff helped to write and illustrate several new techniques for Chapters 3, 5 and 12, and she edited portions of Chapters 7, 10, 11 and 12. A native San Franciscan, she is an award-winning artist and illustrator currently living in Oakland. Carol loves combining Painter with her printmaking, drawing and painting tools, which is an ongoing experiment that she uses in all her work. When she puts down her brush, she loves to garden, accompanied by her cats, and take long walks in the wood with her companion, Heinz. You can see more of Carol's art and illustrations on her website, www.carolbenioff.com.

Linnea Dayton helped to revise Chapters 4 and 5, and she was willing to cheerfully answer questions, offer suggestions and edit galleries and new stories that we wrote. Linnea is principal of Dayton and Associates and is an award-winning author and editor. In addition to being the author and co-author of numerous books—including the best-selling *Photoshop Wow! Books*—she is the Series Editor for all of the *Wow!* books. When she's not cooking up cool recipes for Photoshop in her office by the beach, Linnea enjoys taking her writing work with her as she travels around the world with her husband, Paul, an esteemed marine ecologist.

Please see the Acknowledgments for a more thorough listing of the *Wow!* team contributors.

To my husband, Steven,
for his friendship,
encouragement and understanding;
and to our Creator
from whom all inspiration comes. . .

— Cher Threinen-Pendarvis

John Derry, co-creator of Painter

FOREWORD

My, how time flies. . . here is yet another new edition of both Painter and Cher's companion *Wow!* book. This version represents a bold new chapter in Painter's evolution: a completely new interface. You might say that Painter has a new wardrobe appropriate for the 21ˢᵗ century. However, underneath these spiffy new threads is the same philosophy that has guided Painter since its initial release in 1991: the quest to capture the artist's natural gesture for the sake of personal expression.

Cher's personal perspective with respect to expressive tools comes from a background in traditional art media. She uses this knowledge to create a bridge between traditional and digital tools. And because Painter is not a physical medium, it becomes possible to do things un-dreamed of with traditional tools. Imagine dipping your paintbrush into a photograph, or drawing with an endless string of pearls. With Cher's tutoring, you can choose to be as traditional or avant-garde as you like.

Like art in any medium, imagery created with Painter can look very different depending on the artist using it. *The Painter Wow! Book* is richly illustrated with examples produced by a wide cross-section of expert Painter users. Cher takes these examples and breaks them down into clear step-by-step explanations. This provides the reader with a valuable insight into the artist's creative process. From here it's a short step to applying this knowledge to create one's own unique expression.

John Derry created the powerful image Imagine *using Painter's realistic brushes and industry-standard layers.*

The act of creativity is the transmission of an internal vision to a physical form that can be interpreted by others. Painter is an excellent tool for enabling this creative transmission of ideas and emotions. Thomas Edison said, "Genius is one percent inspiration, ninety-nine percent perspiration." Via *The Painter Wow! Book*, Cher has done most of the perspiring, leaving the inspiration to you. As you read through this book, you'll discover the seeds of inventive visual ideas sprouting from your creative imagination.

It has been a real pleasure to work with Cher throughout the evolution of *The Painter Wow! Book* series. She continually brings a never-ending source of enthusiasm to her efforts. With each new edition, she deftly adds instructional—as well as inspirational— features that get to the heart of Painter's usefulness and utility. You, as the reader of this book, enjoy the direct benefit of her labor of love.

Now, I suggest that you find a comfortable chair, sit down, read on, and prepare to be amazed!

John Derry

Overland Park, Kansas
June, 2003

Groovy was created for the Painter 8 poster by Nancy Stahl.

Susan Levan created Conch Shell *using Painter's Water Color brushes, Pens, Airbrushes, masks and layers.*

Capitola Woodcut *was created by John Derry using Painter's Woodcut features.*

PREFACE

"What is art?" That's a question we've debated for centuries, and with the invention of the desktop computer, we're now asking it in a whole new context. Is it possible to create art digitally? In *The Painter 8 Wow! Book*, Cher Threinen-Pendarvis clearly demonstrates the answer is yes.

Over the years, the creators of Corel Painter developed a program to capture the entire art-making experience by turning traditional tools digital. During the development of Corel Painter 8, we enhanced the user experience while continuing to bring the most realistic natural-media tools to the computer desktop. In *The Painter 8 Wow! Book*, Cher shows you how to be creative and productive with this toolset in meaningful and artistic ways.

Cher's personal and professional experiences as an artist, designer, illustrator, and teacher provide her with a complete understanding of the art-making process. She'll guide you through the steps of conceptualizing and creating compelling images, from composition, layout, and form through to medium, texture, and color.

Whether you are a digital artist, illustrator, graphic designer, photographer, or someone who just wants to have fun with digital painting, *The Painter 8 Wow! Book* is the ideal resource for learning and inspiration.

Tanya Staples

Program Manager, Corel Painter products
June 2003

Mark Zimmer created the original Paint Can *image for the Painter 1.0 program.*

ACKNOWLEDGMENTS

The Painter 8 Wow! Book would not have been possible without a great deal of help from some extraordinary people and sources.

I am grateful to each of the talented Painter artists who contributed their work and techniques; their names are listed in Appendix D in the back of the book.

Heartfelt thanks go to my friend and colleague Carol Benioff for collaborating with me to create new art and tutorials for the book and for helping to edit chapters. Warmest thanks go to Linnea Dayton, the *Wow!* Series Editor and a long-time friend and colleague. During all *six* editions, her inspiration, wisdom and encouragement proved invaluable. My special thanks go to Dave Awl for his careful copy editing and helpful advice.

Sincere thanks go to my friends at Peachpit Press, especially Ted Nace for his inspiration, Nancy Ruenzel for guidance, Cary Norsworthy—our *Wow!* Peachpit editor—for her advice, William Rodarmor for his editing suggestions (which were often generously spiced with humor), Lisa Brazieal for her helpful production advice, Suki Gear and the rest of the publishing team for their support. Thank you Peachpit, for giving me the opportunity to write this book.

A big "thank you" goes to the creators of Painter: Mark Zimmer, Tom Hedges and John Derry, for creating such a *Wow!* program with which we artists can enjoy limitless creativity. My heartfelt thanks go to our special friend John Derry for his inspiration, enthusiasm and encouragement during all editions of this book.

My warmest thanks go to Tanya Staples and Roe J. McFarlane, the Program Manager and Product Manager for Painter products, for their support; I'm also grateful to the Painter 8 development, quality assurance and documentation teams.

Pouring it on with Painter was created for the Painter 3 poster by John Derry.

John Derry created this illustration for the Painter 4 poster.

Phoenix and Painter 7 at Mount Fuji *was created for the Painter 7 poster by Cher Threinen-Pendarvis.*

© COREL CORPORATION

© COREL CORPORATION

John Derry and Adrian Garcia created the Paint Can *image for the Painter 8 package.*

I'd also like to thank the companies who supplied the *Wow!* book team with supporting software and hardware during the development of the book. I'm grateful to Adobe Systems for supplying me with Photoshop, Illustrator, Premiere and GoLive; so I could demonstrate how nicely these programs work with Painter.

Thanks to Wacom for their great pressure-sensitive tablets and to Epson for color printers for the testing of printmaking techniques, and to ColorVision, makers of color calibration software.

Thanks to Corbis Images, PhotoDisc and PhotoSpin for their support during all editions of the book; these "stock on CD-ROM and Web" companies allowed us to use their photos for demonstration purposes in the book. I am also grateful to the other companies who provided images or video clips for *The Painter 8 Wow!* CD-ROM; they are listed in Appendix A in the back of the book.

I'm grateful to Linnea Dayton, Jack Davis, Victor Gavenda and Shawn Grunberger for their helpful technical reads. My warmest thanks go to Carol Benioff for sharing her expertise in traditional and digital printmaking, and Steven Gordon for his experience with terrain maps. Special thanks also go to Dorothy Krause and Bonny Lhotka for sharing their knowledge of experimental printmaking; Jon Lee and Geoff Hull of Fox Television for sharing their experience in designing for broadcast television; Cindy and Dewey Reid of Reid Creative for sharing their expertise in animation and film; and Lynda Weinman for sharing her knowledge about designing graphics for the Web.

I'd like to thank my co-workers "behind the scenes" on the *Wow!* book team. Warmest thanks go to Jill Davis for her brilliant book design; William Rodarmor for copy editing and proofreading; Cristen Gillespie for her careful indexing; and PageMaker whiz Jonathan Parker for his production and prepress expertise. Jonathan's calm assurance during the deadlines of all six editions of this book was much appreciated!

My special thanks go to Heidi Jonk-Sommer and Victor Gavenda at Peachpit Press for their work on the *Painter Wow!* CD-ROM.

A heartfelt thank you to these special "co-workers": to my husband, Steve, for his encouragement, healthy meals and reminders to take surfing breaks during the project; and to our cats, Soshi, Pearl, Sable and Marika, the close companions who keep me company in the office and studio. A warm thanks to our sister-in-law Joy Young and dear friends Lisa Baker, Julie Klein and Donal Jolley, who shared sincere encouragement and prayers. Thanks for checking in with me while I worked!

Finally, I would like to thank all the other family, friends and colleagues who have been so patient and understanding during the development of six editions of this book.

— Cher Threinen-Pendarvis

CONTENTS

Welcome

WELCOME TO *PAINTER 8 WOW!*

SOME PEOPLE EMPHASIZE THE DIFFERENCES between traditional and digital art tools—almost as if "real" art and the computer are not compatible. But during the early development of this book, we discovered many working artists who had bought computers specifically because they were thrilled by the promise of Painter. It seemed logical that *The Painter Wow! Book* should become a bridge connecting conventional tools and techniques with their electronic counterparts. Early chapters of the book, in particular, touch on color theory, art history and conventional media, and explain how to translate foundational art theory using Painter's tools.

This book addresses the needs of a wide variety of creative professionals: artists making the transition from traditional to digital media; photographers looking to expand their visual vocabulary; screen or print graphic designers hunting for special effects to apply to type and graphics; even creative explorers out for some fun. For those of you with a long history in a traditional art form and a short history with computers, we've done our best to guide you through Painter's interface, making it as simple as possible for you to achieve the results you want. And if you've spent more time with a keyboard and mouse than you have with an artist's palette and paintbrush, you may learn a lot about conventional art terms and techniques as you read the book.

The creative team that invented Painter—Mark Zimmer, John Derry and Tom Hedges of Fractal.com are famous for their creativity. John Derry of the original team consulted with the innovative Corel development team during the creation of Painter 8. Along with exciting new natural-media tools such as Digital Water Color and other useful new features such as the full-featured Brush Creator, Corel has made significant changes to the interface that make Painter more streamlined and much easier to use.

Water Color brushes and layers in Painter 8 let you paint with realistic watercolor washes that can be smooth or runny, as show here in African Violet.

Hillside Lake *was created using the Liquid Ink brushes and layers with which you can create images with thick, sticky ink.*

Commissioned by London's Watch Magazine, Fiona Hawthorne used Painter's expressive brushes to create this glamorous illustration for a page devoted to the Patek Philippe Twenty 4 watch.

WHAT'S NEW IN PAINTER 8?

To make *The Painter 8 Wow! Book* complete and up-to-date for Painter 8, we've revised every page. And we've expanded the book—adding brand-new techniques, new real-world tips, and galleries that specifically profile features added in version 8. Here's a quick overview of some of Painter's exciting new features and a description of where in this book you can find information about them.

Among the changes that make Painter easier to use are these: Painter 8 features a **redesigned interface:** The new vertical **Toolbox** allows you to choose tools and art materials easily—you can choose primary and secondary colors, and you can enjoy access to the papers, gradients, patterns, nozzles and looks libraries using the new **Content Selectors.** The new context-sensitive **Property Bar** allows you to change settings for tools quickly. Painter's new **Mixer palette** lets you mix colors interactively, and the helpful new **Tracker palette** remembers brush categories and variants, making it easy to return to a brush you recently used by choosing it in the Tracker palette.

Painter's new **Brush Creator** includes three tabs, the **Stroke Designer,** which makes creating your custom brushes easier, the **Transposer,** which allows you to combine the functionality of two of your favorite brushes into a new brush, and the **Randomizer,** with which you can choose an existing brush variant and have Painter randomize the properties to create a new variant.

An area of the program that's most likely to change the way you work is Painter 8's **improved Photoshop compatibility**, including the ability to import and preserve layers, layer sets, layer masks and channels from Photoshop files. Painter's industry-standard **masks and layers** model will be familiar to users of Adobe Photoshop. With Painter, you can make selections and save them as masks into the **Channels palette,** much like saving selections as masks into the Channels palette in Photoshop. Painter's layers operate much like Photoshop's layers, and are true transparent layers (with Preserve Transparency) that you can paint on with most any brush. You can also use a selection with any layer you target, and add a **layer mask** to a layer. Additionally, Opacity and Compositing Methods controls are included in the **Layers palette.**

Painter 8 boasts exciting new natural-media features, including **Digital Water Color,** with dozens of new brushes to use with the medium. Digital Water Color is a simple, transparent medium you can use to paint on the Canvas or on a default layer, and you can brush on washes that are smooth, diffused, or grainy. See "Painting With Digital Water Color" on page 85 and "Coloring a Drawing Using Digital Water Color" on page 86 for information about using these new tools in a creative way.

The new **Brush Selector Bar** replaces Painter's Brushes palette; it allows you to choose brush categories and variants. Users

Athos Boncompagni used Painter 8's Chalk, Pastels, Pencils and Pens variants while creating this wrapping paper design.

©CDM—(ITALY)

You'll learn real applications for Painter's tools in the Basics sections of each chapter.

Each chapter includes step-by-step technique sections.

will be pleased to find the new Brush Selector Bar stocked with hundreds of brand-new **brushes** that paint more naturally than ever before—and faster, too. The new **Acrylics** and **Oils** brushes paint with more sensitivity: For instance, the **Wet Soft Acrylic** variants can lay down color or subtly smear it, and the **Thick Opaque Acrylic** variants allow you to apply thicker paint with crisper edges on the brushstrokes; the new **Smeary Fine Camel** variants of Oils offer both the feel of wet paint and thick-and-thin finesse while painting. Additionally, new grain-sensitive brushes such as the **Square X-Soft Pastel** and **Sharp Pastel Pencil** variants of **Pastels** offer a realistic dry-media experience. New **Blenders** variants, such as the **Round Blender Brush** allow you to blend paint, while revealing bristle marks. The program also includes many more **realistic cloning brushes** such as the new **Bristle Oils** and **Thick Camel Cloner.**

Users will appreciate Painter 8's new **Sketch** feature which allows you to generate a pencil drawing from a photo, including controlling the paper grain that you apply to the sketch image.

DO YOU USE MAC OR WINDOWS?

Painter works similarly on Macintosh and PC/Windows platforms. We've taken the path of least resistance by using primarily Macintosh OS X screenshots. (Just to make sure of our techniques, though, we've tested them under Windows 2000, and we've included key commands for both Mac and Windows users.) The few differences between running Painter on Mac and PC are covered in Chapter 1.

ARE YOU A BEGINNER OR A POWER USER?

If you're new to Painter, welcome! We've worked very hard to make this edition of *Painter Wow!* more friendly to beginners by adding more cross-references and by including complete, unabbreviated directions to the techniques in the book. We've also added more basics to the chapter introductions. For intermediate and advanced users, we've included new power-user tips throughout and added many new techniques and inspiring galleries.

We've assumed that you're familiar with the basic Mac or Windows mouse functions and that you know how to open and save files, copy items to the clipboard and navigate through the Mac's hierarchical file system or through Windows directories. We suggest reading Chapter 1, "Getting To Know Painter," Chapter 4, "Selections, Shapes and Masks," and Chapter 5, "Using Layers," before jumping into the more advanced techniques. It's also a good idea, though it isn't essential, to have worked with the *Painter 8 User Guide* and to have completed tutorials that come with the program.

HOW TO USE THIS BOOK

In Chapters 2 through 12, the information we're presenting generally progresses from simple to complex. We've organized these

SAMPLING PAINT

You can temporarily switch to the Dropper tool and sample colors by holding down the Ctrl/⌘ key while you're using many of Painter's other tools.

4

Each chapter includes an inspiring gallery of professional work.

5

You'll find helpful resources in the Appendixes.

chapters into four types of material: "Basics" sections, techniques, practical tips and galleries. In addition, useful hardware, software and other resources are listed at the back of the book.

1 The **Basics** sections teach how Painter's tools and functions work, and give real-world applications for the tools. *The Painter 8 Wow! Book* wasn't designed to be a replacement for the *Painter 8 User Guide* that comes with the program. We've focused on the tools and functions that we think are most useful. In some cases we've further explained items addressed in the manual, and, where important, we've dug deeper to help you understand how the tools and functions work. In other cases, we've covered undocumented functions and practical applications, either shared by contributing artists or uncovered in our own research.

2 Within each **Technique** section, you'll find step-by-step, real-world methods that give you enough information to re-create the process yourself. In the *Wow!* format, pictures illustrating the stages of the process are positioned alongside the appropriate step in the project. Browse the pictures in the art column within a technique for a quick overview of the development of an image. We've done our best to give you enough information so you won't have to refer to the manual to follow the steps.

3 The **Tips** are easily identified by their gray title bar. We've placed them in the Basics and Technique sections where we thought they'd be the most helpful. But each tip is a self-contained tidbit of useful information, so you can learn a lot very quickly by taking a brisk walk through the book, reading only the tips.

4 The **Galleries** are there for inspiration, and one appears at the end of every chapter. With each gallery image, you'll find a short description of how the artwork was produced.

5 No book is an island, so in the **Appendixes** in the back of this one, we've included lists of other resources for your use. If you want to contact a vendor, an artist, or a fine art print studio, or locate an art-related book or other publication, you'll find the information you need there.

The Painter 8 Wow! Book was created to share useful techniques and tips and to provide creative suggestions for using the program. We hope that you'll use it as inspiration and a point of departure for your own creative exploration. Above all, don't be overwhelmed by Painter's richness. . . Just dig in and enjoy it!

—Cher Threinen-Pendarvis

Painter Wow! Web site: www.peachpit.com/wow/painter

Cher Threinen-Pendarvis's Web site: www.pendarvis-studios.com

GETTING TO KNOW PAINTER

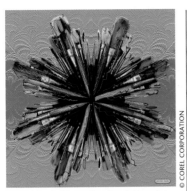

John Derry's illustration, Brush Mandala, was inspired by the artist Peter Max. Derry created it for the promotion of Painter 8 using a variety of brushes and special effects such as Effects, Esoterica, Blobs and Apply Marbling. To create the mirrored group of paintbrushes, he used Painter's Kaleidoscope dynamic plug-in. Derry also painted spontaneous brushstrokes using the Smeary Flat variant of Oils and the Smooth Ink Pen variant of Pens.

SIT RIGHT DOWN AND POWER UP! This chapter explores Painter's basic needs and functions, as well as its unique strengths. If you're new to Painter, you'll benefit the most from this chapter if you've already spent some time with the *Painter 8 User Guide* that ships with the program.

PAINTER'S REQUIREMENTS FOR MAC AND PC

Here are Painter's *minimum* requirements: If you use a Macintosh you'll need at least a G3 running System 9.2.2 or OS X (version 10.2 or later) with a minimum of 128 MB of application RAM. To run Painter on Windows 2000, or Windows XP, you'll need a Pentium 200 or higher processor with at least 128 MB of application RAM. For both platforms, a 1024 x 768 display with 24-bit color are recommended, and a hard disk with approximately 200 MB of free space is required to perform an installation.

When you open an image in Painter—for example, a 5 MB image—and begin working with it, Painter needs three to five times that file size in RAM in order to work at optimal speed—in our example, that would be 15–25 MB of RAM. Opening more than one image, adding layers or shapes, or increasing the number of Undos (under Edit, Preferences, Undos in Windows and Mac 9.2.2, and under Corel Painter 8 on Mac OS X) adds further demands on RAM. When Painter runs out of RAM, it uses the hard disk chosen under Edit, Preferences, General in Windows and Mac 9.2.2 and under Corel Painter 8 on Mac OS X) as a RAM substitute. This

ABOUT LAYERS AND SHAPES

Layers and *shapes* are image elements that are "stacked" above the Painter image canvas. Both layers and shapes can be manipulated independently of the image canvas—allowing for exciting compositing effects.

This Wacom 6 x 8 Intuos2 pressure-sensitive tablet with stylus is versatile and easy to use. The Intuos2 tablets offer pressure-sensitivity, as well as tilt and bearing, and allow you to paint more expressive strokes with Painter's brushes that can sense the pressure you apply, and the rotation of your hand as you draw.

Choosing a partition for the Temp File Volume

"scratch disk" holds the Painter Temp file you may have seen. Since hard disks operate much slower than RAM, performance suffers—even if you have a fast hard disk.

Ideally, to work with Painter, you would use a computer with a speedy processor; a large, fast hard disk; and lots of RAM. In addition, you'll want a large, 24-bit color monitor—probably no less than 17 inches—and perhaps a second monitor on which to store palettes. Also highly recommended—some would say *essential*—is a pressure-sensitive drawing tablet with a stylus. Not only is it a more natural drawing and painting tool than a mouse, but many of Painter's brushes have a lot more personality with a pressure-sensitive input device.

Mac memory allocation. Mac OS X allows Painter to use as much RAM as it needs. On a Mac running OS 9.2.2, you need to allot maximum RAM to Painter. First quit all open applications. In the Finder, under the Apple menu, choose About This Macintosh and write down the number next to Largest Unused Block. This is the total amount of RAM in which you can run applications. Subtract 500 or 1000 K from this number (as a buffer). Now, in the Painter folder, click once (not twice!) on the Painter application icon to select it rather than launch it, and choose File, Get Info. Enter the result of your math in the Preferred Size box. This method won't let you open any other applications of significant size while Painter is running, but it means you can use nearly all available RAM while you're in Painter.

Windows memory allocation. To make maximum RAM available for your Windows-based PC, choose Edit, Preferences, Windows to access the Windows Preferences dialog box. Under Physical Memory Usage click the "Maximum Memory for Painter" button. Quit all applications and relaunch Painter. Painter will run faster if you let Windows manage the virtual memory scheme this way.

FILE SIZE AND RESOLUTION

If you're new to the computer, here's important background information regarding file sizes: Painter is primarily a *pixel-based* program, also known as a *bitmap*, *painting* or *raster* program, not a *drawing* program, also known as an *object-oriented* or *vector* program. Drawing programs use mathematical expressions to describe the outline and fill attributes of objects in the drawing,

On the Mac in System 9.2.2, you can use the Finder's File, Get Info window to set the memory allocation for the program.

Setting the Maximum Memory for Painter in Windows

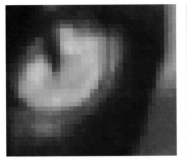

This scan of a photograph is a pixel-based image. Enlarging it to 1200% reveals the grid of pixels.

Using Painter's cool new Sketch effect, you can generate a black-and-white sketch from a photo. Open an image with good contrast, then choose Effects, Surface Control, Sketch. In the dialog box, move the Grain slider to the right to add more grain and leave the Sensitivity slider at a lower range if you'd like to pick up primarily the edges.

We increased the Sensitivity to 1.40 to pick up lines from the photo background. We set the Grain setting at 1.40 to add richer paper grain to the sketch.

The black-and white "sketch" image

while pixel-based programs describe things dot-by-dot. Since mathematical expressions are more "compact" than dot-by-dot descriptions, object-oriented files are generally smaller than pixel-based files. Also, because its components are mathematically described, object-oriented art can be resized or transformed with no loss of quality. Not so with Painter, Photoshop and other pixel-based programs. Increasing the size of most images in these programs means that additional pixels must be created to accommodate the larger size by filling in spaces as the existing pixels spread apart. As a result of these interpolated (manufactured) pixels, resized images can lose their crispness.

There are ways of working around this "soft image" dilemma. One solution is to do your early studies using a small file size (for instance, an 8 x 10-inch image at 75 pixels per inch), then start over with a large file to do final art at full size (for instance an 8 x 10-inch file at 300 pixels per inch). Another approach is to block in the basic form and color in a small file, then scale the image up to final size (using Canvas, Resize) to add texture and details (textures seem particularly vulnerable to softening when enlarged). You'll notice that many of the artists whose work is featured in this book use another efficient method: They create the components of a final piece of art in separate documents, then copy and paste (or drag and drop) the components into a final "master" image. Painter offers yet another solution for working with large file sizes—composing with reference layers (small "stand-in" versions of larger images that are kept outside the document). Because data for the large image is not kept in the working file, performance improves. "Using Reference Layers" on page 182, tells more about this feature.

Painter's vector capabilities. Although it's primarily a pixel-based program, Painter does have some object-oriented features—type, of course, and shapes, shape paths and outline-based selections. Painter's shapes exist as layers above the image canvas; they are mathematically described outlines with stroke and fill attributes. And Painter's selections (areas of the image designated for work) are versatile; they can be used as pixel-based selections (similar to Photoshop's selections), or they can be transformed into outline-based selections or converted into shapes. (Other elements in Painter—the image canvas, masks and image layers—are pixel-based.) Chapters 4 and 5 tell more about selections and shapes.

Here are two ways to make quick copies without going through the clipboard and using valuable RAM. To make a copy of your entire document, use File, Clone. (This is also a quick way to make a "flat" copy with the layers in the document merged.) To quickly duplicate a layer, select the layer in the Layers palette, choose the Layer Adjuster tool, press the Alt/Option key and click in the image to make a copy in register, or drag off a copy into another area of the document.

Expressing width and height in pixels in the New dialog box keeps the file size the same, regardless of how you change the resolution.

Whether the Constrain File Size checkbox in the Canvas, Resize dialog box is checked or unchecked, if you're using pixels as the units, the file size stays the same, regardless of how you change the resolution.

In the Preferences, Save dialog box, you can choose to have Painter ask if you want to Append a File Extension when you save the file, and to prompt you to check the Color Space when saving as well.

Click the Browse button in the Open dialog box to preview all of the images in a folder. The watercolor studies in Mary Envall's "Lilies" folder are shown here. (Some files may not have a preview—for example, some PICT or JPEG files created by other programs.)

Pixels and resolution. There are two commonly used ways of describing file sizes: in terms of their pixel measurements, or in a unit of measure (such as inches) plus a resolution (pixels per unit of measure). An image is a fixed number of pixels wide and tall—like 1200 x 1500—or a measurement combined with a resolution—4 x 5 inches at 300 ppi (4 x 300=1200, and 5 x 300=1500), so both files are these dimensions. (Either way it's expressed, this flat full-color file is 7 MB.) If you use pixels as a measurement for Width and Height in the New dialog box, notice that changing the numbers you type into the Resolution box doesn't change the file size. But increasing or decreasing the number of pixels in the Width and Height fields in the New dialog box or the Canvas, Resize box will add (or reduce) pixel information in the picture.

OPENING FILES

Images in Painter are 24-bit color, made up of RGB (red, green and blue) components consisting of 8 bits each of color information. Painter will recognize and open CMYK TIFF and grayscale TIFF images as well as layered Photoshop format files in CMYK, but it will convert both CMYK and grayscale files to Painter's own RGB mode. CIE LAB, Kodak Photo CD format and other color formats will need to be converted to RGB in a program such as Adobe Photoshop or Equilibrium's Debabelizer before Painter can read them.

SAVING FILES

Painter offers numerous ways to save your image under File, Save or Save As. If you've created an image with a mask to hide some parts of the image and reveal others (Chapter 4 tells about masks), some of the formats will allow you to preserve the mask (by checking the Save Alpha box in the Save or Save As dialog box), while others won't. Here's a list of the current formats that includes their "mask-friendliness" and other advantages and disadvantages:

RIFF. Thrifty (files are saved quite small) and robust (allows for multiple layers), RIFF (Raster Image File Format) is Painter's native format. If you're using elements unique to Painter, such as Water Color Layers, Liquid Ink layers, reference layers, dynamic layers,

You can preserve layers in files by saving in either RIFF or Photoshop format, but RIFF (even uncompressed) is usually significantly smaller. Rick Kirkman's 663 x 663-pixel image with 150 layers weighs in at 1.7 MB as a compressed RIFF, 6.1 MB as an uncompressed RIFF, and 7.1 MB when saved in Photoshop format.

To create Zorro's Gone, Janet Martini used several of Painter 8's brushes and effects, including Shells sprayed with the Image Hose and a fill using the Flying Blackbirds pattern. She colored the birds white using the Graphic Paintbrush variant of F-X. To complete the image, she added a Woodcut look by choosing Effects, Surface Control, Woodcut.

shapes, or mosaics, saving in RIFF will preserve them. (Water Color Layers, Liquid Ink layers, reference layers, dynamic layers and shapes are described in depth in Chapter 5; mosaics are described in Chapter 7.) If you have *lots* of free hard disk space, check the Uncompressed box in the Save dialog box when you're saving in RIFF: Files will become many times larger, but will save and open much more quickly. Few other programs recognize RIFF, so if you want to work with a Painter image in another program, save a copy in a different format.

Photoshop format. Saving files in Photoshop format gives you nearly all the flexibility of RIFF, and is ideal if you frequently move data between Painter and Photoshop. When you use Photoshop to open a file saved in this format, Painter's layers become Photoshop layers (Chapter 9, "Using Painter with Photoshop," contains more information about working with Painter and Photoshop); Painter's masks (explained in depth in Chapter 4) become Photoshop channels; and Painter's Bézier paths translate perfectly into Photoshop's paths and subpaths, appearing in Photoshop's Paths palette.

TIFF. Probably the most popular and widely recognized of the bitmap file formats, TIFF allows you to save a mask with your image (check the Save Alpha checkbox). Unfortunately, unlike Photoshop, Painter's Save As dialog box gives you no option to compress the TIFF file—the Uncompressed checkbox is checked and grayed-out.

PICT. PICT is the format of choice for many Mac multimedia programs and other on-screen display. Painter's PICT format lets you save a single mask (but not layers), and save a Painter movie as a sequence of numbered PICT files to export and animate in another program (described in Chapter 10, "Multimedia and Film with Painter"). Painter also opens PICT files very quickly.

JPEG. When you save a file in JPEG format, a dialog box will appear with four choices: Excellent, High, Good and Fair. You'll

Here are some hints for working with Painter in a CMYK production environment. If you're starting with scanned images, scan them in RGB instead of CMYK—RGB has a significantly broader color gamut. If possible, avoid importing your image into another program (like Photoshop) to convert it to CMYK until you're ready to print, since you lose colors when you convert from RGB to CMYK. And, it's a good idea to save a copy of the RGB image before converting in case you want to convert it again with different RGB-to-CMYK conversion settings.

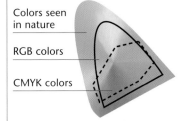

Colors seen in nature

RGB colors

CMYK colors

Relative sizes and extents of color gamuts

Janet Martini began Crane Crashes into Chip, *by scanning a copyright-free drawing of a crane from a Dover clip art book. She copied the scan and pasted it into her image, then she used Painter's Image Hose to spray a few poker chips onto the illustration. Next, she pasted in her signature "chop" image, which she'd drawn using a Pens variant. To paint the bright pink, yellow and green areas, she used the Graphic Paintbrush variant of F-X. Finally, to create a higher-contrast look, she used the Effects, Surface Control, Woodcut feature.*

get the best-looking results by choosing Excellent. The advantage of saving a file in JPEG format is that you get superb space savings: A JPEG file is usually only one-tenth as large as a TIFF file of the same image if you choose Excellent, and only one-hundredth the size if you choose Fair. The drawbacks: no mask, layers or paths are saved, and the compression is a lossy compression—which means that some data (color detail in the image) is lost in the compression process. While JPEG is a good way to archive images once they're finished (especially images that have no sharp edges), many artists prefer not to use JPEG because it alters pixels. Don't save a file in JPEG format more than once—you'll lose more data every time you do so.

JPEG is also useful for preparing 24-bit images with the tiny file sizes that are needed for graphics used on the World Wide Web. (See Chapter 11 for more information on using JPEG in projects created for the Web.)

GIF. GIF is the graphics format of choice for most non-photographic images on the World Wide Web. Like TIFF, PICT or JPEG, saving in GIF format combines layers with the background. It also reduces the number of colors to a maximum of 256, so remember to Save As in a different file format first, if you want to be able to access the original image structure again. When you save in GIF, a dialog box appears that gives you a number of options for saving your file. Click the Preview Data button to see how your choices will affect your image. For more information about using Painter's GIF format turn to Chapter 11, "Using Painter for Web Graphics."

EPS. Saving in this format drops layered elements into the background and ignores masks, so it's best to choose Save As in another format if you'll want to make changes to your document at a later time. Saving in EPS format also converts the file into a five-part DCS file: four separate files for the four process printing colors, and a fifth file as a preview of the composite image. Check the *Painter 8 User Guide* for a complete explanation of the EPS Options dialog box.

PC formats. BMP, PCX and Targa are formats commonly used on DOS and Windows platforms. BMP (short for "bitmap") is a Windows-based graphics file format, and PCX is the PC Paintbrush native format. Neither of these two formats supports shapes or masks. Targa is a popular format used for creating sophisticated 24-bit graphics. The Targa format is often used (in place of PICT) when preparing numbered files for import into Windows animation applications.

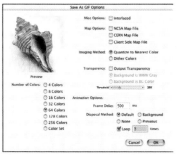

The Save As GIF Options dialog box includes GIF Animation Options. To learn about creating a GIF animation step-by-step, turn to "Making a Slide Show Animation" on page 334.

A Rose for Anne, a detail of which is shown here, was painted with several of Painter's Oils brushes, including the Round Camel-hair and Smeary Flat. The final illustration appears on the front cover of this book.

Movie formats. Movies in Painter (described in Chapter 10, "Multimedia and Film with Painter") are saved as frame stacks, but you can choose Save As to export the current frame of your movie, export the entire frame stack as a QuickTime or AVI (on the PC) movie, or export the entire Frame Stack as numbered PICT files. See Chapter 10 for more about multimedia formats.

PAINTER BASICS

Here's a guide to some of Painter's basic operating procedures.

Navigating the Painter 8 Workspace. The workspace has been redesigned for Corel Painter 8, and it's leaner and easier to use. The Content Selectors in the Toolbox and the context-sensitive Property Bar allow you to choose tools and change settings quickly.

Painter's Menus, Palettes and Document Window

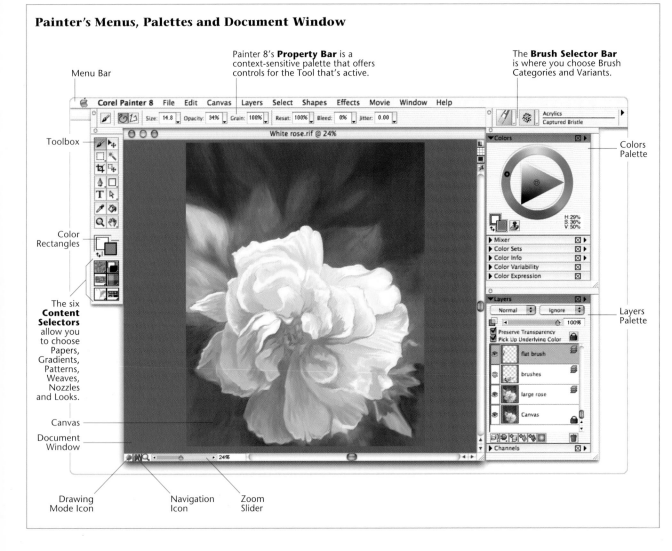

Menu Bar

Painter 8's **Property Bar** is a context-sensitive palette that offers controls for the Tool that's active.

The **Brush Selector Bar** is where you choose Brush Categories and Variants.

Toolbox

Color Rectangles

The six **Content Selectors** allow you to choose Papers, Gradients, Patterns, Weaves, Nozzles and Looks.

Canvas

Document Window

Colors Palette

Layers Palette

Drawing Mode Icon

Navigation Icon

Zoom Slider

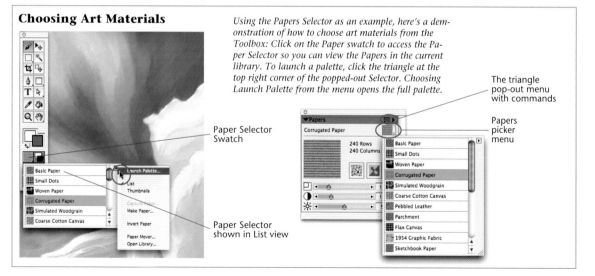
Using the Toolbox. Painter's slick, redesigned Toolbox features mark-making tools, and tools with which you can draw and edit shapes, view and navigate a document and make selections. In addition to the Color Rectangles, you'll also find the Content Selectors near the bottom of the Toolbox.

Painter's Toolbox

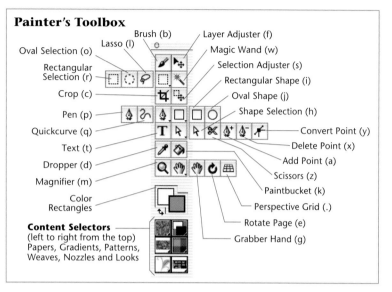

Accessing art materials using the Content Selectors. Previous versions of Painter used a drawer-like container to hold materials. In Painter 8, swatches for Papers, Gradients, Patterns, Weaves, Looks (a combination of a brush and a paper, for instance) and Nozzles (images that are sprayed using the Image Hose) are easy to choose from the Toolbox. Each Content Selector has a triangle menu that pops out a menu with which you can access commands, like launching a full palette or loading an alternate library of materials.

Choosing Art Materials

Using the Papers Selector as an example, here's a demonstration of how to choose art materials from the Toolbox: Click on the Paper swatch to access the Paper Selector so you can view the Papers in the current library. To launch a palette, click the triangle at the top right corner of the popped-out Selector. Choosing Launch Palette from the menu opens the full palette.

Using the Brush Selector Bar. The Brush Selector Bar, which is located to the right of the Property Bar at the top of the Painter workspace, offers an open list of thumbnails for both brush categories and their variants. (For more information about using the Brush Selector Bar, turn to the beginning of Chapter 3.)

The Brush Selector Bar

In the Brush Selector Bar click the Brush Category icon to open the picker, then click on the tiny triangle to the far right of the Brush Category menu to open the pop-out menu, which will allow you to switch from List view (shown here) to Thumbnail view. Click on a name in the list to choose a new Brush Category.

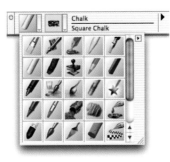

The Brush Selector Bar, showing the Brush Category picker open, to display the Brush Category Thumbnails. Click on a Thumbnail to choose a Brush Category.

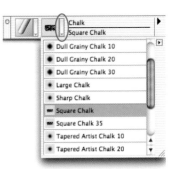

Clicking on the triangle to the right of the Brush Variant icon in the Brush Selector Bar will open a pop-out menu, which allows you to choose a variant—in our case, the Square Chalk variant of Chalk. The Brush Variant menu can be displayed using the List view (shown here), or Stroke view.

Menus

Many of Painter's menus include keyboard shortcuts

Palettes

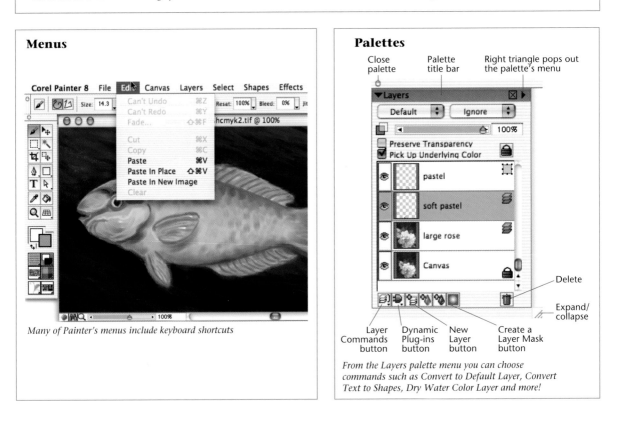

From the Layers palette menu you can choose commands such as Convert to Default Layer, Convert Text to Shapes, Dry Water Color Layer and more!

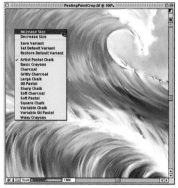

By right-clicking the mouse in Windows, or by pressing the Control key and clicking on a Mac with a one-button mouse, you can access helpful context-sensitive menus like this one, which appears when a Brush is chosen.

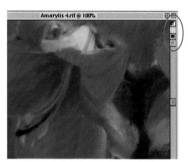

The Tracing Paper, Grid Overlay, Output Preview and Impasto icons reside at the top of Painter's vertical scroll bar.

A. Rafinelli Vineyard by Cher Threinen-Pendarvis. The Drawing Mode icons will pop up if you click the icon in the lower left corner of the image window. They are, from left to right: Draw Anywhere, Draw Outside and Draw Inside. To read more about them, turn to Chapter 4.

Screen management shortcuts. Like other programs, Painter offers lots of shortcuts designed to cut down on your trips to the menus, palettes or scroll bars. To *scroll* around the page, press and hold the Spacebar (a grabber hand appears), then drag on your image. To *zoom in* on an area of your image at the next level of magnification, hold down Ctrl/⌘-Spacebar (a magnifier tool appears) and click in your image. Add the Alt/Option key to *zoom out*. (You can also use Ctrl/⌘-plus to *zoom in* one magnification level and Ctrl/⌘-minus to *zoom out*.) These are the same zooming shortcuts used in Photoshop and Adobe Illustrator.

To *rotate the page* to better suit your drawing style, press Spacebar-Alt (Windows) or Spacebar-Option (Mac) until the Rotate Page icon (a pointing finger) appears, and click and drag in your image until the preview shows you the angle you want. (The Rotate Page command rotates the view of the image only, not the actual pixels.) Restore your rotated image to its original position by holding down Spacebar-Alt or Spacebar-Option and clicking once on the image.

Another frequently used screen-management shortcut is Ctrl/⌘-M (Window, Screen Mode Toggle), which replaces a window's scroll and title bars with a frame of gray (or toggles back to normal view).

Context-sensitive menus. Painter boasts context-sensitive menus that make it easier to change the settings for a brush, or even quickly copy a selection to a layer. Context-sensitive menus are available for all of Painter's tools and for certain conditions, such as for an active selection when a Selection tool is chosen. To access a context-sensitive menu, right/Ctrl-click.

Helpful icon buttons. Just outside the Painter image window are two sets of very helpful icon buttons. At the top right on the Painter Window scroll bar are four toggle buttons: the Tracing Paper icon (allowing you to turn Tracing Paper on and off), the Grid Overlay icon (which turns the Grid View on and off), the Color Correction icon (to toggle between the full-color RGB view and a preview of what your image will look like when printed) and the Impasto effect icon (which you can click to hide or show the highlights and shadows on thick paint). For a step-by-step technique using Tracing Paper, see "Cloning and Tracing" on page 98; see page 15 for a information about using Grid Overlay. Turn to Chapter 12, "Printing and Archival Concerns," for information

SEEING THE WHOLE PICTURE

If you're working with an image too large to fit within your screen, choose Window, Zoom To Fit, or double-click on the Grabber tool in the Toolbox. Painter will reduce or enlarge the magnification to fit the window size.

HIDE AND SHOW PALETTES

To hide all of Painter's open palettes press the Tab key. The key command works as a toggle—press the Tab key to show the palettes again.

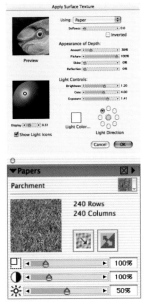

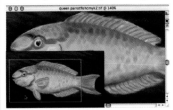

The Apply Surface Texture dialog box Preview window, here shown Using Paper (top), updates when a new choice is made in the Papers palette (bottom).

VARIABLE ZOOM

The continuous, variable zoom function in the left corner of the Painter image window includes a Scale slider, and you can also specify an exact zoom factor using the text field. Click the binocular icon to its left to access the Navigator, and pan around your image.

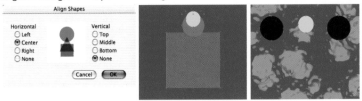

Clicking the Navigation icon (the binoculars) opens a window, in which you can see the area you are viewing in relationship to the entire image.

about Painter's Output Preview; Impasto is covered in Chapter 3, "Painting with Brushes."

In the left corner of Painter's window frame is an icon that pops up the three Drawing Mode icons, which allow you to control where you paint—anywhere in the image, outside of a selection, or inside of a selection. Turn to the beginning of Chapter 4, "Selections, Shapes and Masks," to read more about the Drawing Modes.

Interactive dialog boxes. In most programs, clicking to make choices outside of a dialog box will reward you with an error beep, but Painter's interactive dialog box design encourages you to continue to make the choices you need. As an example, you can open a piece of artwork or a photo, then choose Effects, Surface Control, Apply Surface Texture and click and drag in the Preview window until you see a part of the image that you like. If you then choose Paper in the Using pop-up menu you can go outside the dialog box to choose a different paper (even a paper in another library) from the Papers Selector (in the Toolbox) or from the Papers palette. You can even move the Scale, Contrast and Brightness sliders in the Papers palette and watch as the Preview image in the Apply Surface Texture dialog box updates to reflect your choice. When you've arrived at a result that you like, you can click OK in the Apply Surface Texture dialog box. The Effects, Surface Control, Color Overlay dialog box and the Effects, Surface Control, Dye Concentration dialog box behave in a similar way, allowing you to choose different papers like the Apply Surface Texture dialog box, or you can choose Uniform Color in the pop-up menu and test different colors from the Colors palette before you click OK. The Edit, Fill dialog box (Ctrl/⌘-F) is also interactive, giving you the ability to preview your image before it's filled with the current color, a pattern, a gradient or a weave.

ALIGNING SHAPES AND LAYERS AUTOMATICALLY

The Align dialog box (Effects, Objects, Align) is helpful for lining up shapes or layers (or a combination of the two). To align a series of items, start by selecting the Layer Adjuster tool, pressing the Shift key and clicking on each item's name in the Layers palette. When all the items are selected, go to the Effects menu and choose Objects, Align, and choose your settings. The dialog box preview will update to show you how your choice of Horizontal and Vertical options will affect alignment of the objects, and you can click OK to accept, or Cancel. The elements below in the center, are aligned using Horizontal: Center and Vertical: None. The elements below on the right, were aligned using their tops. The settings were Horizontal: None and Vertical: Top.

The Objects, Align dialog box with settings for the shapes in the center illustration above

Positioning the baseline of text with the help of the Ruler and Horizontal Guides created by clicking the Vertical ruler. The circled items here are the Ruler Origin field (top) and a triangular guide marker (bottom).

Using the Grid Overlay to help when positioning text

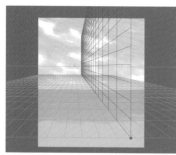

The Perspective Grid feature allows you to set up a one-point Perspective Grid, which is useful as a guide while drawing.

Measuring and positioning elements. The Ruler, Guides, Grid Overlay and Perspective Grid can help you measure and position shapes and layers. The commands for these features reside in the Canvas menu. They are especially helpful for aligning text and selections.

To set up a guide using precise measurements or to change the default guide color, double-click on the Ruler to access the Guide Options. Double-click on a triangular marker on the Ruler to access options for an individual guide. Delete guides by dragging their triangles off the document window or by pressing the Delete All Guides button in Guide Options.

To easily measure the exact *width* of an item, try moving the Ruler Origin. Press and drag it from the upper-left corner of the Ruler, where the horizontal and vertical measurements meet, to the left end of the item you want to measure. Then see where the right end falls on the ruler.

The Grid Overlay is useful for aligning items. Choose Canvas, Grid, Show Grid or click on the checkered Grid icon above the scroll bar. To change the grid's appearance (for example, to create a grid of only horizontal lines), choose Canvas, Grid, Grid Options and adjust the settings.

The Perspective Grid is useful both for aligning items and for setting up a grid that is helpful when drawing. Choose Canvas, Perspective Grids, Show Grid to display a grid. You can adjust the grid using the Perspective Grid tool from the Toolbox by dragging the vanishing point and horizon line or the forward edge of the grid. Choose Canvas, Perspective Grids, Grid Options to adjust the settings and to save your own presets.

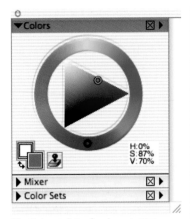

The Colors palette showing a custom grouping including the Mixer and Color Sets palettes

When you make a brushstroke in the Preferences, Brush Tracking dialog box, Painter adjusts the range of pressure-sensitivity based on your stroke.

THE GHOST OF A BRUSH

To view Painter's brush footprint cursor, turn on the "Brush ghost when possible" checkbox in the General Preferences dialog box.

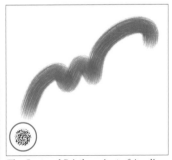

The Captured Bristle variant of Acrylics shows the "brush ghost" or footprint of its captured dab.

CUSTOMIZING YOUR WORKSPACE

Painter makes it easy to customize your workspace. To move a palette grouping to another part of the screen, drag the title bar at the top of the palette. You can also move up or down within a palette group, and remove or add palettes to a group. To see this work easily, click on a blank area of a palette title bar and drag it up or down. For instance, we rearranged our Color palettes in this order: Colors, Mixer and Color Sets, eliminating the other palettes from the group by clicking the white "x" box near the right end of the title bar.

To save your palette layout permanently, choose Window, Arrange Palettes, Save Layout, and when the Save Layout dialog box appears, name your palette grouping and click OK. As your needs change, it's easy to rearrange the palette group. Then to restore a saved layout, choose Window, Arrange Palettes and choose the saved layout from the menu. To delete a layout, choose Window, Arrange Palettes, Delete Layout and choose the layout you want to remove from the list. To return to Painter's default palette arrangement, choose Window, Arrange Palettes, Default.

SETTING PREFERENCES

Painter's Preferences (under the Edit menu, in Windows or Mac 9.2.2, or the Corel Painter 8 menu in Mac OS X) go a long way in helping you create an efficient workspace. Here are a few pointers:

Brush Tracking. Before you begin to draw, it's important to set up the Brush Tracking so you can customize how Painter interprets the input of your stylus, including parameters such as pressure and speed. Choose Edit, Preferences, Brush Tracking (OS X users, choose Corel Painter 8, Preferences, Undo) and make a brushstroke with your stylus using typical pressure and speed. Painter accepts this as the average stroke and adjusts to give you the maximum amount of range and pressure-sensitivity based on your sample stroke. Previous versions of Painter did not remember Brush Tracking settings when you quit the program, but Painter 8 will remember your custom settings until you change them.

Multiple Undos. Painter lets you set the number of Undos you want under Edit, Preferences, Undo. (OS X users, choose Corel Painter 8, Preferences, Undo.) The default number of Undos is set to 32. It's important to note that this option applies cumulatively across all open documents within Painter. For example, if the number of Undos is set to 5 and you have two documents open, if you use 2 Undos on the first document, you'll be able to perform 3 Undos on the second document. And, since a high setting for the number of Undos can burden your RAM and scratch disk—because the program must perform a save for each Undo—unless you have a good reason (such as working on a small sketch where you'll need to make many changes), it's a good idea

You can open alternate libraries using each of the six Content Selectors in the Toolbox. For instance, click the Paper Selector in the Toolbox and when it opens, click the right triangle to open the pop-out menu and choose Open Library.

to set the number of Undos at a low number, such as 5.

Palette Preferences. You can choose which palettes are displayed by choosing their names from the Window menu, which makes it easy to configure Painter to save valuable screen real estate. The Preferences, Palettes dialog box offers controls for Autoscroll (lets you automatically scroll through a palette with several elements), Snapping Behavior (how palettes in a group are laid out) and Snapping Tolerance (how close one palette needs to be to another before it's snapped into the group).

The General Preferences dialog box lets you specify default libraries, cursor type and orientation, Temp File Volume (location of the scratch disk) and Units, among other features.

Painter 8's General Preferences dialog box, with the Drawing Cursor set for our right hand and Brush Ghost enabled

The open Papers Selector showing Painter's default Paper Textures library, and the path to the menu where the Open Library command is chosen

The open Papers palette showing the path to the menu where Open Library is chosen

ORGANIZING WITH LIBRARIES AND MOVERS

Painter uses *libraries* and *movers* to help you manage the huge volume of custom textures, brushes and other items that the program can generate. Libraries are the "storage bins" for those items, and movers let you customize those bins by transferring items into or out of them.

How libraries work. Every palette that includes a resource list of materials has an Open Library (or Load Library) command. Let's use the Papers palette as an example. Choose Window, Show Papers. Click the right triangle on the palette title bar to access the pop-out menu, and choose Open Library to display a dialog box that lets you search through folders on any hard disk until you find the library you want; then double-click to open it. (Although you can load libraries directly from a CD-ROM—like the Painter 8 CD-ROM, the Painter 8 CD 2 CD-ROM or the Wow! CD-ROM—it's more reliable to copy the libraries from the CD-ROM into your Painter application folder.) Fortunately, Painter is smart enough to show only libraries that can be opened in the palette you're working from. For instance, if you choose the Open Library command from the Papers Selector or from the Papers palette, you'll see Papers libraries only, not the Gradients or Patterns libraries.

Using movers to customize your libraries. If you find that you're continually switching paper texture libraries, it's probably time to use the Paper Mover to compile several textures into a single custom library for your work. For instance, you can create a Paper texture library containing favorite textures that work well with Painter's grain-sensitive Chalk and Pastel brushes and the Wow! Chalk Brushes library on the *Painter 8 Wow!* CD-ROM—

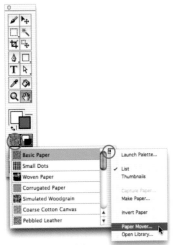

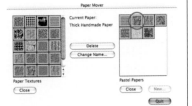

The open Papers Selector showing Painter's default Paper Textures library, and the path to the menu where the Paper Mover choice is located

Dragging an item from the default Paper Textures library into the newly created Pastel Paper Textures library

Painter 8's new context-sensitive Info palette (Window, Show Info) offers an image-size preview, document dimensions, X and Y cursor position and unit information, such as pixels, inches and resolution. The Info palette also displays the RGB and HSV information. To see these values, choose the Dropper tool and click in the image.

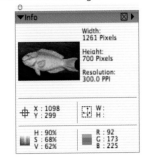

such as Corrugated Paper, Thick Handmade Paper, Rough Charcoal Paper (from Painter's default Paper Textures library), Ribbed Deckle, Rough Grain and Light Sand (from the Drawing Paper Textures library) and Coarse Pavement (from the Relief Textures library). The Drawing Paper Textures and Relief Textures libraries can be found in the Paper Textures folder, on the Painter 8 CD 2 CD-ROM.

Here's how to build this custom paper library: In the Toolbox, click the Papers Selector, and open its pop-out menu. Choose Paper Mover. (You can also access the Paper Mover via the pop-up menu on the Papers palette.) In the Paper Mover, create a new, empty Papers library by clicking on the New button on the right side of the mover, then name your new Papers file and save it. (We named ours Pastel Paper Textures.) To copy a texture from the left side of the mover (your currently active library) into the new library, select a texture's icon on the left side of the mover. The name of the selected texture will appear in the center of the mover window; drag the texture icon from the original library (left side) and drop it into the new library (right side).

Continue adding textures to the new library in this fashion. We selected the three textures from the default Paper Textures library and dropped their icons into the new Pastel Paper Textures library. Next, we added the Ribbed Deckle, Rough Grain and Light Sand textures from the Drawing Paper Textures library to our new library. To add a texture from another library to your new library, click on the left-hand Close button, then click again when it changes to an Open button and open the next library that you want to draw from. (Don't forget the libraries on the

You can make new script libraries to store some of your automated special effects (and reduce the size of the Painter Script Data file, where the default scripts are stored). In the Scripts palette, click the right triangle to open the menu and choose Script Mover. The Painter Script Data file will open on the left side of the mover. Click the New button on the right side of the mover to make a new library and name it and save it when prompted. Select the scripts you want to copy, and drag and drop them into the new library. When you've finished copying, delete the items you've copied from the Painter Script Data file (by clicking on them and pressing Delete), to keep file size trim. (For more information about effects scripts, see Chapter 10.)

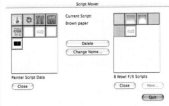

Using the Script Mover to import scripts saved in the Painter Script Data file (left side) into a custom library of special effects scripts (right side)

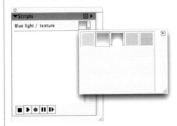

The Scripts library containing special effects "macros" that can be applied to images

For this illustration of a Queen Parrotfish, we laid in color for an underpainting with the oil-painting brushes (including the Round Camelhair variant of Oils), then we added texture to areas of the image by painting with grain-sensitive brushes (the Square Chalk variant of Chalk, for instance) over the Laid Pastel Paper loaded from our custom Pastel Paper Textures library.

Wow! and Painter 8 Application CD-ROMs!) We selected the Coarse Pavement texture from the Relief Textures library and dragged and dropped it to our new library. When you've finished, click Quit. Now open your new library by choosing Load Library from the triangle pop-out menu on the right side of the Papers Selector's list menu. If you want your new library to open every time you launch Painter, choose Edit, Preferences, General (OS X users, choose Corel Painter 8, Preferences, Undo), and type its exact name in the Papers box.

All movers work in the same way, so you can follow the above procedure to, say, create a new Patterns library that contains the only five patterns that you ever use. (See "Creating a Seamless Pattern" in Chapter 7 on page 260 for an example of building a new pattern and using the Pattern Mover.)

LOADING AN ALTERNATE BRUSH LIBRARY IN PAINTER 8

To load a different brush library in Painter 8, first copy it into the Brushes folder within the Painter application folder, then click the triangle menu on the right side of the Brush Selector Bar and choose Load Library. When the Brush Libraries dialog box appears, navigate to the brush library and click Open. (We chose the Wow! Chalks.) When the Brush Libraries dialog box reappears, click the Load button. The new brushes will now be visible in the Brush Selector Bar.

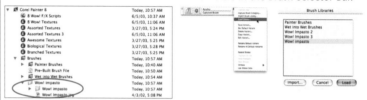

The open Corel Painter 8 application folder (shown in Mac OS X), with the Brush Libraries organized in the Brushes folder; choosing Load Library from the Brush Selector Bar pop-up menu; selecting the Wow! Impasto library in the Brush Libraries dialog box, and then clicking the Load button.

IMPORTING OLDER BRUSHES

In Painter 8 you can import favorite brushes that were created in earlier versions of Painter. These brushes must first be converted to the new brush model, and this is done by choosing Import Brush Library from the pop-out menu on the right side of the Brush Selector Bar. Early Water Color brushes were not built to work with Painter 8's Water Color layers or new Digital Water Color. They can be imported, but will not perform the same as in the earlier version because they were designed to work with the old Wet Paint layer on the Canvas.

The open Corel Painter 8 application folder (shown in Mac OS X), with the 6 Wow! Chalk brushes library (created in Painter 6), copied into the Brushes folder. After choosing Import Brush Library from the Brush Selector Bar's pop-up menu, we selected the 6 Wow! Chalk brushes library in the Select Brush Library dialog box and clicked the Open button, which opened the Brush Libraries dialog box. Then we chose the newly converted 6 Wow! Chalk brushes 1 library from the list and clicked the Load button.

3RD-PARTY FILTERS & PAINTER

You can use third-party filters with Painter by installing them in the Painter application folder within the Plugins folder. Painter will automatically load them the next time you launch the program. To use third-party filters that are stored outside the Painter application folder, you can set up a Shortcut (Windows) or an Alias (Mac) for the plug-in folder to access it: To create a Shortcut, choose the folder containing the plug-in in My Computer or Windows Explorer. Then choose File, Create Shortcut. To create an Alias on the Mac, select the folder on the desktop and choose File, Make Alias. Move the Shortcut or Alias into the Plugins folder in the Painter application folder and restart Painter to see the new filters, which will appear at the bottom of the Effects menu.

THE POWER
OF COLOR

Don Stewart used reds, oranges and
yellows to depict fall afternoon light in
Hunting Dad, *as shown in this detail. To
see more of Stewart's work, turn to the
gallery at the end of Chapter 3.*

Colors bar
Color (Hue) ring
Saturation Value
triangle
Color
rectangles
HSV/RGB
color readout

*The Standard Colors picker with Hue ring,
opened by expanding the Colors palette bar*

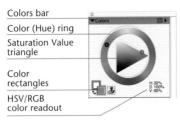

Hue Indicator Bar

*The Colors picker command menu opens so
you can switch between the Standard and
Small Colors pickers*

"COLOR, THE FRUIT OF LIGHT, is the foundation of the painter's
means of painting—and its language." Abstract painter Robert
Delaunay's observation mirrors our own appreciation of color as
an expressive and essential element of the visual arts. Getting the
most out of Painter's powerful color tools is an important first
step for those of us who work with "the fruit of light."

HUE, SATURATION AND VALUE

Painter's interface for choosing color is built around a model that
uses *hue, saturation* and *value* (HSV) as the three basic properties
of color. The program is designed so that you'll typically first
choose a hue, then alter it by changing its saturation or value.
Painter's Standard Colors picker and Small Colors picker are
designed to work with these properties, but the program also
allows you to work in RGB (red, green, blue) color space if you
prefer. Clicking the triangle on the left end of the Colors palette
bar (Window, Show/Hide Color Wheel) opens the HSV Colors. To
switch between Standard and Small Colors pickers, click the triangle at the top right of the Colors bar to access the pull-down
menu. To view RGB values rather than HSV, choose RGB Color by
clicking the triangle on the Colors bar. To open the Color Info
Palette where you can specify color using RGB sliders, click the
triangle at the top right of the Color Info palette bar.)

Hue. The term *hue* refers to a
predominant spectral color, such
as red or blue-green. Hue indicates a color's position on the
color wheel or spectrum, and also
tells us the color's temperature. A

QUICK SWITCH TO RGB

Click on the HSV color readout on the
Standard or Small Colors picker to
show color readings in RGB mode.
Click again to switch back to HSV.

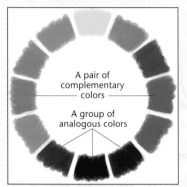

The Color Info palette with Red, Green and Blue sliders. (We moved the Color Info palette nearer to the Colors picker in the nested palette. To move it, drag the Color Info title bar.)

A pair of complementary colors

A group of analogous colors

A pigment-based color wheel

PRIMARY/SECONDARY COLORS

Two overlapping rectangles display the current Primary and Secondary colors. To exchange the Primary and Secondary colors in the Colors picker, click the "Swap" icon, or press the Shift and X keys.

Saturating a color

Desaturating a color

Creating a shade of a color

Creating a tint of a color

red-orange hue is the warmest color; a blue-green hue is the coolest. (Keep in mind, though, that temperatures are relative. Blue-violet is a cool color, but it warms up when it's placed next to blue-green.)

In the traditional pigment-based color system, red, yellow and blue are *primary* hues—colors that cannot be obtained by mixing. *Secondary* hues—green, orange and violet—are those colors located midway between two primary colors on the color wheel. Yellow-green, blue-violet and red-orange are examples of *tertiary* hues, each found between a primary and a secondary color.

Analogous hues are adjacent to each other on the color wheel and have in common a shared component—for instance, blue-green, blue and blue-violet. *Complementary* hues sit opposite one another on the color wheel. Red and green are complements, as are blue and orange. (Painter's Hue ring and bar are based on the RGB components of the computer screen, they don't exactly match a traditional pigment-based color wheel.)

To change hues in Painter's Standard Colors picker, drag the little circle on the Hue ring or click anywhere on the ring. Dragging and clicking also work with the Hue bar in the Small Color picker.

Saturation. Also known as *intensity* or *chroma*, *saturation* indicates a color's purity or strength. The most common way of changing a color's saturation is by adjusting the amount of its gray component. In the Color triangle, move the little circle to the left to desaturate a color, or to the right to saturate it. Fully or very saturated colors—those at or near the tip of the Color triangle—won't print the way they look on the screen. If you want to see colors closer to their printed equivalents while you paint, the Canvas, Color Management command can help. (See the "Color Management" tip on page 28 of this chapter and the *Painter 8 User Guide.*)

SAMPLING PAINT

While you're using many of Painter's other tools, you can temporarily switch to the Dropper tool and sample colors by holding down the Alt/Option key.

USING THE COLOR MIXER

New in Painter 8, the Color Mixer allows you to mix color as an artist would mix paint on a palette. Begin by clicking on one of the colors at the top of the palette (or choosing a color in the Color picker), and dab the colored paint onto the Mixer Palette using the palette's Brush tool. Add a second color and use either the Brush or the Palette Knife (selected in the illustration), to mix the two colors as we did here.

We mixed colors using the Palette Knife tool in the Color Mixer. The pop-out menu allows you to save Mixer Colors, add them to a Color Set, and more.

An example of atmospheric perspective. The illusion of distance is enhanced in this detail of Along Tomales Bay *because the distant hills are painted with reduced saturation and less value contrast.*

As you can see in this detail of 1872, *Richard Noble used saturated color, clear detail and strong contrast to paint a bright morning. To see more of Noble's work turn to the galleries at the end of Chapters 2 and 3.*

A study in value contrast, based on a drawing by Michelangelo

Value. A color's lightness or darkness is its *luminance* or *value*. To create a *tint* of a color (lightening it, or increasing its value), move the little circle higher in the Color triangle. To create a *shade* of a color (darkening it, or decreasing its value), move the little circle lower in the Color triangle.

PUTTING HSV TO WORK

Here are several practical suggestions and creative solutions for solving artistic problems using hue, saturation and value.

Reduce saturation and value to indicate distance. Artists have been creating *atmospheric* (or *aerial*) *perspective* in their work for thousands of years. The wall paintings of Pompeii in the first century B.C. show this technique. Hills we see in the distance have less intensity than nearer hills, and they also have less variation in value. This effect increases in hazy or foggy conditions. To depict this in your art, you can reduce the color saturation and value range as the landscape recedes from the foreground.

Use saturation to indicate time of day. At dawn or dusk, colors appear to be less saturated, and it becomes more difficult to distinguish colors. At noon on a bright sunny day, colors seem saturated and distinct.

Use color temperature to indicate distance. The eye puts warm colors in front of cool colors. For example, orange flowers in the foreground of a hedge appear closer than blue ones.

Create drama with light-to-dark value contrast. Baroque and Romantic period artists as diverse as Caravaggio, Zurbarán, Géricault and Rembrandt are known for their use of extreme light-to-dark contrast. They accomplished this by limiting their palette to only a few hues, which they either tinted with white or shaded by adding black. A close look at the shadows and highlights that these artists created reveals complex, modulated tone. Digital artists can use Painter's Apply Lighting feature (from Effects, Surface Control) to add a dramatic splash of contrast to an image and also to unify a painting's color scheme, although achieving genuine tonal complexity requires additional painting.

Use complementary colors to create shadows. The Impressionists Monet, Renoir and Degas frequently avoided the use of black in the shadow areas of their paintings. They embraced a more subjective view of reality by layering complementary colors to create luminous shadows.

Neutralize with a complement or gray. One way to tone down a hue is to paint on top of it with a translucent form of its complement. El Greco painted his backgrounds in this manner to draw attention to more saturated foreground subjects. Try painting with a bright green hue, then glaze over it with a reduced opacity of red. The result will be an earthy olive. You can also

To paint dramatic billowing clouds in View From Point Loma, *shown here as a detail, we blended color by using the Grainy Water variant of the Blenders.*

Simultaneous contrast at work. Notice how the gold looks brighter next to the dark blue than it does next to pink.

A landscape with figures, based on Mahana no atua (The Day of the God) *by Paul Gauguin*

neutralize a hue using shades of gray, as did the French artist Ingres. Although he often limited his palette to red, blue, gold and flesh tones, he created the illusion of a larger palette by adding varying proportions of gray and white.

Blending, pulling and thinning colors. Subtle changes in hue and saturation take place when colors are blended in a painting. You can use the Just Add Water, Grainy Water or Smudge variant of the Blenders brush (from the Brush Selector Bar) to blend, for instance, two primary colors (red and blue) to get a secondary color (violet). For a more dramatic blending, you can pull one color into another by using the Smear variant of the Blenders brush. Artists using traditional tools often thin paint by mixing it with an extender. In Painter, you get a similar effect by reducing a brush's Opacity in the Property Bar.

Draw attention with simultaneous contrast. If two complementary colors are placed next to one another, they intensify each other: Blue looks more blue next to orange, and white looks more white next to black. In the 1950s, Op artists used the principle of simultaneous contrast to baffle the eye. Advertising art directors understand the power of simultaneous contrast and use it to gain attention for their ads.

Use a family of colors to evoke an emotional response. You can create a calm, restful mood by using an analogous color theme of blues and blue-greens. Or develop another family of hues using reds and red-oranges to express passion and intensity. You can also use a color family to unite the elements of a composition.

Create your own color world. Post-Impressionist Paul Gauguin (among others) created a powerful, personal color language by combining several of the above techniques. He used warm, bright colors to bring a subject forward in his composition, and used cool, dark colors to convey distance and mystery. He also made the bright foreground colors seem brighter by surrounding them with darker, more subdued colors.

In addition to choosing color from the Color pickers you can sample color from an image by clicking with the Dropper tool, or, you can paint with color from another image (or clone source). To see how cloning color works, begin by making a clone. Open a file and choose File, Clone. In the Brush Selector Bar, choose the Impressionist Cloner variant of the Cloners. You can paint over the imagery, or you can delete the contents of the file and clone onto the blank canvas from the original. To read more about cloning, turn to "Cloning and Tracing" in Chapter 3.

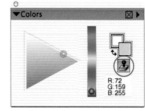

When the Clone Color box is checked, the Standard and Small Colors pickers are disabled

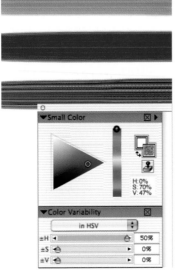

These brushstrokes were painted with the Round Camelhair variant of the Oils with the following settings in the Color Variability palette: top brushstroke, Hue slider only set to 50%; middle, Saturation slider only set to 50%; bottom, Value slider only set to 50%.

These brushstrokes were painted with the Diffuse Grainy Camel (top) and the Wash Bristle (bottom) variants of Water Color with a Hue variability of 10%.

These brushstrokes were painted with the Scratchboard Rake variant of the Pens with an increased Hue variability of 10% (top) and 50% (bottom). Each "tine" of this Rake brush can carry a different color.

PAINTING WITH MULTIPLE COLORS

Painter's Brushes palette has several brushes that can paint with more than one color at a time if you use the settings in the Color Variability palette (Window, Show Color Variability). Brushes with the Rake or Multi stroke type or the Bristle Spray, Camel Hair or Flat dab types have the capability to paint with multiple colors. The Van Gogh variant of the Artists brush and the Round Camel Hair variant of the Oils are examples.

Randomize colors with Color Variability. To see how multicolor works, open the Color Variability palette by clicking the triangle on the Color Variability bar. (Make sure that "in HSV" is chosen in the pop-up menu.) From the Brush Selector, choose the Round Camelhair variant of the Oils; its Camelhair dab type has the potential to carry a different color on each brush hair. Choose a color in the Color picker and begin painting. Then experiment by adjusting the Hue (± H), Saturation (± S) or Value (± V) slider in the Color Variability palette and painting again.

For transparent Water Color washes with variable color, try the Diffuse Grainy Camel and the Wash Bristle. Both of these brushes have the potential to carry a different color in each brush hair.

Also try the Scratchboard Rake variant of the Pens. The Scratchboard Rake incorporates the Rake stroke type; each "tine" of a Rake brush can paint with a different color. In the Color Variability palette, set Hue to 10% (for a subtle variation) or much higher (for a rainbow-like effect) and make brushstrokes on your image.

Using Color Variability based on a gradient. With Painter, you can paint with multiple colors from a gradient instead of using completely random Color Variability. To begin, set all the Color Variability sliders to 0; open the Color picker and set up the colors for a two-point gradient by clicking on the front color rectangle and selecting a color, then clicking on the back color rectangle and selecting a color. Open the Gradients palette by choosing Window, Show Gradients. In the Gradients palette, choose Two-Point from the pop-up menu. From the Brushes Selector Bar select Oils category and the Opaque Bristle Spray variant. In the Color Variability palette, choose From Gradient from the pop-up menu, then make brushstrokes on your image. If the brush does not immediately paint using the Color Variability from the gradient, click the little circle in the Color picker to help it to update.)

> ### COLOR VARIABILITY CAUTION
>
> Painter remembers the changes when you try out Color Variability, and this may cause confusing results later. After you've finished using Color Variability, set the Color Variability pop-up menu to "in HSV" and restore the Hue, Saturation and Value sliders to 0.

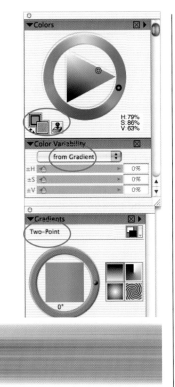

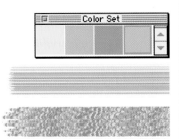

Brushstrokes painted with the Smeary Flat (above) and the Dry Ink (below) variants of the Brushes using Color Variability based on the Color Set shown here.

Brushstroke painted with the Opaque Bristle Spray variant of the Oils using Color Variability based on the current gradient.

Using Color Variability based on a color set. You can create a special Color Set containing a few colors and then use those colors when painting. Begin by opening the Color Variability palette; set Color Variability to "in HSV" and the ± H, ±S, and ±V sliders to 0. Open the Color Set palette and choose the Library Access button (the one with the picture of the Grid). The Color Sets palette will now be empty; it's ready for you to begin adding colors. Choose a color in the Color picker. Click on the Add Color to Color Set button (the "Plus"), to add the chosen color to the Color Set. Continue to select and add more colors by using the Colors picker and clicking the "Plus" button. Choose the Smeary Flat variant of the Oils, and in the Color Variability palette, set Color Variability to "from Color Set." Paint brushstrokes on your image. To learn more about color sets turn to "Keeping Colors in Color Sets," on page 29 and to "Capturing a Color Set," later in this chapter.

Change colors with stylus pressure. Use your pressure-sensitive stylus to paint in two colors. Start by choosing the Acrylics category and the Captured Bristle variant. In the Color Expression palette choose Pressure from the Controller pop-up menu. In the Colors picker, click on the front color rectangle and choose a bright blue color. Click the back color rectangle and select a rose color. If you paint with a light touch, you'll be painting in rose. If you press heavily, the stroke turns blue. (If the balance between the two colors seems uneven, choose Edit, Preferences, Brush Tracking (on the PC and on the Mac in 9.2.2) and Corel Painter 8, Preferences, Brush Tracking (in Mac OSX). Make a typical brushstroke in the Scratch Pad area, click OK, and try the graduated version of the Captured Bristle variant again.)

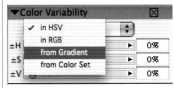

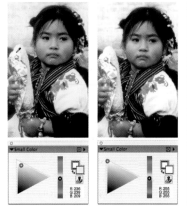

Before and after: Sampling in the image with the Dropper to determine the color cast of a bright highlight on the aluminum foil reveals these values: Red: 227, Green: 241, and Blue 213 (left); the corrected image (right) with pure white highlights shows Red, Green and Blue values of 255.

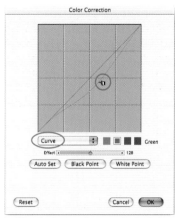

Pulling the Green color curve in the Color Correction dialog box to lessen the green cast in the image above. Light colors are represented at the upper right and dark colors in the lower left. The biggest change in color occurs at the point where you pull the curve. If you pull the dot, the color you sampled will be affected most. The Effect slider controls how much of the curve will change when you pull on it. Move the slider to the right to affect a broad range of tones. Move the slider to the left to affect a narrower range of tones.

MAKING COLOR ADJUSTMENTS

Painter offers several ways to modify color in scanned photos or in your art work *after* you have created it. To see the results of your choices in many of the dialog boxes that are involved in color adjustments, you'll need to click and drag in the Preview window.

Correct Colors. Do you see an unnatural color cast in your image? The Correct Colors, Curve feature can help you fix this problem. This feature is especially useful when working with scanned photos, for instance.

To adjust an image so that the brightest highlights are pure white, begin by analyzing the color cast. (To ensure that the front Color rectangle in the Colors picker will show the color you are about to sample, make sure that "in HSV" is chosen from the pop-out menu in the Color Variability palette.) Use the Dropper tool to sample a bright highlight in your image. In the Color picker, click

COMPLEMENTARY COLORS

The Curve mode of the Color Correction dialog box (Effects, Tonal Control, Correct Colors, Curve) and some other dialog boxes let you increase or decrease the Red, Green and Blue components of color. You can also adjust cyan, magenta and yellow by applying the opposite adjustments to their complements—Red, Green and Blue. To decrease yellow, increase blue; to decrease magenta, increase Green; and to decrease cyan, increase Red.

on the HSV values box to toggle to RGB values. Check the RGB values in the Color picker. In our example (shown at the left), the color and numbers show that the unwanted color cast is green, because the G value is higher than the R and B values. A bright white should have R, G and B values of 255 in the Color picker. Choose Effects, Tonal Control, Correct Colors and choose Curve from the pop-up menu in the Color Correction dialog box. Curve will allow you to adjust the individual RGB values. Click on the small square icon for the color that you want to adjust. (We clicked on the Green color icon—to constrain the adjustment to *only* the green values in the image.) Then, position the crosshair cursor over the diagonal line, and when you see the hand cursor appear, pull down and to the right. Pulling down (as shown) will decrease the selected color in the image. Click the Reset button to try out another adjustment without leaving the dialog box.

Adjust Colors. To change the hue, saturation or value of all of the colors in an image, choose Effects, Tonal Control, Adjust Colors. Experiment with the sliders and view the changes in the Preview window. Adjust Colors is also useful for quickly desaturating a full-color image—making it look black-and-white. To desaturate an image, move the Saturation slider all the way to the left.

Adjust Selected Colors. You may want to make color adjustments in particular color ranges of your image. Painter's Adjust Selected Colors feature lets you make dramatic changes (turning a

Using Adjust Selected Colors to neutralize a bright blue

blue sky yellow) or more subtle ones (removing the red cast from a subject's face). Choose Effects, Tonal Control, Adjust Selected Colors. When the dialog box opens, click in your image (*not* in the Preview window) on the color you want to change. Adjust the Hue Shift, Saturation and Value sliders at the bottom of the dialog box. When the targeted color is changed to the color you want, use low settings on the Extents sliders to limit the range of colors that are adjusted. Use the Feather sliders to adjust transitions between colors: 100% produces soft transition, 0% gives abrupt ones.

Color Overlay. Found under Effects, Surface Control, the Color Overlay dialog box lets you tint an image with a color using either a Dye Concentration model (which applies *transparent* color) or a Hiding Power model (which covers the image with the *opaque* color). With either model you can add texture by choosing Paper in the pop-up menu, as we did in the illustration at the left. When using the Dye Concentration model, adjust the Amount slider to control the density of the color from 0% for no effect to 100% or –100% for full transparent coverage. The Hiding Power model operates differently. You can add color using a plus value, or pull color out of an image using a minus value. Try this to see how it works: open a new image and use the Rectangular Selection tool to make a selection. Choose a yellow-green in the Color picker (approximately H 58%, S 92%, V 43%). Fill the selection using Effects, Fill, Current Color. Choose yellow in the Color picker (ours was H 50%, S 94%, V 70%) then choose Effects, Surface Control, Color Overlay, Using Uniform Color and Hiding Power. Move the Opacity slider to 100% to see the yellow completely cover the yellow-green. Finally, move the Opacity slider to –100% to the see some of the yellow disappear from the original green.

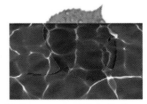

In this image, we applied the Darken composite method to the leaf layer.

Dye Concentration. With Effects, Surface Control, Dye Concentration you can add or remove pigment from your image. Setting the Maximum slider above 100% increases the density of the existing pigment. When you choose Paper in the Using menu, the Maximum slider controls the amount of dye on the peaks and the Minimum slider controls the amount of dye in the valleys of the texture.

PHOTO: PHOTODISC

We added colored texture to this photo with Color Overlay.

Susan LeVan used Effects, Tonal Control, Negative on the left side of the background of Guardians *as shown in this detail. After creating the negative side of the image, she drew over portions of the left side to make the character unique.*

Negative. Creating a negative of all or part of an image can have dramatic, artistic purposes—such as in the detail of Susan LeVan's illustration, at left. Choose Effects, Tonal Control, Negative to convert your image or a selected part of it.

Output Preview and Video Colors. Your monitor can display more colors than can be reproduced in the four-color printing process, and if you are creating images for video, some highly saturated colors will not make the transition from computer to video. It's a good idea to convert your out-of-gamut colors while you're in Painter so there won't be any surprises. Choose Canvas, Color Management or Effects, Tonal Control, Video Legal Colors, depending on whether your image is destined for paper or video. For more information about output for printing, turn to Chapter 12, "Printing and Archival Concerns."

COLOR MANAGEMENT

Painter 8 ships with a color management system that can help to ensure color consistency and the quality of output. Earlier versions of Painter have supported color management through the Kodak Color Management System (KCMS), and the controls have been improved with Painter 8.

The color management system allows you to move files between Painter, Photoshop and other programs while keeping the color consistent and to see an on-screen preview of how your color will look when printed on a specific device. Once it's been set up, the preview can be toggled on and off as you work. Access the Color Management dialog box by choosing Canvas, Color Management. You'll find controls that will help you to set up color matching between devices including a scanner, digital camera, your monitor and composite printer or proofer. To learn more about Painter's color management system, turn to "Color for Printing" in Chapter 12.

MORE COLOR TOOLS

Adding color with Gradations. Painter's powerful Gradients palette lets you fill selected areas with preset gradations or ones that you've created. (See "Adding Color and Gradations to Line Art" later in this chapter.) You can also colorize an image with a gradation using Express in Image from the pop-up menu at the right side on the Gradients palette. To see an example of this technique, turn to "Creating a Sepia-Tone Photo" in Chapter 6.

This is how Painter's Spectrum gradient appears in the Gradient Editor. When you click a square hue box above the Gradient the Color Hue pop-up menu appears. Here it's set to Hue Clockwise, resulting in a tiny spectrum below the square hue box.

The gradient editor is a powerful tool for creating custom color ramps. You can't use this tool to alter all of Painter's existing gradations. However, it is used primarily for creating new ones. Choose Window, Show Gradients to open the palette, then click the right triangle, and choose Edit Gradient from the pop-up menu to bring up the gradient editor. Select one of the triangular color control points and choose a color from the Color picker. The color ramp will update to reflect your choice. Add new color control points by clicking directly in the color bar; the triangular control points are sliders that can be positioned anywhere along the ramp. To delete a control point, select it and press the Delete

Linda Davick uses gradient fills to give her illustrations depth, as shown here in Mice. *Read about Davick's technique in "Adding Color and Gradations to Line Art" on page 30 of this chapter.*

CONSTRAINING BUCKET FILLS

You can use the Paint Bucket to fill an entire area of your image by clicking the Paint Bucket within the area, or you can constrain the fill into a rectangle. To create a rectangular filled area, press, hold and drag a marquee with the Paint Bucket. When you release the mouse or lift up on your stylus, the area will fill with color.

In H is for Hell-bent Haddocks *(shown here as a detail), Keith MacLelland used the Paint Bucket to create a background of filled squares. To see more of MacLelland's work, turn to the galleries in Chapters 2 and 3.*

key; click on the gradient bar to add a new control point. Clicking on any of the squares above the gradient displays the Color menu; experiment with the options available there to get quick rainbow effects in the section of the gradient indicated by the square. To store the new gradient in the Gradients palette, choose Save Gradient from the pop-up menu on the right end of the Gradients palette.

Coloring images. You can color images or selected parts of images using either Effects, Fill (Ctrl/⌘-F) or the Paint Bucket tool. The Fill command lets you fill your image with a color, a gradient, a clone source (if one is available), a pattern (if no clone source is available) or a weave. The Paint Bucket gives you the same fill options. (The Paint Bucket options appear on the Property Bar when you select the Paint Bucket tool.) Cartoonists and others who fill line art with color will want to explore the Lock Out Color feature (to preserve black line art, for example) made available by double-clicking on the Paint Bucket tool icon in the Tools palette. For more information about Lock Out Color and Cartoon Cell fills, see the *Painter 8 User Guide*.

Keeping colors in Color Sets. Painter can store your most frequently used colors in a Color Set. Painter Colors is the default set. Switch Color Sets by clicking on the Library button in the Color Set palette. You'll find more Color Sets (including several Pantone sets) in the Color Sets folder on the Painter 8 application CD-ROM. For more about Color Sets, turn to "Capturing a Color Set" on page 38. 🖌

NAMING AND FINDING COLORS

To name your colors so you can search for them by name, double-click on the color in the Color Set palette that you want to name, type a name and click OK. To view color names, click the right triangle on the Color Set bar and choose Display Name. To search for a named color in a set, click the Find Color in Color Set button (the binoculars near the top of the Color Set section).

	yellow
	orange
	purple
	blue

A Set with names displayed

RESTORING DEFAULT COLORS

To restore the default Color Set (called Painter Colors) after you've used or created another Color Set, choose Open Color Set from the pop-out menu and find the Painter Colors file in your Painter 8 folder on your hard disk.

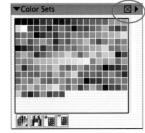

The Color Sets palette with Painter Colors as the current color set

Adding Color and Gradations to Line Art

Overview *Draw line art with the 1-Pixel Pen variant; use the Paint Bucket to fill areas with flat color and gradations; add highlights with the Airbrushes.*

LINDA DAVICK

Line art created with the 1-Pixel variant of the Pens brush, shown here as a detail

Filling the drawing with flat color

FILLING LINE ART WITH COLOR AND GRADATIONS is slick and efficient in Painter, using what children's book illustrator Linda Davick calls "the coloring-book technique." Davick employed the Paint Bucket tool when creating the illustration *Fish Fry* for Debbie Smith's *Beauty Blow-Up*.

1 Creating a black-and-white line drawing. From the Brush Selector Bar palette, choose the Pens, 1-Pixel variant. Choose Window, Show Brush Creator and in the General pane of the Brush Creator choose the Flat Cover subcategory. Flat Cover lets you draw a solid-color line, creating the necessary barriers for this technique that fills all neighboring pixels of the same color. Choose black in the Color picker and draw your line art, making sure all your shapes are completely enclosed with black lines. If you need to correct your work, switch the color to pure white in the Colors picker and erase.

2 Filling with flat color. To test color choices and tonal values, you can fill areas of your illustration with flat color. First open the Color Variability palette, choose "in HSV" from the pop-up menu and set the ± H, ± S and ± V sliders to 0. Choose the Paint Bucket tool, and in the Property Bar, click the Fill Image button and under the Fill menu Current Color. Turn off Anti-Alias. Choose a color, then click in the area of your drawing that you want to fill. Since the Paint Bucket fills all neighboring pixels of the same color, you can refill by choosing another color and clicking again. If you're filling small areas, it's important to know that the Paint Bucket's "hot spot" (where it fills from) is the tip of the red paint in the icon. Davick filled all areas except Zuba's (the pink poodle), face using this method.

3 Adding color ramps. To fill the background with a gradation, open the Gradients palette (Window, Show Gradients). Choose

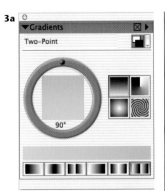

3a

Setting up the Two-Point linear gradient for the sky behind Zuba

3b

Filling the background with the gradient

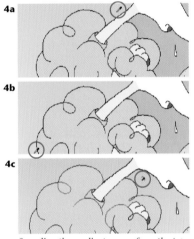

4a

4b

4c

Sampling the gradient across from the top of the area to be filled (a); sampling across from the bottom of the area to be filled (b); filling the area with the gradation (c). Repeat this process for each flat color (negative) area to be filled.

5

Adding dimension to Zuba's hair using the Digital Airbrush inside a selected area

Two-Point from the pop-up menu (top right of the palette) and click the Linear Gradient button (from the four Types buttons to the right of the direction ring), and set an angle for your fill by rotating the red ball around the direction ring. In the Color picker, choose colors for both the front and back Color rectangles. (Click on the front Color rectangle and select a color, then click on the back Color rectangle and select a color.) With the Paint Bucket chosen, in the Property Bar, click the Fill Image button, and from the Fill menu, choose Gradient. Finally, to apply the gradation, click in the area that you want to fill. Davick filled the largest background sky area with a linear gradation.

4 Duplicating color ramps. To duplicate the large background gradation in each of the smaller background shapes—to the right of Zuba, and under the ants—Davick created a new gradation using color sampled from areas in the background gradation. She then filled the smaller background shapes with the new gradation. If you need to do this on the "negative" shapes in your image, first check the Color picker to make sure that the Color rectangle that contains the starting color of your original gradation is selected. Choose the Dropper tool and position it over the gradation in your image at approximately the same height as the top of the negative area that you want to fill. Click in the gradation to sample the color. To sample the bottom portion of the gradation, select the other Color rectangle, then position and click the Dropper at about the same height as the bottom of the area to be filled. Click in the negative area using the Paint Bucket to fill with the new sampled gradation. (If you need to refill, undo the fill—Edit, Undo Paint Bucket Fill—before you fill again.)

5 Painting airbrush details. Davick finished the piece by painting with the Digital Airbrush variant of the Airbrushes within roughly circular selections to add details to Zuba's face and fur. You can make roughly circular selections using the Lasso tool by choosing the Lasso tool and dragging in your image. (To read more about selections, turn to the beginning of Chapter 4, "Selections, Shapes and Masks.") Now use the Digital Airbrush to add dimension. Paint along the edge of the animated selection marquee. Davick used the same Airbrush with unrestricted strokes to add other details in other areas, such as on the cat's face and paws. 🖌

Coloring a Scanned Illustration

Overview *Scan a traditional black-and-white pen drawing; clean up the scanned line art; use the Paint Bucket to fill areas with flat color; create texture and energy with a variety of brushes.*

WENDY MORRIS

The raw scan of the Rapidograph pen drawing

WENDY MORRIS'S WHIMSICAL DRAWING STYLE appears to be a quick, spontaneous expression; but her illustrations begin by drawing carefully with traditional pen and ink. In Morris's *Beeman*, the sky is vibrant and charged with frenetic bee energy. *Beeman* was colored with Paint Bucket fills and a variety of brushes.

1 Creating a pen drawing and scanning. Morris chose a bright white recycled drawing paper with a smooth finish and created a black-and-white line drawing using a conventional Rapidograph pen. She intended to use the *Beeman* illustration for a 6 x 8-inch greeting card design that would be printed with off-set lithography so she scanned the line drawing using grayscale mode at 100% magnification with a resolution of 300ppi. She saved the scan as a TIFF file and opened it in Painter, which automatically converted the grayscale art to RGB. To learn more about scanning and resolution, see Chapter 1, "Getting To Know Painter" and Chapter 12, "Printing and Archival Concerns."

2 Cleaning up the scan. Morris adjusted the contrast of the scanned line work using Brightness/Contrast. To make the adjustment on your scan, choose Effects, Tonal Control, Brightness/

Adjusting the Brightness and Contrast "beef up" the line work

2b

Cleaning up specks of black on the scan

3a

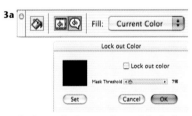

Setting up the Property Bar and the Lock Out Color dialog box to make Cartoon Cel fills

3b

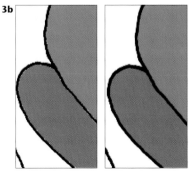

Color fills with halos (left), and color fills made with the Cartoon Cel method, showing no halos (right)

Contrast. When the dialog box appears, you can thicken or thin the line work by moving the Brightness slider (the bottom one of the two) to the left or to the right, respectively. Then, to get rid of any fuzziness along the edge that resulted from the Brightness change, increase the Contrast by moving the top slider to the right. (Keep in mind that moving it too far to the right can create a pixelated edge rather than a smooth one.) Each time you move one of the sliders, you can see the tonal adjustment on your image.

Then Morris cleaned up the specks of black on the scan by choosing white in the Colors palette, and touching up areas with the Pen and Ink variant of the Pens found in Ver 5 Brushes, in the Brushes folder on the Painter 8 Application CD-ROM. (To read about loading libraries, turn to "Libraries and Movers" in Chapter 1, "Getting To Know Painter.") She switched to black color, and used the pen to repair any breaks in the black lines. (The lines must be completely solid to constrain the Paint Bucket fills that follow in Step 3.)

3 Filling areas with flat color. After Morris had adjusted the contrast of the line art, to establish the color theme, she used the Paint Bucket tool to fill the flower petals, stems and sky with flat color. When the Paint Bucket is used to fill areas within scanned black-and-white line art, halos (partially unfilled areas) can appear along the edges of the anti-aliased black lines. In Painter 8 there are at least two ways to prevent these halos: One approach involves layering a copy of your original line work over a thinned version of the lines and filling the thinner version with color. This way any halos that develop on the layer below will be hidden by the original, thicker lines in the layer above. This method is easy to understand and carry out, and it makes it easy to change colors later if you want to. The technique is described in the "Trapping Fills Using a Transparent Layer" tip on page 35. However, if you feel that using extra layers would get in the way of the "painterly" experience of applying color to a single layer of canvas, the Cartoon Cel method may be the technique for you. It works by allowing the fill color to "seep into" the anti-aliasing pixels at the edge of the line work, leaving no halo. This method is described next.

There are three essential parts to the Cartoon Cel fill method: (1) making a selection based on luminance, (2) setting the Paint Bucket's Mask Threshold and filling criteria and (3) choosing a color and filling.

First select the black lines in the image using Select, Auto Select, Using Image Luminance, and click OK.

Second, in the Tools palette, double-click the Paint Bucket to open the Lock Out Color dialog box and set the Mask Threshold low—moving the slider to a point between 7% and 14% usually works well. Click OK to close the dialog box. In the Property Bar, click the Cartoon Cel button, and under the Fill menu, choose Current Color.

3c

The petals and stems filled with color

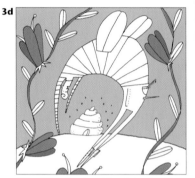

3d

After filling the sky with a flat color fill

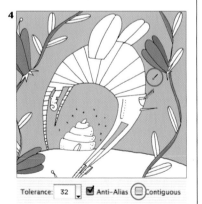

4

| Tolerance: | 32 | ☑ Anti-Alias | ◉ Contiguous |

Using the Magic Wand to select the sky. This detail of the Property bar shows the Contiguous box unchecked.

Third, open the Color Variability palette, choose "in HSV" from the pop-up menu and set the (± H), (± S) and (± V) sliders to 0. This will allow you to choose a flat color in the Colors section. After choosing a color, click with the Paint Bucket in one of the white spaces enclosed by the black lines. Then examine the resulting color fill. (To get a better look at the edge, you can choose Select, Hide Marquee. You can also zoom in by clicking on the image with the Magnifier tool.) If the fill has overrun the lines, the Mask Threshold is set too low. On the other hand, if you see a halo at the edge, the setting is too high. If you need to refill, first undo the fill—Edit, Undo—and then change the Mask Threshold setting and fill again. Once you have a satisfactory fill, you should be able to use the same Mask Threshold setting throughout your drawing.

Morris filled the flower petals with three shades of a purple-pink color. Then she filled the stems and sky with other colors.

4 Making a selection with the Magic Wand. In preparation for the next step, when she planned to paint lively brushstrokes across the sky, Morris isolated the entire sky area (based on its color) by making a selection using the Magic Wand. To select all of the blue sky areas at once, she chose the Magic Wand in the Tools palette, unchecked the Contiguous check box on the Property Bar, and clicked on a blue sky area in her image. To read more about the Magic Wand and selections, turn to the beginning of Chapter 4, "Selections, Shapes and Masks."

5 Painting with brushes. Morris used the Dropper tool to sample sky color in her image, then she used the Variable Flat variant of the Oils to paint "helter-skelter style" brushstrokes across the sky. The Variable Flat incorporates enhanced Color Variability, which allowed the value of the color to change subtly as she painted. For more subtle brushstrokes, she lowered the opacity using the Opacity slider on the Property Bar.

6 Adding texture and details. After completing the flat color fills and the brushwork in the sky, Morris used the Dirty Marker variant of the Felt Pens to modulate color in the plant stems, then she used a low-opacity Digital Airbrush variant of the Airbrushes to paint soft shadows on the leaves and stems. To add texture to the ground, she used the Scratchboard Rake variant of the Pens.

Next, Morris added movement and energy to the bee swarm and the beeman's stinger. She chose black in the Colors section and used the Pixel Dust variant of the Pens to paint spiraling strokes behind the bee's stinger and above the hive. (The Pixel Dust pen is located in the Ver 5 Brushes library, on the Painter 8 Application CD-ROM.)

5

Painting on the sky with free brushstrokes

6a

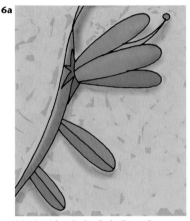

Morris airbrushed soft shadows along edges of the foliage.

6b

The image with fills and brushwork texture, prior to adding Pixel Dust to the bee swarm

Morris finished the piece using the Digital Airbrush to add more highlights and shadows to the bee, plants and flowers. She airbrushed a soft drop shadow along some of the edges on the beeman and the flowers. For more subtle brushstrokes, she lowered the opacity of all of the brushes (except the Pixel Dust pen), using the Opacity slider on the Property Bar. The completed illustration can be seen at the top of the page 32.

TRAPPING FILLS USING A TRANSPARENT LAYER

This method of coloring line art uses a transparent layer that contains slightly thicker lines to trap, or hide the edges of, the fills on the image canvas below. First, correct the contrast of your line art using Effects, Tonal Control, Brightness/Contrast, and retouch any black specks, as described in step 2 of "Coloring a Scanned Illustration" on pages 32 and 33.

Select the black line art by choosing Select, Auto Select, Using Image Luminance. When the selection marquee appears, hold down Alt/Option (to copy), and choose Select, Float to make a transparent layer containing only the line art. (Layer 1 will appear in the Layers section of the Objects palette.) In the Layers section, turn off the visibility of the Layer 1 by clicking its eye icon off, then target the Canvas layer by clicking on its name. Make the lines thinner on the canvas, by choosing Effects, Tonal Control, Brightness/Contrast, and moving both sliders to the right enough to thin the lines but not enough to make breaks in them (you may have to experiment with settings, depending on the thickness of your lines).

Now choose the Paint Bucket tool, and in the Property Bar, click the Image button and from the Fill menu choose Current Color. In the Color picker, choose a new color, then click the Paint Bucket in a white area of the canvas. To complete the "trap" on your fill, toggle Layer 1's visibility back on by clicking its eye icon, and choose Multiply in the pop-up Composite Method menu at the top of the Layers section. You can inspect the result with the Magnifier tool. (To read more about Layers, turn to Chapter 5, "Using Layers.")

The Layers palette

Image canvas showing the flat color fills with "halos"

Image with Layer 1 in Multiply mode and with its visibility turned on

Coloring a Woodcut

Overview *Create black-and-white art; tint the art with sepia; float it and apply the Gel Composite Method; view the black-and-white art as you add a colored texture and brush work to the original canvas layer.*

Phillips' black-and-white drawing

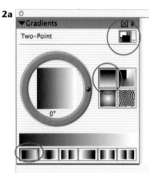

Setting up the gradient

Applying Express in Image

HERE'S A CREATIVE WAY TO ADD COLOR to black-and-white art, a favorite technique of artist Chet Phillips. To paint *Wild Life*, Phillips used the Gel Composite Method, which makes the white areas of a layer appear transparent. He colored the image using a limited palette of browns and warm grays, with accents of green and gold.

1 Creating black-and-white art. Phillips created a black-and-white drawing in Painter as follows: Start a new document with a white background. Choose black for the front color square in the Colors picker, then choose Effects, Fill (Ctrl/⌘-F) using Current Color. Click OK. Use white and the Scratchboard Tool variant of the Pens to "etch" into the black fill, with the look of a rough woodcut in mind.

2 Tinting the line art sepia. Phillips tinted the black lines with a subtle dark brown to warm up the line drawing. To give your drawing a sepia color in Painter, choose a very dark brown in the Color picker, and set up the Gradients palette to apply a two-point gradient to your image as follows: If the Gradients palette is not open, choose Window, Show Gradients. Choose the Two-point gradation from the resource list menu. On the palette front, click the Linear Gradient button and choose the Left to Right direction button. To apply the gradient, click the right triangle on

3a

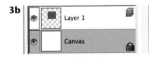

The Layers palette showing the active line drawing layer

3b

The Canvas layer is selected

4a

Using the Paint Bucket tool to fill the selected area of the Canvas

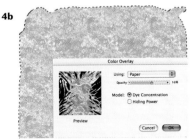

4b

Applying Color Overlay to add a colored texture to the Canvas

5

Using the line art as a guide, Phillips added color to the animals on the Canvas.

the Gradients palette and choose Express in Image. Accept the default settings and click OK.

3 Making a layer with transparent white areas. Select All (Ctrl/⌘-A), choose the Layer Adjuster tool and click once on the image to float it. The image is now floating over a white background. In the Layers palette, choose Gel from the Composite Method pop-up menu. This method makes the white areas of the layer transparent, which will allow any color you will add to the background in Steps 4 and 5 to completely show through without affecting the black in the layer.

4 Adding color and texture to the background. Phillips created a textured ground with an irregular edge to use as a basis for applying color with pastels.

Before beginning to color your background, click the Canvas layer's name in the Layers palette. This makes sure that you'll be working on the background. (To view either layer without the other, toggle the eye icon to the left of the layer name.)

To make an irregular-edged area, choose the Lasso tool from the Tools palette and press, hold and drag to create an irregular selection boundary, which will constrain the colored fill. (For more about selections, turn to Chapter 4, "Using Selections, Shapes, and Masks.")

Choose a very light cream color in the Color picker, and select the Paint Bucket tool in the Tools palette. In the Property Bar, click the Fill Image button; from the Fill menu choose Current Color; and turn on Anti-Alias (for a smooth edge on the edges of your filled area). Click inside the selected area with the Paint Bucket.

After applying the cream color, Phillips added a transparent colored texture. Begin by choosing a dark brown color in the Colors picker and a texture in the Papers palette (Window, Show Papers) (Phillips used the Nice Surface texture from the Etched and Eroded library on the Painter 8 Wow! CD-ROM). Choose Effects, Surface Control, Color Overlay. In the Using menu choose Paper, click the Dye Concentration button and set the Opacity at about 16%. Click OK. Now, deselect the area by choosing Select, None. (Ctrl/⌘-D)

5 Painting on the background. To render the background, Phillips chose a color palette that included rich browns, golds and grays. Using the Artists Pastel Chalk variant of Pastels, he took advantage of the brush's texture-sensitive ability to bring out the Nice Surface texture (see step 4), which was chosen in the Papers section. Choose the Pastels category in the Brush Selector Bar and from the variant menu choose Artist Pastel Chalk. Choose Restore Default Variant from the pop-out menu on right side of the Brushes Selector Bar to restore the variant to its default. Now choose a color in the Color picker and begin painting. If you need to edit the black areas, click on the black-filled layer's name in the Layers palette and then paint.

Capturing a Color Set

Overview *Capture color from a reference image using the Dropper; build and customize a Color Set; use the Color Set to paint a new image.*

1a

The reference photograph

1b

The Color Variability palette showing ± H, ± S and ± V set to 0

1c

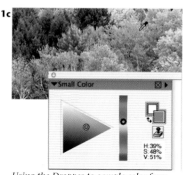

Using the Dropper to sample color from the image

2

Choosing Create New Empty Color Set in the Color Sets palette

IF YOU'RE PLANNING A SERIES OF ILLUSTRATIONS based on the same color theme, you'll find Painter's Color Sets invaluable. Use this technique of sampling color from a photo or painting to quickly build a selective palette of colors as we did here prior to creating the pastel painting *Tienda Verde*.

1 Sampling the color. Open the image that contains the color range you want. Before you begin to sample the color, open the Color Variability palette (Window, Show Color Variability), choose "in HSV" from the pop-up menu and set the (± H), (± S) and (± V) sliders to 0. (This will assure that the colors sampled will be pure color instead of variegated.) Now choose the Dropper tool and click it on a colored pixel in the image. The Colors picker will display the color. If the displayed color isn't the one you want, you can click or drag the Dropper around your image. The Color picker will update to show the new color.

2 Creating a Color Set. Now click on the Color Sets section name to open the Color Sets palette, and click on the Library Access button (the Grid). From the pop-up menu choose Create New Empty Color Set. The Color Set palette now be empty. Click on the Add Color button (the "Plus" in the Color Set section) to add the selected color to the Color Set. Continue to sample and add more colors by clicking the Dropper and the Plus button. To save your colors, click on the right triangle on the Color Sets palette bar and choose Save Color Set from the menu, navigate to the Painter 8 application folder to store your set, name the set and click Save. To use the new Color Set it can be reopened by selecting it in the Painter application folder and clicking the Open button. We named ours "Autumn Color."

3 Arranging the Color Set display. You can change the layout of your colors in the Color Set to fit your drawing environment. To change the shape of the individual color squares, click

3a

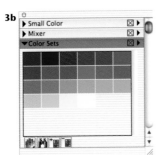

Entering the pixel size in the Customize dialog box

3b

The completed Autumn Color Set

4

Applying colored brushstrokes with the Square Chalk using the Autumn Color Set

on the right triangle on the Color Sets bar and choose Swatch Size to display choices. If you don't see a size that you like, choose Customize. We built our Color Set of 32 x 24-pixel-wide squares.

4 Using your new colors. To paint with the new Color Set, start a new file, click on a color in the set, choose a brush and begin painting. We drew a sketch using a dark blue-gray from our set with the Cover Pencil variant of Pencils, and added brushstrokes in other colors using the variants of the Chalk brush.

AUTOMATIC COLOR SET TOOLS

Painter offers four automatic color set building features: New Color Set from Image, New Color Set from Selection, New Color Set from Layer and New Color Set from Mixer. Using these tools, you can quickly build a color set by extracting every color from an image, selection, layer or the Mixer. (These features are useful if you want to sample every color, but they don't offer quite the same control as sampling individual colors with the Dropper.) To make a color set based on a selected area of your image, begin by opening the Color Sets palette by clicking the Color Sets palette bar name. Open an image, and make a selection (as we did here with the Rectangular Selection tool). In the Color Sets palette, click the Library Access button (the Grid) to display the pop-up menu and choose New Color Set from Selection. Painter will generate the color set. After our color set was made, we displayed the colors in dark-to-light order by clicking the right arrow on the Color Sets palette bar and choosing Sort Order from the pop-up menu, then choosing LHS (Light, Hue and Saturation) from the menu. Automatically generated color sets often have several colors that are very similar. To remove a color, click on it in the working Color Sets and then click the Delete Color From Color Set button (the "Minus") in the Color Sets section. To save your colors, click on the right triangle on the Color Sets palette bar and choose Save Color Set from the menu, navigate to the Painter 8 application folder to store your set, name the set and click Save. To use the new Color Set it can be reopened by selecting it in the Painter application folder and clicking the Open button.

CHER THREINEN-PENDARVIS

An active rectangular selection shown on Forked Path *(top left). Choosing New Color Set from Selection in the Color Sets palette (top right); choosing LHS in the Sort Order menu; Show Grid is enabled in the pop-out menu; and the brightly colored color set (bottom left.)*

■ Artist **Richard Noble** successfully re-creates the look of traditional acrylic using Painter. He generally begins by importing a reference photograph into Painter to use as a template. For these two paintings of Mendocino, he roughed in the color with the Sargent Brush variant of the Artists brush and the Round Camelhair variant of the Oils. Both of these brushes allowed Noble to move paint around on the canvas; he also blended color using the Palette Knife variant (Palette Knives). He added details with Artist Pastel Chalk (Pastels) and a tiny Digital Airbrush (Airbrushes). Noble prints his pieces on canvas, then stretches and finishes them with a clear glaze and touches of acrylic paint.

In *Fog* (above), Noble used a rustic, low-saturation palette and expressive brush work to create the foggy atmosphere. He painted highlights and shadows with subdued color and with looser detail.

In *1872* (right), Noble depicted the bright light of a sunny morning. Using the Sargent Brush and the Round Camelhair, he developed strong light-to-dark contrast. Then he used a small brush to paint fine detail in the shaded areas of the foreground flowers as well as in the sunlit areas of the painting.

■ **Dennis Orlando's** sensitive use of
light combined with layered color in the
shadowed areas in his paintings has
earned him the name "The Modern
Impressionist."

Orlando began *Mission Courtyard Rough*
with the Artist Pastel Chalk variant of
Pastels. To establish a mood of mid-day,
he used saturated colors and a varied
palette with deep shadow colors and
bright highlights. He laid color in with
the Artist Pastel Chalk using increased
Color Variability to create activity in the
color, then he pulled and blended colors
into one another using the Grainy Water
variant of the Blenders brush. In areas

where he wanted to preserve more of the
modulated color, he reduced the Opacity
of the Grainy Water variant, then
continued to blend and pull the color.
For the look of wet paint, he used a
modified Round Camel Hair variant and
the Smeary variants of Oils. These
brushes allowed him to add color and
blend as he painted. Finally, for the look
of wet oil paints and shimmering light in
areas of the painting, he painted smaller
curved brushstrokes using the Smeary
brushes. This brushwork is most evident
in the highlights and in the foliage near
the top of the painting.

■ **Fiona Hawthorne** creates wild and imaginative illustrations with a strong graphic feel and vibrant, saturated color.

Shots magazine commissioned Hawthorne to create **Breaking China** (left) and **Advertising in Korea** (below), for articles focusing on creativity moving forward with technology. She began the illustrations by sketching with the Pens, Pencils and Oils variants. Then she added graphic details.

Keeping in mind the theme of the article (China finding a new creative foundation in a very fast-moving economy), Hawthorne created the bold, expressive illustration, *Breaking China*. For the bright-colored strokes on the buildings, she used the Retro Dots variant of the Graphic Design brushes (loaded from the Brushes folder on the Painter 8 CD 2 CD-ROM). Then to add more texture, she pasted in a few bits of images (for instance, for the image on the TV sets, she scanned her own Deng Xiaoping watch and photos of a TV). She selected the watch element layer and increased its saturation using Effects, Tonal Control, Adjust Colors, then duplicated it several times. Finally, she drew over the scanned elements with the Thick and Thin variant of Pencils so that they matched the brushwork in the illustration.

For *Advertising in Korea*, Hawthorne was inspired by the fact that broadband Internet access at home, the latest mobile phones and 15-second TV commercials are mainstream in South Korea. So she created an image that suggested a link to the new products, ideas and the freedom of youth. She used a large Scratchboard Tool (Pens) to lay int he face, then she sketched a few loose brushstrokes using the Retro Dots variant to suggest the hair and chest. Next, she used the Pen tool to draw shapes for the stars, which she duplicated and scaled. Then she downloaded a picture of the Korean flag to use as a graphic in the necklace. She copied and pasted the flag image into her file as a layer and duplicated it, then positioned the flags using the Layer Adjuster tool.

■ "I want people to see the intricacies of lines, color variations, and the subtle texture patterns that inhabit my paintings," says illustrator **Keith MacLelland**. In his illustrations he communicates the fun he has when creating his art. He began both images by making a sketch in Painter with the Flattened Pencil and 2B variants (Pencils), then refined the drawings using the Scratchboard Tool variant of the Pens, Oils, Blenders and Oil Pastels.

MacLelland created *IT Carnival* (right), for *Philly Tech Magazine*. "The illustration depicts a time when the IT industry was taking hard hits," says MacLelland, "and while some folks kept taking hits, they just would not stay down. There was hope." MacLelland used a palette of pastel colors accented by brighter pink, yellow, red and green colors to help communicate the theme of hope.

To create the feeling of an old carnival poster that showed a history of years of use, MacLelland incorporated a custom texture that he had made from a scan of a piece of furniture he had crackle-painted. To bring out the texture in specific areas (for instance, the clothing), he used a texture-sensitive brush, the Square Chalk variant of Chalk.

For *Scooter Fish* (below), MacLelland also chose pastel colors, accented by thick and thin outlines that he treated with colored texture. To add texture to the lines, he selected the lines based on their color using the Magic Wand, then he lightened them using Effects, Surface Control, Dye Concentration, and applied texture (Effects, Surface Control, Apply Surface Texture, Using Paper). The fish was painted with Oils, Oil Pastel and Chalk variants.

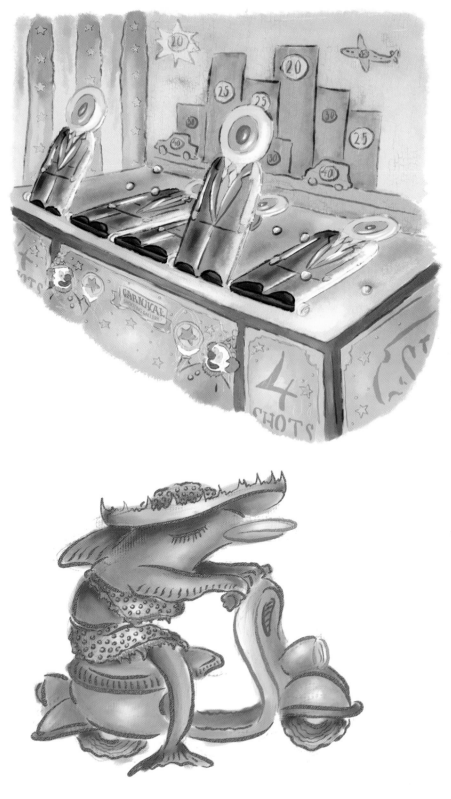

PAINTING WITH BRUSHES

This detailed illustration for Scholastic Press shows Karen Carr's refined digital oil painting technique, achieved by using Chalk, Blenders and Oils variants. See more of Carr's work in the gallery at the end of this chapter.

PAINTER'S BRUSHES ARE THE PROGRAM'S HEART: Without them, Painter would be a lot like other image editors. What sets Painter apart is the way it puts pen to paper and paint to canvas—the way its brushes interact with the surface below them. Here's a primer on getting the most from Painter's brushes.

Painting basics. If you're new to Painter, follow these steps to jump right in and begin painting. Create a new file (File, New). If the Brush Selector Bar is not open, choose Window, Show Brush Selector Bar to open it; or double-click the Brush tool in the Toolbox. (For more brush choices, you can click the tiny arrow to the right of the brush category icon to choose a new brush from the pop-up menu.) Choose Acrylics from the brush category pop-up menu. Then to select a color, choose Window, Show Colors. Click in the Color picker's Hue ring or bar and in its triangle to choose a color for your painting. Click the Paper Selector icon near the bottom of the Toolbox. (It's the top left button in the group of six buttons at the bottom of the Toolbox). Now click the Papers icon to open the Papers list and click a paper swatch to change the texture from Painter's default. Paint a few strokes on the image canvas. Experiment by changing brushes, colors and paper textures as you paint. It's also possible to paint on a layer or a mask instead of the Canvas. Painting on masks is covered in Chapter 4 "Selections, Shapes and Masks, and painting on layers is covered in Chapter 5, "Using Layers."

Brush
category
icon

arrow
to open
brush
category
menu

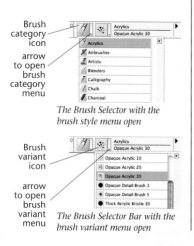

The Brush Selector with the brush style menu open

Brush
variant
icon

arrow
to open
brush
variant
menu

The Brush Selector Bar with the brush variant menu open

YOUR MOST RECENT BRUSHES

Painter's new Tracker palette remembers the most recent brushes that you've used. To open the palette, choose Window, Show Tracker. The brushes that you've used during your current Painter work session will be present in the Tracker window. To choose another brush from the palette, click on it.

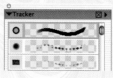

This detail of Roses *shows brushstrokes painted with custom variants based on the Round Camelhair and Opaque Flat variants of the Oils.*

Above: Script drawn with a pressure-sensitive stylus using the Calligraphy variant of Calligraphy. Below: Choosing the Calligraphy variant from the variant pop-up menu.

A lower-opacity brush will allow you to build up color slowly with more sensitivity. This technique was used to paint the coastal hills in Punta San Antonio.

Brush styles. Brush *categories* are shown as the mark-making tool icons on the Brush Selector Bar. To choose a brush category, you can click on the small arrow to the right of the brush category icon to display a pop-up list, then choose a new category, such as the Pens. Brush categories are at the top level of organization for mark-making tools in Painter; they are like the *containers* that hold the individual brushes, pens, chalk and other painting and drawing implements.

Brush variants. Every brush *category* has its own *variants* or varieties, so every time you choose a different brush category, the list of variants changes. Brush variants appear in the pop-up menu to the *right* of the brush category menu in the Brush Selector Bar. For instance, within the Pens are several variants, such as the Smooth Ink Pen, Scratchboard Tool and Thick n Thin Pen. To choose the Smooth Ink Pen variant of the Pens, click the variant pop-up menu and choose Smooth Ink Pen.

Saving and restoring variants. While many artists will be content to use a few of the many brush variants that come standard with the program, others will create dozens of their own. Even if you're an intuitive artist, you'll probably find yourself wanting a custom brush. (In-depth information can be found in "Building Brushes" on page 57.)

When you make modifications to a brush, Painter remembers the custom settings. Still, it's a good idea to save your custom brushes under their own names and to preserve Painter's default brushes. If you've changed settings and want to switch back to the default, choose Restore Default Variant from the triangle menu at the right side of the Brush Selector Bar. To *replace* a default brush with your custom settings, choose Set Default Variant from the triangle menu. **Caution:** After this choice, the only way to restore Painter's original default variant is by reinstalling the Painter Brushes file as described in "Restoring Default Brushes," below.

If you've made changes to a brush variant, and you'd like to store it in the Brush Selector Bar, first check that all your settings

---

RESTORING DEFAULT BRUSHES

To delete *all* cached variants and restore brushes to their original state, hold down the Alt/Option key and from the menu on the right side of the Brush Selector Bar choose Restore Default Variant. (Keep in mind, if you've used Set Default Variant to save your own defaults, this command will restore to the *new* default you set.) To preserve your Painter Brushes with modifications and also have access to the original default set, open your Painter application folder and open the Brushes folder. Rename the Painter Brushes folder. We named ours "Painter Brushes 2." Then to restore the default Painter Brushes from the Painter 8 Application CD-ROM, open the Default Content Files folder on the CD-ROM, open the Brushes folder and copy the Painter Brushes folder into the Brushes folder within your Painter 8 application folder. To replace only a specific brush category, you would open the Painter Brushes folder within your Painter 8 application folder instead of renaming it, then select the category on the Painter 8 Application CD-ROM and copy it into your Painter Brushes folder.

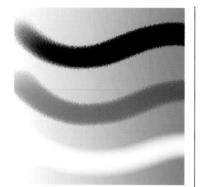

Switch methods to make dramatic changes in brush characteristics. Here we've applied the Waxy Crayons variants of Crayons over a gradient using the default Buildup method (top), Cover method (center) and Eraser method (bottom).

The Gritty Charcoal variant of Charcoal was applied using various Subcategory settings: the anti-aliased default Grainy Hard Cover (top); the pixelated Grainy Edge Flat Cover (middle); and the soft-edged Soft Cover (bottom).

Papers

Coarse Cotton Canvas

230 Rows
230 Columns

100%
154%
50%

Controls on the Papers palette allow adjustment of the Scale, Contrast and Brightness of textures, as shown here.

You can quickly check settings for the current brush variant using the Property Bar (Window, Show Property Bar). Settings for the Tapered Flat variant of the Oils category are displayed below. To change brush settings (such as Size) without opening the Brush Creator, click on a the tiny arrow to the left to access the setting pop-up and drag the slider to the right to increase the setting or drag to the left to decrease it.

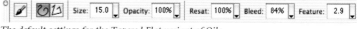

The default settings for the Tapered Flat variant of Oils.

are the way you want them. Then choose Save Variant from the triangle pop-up menu on the Brush Selector Bar, name the variant and click OK. Your new variant will appear in the variant list for that brush category and will stay there, even after you leave the program, until you remove it by selecting it and then choosing Delete Variant from the triangle pop-up menu.

Methods. *Methods* are the backbone of many brush variants, including brushes that users of earlier versions of Painter know and love. To see the method for a specific brush variant, such as the Artist Pastel Chalk, open the Brush Creator palette's General section by choosing Window, Show Brush Creator and then clicking the name of the

THE NEW BRUSH CREATOR

Painter's new Brush Creator includes advanced features for building brushes, including Randomizing and Transposing them. The General section of the Stroke Designer pane is shown in this detail.

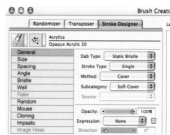

General pane. A brush variant's Method setting controls how the paint will interact with the background and with other paint. For instance, by default the Felt Pens variants use the Buildup method, meaning that overlapping strokes will darken. The Chalk variants use the Cover method by default, which means that strokes—even light-colored ones—will cover other strokes. You can, however, switch the method for the variant that you design. For example, you can save a Cover method variant of the Felt Pens.

Subcategories. While each method gives a radically different effect to a brush, the *subcategories*, or submethods, make more subtle changes, affecting the edges of brush strokes. Subcategories that include the word *Flat* produce hard, aliased strokes with pixelated edges. Those that include the word *Hard* give smoother strokes. Strokes made using *Soft* subcategories appear with feathered edges. Strokes with the word *Grainy* in their subcategory setting will be affected by the active paper texture. Strokes that

Janet Martini added interest to her India *painting—maximizing the interaction between brush and virtual texture in Painter—by exaggerating the size of the texture. Before painting with Water Color and Pens variants, she adjusted the Scale slider in the Papers palette.*

contain the word *Edge* give a thicker, stickier look; *Variable* refers to strokes that are affected by tilt and direction.

Paper textures. "Grainy" brush methods will reveal the paper texture you've selected in the Papers palette. You can use Painter's standard papers or create your own (see "Applying Scanned Paper Textures," on page 104). Adjust the Grain slider on the Property Bar to vary the intensity of the grain revealed by your brushstrokes. For most of Painter's brushes, a lower Grain setting means that *less of the color will penetrate the grain*, so your strokes will actually look grainier (See "Grain Penetration" below.)

CONTINUOUS-STROKE BRUSHES

Using *continuous-stroke* technology, many of Painter's brushes paint faster than dab-based brushes. These brushes render brushstrokes using a bundle of continuous, anti-aliased one-pixel lines. Because the stroke is composed of continuous lines instead of overlapping dabs, the computed brushes can produce smoother, more realistic brushstrokes than dab-based brushes can. Additionally, each brush hair has the ability to carry its own well of color. When an artist uses a traditional brush, the bristles often get contaminated by the colors of wet paint on the canvas. When the brush touches a neighboring color, it affects the paint along the edges of the new brushstroke. When using traditional media, artists often use this technique to mix color on a conventional color palette, or on the canvas itself. In Painter this technique is known as *brush loading*. Some brushes (the Round Camelhair and the Tapered Flat variants of the Oils, are examples) have this capability built into them. When painting with dab-based brushes without the built-in loading capability, you can activate Brush Loading. Open the Brush Creator palette by choosing Window, Show Brush Creator (Ctrl/⌘-B), click the Stroke Designer tab and then click on the Well. In the Well window, enable the Brush Loading checkbox. (You can also activate Brush Loading for brushes created in earlier versions of Painter.)

In addition to speed and brush-loading features, Painter incorporates advanced input technology (such as tilt and bearing) from

Detail of Agave Shawii, *painted with the Round Camelhair variant. The Round Camelhair allows for more color "activity" when painting because each brush hair can paint with its own color. For more information turn to "Painting With Multiple Colors" on page 24 of Chapter 2.*

Curling Tendrils created using Painter's Pattern Pen

These quick sketches of Little Doll *were drawn using the Cover Pencil variant on Italian Water Color paper with a Wacom pressure-sensitive tablet and stylus and a laptop.*

pressure-sensitive tablet manufacturers such as Wacom. Most brushes in Painter are able to take advantage of this capability.

Rendered dab brushes. These brushes are very responsive and smooth and they have the ability to paint with characteristics such as a gradients or a patterns in addition to color. The Smooth Ink Pen and Grad Pen variants of the Pens use rendered dabs. For more detailed information about using rendered dab types turn to "Building Brushes" on page 57.

Pattern Pen brushes. In addition to painting with color, Painter includes several kinds of media application—for instance, brushes that paint with gradients or patterns. To make a sketch like the Curling Tendril example at the left, in the Brush Selector Bar, choose the Pattern Pens category and the Pattern Pen Masked variant. Click the Pattern Selector near the bottom of the Toolbox, choose Curling Tendrils from the list, and make curved strokes with the Pattern Pen on your image. (For more information about special-effects brushes that paint using a pattern or other source, turn to "Building Brushes" on page 57, and to Chapter 7, "Exploring Special Effects.")

EMULATING TRADITIONAL TECHNIQUES

Here's a brief description of several traditional art techniques and how to re-create them in Painter. One or two techniques for each medium are outlined as a starting point for your own experimentation. But there are a number of ways to obtain similar results.

Pencil. Pencil sketches using traditional materials are typically created on location. Tools include soft-leaded graphite pencils (HB to 6B), various erasers and white paper with a smooth to medium grain. To create a pencil sketch in Painter, select an even-grained paper texture such as Basic Paper and choose the Pencils category, 2B Pencil variant. Select a black or dark gray and begin sketching. To paint a light color over dark—for instance, to add highlights—choose a white color and draw with the Cover Pencil variant. For more about working in pencil, see "Sketching with Pencils" on page 64.

Colored pencil. Conventional colored pencils are highly sensitive to the surface used: Layering strokes with light pressure on a smooth board will create a shiny look, while a rougher surface creates more of a "broken color" effect (strokes that don't completely cover the existing art). To closely match the grainy, opaque strokes of a soft Prismacolor pencil on cold-pressed illustration board with Painter, select a fine-or medium-grained paper such as Plain Grain (found in the Drawing Paper Textures library in the Paper Textures folder on the Painter 8 CD2 CD-ROM). Choose the Colored Pencils variant of Colored Pencils. Switch the Method from Buildup to Cover and change the Subcategory to Grainy Edge Flat Cover. See "Drawing with Colored Pencils," later in this chapter for a full description of this technique.

The Artist Pastel Chalk variant of Pastels and the Large Chalk variant of Chalk were used on a rough texture to paint Coastal Meadow.

For this Harp Shell *study, a Conte variant was used to draw on custom-made Laid Pastel Paper.*

This charcoal study after Raphael Sanzio was drawn with the Hard Charcoal and Soft Charcoal variants (Charcoal), then blended with the Just Add Water variant (Blenders).

Pastel. Pastels encourage a bold, direct style: Edgar Degas preferred pastels for his striking compositions because they simultaneously yield tone, line and color. A great variety of hard and soft pastels are used on soft or rough-grain papers. Pastel artists often use a colored paper stock to unify a composition.

Use Painter's Chalk, Pastel and Oil Pastel brushes to mimic traditional hard or soft pastels, and if you want to use a colored paper, click on the Paper Color box (in the New dialog box) as you open a new document and choose a color. The Chalk and Pastel variants are among Painter's most popular; turn to "Blending and Feathering with Pastels," and "Painting with Pastels" later in this chapter for two different techniques for using them.

Conté crayon. Popular in Europe since the 1600s and used today for life drawing and landscapes, Conté crayons have a higher oil content than conventional chalk or pastel; as a result, they work successfully on a greater variety of surfaces.

To get a realistic Conté crayon look in Painter, choose the Conte style and the Tapered Conte variant. Reveal more paper grain in the brushwork by moving the Grain slider in the Property Bar to 8%. Begin drawing. This Conté variant works well over the Laid Pastel Paper texture. To blend color while revealing the paper texture, choose the Smudge variant of the Blenders brush.

Charcoal. One of the oldest drawing tools, charcoal is ideal for life drawing and portraiture in *chiaroscuro* (high value contrast) style. Renaissance masters frequently chose charcoal because images created with it could be transferred from paper (where corrections could be made easily) to canvas or walls in preparation for painting. To create a charcoal drawing in Painter, select a rough paper (such as Charcoal Paper) and a Hard Charcoal Pencil variant of Charcoal. Create a gestural drawing, then blend the strokes—as you would traditionally with a tortillion, a tissue or your fingers—with the Smudge variant of the Blenders. For a smoother result with less texture try blending with the Just Add Water variant of Blenders. Finish by adding more strokes using the Gritty Charcoal variant of Charcoal.

BRUSH RESIZE SHORTCUT

To resize your brush on the fly, press Ctrl-Shift-Alt (Windows) or ⌘-Shift-Option (Mac). You will see the cursor change to cross hairs. Drag to create a circle the size of the brush you want.

Brushstrokes made using the Opaque Acrylic 30 variant of Acrylics. In the upper left, its default size; upper right, the resized brush "ghost" cursor; lower right, a stroke made with the resized brush.

To draw Crab, *a spot illustration, Mary Envall used the Smooth Ink Pen and Scratchboard Tool variants of the Pens. Both of these Pens use Painter's rendered dabs.*

Kathy Blavatt created Heart *using Painter's Liquid Ink brushes.*

In Tiger Kitty, *Chet Phillips used the Scratchboard Tool variant of the Pens.*

Pen and Ink. Many artists use Painter's Pens variants to draw editorial and spot illustrations. To create a black-and-white pen- and-ink drawing in Painter, choose the Fine Point variant of the Pens and choose 100% black in the Color picker. Sketch your composition. To draw with lines that are expressively thick and thin based on the pressure you apply to your stylus, switch to the Smooth Ink Pen. To etch white lines and texture into black areas of your drawing, select pure white in the Color picker and draw with the Fine Point or Smooth Ink Pen. For a sense of spontaneous energy try drawing with the Nervous Pen.

Thick ink and resists. When you start to paint with Painter's Liquid Ink, a special Liquid Ink layer is created. With Liquid Ink you can use the thick, viscous ink to paint graphic flat-color art and to paint thick, impasto-like brushstrokes as well. For smooth-edged strokes try the Smooth Camel variant. To paint textured brushstrokes, experiment with the Sparse Bristle and Coarse Camel variants. To erode Liquid Ink you've already laid down, choose a Resist variant, such as the Graphic Camel Resist. Brush over the area of ink you want to erode. You can also apply a resist and then paint over it. The resist will repel brushstrokes made with a regular Liquid Ink variant, until repeated strokes scrub the resist away. To see how to add volume to a Liquid Ink drawing, target the Liquid Ink layer in the Layers palette (Window, Show Layers) and press the Enter key. Move the Amount slider to 50%, and click OK. For more information about using Liquid Ink, turn to "A Liquid Ink Primer" later in this chapter.

Scratchboard illustration. Scratching white illustrations out of a dark (usually black) background surface became popular in the late 1800s. Illustrations created in this manner often contained subtle, detailed tone effects, making them a useful alternative to photographic halftones in the publications of that era. Modern scratchboard artists use knives and gougers on a variety of surfaces, including white board painted with India ink. To duplicate this look in Painter, start with the Flat Color variant of the Pens and increase its size in the Property Bar. Choose black from the Color picker and rough out the basic shape for your illustration. To "scratch" the image out of the shape with hatch marks, switch to white and change to the Scratchboard Tool variant. Use the Scratchboard Rake to draw several lines at once. Turn to Chapter 5's gallery to see Chet Phillips's Painter-generated scratchboard work.

Calligraphy. With the exception of "rolling the nib" and a few other maneuvers, you can imitate nearly all conventional calli-

A glazing technique was used for a watercolor portrait study of Sabina Gaross.

Cloudy Day on Kauai *was painted with the Runny Wash Bristle, Wash Camel, Fine Camel and Diffuse Camel variants of Water Color. On the trees, highlights were brought out using the Eraser Dry variant and foreground texture was added with the Eraser Salt.*

Study of a Nude *after Rembrandt van Rijn. We sketched with the Fine Point variant of Pens, then added translucent washes using the Wash Camel variant of Water Color.*

graphic strokes in Painter. To create hand lettering similar to the example on page 45, choose the Calligraphy variant of Calligraphy and begin your brush work. To make guides for your calligraphy, select Canvas, Rulers, Show Rulers and drag guides out from the rulers, or you can use Painter's Grid overlay (choose Canvas, Grid, Show Grid). If you want a rougher edge to your strokes, try switching to the Thin Grainy Pen 10 variant of Calligraphy, which has a flatter "nib."

Watercolor. Landscape artists like Turner and Constable helped popularize watercolors in the nineteenth century. The medium's portability lends itself nicely to painting on location. Traditional watercolor uses transparent pigment suspended in water, and the paper is often moistened and stretched prior to painting.

Painter lets you achieve many traditional watercolor effects—without paper-stretching! There are now *two* watercolor mediums in Painter, Water Color and Digital Water Color. Painters who have worked with traditional watercolors may find themselves more at home with Water Color, even though it's a bit more challenging to use. In contrast to Digital Water Color, Water Color employs a special Water Color media layer. Here, the pigments can realistically blend, drip and run. To paint with Water Color, choose the Wash Bristle variant of Water Color, a rough paper (such as French Water Color) and a light-to-medium color, and begin painting. (If the color painted is too intense, reduce the Opacity in the Property Bar.) To remove only the color painted with Water Color variants, use the Eraser Dry variant of Water Color. For more about Water Color turn to "A Painter Water Color Primer" on page 72.

Digital Watercolor operates like most of Painter's other painting tools—you can choose a brush and begin to paint on a standard layer or on the canvas. (Users of Painter 6 and previous versions will recognize similarities between the earlier watercolor and the new Digital Water Color). Many beautiful transparent painting effects can be achieved with Digital Water Color, which is easier-to-use and to correct than Water Color. Choose the New Simple Water variant of Digital Water Color and make brushstrokes on your image. To blend color, stroke over the area with a low opacity New Simple Water brush. For strokes that reveal bristle marks, try the Coarse Dry Brush or the Coarse Mop Brush. Turn to pages 84–87 for step-by-step techniques using Digital Water Color.

Pen and wash. Tinted, translucent washes over pen work has been a medium of choice of Asian painting masters for many centuries. Painter's Water Color layers let you add a wash to any drawn (or scanned) image without smearing or hiding the original image. Choose the Soft Camel or Wash Camel variant of Water Color and pick a color (it works best to build up color beginning with very light-colored washes). Choose an even, medium-textured paper (such as Basic Paper) and begin painting on top of line work.

To paint Porcelain Morning Glory, *Kathy Blavatt used several Airbrushes variants.*

THE VANISHING SURFACE

Applying Surface Texture to an empty canvas is a good way to give an entire surface a texture, but it will be covered as you paint if the brush you're using doesn't show grain (doesn't have the word "grainy" in its subcategory). Some artists apply Surface Texture before *and* after they paint.

This detail of Nancy Stahl's Sappi Portrait *shows her gouache technique. To see the full image and read about her illustration, turn to "Painting With Gouache," later in this chapter.*

Airbrush. The trademark of most traditional airbrush work is a slick, super-realistic look; photo retouching is a more subtle use of the tool. A traditional airbrush is a miniature spray gun with a hollow nozzle and a tapered needle. Pigments include finely ground gouache, acrylic, watercolor and colored dyes, and a typical support surface is a smooth illustration board. Airbrush artists protect areas of their work from overspraying with pieces of masking film, or flexible friskets cut from plastic.

In Painter, choose one of the Airbrushes variants and begin sketching or retouching. To get the most from the tool, make selections with the Lasso tool and use them to limit the paint just as you would traditional airbrush friskets.

Several of Painter's Airbrushes (such as the Fine Spray, Pixel Spray and Graffiti variants) spray paint onto the image canvas differently than earlier Airbrushes. These Airbrushes take advantage of new input technology available from tablet-and-stylus manufacturers such as Wacom. They respond to angle (tilt) and bearing (direction). For instance, as you paint, particles of color land on the image canvas reflecting the way the artist tilts the stylus. And with Painter's Fine Wheel Airbrush variant, you can adjust the flow of paint by adjusting the wheel on a special Airbrush stylus. For those accustomed to the Airbrushes in earlier versions of Painter, the Digital Airbrush variant is most similar to these. Turn to "Selections and Airbrush" in Chapter 4 and the gallery in Chapter 8 to see John Dismukes's masterful airbrush work using selections and layers.

Gouache. Roualt, Vlaminck, Klee and Miro were a few of the modern artists who experimented with this opaque watercolor, used most frequently in paintings that call for large areas of flat color. Gouache contains a blend of the same type of pigment used in transparent watercolor, a chalk that makes the medium opaque, and an extender that allows it to flow more easily. For an expressive, opaque color painting brush, try the new Flat Opaque Gouache variants; for a more subtle semi-transparent look, use the Wet Gouache Round variants.

Oil paint and acrylic. These opaque media are "standards" for easel painting. Both can be applied in a thick impasto with a palette knife or stiff brush. (Impasto is a technique of applying paint thickly.) They can also be *extended* (thinned) with a solvent or gel and applied as transparent glazes. They are typically applied to canvas that has been primed with paint or gesso.

Try the following methods to get the look of acrylic in Painter. For a technique that incorporates the texture of brush striations and a palette knife, begin by choosing the Flax Canvas paper texture from the Paper Selector (located near the bottom of the Toolbox) and an Opaque Acrylic variant of the Acrylics and then start painting. Blend colors using short strokes with a Round Blender

This detail from Amaryllis *was painted with the Opaque Bristle Spray and Smeary Bristle Spray variants of Oils, then blended with the Smudge variant of Blenders.*

Coast *by Richard Noble is an example of the artist's digital acrylic technique.*

Chelsea Sammel used Impasto brushes to add thick paint to Dying Orchids, *a detail of which is shown here. To read about her painting process step-by-step, turn to "Working with Thick Paint," on page 114.*

Brush variant of Blenders. To subtly bring out the Flax Canvas texture, try blending with the Grainy Water variant of Blenders. To scrape back or move large areas of color on the image canvas, use a Smeary Palette Knife variant of the Palette Knives. When working on smaller areas of your image, adjust the size of the Palette Knife variant using the Size slider on the Property Bar.

For an oil painting technique with the feel of wet paint on canvas, use the Sargent Brush variant of the Artists brush. The Sargent Brush allows you to move color as well as apply it. As you pull the Sargent Brush through pools of color on the image canvas, the brush carries some of the neighboring color with it as you paint.

For a painting method that emphasizes the texture of canvas, begin by choosing the Coarse Cotton Canvas texture from the Paper Selector. Now choose the Opaque Bristle Spray variant of the Oils and lay color into your image. To smear existing paint as you add more color, switch to the Smeary Bristle Spray variant. To reveal the texture of the image canvas, while you blend colors, switch to the Smudge variant of Blenders. For yet another digital oil method, see Dennis Orlando's version of a traditional oil look in "Painting With Oils," later in this chapter; to see more examples of Richard Noble's digital acrylic paintings, turn to the gallery in Chapter 2, "The Power of Color."

To get textured brushstrokes (a "3D paint" look) with any of these methods when you're finished, choose Effects, Surface Control, Apply Surface Texture. Choose Image Luminance from the pop-up menu, and an Amount setting of 20–30%. If you want to mimic the look of acrylic paint extended with a glossy gel medium, drag the Shine slider to 100%. To get a semi-matte finish, move the Shine slider to between 20% and 30%.

Painting with realistic Impasto. Impasto gives you the power to show the texture of brushmark striations and the thickness of paint itself with realistic highlights and shadows as you paint. Impasto brings thick paint to the tip of your stylus! When you choose a variant of the Impasto brush (such as the Opaque Round) in Painter 8's Brush Selector Bar, the Impasto effect is automatically enabled. You can use Impasto on the image Canvas, or on added layers.

Here's an Impasto primer: Create a new blank file (File, New). To activate Impasto, choose an Impasto brush (such as the Round Camelhair variant) from the Brush Selector Bar. Make brushstrokes on the image canvas. To toggle the Impasto effect on and off, you can click the small paint splat icon in the upper right of Painter's scroll bar. (This toggle does not affect the dimensionality created with the Apply Surface Texture command described on the "Oil paint and acrylic" section above.) To read more about painting with Impasto, turn to "Brushing Washes Over 'Live' Canvas" and "Working With Thick Paint," later in this chapter.

In Three Trees, *Chelsea Sammel mixed media while painting. As shown in this detail, she used modified Chalks and Oils brushes—the Smeary Bristle Spray; Blenders—the Coarse Smear; and finally the Oil Pastels and a modified Sharp Chalk variant (Chalk) to define details.*

In Harley, *Richard Noble blended color with a variant of Blenders to get the look of conventional acrylic.*

To complete Speedy Persimmon, *Janet Martini mixed media using the Calligraphy variant of the Pens on top of Water Color variants and Oil Pastel strokes*

Mixed media. You can create media combinations in Painter that would be impossible (or at least very messy!) in traditional media. Try adding strokes with a Water Color or Pencils variant atop Oils, or use a Pens variant on a base you've painted using the Chalk or Gouache variants. See how artists Phil Howe and Janet Martini combined media in the two paintings at the left.

Mixed media painting with a liquid feel. Painter offers several brushes that are reminiscent of wet paint on canvas—for instance, the Sargent Brush variant of the Artists brush, which can both lay down color and smear it, and the Palette Knife variants, which can move large areas of color. Painting with these new brushes is a very tactile experience, as you learned if you experimented as described on page 53.

In the *Paths to Water 4* study shown on page 55, we sketched in color with the Square Chalk variant of Chalks on a rough paper. Then we switched to the Sargent Brush variant of the Artists brushes to apply more painterly strokes. To blend areas of the foreground and mid-ground we used the Grainy Water variant of Blenders, then we used the Smeary Palette Knife variant of the Palette Knives to expressively pull color in the sky. To paint and blend using these brushes, choose the Sargent Brush and a color, and begin painting. When you are ready to pull and blend paint, switch to the Palette Knife. Try reducing its Opacity in the Property Bar for a more subdued effect.

The Blenders and Distortion variants are also helpful blending tools. To create *Zinnias*, shown on page 55, we used the Bulge variant of the Distortion brush to enlarge the pink flowers, and the Coarse Smear variant of Blenders to pull pixels and add diffused texture to the edges. Then we used the Marbling Rake variant of Distortion to add linear texture and to pull pixels up and around the image to create a sense of movement.

Erasing techniques. Painter provides several ways to simulate traditional erasing and scratch-out techniques. *Lighten* an area of an image by using the Bleach variant of the Erasers, lowering the Opacity slider in the Property Bar to 5% for improved control. (You can also use the Dodge variant of the Photo brush to lighten color.) Use the Thin Grainy Pen 10 variant of the Calligraphy brush and white or a light color to *scratch out* pigment from a pastel or oil painting; to create strokes with more subtle texture, switch to the Thin Smooth Pen 10 variant of Calligraphy. Use the Eraser Dry variant of the Water Color brush to pull up pigment from a "wet" painting done with Water Color variants (similar to *sponging up* a traditional water-color). For a more subtle result, lower the Opacity slider (in the Property Bar) to 40%. Try the

LIQUID BRUSH STRENGTH
To control the strength of the Bulge, Pinch, Smear and Turbulence variants of the Distortion brush, adjust the Opacity slider in the Property Bar.

In this detail from a study for Paths to Water 4, *Palette Knife variants were used to pull and spread color in the clouds and sky.*

You can paint Impasto on layers and then set Composite Depth on each layer (in the Layers palette), to raise or excavate the paint, as described on pages 115–116. (The Composite Depth option will have no effect if you've used Impasto on the Canvas instead of on added layers.)

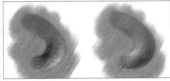

We painted each rust brushstroke on a separate layer with the Opaque Round variant of Impasto. Then we used Composite Depth controls, Subtract (left) and Add (right), to excavate the left stroke and raise the right stroke.

For Zinnias, *we painted over a photo with Pastel variants, completely covering it with colored strokes. Then we used Distortion and Blender variants to distort the flowers, add texture and emphasize the focal point.*

Bleach Runny variant of Water Color to leach color from an area, while creating a drippy texture. To pull color out of areas when using Painter 8's new Digital Water Color, use the Wet Eraser, and for picking color out of smaller areas, try the Pointed Wet Eraser variant of Digital Water Color.

Painting with texture. The Add Grain variant of the Photo brush is just as useful for painting as it is for photo manipulation, because it literally puts texture on the tip of your brush. You can switch textures at any time during the painting process by changing the selection in the Papers palette. For best results, use very light pressure on the stylus. Make a few marks in the document to preview the effect. For a more subtle look, try lowering the Opacity and Grain settings in the Property Bar.

Painting with special effects. Painter offers intriguing special-effects brushes that allow you to paint with fire, glows, fur, sparkly fairy dust, hair spray, neon, striped strokes, shattered glass and more! In the detail of *Creative Journey* shown on page 56, Brian Moose used the Glow variant of the F/X brush to make the paintbrush tips in his image smolder with a fiery glow.

Painting with the Fire and Glow variants works best on a dark area of your image. To paint semi-transparent flames, choose the Fire brush variant of the F/X brush. For a subdued fire effect that you can build up gradually, with a light pressure on the stylus, choose a very dark orange color with a value (V) of l0–15% in the Color picker. Make short strokes in the direction you want the flames to go. For realism, vary the size of the brushstrokes. Change the size of the brush using the Size slider in the Property Bar, then

When you work with Impasto, the depth and lighting information is stored in a way that allows you to change it for the entire image—as many times as you like, for both past and future Impasto brushstrokes. To demonstrate this flexibility, select an Impasto variant (such as Texturizer-Heavy) and a color, and paint on your image. Next, choose Canvas, Surface Lighting, and when the dialog box opens, increase the Shine (for more glossy paint); increase the Amount (to make the paint look thicker) and experiment with other settings in the Appearance of Depth and Light Controls sections. Also try toggling Impasto off and on using the Enable Impasto checkbox. To clear (delete) the effect entirely, choose Canvas, Clear Impasto. Clearing Impasto is useful if you want to completely start over with new Impasto. Also, if you decide not to keep the Impasto effects in your image, clearing can save memory.

The Impasto Lighting dialog box allows you to dynamically set Appearance of Depth and Light Controls for Impasto brushstrokes in the entire image.

Brian Moose used the Glow brush variant of the F/X brush to make the brush tips burn in his painting Creative Journey, *a detail of which is shown here.*

To paint this study for Cutting Back at Rincon, *we used the Pens, Brushes and Airbrushes variants to paint on transparent layers. After drawing the line sketch on its own layer, we created a second layer for the color work. Using low-opacity color, we painted on the "color" layer to build up brushstrokes without altering the image canvas or the layer with the line sketch. We finished by dragging the line sketch layer to the top of the Layers palette, placing it on top of the color layer.*

paint more brushstrokes using a light pressure on the stylus.

PAINTING ON LAYERS

Painter lets you paint (and erase) not only on the program's canvas, but on transparent layers above it. A *transparent layer* is similar to a piece of clear acetate that hovers above the image canvas. When you paint on a transparent layer with a brush, in the clear areas you can see the canvas underneath, as well as color on other layers that you may have stacked up. You can also change the stacking order of the acetate sheets. If you work with Adobe Photoshop, you'll find Painter's transparent layers familiar.

To add a new layer to an existing file, open the Layers palette (Windows, Show Layers) and click the left triangle on the Layers section bar to open this section. Click the right triangle on the section bar to access the Layers palette's pop-up menu, and choose New Layer. To paint on the new layer, choose any brush except a Water Color or Liquid Ink variant, target the layer in the Layers section and begin painting.

Layers offer great flexibility to digital illustrators. Some artists prefer to draw each item in an image on its own layer, which isolates the item so that it can be repositioned or painted on as an individual element. Transparent layers are also useful when creating *glazes*—thin, clear layers of color applied over existing color. (Turn to Chapter 5, "Using Layers" to read more about painting and compositing techniques.)

PICKING UP COLOR

To bring color from underlying layers into a upper layer that you're painting on (and mix color on the active layer), turn on Pick Up Underlying Color in the Layers section.

THE LOOKS YOU LIKE

If you like the look of a particular brush-and-paper combination (for instance, a Square Soft Pastel variant of Pastels on Corrugated Paper), save the combo as a Brush Look so you can quickly call it up when you want to use it again. Before you can save a new Look, in Painter 8 it's necessary to select an area of an image that can be used as an icon for the Brush Look. In the Toolbox, choose the Rectangular Marquee tool and drag in the image to make a selection. Select the texture from the Paper Selector (near the bottom of the Toolbox) and the brush variant from the Brush Selector Bar. In the Toolbox, click the Looks Selector and choose New Look from the triangle pop-up menu. Naming your New Look saves it to the current Brush Look library, which is located in the Looks Selector in the Tools palette. Open the Looks Selector by clicking the Looks icon. To paint with your new Brush Look, select it from the pop-up menu.

A brushstroke painted with the Pattern Pen brush, Pattern Pen Masked variant (over a dark blue background) using the Wave Mosaic pattern as the Source. This look can be accessed by clicking the Looks Selector (near the bottom of the Toolbox), and choosing Wave Mosaic Pen.

Building Brushes

Overview *Creating these custom brushes will give you insight into the workings of the Brush Creator.*

When building new brushes, you'll spend most of your time using the Stroke Designer tab of Painter 8's new Brush Creator (described on pages 57–61). The Brush Creator offers many new features for customizing brushes including the updated Stroke Designer (above) and the new Transposer and Randomizer functions (described on pages 61–63). The Brush Creator has its own main menu at the top of the screen. To jump back and forth between the Brush Creator and Painter, simply click in the working windows of either.

PAINTER SHIPS WITH MANY NEW BRUSHES, and makes customizing them even easier than before. The new Brush Creator offers many new features for customizing brushes, including the revamped Stroke Designer (shown at left) and the new Transposer and Randomizer functions. The Transposer allows you to blend components of two existing Painter brushes and choose which blend you want. With the Randomizer you can choose a brush and have Painter create twelve variations.

If you like trying new brushes but don't want to build them, check out the Brush libraries on the Wow! CD-ROM in the back of this book—you'll find the brushes shown on these pages and more. But if you enjoy creating your own brushes, read on. *Roses*, above, was painted with several of the custom brushes described here.

DAB TYPES

In Painter, brushstrokes are built from *dabs*. You can switch dab types by opening the Brush Creator (Ctrl/⌘-B), selecting the Stroke Designer, and in its General section, selecting a new dab from the Dab pop-up menu.

Painter has 23 dab types, which fall into two general classifications: *Dab-based* brushes (such as the brushes in earlier versions of Painter) and brushes created with *Continuous Stroke* dab types. The main difference lies in how brushstrokes are created from the dabs as described in "Dab-Based Dab Types" (below) and "Continuous Stroke Brushes" on pages 58–60.

Dab-Based Brushes

For brushes that are *dab-based*, you can think of the dab as the footprint for the brush—a cross-section of its shape. The brush lays down a series of dabs of color to make a stroke. If the spacing is set tight the stroke will appear to be a continuous mark. If the

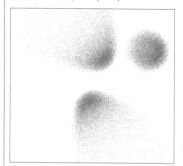

Choosing the Circular dab type in the General section of the Stroke Designer within the Brush Creator

The Fine Spray variant of the Airbrushes is sensitive to the amount of tilt and to the bearing (which direction the stylus is leaning) and sprays conic sections—similar to a beam of light projected onto the canvas—just like a traditional airbrush. Holding the stylus upright sprays a smaller, denser area of color (top right). Tilting the stylus sprays color wider and farther (top left). And holding down Alt/Option redirects the spray (bottom).

spacing is loose, the stroke will be a series of footprints with space between them.

Circular. Many of Painter's brushes use this round dab type. (Don't be fooled by the term *Circular*; even if you change a brush's Squeeze setting in the Angle section of the Brush Controls palette so that its footprint looks elliptical, it's still a Circular brush.)

Single-Pixel. Just as it sounds, this is a 1-pixel-wide brush.

Static Bristle. Since Static Bristle brushes are made up of several "hairs," they have a rich potential. You can make adjustments in Bristle Thickness, Clumpiness and other settings in the Spacing and Bristle sections of the Stroke Designer tab (Brush Creator).

Captured. You can capture any area of a document to act as the footprint for a Captured brush. Use the Rectangular Selection tool and draw a marquee (press the Shift key if you want to constrain the selection to a perfect square) around a mark or group of markings. With the Brush Creator open, choose Brush, Capture Dab; the brush footprint will appear in the Size section of the Brush Creator's Stroke Designer tab.

Continuous-Stroke Brushes

Brushes using *Continuous Stroke* dab types produce smoother-edged, more responsive brushstrokes because the strokes are computed as continuous anti-aliased 1-pixel lines during the stroke. Each line represents an individual brush hair.

Camel Hair. With Camel Hair dabs, you can build brushes with circular-shaped dabs that paint brushstrokes with obvious bristle marks. Brushes using the Camel Hair dab type (the Round Camelhair variant of Oils, for example) are capable of painting very smoothly, and they can carry a different color on each brush hair.

Flat. Like it sounds, a flat dab is used to create a flat-tipped brush. With brushes using the Flat dab type, you can paint wide or narrow strokes, depending on the way you hold and move the stylus. The Opaque Flat variant of Oils is an example.

Palette Knife. With Resat set low in the Well section of the Stroke Designer (Brush Creator), you can use brushes with Palette Knife dabs to scrape paint or move it around on the canvas. The Loaded Palette Knife and Smeary Palette Knife variants (Palette Knives) are examples.

Bristle Spray. With many brushes that use Bristle Spray dabs (such as the Opaque

Click on the brush footprint in the Size section's Preview window to switch the view between "hard" (showing the maximum and minimum sizes) and "soft" (showing bristles).

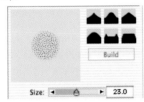

The Size section of the Stroke Designer (Brush Creator) palette showing a "soft" view of a Static Bristle dab used to create the Feathering Brush described on page 62.

Choosing the Rake stroke type in the General section of the Stroke Designer (Brush Creator).

Bristle Spray variant of Oils), the bristles will spread out on one side of the brushstroke as you tilt the stylus.

Airbrush. Like Bristle Spray, Pixel Airbrush and Line Airbrush dab types, Airbrush dabs spray conic sections, and they "understand" Bearing (which direction the stylus is leaning) and Angle (amount of tilt). (See "Redirecting the Spray" on page 58.)

Pixel Airbrush. Brushes using this dab type work like brushes using the Airbrush dab type. With the Pixel Airbrush dab type, however, the individual droplets *cannot* be adjusted using the Feature slider.

Line Airbrush. Brushes using the Line Airbrush dab type (such as the Furry Brush variant of F/X) spray lines instead of droplets.

Projected. The Projected dab-type brushes spray conic sections, similar to the Airbrush dab type, but without the responsiveness. For now, we recommend constructing brushes with the Airbrush and Pixel Airbrush dab types rather than a Projected dab type.

Rendered. In addition to painting with color, brushes built using Rendered dabs can contain a pattern or gradation as a Source. The Graphic Paintbrush variant of F/X is an example. To change the Source used by a Rendered dab brush, use the Source pop-up menu in the General section of the Stroke Designer (Brush Creator).

Water Color dab types. The five Water Color dab types were created for painting on Water Color media layers. These dabs are based on several of the rendered dab types discussed earlier—the Camel Hair, Flat, Bristle Spray, Palette Knife and Airbrush. For

For brushes with Airbrush dab types, you can use the Feature slider in the Property Bar to control the size of droplets. With a higher Feature setting, Airbrush dabs spray larger droplets.

Several of Painter's Airbrushes—the Coarse Spray, the Fine Spray and the Graffiti variants, for example—allow media to pool when the stylus (or mouse) is held down in one position. In contrast, the Digital Airbrush and Inverted Pressure variants must be moved before they apply color to the image. To enable these two variants to apply color at the first touch, turn on Continuous Time Deposition in the Spacing section of the Stroke Designer tab. (Window, Show Brush Creator.)

Brush Loading enables a brush to carry a unique color in each brush hair. Many of Painter's brushes have this capability already built into them—for instance, the Variable Round variant of the Oils. (When Brush Loading is built into a brush, the Brush Loading checkbox is grayed out in the Well section of the Stroke Designer.) To allow a static bristle brush (such as the Captured Bristle variant of the Oils) or a dab-based brush from an earlier version of Painter to use Brush Loading, open the Well section of the Stroke Designer and turn on Brush Loading.

When changing settings for a brush, sometimes typing numerals into the fields is easier than trying to hit a point on the slider.

Most of the settings in the Stroke Designer's windows can be typed in, as shown here in setting Brush Scale in the Rake section.

If you'd like to adjust the orientation of a Calligraphy pen for right or left-handed work, open the Angle pane of the Brush Creator's Stroke Designer within the (Window, Show brush Creator.) Drag the Angle slider, to set the angle you want, and make a test stroke in the Preview window.

more information about working with Water Color, turn to "A Painter Water Color Primer," on page 72 of this chapter.

Liquid Ink dab types.

Designed for painting on Liquid Ink media layers, there are five Liquid Ink dab types. They're based on several of the rendered dab types: the Camel Hair, Flat, Bristle Spray, Palette Knife and Airbrush. To read more about Liquid Ink, turn to "A Liquid Ink Primer," on page 117.

STROKE TYPES

The *stroke* is the way a dab is applied over a distance. You can switch Stroke Types using the pop-up menu in the General section of the Stroke Designer (Brush Creator).

Single. Just as it sounds, Single stroke-type brushes have only one stroke path. Because of this, they're fast. If you use a Static Bristle, a Flat or a Camel Hair dab type, you can create a fast Single stroke-type brush with a lot of complexity. Most Painter brushes incorporate the Single stroke type.

Multi. Painter's computation-intensive Multi stroke-type brushes can paint sensitive multicolored strokes, but are the least spontaneous of the program's brushes. (The Continuous-Stroke dab-type brushes on pages 58–59 provide a much more responsive way to paint with multiple colors.) Try drawing a line with the Gloopy variant of the Impasto. Instead of a stroke, you'll see a dotted "preview" line that shows its path; the stroke appears a moment later. Multi brushes are built from several randomly distributed dabs that may or may not overlap. The Gloopy variant of Impasto is an example of a Multi stroke brush in the Painter 8 default brush library. But lovely, variable strokes can be made using custom Multi brushes. To spread the strokes of a Multi-stroke brush, increase the Jitter setting in the Random section of the Brush Creator's Stroke Designer tab.

Rake. The Rake stroke type is like a garden rake; each of the evenly spaced tines is a bristle of the brush. Painter gives you con-

When you want to design and capture a brush, start by opening a variant that's close to the effect you want. That way you'll have fewer adjustments to make.

Do you want a brush to pull and smear color? A low Resat and a high Bleed setting (in the Well section of the Stroke Designer) will work with Brush Loading to allow the brush to smear pigment while applying it. Choose the Variable Flat variant of the Oils, and in the Well section, set Resat at 5% and Bleed at 80%. To see the colors mix, choose a new color in the Colors picker and drag the brush through existing color on your image.

To make a brush that applies color when you use a light touch and scrubs underlying color when you use heavier pressure, in the Well section of the Stroke Designer, set Resat low and in the Resaturation Expression pop-up menu, turn on the Invert box.

You can add settings to any brush that will allow it to paint with thick Impasto paint. To set up a brush for Impasto, begin by choosing a brush (such as a Bristle Oils variant of the Oils). We used these settings in the Impasto section of the Stroke Designer to build a Bristle Oils Impasto brush: Draw To, Color and Depth; Depth Method, Uniform; Depth, 180%; Smoothing, 120% and Plow, 100%. To save your variant, from the Brush Creator's Variant menu choose Save. To read more about Impasto turn to "Painting with realistic Impasto" on page 53 and to "Working with Thick Paint," later in the chapter.

Painting thick Impasto brushstrokes with the custom Bristle Oils Impasto brush

Using Impasto, you can add brushstrokes that have 3D texture but that don't alter the color in the image—like painting with thick, clear varnish. Select any Impasto variant and in the Draw To pop-up menu in the Impasto section of the Stroke Designer, select Depth.

trol over the bristles; for instance, you can make them overlap, which makes it possible to create wonderfully complex, functional brushes. And you can change the number of Bristles (keeping in mind that fewer bristles make faster brushes). In the Rake section of the Stroke Designer, you can also adjust the way the bristles interact. To try out an existing Rake brush, paint with the Van Gogh variant of the Artists brush.

Hose. The Hose stroke type sprays a variety of images when you paint each stroke. To read about painting with the Image Hose, turn to "Creating a Tidepool" in Chapter 7 of this book and to "The Image Hose" chapter in the *Painter 8 User Guide*.

MAKING BRUSHES USING THE STROKE DESIGNER

For the custom brushes that follow, we used the Stroke Designer window of the Brush Creator. Open it by choosing Window, Show Brush Creator, or by pressing (Ctrl-⌘-B and clicking the Stroke Designer tab.

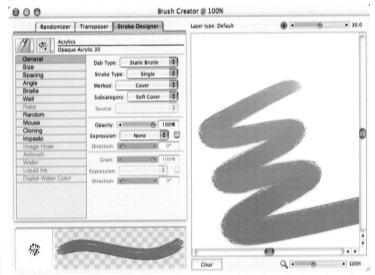

Painter 8's new Brush Creator, with the General section of the Stroke Designer shown here. The Stroke Designer contains controls for building highly customized and sophisticated brushes.

For each of the custom brushes, we started with an existing Painter brush, and we radically modified its character by making adjustments that affect brush behavior. After you've created the brush (and perhaps made further modifications on your own), you can save your variant. Choose Variant, Save from the Brush Creator's menu at the top of your screen, to save it under a new name into your current palette. After saving your custom variant, restore the default settings for the Painter brush by selecting the variant you began with and choosing Variant, Restore Default from the menu.

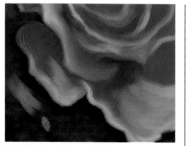

Modulating color on the background with the Soft Oils brush

Using the Feathering brush to layer color on the flower petals and background

Brushstrokes made with the Soft Runny Wash Water Color brush

Brushstrokes made with the Thick Bristle Liquid Ink brush

Try these brushes on images of 1000 pixels square or less. If you work with larger files, you'll want to proportionally increase the Size slider settings that we list here. When a Circular or Static Bristle dab type is used, you'll also want to optimize the Spacing and Min Spacing in the Stroke Designer's Spacing section to accommodate the larger size. If you have trouble setting exact numbers with the sliders, try typing the number into the field to the right of the slider. Hit the Enter key to accept the number you've typed. And don't think your computer has crashed if nothing happens for a while when you try to paint: Painter is working away, building a very complex brush.

To make room for more brushes, we've shortened our descriptions of how to make the brushes. For instance, "*Well:* Resat, 80%" means, "In the Stroke Designer's Well section set Resaturation to 80% but leave all other sliders at their default settings." The palette sections you will use are found in the Stroke Designer. For a full description of the functions of the controls in each of the sections, you can refer to Painter's *User Guide*, although painting with the brush after you make each adjustment will teach you a lot, too. **Caution:** Before starting a brush recipe, restore the default settings for the starting brush by choosing Variant, Restore Default from the main menu above the Brush Creator.

Soft Oils Brush. This Single stroke-type brush was created to feel like a traditional soft, flat brush with long bristles.

Start with the default Opaque Flat variant of the Oils. *Size:* Size, 31.2; Min Size, 42%; Feature: 5.1. *General:* Opacity, 100%; Opacity Expression, Pressure. *Well:* Resaturation, 70; Bleed, 40. *Size:* Size Expression: Pressure; *Random:* Jitter 0.05. In the Color Variability palette (Window, show Color Variability), ±H, 1; ±V, 3.

Feathering Brush. Created for feathering over existing color to add interest and texture, this Single stroke, Bristle brush paints tapered strokes quickly. Increase pressure to widen the stroke.

Start with the default Captured Bristle variant of the Acrylics. *Size:* Size, 23.0; Min Size, 30%; *Size:* Size Expression, Pressure. *General:* Opacity, 9. *Spacing:* Spacing, 9. *Well:* Resaturation and Dryout, maximum; Bleed, 0; *Bristle:* Thickness, 40; Clumpiness, 0 (for smooth strokes), Hair Scale, 515%. In the Color Variability palette, ±H, 1; ±V, 2.

Soft Runny Wash Water Color. This round Water Color brush paints smoother runny washes with soft edges.

Start with the default Runny Wash Bristle variant of Water Color. *Water:* Pickup, 11%; Dry Rate, 10%; Evap Thresh, 83%; Cap Factor, 0. Turn on Accurate Diffusion.

Thick Bristle Liquid Ink. This Liquid Ink brush paints a large volume of Liquid Ink with thick bristles. To access the volume setting, click on the New Liquid Ink Layer button at the bottom of the Layers palette (opened by choosing Window, Show Layers), then double-clicking on the new layer's name in the palette and increase the Amount setting to about 80%.

In the Brush Creator, start with the default Smooth Bristle variant of Liquid Ink. *Liquid Ink:* Volume, 403%; Bristle Frac, 60%; Rand Br Vol, 86%.

MAKING BRUSHES USING THE TRANSPOSER

For the custom brushes that follow, we used the Transposer window of the Brush Creator. Open it by clicking the Transposer tab.

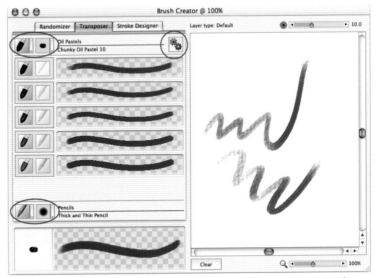

The Transposer window of the Brush Creator allows you to blend the components of two existing Painter brushes. Settings for the Oil Pastel Pencil are shown.

Oil Pastel Pencil. This pencil allows you to sketch while smearing color and revealing grain. In the Transposer's top category pop-up menu choose Oil Pastels, and in the variant pop-up menu choose Chunky Oil Pastel 10. In the Transposer's bottom category pop-up menu choose Pencils, and choose Thick and Thin Pencil as the variant. Next, click the Transpose Current Selection button (the Gears button) and then click the center choice.

Grainy Charcoal. This charcoal allows you to softly sketch with Charcoal while revealing more grain. In the Transposer's top category pop-up menu choose Charcoal and also choose Charcoal for the variant. In the Transposer's bottom category pop-up menu choose Chalk, and choose Blunt Chalk 10 as the variant. Next, click the Transpose Current Selection button (the Gears button) and then click the center choice.

Wet Bristle Oils. This brush allows you to paint while subtly smearing color. In the Transposer's top category pop-up menu choose Acrylics, and choose Wet Soft Acrylic 20 as the variant. In the Transposer's bottom category pop-up menu choose Oils, and choose Bristle Oils 20 as the variant. Next, click the Transpose Current Selection button (the Gears button), and then click the center choice.

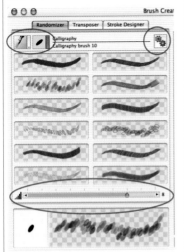

Sketching with Pencils

Overview *Draw a loose sketch with Pencils variants; scribble and crosshatch to develop tones; brighten highlights with an Eraser.*

CHER THREINEN-PENDARVIS

Making a stroke in the Brush Tracking window

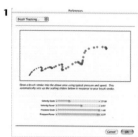

The loose composition sketch

Adding tones to the background and values to the faces

Darker tones and more texture have been added to the background and the faces.

LOOSE, EXPRESSIVE SKETCHES CAN BE DRAWN with the Painter's Pencils variants, with a look that's similar to traditional tools, as shown in this drawing of *Soshi and Pearl.*

1 Setting Brush Tracking. Pencil sketching often involves rapid, gestural movements with the stylus so it's important to set up Brush Tracking before you begin to sketch. With Brush Tracking you can customize how Painter interprets the input of your stylus, including parameters such as pressure and how quickly you make a brushstroke. Choose Edit, Preferences/Corel Painter 8, Preferences, Brush Tracking and make a representative brushstroke in the window.

2 Beginning to sketch. Create a new image file (File, New). (Ours measured 1100 x 600 pixels). Click OK. In the Papers section of the Art Materials palette, select an even-textured paper such as Basic Paper and select the Pencils category, 2B Pencil variant in the Brush Selector Bar. The default 2B Pencil uses the Buildup method, which means that color you draw is semitransparent and will darken to black, just like when you draw with a conventional 2B graphite pencil. Select a dark gray in the Color picker and draw a line sketch that will establish the negative and positive shapes in your composition.

3 Building tones and modeling form. To bring the subjects forward in the picture frame, add dark values behind them. Make crosshatched strokes with the 2B Pencil to create the darker tones. Keep your strokes loose, and gestural. Lively stroke patterns will add texture interest to your drawing. To model the faces and bodies of the cats, we used the Oily Variable Pencil, which smeared the pencil slightly as we scribbled and crosshatched. The Oily Variable Pencil incorporates the Cover method, which means that the color you draw is opaque; a lighter color will paint over a darker color.

For highlights, choose white in the Color picker and switch to the Cover Pencil variant in the Brush Selector Bar. The Cover Pencil is ideal for adding highlights because it covers previous strokes without smearing. To clean up areas, choose the Eraser variant (Erasers). A tiny Eraser also works well for brightening highlights.

Drawing with Colored Pencils

Overview *Create a sketch with the Sharp Colored Pencil variant; use the Cover Colored Pencil to further develop the drawing; adjust Color Variability settings for a more active color effect.*

CHER THREINEN-PENDARVIS

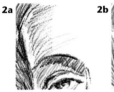

1

The line sketch drawn with Colored Pencils

2a   **2b**

Developing values   *Adding color*

3

Building dimension using increased settings in the Color Variability palette and strokes that follow the form

YOU CAN MODIFY THE COLORED PENCIL variant and get a broken color effect (where the color only partially covers the background or underdrawing) by brushing lightly across a textured surface.

1 Starting with a sketch. To work at the same size we did, open a new 883 pixel-wide file with a white background. Click the Paper Selector near the bottom of the Toolbox, choose Basic texture and select a dark brown color in the Color picker. From the Brush Selector Bar, choose the Colored Pencils category and the Sharp Colored Pencil variant, then draw a portrait sketch.

2 Developing value and adding color. Now choose the Cover Colored Pencil 5 variant of Colored Pencils from the Brush Selector Bar. Use this brush and a lighter brown to develop values throughout the sketch. Choose a skin color (we chose a tan for this portrait of Steve Pendarvis) and apply strokes with a light touch to partially cover some of the brown sketch. Follow the form with your strokes, switching colors and brush sizes as you draw.

3 Building dimension. To give a shimmery look to the color as it's applied, drag the Hue (± H) and Value (± V) sliders in the Color Variability palette to 3%. Using a light touch to allow the underpainting to show through, apply a fresh layer of strokes in the areas of strongest color (in our drawing, the forehead and nose shadows and the hair). 🖐

COLORED PENCIL WASHES

If you're using Colored Pencils on rough paper, you can create a wash effect. Choose the Grainy Water variant of the Blenders, reducing Opacity and Grain penetration in the Property Bar to 40% or less. Stroke over your pencil work to blend colors while maintaining texture on the "peaks" of the paper grain.

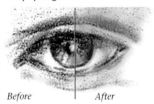

Before   *After*

Making Sketchbook Studies Using Pens

Overview *Start with gestural drawing; build the forms with crosshatching; clean up with an Eraser.*

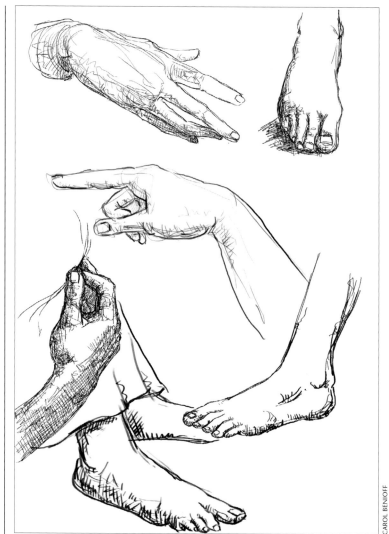

CAROL BENIOFF

1

Drawing the first gestural lines with the Croquil Pen variant

2

Adding defining lines to the gesture drawing and removing some of the lines with an Eraser variant

USING THESE SIX DIFFERENT PEN VARIANTS, it's easy to create quick studies with a variety of looks. The Pens resemble their traditional counterparts, but unlike the conventional pens they emulate, Painter's Pens do not spatter, and you can erase their ink. Carol Benioff used the Pens to draw these black-and-white studies.

Studies from Leonardo da Vinci. Benioff began by finding good reproductions of Leonardo da Vinci's drawings to use as a reference. Then she created a new 7 x 9-inch image in Painter at 300 pixels-per-inch.

1 Making a gesture drawing. She chose the Croquil Pen 5 and she sketched a gestural drawing, mapping out the shape of the hand.

2 Defining lines. Benioff drew over the gesture drawing with more definitive lines. She removed lines that she no longer

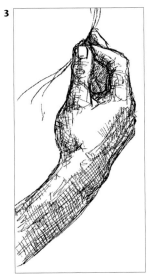

3

needed using a Pointed Eraser variant of Erasers. Next, she built up the tones and form with short, quick strokes.

3 Completing the study. Using a combination of crosshatching and curving lines, she created the highlights and shadows that gave the hand its definition. The study had the scratchy feel of the traditional croquil pen without the splatters.

4 Using the Smooth Round Pen. Turning to another drawing by Leonardo to use as her model, Benioff then selected the Smooth Round Pen 1.5 variant of Pens. It had the delicate quality that she wanted to create thin expressive lines. She drew this study using long gestural strokes.

5 Using the Thick and Thin Pen. For her fifth study, Benioff selected the Thick n Thin Pen 3. The bold quality of line the pen produces helped to create a clean and simple drawing. She added a suggestion of shading, which she sketched using short squiggles and a bit of crosshatching.

6 Using the Ball Point Pen. For this study of a foot, Benioff chose a Ball Point Pen variant. This gave her an even-weighted medium line. She built up the form using overlapping scribbles and crosshatching.

Completing the study with crosshatch and gestural strokes

4

Study of a hand drawn with a Smooth Round Pen in short curving strokes

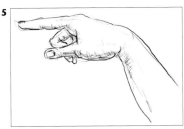

5

Hand drawn with the Thick n Thin Pen

7

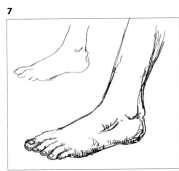

The beginning gesture drawing and the completed sketch of a foot using the Reed pen variants.

8

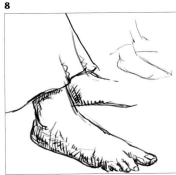

7 Using the Reed Pen. In this drawing of a foot Benioff selected the Reed Pen 5 for its strong, thick-to-thin lines. First she drew a quick gestural outline. Then she used long, smooth strokes to define the contours. Sizing the pen nib down to 3.7 from 7 pixels in the Property Bar, she continued to draw short, curving strokes to indicate the form and shadow.

8 Using a Bamboo Pen. For a strong, clear line Benioff chose the Bamboo Pen 10, sizing it down to about 3 pixels. Again she started with a simple gestural outline, then used short, smooth lines to add the contours. She finished the sketch with short straight lines to add definition to the form and to indicate shadows.

6

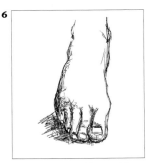

Study of a foot using the medium weight line of the Ball Point Pen 1.5

The first gestures and the finished sketch of two feet, using the Bamboo Pen 10 resized to about 5 pixels using the Size slider on the Property Bar.

Blending and Feathering with Pastels

Overview *Set up a still life, sketch from life with pastels; build color and form; blend the painting; add feathered brushstrokes to finish.*

CHER THREINEN-PENDARVIS

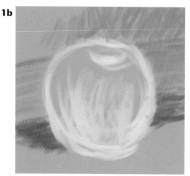

1a

Choosing a paper color

1b

Loosely sketching with the Artist Pastel Chalk variant of Pastels

FEATHERING—THIN, PARALLEL STROKES over a blended underpainting—is a traditional pastel technique that yields texture and freshness. Because the feathered finishing strokes remain unblended on the painting's surface, the viewer's eye must work to blend the colors. Here is an example of optical color blending.

1 Starting with a sketch on colored paper. We set up a still life on a table in the side light of a window, arranging the cloth so that diagonal folds would lead the eye into the composition and give the painting more depth.

When we were satisfied with the still life design, we opened a new file (File, New: 3 x 3.3 inches x 300 ppi) with a rust-colored background. To set the Paper Color, click the Paper Color preview in the New window and choose a color in the Colors dialog box. To select a new hue, or adjust its saturation, click or drag in the color wheel. To make the color darker or lighter, adjust the value slider on the right side of the window. When you have a color that you like, click OK to accept it. Now click the Paper Selector near the bottom of the Toolbox and select Speckled Laid paper texture. Pick a color to sketch with from the Color picker (we began with a golden yellow). Select the Artist Pastel Chalk variant of Pastels from the Brush Selector Bar. For a more sensitive response when using your stylus, choose Edit, Preferences/Corel Painter 8, Preferences, Brush Tracking and make a representative brushstroke in the window, and click OK. Begin to roughly sculpt

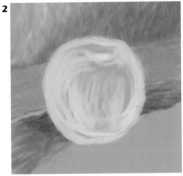

2

Painting angled strokes of varied color on the background

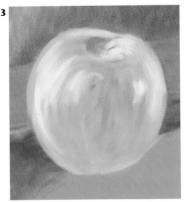

3

Blending color on the apple using the Grainy Water

4

Using feathered strokes to bring out highlights and color variations on the apple

the shape of the apple and suggest a horizon line (in our case, the angled table top) and then rough in the background, choosing new colors as needed.

2 Blocking in color over the sketch. Still working with the Artist Pastel Chalk, lay in more color over your sketch, allowing your strokes to follow the direction of the form.

3 Softening brush work. Select the Grainy Water variant of Blenders, and blend areas of color, again following the direction of the form. To blend while revealing more paper texture, blend colors with the Smudge variant of Blenders.

4 Building the underpainting. Using the Artist Pastel Chalk variant, add color and value to your sketch. To smear existing paint as you add new color, try one of the Soft Oil Pastel variants of Oil Pastels. We also used the Grainy Water variant of Blenders again to selectively blend areas. Layer the color and blend the underpainting until you're pleased with the form. We quickly added brown and purple colors to the background using angled brushstrokes. Then we painted more varied greens on the table cloth, and gave the wrinkles in the cloth more dimension.

5 Adding feathered strokes and detail. To create thin, textured strokes on top of the blended forms, choose the Tapered Pastel 10 variant and reduce its Size to 4.2 using the Size slider in the Property Bar. Stroke with this brush in the direction of the form. In our example, feathering is most noticeable in the highlight areas of the apple, in the reddish color overlaid over the apple's golden color, and in the foreground table cloth. Finish the piece by using Grainy Water to soften the feathering in the shadow areas. (To do the final blending touches, we lowered the Grainy Water variant's Opacity to 40% using the Opacity slider in the Property Bar.) We also used a tiny Soft Pastel Pencil 3 to deepen the shadow under the apple.

5a

Adding more texture and shadow to the table cloth

5b

The apple with the shadows more defined and with deeper reddish colors added

Painting with Pastels

Overview *Rough out a color composition; add layers of color with a custom Round Soft Pastel; blend colors with Blenders brushes; add highlights and details with the Sharp Chalk; use "scumbling" for texture to finish.*

CHER THREINEN-PENDARVIS

Sketching in color with the Sharp Chalk variant of Chalk

Blending the hill and sky using the Smudge variant of the Blenders brush

Adjusting the settings in the Property Bar

2b

Painting the sunlight shining over the ridge with a custom Round Soft Pastel and yellow color

INSPIRED BY THE SPARKLING LIGHT on a moist, breezy morning, *Agave Meadow* was painted from memory using Painter's Pastel, Chalk and Blenders variants, although we occasionally referred to detailed colored pencil sketches made on location. To achieve the soft atmosphere, we painted layers of color with Pastel variants, blended color with Blender brushes, and added details and broken color to finish the painting.

1 Starting with the drawing. Choose a photo or a sketch of a landscape to use as a reference and open a new file. We started with a 30 x 19.5-inch file at 120 ppi.

Next, choose a color in the Color picker. (If the Color picker is not open, open it by pressing Ctrl/⌘-1). Click the Paper Selector icon (near the bottom of the Toolbox) and choose a medium-grained paper, such as Sketchbook Paper texture. Select the Chalk category in the Brush Selector Bar, choose the Sharp Chalk variant and begin sketching. To keep the freshness and energy of a sketch while you draw, don't get bogged down with details. We also used the Artist Pastel Chalk variant of Pastels to add crosshatching to the hills and the Smudge variant of Blenders to blend colors.

2 Building a custom Pastel variant. When you've finished sketching your composition and you're ready to layer color in the underpainting, create a midsized, soft Pastel variant: First choose the Round Soft Pastel 10 variant of Pastels. In the Property Bar, set the Size to 12.0, and lower the Opacity to 30%. A lower opacity will allow you to build up color slowly with more sensitivity. To save this custom brush as a variant, choose Variant, Save Variant from the triangle pop-up menu on the right side of the Brush Selector Bar. Name your variant and click OK. The new name will appear in the Brush Selector Bar under the Pastels category. Choose a color and begin painting. We adjusted our new variant's size and opacity as we worked, switching to a 50% opacity, for instance, when painting the sunrise light shining over the ridge of the hill.

3

Using the Grainy Water variant to "melt" the hill separation, and create a subtle line

4

Using the custom Soft Pastel variant to paint "windy" hatching strokes on the hills

5

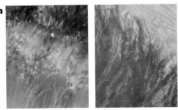

Scumbling on the path with the Hard Square Pastel 40 variant

6a

Drawing the foreground grass blades and details on the acacia with the Sharp Chalk

6b

Painting the highlights on the agave plants using the Artist Pastel Chalk variant

3 Blending colors. To achieve a smooth look with traditional pastels, you rub them with precise blending tools like a tortillion or a blending stump. Use the Just Add Water, Grainy Water, and Smudge variants of the Blenders brush to mimic these traditional tools. A few hints about these blenders: The Just Add Water uses the Soft Cover subcategory, and blends smoothly without texture; Grainy Water use Grainy Flat Cover and blends showing a hint of texture; Smudge uses Grainy Hard Cover and reveals more texture as it blends color. Begin blending, and experiment with these brushes and various brush sizes while you work.

4 Achieving a feeling of movement. Select the Pastel variant you created in Step 2. Imagine the wind blowing over your landscape, and apply light strokes over the hills in your painting, as if your strokes were blown by the wind. We switched to a rougher paper texture (Coarse Cotton Canvas texture), then added gold, rust-colored and blue strokes to the mid-ground hills and lighter blues to the sky. We covered most of the rolling coastal hills with soft, linear brushstrokes.

5 Scumbling for more texture. Artists using traditional media will often finish a pastel drawing by brushing the side of the pastel lightly along the peaks of the rough art paper. This technique, called *scumbling*, causes colors to blend optically and adds texture. To scumble electronically, select the Hard Square Pastel 40 variant from the Brush Selector Bar and adjust Opacity to 25% in the Property Bar. Choose a rough paper, such as Coarse Cotton Canvas. Apply strokes lightly using a color sampled from your image with the Dropper. We used scumbling to complete the sky and clouds and to show subtle reflected light on the foreground path. To add a semi-transparent texture to the plant life in the foreground, we switched to the custom low-opacity Round Soft Pastel variant.

6 Finishing with fine details. After adding the scumbling, we added fine details, such as the thin foreground grass blades and the planes of the agave leaves that were illuminated by full sunlight.

To draw grass blades we chose the Sharp Chalk variant and a light greenish-gold color in the Color picker. Before we began to paint, we opened the Color Variability palette (Window, Show Color Variability) and adjusted the Value (± V) to 4% so the color would vary slightly as we painted. We painted thin, slightly curved strokes (keeping the wind direction in mind). We made a few strokes overlap and adjusted the size of the strokes using the Size slider on the Property Bar.

To enhance the focal point of the painting, we painted bright highlights on the sides of the agave leaves that were catching the direct morning sun. For the highlights we chose a light golden yellow, and painted curved strokes with the Artist Pastel Chalk, using it at its full opacity.

A Painter Watercolor Primer

Overview Here you'll find the basics for painting with Painter's Water Color brushes and layers.

CHER THREINEN-PENDARVIS

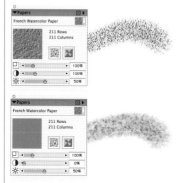

Two brushstrokes painted with the Diffuse Grainy Camel variant of Water Color: 100% Contrast, the default (top), and painting with 0% Contrast (bottom)

PAINTER 8 FEATURES TWO KINDS OF WATERCOLOR: Water Color layers and Digital Water Color. This primer covers Water Color Layers. Digital Water Color, which is simpler to use and doesn't require a special layer, is covered on pages 84–87.

Water Color media layers provide artists with an experience that's surprisingly like traditional watercolor. The Water Color layer is a simulation of a transparent wet medium containing suspended pigment. This makes it possible to create smooth, transparent washes and then diffuse color into existing wet paint to blend, as a traditional watercolorist would.

Red Hibiscus (above), is one of a series of flower studies painted using the technique presented step-by-step in "Combining Wet-into-Wet and Glazing on Layers" on page 80. But before you start using Water Color, reading these four pages will help you to understand how to achieve the results you desire.

Controlling Water Color. You can control the wetness, drying time, direction in which your wash will run and many other techniques that you're able to achieve using conventional watercolor tools. The most important settings for Water Color are in the Stroke Designer tab of the Brush Creator (the General, Size, and Water sections); the Papers palette; and the Layers palette. When you make a brushstroke with a Water Color brush, a Water Color layer is automatically generated in the Layers pal-

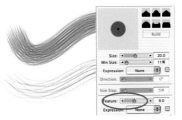

These two brushstrokes were painted with the Dry Bristle brush. The top stroke uses the default brush settings. For the bottom stroke, the Feature size was increased to 8.0 in the Size section of the Brush Stroke Designer tab in the Brush Creator, which resulted in a brushstroke with fewer brush hairs.

The Water section of the Brush Stroke Designer (Brush Creator) contains controls for modifying Water Color brushes.

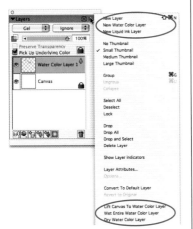

The menu on the right side of the Layers palette bar offers useful options for working with Water Color layers: New Water Color Layer, Lift Canvas to Water Color Layer, Wet Entire Water Color Layer, and Dry Water Color layer.

ette. Water Color layers can be targeted in the Layers palette and edited like other layers. Chapter 5 tells about working with layers.

In the General section of the Stroke Designer (within the Brush Creator), the Water Color dab types are displayed in the Dab Type pop-up menu. A dab type determines the shape of the brush—for instance, Water Color Flat and Water Color Camel (round). Most of the Water Color brushes use continuous-stroke technology, which means that brushstrokes are painted using brush hairs that are a set of anti-aliased 1-pixel lines. You'll find more information about dab types in "Building Brushes" on page 57 of this chapter.

In the Size section of Stroke Designer, you'll find the Feature slider, which determines the density of the brush hairs in the continuous-stroke brushes. **Note:** A very low Feature setting (producing more densely packed brush hairs), takes greater computing power and this can slow down the performance of a Water Color brush.

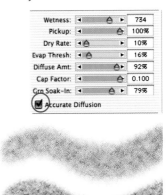

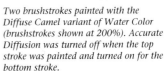

Two brushstrokes painted with the Diffuse Camel variant of Water Color (brushstrokes shown at 200%). Accurate Diffusion was turned off when the top stroke was painted and turned on for the bottom stroke.

In the Water section of the Stroke Designer, *Wetness* works with Evaporation Threshold to control the amount and spread of the *water* and *dye*. A low Evaporation Threshold will allow more spread; higher values will cause less spread. A high Wetness setting will blur the individual bristle marks and (with a high Diffusion Amount setting) increase the spread of the stroke, but it may make the performance of the brush lag. *Pickup* controls the amount of existing paint that gets moved when a new brushstroke paints over existing pigment. High Pickup rates cause wet edges or puddles, which can be desirable. The *Dry Rate* controls the length of time the water and pigment take to settle. A high Dry Rate will keep a brush with high Diffusion Amount settings from spreading as far, because the stroke will dry before it has had time to diffuse. A low Dry Rate value will allow more time for spread. *Evaporation Threshold* controls the amount of *water* that can diffuse. (In traditional watercolor, evaporation is the rate in which liquid is sublimated into the atmosphere.) *Diffusion Amount* controls the

A smooth wash (top), and thick and thin flower petal shapes (bottom), painted with the Wash Camel variant of Water Color

A smooth stroke painted The Wash Bristle (top) and diffused strokes with wet edges, painted with the Wet Bristle (bottom). The variation in color is caused by pigment buildup.

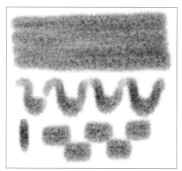

These soft-edged washes and brushstrokes were painted with the Diffuse Flat.

These crisper, expressive strokes were painted with the Wash Pointed Flat.

amount of *pigment* that can diffuse. *Capillary Factor* and *Grain Soak-In* affect the amount of pigment that settles in the valleys of the paper grain. Setting both of these controls to 0 will minimize grain effects. Also, very low Capillary Factor and Grain Soak-In settings will allow a runny wash to spread more smoothly. A high Capillary Factor (with a low Grain Soak-In setting) will create a "stringy" drip texture in the runny wash.

GETTING TO KNOW THE WATER COLOR BRUSHES

Here are some suggestions for how to paint traditional-looking brush work using Painter's Water Color brushes. Even if you're familiar with using a stylus and Painter's other brushes, try these exercises and experiment with all of the water color brushes. You may enjoy discovering a new kind of expressive brushstroke!

Versatility with Camel brushes. The most versatile of all the Water Color brushes, the Camel brushes, are round. In addition to painting various kinds of washes, most Camel brushes allow you to paint brushstrokes that can be thick and thin, depending on the pressure applied to the stylus. Other Camel brushes allow you to apply drippy washes (Runny Wash Camel and Runny Wet Camel), while the Diffuse Camel paints strokes that have soft, feathery edges.

Choose the Wash Camel variant and paint a smooth wash area. Apply even pressure to your stylus, and make a horizontal stroke, then carefully paint a second horizontal stroke below it, just slightly overlapping the first stroke. The diffusion in the stroke edge will help make a smooth transition between the strokes. Before painting thick to thin strokes, set Brush Tracking (Edit, Preferences/Corel Painter 8, Preferences, Brush Tracking, make a representative brushstroke in the window, and click OK). Using the Wash Camel, press harder to paint the thicker area of the shape, then gradually reduce pressure on the stylus, finally lifting your stylus as you complete the stroke.

Expressive brush work with Bristle brushes. These Water Color brushes paint just like brushes with real bristles because they're sensitive to tilt and rotation of the stylus. As you tilt your stylus, the bristles of the brush spread or splay out as you rotate your hand through the stroke. To paint a wash that has the texture of soft bristle marks, try the Wash Bristle brush. For a wet-into-wet effect with subtle bristle marks and pools at the stroke edges experiment with the Wet Bristle.

Thick and thin strokes with the Flat brushes. Look for brushes with the word Flat in their name; the Diffuse Flat and Wash Pointed Flat are examples. With Flat-tipped brushes, you can paint wide or narrow strokes, depending on the way you hold the stylus and how much pressure you apply. When trying the strokes that follow, position your stylus with the button facing up (away from you). To paint a fuzzy wash with the Diffuse Flat (as in the image on the left), pull the brush straight across your image using even pres-

The Fine variants are useful when painting expressive, linear brushstrokes, as in the sketches of the eye and grasses shown here.

We painted this cloud study using the Runny Wash Bristle and Runny Wet Camel to paint the clouds, the Wash Camel and Fine Camel variants to paint the water and the Diffuse Camel to soften a few edges.

For this foliage study we created texture in the foreground with a small Splatter Water brush.

As a final touch to Pink Orchid, we used the Eraser Salt variant of Water Color to sprinkle light speckles on the tops of the petals

sure. To make the thin lines, pull down. To make a curved, thin-to-thick wavy line, use light pressure on your stylus for the thin top areas, and more pressure as you sweep down and rotate the brush.

For flat brushstrokes with crisper edges and more thin-to-thick control, try the Wash Pointed Flat. For a thin-to-thick sweeping curved stroke, begin the thin portion with very light pressure on your stylus, and as you sweep downward rotate your stylus slightly (changing the button orientation) and apply more pressure. To make a thick, even stroke, pull the stylus sideways relative to the button, using even pressure. For the thin lines, apply even pressure and pull in a direction toward or away from the button.

Adding detail with the Fine brushes. The Fine variants of the Water Color brush are good for painting details, and for calligraphic line work. The Fine Camel and Fine Bristle are similar to "rigger" or "line" brushes, which are used to paint expressive line work in traditional watercolor.

Painting runny washes using the Runny brushes. The *Runny* variants (the Runny Wash Bristle and the Runny Wash Camel, for instance), are useful for painting drippy wet-into-wet washes, where the colors run together and blend, but they don't displace the underlying color. The *Runny Wet* variants, however, will run and move existing color as the new pigment travels. The Runny Wet brushes are useful if you want to add a darker wet-looking edge to the bottom of a cloud, for instance.

For all of the Runny Wash and Runny Wet brushes, the Wind Direction and Force settings determine the direction of the run and how far a wash will run, much like tipping your watercolor board when working in the field. To paint a Water Color Runny wash that moves only a little ways, lower the Force setting.

While painting the clouds in the illustration on the left, we laid varied sky colors in using the Runny Wash Bristle and Runny Wet Camel. To soften some of the runny edges, we dotted in more color using the Diffuse Camel, applying color with short dabbing strokes. Then we painted the water with the Wash Camel and Fine Camel variants, again softening areas with the Diffuse Camel.

Adding spatter effects. With the Splatter Water variant, you can add dots of diffused color to your paintings. This is especially effective when painting foliage. Paint some wash areas using the Wash Camel or Wash Flat, and varied colors of green. Now choose the Splatter Water variant and a slightly different color. Paint a few dots of color, then change the color slightly in the Color picker and add a few more diffused color dots, changing the size of the brush as you work.

Also, you can add varied, light speckles to your images (as we did in the image on the left), with the Eraser Salt variant of Water Color. To follow the step-by-step technique used for painting the orchid, turn to "Wet-Into-Wet Water Color" on page 76.

Wet-into-Wet Watercolor

Overview *Make a "pencil sketch"; loosely paint smooth washes with Water Color brushes to build up varied color; add subtle wet-into-wet bristle marks; add details to the image and create a speckled texture using Salt.*

CHER THREINEN-PENDARVIS

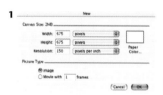

Starting a new file for the Orchid painting

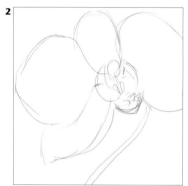

The pencil sketch drawn in Painter using the 2B Pencil variant of Pencils

PINK ORCHID, A LOOSE DIGITAL WATER COLOR STUDY, was painted from life in Painter with a Wacom Intuos pressure-sensitive tablet and stylus. Water Color wet-into-wet techniques were used, then details and texture were added. *Wet-into-wet* is a traditional technique that can be simulated using Painter's Water Color technology. Wet-into-wet is the most fluid way to apply color, as it involves keeping the paper wet while new color is applied, so new colors blend with existing moist paint. With Water Color layers, you can paint with Water Color brushes that apply pigment that will percolate and diffuse into the paper grain, paint washes that actually run and blend into existing wet paint, and you can paint transparent glazes.

1 Setting up and opening a new file. For the best performance, Macintosh users may need to increase the RAM that is allotted to Painter when working with Water Color.

Begin by creating a new file with a white background (File, New). In the New dialog box, click the Image button. For a square format, set the Width and Height at 675 x 675 pixels. Click OK. (The brush sizes that you'll use will depend on the pixel size of the document.)

2 Making a pencil sketch. Select a natural-looking grain (such as French Water Color) by clicking the Paper Selector near the bottom of the Toolbox and choosing from the menu. Choose a neutral gray color in the Color picker and select the 2B Pencils

3a

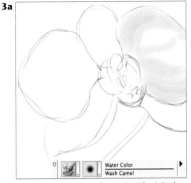

Painting smooth washes using the Wash Camel variant

3b

An active Water Color layer shown in the Layers palette

3c

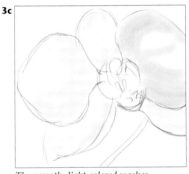

The smooth, light-colored washes

4a

Using the Wash Camel variant to add deeper colors

SETTING BRUSH TRACKING

It's a good idea to set up Brush Tracking before you begin a Water Color session because it will increase expressiveness in Painter's brushes and make smoother strokes. With Brush Tracking you can customize how Painter interprets the input of your stylus, including parameters such as pressure and how quickly you make a brush stroke. You'll notice the more sensitive control of the Water Color brushes, especially with brushes such as the Diffuse Camel and Fine Camel variants. From the Painter 8 menu choose Preferences, Brush Tracking, make a representative brush stroke in the window, then click OK.

Making a brush stroke in the Brush Tracking window

variant of Pencils (in the Brush Selector Bar) to draw your line sketch. We set up our blooming orchid plant next to the computer and sketched from life.

3 Painting the first washes. The brush work in the *Pink Orchid* study is loose and spontaneous. As you prepare to begin adding color, make a few loose, practice brushstrokes. (You can always undo the brushstrokes by pressing Ctrl/⌘-Z, or you can delete your practice Water Color layer by selecting it in the Layers palette and clicking the Delete button on the palette).

Plan to work from light to dark as you add color washes to your painting. Choose a light color in the Color picker (we chose a light lavender-pink). In the Brush Selector Bar, choose the Wash Camel variant of Water Color. (When you select a Water Color brush and make a brush stroke on your image, Painter will automatically create a new Water Color layer in the image.) When you apply a light, even pressure on your stylus, the Wash Camel will allow you to lay in the wash areas smoothly. The slight bit of diffusion built into the brush will help the brush strokes to blend subtly as

STRATEGIC AREAS OF WHITE

Don't feel like you have to cover every inch of your image with color. Leaving strategic areas of white will add to the beauty and give your painting a feeling of dappled light.

you paint. When you make a new stroke, place it next to the previous stroke so that it barely overlaps. Try not to scrub with the brush or paint over areas too many times, unless you want to darken the area. Painter's Water Color operates like traditional transparent Water Color.

Paint with strokes that follow the direction of the forms in your subject. Complete the lightest wash areas, leaving some of the "white of the paper" showing through for the highlights.

4 Building up the midtones on the flower. Using medium-value colors, begin to develop your midtones, painting lighter

4b

Continuing to develop the mid tones with the Wash Camel variant

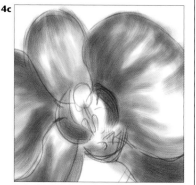

4c

Painting bristle marks with the Dry Camel variant. The reddish color was added with the Wash Camel variant.

5

The drippy washes on the lower petals were painted with the Runny Wash variants of Water Color

colors first, then adding darker tones to continue to develop the form. Keep your light source in mind and let your strokes follow the direction of the forms. To resize the brush, or change its Opacity as you work, use the Opacity slider on the Property Bar. We added deeper colors of lavender-pink, while keeping the brushwork loose.

We continued to gradually build up deeper color. As we completed the midtones stage, we switched to the Dry Camel variant of Water Color, which allowed us to add a little more brush stroke texture over some of the wash areas and at the ends of the strokes, while still allowing the new strokes to blend as wet-into-wet.

5 Painting wet-into-wet runny washes. Painter offers dynamic brushes that allow you to emulate various traditional Water Color *run* effects. For a smooth runny wash that will not displace the underlying color, use one of the Runny Wash variants. Choose a slightly different color in the Color picker and dab the new color on to areas with existing color. Using the Runny Wash Camel and Runny Wash Bristle, we applied brighter pink and magenta colors (using short dabbing strokes) on the deeper color areas of the flower petals. Then we added deeper pink and reddish colors to the interior of the orchid. The Runny Wash variants allowed the new color to mix with existing color without moving the existing color.

The *Runny* variants of Water Color (the Runny Wash Bristle and the Runny Wash Camel, for instance), are useful for painting *wash runs*, where colors run together and blend, but don't displace the underlying color. This is similar to a glazing effect. The *Runny Wet* variants, however, will run and displace existing color on the image as the new pigment travels. Often the Runny Wet brushes will leave a lighter area because the Wet variants cause leaching of the existing pigment. The Runny Wet brushes are useful if you want to add darker wet-looking edges to foliage or when painting a sky with rain clouds.

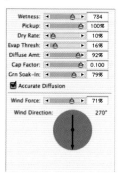

The default Runny Wet Bristle variant of Water Color paints strokes that run vertically down the image and move existing color. The Dry Rate is set at 10%, allowing lots of time for the pant to run, the Wind Direction is set to 270°, and the Force setting (71%), makes the washes drip a long way. The high Pickup rate allows the brush strokes to move existing color.

Keep in mind that Painter 8's Water Color is based on traditional Water Color painting. With traditional water color, an artist plans on time for the paint to spread, run and dry, and this time is often used to analyze and improve the composition of the painting. Painter's new Water Color technology uses a lot of computing power. It takes time for the digital pigment to diffuse and settle on the image, not unlike traditional water color.

6

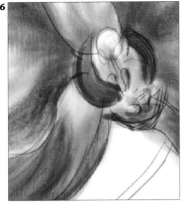

Lightening an area in the center of the flower with the Eraser Dry variant of Water Color

7

Adding soft detail to flower stamen and highlights and shadows to the stem with the Fine Camel variant of Water Color

8

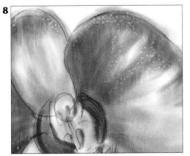

Sprinkling "salt" on the upper area of the orchid using the Eraser Salt variant of Water Color

6 Editing a Water Color layer or the sketch. It's not possible to use a variant of the Erasers brush on a Water Color layer, and you can't use a Water Color Eraser or Bleach variant on the Canvas, or on an image layer. To softly remove color on a Water Color layer, choose the Eraser Dry variant of Water Color and choose white in the Color picker. In the Layers palette, click on the name of the Water Color layer you wish to edit and brush over the area you'd like to lighten. We used the Eraser Dry variant to brighten the highlights on the flower petals and the stamen.

If you'd like to edit your pencil sketch, target the Canvas in the Layers palette and switch to the Eraser variant of the Erasers and brush over the area that you'd like to erase.

7 Painting details. If you want very crisp details, it's a good idea to paint detail work on a separate layer, but in this case we stayed on the same Water Color layer because we wanted to preserve the softer wet-into-wet look. Add crisper edges to areas that need definition using a small Fine Camel variant (6–8 pixels). To reduce the Size of the Fine Camel variant, use the Size slider in the Property Bar. If the Fine Camel seems too saturated for your taste, lower the Opacity to about 20%, using the Opacity slider in the Property Bar. If you'd like softer edges, experiment with the Wash Camel and the Diffuse Camel variants, using a small size (about 6–8 pixels). Make expressive strokes, varying the pressure on the stylus. To paint expressive details, we used the Fine Camel variant to add curved brush strokes and to paint small areas of color on the interior of the orchid. To deepen color and break up a few of the edges, we dabbed a little more color on using the Runny Wash Camel variant. We also painted highlights and shadows on the stem using the Fine Camel variant.

8 Adding color modulation and texture. To add a little more activity in the color, we loosely added a few more bristle marks using the Dry Bristle variant. Finally, we added a light speckled texture using the Eraser Salt variant of Water Color. To add bleached speckles on your image, choose the Eraser Salt variant and scrub the brush over the area you want to add speckles to. For smaller salt particles, reduce the brush Size using the Size slider in the Property Bar. To keep a spontaneous hand-done look, we retained the original sketch drawn with the 2B Pencil in the image.

ERASING WATER COLOR

You can lighten areas of color using the Eraser variants of Water Color. To smoothly erase color, choose white in the Color picker and choose the Eraser Dry variant of Water Color. Stroke over the area that you'd like to remove.

USE THE OPACITY KEYS

To change the opacity of your brushstrokes without using the Property Bar's Opacity slider, use these keyboard shortcuts: Press 1 for 10% Opacity, 2 for 20%, and so on (press 0 for 100% Opacity).

Combining Wet-Into-Wet and Glazing on Layers

Overview *Draw a tight pencil sketch; brush in soft wet-into-wet washes; paint glazes on separate layers; add texture and crisp details.*

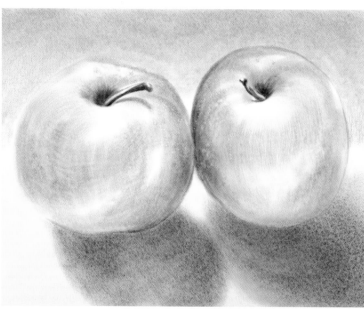

TWO COMMON TRADITIONAL WATERCOLOR techniques that can be simulated with Painter are *wet-into-wet* and *glazing.* Wet-into-wet creates a softer-edged look—the painting surface is kept wet as new color is applied, so new paint blends easily with old. Glazing involves applying transparent washes of watercolor; colors are usually built up in layers from light to dark.

Before beginning *Two Green Apples,* we arranged the apples in the natural light of a window near the computer, and chose a close-up view of our subject to emphasize subtle details. We began the painting with a tight pencil sketch in Painter and used transparent glazes to build layers of color and value, progressing from light to dark. As the painting progressed, we added more Water Color layers so that we could edit the wet-into-wet brush work separately without disturbing underlying color.

1 Drawing a tight pencil sketch. Create a new file with a white background by choosing File, New. (Our image measured 1200 x 850 pixels.) Before beginning your sketch, choose an even-textured paper (such as French Water Color or Basic Paper) from the Papers Selector (near the bottom of the Toolbox) and choose a dark gray in the Color picker. Now select the 2B Pencil variant of Pencils from the Brush Selector Bar and begin sketching. While drawing, we carefully explored the shapes and forms of the apples and we established the light source. (Turn to "Sketching With Pencils" on page 64 to read more about working with Pencils in Painter.)

Because we planned to use the sketch as a guide, we wanted to be able to turn its visibility on and off and adjust its opacity as needed, so we decided to float the sketch onto a layer. To put your

1

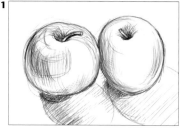

The pencil sketch drawn using the 2B Pencil variant of Pencils

2a

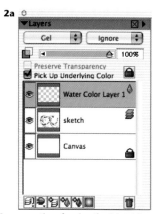

The Layers section showing the "sketch" layer and the active new Water Color layer

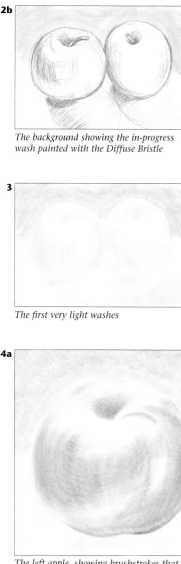

2b

The background showing the in-progress wash painted with the Diffuse Bristle

3

The first very light washes

4a

The left apple, showing brushstrokes that wrap around its form

4b

The apples with light washes established and midtones in-progress

sketch onto a layer, choose Select, All (Ctrl/⌘-A), and Select, Float. To lower the opacity of the layer, click on the layer name in the Layers palette, then adjust the Opacity slider to about 25%. If the Layers palette is not open, choose Window, Show Layers. (For more information about layers, turn to Chapter 5, "Using Layers.")

2 Painting the background. When you choose a Water Color brush and touch your stylus to the tablet, a Water Color layer will automatically appear in the Layers palette. You can choose to paint your entire painting using only one layer (which is beneficial if you want a natural wet-into-wet look). Or you can choose to paint different stages of the painting on separate layers as we did. When creating a tight illustration (such as the apples shown here), using several layers can give you better control over separate brush work, but some of the effect of overall wet-into-wet may be sacrificed.

When painting the background, we carefully painted around the shapes of the apples. Choose the Diffuse Bristle variant of Water Color in the Brush Selector Bar. When you apply a light pressure on your stylus, the Diffuse Bristle will allow you to smoothly lay in soft-edged washes. The Diffuse Bristle incorporates diffusion, which helps overlapping brushstrokes to subtly blend. Try not to cover every inch of your background with color. Leaving areas of white will add texture and interest to your painting. (We left some white paper showing in the top areas of the painting.)

3 Painting the first light washes. Add a new Water Color layer by choosing New Water Color layer from the menu that pops out from the upper right corner of the Layers palette. As you add color washes to your painting, plan to work from light to dark as much as you can. Choose a very light color in the Color picker and use the Diffuse Bristle variant of Water Color. Using the light color, block in large areas and begin to establish the roundness of the forms. Establish the cast shadows and foreground also by painting light washes.

4 Adding richer color and tonal values. For the deeper tones, add another new Water Color layer, as you did in step 3. Working on the new layer, build up medium-value colors, then gradually add darker tones that will sculpt volume. Keep your light source in mind as you paint, and let the brushstrokes follow the direction of the forms. Resize the brush, or change its Opacity as needed using the sliders on the Property Bar. Remember to preserve the white areas that will be kept as bright highlights. To render the volume of the left apple, we painted curved vertical strokes in the shadowed areas. Then we added a few curved horizontal brushstrokes. We also used medium tones of brown to begin to paint the stems.

4c

The midtones and some darker tones in the shadows

5

The speckled texture is visible in this detail of the two apples

6

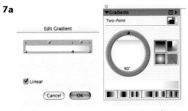

The fine details on the apple stems and their cast shadows added.

7a

Setting up the custom two-point gradient

7b

In this example, the painted blue background layer is hidden. The gradient is applied to the Canvas (left); the texture applied is applied (right).

5 Adding subtle wet-into-wet texture. Working on the Water Color layer that contains the midtones, we used a grain-sensitive brush to paint subtle texture in the shadow areas of the apples. The Diffuse Grainy Camel paints soft-edged washes while bringing out the texture chosen in the Papers section. Choose the Diffuse Grainy Camel. Now sample color from the image by pressing the Alt/Option key to temporarily switch from the Brush to the Dropper, then paint using short dabbing strokes to "bleed" color variation and subtle values into the shadows. We sampled color several times while we painted over the shadow areas. For the light-colored speckles on the apples, we used a small Splatter Water variant of Water Color.

6 Painting details. To keep detail crisp, add a separate layer for your detail work (as described in step 3). In areas that need more definition, paint crisper edges using a small Fine Camel brush (4–5 pixels). If the Fine Camel seems too saturated for your taste, lower its Opacity to about 20% using the slider in the Controls: Brush palette. For more subtle edge effects, try experiment with the Soft Camel and the Diffuse Camel variants, using a small size (about 6–8 pixels). To complete the study, we used the Fine Camel variant to darken the edges of the shadows under the apples.

7 Adding a gradient with water color texture. Our painting needed more depth. To quickly add deeper color to the image background, as detailed below, we filled the Canvas with a blue-to-white gradient, then we floated it to a Water Color layer and applied a Water Color texture effect.

To fill the Canvas with a gradient, target the Canvas by clicking on its name in the Layers palette. Choose the Dropper and click on a rich blue in the background area behind the apples. Open the Gradients palette by choosing Window, Show Gradients and choose Two-Point from the resource list menu. To edit the gradient so that the blue is concentrated near the top of the image, with white below, choose Edit Gradient from the menu that pops out from the right side of the Gradients palette bar. In the Edit Gradient dialog box, click on the colored ramp to add another color control point where you'd like it. With the new control point active, choose white in the Color picker. Click OK. For more information about gradients turn to Chapter 2, "The Power of Color." In the Gradients section, drag the Gradient Ring to position the Gradient Preview with the blue at the top. When the gradient is the way you like it, choose Effects, Fill, Fill With Gradient.

To give the gradient on the Canvas a water color texture, lift it to a Water Color layer by choosing Lift Canvas to Water Color Layer from the menu on the right side of the Layers palette. You can now apply a Water Color-like texture to the new layer that is

7c

Choosing Wet Entire Water Color Layer from the Layers palette menu

8a

Blocking in the cast shadows using the Wash Bristle

8b

The in-progress cast shadows showing some of the brush work added with the Grainy Wash Bristle

8c

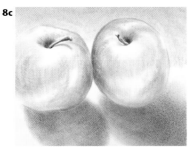

The final cast shadows after the Wet Entire Water Color layer effect was applied

based on the characteristics of the Water Color brush chosen in Brushes palette. If the brush chosen is texture-sensitive, the paper texture chosen in the Papers Selector will also contribute to the effect. Select the Grainy Wash Camel variant. With the new Water Color layer active, choose Wet Entire Water Color Layer from the menu on the right side of the Layers palette bar.

8 Completing the cast shadows. We carefully studied the subtle graduated tones in the cast shadows created by the light from the window. In areas where they overlapped, darker-toned curved shapes were created. The shadows gradually became lighter as they progressed toward the foreground.

Working on a new Water Color layer so that we could edit the shadows separately from the rest of the image, we gradually developed the deeper tones in the cast shadows as follows: Add a new Water Color layer using the process in step 3. Choose the Wash Bristle variant and a blue-gray color in the Color picker, which will work well with the blue you've chosen for your background. Block in the basics shapes, then to add more texture in the deeper-colored areas, switch to the Grainy Wash Bristle and gradually add to the deeper tones.

To melt the new work into the old, wet the cast shadow layer: With the Grainy Wash Bristle still selected, choose Wet Entire Water Color Layer from the menu on the right side of the Layers palette bar.

LIFTING ART ON THE CANVAS TO A WATER COLOR LAYER

With Painter's Water Color technology, any existing artwork or photograph on the Canvas layer can be turned into Water Color, as follows:

1 Open an image that contains artwork on the Canvas layer. From the pop-out menu on the right side of the Layers palette bar, choose Lift Canvas to Water Color Layer

2 Choose a texture in the Paper Selector. Some brushes (such as the Grainy Wash variants) are grain-sensitive and apply nice texture effects.)

3 In the Brush Selector Bar, choose a Water Color brush whose characteristics you'd like to apply to your image.

4 Choose Wet Entire Water Color layer from the pop-out menu on the right side of the Layers palette bar, and watch as Painter applies Water Color to your image! In the Layers section, when the animated water drop to the left of the Water Color layer name stops dripping, the effect is complete.

After lifting this pastel drawing to a Water Color Layer, we added to the texture on the image by using the Grainy Wash Camel variant of Water Color to "wet" the Water Color Layer.

Painting With Digital Water Color

Overview *Scan a pencil sketch; use it as a guide while painting contours using a brush; apply colored washes to the sketch with brushes; add final highlight detail to the dried image with an Eraser.*

1

The sketch made using pencils and paper

2

The contours painted using the Pointed Simple Water variant

3a

Light washes painted with the New Simple Water variant

WITH PAINTER'S DIGITAL WATER COLOR, you can paint wet-into-wet and add smooth glazes of thin transparent color on the Canvas or on a standard layer. For wet-into-wet, the painting surface is kept wet as new color is applied, so new paint blends easily with existing paint. The process of layering washes using Digital Water Color is similar to using Painter's Water Color layers (covered on pages 72–83). The pigment colors are usually built up in layers from light to dark, but the effects are not as realistic as those that can be achieved with Painter's special Water Color media layers. Digital Water Color is simpler and quicker to apply, and thus it's ideal for quick studies.

1 Sketching and scanning. We began *Aloe Medusa*, one in a series of plant studies, by sketching with conventional pencils in our sketchbook. We carefully observed the subject while making the drawing, and added such details as the shadow lines along the edges of the leaves. Then we scanned the pencil drawing at 300 ppi, a resolution suitable for offset printing.

2 Setting up and painting contours. Because we planned to remove the pencil sketch after the painting was roughed out, we painted a contour drawing using a color that would appear in the final image. The contours would help to define the edges of some of the forms in the study. Before beginning to paint, put your scanned sketch on a layer by choosing Select, All (Ctrl/⌘-A) and Select, Float. So the white areas in the sketch will appear transparent, set the Compositing Method for this layer to Multiply in the Layers palette. Now target the Canvas by clicking on its name in the Layers palette. Choose a color that will appear in the light-to-mid-tone areas of your painting (we chose a rich golden color) and select the Pointed Simple Water variant of Digital Water Color in the Brush Selector Bar. When you paint using a Digital Water Color brush, the layer's Composite Method will automatically change from

3b

Building up tones using slightly darker washes

3c

Painting soft, diffused washes behind the leaves for a background

4a

Painting crisper washes on the leaves and beginning to build up the forms

4b

Adding deeper tones to the interior of the aloe using the New Simple Water variant

5

Adding detail to the edges of the leaves

Default to Gel to give the look of transparent washes. Sketch the contours with the brush expressively, applying more pressure to your stylus when you want a thicker line and less for a thinner line. When wet-into-wet washes are added in the next step, the colors will mix at the edges of the contour lines.

3 Adding the first washes. We used highlight colors for the first washes. Choose very light colors and block in the large areas with the New Simple Water variant of the Digital Water Color. (This brush will allow you to add color and will subtly smear it into existing pigment.) After the lightest washes are laid in, use the New Simple Water variant to add a slightly darker series of washes with more detail, as we did before developing the midtones in the next step. We also began to layer deeper blues for the background behind the leaves. We pulled the strokes out from the center of the plant to accentuate the focal point. (At this point, we removed the pencil sketch by selecting its name in the Layers palette and clicking the Delete button at the bottom of the Layers palette.) To paint a soft, diffused background, choose the Coarse Water brush and use light pressure on your stylus as you apply the strokes to gradually build up the deeper tones. For a smoother effect, try the Soft Diffused Brush.

4 Building form and midtone values. Choose medium-value colors and develop your midtones, applying lighter colors first, then darker ones to create form. Keep your light source in mind and let your strokes follow the direction of the forms. We added the larger intermediate-value shapes and some of the shadows. Then we added deeper greens and teals to the interior of the aloe to enhance the focal point, while remembering to leave areas of the "paper" white to preserve the highlights.

5 Adding texture, details and blending. Next, we used the Coarse Mop Brush (Digital Water Color) to paint soft, striated strokes onto the background. To softly blend areas of the background, we used a lower-opacity New Simple Water variant. After completing the blending, we dried the painting, by choosing Dry Digital Water Color from the pop-up menu on the right side of the Layers palette. Then we used a small Pointed Simple Water variant to brighten the green and golden yellow details on the interior of the aloe. We added linear details to the leaves and deepened shadows, adjusting the Opacity and Size of the brush in the Property Bar as we worked. We worked carefully to develop subtle layers of color and contrast. To bring the aloe forward more in the composition, we used the New Simple Water variant to paint loose strokes of deeper blues behind the plant. Then we diffused the paint on the layer by choosing Diffuse Digital Water Color from the pop-up menu on the Layers palette. To finish, we sharpened areas of the painting that needed definition using a tiny Pointed Simple Water brush. Finally, we defined the highlights along the edges of the leaves with a tiny Pointed Eraser variant of the Erasers.

Coloring a Drawing Using Digital Water Color

Overview *Create a drawing using traditional pencils and paper; scan the drawing; put the drawing on a layer; use Painter's Digital Water Color brushes to hand-color the drawing.*

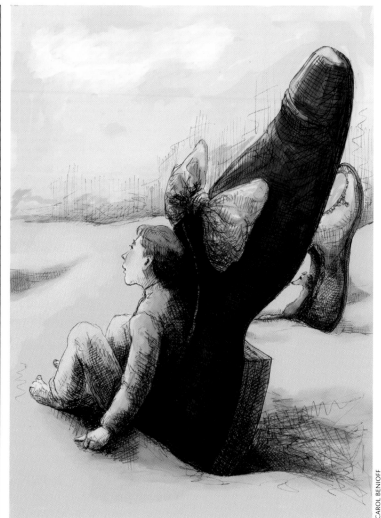

CAROL BENIOFF

The scanned drawing along with Benioff's custom color set

The drawing on a layer with its Composite Method set to Multiply in the Layers palette

CAROL BENIOFF TAKES ADVANTAGE of the quick and fluid qualities of the Digital Water Color brushes in *On the Beach*, one of a continuing series of prints and drawings using shoes as the motif.

1 Preparing to paint. Benioff drew the two shoes on the beach with a 2B pencil on acid-free bristol board. Then she scanned the drawing at 300 pixels-per-inch and opened the image in Painter. Next, she opened one of her custom color sets by choosing Window, Show Color Sets, clicking on the right arrow of the Color Set palette and choosing Open Color Set. For the paper texture, Benioff chose Thick Handmade Paper from the Paper Selector near the bottom of the Toolbox.

2 Putting the drawing on a layer. After she opened her scanned pencil drawing, Benioff selected the entire image (Select, All), then put the drawing onto a layer by choosing Select, Float.

For painting the sky, Benioff chose the variants Wash Brush, Soft Broad Brush, Soft Round Blender and the Pure Water Brush.

Using short quick strokes, Benioff painted the shoe using the Broad Brush, Fine Tip Water and Fine Mop Brush variants of Digital Water Color.

Benioff mixed colors in the Mixer palette.

To make the white areas of the drawing appear transparent in the next step, she set the Composite Method for the layer to Multiply in the Layers palette. Then she clicked on the Canvas in the Layers Palette to make it active so she could begin her painting.

3 Painting the sky and the beach. To add the first washes of color, she chose the Brush Tool in the Toolbox and chose the Wash Brush variant of Digital Water Color in the Brush Selector. Using large sweeping strokes she began painting the sky, resizing the brush from 50 to 90 pixels in the Property Bar as she worked. She also used the Soft Broad Brush sized to 40 pixels, the Soft Round Blender with its Wet Fringe set to 0% in the Property Bar (with its Size ranging from 40 to 70 pixels), and the Pure Water Brush sized to 40 pixels. These combinations of brushes gave her the smooth translucent look that she wanted. As she was painting, she chose varying hues of blues, greens, ochres and pinks from her custom Color Set.

4 Painting the shoes. For the shoes, Benioff wanted to add the textured brushstrokes of more intense color. So she chose the Broad Water Brush and set its Wet Fringe set to 0% in the Property Bar. She likes this brush's ability to lay down color and blend with underlying colors. She painted with short, quick strokes, resizing the brush from 9 to 15 pixels and changing its percentage of Opacity in the Property Bar. For fine detail in the image, Benioff used the Fine Tip brush with its opacity set to 6%. She selected the Fine Mop brush to add a more watery feel.

5 Mixing colors. When Benioff's Color Set did not have the color she wanted, she switched over to the Color Mixer palette (Window, Show Mixer). With her current color selected she selected the Apply Color tool in the Mixer palette, painted a stroke,

The final watercolor image without the pencil drawing layer

then selected another color from her custom Color Set and mixed them on the palette. Clicking on the Sample Color Tool in the Color Mixer palette, she then could select a new color from her mix. Another option she uses is the Eye Dropper from the Toolbox (the Alt/ Option key) to pick up newly mixed colors in the image.

6 The final touches. For the last washes of translucent color in the figure, beach and sky, she used the Wash Brush with its Opacity turned down to 2%.

Painting with Acrylics

Overview Paint a rough sketch; build up form and color; enrich the final colors with glazing.

The beginning sketch with the Dry Brush

Using and adjusting a custom Color Set to define the color palette

The Wet Soft Acrylic brush both paints and blends the colors

CAROL BENIOFF

PAINTING THIS *PORTRAIT OF HEINZ*, Carol Benioff was pleased to be able to use the Acrylics brushes straight out of Painter 8's box. She used a direct method of painting on the canvas with no preliminary drawings. This enabled her to finish the portrait in one sitting, even though Heinz has difficulty sitting still for long.

1 Roughing out the painting. Create a new document with a white background color. (Benioff created a 7 x 9-inch image at 300 pixels-per-inch.) Starting with the Dry Brush 10 variant of Acrylics, Benioff began to draw out the shapes using a neutral green. Then, she switched to the Wet Acrylic 20 variant, varying the size from 10 up to 62 pixels in the Property Bar as she roughly laid out the shapes and colors.

2 Selecting the colors. To ensure she is using colors that will print the way she wants them, Benioff makes her own custom Color Sets. (For information about making a Color Set that includes printable colors, see Chapter 12.) From the start, she

4

Adding depth and detail with the Dry Brush and Wet Acrylic variants

5a

The final painting before the translucent glazes of color were added

5b

Detail of the face before glazing

opened her own Color Set by choosing Window, Show Color Set. Then she clicked on the right arrow of the Color Sets palette and selected Open Color Set. To quickly modify the colors as she painted, she also opened the Color Info palette, where you can adjust the current selected color with RGB sliders.

3 Working with the paint. Benioff continued to work with a combination of Dry Brush and Wet Acrylic variants. She selected soft hues of blue so the back wall would sit behind Heinz's face and the back of the chair. She used the Wet Soft Acrylic brush in various sizes to push and smear the paint to a greater degree. She found that Dry Brush variants worked best for the details, and also provided her with the ability to scumble. To scumble, use a light pressure on the stylus and brush lightly across the peaks of the paper texture. With scumbling, colors blend optically and texture is added.

4 Defining form. Switching between the Dry Brush and the Wet Acrylic brush, she built up the form with contrasting colors both in the highlights and shadows. Benioff helps keep the painting lively with the push and pull of contrasting colors, strong lights and darks, and loosely drawn paint strokes.

5 Tying it all together. With the three variants of the Acrylic brushes Benioff was able to quickly complete her painting. She enlarged a Wet Acrylic variant to more than 60 to do more work on the background. She deepened the shadows, creating more contrast. Benioff then moved in close and painted with the smaller Wet Acrylic and Dry Brush, bringing out the details of the face. She then concentrated on the lights and darks of the shirt to create the illusion of it draping around his neck.

6 Glazing to add richness and depth. Benioff loves the depth and richness that happens with laying thin washes of translucent color over an existing painting. This technique, called

6

glazing, is one that she has used in traditional mediums and in most of the work she has done with Painter. The brush category of Acrylics comes with its own built in glazing variants called Glazing Acrylic. She used these variants in varying sizes up to 60 to glaze in the shadows, adding richness to the color and helping the shadows recede.

Detail of the face after multiple glazes of blues and deep purple were applied

Painting with Gouache

Overview *Create a finely grained surface; begin with a scanned sketch; sculpt highlights and details using Oils, Gouache and Impasto variants; pull color with a Palette Knife.*

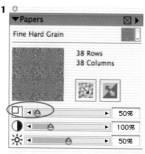

Scaling the Fine Hard Grain texture to 50%

Stahl's sketch drawn with the Smooth Ink Pen variant

ARTIST NANCY STAHL HAS WORKED WITH TRADITIONAL gouache on illustration board since 1976. When she began to work with the computer, her clients would accept her digital art only if the quality matched her conventional style. After much experimentation with Painter's brushes and surfaces, she has been able to fully re-create the effects in her traditional work, evident in *Sappi Portrait,* above.

1 Emulating a traditional gouache surface. Stahl's favorite traditional gouache support is a Strathmore kid finish illustration board. The kid finish is soft and allows for a smooth application of paint. To create a surface for gouache similar to Stahl's, begin by choosing Window, Show Papers to open the Papers palette. Choose the Fine Hard Grain texture. To make the surface even

3a

Sculpting the forms of the eye and brow area using the Camelhair Medium

3b

The completed color study

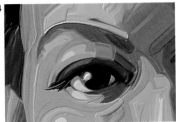

4

The Impasto painting of the eye and brow area is shown in this example

5

Using a tiny Palette Knife (Impasto) to pull color in the hair and background

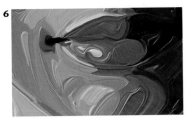

6

Using the Palette Knife (Impasto) to add linear accents and paint texture on the lips and chin

smoother, scale it to 50%. This finely textured surface is most noticeable when used for painting the hair in Step 3.

2 Beginning with sketches. Stahl began by using traditional pencils and paper to draw a black-and-white study to establish the composition and work out values.

In Painter, she created a new file that measured approximately 1200 x 1900 pixels. Stahl drew an expressive sketch with the Smooth Ink Pen variant of Pens. Begin by creating a new file similar to the size of Stahl's, select the Smooth Ink Pen variant and set the Size to 4.0 in the Property Bar. Choose a dark color and begin sketching.

3 Painting teardrop shapes. For the color study, Stahl used two brushes, a fast, sensitive brush with grainy edges to rough in color (the Broad Cover Brush 40 variant of Gouache sized to 25 pixels) and a modified Round Camelhair variant, to paint tear-drop shapes suggesting highlights in the hair and to sculpt the facial features. The controls needed to build Stahl's modified Round Camelhair brush are located in the Property Bar.

In the Brush Selector Bar, choose the Round Camelhair variant, and in the Property Bar, set Feature to 1.3. (Lowering the Feature setting "tightens" the bristles in the brush, giving the strokes a smoother, crisper edge with fewer bristle marks, similar to using a soft traditional brush loaded with paint on a smooth surface.) In the Property Bar, set Resat to 65% and Bleed to 8% (increasing the Resat setting allows the brush to paint with more of the current color, with less mixing of colors on the image canvas). From the Brush Selector Bar's triangle pop-up menu, choose Save Variant, name your variant (Stahl named hers Camelhair Medium) and click OK. Stahl varied the size of her brush while she worked.

4 Building up thick paint. For the look of thicker paint, Stahl used Impasto brushes. To quickly make a copy of her color study, she chose File, Clone. She saved the clone image using a new name, to preserve the color study, then she painted directly over the copy of the color study using various Impasto brushes, including the Opaque Flat and Round Camelhair. When she wanted to reveal bristle marks, she used the Opaque Bristle Spray (Impasto). To pull color with a flat-sided tool that would give the features a sculpted look, she used a small Palette Knife variant (Impasto).

5 Pulling and blending. Stahl used varying sizes of the Palette Knife variant of Impasto to blend and pull colors in the background and on the shoulders. To paint curls in the hair and achieve an oily look, she used the Distorto variant of Impasto.

6 Finishing touches. To finish, Stahl added linear accents on the model's eyes, lips, nose and chin using a small Palette Knife (Impasto) and she painted a few thick bristle marks on the background and hair using Opaque Bristle Spray (Impasto). 🖌

Painting an Expressive Oil Study

Overview *Open a new file and sketch using a Bristle Oils variant; paint using Oils brushes that can both apply color and smear it; complete the study using Oils and Blenders variants.*

CHER THREINEN-PENDARVIS

1

We painted a loose sketch in color using the Bristle Oils variant of the Oils, sized to about 10 pixels.

2a

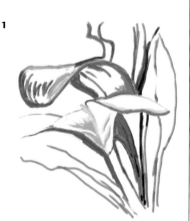

Painting color over the sketch

PAINTER'S OILS BRUSHES ENCOURAGE SPONTANEITY and quick gestural painting because they make expressive, smooth strokes and thus make possible a more tactile painting experience. For this color study, *Calla Lily and Ti,* we sketched using the Bristle Oils variant. Then we laid in color using the Smeary Bristle Spray and a Medium Bristle Oils variant. To blend and pull color we used a modified Medium Bristle Oils brush, that can both apply color and smear it like traditional wet oil paints. To build up more color activity in some areas, we painted glazes using a low-opacity version of the modified Medium Bristle Oils brush. We added final details using small Round Camelhair (Oils) and Round Blender Brush (Blenders) variants.

1 Setting up and making a sketch. Open a new file (our file measured 1300 x 1500 pixels). Before you begin your sketch, open the Papers palette by choosing Window, Show Papers. Click the Paper Selector (near the upper right corner) and choose Coarse Cotton Canvas from the pop-up menu. For a finer canvas effect, scale the paper to 50% using the Scale slider on the Papers palette. In the Brush Selector Bar, choose the Bristle Oils 20 variant of the Oils, and reduce its Size to about 10 pixels (using the Size slider popped out of the Property Bar). We chose the Bristle Oils because of

2b

Roughing in colors to show the afternoon sunlight on the leaves

3

The Medium Bristle Oils 25 chosen in the Brush Selector Bar (top) and the new settings in the Property Bar

4

Using the modified Medium Bristle Oils to add more brushstrokes and smear areas on the leaves and flower

5

Using a tiny Round Camelhair brush to define edges of the leaves and to add striated highlights and shadows on the calla lily and under the leaves

the sensitivity of this tool when used with a stylus—with it you can make expressive, thick and thin strokes that reveal bristle marks. Now select a mid-toned color in the Color picker to begin your sketch. As you sketch, develop the contours of the shapes in your image.

2 Developing the underpainting. The brushes we used for the underpainting, the Smeary Bristle Spray and Medium Bristle Oils, have unique qualities. By varying pressure on the stylus, you can add new color, or subtly mix color as you paint. This gives the feeling of painting with conventional wet oil paints.

We established a general color theme by laying in color—greens, purples, blues and yellows—directly over the sketch. Using the Medium Bristle Oils, and Smeary Bristle Spray (also Oils), we loosely blocked in color. We purposely left some of the white from the canvas showing to help retain the loose quality of the study.

3 Modifying a brush. In preparation for the blending and glazing work in Step 4, we modified the Medium Bristle Oils to accentuate its smeary capabilities as follows: Choose the Medium Bristle 25 variant of the Oils and in the Property Bar, reduce the Resaturation to 25% and increase the Bleed to 40%. Now choose a color. Using your stylus, paint a few brushstrokes on your image using firm pressure, then select a new color and apply more brushstrokes over the original strokes using very light pressure. As you drag this brush through a pool of color while using light pressure, you'll notice the brush picks up a small amount of the existing color from the canvas. Resize the brushes as you work using the Size slider in the Property Bar.

4 Blending and glazing. After painting the foreground, we wanted to create an atmosphere of afternoon light shining on and through the leaves by painting a subtle separation between the foreground calla lily and ti leaf, the mid-ground leaves and the background wall. We used the new smeary version of the Medium Bristle Oils brush to modulate deeper blues, purples and grays into the mid-ground and background areas. To make the background recede more, we softened the focus in some areas using a Round Blender Brush (Blenders). Next, we used a low Opacity version of the smeary Medium Bristle Oils brush and lighter yellow and orange colors to brighten the backlit areas in the foreground and mid-ground leaves. To lower the opacity of the brush, move the Opacity slider on the Property Bar to the left.

5 Adding details. To finish, we modulated the highlight areas on the foreground ti leaf and calla lily using the new Medium Bristle Oils and a Round Blender Brush; we used a tiny Round Camelhair brush to define the edges of the calla lily and to brighten areas where sun was shining on the leaves; we built up more detailed, striated shadows under the ti leaves.

Painting with Oils

Overview *Create a sketch with a Pencils variant; add color to the underpainting with the Smeary Bristle Spray brush; use an Impasto brush to build up the look of oils.*

INSPIRED BY THE WILD WATER FLOWERS OF SUMMER that seem to emerge magically in the natural ponds of Bucks County, Pennsylvania, artist Dennis Orlando captures an exquisite harmony between the circular shapes of the lily pads, the flowers and water reflections in *Lily Pads.* Strong intersecting horizontal and vertical thrusts, color harmony that leads the viewer's eye to follow the composition around the image, and sensitivity to light and shadow all combine to give this well-designed composition its power.

1 Drawing the sketch. Orlando set up a new 6 x 7-inch document with a resolution of 300 ppi and a white Paper Color. He modified a Pencils variant and used it to trace the lily pads and flowers. To create his custom variant, select the Thick and Thin Pencil variant (Pencils). Open the Brush Creator (Ctrl/⌘-B). In the Brush Creator's Stroke Designer tab, click on the General section and change Method to Cover and Subcategory to Grainy Soft Cover. Next, in the Property Bar, drag the Size slider to 2.0. Select Basic Paper in the Papers Selector and choose a color in the Colors picker (Orlando started with a neutral gray) and begin sketching.

1

Orlando's pencil drawing

Laying the first color with the Smeary Bristle Spray

Laying in, pulling and blending color

Creating color activity while painting the reflections

Adding brushstrokes with highlights and shadows using an Impasto brush

2 Developing the underpainting. Before you begin to paint in color, open the Color Variability palette, and set Hue (± H), Saturation (± S) and Value (± V) to 0. Once Orlando felt the composition worked nicely, he began to loosely block in color (on top of the pencil drawing) using the Smeary Bristle Spray variant of the Oils. The Smeary Bristle Spray variant allowed him to quickly lay in color while moving it around on the image, like wet-into-wet oil paint. Orlando continued to work color around the entire composition and to define elements and give the painting its overall tonal value and weight. When the underpainting was complete, the color palette and the direction of light were established.

3 Using Color Variability in the water. One of Orlando's "electronic oil" trademarks is activity in the color. He achieves this by adjusting the Color Variability settings for certain brushes. To recreate the active color look he achieved in the water reflections, start with the Smeary Bristle Spray variant of the Oils. Choose a dark gray-green, then open the Color Variability palette and adjust the Color Variability sliders: set Hue (± H) to 10, Saturation (± S) to 5 and Value (± V) to 10. Name and save this variant (from the triangle pop-up menu on the right side of the Brush Selector Bar, choose Variant, Save Variant, enter a name and click OK). After saving the custom variant, restore the default Smeary Bristle Spray brush to its original settings, by choosing Variant, Restore Default Variant from the same menu on the Brush Selector Bar. Begin painting. Using the Size slider in the Property Bar, Orlando changed to a smaller brush size when working close to the lily pads in order to preserve their shapes.

4 Emulating thick, traditional oils. Painter's Round Camelhair variant of Impasto lets you smear existing "pixel paint" to get the same look that you would get by pushing thick, conventional oils around a canvas. As the painting continued to evolve in the final step, Orlando switched to the Round Camelhair variant of Impasto. He used this variant to paint over the loose color (applied in Steps 2 and 3), choosing colors and pulling the visible brushstrokes to follow the natural curves and rhythms of the flowers, pads and water. He used the Impasto brush work to add texture and dimension, as well as to unify the quality of the entire composition.

   To apply thick paint while subtly blending strokes with existing color on the image, begin by selecting the Round Camelhair variant of Impasto. In the Size section of the Property Bar, adjust the Size slider to the size brush you need (Orlando chose 18.5, then varied his brush size slightly by changing stylus pressure as he painted). With the Dropper tool, sample a color from the area you want to paint, or hold down the Alt/Option key while you're using the brush to temporarily switch to the Dropper. Use the brush to make short, crisp strokes that pull color from one area of your painting into another.

Sculpting a Portrait

Overview *Make a sketch; block in color with Chalk variants; blend and sculpt the forms; refine the composition.*

The sketch on a warm-toned paper color

Loosely blocking in mid-tone color

Sculpting the facial features

RICHARD BIEVER LOVES THE EXPRESSIVE FREEDOM he enjoys while working with Painter and a pressure-sensitive tablet and stylus—the natural brushstrokes, the sensitivity, the happy accidents of two colors blending together or a bit of canvas showing through. Biever's painting *The Parable,* a portrait of Jesus Christ, was painted using Painter's Chalk and Distortion variants.

1 Sketching on a colored ground. To begin the portrait with a warm tone, Biever began a new file (about 3000 x 3500 pixels) with a sand-colored paper color. He chose the Sharp Chalk variant of Chalk in the Brush Selector Bar, a dark neutral color in the Color picker and Basic Paper in the Papers Selector. Using the Sharp Chalk, he sketched loosely, indicating the general position of the facial features and shape of the head.

2 Blocking in color and blending. Next, Biever blocked in the base tones using the Square Chalk variant (Chalk). Using the Size slider on the Property Bar, he enlarged the Square Chalk to make thicker strokes. Using broad strokes of color, he established the planes of the face and set the general tone of the painting and the angle and color of light on the face. (Biever wanted the feeling of natural sunlight, outdoors.) He worked from dark to light, roughing in general shapes using mid-toned color to sculpt the facial structure, letting his brushstrokes follow the direction of the forms. (He planned to add the highlights last.) Using the Marbling Rake variant of Distortion, he began to blend color and build up form.

3 Blending and sculpting. Continuing to use the Marbling Rake, Biever began to develop the feeling of oil paint. To achieve

4a
Roughing in the left hand

4b
The left hand and more canvas added

5
The completed face after the contrast was adjusted

a smoother stroke, he reduced the Size and Opacity of the brush using the sliders in the Property Bar. For more smear, he lowered the Resat using the slider on the Property bar. Then he opened the Brush Creator (Ctrl/⌘-B), and in the Stroke Designer tab's Rake section, he reduced Brush Scale. The Marbling Rake gives an illusion of oil paint texture. You can lose the paper texture with the Rake, but through careful stroking Biever left bits and pieces of the canvas showing through. He continued to refine the face using the Large Chalk (Chalk), while mixing and pulling color with the Marbling Rake.

4 Painting the hands and emphasizing the face. To emphasize the telling of a story, Biever roughed in the hand on the left. To balance the composition and give the picture more room, he added to the canvas using Canvas, Canvas Size. After he had rendered the right hand also, he selected them using the Lasso tool, floated them (Select, Float) and repositioned them using the Layer Adjuster tool. Then, he dropped the layer by choosing Drop from the Layer Commands menu on the bottom of the Layers palette. (To learn about using selections and layers, turn to Chapters 4 and 5.)

Using lighter colors, Biever brought out highlights in the face and hands using small Chalk variants. To emphasize the face even more, he painted over the tunic with the Large Chalk and lighter color, again blending with the Marbling Rake.

5 Adding final details and more texture. To enhance the highlights and shadows in the portrait, Biever increased the contrast using Effects, Tonal Control, Brightness/Contrast.

Then for *more* atmosphere, he added a papyrus texture from an Art Beats CD-ROM, copying and pasting the texture into the file as a layer. Using the pop-up menu on the Layers palette, he set the Compositing Method to Soft Light. He blended the texture into the hair and beard, creating a dusty feel. To blend a texture into your painting, target the texture layer in the Layers palette, then click on the Layer Mask button. The new Layer Mask will appear in the Channels palette. Choose the Digital Airbrush (Airbrushes) and black color. Spray over the area of the image that you want to hide. (To read more about working with masks and layers, see Chapters 4 and 5.)

Cloning and Tracing

Overview *Open a reference image; make a clone; delete the contents of the clone; use tracing paper to aid in tracing the original image; add detail using Cloning brushes.*

CHER THREINEN-PENDARVIS

PHOTO: CORBIS

The original photo

Sketching in the clone using Tracing Paper

Selecting the sky with the Magic Wand

WHEN THERE ISN'T TIME to draw from scratch—or if drawing from life isn't your fancy—Painter's cloning and tracing paper features make it easy to use a photo or other existing art as a reference for a new illustration.

1 Selecting an image and making a clone. In Painter, start by opening a reference image (such as a painting or photo). To make a clone, choose File, Clone. The new clone will be linked to the original file—its clone source. The cloning process maps the clone (the destination image) directly to the original (the source image), pixel-by-pixel. Leave the original image open.

2 Tracing and sketching. Working with Tracing Paper in Painter is similar to using a conventional light table. In preparation for using the Tracing Paper function, select all (Ctrl/⌘-A), and delete the contents from the clone canvas (Backspace/Delete). Turn on Tracing Paper by clicking the Tracing Paper icon at the top of the scroll bar or choose Canvas, Tracing Paper (Ctrl/⌘-T). The original image will appear "screened back," ready to be traced with a brush.

Click on the Paper Selector (near the bottom of the Toolbox) and choose a paper texture from the pop-up list. We alternated between Basic Paper and Smooth Handmade Paper textures. Open the Color picker (Window, Show/Hide Colors). Click in the Hue ring or Hue bar to choose a hue, and in the color triangle to select a tint or shade of the color. We chose a warm gray for our sketch.

Open the Brush Selector Bar (Window, Show Brush Selector), and choose a brush for instance, the Fine Point variant of Pens. (You do not need to use a cloning method brush to sketch using Tracing Paper.) Begin painting using the clone source

3b

Filling the sky with imagery from the source image

3c

Adding grainy strokes to the sky and foliage using the Chalk variants

4

To add crispness to the soft illustration we cloned in a few details from the original.

5

Cloning the border. Notice the crosshair denoting the sampled area.

image as a guide. To toggle Tracing Paper on and off as you work, press Ctrl/⌘-T. We drew a solid line to outline the building, using the Fine Point variant of Pens.

3 Making a selection and filling. Next, we selected the white sky above the solid line with the Magic Wand. (In the Property Bar, we set the Tolerance to 1 and turned on Contiguous, so that only the white pixels would be selected in the sky area.) We saved the selection by choosing Select, Save Selection, New, to save it as a mask that we could use later. Then we chose Effects, Fill, Clone Source to bring the color from the original image into the selected sky. (For more information about selections, turn to Chapter 4.) With the selection still active, using shades of blue, we painted grainy strokes over the filled sky with the Large Chalk variant of Chalk, and then dropped the selection (Ctrl/⌘-D).

4 Adding details with brushes. After painting the foreground foliage with greens and black using the Smooth Ink variant of Pens, we switched to the Large Chalk to add loose curved strokes of white to denote highlights on the foliage. Then, changing the brush size in the Property Bar as we worked, we added more strokes to the foliage in various shades of green, some imported from the original image using Clone Color. To brush detail from the original image onto your illustration, choose a cloning brush variant. We used the Chalk Cloner variant of the Cloners to add detail to the door of the mission. You can change almost any Painter brush into a cloning brush by changing its method to Cloning in the General section of the Stroke Designer (Brush Creator).

5 Cloning a border with a chalky edge. In preparation for adding a rough-edged border, we increased the canvas size of the file (Canvas, Canvas Size) by 20 pixels on all four sides. (When you change the size of your canvas, Tracing Paper will no longer be available unless you also change the source image to the same pixel size.) We added the border by sampling imagery and making rough strokes along the edge using the Chalk Cloner. To clone from one point to another within an image (much like using the Rubber Stamp in Photoshop), select a source point in your image (Alt/Option-click). Reposition the cloning brush in your document and stroke to bring the imagery into the area. Reload the cloning brush as necessary as you work around the edge. 🖐

CLONING FROM ONE UNRELATED IMAGE TO ANOTHER

To clone from one unrelated image to another (to map pixel for pixel, or to use the Tracing Paper function), the two images must have exactly the same pixel dimensions. Open two images that are the same size and choose one image for your destination image. Choose File, Clone Source, and designate the second image as the clone source. Use a Cloning brush to bring imagery into the destination image, in exactly the same position as in the source. To continue to clone or use Tracing Paper, the source image must be left open.

Coloring and Cloning

Overview *Scan a pencil sketch; clone it; tint it and add texture; restore from the original by cloning; add color with the Airbrush, Chalk and Water Color brushes.*

PHILIP HOWE

The original pencil illustration, scanned

Adding a tint and a texture to the clone

Using a Cloning method brush to partially restore the gray tones of the original

MUCH OF THE BEAUTY of illustrator Philip Howe's work lies in his seamless, creative blending of the traditional with the digital. In a spread for *Trailblazer* magazine—a detail of which is shown here—Howe combined hand-drawn calligraphy, a photo of two slides, a photo of a watercolor block (for the background), and his own pencil sketches, colored to simulate traditional watercolor.

1 Starting with a sketch. Howe began by sketching the various birds in pencil on watercolor paper. He scanned the images on a flatbed scanner, saving them as grayscale files in TIFF format. Each bird image was 4 to 5 inches square and 300 ppi.

2 Modifying a clone. Open a grayscale scan in Painter. Choose File, Clone, to clone your scan, giving you an "original" and a clone. Keep the original open—you'll want to pull from it later. Howe added a color tint and a texture to the clone of the scanned bird. To add a tint, choose a color in the Color picker (Howe chose a reddish brown), then choose Effects, Surface Control, Color Overlay. Select Uniform Color from the pop-up menu, set Opacity to 30%, click the Dye Concentration button and click OK. To add texture, select a paper texture (Howe chose Basic Paper) from the Paper Selector near the bottom of the Toolbox, and choose Effects, Surface Control, Apply Surface Texture. Select Paper from the Using menu, set Amount to 50% and set Shine to 0%. Click OK.

3 Restoring from the original. Howe used Painter's cloning capabilities to replace most of the tint and texture in the bird's body with the light gray tones of the original. In the Brush Selector Bar, choose the Cloners category, and the Soft Cloner variant. In the Property Bar, try lowering this cloning brush's Opacity for more sensitivity. (The Soft Cloner sprays soft color, similar to an aitbrush.) Once you've arrived at the opacity you like, paint on the portion of your image that you want to restore. The original will automatically be revealed in the area covered by your strokes.

4 Adding color tints with an Airbrush. To achieve the effect of traditional airbrushing with transparent dyes or watercolor

Applying color tints with the Digital Airbrush in Buildup method

Using a Large Chalk variant to add color to the background

Applying watercolor accents with the Splatter Water variant

Another spot illustration from the Trailblazer spread. Howe used the same brushes and technique for all illustrations.

pigments, Howe used two versions of the Digital Airbrush variant of Airbrushes. The first Digital Airbrush (using the default Cover method), allowed a light color to cover a darker one. In the Property Bar, he reduced the Opacity setting to between 5% and 10%. He used this low-opacity brush to carefully lay in the golden brown tones on the bird's back. Howe's second airbrush used the Buildup method, which applied color transparently. The Buildup method allowed him to use a slightly higher Opacity (between 10% and 20%) to achieve richer color while preserving the intensity of the pencil sketch. To make a "transparent" airbrush similar to Howe's, choose the Digital Airbrush variant of Airbrushes in the Brush Selector Bar. To change its method from Cover to the Buildup Method, open the Brush Creator (Ctrl-⌘/B) and in the Stroke Designer, choose the General section, change the Method pop-up menu to Buildup, and the subcategory pop-up menu to Soft Buildup.

5 Cloning again and brushing with Chalk. Howe uses the Clone feature like a flexible "Save As" command. When he's ready to move on to the next phase of an illustration, he often makes a clone and uses the original as "source material." Here, when he had colored the bird to his satisfaction, he chose File, Clone. If he over-worked an area in the new clone, he restored it by cloning in imagery from the previous version by opening that version and designating it as the "source" by choosing File, Clone Source. Then he painted with a cloning brush to restore the area.

Howe switched to the Large Chalk variant of Chalk and began to paint loose, gestural strokes on the image background around the bird using two similar green hues. He changed the size of the brush as he worked by making adjustments in the Property Bar.

6 Adding tints and texture. To add a finishing touch without muddying his existing color work, Howe used transparent washes to add more depth to the color on the bird's head and other areas. To paint washes, use the Wash Camel variant of Water Color. (As you paint, a Water Color layer will be generated in the Layers palette, keeping these brushstrokes separate from the Canvas). Now, sample color from the bird and background using the Dropper tool, switch to the Splatter Water variant and paint a "water drop" effect on the background. To combine the selected Water Color layer with the Canvas, click the Layer Commands button at the bottom of the Layers palette and choose Drop.

Merging the files. Using the Lasso, Howe drew a loose selection around the bird, then he chose Select, Feather and feathered it 30 pixels. Then he opened the 17 x 11-inch main image and used the Layer Adjuster tool to drag and drop the bird into the main image. To blend the bird layer with the background, he set its Composite Method in the Layers palette to Multiply.

Spontaneous Mixed Media

Overview *Add a colored gradient to a new document; block in color with Oils variants; blend and smear the paint; add textured brushstrokes and detail with Chalk and Conté variants.*

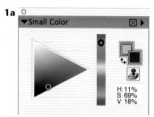

Setting up the Colors picker

The gradient background

Painting pastel colors onto the sky

Adding more color with Oils variants

THE OILS, CHALK AND BLENDERS VARIANTS are among Painter's most responsive tools, and mixing the media is a natural match for artist Chelsea Sammel's spontaneous style. She painted *Three Trees* from her imagination while working in her studio.

1 Building a colored background. Pastel artists sometimes prepare a support by painting first with acrylic or oil paints. Sammel created a colored background by filling the image with a dark-to-light purple gradation to suggest a sky. To start as Sammel did, create a new document (1200 x 800 pixels) with a white paper color. In the Color picker choose a dark purple color for the Primary Color Square. Click on the Secondary Color Square and set it at a lighter purple color. Open the Gradients palette (Window, Show Gradients). Choose Two-Point from the resource list menu and set the Preview Window wheel to 90°. To fill the canvas with the gradient, choose Effects, Fill, Fill With Gradient. (For more information about using Gradients, turn to Chapter 2.)

2 Adding colored brushstrokes. Sammel quickly roughed cream, peach and light green colors onto the image—directly over the gradient—using the Smeary Bristle Spray and Round Camel-hair variants of the Oils. Then she blocked in the distant trees and meadow using rich greens and browns, and added a few strokes of darker color to suggest shadow.

3 Blending paint and adding more color. Traditional artists often use palette knives to move paint around on the canvas surface. To scrape back and blend areas, Sammel used the Tiny Palette Knife variant of the Palette Knives. Switching between the Smeary Bristle Spray and Palette Knife variants of the Brushes, she painted and scraped back, pulled and blended colors, adding expression and movement to the sky and background hills.

3

Pulling and blending paint

4

Adjusting the settings for Tapered Chalk in the Size section of the Stroke Designer

5a

Adding color to the meadow with the custom Tapered Chalk variant

5b

The painting with the trees in progress

5c

Using the Tapered Chalk to add deeper color to the sky

For the look of grainy pigment, Sammel also blended areas with the Coarse Smear variant of Blenders. She chose a coarse laid texture in the Papers Selector, for example Speckled Laid Paper. (To choose a paper, click the Paper Selector icon near the bottom of the Tools palette, and select a paper from the menu.) To bring out the paper texture, she blended areas of her image using the Smudge variant of Blenders.

4 Building custom chalk variants. Sammel likes Painter's default Chalk and Pastel variants and makes only minor adjustments to their settings. She works quickly and spontaneously, creating a few variants on the fly and switching frequently among them. To create her Tapered Chalk, choose the Tapered Large Chalk 30 variant of Chalk. Open the Brush Creator by choosing Window, Show Brush Creator (or type Ctrl/⌘-B). Click the Stroke Designer tab and open the Size section by clicking its section bar; set Size to 36.5 and Min Size to 40%. Also in the Size section, in the Expression pop-up menu, set Size to Pressure. This setting, combined with a moderate Min Size setting, creates more taper at the end of each stroke. To save the variant, choose Variant, Save Variant from the Brush Creator's variant menu, then name your brush and click OK. To create Sammel's Conté Crayon, start with the Tapered Conte 15 variant of Conte. Again in the Brush Creator's Stroke Designer, change Size to 9.4 and Min Size to 50% in the Size section. In the Expression pop-up menu, set Size to Pressure. For a less grainy stroke (in the General section), drag the Grain slider to 13% in the Property Bar. Save the variant.

5 Adding color and texture with the chalks. Sammel added color to the grass with the Tapered Chalk variant. She used the same variant to begin the foreground trees, drawing dynamic, angled strokes, in a very dark brown-black color so that the trees would contrast with the rich-colored background. Next she brushed a deeper blue onto the sky. Then she switched to the Conte Crayon variant and added a few strokes of complementary blues, greens, golds and oranges to the distant foliage.

5d

Finally, she chose the Smudge variant of Blenders and smudged areas of the background and meadow. She finished the image by using the Soft Oil Pastel variant of Oil Pastels to add a few lighter brushstrokes on the trees and grass.

Adding more highlight color to the branches using the Conte Crayon variant

Applying Scanned Paper Textures

Overview *Scan a textured paper; open the file in Painter and capture the texture; use a grain-sensitive brush and Painter's special effects to apply the texture to your image.*

CORRINE OKADA

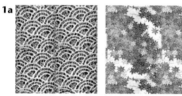

The scanned paper textures: rice paper (left) and maple leaf (right)

1b

Brightness/Contrast

Reset   Cancel   Apply

Increasing the contrast of the paper scan

2a

▼ Papers
Simulated Woodgrain

Capture Paper...
Make Paper...
Invert Paper
Paper Mover...
Open Library...

Capturing a selected area of the paper scan

2b

Save Paper

Save As: maple leaf

Crossfade ◄ ░ ► 16.00

Cancel   OK

Saving and naming the new paper texture

WHILE PAINTER OFFERS A SEEMINGLY ENDLESS assortment of paper grains, many artists still choose to create their own surfaces. They draw from many sources: video grabs, scanned photos, texture collections on CD-ROM, scans of natural objects (leaves or richly grained wood), scans of papers or patterns and images drawn in Painter. They also generate their own seamless textures with Painter's Make Paper and Make Fractal Pattern features.

When Corrine Okada first began using Painter, she scanned her extensive paper collection, capturing the images in Painter and saving them into her own texture libraries. Her skill in applying these custom textures is evident in *Crane Maiden*, a CD-ROM cover commissioned by Silicon Graphics.

1 Scanning the papers. Okada scans her papers on a flatbed scanner in grayscale mode. She scans an 8 x 10-inch area at 300 ppi. If you're scanning a thin, light-colored sheet—like the piece of lacy rice paper that Okada scanned for this job—you may want to place a sheet of black paper behind it to create more contrast. Okada also scanned a sheet of Japanese maple leaf paper.

You'll have more flexibility when you apply the texture if the scan you apply has good contrast and a broad tonal range. So open your scanned texture and choose Effects, Tonal Control, Brightness/Contrast. Drag the top slider to the right to increase contrast. If necessary, adjust the lower slider (Brightness) and then click Apply.

2 Capturing the texture. Use the Rectangular Selection tool to isolate an area of your image. Start by selecting an area of about 200 x 200 pixels. Open the Info palette (Ctrl-⌘-7). Read the

3a

Detail of the Rice Paper texture brushed behind the head

3b

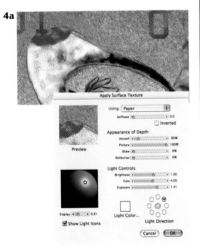

Detail of the Rice Paper texture brushed onto the kimono

4a

Applying a Surface Texture using Painter's Rice Paper texture

4b

The Maple Leaf texture on the brushstroke (applied with Surface Control effects) and the computer monitor (applied with the Gritty Charcoal variant of Charcoal)

Width and Height dimensions in the Info palette. The repetition of your pattern may be too obvious if your selection is much smaller. Open the Papers palette (Window, Show Papers). Choose Capture Paper in the Papers pop-up menu (opened by clicking the triangle on the right side of the Papers palette). For the smoothest results, leave the Crossfade setting at 16. Name your paper and click OK. A picture of the texture will appear in your current Paper library.

3 Applying grain with brushes. Painter lets you apply textures in two ways: with a brush or as a special effect. Okada used both of these methods (within selections and on layers), in this piece. To brush the Rice Paper texture behind the woman's head, she first inverted the texture by checking the Invert Paper box in the Papers palette. She selected the area behind the head, then brushed the texture into the selected area using the Gritty variant of Charcoal and a white color. Okada selected a purple color to brush the same texture (with Invert Paper turned off) onto the woman's kimono. Near the end of the project, she used the same brush to apply the Maple Leaf texture onto the computer screen in blue, yellow and white.

4 Special effects with grain. To create a subtle woven look across the entire image, Okada overlaid texture on the image. She began by selecting a Rice Paper texture in the Papers palette. Then she chose Effects, Surface Control, Apply Surface Texture. In the Using menu she selected Paper, and set the Amount at 30% and the Shine at 0 and clicked OK.

To add color, value and texture to the brushstroke that sweeps across the lower half of the image, Okada applied multiple special effects using the Maple Leaf texture. She selected, then floated the brushstroke, and used Color Overlay, Apply Lighting, and Apply Surface Texture (all under Effects, Surface Control) a few times each with various settings to get the effect she wanted.

Combing Oil Pastels, Texture and Blending

Overview *Start from a pencil sketch; build a drawing using multiple variants of the Oil Pastels combined with different paper textures; blend them with Blenders variants.*

CAROL BENIOFF

1

The scan of the pencil sketch

2a

Using Invert Paper Texture to create the texture for the flooring

2b

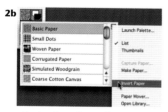

Paper selection from the Toolbox, and Invert Paper Texture option

THE OIL PASTELS ARE A VERY VERSATILE set of tools—their strokes, their blending capability and their responsiveness to paper textures all add to the tactile feel of this illustration of toys painted by artist Carol Benioff. She also used Blenders variants, with which you can smear, ripple, add texture, and blend your drawing.

1 Starting with a pencil sketch. Benioff started by drawing a simple composition of toys on a floor with traditional pencils and paper. Then she scanned the drawing at 300 pixels per inch and opened it in Painter. She started drawing directly over the pencil drawing with the Chunky Oil Pastel 10 variant, resized to 5 pixels using the pop-out Size slider on the Property Bar.

2 Picking different papers. Next, Benioff began sketching the stuffed dog. First, she selected the Pebbled Leather texture in the Paper Selector near the bottom of the Toolbox. The paper mimics the dog's nubby blue fabric. With the Chunky Oil Pastel she drew colored strokes which revealed the pebbly paper, and she blended the new color with colors picked up from underneath. For the floor, she switched to the Simulated Wood Grain texture and to a Soft Oil Pastel variant—with the Grain turned down to 10% in the Property Bar—to reveal more of the texture. She chose a dark ochre color and with swift strokes roughed out parts of the floor. Then she opened the Papers palette (Window, Show Papers), and clicked on the Invert Paper button. She selected a light ochre and again drew on the floor with quick strokes. Because she had inverted the paper texture, she was now drawing into the recesses of the paper with the lighter color. The Soft Oil Pastel is designed

3a

The jacks are drawn with Oil Pastel variants on Smooth Handmade Paper. The ball is drawn with Chunky Oil Pastel on Coarse Cotton Canvas.

3b

1954 Graphic Fabric is the texture for the jack-in-the-box, drawn with the Round Oil Pastel; and the wallpaper, drawn with the Variable Oil Pastel.

4

The bear was drawn with Chunky Oil Pastel on Corrugated Paper, with the paper texture inverted and lighter colors to add depth to the grain.

5

Using Blenders variants as the final touch

so the amount of resaturation and bleed are controlled by the amount of pressure you apply. Benioff varied the pressure on the stylus as she painted to control how much of the paper texture was revealed or covered by the pigment. For more information about Resaturation and Bleed, turn to Building Brushes on pages 57–63.

3 Using smooth and coarse textures. To achieve the dull metal sheen on the jacks, Benioff chose the Oil Pastel 10 variant and sized it to 4 pixels. To modify the Oil Pastel so it would lay down less color and blend more with the underlying colors, she reduced the Resat to 10% and set the Bleed at 80% in the Property Bar. Then she chose the Smooth Handmade Paper, for a more subtle paper texture effect. To paint the ball and simulate the rough-textured rubber, she picked Coarse Cotton Canvas in the Paper Selector, and switched back to the Chunky Pastel which reveals the paper texture as well as blending with the colors underneath.

Next, she painted the box, the jack-in-the-box's clothing and the striped wallpaper using the 1954 Graphic Fabric texture and different Oil Pastels. For the wallpaper and the jack-in-the-box's clothing Benioff used the Variable Oil Pastel variant in a variety of sizes; for the box she selected the Round Oil Pastel. She clicked on the Straight Line Strokes button in the Property Bar when she drew the straight lines in the wallpaper.

4 Using inverted texture. To paint the stuffed bear's well-worn fur she used a Chunky Oil Pastel over Corrugated Paper texture. She mapped out the lights and darks of the forms. Then she clicked on the Invert Paper button in the Papers palette and selected lighter shades of browns to draw into the recesses of the paper. By varying the colors, pressure and strokes she was able to paint mottled textures on the bear.

5 Blending and smearing color. To complete the study, Benioff used a variety of the Blenders brushes on different areas of her drawing as follows: For the dog, she chose an Oily Blender, and pushed and pulled the existing color. For the ball, she switched to a Coarse Oily Blender, with the Coarse Cotton Canvas paper selected. (This pushed and pulled the paint and blended the strokes, while still revealing the paper texture.) For the jacks, she used a Detail Blender, which maintained their dull metallic shine, but smoothed out some rough edges. For the jack-in-the-box's clothing she used a Coarse Smear blender. On the box she used Just Add water to bleed and blur the rough-edged strokes. With the Bear she selected a Grainy Blender and the Corrugated Paper texture to soften the transitions from light to dark while keeping the texture. Next, she chose French Watercolor Paper and used a Grainy Water on the bunny. Finally, she used the Runny variant of Blenders to create a rippling effect on the floor.

Applying Rich Textures with Custom Brushes

Overview *Scan a traditional pencil sketch; modify brushes to include enhanced color and grain settings; paint rich color with varied textures using the custom brushes.*

DON SEEGMILLER

1a

The scanned pencil sketch

BY SKILLFULLY USING COLOR WHILE PAINTING with custom brushes and textures, Don Seegmiller created a dark and comically ominous atmosphere for *Strange High House*, painted from the imagination. He used somber colors in the highlight and shadow areas of the painting and developed a rich layering of multiple textures, applied with modified brushes that included increased color variability and enhanced grain settings.

Seegmiller, whose traditional oil paintings can be found in both private and public collections, has worked as an art director for innovative gaming development companies. He also teaches illustration at Brigham Young University.

1 Sketching, scanning and equalizing. Seegmiller began by sketching with conventional pencil in his sketchbook. He scanned the pencil drawing at 300 ppi, a resolution suitable for offset printing. Because he likes working with a high-contrast version of the sketch, he removed the grays from the scan. To increase the contrast in your sketch, as Seegmiller did, choose Effects, Tonal

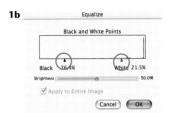

1b

Equalize

Black and White Points

Black 26.4%   White 21.5%

Brightness ▬▬▬▬▬▬▬▬▬▬▬ 50.0%

☑ Apply to Entire Image

Cancel   OK

Using Equalize to give the sketch more contrast

▼ Color Variability   ☒

in HSV

±H ◄ △ ► | 8%
±S ◄ △ ► | 8%
±V ◄ △ ► | 11%

Painting the sky in the clone with a modified Water Color brush, using these Color Variability settings. Tracing Paper is turned on to view the original scan of the pencil sketch

The study with soft watercolor background and the embellished sketch

Control, Equalize. When the Equalize dialog box appears, move the black point marker and the white point marker under the histogram closer together to eliminate the gray tones. Move them right or left to affect the line thickness and quality. You'll be able to preview the adjustment in your image before you click OK to accept.

2 Painting the background. Prior to painting with color, Seegmiller made a quick duplicate of his sketch to preserve the original, using Painter's cloning process. To make a clone, choose File, Clone.

Seegmiller planned to paint washes on the sky using a modified Water Color variant. He chose Pavement texture in the Papers palette because he likes its coarse, uneven look. Then he chose a soft blue in the Color picker and a modified Water Color brush in the Brush Selector Bar. The custom brush included enhanced Color Variability and Grain settings so that he could subtly paint the sky with varying colors of blue while revealing the texture.

To make a brush similar to Seegmiller's, choose the New Simple Round Wash variant of Water Color, then open the Color Variability palette by clicking on its section name. Adjust the sliders using these settings: ±H8 %, ±S8 %, and ±V11 %. Open the Brush Creator by pressing Ctrl/⌘-B. (All of the modifications will be made in the Stroke Designer tab of the Brush Creator.) In the General section of the Stroke Designer tab, move the Grain slider to 75%, to allow more grain to show as brushstrokes are applied. In the Size section, increase the Size to 59.1. To avoid seeing circles (individual brush dabs as you paint) when using the larger brush size, decrease the spacing between the brush's dabs. In the Spacing section, move the Spacing slider to 14% and the Min Spacing slider to 0.5. To save your new Water Color brush (instead of leaving the new settings in the default Simple Round Wash brush), choose Save Variant from the Brush Selector Bar's triangle pop-up menu. When the Save Variant dialog box appears, type in a name for your brush and click OK. To restore the Simple Round Wash brush to its default settings, select the variant and from the Brush Selector Bar's triangle pop-up menu choose Restore Default Variant.

Using a soft touch on the stylus, Seegmiller painted brushstrokes over the sky. He changed color as he worked, choosing low-saturation blues, purples, browns and grays in the Colors section. (When you paint with a Water Color brush, a Water Color layer is generated, keeping the Wet Paint separate from the image Canvas. To read more about painting with the Water Color brushes and layers, turn to "A Painter Water Color Primer," earlier in this chapter.)

3 Strengthening the sketch. After establishing the sky, Seegmiller used a modified Pencils variant to embellish areas of the pencil sketch in his working study. (Drawing with the Pencils variants will not interrupt the wet Water Color brushstrokes.) His modified Pencil incorporates the Grainy Hard Buildup subcategory, and enhanced Grain settings, making it very sensitive to the Paper

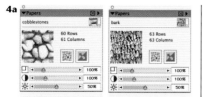

Seegmiller switched between custom-made Cobblestones and Bark textures

Using a modified Square Chalk variant to paint layers of custom-made Cobbles and Bark texture onto the cliff areas

Adding warmer, lighter tones to the top house and its windows

grain chosen in the Papers section. To build a Sketching Pencil similar to Seegmiller's, begin by choosing the 2B Pencil variant. In the General section of the Brush Creator's Stroke Designer, change its Dab Type to Single-Pixel, then set the Opacity slider at 69% and the Grain slider at 24%. Open the Random section of the Stroke Designer and increase Jitter to 0.95 to make the brushstrokes uneven. Increasing Jitter also broadens the stroke slightly. Now choose a fine, even-textured paper (such as Italian Water Color) in the Paper Selector.

After drawing over certain areas, Seegmiller added more intensity to the pencil sketch by selecting the drawing in the original image, then choosing Select, All, and copying and pasting it into the working study. In the Layers palette, he set the Composite Method for the layer to Multiply, then he dropped it to the image canvas by clicking the Layer Commands button at the bottom of the Layers palette and choosing Drop. (Multiply mode makes the white areas of the image clear, while preserving the dark areas.) To read more about Layers and Composite Methods, turn to the beginning of Chapter 5, "Using Layers."

4 Using a custom chalk to build up textures on the cliffs.

Seegmiller used a modified Square Chalk to paint custom textures (primarily the Cobblestones and Bark textures) onto the cliffs. (Seegmiller creates custom textures from scans of his own photos or by painting in Painter, then capturing the elements as paper textures. To read more about paper textures, turn to "Applying Scanned Paper Textures," earlier in this chapter.) He built up layers of texture subtly. While painting with the custom Chalk, he strengthened and lightened areas in both the sky and cliff areas. While he worked, he continually changed paper textures in the Paper Selector and applied the textures using slightly different colors.

To build Seegmiller's custom Chalk, begin by selecting the Square Chalk variant of Chalk in the Brush Selector. In the Color Variability palette, move the sliders to these settings: ±H5 %, ±S7 %, and ±V10 %. Now set the Grain very low in the Property Bar: Move the Grain slider to 8%, to allow the Chalk to reveal more grain. To save your new custom Chalk without modifying settings for the default Square Chalk, choose Variant, Save Variant from the menu on the right side of the Brush Selector Bar. Restore the Square Chalk vari-

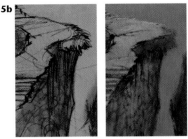

5b

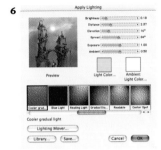

Using the custom Warm Fuzzy brush to add soft tones to the cliffs and path

6

Modifying the Gradual light

7a

The glow added to the window

7b

The highlights added to the roofs, and glows to the lights and the moon

ant to its default settings (select the Square Chalk, and from the Brush Selector Bar menu choose Variant, Restore Default Variant).

5 Establishing the center of interest. Seegmiller began to develop the feeling of light he envisioned for the house and high cliffs. He used another custom brush, the Warm Fuzzy, to achieve a softer feeling in some of the areas of the cliffs and edges of the path. Seegmiller's Warm Fuzzy brush paints with natural, "fuzzy-looking" strokes that made it a good choice for suggesting the texture of vegetation on the cliffs. To build the Warm Fuzzy, begin by choosing the Opaque Round variant of the Oils. In the Size section of the Stroke Designer (Brush Creator), change Size to 6.7, Min Size to 100% and Feature to 4.4 (to spread the Bristles). In the Expression controls change Size and Opacity to Pressure. In the General section change Opacity to 68%; in the Well, set Resat, Bleed, and Feature to None. Finally, an important ingredient that adds a more natural look: In the Random section, increase Jitter to 0.43.

Using his Warm Fuzzy brush, Seegmiller added warm oranges and yellows to the two small windows to act as a balancing element against the purples, blue, grays and browns. He also added rusty-brown highlights to the roofs on the higher house to create the center of interest. He worked his way down the cliffs and added more subtle colors and texture to the houses and rocks.

6 Adding to the atmosphere and focal point. Seegmiller believes that Apply Lighting is one of the finest tools that Painter offers to change the complexion of an image without painting over underlying work. He used lighting to add atmosphere (for a more ominous feeling) and to create a soft vertical gradation from dark-to-light in the image (to strengthen the focal point). To create a custom light similar to Seegmiller's, choose Effects, Surface Control, Apply Lighting. When the dialog box appears, choose the Gradual light. Make these changes to the light: Click on the Light Color square and in the Select Light Color dialog box, choose a light blue-gray. Reduce Brightness by moving its slider to 0.18. Leave other settings at their defaults. To save your light, click the Save button, name your light and click OK. Then click OK to apply the light. To learn more about Apply Lighting, see the beginning of Chapter 7, "Exploring Special Effects."

7 Refining the painting. Seegmiller continued to add fine color detail over the entire image, particularly on the buildings, cliffs and path, while maintaining color harmony throughout the image. He added a small lamp outside the tunnel by the bridge, then embellished the lights in the windows and the lantern using the Glow variant of the F/X brush. He also used the Glow brush to lighten the moon. Using a tiny version of the Warm Fuzzy brush, he also added highlights along the roof edges of the buildings to give them a feeling of light from the moon. (For more about the F/X brushes see Chapter 7.)

Brushing Washes Over "Live" Canvas

Overview *Open a new file and use an Impasto brush to emboss texture into the image canvas; paint color washes over the canvas with brushes.*

STANLEY VEALÉ

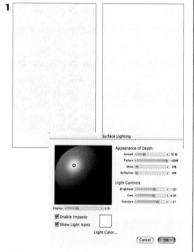

Surface Lighting

The canvas with the default Impasto Lighting settings (left) and with the reduced Amount and Shine (right), as set in the Impasto Lighting dialog box.

2a

Choosing the Wet Bristle variant of Impasto in the Brush Selector Bar

ON TRADITIONAL CANVAS YOU CAN USE OIL PAINT mixed with linseed oil and turpentine to brush washes over the surface without obliterating the canvas grain. With Painter's Impasto feature you can do something very similar, with the added advantage of being able to emphasize or de-emphasize the grain by changing the angle or intensity of lighting on the canvas. Using the Impasto feature to "emboss" the canvas will keep the grain "live" and changeable throughout the painting process. To paint *Ashanti,* a still-life study of an African wood carving, artist and designer Stanley Vealé used a unique method that allows the canvas texture to always show through the brushstrokes.

1 Embossing the canvas. Begin by creating a new file the size and resolution you need. (Vealé's file was 800 pixels square.) In the Papers Selector, choose the Coarse Cotton Canvas texture. (Considering the 800-pixel file size, Vealé left the Scale of the Coarse Cotton Canvas texture at 100% in the Papers palette.)

Vealé used the Grain Emboss variant of Impasto to "emboss" the Raw Silk texture values into the image canvas without adding color. Select the Grain Emboss variant of Impasto and paint wide strokes all over the image so that the paper texture is embossed into the image. You can reduce or increase the effect of the texture by choosing Canvas, Surface Lighting, and adjusting the Amount slider to your liking. Because the default Impasto Lighting settings seemed too coarse and shiny, Vealé reduced the Amount to 51%, and for a matte finish on the canvas, he set the Shine at 0.

2 Customizing a brush. Vealé likes the Wet Bristle variant of Impasto because of its bristle marks and how it scrubs existing paint when you apply pressure on the stylus. However, if he used the

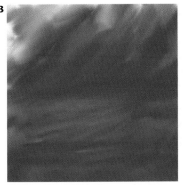

2b

Changing the Impasto settings in the Stroke Designer tab of the Brush Creator for the Wet Bristle variant copy

3

Applying glazes to the image canvas

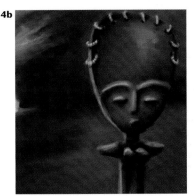

4a

The figure study in progress

4b

Vealé painted reflected light on the face of the Ashanti figure.

default Impasto Wet Bristle, the brush would paint with depth as well as color, eventually covering the embossed texture applied in Step 1. So he modified a copy of the Wet Bristle so that it would apply only color to his image, as follows: Select the Wet Bristle variant of Impasto and copy it to the Oils category by choosing Copy Variant from the triangle pop-up menu on the right side of the Brush Selector Bar. When the Copy Variant dialog box appears, choose the Oils category from the pop-up menu and click OK. Now choose the Wet Bristle copy from the Oils category. Open the Brush Creator (Ctrl/⌘-B), and its Stroke Designer tab. In the Impasto section, change the Draw To pop-up menu to Color. Then choose Set Default Variant from the Variant menu in the Brush Creator to make the change permanent for the new Wet Bristle variant.

3 Painting colored washes. Using a light touch on the stylus, and the new Wet Bristle brush, Vealé freely brushed loose washes of color over the image canvas, suggesting a subtle horizon line and a glowing campfire in the background.

Choose your new Wet Bristle variant and paint brushstrokes on the image. The brush applies paint when you press lightly, but scrubs underlying paint when you press hard. (You can also achieve good washes with other brushes, such as the Smeary Round and the Variable Flat variants of the Oils.)

4 Setting up a still life and painting the figure. Vealé set up a conventional light to shine from behind the figure that served as his model and another to reflect light onto its face. Then he carefully studied the Ashanti figure's form, and painted it directly on the image canvas with a smaller version of the Wet Bristle variant. He built up values slowly, gradually adding more saturated, darker tones to the still life study. Vealé brought out orange tones that were reminiscent of firelight in the background. He added deeper red and brown colors to the sky, and brighter colors and more detail to the bonfire in the background. Then he added stronger highlights and cast shadows to the foreground and to the carving. Finally, to relieve some of the rigidity of the centered composition, he repainted areas of the background to move the horizon up.

Variations. A slightly different effect (shown at right) can be achieved if you choose the new Wet Bristle, and in the General section of the Stroke Designer (Brush Creator), reduce the Opacity of the brush to between 20–40% and set the Opacity Expression pop-up menu to Pressure.

Figure study, by Stanley Vealé

Working with Thick Paint

Overview *Paint a color study; use Impasto brushes to add 3D brushwork to the study; use Surface Lighting to adjust the appearance of the highlights and shadows on the thick paint.*

Sammel's black-and-white pencil study

IMPASTO BRINGS THE TEXTURE OF THICK, LUSCIOUS PAINT to the tip of your stylus. When painting *Dying Orchids,* artist Chelsea Sammel used Painter's Impasto brushes to add the texture of brush marks with realistic highlights and shadows to a color study. Then she scraped back and added more expressive brushwork, bringing more texture and activity to the painting.

1 Designing the still life and making a sketch. Sammel envisioned a composition with strong side lighting in which the orchids appeared to be suspended in space. She designed an airy, asymmetrical flower arrangement with interesting negative space, set up in the natural light of a window.

To begin the sketch, she created a new file that measured 1200 x 1600 pixels. In the Brush Selector Bar, she chose the Colored Pencil variant of the Colored Pencils, and in the Paper Selector, she chose Basic Paper. Then she drew a tight, black-and-white sketch. To sketch as Sammel did, select the Colored Pencil variant

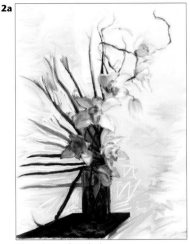

The color underpainting

A detail showing scraped back canvas

Adding texture to the background with the Loaded Palette Knife variant of Impasto

and choose Restore Default Variant from the triangle pop-up menu on the right side of the Brush Selector Bar, to make sure that the Colored Pencil uses the default settings.

2 Creating the color underpainting. She began to lay color directly over the sketch using Round Camelhair variant of the Oils. She painted using warm autumn colors—browns, burnt sienna, golds—and other rich hues.

Traditional artists often add texture and complexity to the surface of their paintings by scraping areas of paint off the canvas. To scrape back areas, Sammel chose the Loaded Palette Knife variant of the Palette Knives. To make a smaller version of the brush, she reduced its size using the Size slider in the Property Bar. Switching between the Round Camelhair and Loaded Palette Knife variants, she painted and scraped back, pulled and blended colors, creating an expressive painting with a lot of movement.

3 Adding textured brushwork. Then Sammel added more interest and activity to the composition by adding textured brushstrokes that did not necessarily follow the lines of the colored paint. She modified the Loaded Palette Knife variant of Impasto, so that it would paint with negative depth, but not color, and she made it smaller. To make Sammel's custom palette knife, choose the Loaded Palette Knife variant of Impasto and set the Size slider in the Property Bar to 11.0. Open the Brush Creator by pressing Ctrl/⌘-B. Click the Stroke Designer Tab to open the Stroke Designer, then click the Impasto section bar to open the Impasto section. In the Impasto section, set the Draw To menu to Depth and the Depth slider to 35%, leaving other settings at their defaults: Smoothing, 77% and Plow, 100%. Save the variant by choosing Save Variant from the Brush Creator's Variant menu, giving it a new name. Then, to preserve the original variant, choose the original Loaded Palette Knife and restore its default settings by choosing Variant, Restore Default Variant.

When she wanted the new palette knife to paint with both color and depth, she modified it to pick up and smear underlying colors. To make this modification, select the new palette knife, and in the Impasto section of the Stroke Designer (Brush Creator), set the Draw To menu back to Color and Depth. To pick up and mix underlying colors more, click on the Well section bar to open the Well section and set Resat to 20%. Save and name the new variant, then reselect the first modified palette knife.

Using warm, creamy colors, Sammel painted loose, gestural brushstrokes over the background. At this point, she exaggerated the strong side lighting and enhanced the negative space in the painting by using the Variable Flat Opaque variant of Impasto with Draw To set to its default Color And Depth to apply more white brushwork to the right side of the image.

4a

Painting details on the orchids

4b

Pulling and blending paint on the flowers with a small Variable Flat Opaque brush (Impasto)

5a

Adding more texture to the foreground using the Texturizer-Fine (Impasto)

4 Painting details on the flowers, vase and table.

Once the background was painted in, Sammel painted over the orchids using the Variable Flat Opaque (Impasto). She added bright highlights to the right side of the orchids and deeper, richer colors to areas in shadow on the flowers, vase and table. As she worked, she frequently modified settings in the Impasto section of the Stroke Designer (Brush Creator) for the Variable Flat Opaque variant. To paint with color and texture, she left the Draw To menu set at Color And Depth; to add textured brushstrokes without adding color, she chose the Draw To Depth setting. To paint brushstrokes with texture based on the current paper texture, she kept the Depth Method set to Paper.

5 Refining the painting.

Sammel used a small Loaded Palette Knife (Impasto) to drag color through the image (especially in the vase), then she added more colored paint using the Dry Ink vari-ant of Sumi-e. To allow the Dry Ink to mix and pull colors on the canvas, she made changes to the Well controls using the Property Bar. She lowered the Resat (to about 20%) and raised the Bleed setting (to about 80%).

She added spattery Impasto texture to the image foreground with the Texturizer-Fine variant of Impasto. Then Sammel brushed over areas that were too "impastoed" using the Depth Equalizer variant (Impasto) at a low Opacity. She lowered the Opacity using the Opacity slider in the Property Bar. Finally, she reduced the overall effect of the Impasto by choosing Canvas, Surface Lighting. For a more subtle Impasto look she reduced the Amount to 75%. 🎨

5b

Painting final details on the vase and flowers using the Loaded Palette Knife (Impasto) and Dry Ink (Brushes) variants

A Painter Liquid Ink Primer

Overview *Here you'll find the basics for painting with the Liquid Ink brushes and layers in Painter.*

CHER THREINEN-PENDARVIS / CREATED FOR COREL CORPORATION

We began this Liquid Ink study of Little Doll *by creating a black line drawing with the Fine Point variant of Liquid Ink on a Liquid Ink layer. Then we added a new layer (by choosing New Liquid Ink Layer from the Layers palette menu), dragged it below the sketch layer in the Layers palette, and added color to the table and background with the Graphic Camel variant. For the cat's fur we created another new layer between the two we already had, and painted using gold and tan colors. For the look of thicker paint on the layer with the fur, we double-clicked the layer's name in the Layers palette and adjusted the Amount slider in the Liquid Ink Layer Attributes dialog box. Then we painted with the Coarse Camel Resist to erode some of the colored ink.*

WITH THE LIQUID INK BRUSHES AND MEDIA LAYERS in Painter, you can paint bold, graphic brushstrokes of flat color, then erode ink with resist brushes or build up thick ink that has three-dimensional highlights and shadows. Like traditional viscous media (printer's ink or the enamel used in jewelry making, for example), Liquid Ink is sticky.

Yellow Pitcher (above), one in a series of studies of 1930s California pottery, was created with the Graphic Camel and Graphic Camel Resist variants on several Liquid Ink layers, so that each color could be kept separate without mixing. Before you start a Liquid Ink painting of your own, reading the next five pages will help you to understand how to achieve the results you desire.

Controlling Liquid Ink. The most important settings for Liquid Ink are in the Property Bar and in several sections of the Brush Creator's Stroke Designer window: the General, Size and Liquid Ink sections of the Stroke Designer; the Layers palette; and the Surface Lighting dialog box, found under the Canvas menu. Painting with a Liquid Ink brush automatically generates a Liquid Ink layer, which is then listed in the Layers palette. Liquid Ink layers can be targeted in the Layers palette and edited like other layers. (Chapter 5 tells more about working with layers.)

RESOLUTION-INDEPENDENT INK

A graphic medium, Liquid Ink is resolution-independent. It's possible to create a Liquid Ink illustration at half size, then double the resolution of the file and retain the crisp edges on the brush work.

In this example, the "e" was drawn after the "S," and the new Liquid Ink stroke melted into the existing ink. The lettering was drawn using the Smooth Flat variant of Liquid Ink. The rough strokes were added using the Graphic Camel.

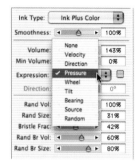

The Volume setting in the Expression section of the Stroke Designer palette allows you to specify which factor controls the Volume of a stroke.

The Liquid Ink section of the Stroke Designer, showing the Type pop-up menu

The Liquid Ink section, showing the default settings for the Graphic Camel

In the General section of the Stroke Designer (Brush Creator), the Liquid Ink dab types are displayed in the Dab Type pop-up menu. A dab type determines the shape of the brush tip—for instance, Liquid Ink Flat and Liquid Ink Camel (Camel brush tips are round). The Liquid Ink brushes use continuous-stroke technology, which means that brushstrokes are painted using brush hairs that form a set of anti-aliased 1-pixel lines. You'll find more information about dab types in "Building Brushes" on page 57.

In the Property Bar (and in the Size section of the Stroke Designer), you'll find the Feature slider, which determines the density of the brush hairs in the continuous-stroke brushes. **Note:** A very low Feature setting (producing more densely packed brush hairs), takes greater computing power, and this can slow down the performance of a Liquid Ink brush.

In the Liquid Ink section of Stroke Designer (Brush Creator), if the Volume Expression controller is set to Pressure, the height of the brushstroke will increase as pressure is applied to the stylus.

Liquid Ink has two basic components: Ink and Color. *Ink* consists of the shape and dimension of the Liquid Ink, giving the medium its sticky, plastic quality and form. The *Color* component is independent of the ink form. In the Liquid Ink section of the Stroke Designer (Brush Creator), the Type pop-up menu includes nine important Color-and-Ink options that dramatically affect the performance of the Liquid Ink brushes. The Type settings themselves are complex and are also affected by slider settings in the Liquid Ink section (described below). A brush of the *Ink Plus Color* type adds new ink using the current color in the Color picker. While the *Ink Only* type affects only the shape of the brushstroke, the *Color Only* type affects only the color component. *Soften Ink Plus Color* alters existing brushstrokes so that the ink changes shape and the colors blend into one another. The *Soften Ink Only* reshapes the ink without changing its color, and *Soften Color Only* blends the Color without reshaping.

Painting with a *Resist* type brush will cause brushstrokes applied over the resist to be repelled. (Scrubbing with a non-resist brush can erode the resist until it is eventually removed.) Using the *Erase* type will remove existing ink and color. *Presoftened Ink Plus Color* works in conjunction with the Volume control settings to build up height as additional brushstrokes are applied.

Liquid Ink has two basic components: Ink and Color. *Ink* controls the shape and dimensionality of the strokes and gives the medium its sticky, plastic quality. *Color* controls color without affecting the shape.

Many of the various settings that control Liquid Ink interact with one another in complex ways. This is what produces the magic of this medium, but mastering the complexity can present quite a challenge. It's a good idea to experiment with the different brushes and types until you get a feel for how Liquid Ink performs.

An active Liquid Ink layer as it appears in the Layers palette. To create a new Liquid Ink layer, click the right triangle on the Layers palette bar and choose New Liquid Ink Layer or click the Create New Liquid Ink Layer button at the bottom of the Layers palette.

For Ocean Waves, *the Coarse Bristle variant of Liquid Ink was used to draw curved strokes with a thick, bristly texture. We used the Coarse Airbrush Resist to add a foamy texture to the water and to suggest atmosphere in the sky.*

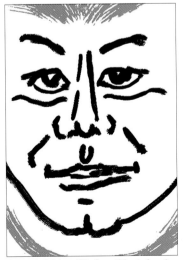

Sumo Ink Man. *We drew this study using a Wacom pressure-sensitive tablet and stylus on a laptop (while watching Sumo wrestlers on TV), with the Graphic Camel and Graphic Bristle variants of Liquid Ink.*

The eight sliders in the Liquid Ink section work in conjunction with each other to create many kinds of Liquid Ink brushstrokes. Because these controls are very complex and interdependent, they're difficult to clearly define. Experiment—dig in and try out the Liquid Ink variants, while keeping an eye on the Liquid Ink section controls. The *Smoothness* slider controls how sticky the ink is. Lower values will create coarser brushstrokes with less self-adhesion. A high Smoothness setting will help to hide the individual bristle marks and will increase adhesion, but it may make the performance of the brush lag. *Volume* controls the height of the brushstroke. Use this setting in conjunction with the Volume setting in the Expressions section of Brush Controls to add height to brushstrokes. (**Note:** To view volume on your image, the Amount setting must be adjusted in the Liquid Ink Layer Attributes dialog box. See the "Turning on 3D Highlights and Shadows" tip below.) The *Min Volume* controls the amount that the volume can vary. (This slider is used in conjunction with the Volume setting in the Expression section.) *Rand Vol* controls the randomness of the volume in a stroke. A low value will create a smoother, less variable stroke. *Random Size* controls randomness of brush hair size within the stroke; again, a lower value will help to create a smoother stroke. *Bristle Frac* controls the density of the bristles. *Rand Bristle Vol* controls the variation in volume of ink laid down by individual bristles, and a low value will make the bristle marks a more even thickness. *Rand Bristle Size* controls variation in the widths of individual bristles. A very low setting will make the bristles more similar in width.

TURNING ON 3D HIGHLIGHTS AND SHADOWS

To view Liquid Ink brushwork with three-dimensional highlights and shadows, double-click the name of the Liquid Ink layer in the Layers palette and increase the Amount (thickness) setting. Click OK. The Liquid Ink medium has no thickness limit. After you have increased the Amount setting, you can use your stylus to paint more Liquid Ink onto the layer, continuing to build up the pile of ink. You can adjust the thickness at any time using the Amount slider in the Liquid Ink Layer Attributes dialog box. (There is no preview in this dialog box. You have to adjust the slider and click OK, then observe the effect on the image.) To change the direction, intensity, or other properties of the lighting, choose Canvas, Surface Lighting, and adjust the settings in the Impasto Lighting dialog box.

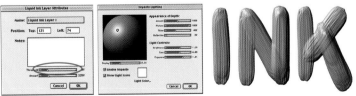

Increasing the Amount setting (left) increased the thickness of the brushstrokes (right). We left the settings in the Surface Lighting dialog box at their defaults.

JOHN DERRY

After drawing black line work using the Fine Point variant, John Derry created a new Liquid Ink layer, and dragged it below the line work layer in the Layers palette. Working on the new layer, he used the Smooth Knife variant to paint broad areas of color onto the background. He created interesting texture by eroding paint with the Coarse Airbrush Resist. For the smooth-edged highlights on the stool, he painted with the Smooth Camel variant.

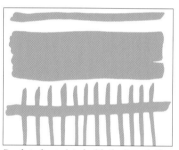

Brushstrokes painted with the Smooth Flat variant of Liquid Ink

Thin-to-thick sweeping curved strokes painted with the Pointed Flat variant of Liquid Ink

WORKING WITH THE LIQUID INK BRUSHES

Here are some suggestions for how to paint using the Liquid Ink brushes in Painter. Even if you're familiar with Painter's other brushes, try out these ideas and experiment with all of the Liquid Ink variants.

Painting coarsely textured brushstrokes. To paint brushstrokes with a coarse, bristly texture, choose the Coarse Bristle variant. You can control the paint coverage by applying more or less pressure to the stylus—a lighter pressure will create a stroke with less paint. The Graphic variants also paint coarsely textured brushstrokes and with better performance, for more spontaneous painting. The Graphic Camel is one of our favorites because it paints expressive, thin-to-thick strokes, with finer texture on the edges of the brushstrokes.

Blended color with smooth brushes. Any Liquid Ink variant with Smooth in its name has a high smoothness setting and will paint just like a brush loaded with very thick, sticky ink or paint. The Smooth Bristle variant's bristles will spread or splay out as you rotate your hand through the stroke, while the Smooth Camel performs like a big, round brush with longer bristles. As you press harder on the stylus, the Smooth Camel will paint a broader stroke. As you paint a new color over existing ink with a Smooth brush, the edges of the colors will subtly blend.

Thick and thin strokes with the Flat brushes. Look for brushes with the word Flat in their name; the Coarse Flat and Pointed Flat are examples. With Flat-tipped brushes, you can paint wide or narrow strokes, depending on how you hold the stylus relative to the stroke direction and how much pressure you apply. When trying the strokes below, position your stylus with the button facing up (away from you). To paint a broad flat area of color with the Smooth Flat (as in the example on the left), pull the brush straight across your image using even pressure. To make the thin lines, pull down. To make a curved, thin-to-thick wavy line, use light pressure on your stylus for the thin top areas, and more pressure as you sweep down and rotate the brush. For flat brushstrokes with sensitive thin-to-thick control, try the Pointed Flat. With this brush, bristle marks will be more visible when heavy pressure is applied to the stylus. For a thin-to-thick sweeping curved stroke, begin the thin portion with

> **MOUSE ALERT!**
>
> Liquid Ink brushes are very responsive to the pressure applied to a stylus. Because of the importance of pressure, many of the brushes do not perform as described here when a mouse is used. For instance, if a resist is painted using a mouse and the Smooth Bristle Resist, you many be able to paint over the resist with the Smooth Round Nib variant using a mouse; in this case the mouse seems to simulate enough pressure to wear away the resist.

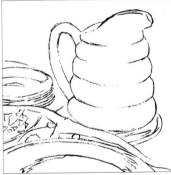

We drew the sketch for Yellow Pitcher *using the Velocity Sketcher variant.*

The Graphic Camel Resist variant was used to erode ink and create highlights in Yellow Pitcher. *A detail is shown here.*

very light pressure on your stylus, and as you sweep downward rotate your stylus slightly and apply more pressure. To make a thick, even stroke, pull the stylus sideways relative to the button, using even pressure. For the thin lines, apply even pressure and pull in a direction toward or away from the button.

Sketching and line work. You can also sketch or draw line work with Liquid Ink. Quick performance makes the Velocity Sketcher ideal for spontaneous sketching. On the edges of the brushstrokes, you'll notice grainy texture.

The *Fine* variants of Liquid Ink are good for painting details and for calligraphic line work. The Fine Point draws like a steel pen with a pointed nib, and the Fine Eraser is ideal for cleaning up edges and for removing small patches of ink.

Painting resists. A *resist* is a substance that can be painted onto a Liquid Ink layer with a Liquid Ink Resist type brush. A resist is capable of repelling ink when the area is painted over by a standard Liquid Ink brush. You can also "scrub away" existing Liquid Ink using a Resist type brush. The Coarse Bristle Resist and the Graphic Camel Resist, for instance, are useful for painting coarse, eroded areas on a Liquid Ink painting. For a smoother resist, try the Smooth Bristle, Smooth Flat or Smooth Camel Resist variant. To erode existing ink and create an interesting speckled texture, use the Coarse Airbrush Resist.

SOFTENING EDGES

Using the Soften Edges and Color variant of Liquid Ink, you can subtly blur areas of ink and color.

Detail of Hillside Lake. *We used Soften Edges and Color to blend the top edge of the purple hill in the midground.*

ADJUSTING LIQUID INK EDGES

You can nondestructively make Liquid Ink brushstrokes appear to expand or contract by adjusting the Threshold slider in the Liquid Ink Layer Attributes dialog box. To see how Threshold works, in the Layers palette, target the layer that you'd like to change and access the Liquid Ink Layer Attributes dialog box by double-clicking the layer's name in the Layers palette (or press the Enter key). To thicken the appearance of the brushstrokes, lower the Threshold value by moving the slider to the left. To give the ink a thinner appearance, raise the Threshold value by moving the slider to the right.

Adjusting the Threshold slider very low (to –49%) thickened the blue ink.

Adjusting the Threshold very high (to 160%) dramatically thinned the blue ink on the sugar bowl.

Encaustic Painting with Liquid Ink

Overview *Use a Liquid Ink brush to paint textured color on a layer; duplicate the layer; make a custom coloring brush; recolor the layer and erode areas; add more layers with new color and texture.*

JOHN DERRY

1a

Painting the yellow square with the Sparse Camel variant of Liquid Ink

1b

The new active Liquid Ink layer shown in the Layers palette

ENCAUSTIC PAINTING INCORPORATES PIGMENTS suspended in wax. It was used by the ancient Greeks who painted the brightly colored statues in the Acropolis and by the Romans for wall murals in Pompeii. Traditional encaustic technique involves heating the wax-based medium and then painting quickly while the wax is still malleable. Delicate layering of transparent color as well as heavy impasto techniques are possible. In Painter, you can create the look of encaustic painting with the new Liquid Ink brushes and media layers.

To create *Chess*, John Derry used Liquid Ink brushes and media layers to emulate encaustic painting. He painted bright colors on Liquid Ink layers, then eroded and scratched out areas to reveal the color and textured brush work on the underlying layers. For the look of thick encaustic paint, he added subtle three-dimensional highlights and shadows to the layers.

1 Creating textured brush work. Begin your Liquid Ink painting by opening a new file with a white background (File, New). To work at the scale of this painting, set the Width and Height at 800 x 800 pixels and click OK.

To paint a background consisting of large, textured strokes, choose the Sparse Camel variant of Liquid Ink in the Brush Selector Bar and choose a bright yellow color in the Color picker. When you've chosen a Liquid Ink brush and you touch your sty-

2

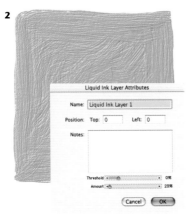

The completed first layer, showing the highlights and shadows on the brush work and the settings in the Liquid Ink Layer Attributes dialog box

3

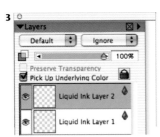

The active, duplicate layer in the Layers palette

4

Choosing Color Only for the Type setting in the Liquid Ink Section of the Stroke Designer

5

The square reddish areas added to the image on the duplicate layer, then partially eroded using a resist brush; shown with both layers visible (left) and with the yellow layer hidden (right).

lus to the tablet, a Liquid Ink layer will automatically be generated and will be listed in the Layers palette. Loosely block in a square shape using the Sparse Camel. Derry purposely painted an irregular edge and left part of the white background as an informal border, which would add to the textural contrast in his image.

2 Turning on thick paint. To add realistic highlights and shadows to the brush work on the yellow layer, double-click its name in the Layers palette. When the Liquid Ink Layer Attributes dialog box appears, increase the Amount setting to about 20% and click OK.

3 Duplicating a Liquid Ink layer. Derry wanted to add different colors while keeping the brushstroke pattern that he had already created. So he duplicated the active yellow layer by choosing the Layer Adjuster tool in the Toolbox, pressing the Alt/Option key and clicking once on the layer in the image. (To read more about working with layers, turn to Chapter 5, "Using Layers.") Once you've duplicated the layer, choose the Brush again in the Toolbox.

4 Making a custom brush for coloring. With some Liquid Ink brushes, you can recolor elements without disturbing the ink (shape, volume and lighting) component that you've painted on a layer. After the layer duplicate was created, Derry modified the Sparse Camel brush so that it would change the color without changing the shape and thickness of the existing strokes. To modify the Sparse Camel as Derry did, open the Brush Creator palette by choosing Window, Show Brush Creator, or by pressing Ctrl/⌘-B. Click the Stroke Designer tab, and open the Liquid Ink section by clicking on the Liquid Ink section bar and in the section's Type pop-up menu, choose Color Only. To save this custom Sparse Camel brush, choose Save Variant from the Variant menu in the Brush Creator, name the new brush and click OK to save it. In addition to saving your new brush, Painter will remember the changes that you've made to the default Sparse Camel brush, so it's a good idea to restore it to its default settings. To return the original Sparse Camel variant to its default, choose Restore Default Variant from the Variant menu in the Brush Creator.

5 Coloring and eroding the duplicated layer. With the duplicate layer active in the Layers palette, choose a new color (Derry chose a bright reddish-pink) and paint over the areas that you want to

6a

The smaller blue squares are added to the image, breaking each of the original four squares into four.

6b

The small green squares are added, so that now each of the four original squares has sixteen parts.

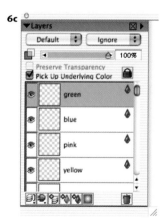

6c

The Layers palette showing the renamed Liquid Ink layers

recolor. To scrape away areas of the layer so that the color from the underlying layer will show through, you can use a Resist type variant or an Eraser type variant of Liquid Ink. Because he likes the texture it creates, Derry scrubbed with the Sparse Camel Resist variant to scrape away the pink upper right and lower left areas to reveal the yellow. Then, to add an eroded texture into areas within the pink squares that he planned to keep, he brushed lightly over them using the Sparse Camel Resist variant.

6 Adding the blue and green squares. To add the blue and green colors to his image, Derry repeated the duplicating, revealing and eroding process in Steps 2 and 3. The blue squares were smaller, so the effect was to break each pink square into four. The green squares were even smaller; the effect was to break up each original square into sixteen.

7 Painting the chess piece. So the castle would look as if it were thicker paint sitting on top of the painted chess board, Derry wanted the direction of the brushstrokes to be different. He created a new Liquid Ink layer by clicking the New Liquid Ink Layer at the bottom of the Layers palette bar. On the new layer, he blocked in the basic shape of the chess piece with the default Sparse Camel using white color, then used the Sparse Camel Resist to erode some of the white paint. For the black areas on the chess piece, Derry duplicated the white layer as he had done for the yellow in Step 3. Then he chose his custom Sparse Camel brush (which used Color Only) and painted black onto the right half of the castle. To finish, he used the Sparse Camel Resist to erode areas of the black layer to expose the white underneath.

7a

The white shape was painted on a new Liquid Ink layer

7b

The black brush work shown in this detail was painted on a duplicate of the white layer

■ Artist **Michela Del Degan** creates illustrations for educational books and multimedia projects and she exhibits fine art work.

Africa and Life is a series of six images, two of which are shown here. The works were inspired by a story that takes place in Africa. In the story, there are three parallel situations: the growth of a tree from a small seed, the growth of love, which brings to life a new being, and the attraction between the sun and the moon. Four main elements—Earth, Wind, Fire and Water—are important in the story. Del Degan began the images using traditional materials: She painted with conventional acrylic on canvas using thick white paint; she chose a piece of watercolor paper and painted bright-colored washes over the background and figures. To define the elements, she used a dark pencil to draw an outline rendering for each composition. Next, she scanned the canvas and the watercolor and pencil studies using a flatbed scanner and saved each scan as a TIFF file. Working in Painter, she opened the scan of the acrylic on canvas and each scanned watercolor and assembled the pieces as layers in six separate files. To combine the acrylic brushwork with the watercolor images, she used Multiply Composite Method in the Layers palette, then she dropped the layers by choosing Drop All from the Layers palette menu. She increased the saturation of each watercolor using the Effects, Tonal Control, Adjust Colors dialog box. She also bumped up the luminosity using the Image Luminance choice in the Adjust Color dialog box. Then Del Degan strengthened the outline drawings using the Soft Charcoal. To retouch areas of the scanned art, she sampled color from the image and used the Soft Charcoal to paint color over the areas. To add a rough paper texture to areas of her images, she used the Grain Emboss variant of Impasto. Finally, to complete the works, she touched up the black outlines using a small Soft Charcoal variant.

■ "I approach painting in Painter the same way I paint conventionally," says **Karen Carr**, an accomplished illustrator who often creates natural history illustrations for educational publishers.

Carr was commissioned by *Scholastic Press* to create the undersea illustration above. She began by sketching with the Chalk variants, then roughed in color using Oils variants. She painted glazes of color over the top of her underpainting just as she does with oil paints. Carr prefers to keep the use of layers to a minimum, because she likes the tactile feel of moving paint around on the

Canvas. To achieve the illusion of light shining down in the upper left, she set up a custom colored light using Effects, Surface Control, Apply Lighting. After blocking in basic color on the dolphin, the fish, and coral using a modified Charcoal variant, she used the Just Add Water variant of Blenders to smoothly blend and render the sea life. She worked back and forth, adding color and blending as she refined the volume of their forms. When she wanted to smudge paint and reveal texture, she used the Coarse Smear and Smudge variants of Blenders.

■ **Karen Carr** was commissioned by *Scientific American* magazine to create ***Temnodontosaur***, a cover illustration representing the work of Dr. Ryosuke Motani, a researcher in the paleobiology department at the Royal Ontario Museum of Toronto. Carr worked closely with Dr. Motani when painting this cannibal of the Jurassic Sea. To begin *Temnodontosaur*, Carr chose an ocean blue color in the Colors picker and then chose Effects, Surface Control, Color Overlay to establish the color theme for the painting. Then, using modified Charcoal variants,

she roughed in color. While painting, she used a wide variety of textures, and she changed the size and opacity of the brushes often as she worked. As Carr began to build up the volume of the animals, she used the Just Add Water (and other Blenders variants) to blend and pull color around on the image. To create the patterns in the water in the upper area, she blended and pulled paint using the Distorto variants of Distortion as well her own custom Blenders variants.

■ An accomplished illustrator who specializes in book illustration, **Don Stewart** used to work on gessoed illustration board with airbrush and colored pencils before he began using Painter. Today he draws on the computer using Painter's tools and brushes that match his traditional ones.

Planters Foundation Books commissioned Stewart to create *Baskim's Lesson* for a children's story poster. Stewart began by choosing a fine-textured paper and drawing a detailed sketch in Painter using Pencils variants. To isolate areas of the image (such as the fox's head and body), he made freehand selections using the Lasso tool and then saved the selections as masks in the Channels palette (Window, Show Channels), in case he needed to use them later. He blocked in basic color using Water Color brushes, and then he dropped the Water Color layer to the Canvas so he could paint on it with other brushes. To build up values, he used the Digital Airbrush variant of Airbrushes and the Smeary variants of the Oils. Then he added highlights, deeper shadows and fine detail using the Colored Pencil variant of Colored Pencils. Stewart sprayed texture on the fox's fur using the Coarse Spray variant of Airbrushes. For the texture on the grass in the foreground, he used Chalk variants and the Coarse Spray and Variable Splatter Airbrushes.

■ *One Nation* was commissioned by *Liberty* magazine for a cover illustration. **Don Stewart** began the illustration by sketching in Painter using Colored Pencils variants on fine-textured paper. To isolate areas of the image (for example, the background behind the figures and frame) so that he could freely paint within the selected areas, he used selections in the same way that he used friskets in tra-

ditional airbrush illustration. To lay in colored washes he used Water Color variants. When he had finished the washes, Stewart combined the Water Color layer with the Canvas by choosing Drop from the Layers palette. Next, he used the Digital Airbrush variant of Airbrushes to paint smoother areas (such as the skin), and to begin to build up tone and value. When the figures were modeled the way he wanted them,

he added highlights and detail using the Colored Pencil variant of Colored Pencils. For more texture on the clothes and chalkboard, he used the Fine Spray and Coarse Spray variants of the Airbrushes. To add coarser texture to the background, he painted with subtly different colors using Chalk variants over a rough texture, then touched up a few areas with the Coarse Spray Airbrush.

■ **Cher Threinen-Pendarvis's**
experience with traditional style in pastel,
watercolor and acrylic translates easily to
digital pastel in Painter.

Paths to Water North (above) is one in a
series of paintings of Sunset Cliffs Natural
Park in San Diego, California. Pendarvis
began the painting by making location
studies using a Powerbook laptop
computer, Painter and a Wacom
pressure-sensitive tablet. Sitting in the
shade near the trees, she began by

creating a new file with a beige
background paper color. She chose a
rough, even-grained paper texture, and
sketched using the Sharp Chalk variant of
Chalk and a dark brown color. Observing
the afternoon light and shadows she
worked on location using the laptop until
she had established the composition,
general color theme and cast shadows in
the study. Later on her studio computer,
Pendarvis added more layers of color
using modified Square Chalk and Large

Chalk variants of Chalk, working over the
entire piece. She blended areas with the
Grainy Water variant of Blenders and
added more textured, directional strokes
with the Chalk variants. As a last step, she
used Effects, Surface Control, Apply
Surface Texture to apply the paper
texture to the entire painting, using
subtle settings.

■ **Cher Threinen-Pendarvis** often makes several color studies for a painting on location, carefully observing how light and atmosphere affect color in highlights and shadows.

An isolated, breathtaking view and unique plant life provided the inspiration for *Agaves on the Edge*. For this painting, Pendarvis began by making several colored pencil sketches—details of the agave plants, the cliffs and the overall seascape—in a traditional sketchbook that she'd carried in her backpack. Later, back at the studio she created a new file in Painter. Using the 2B Pencil variant of

the Pencils and Basic Paper texture, she sketched the composition. She loosely blocked in color directly over the sketch with a Round Camelhair variant of Oils, which she had modified to include a small amount of Color Variability to help to modulate the color. To build up layers of color interest on the hills, cliffs and water, she dabbed small strokes of paint on top using a smaller Round Camelhair brush, then she blended areas of the cliffs, hills and water using the Grainy Water variant of Blenders. Pendarvis added softly colored clouds to the sky using the Square Chalk variant of Chalk,

then smoothed and blended color using the Grainy Water. To add textured highlights to the beach and color interest to the cliffs, she used the Square Chalk and Artist Pastel Chalk (Pastels). To balance the composition, she reworked some of the foreground plants and added soft brushstrokes to the path using the Round Camelhair variant. She also used the Artist Pastel Chalk to feather subtly colored strokes over the painted leaves, to further define their forms and to add color complexity and movement. Finally, she applied highlights to some of the leaves using the Artist Pastel Chalk.

■ Artist **Donal Jolley** usually begins his paintings by shooting reference photos. He roughs in color using the Chalk and Pastels variants, then he uses the Oils variants for more developed brushwork and the Pens variants for tiny details.

For *Storm Chaser*, Jolley opened several of his own ocean and sky photos in Painter and assembled them into a composite by pasting them into his image as layers. When he was happy with the composition, he dropped the layers by choosing Drop from the menu on the Layers palette. Then, he made a clone by choosing File, Clone, and deleted the contents of the clone image by selecting

All (Ctrl/⌘-A) and pressing Backspace/Delete. He saved the clone image by choosing File, Save As, giving it a new name. He kept the original photo open and turned on Tracing Paper in the clone file by pressing Ctrl/⌘-T. Next Jolley added a new layer to his image and used the Square Chalk (Chalk) to paint the larger shapes and to develop the color palette in the painting. He added more layers for the intermediate brushwork and detail. As he developed the painting, he toggled Tracing Paper on and off as he worked. Once the composition was developed, he dropped the layers to the Canvas. For added texture on the sea

foam highlights, he chose Basic Paper texture in the Paper Selector in the Tools palette, and painted over areas using a low-opacity Square Chalk. When painting the waves, Jolley switched to the Round Camelhair and Smeary variants of the Oils. The smeary brushes allowed him to apply new color and blend it with the existing pigment, just like working with wet paint. To soften areas in the water and sky, he blended them with the Just Add Water and Grainy Water variants of the Blenders.

■ **Donal Jolley** began *Deer Flat Memories* by scanning a 30-year-old family photo taken on the Big Sur Coast, near San Simeon. He did not use the colors in the original photograph, but instead chose a palette that came more from memory of the bright, cold morning when the photo was taken. "I painted the cloud cover to show how the clouds rolled in off the water and up the ravines in a relatively even mist, tending to burn off as the morning progressed," says Jolley.

He opened the scanned photo in Painter and made a clone of the photo by choosing File, Clone, deleted the contents of the clone image by selecting All (Ctrl/⌘-A) and pressing Backspace/Delete. He saved the clone image by choosing File, Save As, giving it a new name. Jolley kept the original photo open and turned on Tracing Paper in the clone by pressing Ctrl/⌘-T. Next, he added a new layer to his image on which he would rough in the composition and develop the color theme. Working on the new layer, he used the Sharp Chalk to sketch the composition and the Square Chalk to paint the larger shapes and paint the broad colored areas. As he worked, he constantly changed the sizes of his brushes, and he added more layers as he painted (for the figures in the landscape, for instance) so that he could move elements around. He also added a new layer before he painted the foggy atmosphere—this enabled him to try out different opacities and compositing methods for a more transparent look. Once the composition was developed, he dropped the layers to the Canvas. Then, using the Smeary variants of the Oils he applied new color and blended it with the existing pigment, for a very painterly feeling. This work is especially evident in the receding coastline and atmosphere, and also in the foreground grasses. To soften areas in the ocean and foggy sky, he used the Just Add Water and Grainy Water variants of the Blenders.

■ **Richard Noble** has been an accomplished traditional painter and designer for many years. Today he paints most of his fine artwork in Painter, using techniques that simulate traditional acrylic painting. He typically begins a painting by shooting reference photos and making sketches on location.

For *Garden* (right) and *Coast* (below), two paintings from his Mendocino series, Noble roughed in vibrant, saturated color with the Sargent Brush variant of the Artists brush and the Round Camelhair variant of the Oils. Both of these brushes allowed Noble to move paint around on the canvas. He also blended color using the Palette Knife variant of the Palette Knives and the Distorto variant of Distortion. Using a small Round Camelhair variant, he painted fine details in the shady areas of the foreground foliage as well as in the sunlit areas of the paintings. Noble usually prints his paintings on canvas with light-fast inks and finishes them with touches of acrylic paint. To see two other paintings from his Mendocino series, turn to the gallery at the end of Chapter 2.

■ **Dennis Orlando** is well-known for his Impressionist-style landscape and still life paintings. To create the vibrant look of oil paints in *Views of Monterey Bay*, he layered color using the Artist Pastel Chalk variant of Pastels, the Impressionist variant of the Artists brush and the Smeary variants of the Oils.

Using a palette of earth tones and blues, he roughed out a study for the composition in Painter using the Chalk and Pastel variants, then layered more color to build up an underpainting.

Switching back and forth between the Artist Pastel Chalk and the Grainy Water variant of Blenders, he continued to add color and smudge it. He painted the foreground sand by making short, curved strokes with a modified Smeary Flat variant of the Oils. To help to modulate color, Orlando increased Color Variability for the Smeary Flat variant, moving the ± H (hue) slider to about 15% in the Color Variability palette. His use of enhanced Color Variability is most easily seen in the sky and water. To pull and

mix color in the water, sky and cliffs, he used a large Smeary Bristle Spray variant (Oils) and the Impressionist variant (Artists). Then he added accents of more saturated color to the foreground trees and sunlit areas of the water using a smaller Smeary Bristle Spray variant. Finally, he used tiny Grainy Water (Blenders) and a small Distorto variant (Distortion) to blend and finesse the highlights on the midground cliffs and rocks and the sea foam.

■ Artist **Nancy Stahl** has created award-winning illustrations using gouache and other traditional materials since 1976. Using Painter's brushes and surfaces, she's been able to re-create the effects she achieved in her traditional work, as shown here in *Sax* (above) and *Workbook Man* (right). To learn more about her painting techniques, turn to "Painting with Gouache," on page 90.

Stahl began *Sax* by roughing in a cream-colored background using a modified Broad Cover Brush variant (Gouache). Using a darker color, she sketched the forms of the sax using the Smooth Ink Pen variant of the Pens.

Using custom-made brushes she had built to imitate her favorite gouache brushes, Stahl added color and began to render the forms of the musical instrument. For the look of thicker paint on her study, Stahl used the Opaque Flat and Round Camelhair variants of Impasto to paint very expressive linear strokes on the instrument and behind it. To move the paint around while carving into the existing thick paint, she switched to a small Palette Knife variant of Impasto. To finish, she chose the Opaque Bristle Spray (Impasto) and brightened the highlights in a few areas.

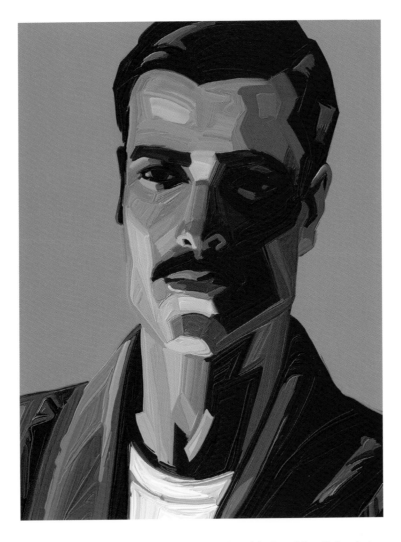

■ For *Workbook Man* (above) **Nancy Stahl** used Painter brushes that imitate her favorite traditional tools.

Stahl began the study by setting up a colored ground for her image. She chose File, New and in the New dialog box, she clicked in the Paper Color square and chose a dark tan paper color. Then she chose a darker color in the Color picker. She used the Smooth Ink Pen variant of Pens to draw a line sketch for the portrait. To block in the basic color theme, while beginning to sculpt the forms of the head, Stahl used a modified version of the Round Camelhair variant (Oils). To add brushstrokes with thicker paint, she switched to the Opaque Flat variant of Impasto. Then, to scrape into the thick paint and move it around, while enhancing the expressive, angular look of the painting, she switched to a small Palette Knife variant of Impasto, and made straighter, angled brushstrokes on the neck and shoulders. To complete her painting, she brightened a few of the highlights on the shirt, nose and chin using the Opaque Flat variant of Impasto.

■ Based in Normandy, France, **Kathy Hammon** is an accomplished artist and educator who works both traditionally and digitally. Hammon's current work with traditional media consists of very large oil paintings on canvas. Her digital paintings also give the viewer the feeling of vast spaces. When she uses Painter she paints directly on-screen, without the use of photographs or scanning. Hammon loves the realistic textures that can be achieved with the Chalk, Pastels, Oil Pastels, Oils, Sumi-e and Blenders variants.

The Whale was inspired by the beautiful whale she saw while sailing in Ecuador. She interpreted this vision as a dream of a whale swimming and jumping during the night. Hammon began the painting by using Oil Pastels variants to paint sweeping brushstrokes and large areas of color. When she wanted to blend one color into another, she used the Just Add Water variant of Blenders. Spontaneously painting, then blending, she worked back and forth, changing the sizes of the brushes as she worked. For the coastline,

she used deeper colors to enhance the dreamy night time scene. To add details to the coastline (the palm trees and volcanoes) she used lighter colors and a small Artist Pastel Chalk variant (Pastels). Then she added more coarse brushstroke details to the hills and trees using the Dry Ink (Sumi-e). To complete the seascape, Hammon used a modified Artist Pastel Chalk variant to add texture and redefine the edge of the whale's tail. She also added a few small highlights to the distant hills.

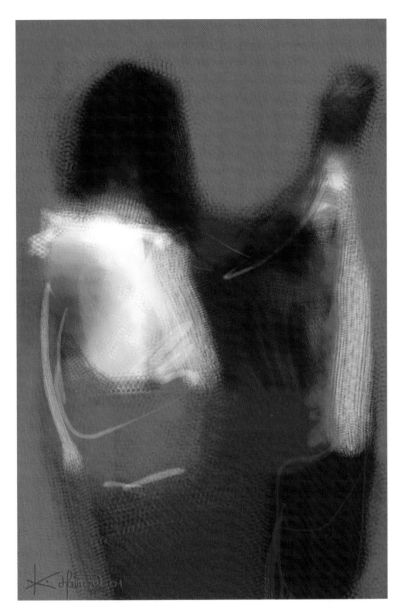

■ **Kathy Hammon** painted *Goodbye* to honor the memory of her father Jacques. The painting depicts a woman with one hand raised, waving goodbye.

For *Goodbye,* Hammon began by using Oil Pastels variants to quickly rough in large areas of color for a background. Then she chose the Round Camelhair variant of Oils, which allowed her to apply more colors while subtly blending with the underlying color. She worked back and forth, switching between the Oil Pastel and Round Camelhair brushes. To blend more smoothly she used the Just Add Water variant of Blenders. Next, she loosely sketched the outline of the figure using a small Dry Ink variant of Sumi-e. To add more texture she used a custom Artist Pastel Chalk variant. Then, using the Dry Ink and a very light blue-gray color, she painted thicker brushwork around the figure, to set her apart from the background. To complete her painting, Hammon used the Artist Pastel Chalk variant of Pastels and a white color to add a few more accents and to strengthen the highlights.

■ Artist **Carol Benioff** created *Doves* for a holiday card. She wanted to create an image that spoke of coming together for peace.

Benioff began the image by drawing a rough sketch of the doves and a rough sketch of the interlocked hands using pencil and paper. She also created a tighter pencil drawing of the doves. She scanned all three drawings, pasted them into a composite image in Painter and then played with the positioning and scale of the drawings. She kept all of the elements on layers over a blank canvas so she could keep each element separate as she developed the image. She set the Composite Method of the drawing layers to Multiply so they would appear to be one image and the white in the drawings would be transparent. Benioff opened the Papers palette (Window, Show Papers) and chose Basic Paper. Then she used the Square Chalk (Chalk) and the Artist Pastel Chalk (Pastels) to add color to the interlocking hands. She used the same color on the background. She developed a rich textured surface behind the doves and hands by layering different color and texture as follows: First she inverted the paper texture by clicking the Invert Paper button in the Papers palette, selected white as the color and went over the background to give it a grainy look. Then she went back and forth, working with three pastel colors until she had built up the rich, grainy texture. Next, she used a modified Wash variant of Water Color and hand colored the dove drawing. (A new Water Color Layer is created when you begin to paint with a Water Color brush.) She also used the same Wash variant to paint light ochre and Prussian blues. She loosely brushed on the washes and let the paint diffuse, bleeding outside of the lines in the pencil sketch. When she had finished this layer, she set its Composite Method to Darken in the Layers palette. To add depth to the background around the interlocking hands, Benioff used the modified Wash variant again to paint long, broad strokes, adding glazes of varying colors to her image. She also set the Composite Method of this layer to Darken. Finally, she flattened the image by choosing Drop All from the Layers palette menu. She saved the image as a PSD file, which she opened in Photoshop to prepare for offset printing.

■ *Shadow Play 6, by* **Carol Benioff**, is one in a series of self-promotional pieces using the theme of shadows.

Benioff started by drawing with pencils and paper. She completed eight drawings, and scanned them all into the computer. Then she played around with different combinations of the eight images. For this piece, she repeated the same image smaller and lighter. Hints of the smaller images are visible behind the horse. With her sketches in place, she painted large washes of light colors for the background using her own set of glazing brushes, which were based on the Simple Water variant of Digital Water Color. To paint textured color on the figures and the rug she used the Square Chalk (Chalk) over a rough watercolor paper texture for areas of intense color. She also used the Nervous Pen variant of Pens in the background to break up the color and add more interesting texture. To add detail to the faces, she used a custom sketching pencil which is like the 2B Pencil variant of Pencils with the method set to Soft Cover in the General section of the Stroke Designer (Brush Creator). When she had finished, she combined all of the layers by choosing Drop All from the Layers palette menu. She saved her image as a PSD file and opened it in Photoshop to prepare it for offset printing.

SELECTIONS, SHAPES AND MASKS

Horsepower Heart. Artist Chet Phillips began by making a black-and-white drawing with the Scratchboard Tool variant of the Pens. Then, working on top of the scratchboard drawing, he used the Pen tool to draw shapes and converted each shape to a selection (Shapes, Convert to Selection). After making each selection, he saved it as a mask (Select, Save Selection). Next, Phillips turned the entire scratchboard drawing into a separate layer by choosing Select, All and then Select, Float, and set its Composite Method to Gel. Working on the now blank image canvas, he loaded each of his masks in turn (Select, Load Selection), and applied tints to the selected areas using Effects, Fill. Then he painted colored details with the Airbrushes. Because the scratchboard layer was in Gel mode, the white areas were clear, allowing the color on the image canvas to show through.

TO GET THE MOST FROM PAINTER, you need to invest some time in understanding how the program isolates portions of images so you can paint them, apply special effects, or otherwise change them without affecting the rest of the image. Much of the program's power is tucked into the complex area of *selections*, *shapes* and *masks*.

WHAT IS A SELECTION?

A *selection* is an area of the image that has been isolated so changes can be made to the contents only, or so the area can be protected from change. There are two kinds of selections in Painter: outline-based and pixel-based. Like a cookie cutter, an *outline-based* selection sharply defines the area it surrounds. But unlike cookie cutters in the real world, an outline-based selection border in Painter can be freely scaled or reshaped. Outline-based selections can be made by dragging with the Lasso tool (for free-hand selecting), the Rectangular Selection tool or the Oval Selection tool.

If Painter's outline-based selections are like the outlines produced by cookie cutters, then *pixel-based* selections are more like painted resists. Pixel-based selections make the selected areas fully or *partially* available for change or copying, with the degree of availability determined by the nature and "thickness" of the "resist material." Pixel-based selections can be made by selecting based on the color or tone of pixels, rather than by an outline you draw. The Magic Wand tool makes pixel-based selections; they can also be made with the Auto Select and Color Select commands from the Select menu.

The perimeter of either kind of selection is indicated by an animated border, the selection marquee. A selection is temporary. If

The selection tools are located near the top of the Toolbox. Some tools share a space in the Toolbox with other tools, as shown here in pop-out view. (The Rectangular Selection, Oval Selection and Lasso are shown popped out on the left; the Magic Wand is shown on the right.)

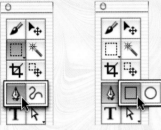

The shape-drawing tools are the Pen and Quick Curve (left), which share a Toolbox space, and the Rectangular Shape and Oval Shape (right), which also share a space.

USING ANTIALIASING

Antialiasing renders a smooth selection edge, preventing jagged, pixelated edges. All of Painter's selection tools make smooth-edged selections. The Magic Wand is the one tool that gives you a choice—just uncheck the Anti-Alias checkbox on the Property Bar if you want to make a jaggy-edged selection.

To isolate an area of the canvas for filling with blue, the Oval Selection tool was used. This extreme close-up shows the antialiasing of the edge after filling. At normal magnification, the antialiasing makes the edge look smooth.

you choose Select, None (Ctrl/⌘-D) or accidentally click outside the selection marquee, the selection will be lost, unless you have stored it in the Selection Portfolio palette or saved it as a mask in the Channels palette or converted it to a shape. (The Selection Portfolio is described on page 145, the Channels palette is covered on page 153 and shapes are described next.)

WHAT IS A SHAPE?

A *shape* is similar in construction to an outline-based selection, but it has stroke and fill characteristics. (This chapter tells about how to draw shapes and how they are related to selections. The stroke and fill attributes of shapes, their layering capabilities and their relationship to layers, are covered in Chapter 5.) Shapes can be created with the Rectangular Shape, Oval Shape, Pen or Quick Curve tool. As soon as a shape is drawn, it is automatically stored in the Layers palette. (The Layers palette can be used to control how shapes are used in the image, as described in Chapter 5.)

Shapes can be used as independent elements in an illustration, or a shape can be converted to a selection and then used to isolate an area of the image. When you convert a shape to a selection (Shapes, Convert To Selection), its name disappears from the Layers palette and an animated selection marquee appears on the image. **Beware:** If you convert a shape to a selection, it will be permanently lost if you deselect it before you either convert it back to a shape, store the selection you made from it, or choose Edit, Undo (Ctrl/⌘-Z) or Select, Reselect (Ctrl/⌘-R).

WHAT IS A MASK?

Unlike a shape, which is stored *outline* information, a *mask* is stored *pixel-based* information. Masks can store 8-bit grayscale information, which means that complex image information such as a painting, a photo or a graphic can be saved and then loaded

RESTORING A SELECTION

If you've made a selection and have deselected it—either by accident or to work outside of it—and then want to use it again, choose Select, Reselect (Ctrl/⌘-R).

CONTEXT-SENSITIVE MENUS

Painter offers context-sensitive menus that allow access to helpful commands. For instance, click within an active selection while pressing the right mouse button on the PC (or the Ctrl key on the Mac) to display a list of commands that are useful for working with selections.

The context-sensitive menu for an active selection appears at the spot where you right/Ctrl-click

The Property Bar for each of the shape-drawing tools has buttons for access to the other shape-drawing tools. It also has a button for transforming the current shape to an outline-based selection. This button will work only if the shape is closed—that is, if it has no gaps.

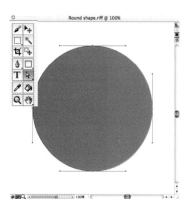

This shape has been selected with the Shape Selection tool (shown chosen in the Toolbox) and shows its control points and handles.

PRECISION DRAWING SETUP

If you're drawing shapes and you find that the stroke and fill obscure your view and make it hard to see the outline, simply uncheck the Fill and Stroke boxes in the Property Bar.

---

as a selection. Painter's 8-bit masks allow 256 levels of opacity. When a mask is loaded as a selection, in areas where the mask is black, the selection completely protects the pixels of the image from change; where the mask is white, the pixels are fully selected and exposed to brushstrokes; gray areas of the mask result in partially selected pixels. The protective mask can be "thinned" or even completely removed pixel by pixel. Masks allow complex image information to be used as a selection. Another way to use a mask, besides loading it as a selection, is to choose it when applying the functions in the Effects menu, such as Tonal Control, Adjust Colors and Surface Control, Apply Surface Texture. Masks also provide a way of permanently storing selection information until you need to use it. The Channels palette not only stores masks but also controls operations such as turning them on and off so they can be used as selections. (The Channels palette is described on page 153.)

CREATING OUTLINE-BASED SELECTIONS AND SHAPES

You can make an outline-based selection or a shape in a number of ways. One way, as mentioned earlier and described in more detail here, is to draw it with one of the selection or shape tools:

Rectangular and Oval Selection tools. Drag to make selections with these tools. To constrain the Oval or Rectangular Selection tools so they select perfect squares or circles, begin dragging and then hold down the Shift key to complete the drag.

Lasso tool. The Lasso tool is good for making quick, freehand selections. Choose the Lasso and carefully drag around the area that you want to isolate.

Rectangular and Oval Shape tools. Drag with these tools to create rectangular and elliptical shape layers. Hold down the Shift key as you drag with the tool to draw a perfect square or circle shape.

Pen tool. Choose the Pen tool for precise drawing using a combination of straight lines and curves. Click from point to point to create straight line segments; to draw curves, press to create a curve point and drag to pull out handles that control the curves. To complete an outline drawn by the Pen, close the shape by connecting to the origin point or by pressing the Close button on the Property Bar.

Quick Curve tool. Drag with the Quick Curve tool to draw freehand shapes. Like the Pen, the Quick Curve has a Close button on its Property Bar.

WHERE'S THE PATH?

If you switch from the Pen to another tool (such as the Brush), and your paths seem to disappear, you can bring them back into view by choosing the Pen, the Quick Curve tool, the Shape Selection tool or a shape-editing tool (Scissors, Add Point, Delete Point, or Convert Point).

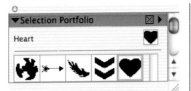

Choosing a heart-shaped path in Painter's Selection Portfolio palette, opened by choosing Window, Show Selection Portfolio

These type shapes were set with the Text tool and converted to shapes (choose Convert Text to Shapes from the pop-up menu on the right side of the Layers palette). They were then selected with the Layer Adjuster tool (top), converted to a selection (Shapes, Convert To Selection) and then used to fill areas of the image canvas by choosing Effects, Fill (bottom).

When this bird, drawn in Adobe Illustrator, was copied and pasted into Painter, it came in as a compound shape. To read about how the drop shadow was added turn to page 164.

In addition to drawing them by hand, here are some other ways of making an outline-based selection or a shape:

Transforming a pixel-based selection. Change a pixel-based selection to an outline-based selection by choosing Select, Transform Selection. (See page 148 for information about converting soft-edged pixel-based selections to outline-based.)

Using the Selection Portfolio. Drag a stored selection from the Selection Portfolio palette into your image. (If you use a lot of custom paths in your work, you may want to create custom libraries as described in the "Libraries and Movers" section of Chapter 1.)

Converting text. Convert a text layer to shapes by choosing Convert Text To Shapes from the Layers palette's pop-out menu. (For more information about type, turn to Chapter 8 "Working With Type in Painter.")

> ## AI IMPORTING ALERT!
>
> There may be problems with importing Illustrator files created in early versions of Freehand and Illustrator (prior to version 7 of the programs). So if you have an older file you want to use, open it in version 7 or later and resave it for version 7 compatibility. When working in Illustrator 10, for best results, save the file in AI format with Illustrator 7 or 8 compatibility.

Importing PostScript art. Import EPS paths as shapes from a PostScript drawing program. Painter supports two ways to import shapes, such as preexisting EPS clip art or type set on a curve and converted to outlines in a PostScript drawing program. The first option (File, Acquire, Adobe Illustrator File) creates a new file, importing the EPS outlines—with their strokes and fills—into Painter as shapes. To add the shapes to an existing Painter file, copy and paste the shapes from the new file into your working composition.

The second option allows you to copy outlines with strokes and fills from a PostScript program to the clipboard and paste them into your Painter file. The outlines will be imported into your document as shapes and will appear in the Layers palette. Objects such as the converted letters "O" and "A" that have a *counter,* or hole, in them will come into Painter as compound shapes, preserving the holes.

MOVING SELECTIONS AND SHAPES

For both pixel-based and outline-based selections, you can move the selection boundary without moving the pixels it surrounds. This gives you a great deal of flexibility in positioning the selection boundary before you use it to change the image. To move a selection boundary without moving any pixels, choose the Selection Adjuster tool and put its cursor inside the animated selection boundary; dragging will move the selection boundary. This works for both pixel-based and outline-based selections. To move the

Use the arrow keys on your keyboard to move selections or shapes by one screen pixel at a time. (Before attempting to move a selection, choose the Selection Adjuster tool; prior to moving a shape, choose the Layer Adjuster tool.) Since the distance moved is a screen pixel and not a fixed distance, zoom out from the selection or shape if you want to make coarse adjustments and zoom in for fine adjustments. Arrow-key nudging is especially useful for kerning type that has been converted to shapes.

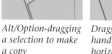

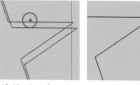

Alt/Option-dragging a selection to make a copy

Dragging a side handle to scale horizontally

Shift-dragging one of the corner handles to scale proportionally

Using a corner handle and the Ctrl/⌘ key to rotate

selection's contents, drag with the Layer Adjuster tool instead of the Selection Adjuster; this turns the selected area into a new layer. The Layer Adjuster can also be used to move shapes: Click the name of the shape in the Layers palette and then use the Layer Adjuster tool to drag the shape.

RESHAPING SELECTIONS

Painter allows an outline-based selection border or a shape to be transformed—scaled, skewed or rotated—without altering the image. It can also be expanded, contracted, smoothed, or made into a selection of its border area only. Selections made with the Lasso or Rectangular or Oval Selection tools, as well as selections converted from shapes, are automatically outline-based and thus can be transformed. Selections made with the Magic Wand or loaded from masks must be converted to outline-based information before they can be scaled, skewed or rotated. To convert a pixel-based selection to an outline-based selection, choose Select, Transform Selection. To convert a selection stored as a mask in the Channels palette to an outline-based selection, load the selection (Select, Load Selection) and then transform it.

Whether it was outline-based from the beginning or it was made by transforming, a selection needs to be displaying its bounding box handles in order to be transformed. To display the handles for the currently working selection, the Selection Adjuster tool has to be chosen. Once the bounding box handles are visible, you can move the selection, or scale, skew, or rotate its outline, or change it using commands under the Select, Modify menu to widen, contract or smooth it, or make a selection around its border.

Since outline-based selections are based on mathematical information, they can undergo all of the following transformations, carried out with the Selection Adjuster tool, with no loss of edge quality. (These transformations don't work on pixel-based selections; a pixel-based selection has to be converted to an outline-based selection first, as described above.) Display the eight bounding box handles as described above and then:

To duplicate, hold down Alt/Option (a tiny "plus" will appear next to the cursor); drag and release to add a copy to the selection.

To scale, position the tool over one of the corner handles; when the cursor changes, drag the handle. To *scale proportionally,* hold down the Shift key as you drag. If you want to *resize only horizontally or vertically,* drag on the center handle of the top, the bottom or a side.

To rotate, use a corner handle, adding the Ctrl/⌘ key as you position the cursor. Be sure you see the curved arrow cursor around the handle before dragging to rotate. **Be careful:** Don't

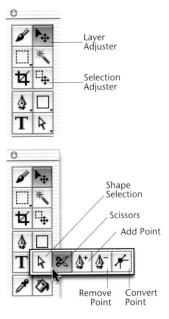

Layer Adjuster

Selection Adjuster

Shape Selection

Scissors

Add Point

Remove Point

Convert Point

The Layer Adjuster and Selection Adjuster tools can move, rotate, scale and skew shapes and outline-based selections, respectively. The shape-editing tools that share a space on the Toolbox are used for reshaping shapes in a more detailed way.

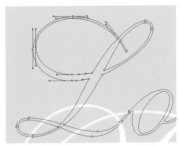

This path has handles showing and is ready to be manipulated with the Shape Selection tool.

start dragging until you see the curved arrow cursor, because the Ctrl/⌘ key is also used to temporarily turn the Selection Adjuster tool into the Layer Adjuster tool—the pointing-finger cursor. If you're trying to rotate the selection boundary, don't drag with the pointing finger! If you do so accidentally, the contents of the selection will be moved, but you can recover by pressing Ctrl/⌘-Z.

To skew, press Ctrl/⌘ while positioning the cursor over a center handle on the side, top or bottom, and then drag. **Be careful:** Don't start dragging until you see the slanted arrow cursor across the handle. If you're trying to skew the selection boundary, don't drag while the cursor is a pointing finger! If you do so accidentally, you can recover by pressing Ctrl/⌘-Z.

RESHAPING SHAPES

The Layer Adjuster tool can scale, rotate and skew shapes in much the same way the Selection Adjuster works with outline-based selections. In addition, shapes can be modified in more detail with the shape-editing tools, which share a space in the Toolbox. The Shape Selection tool (hollow arrow) and the other shape-editing tools allow you to adjust individual anchor points and control handles to modify shapes.

The Shape Selection tool works much like its counterpart in Adobe Illustrator, by clicking the outline of a shape to show its control points, then dragging a point or path segment to change its position. You can also use it to click on an individual point so it will show its handles, and then drag a handle to adjust the curve.

The Scissors, Add Point, Remove Point and Convert Point tools will also be familiar to Illustrator users. For instance, the Scissors tool allows you to cut a path segment. To add a new anchor point, click with the Add Point tool. To delete an anchor point, click on it with the Remove Point tool.

Because it's so easy to convert an outline-based selection to a shape and vice versa (see page 150), you can easily modify an outline-based selection by converting it to a shape, editing it with the shape-editing tools, then converting it back to a selection.

SELECTING AND MASKING BY COLOR

In addition to the selection-outlining tools described on pages 145–147, Painter also offers useful tools and procedures for making selections and masks based on the color in your image rather than on an outline you draw.

Magic Wand. Painter's easy-to-use Magic Wand is a real production time-saver. The Magic Wand lets you select an area of your image based on color similarities of contiguous (touching) or noncontiguous pixels. This is especially useful for selecting a

The Property Bar for the Magic Wand lets you set the Tolerance, or size of the color range, you want the Wand to select. You can also choose whether to select only those pixels that are connected as a continuous patch of color that touches the pixel you click; for this option, Contiguous should be turned on (checked in the Property Bar). To select all pixels within the color range, both touching and not touching, turn off the Contiguous option.

Our goal was to generate a selection for the sky in this photo. We chose Select, Color Select and clicked in the image to sample the color we wanted to isolate. We adjusted the H, S and V sliders until the red mask covered only the sampled color in the preview window, then clicked OK to activate the selection. Alternatively, you can use New From Color Range (from the pop-out menu of the Channels palette) to accomplish the same thing, except as a mask rather than a selection; the mask is automatically stored in the Channels palette.

uniformly colored element in an image, without having to draw around the area with the Lasso or Pen tool. To select a wider range of color, increase the Tolerance number in the Property Bar before you use the Wand. To make a smooth-edged selection, make sure the Anti-Alias box is checked before you make the selection.

To add areas of similar adjacent color to the selection, reset the Tolerance higher, then hold down the Shift key and click inside the existing selection. To shrink your selection by reducing the range of the colors it's based on, Alt/Option-click within the selection on the color you want to eliminate (you may want to set the Tolerance lower first). To remove a range of colors from a selection, Alt/Option-drag in the area. To add areas of similar color that are not adjacent (like Select, Similar in Photoshop), turn off the Contiguous checkbox in the Property Bar, and continue adding areas of non-contiguous color by Shift-clicking on other areas of the image. To turn off the nonadjacent mode, turn on Contiguous again.

Once the Magic Wand has produced the pixel-based selection you want, you can store it as a mask by choosing Select, Save Selection or by clicking the Save Selection as Channel button at the bottom of the Channels palette.

Color Select. Painter also offers an automated procedure for isolating parts of images based on color. It does something similar to the Magic Wand in non-Contiguous mode. In one way you have more control than with the Magic Wand because "Tolerance" is separated into three components (hue, saturation and value) and you can choose to partially select colors outside the range. The difficulty with this selection method is that it's hard to control the smoothness of the edges, and they tend to be somewhat rougher than an antialiased Magic Wand selection. To generate a rough-edged pixel-based selection based on a range of color, choose Select, Color Select. When the Color Select dialog box opens, click in the image on the color that you want the range to center around. In the Color Select dialog box adjust the H (Hue), S (Saturation) and V (Value) Extents sliders to control the range of each of these properties sampled in the image. Experiment with adjusting the Feather sliders to partially select the other colors in the image. To reverse the mask to a "negative," enable the Inverted checkbox. Click OK to complete the selection.

To save your Color Select selection, you can use Select, Save Selection or click the button in the Channels palette as described above for the Magic Wand. But the Channels palette also provides a way to make and store a color-based mask directly, as described next.

New from Color Range. In the Channels palette's pop-out menu, choose New from Color Range. In the Color dialog box (which works the same as the Color Select box described above) you can then make the same Extents, Feather and Invert choices.

Killdeer *by Mary Envall. To create this wildlife illustration—featuring a black-and-white ink drawing floating on top of colored, textured paper—Envall began by making a black-and-white scratchboard drawing in Painter. To drop the white background out behind the drawing she made an automatic selection, choosing Select, Auto Select, using Image Luminance. She floated the active selection by clicking on it with the Layer Adjuster. Next, she filled the background (the Canvas) with a colored texture, using Effects, Surface Control, Color Overlay using Paper and Dye Concentration.*

OTHER PIXEL-BASED SELECTING AND MASKING OPTIONS

Two powerful functions—Auto Select and New From (short for "New Channel From")—create a selection or mask based on color or on tonality (brightness values, or shades of light and dark). When you choose Select, Auto Select or choose New From from the Channels palette's pop-out menu, a dialog box opens that gives you a choice of Paper, which bases the selection or mask on the tonality of the currently selected Paper texture; 3D Brush Strokes, which is useful when you are "cloning" a painting from an image; Original Selection, which can be used to copy a selection from one file to another; Image Luminance, which bases the selection or mask on the lights and darks in the current image; Original Luminance, which is useful for importing an image into a channel so it can serve as a mask; or Current Color, which creates a selection or mask based on the current primary color. The dialog boxes for Auto Select and New From are identical, with the exception that Auto Select creates a pixel-based *selection* whereas New From creates and stores a *mask*. Both have an Invert checkbox for reversing the selection or mask, as described in the "Doing the Opposite" tip below.

To practice generating a mask based on the brightness values in an image, try this: Create a new file (Ctrl/⌘-N) with white as the Paper Color. Double-click the primary (forward) color square in the Toolbox and when the Color Picker opens, choose black. From the Brush Selector Bar (opened by choosing Window, Show Brush Selector Bar), choose the Scratchboard Tool variant of the Pens. Make a sketch, and then generate a mask for your sketch by choosing New From (Ctrl/⌘-Shift-M) using Image Luminance; click OK. The mask will appear in the Channels palette, targeted and with its eye icon turned on, and you will see the mask as a red overlay. You can edit it by painting on it with a brush. Current Color is the only option for Auto Select or New From that produces a completely jagged selection or

Susan LeVan used Painter's New From, Current Color feature to make rough-edged masks for brushstrokes shown in this illustration Covering Home, *created for* Becoming Family *magazine.*

REMEMBERING SETTINGS

Like some other dialog boxes in Painter, the Color Select and Color boxes remember the settings you used last, rather than reverting to default settings. So when the dialog box opens, it shows the most recent settings. The Color Select and Color boxes have a "shared memory": If you open one of these dialog boxes, it "remembers" the last settings you made in either box.

DOING THE OPPOSITE

The Color Select dialog box has an Inverted checkbox that you can use to control whether the color you click on defines the selected area or the unselected area. Likewise, an Inverted box in the Color dialog box lets you choose whether the color you click is the masked or unmasked area of the mask you generate. This "reversing" function is also found in the Invert button of the Auto Select and New From dialog boxes.

PHOTO: CORBIS IMAGES

To vignette this photo, we began by making an Oval selection. We scaled the selection using the Selection Adjuster tool, then applied a feather of 15 pixels (Select, Feather) to soften the edge. Next, we reversed the selection by choosing Select, Invert. We chose Edit, Clear to delete the background, leaving the vignetted edge against white.

MIDDLE OF THE ROAD

When you use the Select, Transform Selection command on a soft-edged selection, Painter draws an outline-based selection using the 50%-transparency boundary. For instance, if you make a hard-edged selection with the Rectangular Selection tool, then feather it (Select, Feather) and transform it (Select, Transform Selection), the result will be a hard-edged selection, but with rounded corners.

To show the difference between a hard-edged and a feathered selection, the original rectangular selection was filled with blue, then feathered 20 pixels and filled with a rose color (left). Then the selection was transformed to an outline-based selection and filled with yellow, revealing the new rounded hard edge (right).

mask, with no edge-smoothing or antialiasing at all. For an example of Auto Mask using Current Color, turn to "Auto-Masking with Color" on page 169.

FEATHERING

Feathering a selection softens its edge. This is useful for vignetting an image or for blending a selected area into a background. To see feathering at work, drag a selection from the Selection Portfolio into your image. Choose Select, Feather, and type 20 into the field to define the extent of the feather; click OK. Now choose Effects, Fill, then select one of the options and click OK. Note the soft edges of the filled selection. The feather is always built both inward and outward from the selection boundary. Applying the Select, Feather command to an outline-based selection changes it to a pixel-based selection.

CONVERTING SELECTIONS, SHAPES AND MASKS

Outline-based and pixel-based selections have entirely different origins, but there is some degree of interchangeability.

To convert a pixel-based selection into an outline-based selection so you can transform the outline (scale, skew or rotate) using the Selection Adjuster tool, choose Select, Transform Selection. To convert a mask into an outline-based selection so you can transform it, first load the mask as a selection: In the Channels palette, click the Load Channel as Selection button at the bottom of the palette. In the Load Selection dialog box, choose the appropriate mask, make sure the Replace Selection button is chosen and click OK. This turns the mask into an active selection. Then you can choose Select, Transform Selection. (When a selection is loaded from a mask and transformed, the mask in the Channels palette remains unmodified unless you replace it using the Save Selection, Replace Mask command.)

To convert an outline-based selection into a mask and save it in the Channels palette as pixel-based information instead of outline information, choose Select, Save Selection or click the Save Selection as Channel button at the bottom of the Channels palette. (You might want to make this kind of conversion in order to edit the mask by painting on it, then load the modified mask as a selection again.)

To convert a shape to a selection so can you use it to isolate an area of the image canvas, select the shape by highlighting its name in the Layers palette, and choose Shapes, Convert to Selection. (The tools that draw and edit shapes and selections have a Convert to Selection button on the Property Bar, allowing quick conversion of a shape you make or edit with one of these tools.)
Remember: If you convert a shape to a selection, the shape is no longer stored in the Layers palette, and it will be lost when you

We set this Adobe Woodtype Ornament using the Text tool. We Alt/Option-dragged with the Layer Adjuster tool to make a copy of the text ornament. To convert it to shapes, we chose Convert Text to Shapes from the Layers palette's pop-out menu. Next, we converted the copy into an active selection (Shapes, Convert to Selection) for treating the image canvas. To add the colored texture, we chose Effects, Surface Control, Color Overlay, Using Paper, Hiding Power with a pavement-like texture.

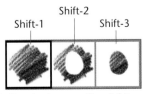
deselect—unless you have stored it in the Selection Portfolio (described in "Saving Selection Outlines" below) or in the Channels palette as a mask (as described earlier in this section), or unless you convert it back to a shape (as described next).

To convert the current selection into a shape so you can store it in the Layers palette, or edit its outline (using anchor points and control handles), or fill and stroke it (using the Shapes, Set Shape Attributes dialog box), choose Select, Convert to Shape. Alternatively, all of the selection tools have a Convert to Shape button on the Property Bar for quick conversion when one of these tools is active.

SAVING SELECTION OUTLINES

Use the Selection Adjuster tool to drag outline-based selections to the Selection Portfolio to store them. If you want to save shapes into this library, first convert them to selections (Shapes, Convert To Selection) and then drag them to the Selection Portfolio. If you're very organized, you might create multiple selection libraries for different jobs. To swap outlines between libraries or to set up a new, empty palette, you can use the Selection Mover, accessed by clicking the triangle in the top right corner of the Selection Portfolio palette, to open the palette's pop-out menu.

Use File, Export, Adobe Illustrator™ File to export shapes to PostScript drawing programs. We successfully exported simple shape objects as well as more complex objects that included blends and compounds, opening them in Illustrator 7, 8 and 9.

SELECTIONS AT WORK

Once you've made or loaded a selection, you can choose to draw outside of it instead of inside, or use it to isolate areas of the image canvas or a layer when applying special-effects procedures found in the Effects menu.

Inverting a selection. If you want to apply a fill or effect to the *outside* of your active selection, use Select, Invert beforehand. This procedure reverses the current selection. It's often useful to save a selection as a mask in the Channels palette, then save the inverse of it; for instance, save an element, then save the background, also as a mask. This inverting process can also be used for painting outside a selection, but there's a more efficient way to control painting, described next.

Using the Drawing icons. The Drawing icons are found in the bottom left corner of an active document's window. Take the name "Drawing icons" literally; they affect *drawing and painting actions only,* not fills or other effects. A fill or effect is always constrained to the inside of an active selection, regardless of which Drawing icon you choose. Several of the techniques in this chapter demonstrate how these icons work, and you can refer to

To make a selection isolating the large dahlia in this photo, we used Select, Color Select, then used the Lasso to "clean up" the selection border—pressing the Alt/ Option key to subtract from the selection— to exclude the smaller flower.

PHOTO: CORBIS IMAGES

"Selecting a Drawing Mode" in Chapter 12 of the Corel Painter 8 *User Guide* for a detailed explanation.

Stroking a selection. In Painter, you can use any brush variant *to stroke an outline-based selection.* Begin by making an outline-based selection, either with one of the outline-based selection tools described earlier in this chapter or by transforming a pixel-based selection to outline-based. The effect is more fun to observe if you choose one of Painter's grain-sensitive brushes. In the Brush Selector Bar, choose the Large Chalk variant of Chalk. Next, open the Papers palette (Window, Show Papers) and choose a texture from the Paper Selector near the upper right corner of the palette. With the selection still active, press the Drawing icon in the bottom-left corner of the image window and choose from the three options: You can choose to have your stroke inside the selection border (Draw Inside), outside of it (Draw Outside), or centered directly on top of it (Draw Anywhere); then go to the Select menu and choose Stroke Selection.

TRANSFORM FIRST. . .

If you'd like to stroke the outline of a pixel-based selection, use Select, Transform Selection to convert it to an outline-based selection before attempting to use the Select, Stroke Selection command.

EDITING SELECTIONS

Painter offers methods for finessing outline-based and pixel-based selections that will be familiar to Photoshop users. (To read about editing masks, see "Using the Channels Palette," on the facing page.)

Adding to a selection. To add to an existing selection marquee, choose a selection tool, then click the Add To Selection button in the Property Bar and click or drag outside of the existing marquee. (A keyboard shortcut for using the button is to hold down the Shift key as you click or drag.) The Add To Selection operation is also useful—it is described on page 154.

Subtracting from a selection. To remove a portion of a selection, press the Subtract from Selection button in the Property Bar (or hold down the Alt/Option key) and drag with a selection tool. The Subtract From Selection and Intersect operations are also useful; they are described on page 154.

The Modify menu. Four commands under the Select, Modify menu—Widen, Contract, Smooth and Border—allow you to change outline-based selections. Widen and Contract allow you to change the size of a selection by a specified number of pixels. The Smooth command is useful for rounding corners and softening jaggedness in a selection. The Border function selects a border area (based on a specified number of pixels) outside the existing marquee.

To create a light-valued border for an image, make a rectangular selection where you want the inner edge of your border; then choose Select, Modify, Border and set the width for the border large enough so it reaches all the way to the edge of the image. Then choose Effects, Tonal Control, Adjust Colors and move the Value slider to the right to lighten the border area.

PHOTO: CORBIS IMAGES

Multiple applications of the Smooth function can turn a perfectly good typeface (Stone Sans, left) into a trendy, avant-garde one. Set type with the Text tool, convert the characters to shapes (choose Convert Text to Shapes at the bottom of the pop-up menu of the Layers palette), convert the shapes to selections (Shapes, Convert To Selection), apply the Smooth operation (Select, Modify, Smooth) and fill them with a color (Effects, Fill). If the characters aren't "smooth" enough yet, undo the fill (Ctrl/⌘-Z), smooth again, and fill again.

The Channels palette. Several useful commands are found in the pop-out menu.

Five buttons at the bottom of the Channels palette offer shortcuts to important commands: From left to right, Load Channel as Selection, Save Selection as Channel, Invert Channel, New Mask and Delete.

MASKS

You can create masks in Painter in several ways: by making a selection and saving it in the Channels palette, by painting directly onto a new blank channel with brushes, by generating masks with procedures such as New From or New From Color Range in the Channels palette's pop-out menu, or by using Boolean operations to calculate new masks from existing ones. To read about New From Color Range turn to "Making a Mask Based on Color" on page 145, and for more information about calculating masks, turn to "Calculating and Operating" on page 154.

USING THE CHANNELS PALETTE

The Channels palette lists all the masks you've made and stored. A Painter file can contain a maximum of 32 of these stored masks. If you'll be doing a lot of work with masks, it's a good idea to get on friendly terms with this palette. Here are some basics:

To view a mask as an overlay on top of the RGB image canvas, open the eye icon to the far left of the mask's name.

To hide a mask, click its eye icon shut.

To view a mask alone in black-and-white, without the RGB Canvas, open the mask's eye icon and close the RGB eye icon.

To view a mask as an opaque overlay, choose Channel Attributes from the pull-down menu of the Channels palette, and move the Opacity slider to 100%. Viewing a mask as an opaque overlay can often help you see defects in the mask, and it may be less confusing than using partial opacity. Adjusting the Opacity slider changes the overlay's onscreen appearance only, and does not affect the actual density of the mask.

To edit a mask, click the mask's name to activate it (the mask's name will then be highlighted). Open the eye icon to the far left of the mask's name.

To change the mask overlay to a color easier to see while making a mask for an orange Garibaldi fish, we changed the overlay color from the default red to yellow by choosing Channel Attributes from the Channels palette's pop-out menu and clicking the Color swatch in the Channel Attributes dialog box.

We used Intersect With Selection to create the filled half-circle (above right). To repeat what we did, begin by making a square selection with the Rectangular Selection tool and Shift key and save it by choosing Select, Save Selection, or clicking the Save Selection as Channel button at the bottom of the Channels palette. View the mask as an overlay (above left) by clicking its eye icon open in the Channels palette, along with the eye for RGB (at the top of the palette). Click the RGB name to target the image canvas, and make a new selection partially overlapping the square with the Oval Selection tool. With this oval selection active, click the Load Selection from Channel button at the bottom of the Channels palette. In the Load From pop-up menu choose the square mask, click the Intersect With Selection button and click OK. Now you can fill the selection (choose Effects, Fill).

PHOTO: CORBIS IMAGES

You can edit the mask by painting on it with any brush except a Water Color or Liquid Ink brush.

To apply a paper grain to a mask, click the mask's name to activate it and use Effects, Surface Control, Express Texture, using Paper. Watch the Preview as you experiment with the Gray Threshold, Grain and Contrast sliders.

To blur a mask so that loading it as a selection will produce a feathered selection, select the mask and choose Feather from the pop-out menu, type a number in the field and click OK.

CALCULATING AND OPERATING

Painter offers Boolean operations, useful functions that help generate new masks that fit perfectly against existing ones. Skillful use of these techniques will save time and effort. To see these functions at work, turn to "Making Masks for Embossing," on page 155.

To edit a mask using a selection, create a selection marquee, and choose Select, Save Selection or click the Save Selection as Channel button at the bottom of the Channels palette. In the Save Selection dialog box, choose the mask you wish to edit from the Save To pop-up menu, and choose the operation you wish to perform.

To replace a mask with the active selection, in the Save Selection dialog box, from the Save To menu, choose the mask you wish to replace, then click the Replace Mask button. This choice "throws away" the original mask.

To edit a selection using a mask, create a selection marquee and choose Load Selection, or click the Load Channel as Selection button at the bottom of the Channels palette. In the Load Selection dialog box, choose the mask you want to use and click a button to add, subtract or intersect; then click OK. The Intersect With Selection button makes a new selection from the intersection of the existing selection and the mask, selecting only the area where the two overlap. 〰

PAINTER AND PHOTOSHOP

To save Painter masks and use them in Photoshop, save a Painter file in Photoshop format. When you open the file in Photoshop, the named masks will automatically appear in the Channels palette. To learn more about using Painter masks and paths with Photoshop (and vice versa) turn to Chapter 9, "Using Painter with Photoshop."

Making Masks for Embossing

Overview *Open a new file with a colored background; set type; convert the type to a shape and the shape to a selection; save the selection as a mask; use the selection to build bevel and background masks; apply special effects to create three-dimensional looks.*

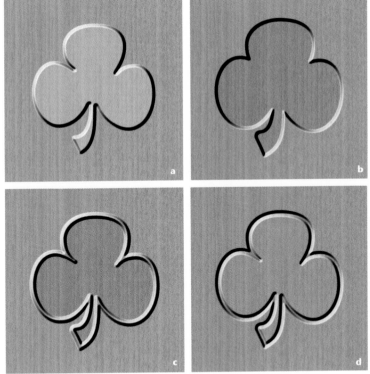

CHER THREINEN-PENDARVIS / PHOTO: ARTBEATS

1

The shape before converting to a selection

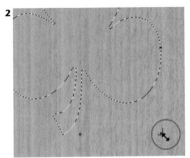

2

Using the Selection Adjuster to scale the selection

PAINTER'S EFFECTS, SURFACE CONTROL MENU contains powerful features for creating three-dimensional artwork needed for an embossed look or for interactive buttons. These features are most effective when combined with a skillful use of selections and masks. To create these tooled wood reliefs, we began with a graphic shape for the face of the graphic. Then we created a series of masks based on the original graphic—a widened face, a bevel and a background—to isolate areas for special effects application. Preparing the masks up front allowed quick previewing of a variety of effects.

1 Setting a shape and converting it to a selection. Create a new file with a light background color, or open a textured background image (we chose Beechwood from the ArtBeats *Wood and Paper* CD-ROM). Choose black (Colors palette), click in the image with the Text tool and type a letter. (Using a 500-pixel-wide file, we set an ornament using the Adobe Wood Type Ornaments font.)

Before you can use the graphic character to isolate areas of the image canvas, you'll need to convert it to a shape, then to a selection. Target the Text layer in the Layers palette and choose Convert Text to Shapes from the bottom of the palette's pop-out menu. Now from the main menu choose Shapes, Convert to Selection.

3

Typing a descriptive name for the mask

4

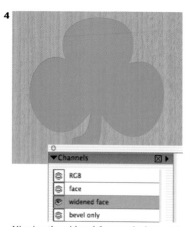

Viewing the widened face mask along with the RGB image

5a

5b

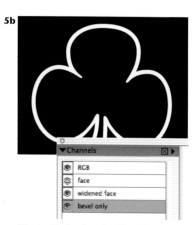

Viewing the bevel mask without the canvas

2 Moving and scaling. Choose the Selection Adjuster tool from the Tools palette. Press inside the selection with the Selection Adjuster tool; you can safely move your selection without distorting it. To scale, drag on one of the selection handles; to scale proportionately, press Shift and drag one of the corner handles (a two-headed diagonal arrow).

3 Saving and naming the selection. Saving a selection permanently stores it in the Channels palette as a mask. The first selection will be the top face of the bas relief, and we will use it to create three masks. To save the selection, choose Select, Save Selection, or click the Save Selection as New Channel button at the bottom of the Channels palette. When the Save Selection dialog box appears, accept the default in the pop-up menu—Save to New. Click OK. The selection is converted from outline-based to mask information. To rename the mask, double-click its name in the channels palette. We named ours "face."

4 Widening the selection. With the "face" selection still active, choose Select, Transform Selection. You can now expand the selection to create a wider boundary around the graphic. Choose Select, Modify, Widen and set the radius by typing a number in the field (we used 10 pixels). Save this new widened selection into the Channels palette, naming it "widened face."

5 Creating new masks using calculations. Next, we created a bevel mask describing the thin area between the outside widened boundary and the original face boundary. Painter offers Boolean operations, calculations in the Save Selection and Load Selection dialog boxes to make the job easier. To build a mask for the bevel, (with the "widened face" selection still active) click the Load Channel as Selection button at the bottom of the Channels palette and choose "face" from the pop-up menu and under Operation, click the Subtract From Selection button to subtract the original face area from the widened face area, and click OK. Then click the Save Selection as Channel button and name the channel "bevel only."

We also built a mask isolating the image area outside of the widened face mask. To do this, load a selection using the "widened face" mask, and then choose Select, Invert. We saved this selection as a mask, naming it "background."

QUICKER LOADING

To save a visit to the Select menu or Channels palette when you'd like to load a selection—press Ctrl/⌘-Shift-G to display the Load Selection dialog box.

MODIFYING SELECTIONS

Only outline-based selections accept commands from the Select, Modify menu such as Widen and Contract. To convert a mask-based selection to path-based information so you can modify it, choose Select, Transform Selection. For more information, turn to "Editing Selections," on page 152.

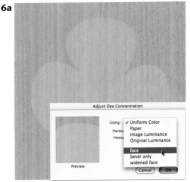

6a

Using Dye Concentration in conjunction with the "face" mask

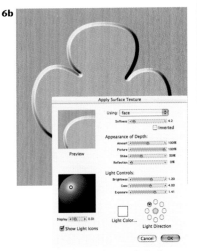

6b

Using the "face" mask to apply Surface Texture to create the embossed face

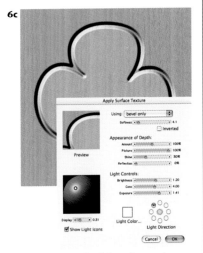

6c

Using the "bevel only" mask to apply Surface Texture for the cut bevel effect

6 Putting the masks to work. Many operations available under the Effects menu in Painter—for instance, Tonal Control, Adjust Colors; Surface Control, Apply Surface Texture; and Focus, Glass Distortion—offer a pop-up menu allowing you to apply the effect using any mask saved in the Channels palette.

MAC OS X GLITCH

In the first release of Painter 8, the "Using" function for the Effects, Surface Control commands (such as Dye Concentration and Apply Surface Texture) doesn't work right. Channels are listed as choices for the Using function, but when you try to choose a channel, it doesn't "load"; instead, the Original Luminance choice is used. Because of this, step 6 of the "Making Masks for Embossing" technique doesn't work with Mac OS X. Until Corel fixes this problem, you can use a different method for step 6:

Load the appropriate channel ("face" or "bevel only") as a selection by choosing Select, Load Selection and choosing the channel. Then apply Effects, Surface Control, Dye Concentration Using Image Luminance. (Experiment with the settings in the Dye Concentration dialog box until you get the result you want.) Then, with the selection still loaded, apply Effects, Surface Control, Apply Surface Texture, again experimenting with the settings.

To **emboss** the face, creating the bas-relief look in image "a" at the top of page 155, you can use the "face" mask to isolate an area of the image to lighten and "raise" above the surrounding surface. Lightening the face of the graphic will enhance the illusion of relief. With no selection active (Ctrl/⌘-D deselects all) click the RGB channel in the Channels palette and the Canvas in the Layers palette. Then choose Effects, Surface Control, Dye Concentration. In the Using pop-up menu, choose the "face" mask; to lighten the area, set the Minimum slider below 100% (we used 80%) and click OK. Now, for the relief effect: To "pop" the graphic face out (creating a convincing 3D effect), choose Effects, Surface Control, Apply Surface Texture. In the Using menu choose "face." Set Softness (we used 4.3), reduce the shine (we used 30%), click the top left Light Direction button and click OK.

To **deboss** the face of the graphic as in image "b" at the top of page 155, you can use the same process described above for embossing, except that for Dye Concentration darken the face area by setting the Minimum slider higher than 100% (we used 125%). And for Apply Surface Texture, click the Inverted checkbox to turn it on.

To create the **beveled** look in image "c" at the top of page 155, use the embossing process described above, but use the "bevel only" channel instead of the "face" channel.

To **carve the beveled area *in*,** leaving the face and background flat (image "d" at the top of page 155), use the debossing process described above, except use the "bevel only" channel instead of the "face" channel. 🖌

Working with Bézier Paths and Selections

Overview *Use the Pen tool to create paths of straight and curved lines; convert the paths to selections; use a custom pencil to draw inside and outside of the selections.*

The logo sketch, including a rough grid

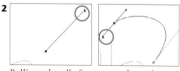

Pulling a handle from an anchor point to prepare for a curved path segment, then pressing and dragging to create the curve

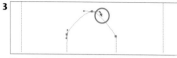

Dragging on a control handle to change the path's shape

CHANGING DIRECTION

While drawing with the Pen, click a second time on an anchor point to create a *cusp* and establish a new direction for the next curve. A cusp is a corner point between two curved line segments, such as the "dent" at the top of a heart shape.

JOHN FRETZ

TO DESIGN A LOGO FOR THE 100-YEAR-OLD Bethany Church in Seattle, John Fretz used a custom pencil to draw inside and outside of selections to create a hard-edged, graduated look similar to his conventional colored pencil illustration style.

1 Sketching the logo. Fretz created a 4 x 4-inch pencil drawing of the logo that included a rough grid aligning the roofs of the houses. He scanned the sketch at 300 ppi and opened it in Painter to use as a template.

2 Creating a path with Bézier curves. The most efficient way to create a combination of curve and straight-line path segments is with the Pen tool. You can set up shape attributes (with no fill or stroke) to produce a skeletal line that will help you see precise lines and curves while you draw: Choose the Pen tool from the Toolbox. In the Property Bar, make sure the Stroke and Fill boxes are *not* checked. Now click to place anchor points for straight-line segments, and press, hold and drag to create anchor points with handles that control curve segments. When you want to close a path, place the cursor over the starting anchor point, and click when you see a small circle designating the origin point, or press the Close Shape button in the Property Bar.

3 Changing the path shape. You can use the Shape Selection tool to fine-tune a path. First, if the anchor points are not showing, click the shape with the Shape Selection tool to show them; to show the control handles for an anchor point, click the point. Move the Shape Selection tool over an anchor point, a control handle, or a curve segment and drag to reposition it. (While drawing with the Pen tool, you can temporarily change from the Pen to the Shape Selection tool by pressing the Ctrl/⌘ key.)

4 Changing the path to a selection. Paths must be turned into selections before you can use them to control where paint is applied on the image. You can convert a path drawn with the Pen

4a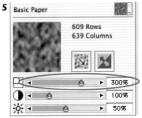

Click on the Convert to Selection button to change the shape into a selection.

4b

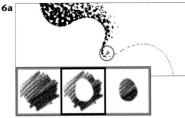

Selections stored as masks in the Channels palette

5

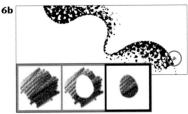

Scaling the Basic Paper texture

6a

Painting outside of the cloud selection using the custom black pencil

6b

Painting inside of the cloud selection

7

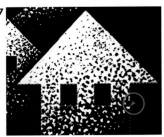

The subtracted selection of the windows protected those areas, keeping them black when Fretz filled the house with white. He used his custom pencil to add black texture over the white fill.

or Quick Curve tool to a selection immediately after drawing it by pressing the Convert to Selection button in the Property Bar. You can also change a path into a selection by selecting the shape in the Layers palette and choosing Shapes, Convert To Selection. In your image, the Bézier curves will turn into a selection marquee. To save and name the selection as a mask in the Channels palette for future use, choose Select, Save Selection. Type into the Name field and click OK. To return to the image canvas, click on RGB in the Channels palette.

5 Creating the pencil and surface. To re-create the graduated effect he gets with conventional pencils on rough illustration board, Fretz built a heavy, grainy pencil. To build a grainy pencil similar to the one Fretz used, choose Window, Show Brush Creator, and then choose the Pencils and the 2B Pencil variant in the upper left corner of the Brush Creator window. In the General section of the Stroke Designer panel of the Brush Creator, modify the variant by switching to the Cover method and Grainy Edge Flat Cover subcategory, and change the Grain setting to 10%. In the Size section, increase the Size to roughly 200 pixels. In the Spacing section, set the Spacing slider at 25% (so the dabs created by the larger pencil will overlap and paint continuous strokes). Now choose black in the Colors palette. In the Papers section, Fretz clicked the Paper Selection swatch and chose Basic Paper because of its even texture, scaling it to 300% using the Scale slider.

6 Drawing in and out of selections. Fretz used the Drawing Modes, three icons located in the bottom left corner of the image window, to paint inside and outside of selections. Begin by loading a selection (Select, Load Selection) and choosing the Brush tool in the Toolbox. To protect the area inside an active selection, click on the middle Drawing button; to protect the area outside the selection, click on the far right Drawing button. Fretz switched back and forth between these two options as he rendered a graduated, even texture using his custom pencil. (You can also use the Select, Invert command to invert an active selection.)

7 Subtracting from a selection. To fill each house with white and leave the windows black, Fretz loaded each house selection and subtracted the window selection from it: Choose Load Selection again and in the Load Selection dialog box, choose a selection and click the Subtract From Selection button to subtract it from the original selected area. Fretz filled the resulting selection with white, then he added black texture to the house with his custom pencil. He continued to add textured, even tone with the black and white pencils until he completed the logo.

Fretz saved the finished image in TIFF format, and to eliminate all grayscale information, he opened the image in Photoshop and converted it from grayscale to a 600 ppi Bitmap image.

Using Selections to Limit Paint

Overview *Make a sketch on a colored ground; draw paths, convert them to selections and store them as masks; paint and apply effects within the selections.*

RAY BLAVATT

Sketching with the Flattened Pencil variant

Adding bolder lines to the sketch

RAY BLAVATT LOVES THE ENERGETIC, EXPRESSIVE line work of fashion illustrators (notably Carl Erickson and Rene Bouche) and political cartoonists (including Jim Borgman and Pat Oliphant). His background is in traditional illustration, but today most of Blavatt's work is in animation. His procedure involves drawing in Painter and then saving the illustrations for animation in Quick-Time format, importing them into Macromedia Flash and eventually exporting his work to VHS tape.

To create *Parisian,* Blavatt began by making a gestural drawing in Painter. Then he drew paths with the Pen tool directly on the sketch and converted the paths to selections so that he would have boundaries to limit paint when he painted fast. Artists familiar with drawing in a PostScript program (as Blavatt is) will like this method of drawing straight and curved line segments with the Pen, then converting the shapes to selections. (To read more about different methods of making selections, turn to the beginning of this chapter.)

1 Sketching on a colored ground. Blavatt opened a new file measuring 1900 x 2100 pixels with a newsprint-colored background. He chose the Brush tool from the Toolbox and chose the Flattened Pencil variant of the Pencils in the Brush Selector Bar. He chose a gold color in the Color picker and Pavement texture in the Paper Selector (loaded from the Painter 6 Textures library on the Painter 8 CD 2 CD-ROM). Envisioning a young woman on a fictitious street in Paris, he sketched quick, gestural strokes to lay out the drawing. He changed the size of the pencil as he worked using the Size slider on the Property Bar. The Flattened

3a

Drawing the path around a building

3b

The Property Bar showing the Convert to Selection button

4

The painting with textured chalk strokes added to the sky, street and figure

5a

Using Dye Concentration to apply a darker tint to the selected background

Pencil incorporates the Buildup method, which allows color to be applied with transparency (overlapping strokes will darken); its Grainy Hard Buildup subcategory creates crisp-edged strokes that are affected by the current paper texture.

2 Emphasizing the line work. Next, Blavatt added darker color and textured, thick and thin lines to the drawing using the Graphic Paintbrush variant of the F-X brush. (The Graphic Paintbrush reminds Blavatt of the Rough Out brush, a favorite he liked using in earlier versions of Painter, although by default the Graphic Paintbrush reveals more paper texture along the edges of the strokes, due to the Grainy Edge Flat Cover method it uses in the Stroke Designer tab of the Brush Creator.) To lay bold strokes over your pencil sketch, choose the Graphic Paintbrush and a dark color in the Color picker. For finer line work, Blavatt sized the brush smaller (to 7.3) using the Size slider on the Property Bar.

3 Drawing paths and converting to selections. So that he could isolate areas of the drawing while painting and applying special effects, he created selections. Because his subject included straight lines (buildings) and smooth curves (the figure and street light, for instance), Blavatt chose the Pen from the Toolbox to draw a path around each building and the figure of the young woman. To draw precise paths, some artists prefer to draw the paths without a Stroke or Fill. But to make it easier to see the path as he was drawing it, Blavatt applied a Stroke. To set up the Pen to automatically stroke paths as you draw them, without filling: In the Property Bar, click as needed to make sure the Stroke checkbox is checked and the Fill box is unchecked; click the Stroke color swatch and choose a color that will show up well against your artwork. Click and drag with the Pen tool to draw a path. (For more information about drawing paths with the Pen tool, turn to "Working with Bézier Paths and Selections," on page 156.)

When the path was complete, Blavatt converted it to a selection. (Click the Convert to Selection button on the Property Bar.) To make a soft selection edge that would help to make transparent color on the edges when he painted or filled, he feathered the selection 8 pixels (Select, Feather). Then he saved the selection as a mask so he could use it later (Select, Save Selection). Each mask was saved in the Channels palette.

4 Adding color and texture. Painting with blues and golds, Blavatt used the Square Chalk variant of Chalk to quickly build up color over the entire image, using a light enough touch on his stylus to reduce opacity and preserve the texture.

5 Enhancing the figure as the focal point. Next, he added details to the blouse and more colored texture to the figure. He chose Select, Load Selection and chose the figure's mask from the Load From menu. When the selection was active, he added

6a

Drawing a path for the beam of light

6b

Airbrushing within the active selection

6c

The completed beam of light

7

The Flattened Pencil variant (Pencils) and the Graphic Paintbrush variant of F-X were used to add final details to the face.

highlights to the woman's blouse using the Bleach variant of Erasers. To deepen color and build shadows, he used the Darkener variant of Erasers. Then he chose a creamy pink color in the Color picker, and with Pavement texture still chosen in the Paper Selector, he used the Square Chalk to gently brush textured highlights over the figure's face, neck and arms. When he'd finished the figure and clothing, he reversed the selection by choosing Select, Invert so he could work on the background while protecting the figure.

To further strengthen the focal point and to enhance the mysterious atmosphere of the city street, he added a dark burgundy "dye" to the background only, while leaving the focal point—the figure—in lighter colors. To add a "dye" to an area of your image, start by loading a selection. To re-create Blavatt's effect, make sure Pavement is the current texture in the Papers Selector. (When Paper is chosen in the Using menu, the luminance of the current texture chosen in the Papers section is used as the means to apply the transparent dye effect.) Then choose a deep red in the Color picker and choose Effects, Surface Control, Dye Concentration, Using Paper. Experiment with the settings. (Blavatt set a Maximum of 488% and a Minimum of 50%.) To scroll around your image in the Preview window, drag in the Preview window. Click OK when you have an effect you like.

6 Airbrushing a beam of light. To balance the composition, Blavatt added a gold beam of light shining from a street light on the left side of the image. First he created a selection to limit the paint: Using the Pen tool from the Tools palette, he drew a path to define the beam of light; he converted the path to a selection by using the Convert to Selection button on the Options bar. For a smooth edge, he feathered the selection to 8 pixels (Select, Feather), then he stored the selection as a mask for safekeeping (click the Save Selection as Channel button at the bottom of the Channels palette). To ensure that the color of the light matched existing color in the illustration, he used the Dropper tool to sample a gold color from the image. Next, he chose the Fine Spray variant of the Airbrushes and used firmer pressure to spray denser color near the light source, then used lighter pressure to fade the spray of color as he painted lower within the selection.

7 Final details. To complete the painting, Blavatt went back over the image and added details: With the Flattened Pencil and a dark color he touched up the woman's eyes; with the Graphic Paintbrush he added more tiny strokes of white at the top of light beam and he strengthened highlights on the woman's hair and blouse collar. Finally, he used the Bleach variant of the Erasers to brighten the highlight on the roof of the background building. 🐾

Selections and Airbrush

Overview *Create a pencil sketch; create PostScript outlines in a drawing program; import outlines and sketch into Painter; add texture and gradient fills within the selections; use the Airbrush to create a metallic look.*

JOHN DISMUKES, CAPSTONE STUDIOS

1a

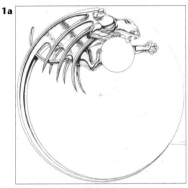

The original pencil sketch

1b

The selected and grouped panther outlines were copied to the clipboard in Illustrator.

2a

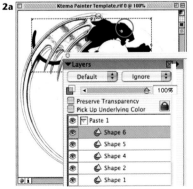

The pasted shapes selected with the Layer Adjuster tool on the image, showing their names in the expanded group in the Layers palette

ARTISTS USING TRADITIONAL AIRBRUSH technique cut friskets out of paper, film or plastic to protect portions of their artwork as they paint. For complex jobs this can become quite a task. That's one of the reasons why John Dismukes of Capstone Studios traded in his traditional tools for electronic ones. For this logo for Ktema, a manufacturer of promotional clothing for the entertainment industry, he started with a pencil sketch, added PostScript paths and brought both into Painter. He turned the paths into selections and used them as friskets.

1 Organizing the elements. Dismukes had a scanned pencil sketch and a PostScript drawing created in Adobe Illustrator, which fit the sketch. The paths included the panther, the wing ribs and membrane, the large and small globes, and the Ktema nameplate. (If you need to import type from Illustrator into Painter, first convert the type into outlines.) Painter has the ability to recognize fill and stroke attributes and groups when PostScript art is imported. To prepare a document for importing into Painter, save a version in Adobe Illustrator 5 (or later) or EPS format.

2 Importing, positioning and scaling. Dismukes opened the original pencil sketch in Painter and began importing the paths into the document. There are two reliable ways to import PostScript outlines into a Painter file: using File, Acquire, Adobe Illustrator File (which creates a new file) or copying from the PostScript program to the clipboard and then pasting into an open file in Painter. For the second method to work, both applications have to be running at the same time. Importing the outlines through the clipboard is fairly fast and always reliable. To do this, select the outlines in Illustrator and copy, then switch to Painter and paste. You'll see a closed group of shapes appear in the Layers palette. Move this shape group into position on the template using

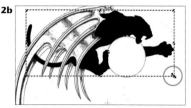

The Layer Adjuster tool changes to an arrow cursor when scaling shapes.

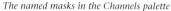

The named masks in the Channels palette

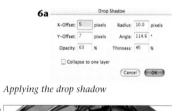

Cloning texture into the membrane selection

Airbrushing highlights on the panther

Applying the drop shadow

6b

The shadow and lens flare are shown in this detail. The 40 MB logo was output as a 4 × 5-inch color transparency at 762 ppi.

the Layer Adjuster tool or the arrow keys on your keyboard. To scale the shapes proportionally, choose the Layer Adjuster tool, hold down the Shift key and drag on a corner handle.

3 Converting, saving and naming. If you have a complex graphic with overlapping shapes, you may want to ungroup the shapes before converting them to selections. This will enable you to save each selection as a mask in the Channels palette so it can be used individually or added to or subtracted from the other selections. To ungroup, first make sure the group is closed (not expanded) in the Layers palette. Then at the bottom of the Layers palette, click the Layer Commands button and from the menu choose Ungroup. To convert a shape to a selection so you can paint or fill it, click on its name in the Layers palette and choose Shapes, Convert To Selection. The shape will disappear from the Layers palette and will become an active marquee on the image canvas. Store the selection in the Channels palette as a mask by choosing Select, Save Selection, then typing a Name and clicking OK.

4 Filling selections. Dismukes created texture within the membrane selection using a Cloners brush and a modified paper texture from a second document. He filled the large globe with a maroon gradient and the small globe with a green gradient. To read more about cloning turn to "Cloning and Tracing" in Chapter 3.

5 Airbrushing. Dismukes's template showed good shadow and highlight detail. Using it as a guide, he began by laying down dark colors, gradually building forward to the white highlights. He used the Digital Airbrush variant of Airbrushes, adjusting only the Size and Min Size in the Size section of the Brush Creator window as he worked.

6 Adding a shadow. Dismukes used a layer to create the panther's drop shadow on the maroon globe. To use the Create Drop Shadow command to do this, you first need to load the selection: Click the Load Channel as Selection button at the bottom of the Channels palette and choose a channel. To load more than one mask at a time as a single selection, load the first selection, then click the Load Channel as Selection button again; in the Load From menu, choose a second selection and for the Operation choose Add To Selection. Continue to Load and Add to your selection until you have all of the elements active. Store this complex selection as a new mask by clicking the Save Selection as Channel button at the bottom of the Channels palette.

To create the shadow, turn the new selection into a layer by clicking on it in your image with the Layer Adjuster tool. Choose Effects, Objects, Create Drop Shadow. Use the default settings or experiment with other settings, then click OK.

As a final touch, Dismukes opened the image in Adobe Photoshop and applied the Lens Flare filter to the green globe.

Working with Hand-Drawn Selections

Overview *Open a scanned drawing as a template; select areas of the image using the Lasso; use selections to constrain brushstrokes, fills and effects.*

STEVE CAMPBELL

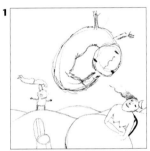

The original pencil sketch

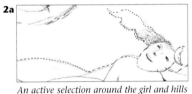

An active selection around the girl and hills

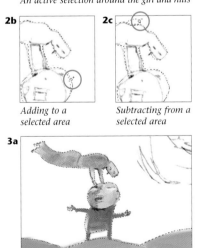

Adding to a selected area

Subtracting from a selected area

Paint applied within a selection

TO ISOLATE AREAS FOR PAINTING, FILLING AND LIGHTING effects in the whimsical *Ægypt*, artist Steve Campbell used the Lasso tool. He painted and applied special effects within each selection, then he unified the piece by applying effects across the entire image.

1 Sketching and scanning. Campbell started with a pencil sketch, which he scanned and opened in Painter and used as a guide for making selections.

2 Creating selections. Campbell created a selection for each element in the drawing. To select with the Lasso tool, drag carefully around the area you want to select, ending at your origin point. You may find it helpful to zoom in on your image while making detailed freehand selections. Press M to switch to the Magnifier tool; then click to zoom in, or press Alt/Option and click to zoom out. (Press L to switch back to the Lasso.) You can also zoom in and out of your image using the Scale slider in the lower left corner of the image window.

Painter's Lasso tool lets you add to or subtract from the currently active selection. To add to the currently selected area, click the Add to Selection button on the Property Bar or hold down the Shift key and then drag with the Lasso. To subtract from the currently selected area, use the Subtract from Selection button on the Property Bar or hold down the Alt/Option key and drag to cut part of the active selection away.

Saving the completed selection as a mask will store it permanently with your image in the Channels palette. To save a selection, choose Select, Save Selection, or click the Save Selection as Channel button at the bottom of the Channels palette.

Painting brushstrokes using clone color

Adding lighting and texture to the sky

Painting details on the face

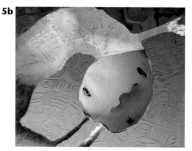

Paper grain texture added to the face

Applying lighting to the tumbler's back

3 Painting inside selections. Campbell loaded individual selections and used various brushes to lay in color within each one. To paint within a selection, first make the selection active: Choose Select, Load Selection (or click the Load Channel as Selection button on the Channels palette).

To begin painting the graduated sky, Campbell made a clone of his painting file (File, Clone), and filled the clone with the Night Sky (a dark-to-light-blue gradient) loaded from the Painter 6 Gradients library. To load a gradient, open the Gradients palette (Window, Show Gradients) and choose from the menu of gradients that pops out from the swatch near the upper right corner of the palette. Or click the little triangle in the upper right corner and choose Open Library from the pop-out menu and navigate to the Gradients library you want. Once you've chosen a gradient, set the angle by dragging the little red ball. Then choose Effects, Fill, Gradient.

Next, Campbell activated the painting file and designated the filled clone as the clone source (File, Clone Source). In the painting file, he loaded the sky selection. He chose the Captured Bristle variant of Acrylics and changed it into a cloning brush (that would sample color from the graduated image while painting in the destination file) by opening the Colors palette (Window, Show Colors) and clicking its Clone Color button (the "rubber stamp"). Using the new Captured Bristle "cloner," he painted angled and curved strokes into the sky selection.

4 Adding effects to the sky. To add a graduated golden tint within the sky selection, Campbell used Effects, Surface Control, Apply Lighting (using a customized version of the Splashy Colors light), then he built up "thick paint." To give your painted image realistic "thick paint" highlights and shadows based on dark and light values in the brushstrokes, choose Effects, Surface Control, Apply Surface Texture, Using Image Luminance.

5 Finalizing the image. To paint the central figure's face, Campbell used the Artist Pastel Chalk variant of Pastels (on top of Basic Paper texture) within the face selection. Then he blended the areas using the Just Add Water variant of Blenders.

After painting the face, he changed its appearance dramatically by applying custom colored lighting and a paper grain effect within the active selection. He used similar procedures to add rich textures and complexity to other elements in the image. To apply a paper texture within a selection, load the selection, and choose Effects, Surface Control, Apply Surface Texture, Using Paper. If you want, you can choose a different paper texture from the Paper Selector (near the bottom of the Toolbox) with this dialog box open.

Finally, to further unify the image, Campbell dropped all selections (Ctrl/⌘-D), and chose Effects, Surface Control, Apply Surface Texture Using Image Luminance with very low settings (Amount 20–30% and Shine 20%).

Making a Color Mask

***Overview** Use New From Color Range and brushes to mask an area of an image; convert the mask to a selection; use Adjust Color to shift the color of the selected area.*

CTP/PHOTO: PHOTODISC

1a

The original photo

1b

The default Color Mask dialog box

1c

Adjusting the sliders to isolate the leaf

COLOR MASK IS ONE OF PAINTER'S most powerful features, letting you create a mask based on a specific color in an image. In the example above, we used a combination of the New From Color Range command and editing with brushes to create masks for individual leaves. We saved the masks in the Channels palette, then used Adjust Color to change the hue and saturation of the individual leaves and the background.

1 Sampling color and adjusting the mask. Open an image and then open the Channels palette. Click the triangle in the top right corner of the palette and choose New From Color Range. When the Color dialog box appears, click in your image (*not* in the preview window) on the color you want to sample (the "center color" of the range of colors to be selected). We selected a color on the tan leaf in the center of the image. To narrow the range of selected colors, drag the H (Hue) Extents slider to the left (we set ours to 10%). Press and drag to scroll the image in the Preview window so you can see how your settings are affecting selection in other parts of the image. Experiment with the S (Saturation) and V (Value) Extents sliders; we got the best results when we reduced the V Extents to 30% to isolate the leaf from darker tan colors in the background water. You may also want to move the three Feather sliders to the left to create harder transitions in your mask. When you're satisfied with the preview of your mask, click OK. Painter will generate a mask based on the sampled color. The mask will automatically appear in the Channels palette.

2 Cleaning up the mask. To view the mask as a red-tinted overlay on top of the image canvas, in the Channels palette make sure the eye icons are open for both the mask and the RGB channel. To edit the mask, click on its name in the palette and choose the Scratchboard Tool variant of Pens in the Brush Selector Bar (it allows smooth painting with opaque "paint"). Choose black for the primary color and paint to add to your mask; paint with white to remove portions of the mask.

The interior of your mask will need to be opaque to completely select your subject. You'll need to view the mask at full opacity to

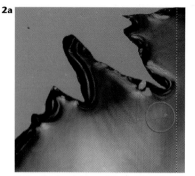

2a

Using the Scratchboard Tool and white paint to erase an area of the mask

2b

Using the Scratchboard Tool to erase the mask from an overlapping leaf. The mask is viewed at a reduced opacity, making both the mask and the image beneath it visible.

2c

The finished mask of the center leaf viewed at 100% opacity

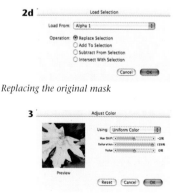

2d

Replacing the original mask

3

Adjusting color within the center leaf selection

identify areas where coverage is not complete so you can paint over any thin spots. To adjust the opacity of the mask overlay, display the Mask Attributes dialog box by double-clicking the mask name in the Channels palette. Move the Opacity slider to 100%; this will have no effect on the actual density of the mask—it's for viewing only.

As a final check for your mask, turn off the eye icon for the mask, and then load the mask as a selection by first clicking the Invert Channel button at the bottom of the Channels palette and then clicking the Load Channel as Selection button. To edit the selection, use the Lasso, clicking the Add to Selection button or the Subtract from Selection button in the Property Bar to draw around the area you want to add or remove. If you edit your selection like this, make sure you replace the original mask in the Channels palette with the edited one: Choose Select, Save Selection; in the Save To menu, choose the mask name, select the Replace Mask option, and click OK.

3 Colorizing with Adjust Color. To make changes to the color within a selection, begin by loading a selection (as above or by choosing Select, Load Selection). With the selection active, choose Effects, Tonal Control, Adjust Colors, Using Uniform Color. Use this feature to change the hue, saturation or brightness in the selected area. If you prefer more radical changes, you can also paint within your selection or apply any of the commands under the Effects menu. 🖌

CLEANING UP MASKS WITH BRIGHTNESS AND CONTRAST

Here's a method for cleaning up masks that can save time and effort when the color of the subject you want to mask also occurs in the surrounding image. Start by making a mask using New From Color Range, clicking to sample the color you need to mask and adjusting the H (Hue), V (Value) and S (Saturation) Extents sliders to create the best mask you can for your subject. Then click OK. To select the mask so you can view it in black-and-white, and manipulate it using commands under the Effects menu, click on the mask name in the Channels palette and click the RGB channel's eye icon closed. Click on the name of the mask, then use Effects, Tonal Control, Brightness/Contrast to bump up the contrast and adjust the brightness to make the gray areas solid black or white. To avoid losing anti-aliasing in the mask, use moderate settings and check the edges of the mask closely.

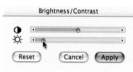

Adjusting settings in the Brightness/Contrast dialog box

The mask before (left) and after (right) adjusting Brightness/Contrast

Auto-Masking with Color

Overview *Use the New From command to generate a mask based on a selected color; load the mask as a selection; paint into the selection with various brushes.*

LEVAN/BARBEE STUDIO

The black-and-white sketch

Choosing the New From command from the Channel palette's pop-up menu

Viewing the new current color mask

WITH PAINTER'S NEW FROM COMMAND you can isolate an area of an image by automatically generating a mask based on color. Once the mask has been created, you can use it to make a selection and fill the area with color or paint into it. When Susan LeVan of LeVan/Barbee Studio created *Man With Buildings*, she used brushes to paint within selections. She used the Current Color setting of the New From command to create jaggy white "halos" around the background scratch marks, giving her piece texture, lightness and air. Repainting a printed, collaged and scanned version of the image produced the result above.

1 Establishing the composition. LeVan began a new document with a white paper color. She chose Basic Paper from the Paper Selector near the bottom of the Toolbox, the Dry Ink variant of Sumi-e and black color to sketch. Prior to drawing, she resized the brush smaller using the Size slider popped out from the Property Bar.

2 Generating and viewing a mask. To create a mask for the black-and-white line drawing, LeVan used the Current Color option for the New From command. To begin, first sample the color from your image with the Dropper tool, which will make that color your Current Color. (LeVan clicked the Dropper on the black line work in her sketch.) To generate the mask, open the Channels palette (Window, Show Channels). Click the triangle and choose New From (or press Ctrl/⌘-Shift-M). In the New From

The Channels palette showing the mask

Painting within the selection with a brush

The Man 3 image   *Scan of the collage*

The image showing details painted on the face, tie and eyes

dialog box, choose Current Color and click OK. In your image, you'll see all instances of the current color masked in red. The mask name, by default Alpha 1, will appear in the Channels palette.

Since New From using Current Color lacks the feathering capabilities of Painter's Color Mask (see "Making a Color Mask," earlier in this chapter), there will be rough, aliased areas at the boundary between the selected and unselected portions of your image. LeVan likes the white "halos" that result when she uses New From for color fills because they accentuate the texture on the background.

3 Loading the mask as a selection. Click the Load Channel as Selection button at the bottom of the Channels palette and in the Load Selection dialog box, choose the Replace Selection button. To view the RGB image and the active selection without the red mask, click the eye icon to the left of the mask to shut the eye thumbnail.

4 Painting and filling within the selection. With the selection active, LeVan changed the black line work to a textured white line by first inverting the selection (Shift-Ctrl/⌘-I) and then choosing Effects, Tonal Control, Negative. Then by inverting the selection again, she used it to protect the linework while she painted flat color areas on the image, as follows: To paint within the selected area of the image canvas with a color, first choose RGB in the Channels palette to target the image canvas. Choose a color in the Colors palette. Then select a brush and paint within the selected area. After painting and filling the large areas of color with the Opaque Flat (Oils) and Dry Ink (Sumi-e) variants, LeVan inverted the selection again (to isolate the line work) and painted it green using the Square Chalk (Chalk).

5 Printing, collaging and scanning. When LeVan had finished painting the flat color on her image, she printed the Man 3 image using a color inkjet printer. Then she painted the print with acrylic paint and added other conventional media—tape and newspaper—to make a collage. When the collage was complete, she scanned it so she could rework it in Painter.

6 Adding rich color and texture. To add richness and complexity to her image, LeVan used New From, Current Color again to mask areas in the face and then painted with the Square Chalk variant. To add more texture, she painted, then repeated painting with New From several times. First she painted in pale yellow, then masked the yellow; then she painted in tan, then masked the tan; and finally she painted in pink.

LeVan then painted more detail: For the tie, eye and mouth she used the Opaque Flat; the magenta splotch outside the head and the ground line were done with the Smeary Flat. Then she drew over the background with the Square Chalk and an orange color. Finally, she drew the buildings with a small Scratchboard Tool variant of Pens. Then to draw the straight lines along the edges of the image, she clicked the Straight Lines strokes button on the Property Bar and clicked from point to point.

■ Bear Canyon Creative commissioned illustrator **Cecil Rice** to paint *The Green Hornet*, one in a series of illustrations for a set of audio book covers entitled *The Golden Age of Radio,* published by Dove Audio. An expert draftsman, Rice painted the portrait in Painter from start to finish using traditional painting theory. He began by gathering references from movies done in the 1930s and 1940s. Then he did three portrait sketches in Painter and presented them to his client. The chosen sketch was based on a still from an old Alan Ladd movie. For the final artwork, Rice used Canvas, Resize to enlarge the sketch to the finished size plus bleed; then he made selections and saved them as masks in the Channels palette so he could use them later. He loaded each channel as a selection and clicked with the Layer Adjuster to put each element on a layer. While painting, he blended the color in the image with Blenders variants and added more color with the Oils, Chalk and Pastels variants. Rice continued to refine the shapes of elements, for instance, the ascot and coat, by editing the masks for those layers. When he was pleased with the figure, he painted the background using the Artist Pastel Chalk variant Chalk. To blend the background, he used Effects, Focus, Soften.

■ A freelance illustrator for more than 15 years, **Rick Kirkman** divides his time between producing cartoons for commercial clients and creating the King Feature Syndicate comic strip *Baby Blues* with partner Jerry Scott.

Kirkman began the cover illustration for *Motherhood Is Not for Wimps* (above) in Painter with black linework using Pencils variants on Basic Paper texture. Kirkman planned to add color using the Airbrushes variants. To protect areas of his image from overspray when he used the Airbrushes, Kirkman first drew Bézier paths using the Pen tool, converted the paths to selections and then saved each selection as a mask, in case he needed to use it later. (To convert a path to a selection and save it, click the Make Selection button on the Property Bar and then choose Select, Save Selection.) To load each mask as a selection, he chose Select, Load Selection, then he sprayed color using Spray variants of the

Airbrushes. For a more textured look in the foreground and the shadow, he used the Coarse Spray and Variable Splatter variants.

After the Painter Illustration was complete, Kirkman saved it as a TIFF file and placed it into an Adobe Illustrator file, where he added the blue panel and type. (Illustrator accepts both RGB and CMYK TIFF files, which makes direct export from Painter possible.)

■ Before he began using Painter, **Don Stewart**, who specializes in book illustration, worked on gessoed illustration board with airbrush and colored pencil. Today he draws on the computer, using Painter's tools and brushes that match his traditional ones.

Fall Blitz (above) was commissioned by *The Front Porch Magazine* as a cover illustration. Stewart began the illustration by sketching in Painter using Pencils variants on medium-textured paper. To lay in colored washes he used Oils variants. Then he isolated areas of his image by making selections with the Lasso (for example, the leaves in the foreground) so that he could paint with Painter's Airbrushes without worrying about overspray. He used the Digital Airbrush to paint smoother areas (the skin, for instance), and to begin to build up tones and value. For more texture, he used the Fine Spray and Coarse Spray variants of Airbrushes. When the figures were modeled the way he wanted them, he added highlights and detail using the Colored Pencils variants. To add texture on the mounds of leaves, he painted with contrasting colors using the Tiny Spattery Airbrush and the Chalk variants over a rough texture.

■ **James D'Avanzo** was a young man with a lot of artistic talent and little physical mobility. He began with very basic computer graphics programs, then moved to CorelDraw, which allowed him the opportunity to create some very sophisticated images. However, it was with Painter that he blossomed as an artist. Using Painter with the Wacom tablet and a multi-button cursor, D'Avanzo painted still lives and imaginary landscapes. The National Muscular Dystrophy association chose his image *Woods* (right) for their Christmas card for 1996.

For *Woods*, D'Avanzo chose a limited palette of deep colors to depict a haunting moonlit night. He blocked in broad areas of color using Airbrushes and Chalk variants. Then he blended paint using the Grainy Water and Just Add Water variants of Blenders. To protect the shapes of clouds and moon from paint, he used the Lasso to make selections. To reverse the selected moon (so that he could paint on the sky while protecting the moon area), he chose Select, Invert. After painting the sky, he dropped the selection (Ctrl/⌘-D). To finish, he added more texture to the moon and clouds by painting a few lighter-colored brushstrokes using the Artist Pastel Chalk variant of Pastels.

D'Avanzo created *Deep Love* (right) using saturated, complementary colors to help communicate the powerful healing of love. To create the background, he used the Lasso, then feathered and painted into the selection to create the illusion of a horizon. He used the same technique for the hand and figure. D'Avanzo worked from background to foreground, painting into the selections with a low-opacity Digital Airbrush variant of the Airbrushes.

■ When **Susan LeVan** created the illustration *Family Tree*, she used brushes to paint within selections. To build rough (not anti-aliased) edges on line drawings and around shapes, and to give her work more texture, she repeatedly used the New From command with the Current Color setting and then painted back into her image.

Le Van created the illustration about family history for her portfolio. To begin, she drew the main elements in black with the Scratchboard Tool and Fine Point variants of Pens. She made masks for areas of the image with New From, Using Current Color feature (located in the triangle pop-up menu on the Channels palette) and filled the selected lines with color (Effects, Fill). Then she used the

Square Chalk variant of Chalk and soft colors to paint grainy strokes within each selection. Le Van painted transparent washes using the Wash Camel and Wet Camel variants of Water Color, then she added more textured brushwork using the Dry Camel variant of Water Color.

For the rectangular shapes, she made selections with the Rectangular Selection tool, and painted into them with the Coarse Spray variant (Airbrushes). Then she added brightly-colored brushstrokes using the Opaque Round and the Smeary Round variants of Oils. To complete the richly textured background, she used the Square Chalk variant to brush color on lightly, and then she repeatedly masked and drew over areas with more layers of color.

artist at 50

■ **Mike Reed** takes an approach to digital illustration that avoids the slick look sometimes seen in art created on the computer. To re-create the traditional look of pastel on rough paper, in *Artist at 50* (above) and *Polar Bears* (opposite), Reed sensitively layered textured color with the Pastels and Chalk variants on top of Wood Shavings paper texture (loaded from Wow! Textures on the Painter 8 Wow! CD-ROM).

For the self-portrait *Artist at 50*, Reed began by making a color study with the Square Chalk variant to establish the theme and general elements in the composition. So he could limit paint while working freely, he built selections, which

he began by drawing shapes with the Pen tool. He drew shapes for the figure and clothing and also added stars, a moon, and abstract shapes in the background. He converted each shape to a selection (Shapes, Convert To Selection), feathered it (Select, Feather) and saved it as a mask in the Channels palette (Select, Save Selection). Reed loaded each selection and colored within it using the Square Chalk; then he brushed lightly over areas with the Square Chalk to paint highlights. He added expressive strokes to the gesturing arm to suggest movement. To finish, he added more texture to the background using the Square Chalk and blue and purple colors.

■ To begin the children's book illustration *Polar Bears* (above) for Scholastic Books, **Mike Reed** sketched the composition in soft blues, grays and purples using the Square Chalk variant of Chalk, painting free brushstrokes on top of the Wood Shavings paper texture (from the Wow! Textures on the CD-ROM that comes with this book). So he could paint freely in some areas while protecting other areas of his composition, he created selections using the Pen tool and then converted each shape to a selection (Shapes, Convert To Selection). Because he wanted the color areas to have soft edges, he feathered each selection (Select, Feather) with a radius of 5 pixels. Then he saved it (Select, Save Selection) into the Channels palette so he could use it later as a mask. To paint a textured gradient on the sky, he loaded a selection he'd made and brushed over the selected area with the Square Chalk using various light blue and rose colors. To give the polar bears' bodies more dimension, he loaded selections and painted with the Artist Pastel Chalk variant of Pastels. To add detail to the fur, he used the Sharp Chalk variant of Chalk. To add the shadows under the bears, he hand-painted "gradations" with soft, grainy strokes. To finish, he painted tighter highlight and shadow details on the faces and bodies of the bears with the Sharp Chalk.

USING
LAYERS

Working in separate source files, we painted elements—the turtle, the fishes and the paint can and brushes—for this Emerald City illustration. Then we painted a mask to silhouette each element. We loaded the selection from each element's mask in turn and used the Layer Adjuster to drag and drop the element into the final composite. After dragging the items in, we used the Layer Adjuster to position them. To create a transparent look on the bottom of the paint can, we created a layer mask for the paint can layer and used the Digital Airbrush variant of the Airbrushes and black paint to paint on the layer mask; the effect was to softly "erase" lower areas of the can as they were hidden by the layer mask.

CHER THREINEN-PENDARVIS

LAYERS ARE ELEMENTS THAT HOVER above Painter's image Canvas, or base layer, providing a great deal of flexibility in composing artwork. You can move, paint on, or apply a special effect to a layer without affecting other layers or the background canvas. So when building images you can try several possibilities by manipulating or repositioning the various elements. Then, when your layers are as you like them, you can drop them onto the canvas, blending them with the background.

In addition to *image* (or pixel-based) *layers,* Painter incorporates other types of "layers": *floating objects, reference layers, shapes, dynamic layers, text layers,* and two *media layers—Water Color* and *Liquid Ink.* The controls for naming, stacking, compositing, and grouping all of these kinds of layers are found in the Layers palette, as described in "Organizing with the Layers palette" on page 188. Each layer in a composite file has a Composite Method that affects how it interacts (or blends) with other layers and with the Canvas.

You can preserve layers by saving your file in RIFF format. Saving in most other formats requires *dropping,* or merging, the layers. However, if you'd like to be able to open a Painter image in

A TIFF-TO-RIFF LIFESAVER

If you save a layered file in TIFF format (a format in which Painter doesn't support layers and floating objects), Painter is smart enough not to automatically drop the layers in your working image. A dialog box will appear, and when you click OK, the program will save a closed copy of your document with layers dropped in TIFF format, but the layers will stay alive in your open working image. Make sure to save in RIFF format before quitting, in order to preserve the image layers, floating objects, reference layers, dynamic layers, text layers, shapes, and Water Color and Liquid Ink layers.

Recognizing items in the Layers palette: Image layers are designated by a stack of rectangles, a floating object by a star, a shape by a circle and triangle, a reference layer by a dotted rectangle with handles, a dynamic layer by a plug icon, a Text layer by a capital "T," a Water Color layer by a blue water drop and a Liquid Ink layer by a black drop of ink. In the Layers palette shown here, the document's Canvas is selected.

USING DRAG-AND-DROP

Here's a quick way to copy a layer or shape into a composite file from a source image. Open both images. In the source image, select the layer or shape by clicking its name in the Layers palette and then drag the item into the composite image using the Layer Adjuster tool.

For this flower illustration, the Wash Bristle and Runny Wash Camel variants of Water Color were used to paint washes on Water Color layers.

Photoshop with layers intact, save the file in Photoshop format. All layers and shapes will be converted to Photoshop layers, with their names and stacking order intact. To read more about working with Photoshop, turn to Chapter 9, "Using Painter With Photoshop."

LAYER OR FLOATING OBJECT?

New *image layers* can be made by selecting an area of the *Canvas* and cutting or copying. But if you select and cut or copy *from a layer other than the Canvas*, you produce a *floating object* associated with the layer you used to make it.

An *image layer* can hold pixels or transparency. When you add a new layer by clicking the New Layer button at the bottom of the Layers palette or by choosing New Layer from the palette's pop-up menu, it's completely transparent until you paint on it. See "Working with Image Layers," below.

A *floating object* is an area of an image layer that has been isolated and lifted from the layer, to create a kind of sublayer. Each layer can have only one floating object at a time. See "Working with Floating Objects" on page 181.

Reference layers can be helpful for assembling large images from several separate source files. A reference layer is a 72 ppi screen proxy (or "stand-in") for an image layer in the current image, or for a placed image that's linked to an image file outside of the document. (See "Using Reference Layers" on page 182.)

Shapes are essentially a resolution-independent kind of layer that can be reshaped or resized without degradation. As described on page 183, shapes are outline-based elements with attributes such as stroke, fill and transparency. Shapes and their attributes are PostScript-based objects. To be able to paint on a shape, adding pixel information, you have to first convert it to an image layer.

Dynamic layers are special hovering devices that allow you to make adjustments to an existing image (by adding an Equalize layer or Brightness and Contrast layer, for example), or to create entirely new effects (for instance, a Liquid Metal layer). You can create a dynamic layer by clicking the Dynamic Plugins button at the bottom of the Layers palette and choosing a plug-in from the pop-up menu (see page 185).

Painter's improved *Text layers* are described on page 187.

Media layers are special layers that allow startling, realistic painting effects. Read about two types of media layers—Water Color and Liquid Ink—on page 187.

All layers take up extra disk space and RAM. You can minimize the need for extra space by floating only what's necessary, and by dropping and combining layers whenever it makes sense.

WORKING WITH IMAGE LAYERS

You can make an image layer by activating the Canvas layer, selecting part of it, then clicking on the selected area with the Layer Adjuster tool. This process cuts the selected area out of the Canvas and turns it into the new layer, leaving behind a hole

To make a new layer by copying an active selection on Painter's image Canvas (similar to choosing Layer, New, Layer Via Copy in Photoshop), make or load a selection in your image, hold down the Alt/Option key, choose the Layer Adjuster tool, and click or drag inside the selected area. To *cut* from the image canvas and turn the selected area into a new layer, click or drag with the Layer Adjuster without pressing the Alt/Option key.

PHOTO: CORBIS IMAGES

If you don't hold down the Alt/Option key when you drag a selection with the Layer Adjuster, you'll leave a hole behind in the Canvas if you then move the newly created layer. Occasionally this is desirable, but most of the time you'll want to use the Alt/Option!

In Painter there can be only one active selection at a time. You can use a selection to edit a portion of any image layer, reference layer, Water Color layer or Liquid Ink layer listed in the Layers palette.

that you can see if you drag the new layer with the Layer Adjuster. Alt/Option-click to *copy* an active selection or to duplicate the entire Canvas. This creates a new layer from the copy but also leaves the original pixels in place on the Canvas. The selection that defines the area to turn into the new layer can be made with any of the selection processes described in Chapter 4.

There are other ways to create an image layer. For instance, all elements pasted into a Painter document come in as image layers, and you can also drag an image layer from the Image Portfolio palette into your image.

An image layer automatically includes a *Transparency mask;* when the layer is active (clicked in the Layers palette) its Transparency mask is available to be loaded to select all the nontransparent areas of the layer (Select, Load Selection). An image layer can also include a *layer mask,* created by clicking the Create Layer Mask button at the bottom of the Layers palette. The layer mask determines what parts of the pixel information on the layer are shown or hidden. You can load the layer mask for the active layer as a selection (Select, Load Selection), just as you can the Transparency mask described above. In contrast to the transparency mask, the layer mask can be directly modified to hide or reveal parts of the layer or to blend layered images with exciting transparency effects as described on page 201.

Here's how to work with image layers once you've created or imported one:

To activate a layer, click its name in the Layers palette. Or choose the Layer Adjuster in the Toolbox, then turn on Auto Select Layer in the Property Bar and click on a visible area of the layer. Either way, the name will be highlighted in the Layers palette to show that the layer is active.

To deactivate a layer, click on another layer. Or choose the Layer Adjuster tool, turn on Auto Select Layer in the Property Bar, and click somewhere in the image where the current layer has no pixels.

To apply a special effect to a layer, make sure it's active (highlighted in the Layers palette, as described above). Then choose from the Effects menu. (Of course, an effect applied to a transparent layer with no pixels on it has no effect.)

To paint on a layer, make sure it's active (highlighted in the Layers palette, as described above). Choose any brush (except a Water Color or Liquid Ink variant) and paint brushstrokes onto the layer. (Water Color and Liquid Ink can paint only on appropriate media layers, which will automatically be created if you try to use these brushes on image layers.) For more information, turn to "Painting on Layers" on page 56 in Chapter 3 and to "Illustrating with Layers," on page 193 of this chapter.

To erase paint you have applied to a layer, making the area "clear" again, you can choose the Eraser variant of the Erasers (in

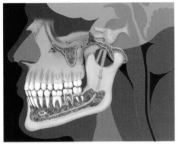

When creating Neural Pathway, *a detail of which is shown here, David Purnell used many layers and shapes. See the complete illustration and more of Purnell's work in the gallery at the end of this chapter.*

A QUICK CANVAS COPY

To quickly float a copy of the Canvas to a layer, choose Select, All, (Ctrl/⌘-A), then hold down Ctrl-Alt (Windows) or ⌘-Option (Mac) and click on the Canvas.

RESTACKING LAYERS

When you create a new layer, it appears at the top of the layer stack. To reposition it in the stack, simply drag its name to the appropriate level in the Layers palette.

the Brush Selector Bar) with 100% Opacity set in the Property Bar, and paint on the layer to "erase."

To hide part of a layer without permanently erasing it, begin by choosing black in the Color picker. Click on the layer in the Layers palette. If the layer doesn't already have a layer mask, click the Create Layer Mask button at the bottom of the palette. Then click the mask thumbnail that will appear next to the image thumbnail for the layer; this activates the mask rather than the layer's image. Choose a brush (such as the Pens, Scratchboard Tool) and paint on the mask with black where you want to hide the layer. If you want to *reveal* parts of the image that you have hidden with the layer mask, paint the mask with white.

The most foolproof way to move a layer is to click the layer's name in the Layers palette to activate the layer, then choose with the Layer Adjuster tool (and make sure Auto Select Layer checkbox is turned off in the Property Bar), and drag anywhere in the image window. To adjust a layer's position a screen pixel at a time, activate the layer and use the arrow keys on your keyboard.

To merge a layer with the Canvas, activate the image layer in the Layers palette and click the Layer Commands button (far left at the bottom of the palette) and choose Drop from the pop-up menu, or click the triangle in the upper-right corner of the palette and choose Drop from that menu. If you want to merge all of your layers onto the Canvas—much like using Photoshop's Flatten Image command—simply choose Drop All from the menu in the upper-right corner (this command is not available through the Layer Commands button). Another option, if you want to keep a layered version but also create a "flattened" one, is to choose File, Clone; a duplicate of the image will appear with all layers merged.

To scale, rotate, distort or flip a layer, activate the layer and choose the appropriate command under Effects, Orientation.

To change the opacity of a layer, click its name in the Layers palette and use the Opacity slider near the top of the palette.

WORKING WITH FLOATING OBJECTS

To reposition a portion of an image layer, Painter uses a *floating object*. Only an image layer can have a floating object, and each layer can have only one floating object at a time. Besides moving part of a layer, you can also use a floating object to isolate part of a layer for editing. The advantage of using a floating object (rather than simply selecting an area of the layer and changing it) is that a floating object can have its own layer mask, which you can use to hide or reveal part of the floating object.

To create a floating object that's cut out from a layer, make a selection, click on a layer's name in the Layers palette and choose Select, Float, or click inside the selection with the Layer Adjuster tool. The floating object will be listed below its parent

If you'll be making several transformations (such as rotations or scaling) to a single layer, like rotating it into place and then scaling it to fit your layout, you need to know that the quality of an image layer can be degraded with every transformation. Instead of using a series of individual transformation commands (such as Effects, Orientation, Rotate and then Effects, Orientation, Scale), consider converting the layer temporarily to a reference layer by selecting it and choosing Effects, Orientation, Free Transform. You can then rotate, scale and skew the reference layer as many times as you like. When you arrive at the result you want, choose Effects, Orientation, Commit Transform. The effect is to transform the actual pixels only once and thus preserve quality.

A reference layer, ready to have Free Transform applied, has eight handles around it.

You can merge several layers at once with the Canvas by Shift-selecting their names in the Layers palette before clicking the Layer Commands button and choosing Drop from the pop-up menu.

layer in the Layers palette, indented to show the relationship. (If you turn off visibility for the floating object by clicking its eye icon, you'll see the hole where it has been cut from the parent layer.)

To make a floating object copy of information on the parent layer (without cutting out), make a selection, press the Alt/Option key, then choose Select, Float, or Alt/Option-click with the Layer Adjuster tool. The floating object "copy" will be listed below its parent layer in the Layers palette.

To recombine a floating object with its parent layer, activate the floating object by clicking its name in the Layers palette and click the Layer Commands button (far left at the bottom of the palette) and choose Drop from the pop-up menu. The floating object will also recombine with its parent layer if you do any of the following: paint or make another selection while either the layer or its floating object is active; paste into the document or drag an item from the Image Portfolio while the floating object is active.

USING REFERENCE LAYERS

If you work with large files and your computer slows to a crawl when you try to reposition a big image layer, consider converting image layers to *reference layers*. Reference layers are 72 ppi proxy, or "stand-in" images. They let you manipulate high-resolution images faster, instead of dragging huge images around your screen. Because you are working with a proxy—and not the actual pixels—you can perform multiple rotations, scaling, skewing and repositioning very quickly. When you've finished all your manipulations, convert reference layers back to image layers; Painter will remember all the manipulations you've made and will carry them out as a single change, with much less loss of quality than if you had made them one by one on the high-resolution file.

To make a reference layer, select an image layer and choose Effects, Orientation, Free Transform. To get ready to operate on the layer, choose the Layer Adjuster.

To scale a reference layer proportionately, press the Shift key and drag on a corner handle with the Layer Adjuster tool to resize as many times as needed to get just the result you want.

To rotate a reference layer interactively, press the Ctrl/⌘ key and drag a corner handle with the Layer Adjuster.

To skew a reference layer interactively, press the Ctrl/⌘ key and drag one of the original four middle handles with the Layer Adjuster tool.

If you're compositing large files, you may want to work with each component file separately, then make a reference layer by importing the image (with its layer mask, if you like) into your composite file using File, Place. When the positioning and transformations of the imported layer are complete, convert the reference layer to an image layer by choosing Effects, Orientation, Commit Transform.

Rick Kirkman created Postal Cat *by drawing shapes, then converting them to image layers so that he could paint on them. Turn to page 196 to read about his technique step by step.*

The opacity of a shape's fill can be set in the Set Shape Attributes dialog box (Shapes, Set Shape Attributes).

To scale, rotate or skew a reference layer numerically, choose Effects, Orientation, Set Transform, and type specifications into the fields. (The skew is set as the Slant, which is found in the Rotation section of the dialog box.)

To turn a reference layer back into an image (pixel-based) layer, choose Effects, Orientation, Commit Transform, or paint or apply an effect to the reference layer, clicking the Commit button when prompted. If you drag a reference layer into the Image Portfolio palette, the full-resolution version is stored in the Portfolio.

WORKING WITH SHAPES

Shapes can be drawn with the Rectangular or Oval Shape tool, or the Pen or the Quick Curve tool. Or they can be made from a selection (converted from a selection using the Select, Convert To Shape command) or imported from a PostScript drawing program such as Adobe Illustrator (this process is described in Chapter 4).

Before modifying a shape, you need to make it active. You can activate a shape just as you would a layer—by clicking its name in the Layers palette or by clicking it with the Layer Adjuster tool, with Auto Select Layer turned on in the Property Bar. Or use the Whole Shape Selection tool (solid arrow, the Shape Selection tool with the Ctrl/⌘ key held down) to select the entire shape so you can move it as a unit, without distorting it, by dragging anywhere on its outline.

To drag off a copy of a shape, you can select the shape with the Layer Adjuster tool, then press Alt/Option and drag.

To scale a shape proportionately, click it with the Layer Adjuster, hold down the Shift key and drag a corner handle.

To rotate a shape, click it with the Layer Adjuster, press the Ctrl/⌘ key and drag a corner handle.

To skew a shape interactively, click it with the Layer Adjuster, press the Ctrl/⌘ key and drag a middle handle.

To scale, distort, rotate or flip a shape, select it in the Layers palette and use one of the choices from Effects, Orientation.

To duplicate a shape and transform the copy, choose Shapes, Set Duplicate Transform. Set up specifications in the Set Duplicate Transform dialog box and click OK. Now when you choose Shapes, Duplicate, the transformation will be applied to the copy.

To modify the stroke and fill attributes of a shape, select it and open the Set Shape Attributes dialog box by choosing Shapes, Set Shape Attributes or by double-clicking on the name of a shape in the Layers palette. To change the fill or stroke color of a shape, click once in the Stroke or Fill color field and choose a new color in the Color picker. (This method lets you select the current color

WHOLE SHAPE SELECTION

To select an entire unfilled shape path, choose the Shape Selection tool (hollow arrow), press the Ctrl/⌘ key to put it in Whole Shape Selection mode, and click on the shape's outline to select all of its anchor points at once, making it possible to move the shape to a new location, undistorted, by dragging anywhere on its outline.

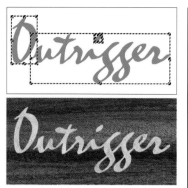

For this restaurant logo, we drew black calligraphy letters on the canvas using the Calligraphy variant of the Calligraphy brush. We made a luminosity mask by choosing the New From command from the Channels palette's triangle pop-out menu and choosing Image Luminance in the New From dialog box. Then we loaded the selection (Select, Load Selection, Alpha 1), and converted the selection to shapes (Select, Convert To Shape). The client planned to use the logo in a variety of ways, so we appreciated that Painter automatically created compound shapes to make the counters transparent for the letter "O," the two descending "g" shapes and the "e." Seen here are the selected filled shapes (top), and the logo applied onto Koa wood texture (bottom), from an ArtBeats Wood and Paper CD-ROM (bottom). To read more about compound shapes turn to "Making a Compound," on the next page or to "Using Shapes," in the Painter 8 User Guide.

without displaying the color wheel. To use the wheel instead, simply *double*-click the Stroke or Fill color swatch in the Set Shape Attributes dialog box.) **A word of warning:** If you paint on, or apply an effect to, a shape—rather than simply changing its stroke and fill—it will be automatically converted into an image layer when you click the Commit button. When this happens, shape attributes (such as resolution independence and control of stroke and fill) are lost.

To convert several shapes into individual image layers, you can Shift-select multiple shapes in the Layers palette and convert the shapes to image layers all at once—as long as they are stroked and filled—using Shapes, Convert To Layer.

To make a single image layer from several shapes, first Shift-select the shapes, then click the Layer Commands button on the left at the bottom of the Layers palette to access the pop-up menu, and choose Group. With the group closed (controlled by the arrow to the left of its name in the Layers palette), choose Shapes, Convert To Layer.

To duplicate, move or transform a group of shapes, you can select the group by clicking its name in the Layers palette and then move or transform it as you would a single shape. (See "Organizing With the Layers Palette" on page 188 to read more about groups.)

To move an individual shape within a group, expand the group by clicking the arrow to the left of the group's name in the Layers palette. Then choose the Layer Adjuster tool and drag the shape; or click it and move it using the arrow keys.

Blending between shapes. To create intermediate shapes between two shapes, Shift-select both shapes in the Layers palette

SHAPES OF A CURRENT COLOR

To automatically fill or stroke a shape with the Current Color chosen in the Color picker as you draw it, set up your Shape preferences: Choose Preferences, Shapes from the Edit menu (for Windows or Mac System 9.2.2) or from the Corel Painter 8 menu (for Mac OS X), check the appropriate checkboxes and click OK.

Setting up the Shape Preferences to automatically fill with the Current Color

A HIDDEN RASTERIZER

You can rasterize PostScript art from Illustrator in Painter and at the same time save a mask for selecting that area later. Choose File, Acquire, Adobe Illustrator File to import the art as shape layers. Target the resulting shapes in the Layers palette and convert them to image layers using Shapes, Convert To Layer. To flatten the image and make a selection, target each layer by choosing its name in the Layers palette and use the Drop and Select command in the Layers palette's pop-out menu. To store the selection for use later, choose Select, Save Selection and save it as a mask in the Channels palette.

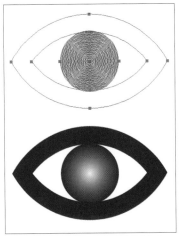

Viewing shape paths (top) and finished objects (bottom). For this filled compound outer object with blended interior object, we began by making a blend. To blend the blue circle with a very small white circle in its center, we selected both circles in the Layers palette, then chose Shapes, Blend and specified 50 steps. To build the compound of the two outer shapes, we Shift-clicked in the Layers palette to target them both and chose Shapes, Make Compound. The Make Compound command cut a hole with the smaller eye shape, allowing only part of the outer fill to be visible.

Detail from Hot Beveled Metal. *Beginning with a text layer, we used a Bevel World dynamic layer to commit the live text to an image layer and to create a 3D effect. Then we layered two more copies of the bevel—we painted on the first copy and we created the glow using the second copy. To learn more about type effects using Bevel World, turn to Chapter 8.*

and choose Shapes, Blend. Make choices in the dialog box and click OK. The *Painter 8 User Guide* contains a complete explanation of the Blend dialog box.

Here's a useful application for Painter's Blend command: If you've imported an image created in Illustrator that has blends but they don't make the transition successfully into Painter, zoom in and count and then delete the interior objects inside the blend using the Shape Selection tool and Delete key. Shift-select the two remaining outside objects in the Layers palette, then choose Shapes, Blend and specify the number of steps to regenerate the blend.

Making a compound. To cut a hole in a shape and reveal the underlying image, make a compound using two shapes: Move a small shape on top of a large one, Shift-select both of them in the Layers palette, and choose Shapes, Make Compound. The top shape will cut a hole in the bottom shape to reveal the underlying image. Compounds are made automatically to create counters in letters when type is set or when type outlines are imported, and also when selections with holes are converted to shapes.

USING DYNAMIC LAYERS

Dynamic layers are special devices that allow you to create a variety of effects. To keep dynamic layers "live" (allowing changes to be made and previewed on the image without becoming permanent), the file can be saved only in RIFF format. Saving in Photoshop format converts the dynamic layers to image layers, freezing the effects in their current state.

Dynamic layers, which are indicated by a plug icon in the Layers palette, fall into three basic categories. The first kind is similar to an adjustment layer in Adobe Photoshop. It allows you to set up a procedure such as a brightness-and-contrast correction or a posterization of the underlying image, without permanently changing the pixels of the image itself. Image correction tools such as Equalize, Brightness and Contrast, and Posterize, as well as special

AUTOMATIC DROP SHADOWS

To apply a drop shadow to a single shape, select the shape in the Layers palette and choose Effects, Objects, Create Drop Shadow. Enter your own specifications, or just click OK to accept Painter's defaults. When the Commit dialog box appears, asking if you'd like to commit the shape to an image layer, click Commit. Selecting a closed group of shapes and choosing Effects, Objects, Create Drop Shadow will apply an automatic drop shadow to each of the individual shapes in the group and will convert the shapes to image layers as well! To convert a group of shapes to a single image layer and make an automatic drop shadow for the new layer, begin by closing the group (click the arrow to the left of the group's name closed). Then select the group's name in the Layers palette, click the Layer Commands button to access the menu, choose Collapse and click Commit All. Then choose, Effects, Objects, Create Drop Shadow, and apply the shadow.

Cool Water Drops. *To add a water droplet effect to this photo (simulating water drops on a camera lens), we used the Liquid Metal dynamic plug-in. First we made a clone of the image (File, Clone). Then we clicked the Dynamic Plugins button on the Layers palette and chose Liquid Metal from the menu. We chose the Clone Source Map type and a high Refraction setting to make the "water" translucent with a blue reflection. Then we clicked and dragged with the Circle tool from the Liquid Metal dialog box to place the drops. A drop can be extended simply by starting to drag with the Circle tool inside the edge of the existing drop.*

effects layers such as Glass Distortion, Kaleidoscope and Liquid Lens fall into this "adjustment" category. To generate a Posterize layer, for example, click the Dynamic Plugins button at the bottom of the Layers palette and choose Posterize from the pop-up menu. Click OK to apply it. The posterization will apply to all image layers, reference layers, shapes and dynamic layers listed below the Posterize dynamic layer in the Layers palette, so if you want it to apply to only certain layers, you can drag it down in the Layers palette. (To read more about Painter's image-correction layers, turn to Chapter 6. For information about creating special effects with this series of dynamic layers, refer to Chapter 7.)

For a second kind of dynamic layer, you choose an image layer and apply a special effect procedure to the selected image layer, the "source image layer," *turning it into* a dynamic layer. The dynamic layer is "live," so you can preview changes and then modify the effect and preview again, or even return the source image layer to its original condition if you choose. Three of the dynamic layers—Bevel World, Burn and Tear—require a source image layer to perform their magic. To make this kind of dynamic layer, activate a layer in the Layers palette (you can select only part of the layer with any selection tool if you like) and choose Bevel World, for instance, from the Dynamic Plugins menu. Make adjustments to the settings and click OK. (If you start with a selection on the image Canvas, clicking Apply will automatically generate a new dynamic layer from the selection.) Read more about these dynamic layers in Chapter 7.

The third type of dynamic layer allows you to build special-effects imagery on a new layer. Liquid Metal falls into this category. To read about exciting techniques using Liquid Metal, turn to Chapter 7, "Exploring Special Effects," and to "Painting with Ice" in Chapter 8.

To change a dynamic layer's appearance, double-click its name in the Layers palette, make changes to the settings in the dialog box and click OK.

To convert a dynamic layer to an image layer, so you can add a layer mask or convert the image layer into a reference layer (to scale it using Free Transform, for instance), click the triangle in the Layers palette's upper-right corner and choose Convert To Default Layer from the menu. The following actions will also convert a dynamic layer to an image layer: transforming using Effects, Orientation (to scale, rotate or skew); applying an effect from the Effects menu (such as Effects, Surface Control, Apply Surface Texture); painting on the layer; applying a dynamic layer special effect (such as applying the Tear special-effect layer to an active Burn layer); or merging a group that includes a dynamic layer.

Clicking the "plug" icon on the Layers palette will reveal the Dynamic Plugins menu.

For this text design, we began by setting small colored text on a layer. Then we made several duplicates by Option-dragging with the Layer Adjuster. We repositioned the text layers using the Layer Adjuster, and set a large black "W" above the other layers. To achieve the inside-out color effect, we set the Composite Method for the large "W" to Reverse Out in the Layers palette.

The Layers palette showing the pop-out menu that includes important commands for use with Liquid Ink and Water Color layers.

Water Color layers and their special brushes were used to paint the illustration Maui North Shore 2.

USING TEXT LAYERS

When you select the Text tool in the Toolbox and begin to set type on your image, the type is set on a new layer that appears in the Layers palette, designated by a "T" icon. Controls for specifying text settings are located in the Property Bar. For in-depth information about using Text layers, turn to Chapter 8, "Working with Type in Painter."

WORKING WITH MEDIA LAYERS

Painter includes two media layers, Water Color and Liquid Ink. Special brushes must be used to paint on each kind of media layer. When the Canvas or an image layer is selected in the Layers palette and you attempt to paint with a Water Color brush or Liquid Ink brush, a new Water Color or Liquid Ink layer is automatically generated. Chapter 3 includes in-depth information about Water Color and Liquid Ink, including "A Painter Water Color Primer" and "A Painter Liquid Ink Primer" as well as step-by-step techniques for using both media.

Using Water Color layers. Painter offers Water Color layers and special Water Color brushes, making it possible to add wet color on separate layers. Water Color layers can be edited using selections to restrict the changes to the selected area. A Water Color layer can also have a layer mask, which can be edited by clicking on the layer mask thumbnail in the Layers palette and targeting the mask in the Channels palette, then editing the mask. (You'll have to choose a different brush to edit the mask, because Water Color brushes don't work on masks.) For a step-by-step technique for using selections with Water Color layers turn to "Masks and Selections for Water Color Layers" on page 199.

Using commands found under the triangle pop-out menu on the right side of the Layers palette, you can stop paint from diffusing on a Water Color layer by choosing Dry Water Color Layer, and you can re-wet a Water Color layer by choosing Wet Entire Water Color Layer. Or you can add the content of the Canvas to an existing Water Color layer as wet paint, or create a new Water Color layer from the Canvas content, also by choosing from this Layers palette menu.

Using Liquid Ink layers. Liquid Ink is a thick, viscous ink medium. A Liquid Ink layer is not pixel-based but resolution-independent. To paint on a Liquid Ink layer, you must use special Liquid Ink brushes found in the Brush Selector Bar. (Choosing a Liquid Ink brush and painting automatically creates a new Liquid Ink layer except when a Water Color layer is active.) A Liquid Ink layer can have a layer mask. To constrain paint to a specific area, make a selection and then target the Liquid Ink layer before painting.

John Derry created Capitola, *a detail of which is shown here, using Liquid Ink layers. Turn to the gallery in Chapter 6 to see the complete illustration.*

For the ultimate in management using the Layers palette, see how Rick Kirkman did it in "Working with Shapes and Layers," on page 196.

In the Layers palette (above), for David Purnell's Molar Cross Section, *he organized some layers in groups and he locked other items so he wouldn't accidentally select them with the Layer Adjuster. Turn to page 213 to see his illustration.*

ORGANIZING WITH THE LAYERS PALETTE

In the Layers palette, Painter assigns sequential names to layers and shapes (such as Layer 1, Layer 2 and so on) in the order they were created. Rename them by double-clicking on a name (or select the name and press the Enter key) to bring up the appropriate dialog box. Enter the name and click OK. So that you can more easily work with underlying items, you can hide layers or shapes by clicking to close the eye icons next to their names. Click the eye open to show an item again.

To lock an item (making it impossible to select it in the image window, even with Auto Select Layer turned on), target the layer in the Layers palette and click the lock icon near the top of the palette. To unlock, click the lock icon again.

Using groups. Grouping layers or shapes is an ideal way to organize related elements in the Layers palette so the palette doesn't take up so much space on the screen. To group layers or shapes, Shift-select the elements in the Layers palette, then click the Layer Commands button at the bottom of the Layers palette and choose Group, or press Ctrl/⌘-G. To ungroup, click the Layer Commands button and choose Ungroup, or press Ctrl/⌘-U. If you want to apply effects (other than Scale, Rotate, Flip or Create Drop Shadow) to a group of layers or shapes, you'll need to open the group, select individual items, then apply the effect. Like individual layers, groups can be hidden or made visible by clicking the eye icon, and they can also be locked.

Using the Image Portfolio. Open the Image Portfolio palette by choosing Window, Show Image Portfolio. To store a copy of an element for later use or for use in another file, hold down the Alt/Option key and use the Layer Adjuster tool to drag it from the image window into the Image Portfolio palette.

PRESERVE TRANSPARENCY

By turning on the Preserve Transparency checkbox in the Layers palette, you can confine your painting and editing to those areas of an image layer that already contain pixels. Turn Preserve Transparency off if you'd like to paint or edit outside the existing pixels—for instance, to feather the edge by applying the Effects, Focus, Soften command, which would spread pixels outside of the original area. Preserve Transparency is not available for Liquid Ink or Water Color layers.

AUTO-SELECTING A LAYER

By choosing the Layer Adjuster tool and turning on Auto Select Layer in the Property Bar, you can click on the visible portion of any layer to select the layer and drag to move its contents.

READY TO COLLAPSE

If you've finished making changes to a group of layers but you still want to keep the group separate from the Canvas, consider clicking the Layer Commands button at the bottom of the Layers palette and choosing Collapse. This feature merges a selected group of default layers into a single default layer and can be a real memory-saver.

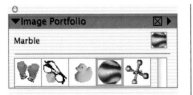

Create an empty image portfolio by opening the Image Portfolio palette (Window, Show Image Portfolio) and choosing Image Mover from the pull-down menu, opened by clicking the triangle on the right side of the Image Portfolio palette bar. In the Image Mover, click the New button to create an empty portfolio, name it, then save it into the Painter application folder. Drag items from the current Image Portfolio into your new Image Portfolio. (To learn more about using Painter's movers and libraries, turn to Chapter 1.)

(To remove the element from the current file as you store it in the Portfolio, use the Layer Adjuster without the Alt/Option key.)

LAYERS AND THEIR MASKS

Layer masks allow for transparent effects. You can edit layer masks using either brushes or special effect commands (such as Effects, Surface Control, Express Texture, with which you can apply a texture to a mask). To view a layer mask, target the layer in the Layers palette, then target the Layer Mask in the Channels palette. For more information, see the "Dropping and Saving a Layer Visibility Mask" tip on this page.

Importing a source file with an alpha channel. Because it's faster to work with fewer layers, many artists assemble pieces of an artwork in source files, then import the pieces into a final composite file. Consider preparing a mask in a smaller source file that you plan to import into a composite (using File, Place) and storing the mask in the Channels palette. When you import the file, in the Place dialog box, check the Retain Alpha checkbox, and click OK to place the source as a reference layer in your document. The imported layer will include the transparency created by the alpha channel mask. To turn the reference layer into an image layer, select it in the Layers palette and choose Effects, Orientation, Commit Transform. (For more information, see "Using Reference Layers" on page 182.)

COMPOSITE CONTROLS

Painter's composite controls can give you nifty special effects with very little effort. With a layer selected in the Layers palette, choose from the Composite Method pull-down menu on the Layers palette. The list includes many of the same blending modes found in Adobe Photoshop, which are listed below the

A VERSATILE MASK EXCHANGE

If you'd like to use a layer mask to make a selection on another layer or on the background Canvas to constrain paint or effects there, here's a way to trade masks back and forth: To copy a layer mask so it becomes a separate mask in the Channels palette, target the layer in the Layers palette, then in the Channels, target the layer mask. Choose Duplicate from the Channels palette's pull-down menu. In the Duplicate Channel dialog box, choose "New" to create a new mask based on the layer mask, and click OK. Now you can activate any layer in the Layers palette and use Select, Load Selection to use the new mask on that layer.

DROPPING AND SAVING A LAYER VISIBILITY MASK

To merge the visible part of an image layer so it becomes part of the image Canvas but at the same time preserve its transparency mask, choose "Drop and Select" from the Layers palette's pull-down menu. A selection will be made from the transparency mask, and you can save it as a mask in the Channels palette by choosing Select, Save Selection.

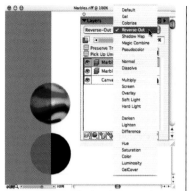

We applied two of Painter's Composite Methods to these marbles floating over a blue-and-white background. The top marble uses Gel and the bottom one uses Reverse-Out.

ones that are unique to Painter. (Not included are Photoshop's Color Dodge, Linear Dodge, Color Burn, Linear Burn, Exclusion, Vivid Light, Linear Light and Pin Light.) "A Visual Display of the Composite Methods" below shows these controls in action.

You'll find Painter's *Composite Depth* pull-down menu near the top of the Layers palette, to the right of the Composite Method menu. Painter's Composite Depth controls work only on impasto paint (see "Painting with Realistic Impasto" on page 53 and "Working with Thick Paint" on page 114 for more information about Impasto). The default Composite Depth method is *Add*. If you paint with an Impasto brush on a layer, *Add* raises the thick paint. *Ignore* turns off the thickness for the paint on the layer, and *Subtract* inverts the paint thickness on the layer, making brushstrokes on this layer excavated rather than raised on the surface. *Replace* changes the paint depth of Impasto on the underlying layer to the applied layer's depth wherever the layers overlap. 🖌

A VISUAL DISPLAY OF THE COMPOSITE METHODS

Painter's Composite Methods (from a menu at the top of the Layers palette) change how a layer interacts with the image underneath. Here a leaf floats over a two-part background. The Default and Normal methods give the same results, as do Shadow Map and Multiply. For complete descriptions of what the modes are doing, refer to Painter's *User Guide,* and *The Photoshop 7 Wow! Book* or Adobe Photoshop's *User Guide.*

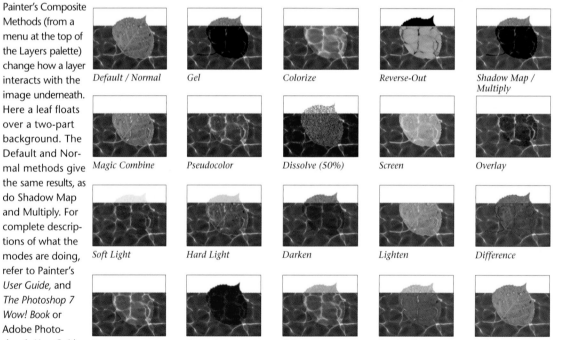

Default / Normal — Gel — Colorize — Reverse-Out — Shadow Map / Multiply

Magic Combine — Pseudocolor — Dissolve (50%) — Screen — Overlay

Soft Light — Hard Light — Darken — Lighten — Difference

Hue — Saturation — Color — Luminosity — Gel Cover

Painting on Layers

Overview *Make practice sketches; set up a reference layer and build a canvas "ground;" sculpt the forms of the head on a layer using tone and color; add transitional tone and detail; apply a canvas texture to the painted layer.*

RON KEMPKE

1

One of the "practice" digital charcoal sketches

2a

The Layers palette with the reference layer active and at a lower opacity

2b

The reference layer at low opacity (left), and the sketch on "canvas" made with the Captured Bristle variant of Acrylics (right)

YOU CAN USE PAINTER'S LAYERS, BRUSHES AND TEXTURES to create a realistic simulation of oil or acrylic paint. Ron Kempke painted *Portrait of Cindy* by painting on layers on top of a canvas "ground."

1 Assembling references and making practice sketches.
Kempke clamped a reference photo to his monitor, so he could easily refer to it when he needed to. He prefers not to clone or to do too much tracing because drawing by hand using the stylus keeps his brushstrokes freer and more expressive. Carefully studying his reference photo, Kempke drew several charcoal sketches in Painter just as a "warm up," working until he had achieved a good likeness of his subject.

2 Setting up layers and a canvas "ground." Kempke began his painting much as a portrait painter might do. But instead of projecting his painting onto a working canvas, he used a 1200 x 1400-pixel scanned photo at reduced opacity in Painter. To set up your on-screen reference, open your scanned image and open the Layers palette (Window, Show Layers). To reduce the opacity of the photo, choose Select, All, then Select, Float. This lifts the image to an image layer, leaving a white canvas underneath. By moving the Opacity slider near the top of the Layers palette, you can fade the reference photo.

Next, Kempke used the Raw Silk texture to add the look of canvas before he started to paint. To build a canvas "ground," target the Canvas in the Layers palette. Apply the Raw Silk paper texture

3a

The shadow shapes are blocked in over the sketch.

3b

The shadow and midtone shapes are more developed in this example.

4

The image with most of the transitional tones and details added

to the image as follows: Open the Paper Selector by clicking the top left square in the group of six at the bottom of the Toolbox. Then find the Raw Silk texture in Painter 7 Textures (loaded from the Painter 8 CD 2 CD-ROM). Choose Effects, Surface Control, Apply Surface Texture, Using Paper. For a subtle canvas effect, reduce the Amount to approximately 20% and Shine to about 10% and leave the other settings at their defaults (Softness, 0; Picture, 100%; Reflection, 0; and Light Direction, 11:00).

Kempke created his painting on a layer above the reference so he could rework certain areas without disturbing the reference. (To add a new layer, click the New Layer button at the bottom of the Layers palette.) He planned to apply surface texture to the brushwork on the layer when he finished it, using the settings above to match the texture on the Canvas. When the painting was finished, the final texture application would perfectly match the existing texture on the image canvas.

Kempke chose a neutral gray in the Color picker and sketched using a modified version of the Captured Bristle variant of Acrylics. He mapped out the proportions of the head with perpendicular lines to locate the eyes, nose, and mouth. He occasionally compared the proportions of his drawing with the reference photo on the layer below, toggling the visibility of the reference layer on and off as he worked by clicking the "eye" icon to the left of the layer name. After he was satisfied with the proportions, he deleted the reference layer by targeting it in the Layers palette and clicking the Delete button. (The photo clamped to his monitor was still available for reference if he needed it.)

3 Adding color and shadow. Kempke sculpted the solid form of the head with simplified shapes of the shadow colors using the Captured Bristle variant. He painted midtones, then blocked in shadow colors in flat tones for the larger masses.

Next, he added transitional tones in the areas between light and shadow. He painted these in flat tones, also, resisting the temptation to blend them with the shadow colors. These transitional tones are among the most intense colors in the portrait.

4 Refining the portrait and adding texture. Kempke added the highlight areas in the face and hair, using broad strokes of color to loosely indicate the features. To bring the head forward by suggesting the space behind it, he added a medium-dark background. Then he added depth and sheen to the hair and loosely suggested the teeth. In areas where he felt there was too much contrast, he added transitional tones and softened edges using a low-opacity brush. (Move the Opacity slider, popped out from the Property Bar, to the left to reduce opacity.) Kempke also added brighter highlights to the eyes and nose. To complete the painting, he added "canvas" to the painted layer using the Apply Surface Texture process described in Step 2.

Illustrating with Layers

Overview *Create sketches using pencil and paper and scan them; combine them into an image with each sketch on its own layer; paint on each layer and on the Canvas; create masks; scan a final pen-and-ink drawing and paste it into the image as its own layer; tint the drawing; add a lighting effect.*

CAROL BENIOFF

1a

The final transformed and layered sketch

1b

The final ink drawing of the dog is targeted and on the top layer in the Layers palette.

PAINTING ON LAYERS BRINGS YOU GREATER CONTROL and flexibility, but to be wildly successful at it, you'll need to change your thinking and painting processes. Painting on layers is like painting one part of your image on one sheet of clear glass, then picking up another sheet of glass and painting another part of your image. It's as if you could cut apart each sheet of glass, put it back together into a new composition, then scale, rotate or skew all of a sheet or just parts of it. And once you've painted and arranged all of your sheets of glass, you can control how their colors and textures mix with each other. For *Homeodog,* Carol Benioff used layers to control how different elements mixed with one another. Benioff created the illustration for the Summer 2003 issue of the ASPCA magazine *Animal Watch.*

1 Working in bits and pieces. Benioff started with a pencil sketch on paper of the dog. Then she used pencils to draw ginkgo leaves, larch needles and a cone flower on three sheets of vellum. She scanned each piece separately, and combined and assembled them into one file in Adobe Photoshop. Opening the final sketch file in Painter, she set the composite method for the four layers to Multiply, which makes all the whites in the image transparent. The dog sketch was the top layer, replaced later with a final ink drawing. The bottom layer was the canvas, which she painted later in the process.

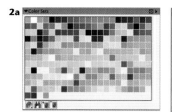

The custom Color Set used for the image

Painting over the pencil sketch with a Wet Acrylic variant on the cone flower layer

The larch needle layer (left), and the gingko leaves layer (right) painted with two variants of the Acrylics

Creating a mask by selecting and masking the white background first. The Background Mask eye icon is open in the Channels palette, and the mask appears as a red overlay.

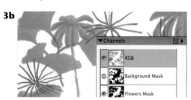

The inverted channel, which will mask out the flowers from the background. The Flowers Mask eye icon is open in the Channels palette and the mask appears as a red overlay.

2 Painting on the layers. Benioff loaded a custom color set: She opened the Color Sets Palette (Window, show Color Set), clicked on the right triangle to access the menu and chose Open Color Set; then navigated to the folder that contained the custom Color Set. Next, she chose Acrylics in the Brush Selector Bar. On the three layers with leaves and flowers, she painted directly into the pencil sketch, letting some of the pencil lines show through. She selected the Wet Acrylic 10 variant to paint the center of the Cone flower, adding yellow and orange colors using short overlapping strokes. Then she painted long, fluid brushstrokes for the petals, using both the Dry Brush 10 and an Opaque Detail Brush in deep pink colors. She blended some of the strokes in the flower and stalk, using the Wet Detail Brush 5 variant. Next she painted around all the edges with white using the Dry Brush 10 variant to give the edges a more painterly look. Benioff used both the Wet Detail Brush 5 and a Wet Acrylic variant to paint the layer with the larch needles. She used the Dry Brush 10 and white color again to add more painterly strokes on the needles, then repeated this process for the ginkgo leaves layer. She changed the size of the brushes as she worked using the Size slider in the Property Bar. Finally, she set the Composite Method for each layer to Multiply in the Layers palette so the colors on the layers would mix with and darken one another and so the whites in the image would appear to be transparent.

3 Masking the flowers and leaves. Next, she planned to paint the background on the Canvas. Benioff did not want the color in the background to mix with the top three layers that contained the flowers and leaves. To keep the elements separate, she created a mask that would prevent her from painting under any of the flowers and leaves. She built a mask for each layer, then combined them into one mask as follows: She chose the Magic Wand in the Toolbox, and in the Property Bar she set Tolerance at 36 and disabled the Contiguous option. Starting with the cone flower layer, Benioff selected the background and then chose Select, Save Selection, naming it Background Mask. She repeated this process for the larch needles layer. When she saved this selection, in the Save Selection dialogue, she chose Save To Background Mask; for the Operation option she selected Add To

Adding to the Background Mask

Mask. She repeated this for the ginkgo leaves. Then she loaded the Background Mask as a selection, and chose Select, Invert, which then selected the flowers and leaves. She saved this selection as a new selection which she named Flower Mask. With the Flower Mask active and

4

Painting the background with the Flower Mask selection active

5

All the layers dropped onto the completed background Canvas

6a

The in-progress illustration with the Canvas, the tint layer and the ink drawing

6b

The colored tint for the dog shown with the Canvas but with the visibility turned off for the ink drawing layer

7

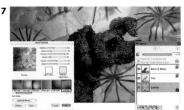

Applying the Soft Globe custom light to the Canvas only

the RGB mask visible in the Channels palette, Benioff selected the Dry Brush 10 and used white paint to fine-tune the mask and black paint to add to the mask.

4 Painting the background. For her canvas texture, Benioff clicked the Paper Selector in the Toolbox and chose Thick Hand-made Paper. Next, she loaded the Flower Mask (Select, Load Selection) and chose Hide Marquee from the Select menu (Ctrl/⌘-Shift-H). To paint the sky, she chose Digital Water Color in the Brush Selector Bar and picked the Soft Diffused Brush variant, set at 30% Opacity in the Property Bar. She added more variation to the colors and transitions using the Soft Diffused Brush variant. She was able to paint broad swaths of color, letting them blend and bleed into each other without visually mixing with the color in the top three layers.

5 Merging the layers. Next, Benioff deleted the pencil sketch of the dog, which was on the top layer. Then she dropped all the remaining layers onto the Canvas by clicking the right triangle on the Layers palette bar and selecting Drop All. She chose the Blenders in the Brush Selector Bar and the Soft Blender Stump 10 variant. She alternated between the 10 and 20 variants, as she softened the edges where all the layers met. To soften some of the edges, she chose the Diffuse Water variant of Digital Water Color and continued to blend and move color along the edges.

6 Coloring the ink drawing. Benioff scanned the completed conventional ink drawing at 266 pixels per inch. She opened the image in Painter, selected the entire image (Select, All or Ctrl-⌘-A), and used the Layer Adjuster tool to drag the image to the top layer of the color file. She set the Composite Method for the dog layer to Multiply in the Layers palette. Benioff then created a new layer under the Dog layer and above the color Canvas by clicking the New Layer button at the bottom of the Layers palette and dragging the new layer into position in the Layers palette. She chose Tinting in the Brush Selector Bar, and the Basic Round variant, and she colored the pen-and-ink drawing by painting with very light colors on the new layer. She left the Tint Layer's Composite Method set to Default, and set the Opacity to 65%.

7 Finalizing the image. To add more atmosphere, she applied a custom lighting effect to the right side of the image. With the Canvas targeted in the Layers palette, Benioff chose Effects, Surface Control, Apply Lighting. She loaded her own library of saved lighting effects, choosing a light called Soft Globe. Then she saved the file and another copy of the image in PSD format to prepare for press.

Working with Shapes and Layers

Overview Draw Bézier shapes in Painter; fill and name the shapes; convert the shapes to layers; paint details on the layers with brushes; add and edit layer masks to achieve transparency; apply textured special effects with Color Overlay, Surface Texture and Glass Distortion.

RICK KIRKMAN

Kirkman's scanned pencil sketch

Setting the Shapes preferences

SHAPES BRING POWER AND VERSATILITY to Painter, saving many illustrators a trip to a drawing program to create Bézier paths for import. With Painter's Pen tool (now similar to Illustrator's) you can completely create and edit Bézier paths, add a stroke and fill, name them, and organize them in the Layers palette. After you draw shapes, you can convert them to layers and add paint and special effects. Rick Kirkman created the illustration above—one in a series of editorial illustrations for *Professional Speaker* magazine—entirely within Painter.

1 Setting up a template. Kirkman began by scanning a pencil sketch, saving it as a TIFF file and opening the scan in Painter. The file measured 2374 x 3184 pixels.

2 Creating shapes. To create your outlines, you can work either in Painter or in a PostScript drawing program. If you plan to trace a template—as Kirkman did—set up shape attributes so that you can draw with a precise skeletal line. For Windows or Mac System 9.2.2, choose Edit, Preferences, Shapes, or for Mac OS X choose Corel Painter 8, Preferences, Shapes, and choose these settings: Under "On Draw," uncheck the Fill and Stroke checkboxes; under "On Close," uncheck the Stroke checkbox and check the Fill checkbox. Using the Pen tool to draw Bézier shape paths,

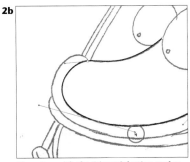

2b

Dragging with the Direct Selection tool to adjust a control handle on a path

3a

Preparing to fill the selected "nose" shape with a flesh color

3b

Applying the flat color fills

4

Painting the shadow on the fish's body using the Digital Airbrush variant

5

The layer mask for the "R piling" layer is targeted in the Layers palette. The heavy black border around the thumbnail shows that the mask, not the image, is targeted.

Kirkman carefully traced his sketch. To make adjustments on the fly while drawing a path with the Pen tool (like adjusting a control handle or anchor point), press the Ctrl/⌘ key to temporarily switch to the Shape Selection tool.

3 Coloring, naming and converting. Before he started drawing each shape, Kirkman clicked the Fill swatch in the Property Bar and chose a color close to the color he would finally use, so the shape would fill with the color when he completed the path. As soon as he had created each shape, he double-clicked its default name in the Layers palette and renamed it. As he worked, he adjusted the opacity of the shapes (using the Opacity slider near the top of the palette), so he could see the layers below more clearly. After he had filled the shapes with color, Kirkman Shift-selected them in the Layers palette and chose Shapes, Convert To Layer.

4 Shading individual layers. To paint on an individual layer, target it in the Layers palette. To create a nice grainy look (similar to colored pencil on kid-finish illustration board), Kirkman chose Basic Paper texture in the Paper Selector and added shading to the clothing using the Fine Spray variant of the Airbrushes. For a smoother look on the man's skin and eyes, he added strokes with the Digital Airbrush variant. Overlapping elements on the layers helped Kirkman create the cast shadows. For example, to paint the shadow under the fish's lips, he targeted the underlying body layer and then airbrushed the shadow directly on it.

5 Editing layer masks. Kirkman added and edited a layer mask on the layer he called "R piling" to achieve a transparent look. To achieve transparency—like Kirkman's—on your layer: Target the layer in the Layers palette, then click the Create Layer Mask button at the bottom of the palette. Click on the new layer mask's thumbnail to target the mask. Next choose black in the Colors palette, choose a soft Airbrush variant (such as the Digital Airbrush) and carefully paint into the mask to partially hide the layer. (See "Melting Text Into Water" on page 201 for a more detailed description of this technique.)

6 Adding details, texture and an irregular edge. Kirkman added the pattern to the tie using Effects, Surface Control, Color Overlay, Using Paper to apply the Op texture (from Crazy Textures,

NAMING AND FILLING SHAPES

To name and add a colored fill (or stroke) to a shape, with the Color picker open (Window, Show Colors) double-click on the shape's name in the Layers palette. Rename the shape in the Set Shape Attributes dialog box and check the Fill (or Stroke) checkbox. With the Fill (or Stroke) color swatch active (outlined by a black and gold box), click in the Color picker. (You can use the Color Sets palette instead of the Color picker if you like.)

PRESERVING TRANSPARENCY

To constrain your painting to stay within the edge of the element on a layer, turn on Preserve Transparency in the Layers palette.

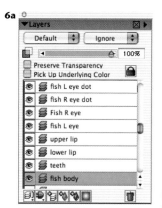

6a

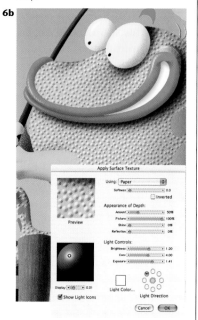

Kirkman targeted the "fish body" layer in the Layers palette before choosing Apply Surface Texture to add texture to the fish's body.

6b

Using Apply Surface Texture to add the 3D texture to the fish

6c

Adding dimension to the fish's teeth by airbrushing along a selection edge

in the Paper Textures folder on the Painter 8 CD 2 CD-ROM). To add details to the water, he used Color Overlay to apply a colored texture using Globes from More Wild Textures (Painter 8 CD 2 CD-ROM), scaling it larger using the Scale slider on the Papers palette. To add more interest to the water, he added Effects, Focus, Glass Distortion, Using Paper with the Blobular texture from Molecular Textures (Painter 8 CD 2 CD-ROM).

Using Effects, Surface Control, Apply Surface Texture, Using Paper, he added a 3D texture to the fish with Random Bubbles (Molecular Textures). He used these approximate settings: Softness, 1.0; Amount, 50%; Shine, 0; leaving other settings at their default values.

The final embellishments he added were the man's mouth, the fish's teeth and the separation of the man's pant legs. To paint these details, Kirkman drew on his many years of experience as a traditional airbrush artist using a technique very similar to traditional airbrush friskets. Using the Pen tool, he drew a shape for each element and converted each shape to a selection by choosing Shapes, Convert To Selection. To save each selection as a mask in the Channels palette after he had converted it, he chose Select, Save Selection. When he wanted to use a selection as a frisket, he chose Select, Load Selection and then chose the appropriate mask from the Load From pop-up menu. When loaded, each active selection acted like a traditional airbrush frisket. For instance, to paint the fish's teeth, he selected the layer containing the teeth, loaded a selection and then airbrushed along the edges of the selection, letting the selection create the hard edge where he needed it. He let the spray from the Airbrush fade out across the selected area. This technique added more dimension and created a rounded, cushiony effect.

Finally, Kirkman created an irregular edge for the background. He used the Lasso to make a loose, freehand selection on the background canvas and turned the selected area into a layer. (Drag with the Lasso and click with the Layer Adjuster). After the area was on its own layer, he reselected the canvas (click on the Canvas name in the Layers palette) and deleted the unneeded background (Ctrl/⌘-A, then Delete), leaving a white border area. Then he clicked on the layer and dragged it to the bottom of the layer hierarchy to serve as a background element, and he renamed it Sky. To give the sky layer a smooth edge, he added a layer mask (using the process described in Step 5) and feathered the mask 3 pixels by targeting the layer in the Layers palette, then targeting the layer mask in the Channels palette, and choosing Feather from the palette's pull-down menu (accessed by clicking the triangle in the top right corner of the Channels palette). After he had feathered the edge, he added a drop shadow based on the Sky layer by choosing Effects, Objects, Create Drop Shadow. To flatten the image, he dropped all layers (choose Drop All from the Layers palette's pull-down menu).

Masks and Selections for Water Color Layers

Overview *Create a pencil sketch; brush in wet-into-wet washes using light colors; add transparent glazes on a new layer; make masks to constrain paint; add final details.*

CHER THREINEN-PENDARVIS / © 2001 COREL CORPORATION

The pencil sketch drawn using the Flattened Pencil variant of Pencils

The Layers palette showing an active Water Color layer and the sketch layer

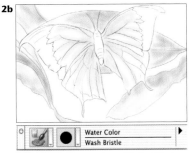

Painting the first washes with the Wash Bristle variant of Water Color

PAINTER'S WATER COLOR MEDIA LAYERS make the medium wonderfully versatile. For *Fairy Tale Butterfly*, we used wet-into-wet techniques, then we painted glazes and details on separate layers. We used masks and selections to limit the paint.

1 Sketching with pencil. With your pressure-sensitive tablet and stylus at the ready, create a new file with a white background, by choosing File, New. In the New dialog box, we set the Width and Height at 1000 x 650 pixels and clicked OK. Before beginning your sketch, click the Paper Selector in the Toolbox and choose a natural-looking grain—for instance, French Watercolor Paper. Choose a neutral gray in the Color picker, select the Flattened Pencil variant of Pencils from the Brush Selector Bar and begin drawing your sketch.

2 Painting the first washes. When the sketch is finished, choose a very light color in the Color picker and choose the Wash Bristle variant of Water Color. With a Water Color brush chosen, as soon as you touch the stylus to your tablet, a Water Color layer will appear in the Layers palette. Block in large areas of color. When you use a light pressure on your stylus, the Wash Bristle will let you paint smooth, even washes with soft edges.

3 Adding deeper color on a new layer. Using several layers can give you better control over separate brush work. (You may have to sacrifice some of the overall wet-into-wet effect.) Add a new Water Color layer by clicking the New Watercolor Layer button at the bottom of the Layers palette. Begin this stage of your painting with medium-value colors, then gradually add darker tones to suggest volume. Keep your light source in mind as you paint. Resize the brush, or change its opacity as needed using the sliders on the Property Bar. At this stage of the painting, we added deeper purples to the wing edges, and gave the veins in the wings more definition. We also added more layers for individual colors.

4 Making masks. To protect the shapes of the butterfly and foreground leaves from the background paint, we made masks, a

3

Layering richly colored washes (left) and defining the wings with deeper color (right)

4

Channels
- RGB
- butterfly
- background
- leaves

The butterfly image with background mask view turned on, showing the butterfly and leaves isolated from the background

5

Painting the background using a selection border to constrain the washes.

6a

Layers

Gel | Ignore

100%

Preserve Transparency
Pick Up Underlying Color

- details
- yellow glazes
- purples
- reds
- light washes
- leaves
- background washes
- sketch

The Layers palette, showing the "Details" layer active

process that serves the same purpose as painting resists in conventional watercolor. To create a mask, you can make a freehand selection using a selection tool such as the Lasso and save it as a mask in the Channels palette by choosing Select, Save Selection. Or you can paint a mask as we did: Target the Canvas in the Layers palette and click the New Mask button at the bottom of the Channels palette. A new black-filled mask will be added to the Channels palette, and a red "film" will appear over your painting. Use the Scratchboard Tool variant of Pens and white to paint, revealing the element (butterfly and leaves, for instance) that you will want to protect when you paint the background in Step 5.

5 Turning the mask to selections and painting the background. Add a new Water Color layer as described in Step 3, this one for the background. Load the mask as a selection, by choosing Select, Load Selection and choosing your new mask in the Load From menu. Now invert the mask (Select, Invert), so that the background is selected and the subject is protected. Lay in the predominant colors using the Wash Bristle. To "bleed" more color variations and value into the shadowed areas, choose the Runny Wash Camel and make short dabbing strokes. To paint with more noticeable wet edges, try the Runny Wet Camel. We painted deeper blue and green colors on the background using the Runny Wash Camel variant.

6 Adding details. Add a new Water Color layer as described in Step 3 for your detail work. Paint crisper edges for areas that need definition using a small Fine Camel brush (approximately 4–5 pixels). If the Fine Camel seems too saturated for your taste, lower its Opacity to about 20%, using the slider in the Property Bar. For more subtle edge effects, experiment with the Soft Camel and the Diffuse Camel variants, using a small size (about 6–8 pixels). Make expressive strokes, varying the pressure on the stylus. To complete the study, we used the Fine Camel variant to add calligraphic details on the butterfly's body and wings. To deepen color and break up some edges, we added a few more wet-edged washes using the Runny Wash Bristle and Runny Wet variants. When the painting is complete, choose Drop All from the Layers palette's pop-out menu.

RUNNING OUTSIDE

If the Wind Force is set high in the Water section of the Stroke Design panel (Brush Creator; Ctrl/⌘-B), a very runny wash (painted with the Runny Wash Bristle, for instance) may creep outside a selection.

6b

The details on the body and wings are nearly complete.

Melting Text into Water

Overview *Use the Text tool to set type over a background; convert the text to selections; float two copies of the type, one to be used as a drop shadow; use feathering, Dye Concentration and a fill to add dimension to the type; add layer masks and paint on them to "melt" the bottoms of the layers.*

1

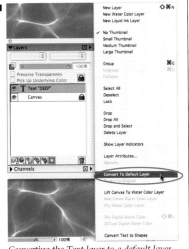

Converting the Text layer to a default layer

2a

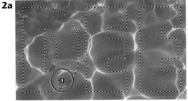

Alt/Option-clicking with the Layer Adjuster on the selection to make a layer

2b

The Layers palette after naming the layers

YOU CAN ACHIEVE A DRAMATIC TRANSLUCENT EFFECT using Painter's brushes to paint on a layer mask of a layer. In the image above, we used the Digital Airbrush variant (Airbrushes) on the lower part of two layers—the type and the feathered shadow behind it—to create the illusion of type melting into water. You can get a similar result using other backgrounds such as clouds, stone or wood.

1 Setting text and converting it to selections. Open an image to use as a background; our photo was 3 inches wide at 225 pixels per inch. Choose the Text tool and select a font and point size in the Property Bar. Procedures such as feathering can erode a thin font, so we chose a font with thick strokes—90-point Futura Extra Bold Condensed. Open the Layers palette (Window, Show Layers). With the Layers palette open, you'll be able to see the text layer appear there when you type. Click the Text tool in the image to place the cursor and begin typing.

To achieve the result in the above image, using the text outlines to float portions of the background, it's necessary to convert the text to a default layer, then to selections. With the Layer Adjuster tool chosen and the text layer targeted in the Layers palette, choose Convert To Default Layer from the pop-out menu on the right side of the Layers palette. Next, reduce the layer's opacity to 0% using the Opacity slider near the top of the Layers palette; the converted text layer will disappear from your image. Choose Drop and Select from the pop-out menu on the right side of the Layers palette; the type will reappear in your image as animated marquees.

To save your selection as a mask so you can use it later, choose Select, Save Selection. Open the Channels palette to see the new mask (named Alpha 1).

With the marquee still active, (in preparation for making the soft shadow layer) choose Select, Feather; we used 15 pixels. Click OK. Now save this selection as a mask by choosing Select, Save Selection. This mask (named Alpha 2) will appear in the Channels palette.

2 Using selections to make layers. To make the two layers needed for this technique, begin with the active feathered shadow

3a

Selecting the text layer mask in the Channels palette

3b

Using Dye Concentration to lighten the text (left) and filling the Shadow layer with a dark blue (right)

3d

The Layers palette showing the Composite Method for the shadow layer set to Multiply

4

Skewing the shadow to add a look of depth

5a

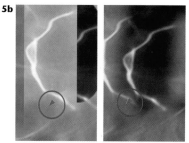

The text layer mask is selected in the Layers palette.

5b

Using the Digital Airbrush variant on the text layer's mask (left) and the shadow layer's mask (with the text layer hidden) to reveal the underlying image

selection (if it's no longer active, you can load Alpha 2 by clicking the Load Channel as Selection button at the bottom of the Channels palette). Choose the Layer Adjuster tool, press the Alt/Option key and click on the active text selection to create Layer 1. (Holding the Alt/Option key makes a copy of the selected area, leaving the background intact.) Click on the Canvas name to deselect Layer 1. Now load the text selection (New Mask 1) by choosing Select, Load Selection; when it appears, Alt/Option-click on it with the Layer Adjuster tool. In the Layers palette, you'll see two items named Layer, followed by a number. Double-click on the Layer 2 name and rename it "text" in the Layer Attributes dialog box. Do the same for the Layer 1, naming it "shadow."

3 Distinguishing the layers. Next, you'll make the text layer stand out from the background. In the Layers palette, click once on the text layer to make it active. Now, change the color of the layer by choosing Effects, Surface Control, Dye Concentration, using Uniform Color and dragging the Maximum slider to 53%. Click OK.

To create a soft, saturated shadow, select the shadow layer in the Layers palette and enable Preserve Transparency (near the top of the palette). Using the Dropper tool, sample a dark color from your image and choose Effects, Fill, Current Color at 100% Opacity. Set the Composite Method of the layer to Multiply in the Layers palette.

4 Offsetting the shadow. Give a greater illusion of depth to the type by nudging the shadow up and to the right using the arrow keys on your keyboard. To make the type appear to stand at an angle to the background, as we did, skew the shadow: With the shadow layer selected, choose Effects, Orientation, Distort. Drag the top center handle of the bounding box down and to the right, check the Better box and click OK. There's no preview of this effect, so it may take a few tries to get the look you want.

5 Painting into the layer masks. To "melt" the lower portions of the letters into the water, you can add layer masks to both text and shadow layers and use a brush to partially erase the layer masks. To add each layer mask, target the layer in the Layers palette and click the Create Layer Mask button at the bottom of the palette.

Choose the Digital Airbrush variant of the Airbrushes. For more sensitivity, check to make sure the Opacity in the Property Bar is set to 9%. Choose black in the Colors palette. Now click the text layer's mask in the Layers palette to target the mask. Brush along the bottom of the letters to make the lower part of the text layer disappear. If you need to restore part of the text, switch to white paint. Then complete the effect by targeting the shadow layer's mask in the Layers palette and brushing black along its bottom. You may find it easier to work on the shadow layer if you hide the text layer temporarily: In the Layers palette, click the text layer's eye icon to close it. When you're finished working on the shadow, click the text's eye icon open again. 🐾

■ "My goal from the outset was to create these works as a gift of consolation and of healing," says **Stephen Crooks**, a New York-based freelance illustrator and designer, speaking of the series of paintings he created in memory of the tragic events of September 11, 2001. All three works depict the same view of New York City, envisioned at different times in the morning as two human figures emerge to replace the stricken buildings.

5:00 AM, (top), captures Manhattan in the predawn hours, and symbolizes the mysterious spirit Crook finds inherent in the people who dwell there.

7:00 AM, (middle), captures the time of day when fragmented sunlight first spills over the city and symbolizes the diversity of New York.

In *10:00 AM*, (bottom), the sun rises high over New York, bathing the skyline in a heavenly glow that symbolizes the spirit of the people of New York, undiminished by tragedy.

Crooks created the basis for the rows of buildings, the figures and water in separate source files. Then he imported the elements into a final layout file as separate layers, so they could be repositioned until he was satisfied with the composition.

With each painting, he began with the sky to establish the light source and color theme. Then he worked from background to foreground on each layer of buildings, using a favorite painting technique of diffusing and toning down the color of each receding layer. This method helped to enhance the illusion of atmosphere. To add to the atmospheric perspective, Crooks also decreased the saturation of the colors of the distant buildings using Effects, Tonal Control, Adjust Colors.

In all three paintings, Crooks combined loose brush work with hard-edged areas using Brushes variants from the Painter 5 Brushes library. (To load the Painter 5 Brushes library, load the Corel Painter 8 CD 2 CD-ROM, open the Brushes folder and copy the Painter 5 Brushes library into the Brushes folder within your Corel Painter 8 application folder. Choose Load Library from the triangle pop-up menu on the Brush Selector Bar, navigate to the Painter 8 application folder and choose Painter 5 Brushes.) He blocked in large areas of color using the Loaded Oils, Coarse Hairs and Big Wet Ink variants of Brushes. Then, to move color around, he used the Brushy variant of Brushes (also from the Painter 5 Brushes library).

■ **Louis Ocepek** is a professor in the Department of Art at New Mexico State University. He created *Summer Reading,* a cover for *Puerto del Sol,* the semiannual international literary journal published by the English Department at New Mexico State University. Ocepek wanted *Summer Reading* to express the perpetual dream many readers have of catching up on their reading on a perfect summer day, sitting in the shade of a big tree.

To heighten the feeling of heat, he used very warm colors in the image. To add to the magical atmosphere, he made the tree very large. He camouflaged many abstract forms in the tree to represent the imaginary worlds of the reader and writer. And he separated the chair from the tree to reinforce the idea of a lone reader, reading peacefully.

After drawing the tree, Ocepek added interest with details from photos of trees he had shot and scanned. He opened the scans and selected, copied and pasted portions of them into his working file, where he positioned them. Then he grouped the layered pieces with the tree drawing layer by Shift-selecting them in the Layers palette, clicking the Layer Commands button and choosing Group from the pop-up menu. Then he merged the grouped layers into a single tree layer by clicking the Layer Commands button and choosing Collapse.

When the tree was almost complete, Ocepek built the chair. He began the chair by drawing shapes with the Pen tool. Then, to convert all of the shapes into a single layer, he Shift-selected them in the Layers palette, grouped them and chose Shapes, Convert to Layer. After turning on Preserve Transparency in the Layers palette, he filled the chair layer with a dark purple color (Effects, Fill, Current Color). Then he painted over the chair with various brushes. Ocepek kept the tree and chair on their own layers to help control their colors and textures so he could preserve the distinction between the two elements in the image.

For a rich, textured look, Ocepek switched paper textures as he painted. To enhance the textured look and to make sure the textures printed clearly in offset lithography, he painted with grain-sensitive brushes—such as the Chalk variants (Chalk). While painting, he slowly built up subtle color, adjusting the Opacity slider on the Property Bar. To create the soft, light auras around the tree and the chair, he selected each layer in the Layers palette and painted it using the Bleach variant of the Erasers. To protect the completed paint on the tree while he added the auras around it, Ocepek loaded a selection he'd saved for the tree (Select, Load Selection). To keep the paint outside each selection on the tree and chair layers, he clicked the Draw Outside (middle) Drawing Mode icon located in the bottom left of Painter's image window before he edited the tree layer. Then he loaded the selection for the chair and edited its layer.

■ **Keith MacLelland** often mixes various media, such as oil paint and pastel, in Painter. He created the mixed media illustration *Friendly Fenway*, for his portfolio.

MacLelland began assembling a photomontage that he could use for reference. He arranged five of his own digital photos—the classic car, statue (hood ornament), sunset, Fenway Park at sunset, and finally his cockatiel Pete in flight—on layers so he could move them around in the composition. When he was happy with the layout he grouped the layers by clicking the Layer Commands button at the bottom of the Layers palette and choosing Group. Then he combined them into one layer by clicking the Layer Commands button again, this time choosing Collapse. Now he could easily lower the Opacity of the reference image using the Opacity slider on the Layers palette, and use it as a template

for tracing. Next, he created a new layer, and using the photomontage for reference, he sketched using the 2B Pencil variant of Pencils on a fine-textured paper. (To add a new layer, click the New Layer button on the bottom of the Layers palette.) Then he added another new empty layer and used the Scratchboard Tool variant of Pens and black color to trace the shapes of each element in the composition. To color the scene, he added another new layer and used custom brushes based on Painter's Oils variants (the Smeary Round, Smeary Flat, Smeary Bristle Spray and Variable Flat) to render the car, hood ornament and building. He also added touches of texture using a modified Oil Pastel variant, as well as the Chalk variants and the Spray variants of Airbrushes. At this point, he returned to the ink drawing layer, chose the Magic Wand in the Toolbox, unchecked the

Contiguous box in the Property Bar, and made a selection of the thick, black ink lines. He set the Tolerance for the Magic Wand in the Property Bar so the selection would grab only the centers of the lines. Then he chose the Layer Adjuster tool and clicked to put the selected lines on their own layer. For a semi-transparent effect, he changed the Composite Method of this layer to Overlay, then used the arrow keys to shift the layer slightly out of register. To give the illusion of a traditionally created piece of art, MacLelland selected the sketch layer and adjusted the Opacity of the layer so the lines looked like a partly erased pencil sketch. As a final touch, MacLelland used Painter's Text tool to create the Chevrolet logo. He added a subtle drop shadow, using the controls in the Text palette (Window, Show Text).

■ *My Uncle* was created by **Athos Boncompagni** for his book *My Monster Family*, which depicts how a child can see the grown-up world. (The 32-page book features a different relative on every page.) He constructed the image on layers to separate pencil and ink drawings from the colored paint.

To begin, Boncompagni created a new file. Because he planned to delete the sketch later, he sketched the composition on a new empty layer using the 2B Pencil variant of Pencils. Then he created another new layer above the sketch and used several Pens variants (including the Fine Point and Smooth Ink Pen) to create an expressive black-and-white drawing. He used the Leaky Pen to add a drippy texture in a few places. Next, Boncompagni deleted the pencil sketch layer by clicking on its name in the Layers palette and clicking the palette's Delete button. For the colored background, he added a new layer, dragged it under the ink sketch layer in the Layers palette and roughed in a soft colors using his own custom brushes that are based on the Smeary variants of the

Oils. After the background was established, he added another layer and laid in brightly colored brushwork over the figures. Then, he added yet another layer—this time above the ink drawing. He turned on Pick Up Underlying Color in the Layers palette so he could pull up color from layers below and smudge it with new color on the new layer. He used a custom brush that was based on the Sable Chisel Tip Water variant (from the Painter 5.5 brushes library). He also applied some strokes using Eraser variants. Finally, he used Pen variants to redefine some of the lines in the ink drawing and to brighten highlights on the colored layers. He also added a few more smudges on the clothing and background using his custom Sable Chisel Tip Water brush and the Blenders variants.

■ While creating *Friends*, **Michela Del Degan** assembled the characters and elements in her scene on several layers. Using layers made it easier to isolate the areas during the coloring process, and also helped her to edit the elements in the composition more easily.

Del Degan began by creating a new file, then clicking the New Layer button at the bottom of the Layers palette to add an empty, new layer. Then she used black color and the 2B Pencil variant of Pencils to draw an outline sketch of the scene. Next, Del Degan strengthened the outline sketch by drawing over it using the Smooth Ink Pen variant of Pens. She also added crosshatch texture and dimension to some of the forms. When the line drawing was as she liked it, Del Degan added a new layer for an element (for instance the yellow character's head

in the foreground) and used the Soft Charcoal variant of Charcoal to apply flat color to the area. She proceeded to add layers and to color the characters in this manner. At this point, Del Degan decided that she wanted a simpler background, so she created a new layer and dragged it under the character layers in the Layers palette list. Using the Soft Charcoal and a gray color, she painted a background wall. When all of the flat color was laid in throughout the image, she turned on Preserve Transparency in the Layers palette to protect the unpainted areas on the layers. Then she used the Charcoal variants to paint shadows and detail on the characters (onto each element's layer). To blend the shadows softly into the existing paint, she used the Smeary Bristle Spray variant of Oils. To give the image more depth, she added drop shadows to

certain elements in the scene, as follows: She targeted a layer in the Layers palette and chose Effects, Objects, Create Drop Shadow and accepted the default settings. The Create Drop Shadow command created a group in the Layers palette that consisted of the colored element and the generated drop shadow. If she wanted to change the position of the shadow, she opened the arrow to the left of the group, targeted the drop shadow layer and moved it using the arrow keys on her key board. To adjust the Opacity of a shadow layer, she used the Opacity slider in the Layers palette. Finally, to complete the image, she retouched and redefined line work in some areas of the illustration using Soft Charcoal variants of different sizes.

■ For this illustration for Glidden Paint company, art directed by Terry Pacifico of the Arras Group, artist **Nancy Stahl** painted on layers using custom brushes she built to imitate her favorite traditional brushes.

Stahl started by photographing herself in the figure's position, then assembled the photo and a sign reference into a rough composition in Painter. She used the composite image as a reference for a line drawing, which she sent to her client for approval.

Using custom-made brushes she had built to imitate her favorite gouache brushes, Stahl painted the figure and the Coca-Cola sign in two separate source files. She completed most of the painting in the source files because the complex brushes performed quicker than they would in a larger composite file. To learn about her painting techniques and custom brushes, turn to "Painting With Gouache," on page 90.

After the figure was complete, Stahl selected it with the Lasso tool and feathered the selection a few pixels by choosing Select, Feather (so the edge of the selection would be smooth). She saved the selection as a mask in the Channels palette by choosing Select, Save Selection. To bring the figure into the sign file, she loaded the selection by choosing Select, Load Selection. To float a copy she pressed Alt/Option and used the Layer Adjuster to drag and drop the copy into the sign painting file. Keeping the sign and the figure on separate layers made it easier for Stahl to add the final details.

ILLUSTRATION: NANCY STAHL / CREATED FOR COREL CORPORATION

■ **Nancy Stahl** created *Groovy* for the promotion of Painter 8 using a variety of tools including Pens, Gouache, Oils, Impasto and F-X variants. She painted each element on a separate layer, so she could move the elements around as she fine-tuned the composition. (To add a new layer, click the Create New Layer button on the bottom of the Layers palette.) She could also change its Opacity using the slider on the Layers palette. To learn more about her illustration work, turn to "Painting with Gouache," on page 90 and to the gallery at the end of Chapter 3.

Stahl began *Groovy* by creating a new file, adding a new empty layer and then drawing a composition sketch with the Smooth Ink Pen variant of Pens and black color. For the "floral" wallpaper on the background wall Stahl used the Furry variant of the F-X brushes to paint abstract flowers that had varied colors and texture. Next, using custom brushes that were based on the Gouache and Oils variants, she rendered the models. She painted short, curved thick-to-thin brushstrokes on the faces, skin and hair

using a custom brush based on the Round Camelhair variant of Oils. For the thick paint on the cake, Stahl used the Opaque Flat and Smeary Bristle Spray variants of Impasto. To smear and carve into the thick paint on the cake, she used a small Palette Knife variant of Impasto. To finish, she switched between the Opaque Bristle Spray and Round Camelhair (Impasto) to brighten the highlights in a few areas.

■ **Cris Palomino** created this portrait of *Xochiquetzal,* the Mexican goddess who is the patron of artists and artisans. Years ago, Palomino had drawn Xochiquetzal on illustration board with pen, brushes and ink. She used this art as a basis for the color illustration in Painter, scanning the black-and-white portrait and opening the scan in Painter. To keep the color separate from the black-and-white drawing on the Canvas, she added a new layer to the file by clicking the Create New Layer button (at the bottom of the Layers palette) and choosing New Layer from the pop-up menu. Then she created a circular selection on the layer and filled it with a sky blue. To give the background depth, she added a purple gradient to the top of the filled circle. (For information about filling with custom gradients, turn to "Adding Color and Gradations to Line Art" on page 30.) Then she dropped the selection (Select,

None or Ctrl/⌘-D). Palomino added a second new layer, on which she established the portrait's predominant colors. Working on the new layer, she used the Digital Airbrush variant of Airbrushes and the Basic Crayons (Crayons) and several Pastel variants (Pastels) to paint Xochiquetzal in color. After the color theme was established, she added another new layer for adding richly colored highlights and shadows. Before painting on this layer, she enabled Pick Up Underlying Color (near the top of the Layers palette) so that she could incorporate color from the underlying color layer as she painted. She used brushes that would smear such as the Oil Pastels, the Smeary variants of Oils and the Tinting brushes. These brushes would have smeared white color into the new paint if Pick Up Underlying Color had not been enabled.

Palomino added another new layer for the finer details and brighter highlights, which she planned to paint using a modified 2B Pencil that incorporated the Soft Cover Subcategory. This Pencil would allow her to paint light color over dark. In the Stroke Designer panel of the Brush Creator, she opened the Size section and set the Size Expression to Pressure. She clicked on the General section and set Opacity Expression to Pressure. Then she saved the custom Pencil by choosing Save from the Brush Creator's Variant menu. Using her new Pencil, Palomino added soft detailing to the feathers of the hummingbird, then painted finer strokes to bring out their crispness. She also used her custom Pencil to add more detail to Xochiquetzal's hair and face, most noticeably in the eyes, eyebrows and lips.

■ Artist **Chet Phillips** painted *Chaos Theory* as one in a series of illustrations for the limited edition book he and his wife are creating entitled *13 Incomplete Chapters of Mysterious Circumstances*. Phillips began by making an expressive drawing using the Scratchboard Tool variant of Pens. Then he floated the entire scratchboard drawing to a layer by choosing Select, All and clicking inside the active selection with the Layer Adjuster tool. Before deselecting the layer, he set the Composite Method to Gel in the Layers palette. Next, Phillips selected the Canvas in the Layers palette and used the Airbrushes, Chalk and Pastels brushes in varying sizes to color the background. He painted the dark blue sky and the water with the Artist Pastel Chalk variant of Pastels. Then he painted the clouds using grainy white strokes, varying pressure on the stylus as he worked. When the coloring was complete, Phillips merged the layers by clicking on the black-and-white drawing layer's name in the Layers palette and choosing Drop from the pop-out menu on the right side of the Layers palette. To see more of Chet Phillips's work, turn to "Coloring a Woodcut" in Chapter 2 and to the gallery at the end of Chapter 7.

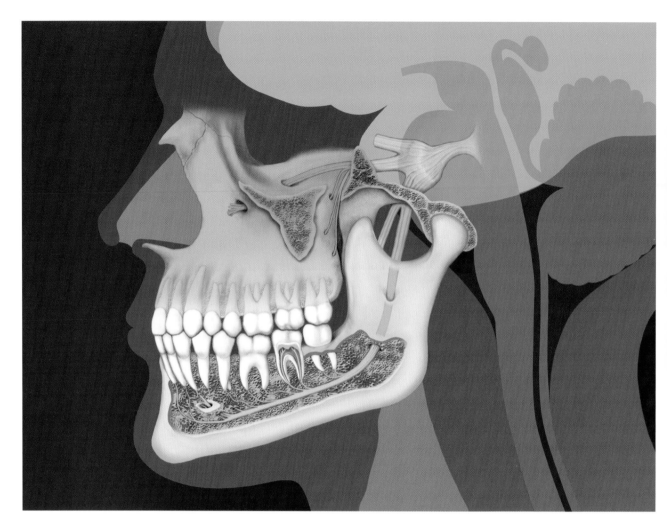

■ Medical illustrator **David Purnell** is proprietor of the New York West Medical Illustration Studio. When creating both of the illustrations on these pages for 3M Dental Products—for posting on the 3M Dental Web site and for printed materials—Purnell used Painter's shapes and layers. The layers helped him to organize elements in his illustration and to keep items separate while he finished the details.

To create *Neural Pathway*, Purnell began by making a line drawing in Macromedia FreeHand and saving it in Adobe Illustrator EPS format. After client approval, he imported the vector line drawing into Painter as shapes by choosing File, Acquire, Adobe Illustrator file. He converted the individual shapes to image layers (Shapes, Convert To Layer) and filled

them with flat color fills by enabling Preserve Transparency in the Layers palette and choosing Effects, Fill With Current Color. One by one, he airbrushed the layers to sculpt the anatomy in the nerves, bones and teeth areas of the illustration. He left the outer areas filled with simple flat color that would not draw focus attention away from the important neural pathway areas.

For the textured cross-section of bone, Purnell used a custom airbrush based on the Variable Splatter variant of Airbrushes. To build a brush that would spray narrower or wider splattery strokes depending on the pressure applied, he changed the Min Size in the Size section of the Stroke Designer (Brush Creator) from the default 0% to 30%. To vary the size of the droplets,

he also changed the Feature setting in the Property Bar as he worked.

To make the bone look even more organic, he used the Distorto variant of Distortion to randomly push and pull areas of the splatter in order to vary its look. To constrain the paint within the element on the layer, he turned on Preserve Transparency in the Layers palette.

Purnell finished the illustration by applying effects: For instance, he targeted the jaw bone layer and applied realistic highlights and shadows based on the gray values in the spatter-airbrushed texture he had painted. He achieved this lighting with Effects, Surface Control, Apply Surface Texture Using Image Luminance, with subtle settings.

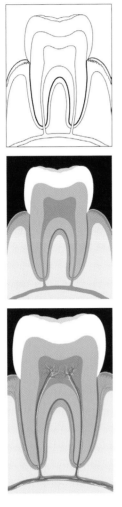

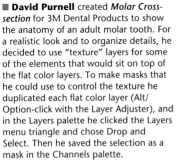

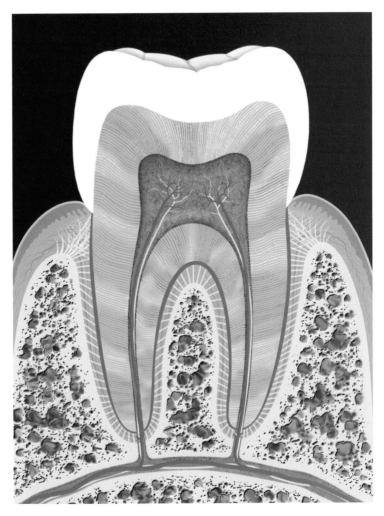

■ **David Purnell** created *Molar Cross-section* for 3M Dental Products to show the anatomy of an adult molar tooth. For a realistic look and to organize details, he decided to use "texture" layers for some of the elements that would sit on top of the flat color layers. To make masks that he could use to control the texture he duplicated each flat color layer (Alt/Option-click with the Layer Adjuster), and in the Layers palette he clicked the Layers menu triangle and chose Drop and Select. Then he saved the selection as a mask in the Channels palette.

To create texture—for instance, the fibrous texture in the pulp chamber—he loaded the selection he had saved (Select, Load Selection). With the pulp selection active, and the pulp texture layer targeted, he was ready to begin applying the texture effect. When working with a selection, he used Painter's Drawing Modes to constrain brushstrokes to the

inside or the outside of the loaded selection. He used Effects, Surface Control, Apply Surface Texture Using Image Luminance (with subtle settings) to bring out texture in the brushwork.

To achieve the cellular look of the odontoblasts on the edges of the pulp chamber, he used the paper texture Random Bubbles (from Molecular Textures loaded from the Corel Painter 8 CD 2 CD-ROM.) He varied the scaling of the texture as he worked from 100% to 30%, using the Scale slider on the Papers palette (Window, Show Papers). To apply the texture onto the layer, he used a custom grainy variant of Airbrushes (based on the Digital Airbrush) that also incorporated variable Opacity and Size. So the brush would reveal grain as he painted, he changed the Subcategory in the General section of the Stroke Designer (Brush Creator) from Soft Cover to Grainy Flat

Cover. To vary the Opacity, also in the General section, he set Opacity Expression to be controlled by Pressure. To vary Size with Pressure, in the Size section (Stroke Designer), he also set Size Expression to Pressure. Then he carefully airbrushed the Random Bubbles texture along the inner edge of the pulp chamber.

For the striations on the dentin layer, Purnell chose a darker ochre color than the solid ochre on the original dentin layer. He made a new "texture" layer as described, then he used a custom Airbrush (which incorporated a Rake stroke type) to draw the striations, keeping in mind the subtle S-curves that are characteristic of the anatomy.

For the textured bone, he used much the same technique as in the *Neural Pathway* piece, painting with his custom Variable Splatter airbrush and Distorto variants, then using Apply Surface Texture.

6
ENHANCING PHOTOS, MONTAGE AND COLLAGE

Michael Campbell created Frances With Hat, *shown here in this detail. See the complete photo-painting in the gallery at the end of this chapter.*

To enhance this portrait, we began by painting a mask to isolate the dancers. To create a shallow depth of field, we used Effects, Tonal Control, Adjust Colors *to desaturate the background and* Effects, Focus, Soften *to blur it.*

PHOTO: CORBIS IMAGES

ALTHOUGH PAINTER BEGAN as a painting program, the features that have been added over the years have turned it into a powerful image processor as well. Many tools are designed *just* for photographers—for instance, dynamic layers that allow you to adjust brightness and contrast, perform posterization, apply glass distortion effects and more! (For the basics of how to work with dynamic layers such as Glass Distortion, turn to page 255.) Painter boasts color reduction features that are useful for working with photographs: *woodcut* and *distress*. (See "Creating a Woodcut from a Photo" on page 236 and "Distressing a Photo" on page 233). Painter also includes brush variants specifically designed for photographers, such as the Scratch Remover and Saturation Add brushes found in the Photo brush category in the Brush Selector Bar. And, of course, when it comes to achieving painterly effects with photographs, Painter has no peer. If you're a photographer, a photo-illustrator or a designer who works with photos and you want to get the most out of Painter, you'll want to pay attention to the following areas of the program.

The Effects menu. Most of Painter's image-altering special effects can be found in the Effects menu. The features under the subheads Tonal Control, Surface Control and Focus are loaded with creative promise for the adventurous digital photographer.

Selections and masks. To alter only a portion of an image, you'll need to become acquainted with Painter's shapes and its selection and masking capabilities. If you're not familiar with the Pen and Lasso tools, turn to "Working with Bézier Paths and Selections" and "Working with Freehand Selections" in Chapter 4.

Painter's powerful automatic masking features—located in the Channels palette—give you a big jump on the tedious process of creating masks to isolate parts of your image. And a bonus: All of Painter's brushes except Water Color and Liquid Ink and the Plug-

To isolate the sky from the buildings in this photo we made a color mask for the sky. (In the Channels palette, click the right triangle to access the pop-up menu, and choose New From Color Range.) Then we used the Scratchboard Tool variant of Pens and white paint to remove from the mask any areas in the photo's foreground that had been selected.

Correcting the tonal range in an image using Effects, Tonal Control, Equalize. To lighten the image overall, we moved the Brightness slider to the right.

in method brushes (such as the Add Grain variant of the Photo brush) can be used to paint directly on a mask. For a detailed description of combining Painter's automatic and painterly masks, turn to "Making a Color Mask," in Chapter 4.

Layers. Chapter 5 gave you an overall look at techniques using layers; this chapter focuses on using layers and masks for photo-compositing and other photo effects—for example, in "Simulating Motion," "Selective Coloring" and "Creating a Montage Using Masks and Layers," later in the chapter.

Dynamic layers. Painter offers dynamic layers that are useful for making adjustments to images. They are: Brightness and Contrast, Equalize, and Posterize. To find these tools, access the Dynamic Plug-ins pop-up menu by clicking the plug icon at the bottom of the Layers palette. Several of the techniques described later in this chapter use dynamic layers. To read more about dynamic layers and how they relate to other elements in Painter, turn to the beginning of Chapter 5.

Cloning. A very powerful and versatile feature, cloning (File, Clone) lets you make multiple copies of an image, alter each copy, then recombine them in various ways while preserving access to the original. Several of the techniques described in this chapter use this or another kind of cloning method.

IMAGE-PROCESSING BASICS

With its strong focus on *creative* image manipulation, Painter has left some *production*-oriented tasks such as color-correcting CMYK images to Adobe Photoshop. But there's no need to move an image from Painter to Photoshop to perform basic image-processing tasks such as sharpening and adjusting brightness and contrast, because Painter has tools that are similar to many of Photoshop's.

Equalizing. Choosing Effects, Tonal Control, Equalize (Ctrl/⌘-E) produces a dialog box with a histogram similar to Photoshop's Levels dialog, which allows you to adjust the tonal range in an image—the difference is that in Painter the image is automatically equalized (an effect similar to clicking on the Auto button in Photoshop's Levels). Move the triangular sliders toward the ends of the histogram to decrease the effect.

Painter also features an Equalize dynamic layer that operates like Effects, Tonal Control, Equalize, but on a copy of your image so you can easily try out different tonal adjustments. To make an Equalize layer, open an image and choose Equalize from the Dynamic Plug-ins pop-up menu at the bottom of the Layers palette. Choose Equalize to generate the dynamic layer. When the Equalize dialog box appears, set the controls as you would for Effects, Tonal Control, Equalize. Using an Equalize dynamic layer you can preview as many changes as you like: Click the Reset button to return your image to its original condition, then apply a new correction.

PHOTO: CORBIS IMAGES

Using a feather setting of 15 pixels, we created a textured edge for this 500-pixel-wide photo. (To make a soft-edged vignette around an image, turn to page 150 in Chapter 4.)

To create a vignette with a textured edge, begin by making a selection with the Oval Selection tool. Use the Selection Adjuster tool to position and scale the selection. Next, apply a feather (Select, Feather). Save the selection (Select, Save Selection). Now for the textured edge: In the Channels palette, select the mask, open its eye icon and close the RGB-Canvas eye icon to view the mask in black-and-white. Select a rough paper texture in the Paper Selector (such as French Water Color), and choose Effects, Surface Control, Express Texture. Adjust the sliders to confine the texture to the soft edge. Click OK. In the Channels palette, click the channel eye icon shut and select RGB. Load the selection (Select, Load Selection). Next, reverse the selection (to select the area outside the oval) by choosing Select, Invert. To clear the background, press the Backspace/Delete key.

Adjusting brightness and contrast. Painter offers two ways to change image brightness and contrast. The first—Effects, Tonal Control, Brightness/Contrast—applies a correction directly to an open image or selection. But if you'd like to preview several Brightness and Contrast options, consider making a Brightness-and-Contrast dynamic layer. Click the plug icon at the bottom of the Layers palette to access the Dynamic Plug-ins menu and select Brightness and Contrast. When the Brightness-and-Contrast dialog box appears, continue to adjust the settings as you preview the corrections in your image. To read more about a Brightness-and-Contrast dynamic layer, see "Making a Selective Correction" on page 224.

Stripping color from an image. There are several ways to turn a color image into a grayscale one in Painter. The quickest way is to desaturate the image using the Adjust Color dialog box. Choose Effects, Tonal Control, Adjust Colors and drag the Saturation slider all the way to the left.

Changing color. While you're using the Adjust Color dialog box, experiment with the Hue Shift slider to change the hue of all of the colors in an image (or a layer or selection). You can get greater control in altering specific colors (turning blue eyes green, for instance) by using Effects, Tonal Control, Adjust Selected Colors. Click in the image to select a color, then drag the Hue Shift, Saturation and Value sliders at the bottom of the dialog box to make the changes. Fine-tune your color choice and the softness of its edge with the various Extents and Feather sliders.

To repair a white scratch on this photo we used a two-step process, beginning with Painter's useful Scratch Remover brush (located in the Photo category, in the Brush Selector Bar). Open a photo you'd like to repair, choose the Scratch Remover variant and for the best results, use a small brush size (we used a 1.7 pixel brush on this 350-pixel-wide image) and a low Opacity setting in the Property Bar (we used 9%). Zoom in to a magnification where you can see the scratch in detail, and carefully paint to blend the scratch into the image. This first step is usually sufficient for images with even color. But the sky in our image was graduated and required more repair. Next, we used a Soft Cloner variant of the Cloners with a small brush size and a very low Opacity, set in the Property Bar. Alt/Option-click to set the clone source to a point near the repair, then gently paint over the repaired area to bring back appropriate colors.

PHOTO: CORBIS IMAGES

The scratched image (left) and the repaired image (right)

Using the Saturation Add brush from the Photo brush library to "pop" the color on the red raincoat, umbrella and reflection

We applied Fine Hard Grain (chosen from the Papers Selector near the bottom of the Toolbox) to this photo with Effects, Surface Control, Dye Concentration Using Paper with the Maximum slider set to 200%.

To "age" this photo, we painted with the Add Grain variant of the Photo brush using the Dry Cracks texture for a crackled look.

The image above was sharpened to produce the result on the right using these settings: Amount, 2.15; Highlight, 90%; Shadow, 80%. A larger image can accept a higher Amount setting.

Painting saturation with brushes. To "pop" the color in a specific area, use Painter's Saturation Add brush, located in the Photo brush category in the Brushes palette. For a more subtle look, lower the Opacity to about 10%.

Adding film grain. Photoshop's Noise filter is a good way to emulate film grain. To get a similar effect in Painter, open the Papers palette by choosing Window, Show Papers and choose an even-textured Paper grain, like Basic Paper or Fine HardGrain. Next, choose Effects, Surface Control, Dye Concentration, Using Paper. Scale the texture in the Papers palette until the grain in the Preview window of the Adjust Dye Concentration dialog box is barely visible—try 50% as a starting point. Try minor adjustments to the Maximum and Minimum sliders.

Adding grain with a brush. Painter offers an exciting pressure-sensitive brush—the Add Grain Brush—that allows you to paint grain onto your images. To begin, choose the Photo brushes icon in the Brush Selector and select the Add Grain variant. Choose a texture in the Paper Selector, scale it if necessary and brush lightly onto your image. For a more subtle effect, reduce the Opacity of the brush in the Property Bar. The Grain Emboss variant of Impasto is also useful for adding a textured, embossed look to an image.

Creating a shallow depth of field. By softening the background of an image, you can simulate the shallow depth of field that you'd get by setting your camera at a low *f*-stop. Select the area you want to soften and feather the selection by choosing Select, Feather to avoid an artificial-looking edge. Then choose Effects, Focus, Soften.

Smearing, smudging and blurring. To smoothly smear pixels in the image, choose the Just Add Water variant of Blenders in the Brush Selector; vary Opacity in the Property Bar between 70% and 100%. To smudge the image, while bringing out the texture chosen in the Paper Selector, choose the Smudge variant of Blenders. For a "wet oil" effect, try the Distorto variant of Distortion. To softly blur an area of the image, use the Blur variant of the Photo brush set to a low Opacity (about 20%).

Sharpening. Painter's Sharpen feature (Effect, Focus, Sharpen) gives you control equivalent to unsharp masking on a drum scanner. (Unsharp masking sharpens the edges of elements in an image.) Use it to give definition to a selected area of interest, or to an entire image as a final step in preparing for output. To sharpen an area in an image using a brush, choose the Sharpen variant of the Photo brush. This brush puts sharpening (very similar to the Effects, Focus, Sharpen command) on the tip of a brush.

Retouching. The Straight Cloner and Soft Cloner variants of the Cloners brush work like Photoshop's Clone Stamp tool (with the Aligned function turned on) to reproduce imagery; use the Alt/Option key as you would Photoshop's Alt/Option key to sample

To add a mysterious gold spotlight to this woman's portrait, we used Effects, Surface Control, Apply Lighting. We modified the Center Spot by changing the Light Color from white to gold. To make the spotlight softer, we decreased the Exposure from 1.00 to .85.

an area (even in another image), then reproduce that image (centered at the point of sampling) wherever you paint. The Straight Cloner variant reproduces imagery without changing it; to clone imagery with a soft edge and low opacity (like an Airbrush) use the Soft Cloner.

ADVANCED TECHNIQUES

It often takes a lot of time and trial-and-error to get cool effects in-camera or in the darkroom. Some third-party plug-in filters do an adequate job of replicating these effects, but Painter gives you more control than you can get with filters alone.

Here's a short guide for using Painter to re-create traditional photographic techniques, starting with simpler, in-camera ones and progressing to more complex darkroom procedures.

Motion blur. You can use the camera to blur a moving subject by using a slower shutter speed or jittering (shaking) your hands while you hold the camera, or you can blur the background by panning with the subject. (See "Simulating Motion" on page 222 to read about a versatile motion-blur technique that involves using an additional layer.)

To create the look of "camera jitter," just as if you had moved the camera while taking a picture, choose Effects, Focus, Camera Motion Blur. When the dialog box appears, drag in the image (not the Preview), to specify the camera's direction and distance of movement. Dragging farther in the image will create a wider blur. To move the origin of the movement along the path of motion, adjust the Bias slider.

Lens filters and special film. To re-create in-camera tinting effects achieved with special films or colored filters, use Effects, Surface Control, Color Overlay. If you want to mimic the effect of a graduated or spot lens attachment (partially colored filters), choose a gradation and fill your image (Effects, Fill) with the gradation at a reduced opacity. (You may need to add contrast to your image afterwards with Effects, Tonal Control, Equalize.)

Shooting through glass. With Painter's Glass Distortion effect or Glass Distortion dynamic layer you can superimpose glass relief effects (using a paper texture or any other image) on your photo. A small amount of this feature adds texture to an image; larger amounts can make an image unrecognizable! To apply the effect directly to your image choose Effects, Focus, Glass Distortion. To make a Glass Distortion dynamic layer for your image, click the plug icon at the bottom of the Layers palette to open the pop-up menu, then choose Glass Distortion. (See Phil Howe's work with Glass Distortion in the gallery at the end of this chapter.)

Lighting effects. Use Painter's Apply Lighting feature (under Effects, Surface Control) to add subtle or dramatic lighting to a scene.

To get the effect of a line conversion, a straight-line screen was applied to a photo with Effects, Surface Control, Express Texture Using Paper and a Line texture set to an angle of 40. (For directions for setting up a Line texture, see Line Screen on the next page.)

For this graphic effect, we applied Painter's Woodcut feature to a photo. See "Creating a Woodcut from a Photo" on page 236 for a step-by-step demonstration of a similar technique.

We posterized this Craig McClain photo using a custom Color Set of "desert" colors and the Effects, Tonal Control, Posterize Using Color Set command.

The original photo of a kelp frond had strong contrast, contributing good detail for this embossed image.

Multiple exposures. Whether created in camera (by underexposing and shooting twice before advancing the film) or in the darkroom (by "sandwiching" negatives or exposing two images on a single sheet of paper), it's easy to reproduce the effect of multiple exposures by using layers or clones in Painter.

Solarization. Painter's Express Texture (Effects, Surface Control) command is a great way to re-create darkroom solarization. Read about a Painter version of a "custom" solarization on page 234.

Line screen. Instead of developing your image in the darkroom onto high-contrast "line" or "lith" paper, try getting a similar effect in Painter. Open the Papers palette by choosing Window, Show Papers, click the right arrow on the Papers palette to access the pop-up menu, and choose Make Paper. In the Make Paper dialog box, choose the Line option and set the Spacing to approximately 10. (You can also adjust the Angle slider if you like.) Store your new texture in the current Paper library by naming it in the Save As field and clicking the OK button. With your new paper chosen in the Papers palette, choose Effects, Surface Control, Apply Screen, Using Paper to get a two- or three-color effect with rough (aliased) lines. Or try Effects, Surface Control, Express Texture, Using Paper to get a broader range of value and smoother, anti-aliased lines. You can also apply screens using Painter's Distress feature. See "Distressing a Photo" on page 233 for a step-by-step demonstration of this technique.

Posterizing an image. Painter lets you limit the number of colors in your image via posterization. To apply a posterization directly to your image choose Effects, Tonal Control, Posterize and enter the number of levels (usually 8 or fewer for best results). You can also perform a posterization using the Posterize dynamic layer. At the bottom of the Layers palette, click the plug icon to open the Dynamic Plug-ins menu and select Posterize from the menu. Click Apply and enter the number of levels. Because the Posterize plug-in layer is dynamic, you can experiment and preview the effect on your image until it's the way you like it.

You can get creative posterization effects by making a Color Set (see "Capturing a Color Set" in Chapter 2) and selecting Effects, Tonal Control, Posterize Using Color Set. This is a great way to unify photos shot under a variety of conditions.

Embossing and debossing. To emboss an image, raising its light areas, choose File, Clone; then Select All and delete, leaving a blank cloned image. Now choose Effects, Surface Control, Apply Surface Texture, and choose 3D Brush Strokes from the Using pop-up menu. To raise the dark areas instead of the light, click the Invert box or change the Using menu choice to Original Luminance. Images with a lot of contrast give the best results, and busy images work better if less important areas are first selected and softened using Effects, Focus, Soften.

Creating a Sepia-Tone Photo

Overview *Use gradient features to tint a color or black-and-white image; adjust the image's contrast and saturation.*

1a

The original photo

1b

Choosing Express in Image

2a

Applying the Sepia Browns gradient

2b

Adjusting the contrast

2c

Neutralizing and warming up the browns

TYPICALLY FOUND IN IMAGES CREATED at the turn of the last century, sepia-tones get their reddish-brown color cast in the darkroom when the photographer immerses a developed print in a special toner bath. You can use Painter's gradation and tonal control features to quickly turn color or grayscale images into sepia-tones.

1 Tinting the image. Open a grayscale or color photo. In the Gradients palette (Window, Show Gradients), select the Sepia Browns gradient from the picker. Choose Express In Image from the triangle pop-up menu at the right end of the Gradients section bar. (Read more about gradients in Chapter 2.) Click OK in the dialog box to tint your image with shades of brown. (You can also use a similar procedure to turn a color image into shades of gray, but make sure the back and front Color rectangles in the Color picker are black and white, respectively, and choose Two-Point in the Gradients palette.)

2 Adjusting the white and black points. If you're working with an image that has poor contrast, you can adjust the white and black points by choosing Effects, Tonal Control, Equalize (Ctrl/⌘-E). When the dialog box appears, the image will be automatically adjusted so that its lightest tones are pure white and its darkest ones are pure black. The automated contrast was too dramatic for our taste, so we lightened the image by moving the Brightness slider to the left.

3 Desaturating the image. We wanted to emulate the mild tinting effect usually used for traditional sepia-tones, so we desaturated the image using Effects, Tonal Control, Adjust Colors, dragging the Saturation slider to the left to –60. Set the Hue Shift at 0% and experiment with the Saturation slider until you see the effect you want in the Preview window. We also adjusted the Hue a slight amount (to 2%) to warm up the browns in the image. ◍

Selective Coloring

Overview *Open a color photo and copy it to a layer; desaturate the layer; paint with a brush to erase areas of the layer mask and reveal the underlying color photo.*

CHER THREINEN-PENDARVIS / PHOTO: PHOTOSPIN

The color photo

Using the Adjust Colors dialog box to desaturate the layer to black-and-white

Painting on the layer mask to reveal the color image underneath

IF YOU WANT TO FOCUS ATTENTION on a particular element in a color photo, you can turn the photo into a black-and-white image and then selectively add color back into it for emphasis. Here's a way to use Painter's layers and brushes to "paint" color on an image.

1 Copying the image. Open a color photo and choose Select, All (Ctrl/⌘-A). Press the Alt/Option key and choose Select, Float. This creates a layer with an exact copy of the original image, in register with the original.

2 Desaturating the layer. Now use the layer to make the image appear black-and-white: Choose Effects, Tonal Control, Adjust Colors, Using Uniform Color, drag the Saturation slider all the way to the left, and click OK.

3 Revealing color in the underlying image. To allow parts of the color image to show through, use a brush to hide portions of the "black-and-white" layer. Target the layer in the Layers palette and add a layer mask by clicking the Create Layer Mask button on the Layers palette. Click on the layer mask thumbnail to target it— you'll see a dark outline around it when it is active. In the Brush Selector Bar, choose a Fine Tip Soft Air variant of Airbrushes and choose black in the Color picker. (To view the layer imagery while editing the layer mask, keep the layer mask eye icon shut.) As you paint with black on the layer mask to hide that area of the mask, the color will appear. If you want to turn a color area back to gray, choose white from the Color picker and paint on the area.

FINE-TUNING YOUR MASK

It's difficult to tell if you've completely covered (or erased) areas when working on a mask with a brush. To view a layer mask in black-and-white, click on the layer mask icon in the Layers palette, and in the Channels palette, open its eye icon. Choose a Fine Detail Air (Airbrushes), and paint directly on the mask to clean it up. (Black creates an opaque mask that hides the layers below; pure white creates no mask, allowing the layers below to show through; shades of gray create a semi-transparent mask.) To switch back to color view, click the layer mask eye icon shut.

Painting on the layer mask using a Fine Detail Air variant of Airbrushes

Simulating Motion

Overview *Open a color photo and copy to a layer; apply Motion Blur to the copy; add a layer mask to the layer; paint with a brush to erase areas of the layer mask and reveal the original photo.*

The original photo

Applying Motion Blur to the layer

Painting the layer mask to hide a portion of the blurred layer

Adjusting the opacity of the blurred layer

CREATING A SENSE OF MOVEMENT for a subject *after* the film is out of the camera is easy with Painter's layers and Motion Blur command. We blurred a layer, then used a layer mask to hide some areas to reveal the untouched image underneath. The benefits of this method over applying effects to selections are that you can control the amount of the effect by adjusting opacity of the layers; you can simultaneously add effects other than a blur (such as lighting and texture); and you are altering a copy while leaving the original intact, and this makes it easy to correct errors.

1 Copying the image. Open a color photo and choose Select, All (Ctrl/⌘-A). Using the Layer Adjuster tool, Alt/Option-click on the image. This creates a layer that's an exact copy of the original image.

2 Blurring the layer. Select the layer by clicking on its name in the Layers palette and choose Effects, Focus, Motion Blur. To get a dramatic blur on our 1500-pixel-wide image, we set Radius to about 72.45, Angle to 5° (to complement the direction the table was moving) and Thinness to 2%. Experiment with different Angle settings for your particular image.

3 Painting on the mask. To allow parts of the original image to show through, target the layer in the Layers palette and add a layer mask by clicking the Create Layer Mask button on the Layers palette. Click on the layer mask to target it—you'll see a dark outline around it when it is active. Use a brush to paint on the layer mask. In the Brush Selector Bar, choose the Digital Airbrush (Airbrushes) and choose black in the Color picker. As you paint the layer mask in the area you wish to hide, the underlying image will appear. If you want to restore an area of the blurred layer, choose white in the Color picker and paint on that area of the layer mask. For an illusion of speed we hid the frontal blur on the table and laptop, leaving trails of motion blur behind them.

4 Adjusting the opacity. To reduce the blur we clicked on the layer (instead of the mask) and made it slightly transparent by lowering the Opacity of the layer in the Layers palette to 75%.

Zooming and Solarizing

Overview *Float a copy of the image, use Painter's Zoom Blur feature to zoom in on an area of the layer; paint the layer mask to accentuate the focal point; make a solarization by changing the Composite Method.*

The original photo of the volleyball players

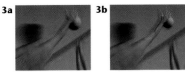

The Zoom Blur dialog box after clicking in the image

The zoom-blurred layer (left) and the mask retouched to reveal the sharp underlying image of the hand and ball (right)

The Opacity and Composite Method settings for the solarization

CHER THREINEN-PENDARVIS / PHOTO: CORBIS IMAGES

WITH PAINTER'S ZOOM BLUR feature you can create zoom and pan effects that rival results you can achieve when shooting with a zoom lens. Here we used Zoom Blur to elongate the subjects, adding to the excitement and illusion of speed during a volley. Afterwards, to add more drama we changed the photo into a mysterious "night scene."

1 Copying the image. Open a color photo and choose Select, All (Ctrl/⌘-A). Choose the Layer Adjuster and Alt/Option-click on the image. This creates a layer with an exact copy of the original image.

2 Blurring the layer. Select the layer by clicking on its name in the Layers palette and choose Effects, Focus, Zoom Blur. To get a moderate blur on our 600-pixel-wide image, we set the Amount to 31%. Set the focal point of the zoom by clicking in the image (not in the Preview). To create the elongated, distorted effect of zooming in, check the Zoom In box. Click OK.

3 Painting on the mask. To enhance the focal point of the image, we painted areas of a layer mask to reveal the underlying image, for instance, the ball and hands. Target the layer in the Layers palette and add a layer mask by clicking the Create Layer Mask button on the Layers palette. Click on the layer mask thumbnail to target it—you'll see a dark outline around it when it is active. In the Brush Selector Bar, choose a Fine Tip Soft Air variant of Airbrushes and choose black in the Color picker. (To view the layer imagery while editing the layer mask, keep the layer mask eye icon shut.)

4 Making a solarization. Next, we created a solarized "night scene" from the image by selecting the layer in the Layers palette, choosing the Layer Adjuster tool and changing the Composite Method to Difference in the Layers palette. To make the layer slightly transparent, allowing the original colored image to show through, we also lowered the Opacity of the layer to 85%.

Making a Selective Correction

Overview *Use a dynamic layer to adjust the brightness and contrast of an image; convert the dynamic layer to an image layer; make a selection; use the selection to remove a portion of the layer.*

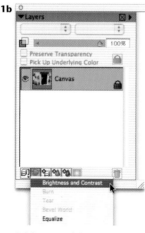

The original photograph

Making a Brightness and Contrast dynamic layer

Increasing the Brightness by moving the lower slider to the right

HERE'S A USEFUL IMAGE-EDITING TECHNIQUE that combines a dynamic layer Brightness-and-Contrast adjustment and a selection. Using a dynamic layer has the advantage of being able to make a correction and dynamically preview the changes on the image without harming the image. To enhance the focal point of this image—shining more light onto the faces—we selectively lightened the shaded window area.

1 Editing brightness and contrast with a dynamic layer.
Open a grayscale or color photo. To make a Brightness and Contrast dynamic layer for your image, click the Dynamic Plug-ins button at the bottom of the Layers palette and from the pop-up menu, choose Brightness and Contrast. A Brightness and Contrast dynamic layer will cover your entire image. (Turn to "Using Dynamic Layers" on page 185 in Chapter 5, to read about the basics of using dynamic layers.)

When the dialog box appears, adjust the sliders and preview the correction in your image. To see more detail on the faces, we moved the Brightness (lower) slider to the right, making the image lighter. We also slightly increased the contrast by moving the Contrast slider (upper) to the right.

We only wanted the Brightness-and-Contrast adjustment to affect the shaded area within the window, so we planned to make a mask and load a selection that we could use to isolate a portion of the layer. To use a selection on a dynamic layer, the layer must first be converted to an image layer. When you've finished making adjustments, convert the dynamic layer to an image layer as follows: Click the right triangle on the Layers palette bar to open the pop-up menu and choose Convert to Default Layer. Next, hide the layer temporarily: In the Layers palette, click the layer's eye icon shut, then click on the Canvas layer's name.

2

The active selection around the window

3a

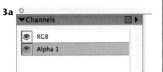

Selecting the mask to view it as a red overlay

3b

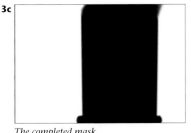

Viewing the mask as a red overlay before editing and feathering

3c

The completed mask

4b

Detail from the final corrected image with more detail in the shaded areas

2 Making a selection and saving it as a mask. In our example, when we were satisfied with the Brightness-and-Contrast adjustment in the window area, the blue wall was too light and flat. In preparation for using only the window area of the adjusted layer, we made a selection of the window area on the image canvas and saved it as a mask. In the Toolbox, choose the Pen tool or Lasso and make a selection. (We drew a shape with the Pen tool and converted it to a selection using Shapes, Convert to Selection.) When you've completed the selection, choose Select, Save Selection to save it into the Channels palette. (For more information about using the Pen tool to create paths with which you can make selections, turn to the beginning of Chapter 4, "Selections, Shapes and Masks" and to "Working with Bézier Paths and Selections" on page 158.

3 Editing and feathering the mask. To get a clear view of the mask as we edited and feathered it, we worked back and forth between viewing it as a red overlay (on the image) and as a black-and-white mask. We used the Digital Airbrush variant of the Airbrushes and white paint to spray soft edges along the top of the window and added a 3-pixel feather to the entire mask to give it a soft transparent edge. If your mask needs editing, select its name in the Channels palette. To view your mask as a red overlay, click both the mask eye icon and the RGB eye icon open. To view the mask in black-and-white, click the RGB eye icon closed. With the mask active you can give it a soft edge by applying feathering as follows: Click the right triangle on the Channels palette bar to open the menu and choose Feather. Type a feather width in the field and click OK. Now shut the mask eye icon and click on RGB in the Channels palette to prepare for the next step.

4 Using the selection to edit the layer. In our example, we used the selection to remove the area on the Brightness-and-Contrast layer outside the window. Now that your mask is complete, load the selection from the mask, as follows: In the Layers palette, click on the Brightness-and-Contrast layer name to select it, and also open its eye icon to display the layer. Now choose Select, Load Selection and choose the mask that you saved (Alpha 1) to isolate the area on the layer. To remove the unwanted portion of the layer, choose Select, Invert and press the Backspace/Delete key. ✐

USING SELECTIONS WITH LAYERS

You can have several masks saved in the Channels palette and choose any one of them to load as a selection to then isolate paint or effects on any image layer. Choose Select, Load Selection and pick the selection you need from the menu. In the Layers palette, click on the name of the layer with which you want to work.

Hand-Tinting a Photo

Overview *Retouch a black-and-white photo; color the image using Tinting brushes and several layers set to Gel Composite Method.*

CHER THREINEN-PENDARVIS

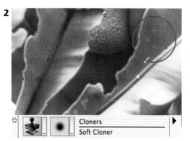

Using Equalize to adjust the tonal range of the black-and-white photo

Repairing scratches with the Soft Cover variant of Cloners

The new layer in the Layers palette, with Composite Method set to Gel

HAND-TINTING IS A GREAT WAY to give an old-fashioned look to a black-and-white print. It also gives the sensitive artist plenty of opportunity to add depth to an image using hues, tints and shades. For this example, *Rell with Bird's Nest Fern,* we hand-colored a portrait of Hawaiian friend Rell Sunn using Painter Tinting brushes, applying transparent color to layers above the image, so we would not disturb the existing photo.

1 Equalizing the image. To preserve shadow detail during tinting, choose a light image without solid shadows, or correct the tonal range after scanning as described below. Because we no longer had the 35mm slide, we scanned an 8 x 10-inch print at 100%, 150 pixels per inch. The print was slightly overexposed, so we darkened it, taking care to preserve detail in the shadows. If your image needs tonal correction, select Effects, Tonal Control, Equalize (Ctrl/⌘-E). Your image will be automatically adjusted when the dialog box appears. For a more subtle result, experiment with spreading the triangular sliders on the histogram; or move them closer together for more contrast. Use the Brightness slider to make the gray tones brighter or darker overall.

2 Retouching scratches. To touch up scratches, use the Magnifier tool to enlarge the area that needs retouching. Using the Brush tool, choose the Soft Cloner variant of Cloners in the Brush Selector Bar. Establish a clone source by Alt/Option-clicking on your image near the area that needs touch-up, then begin painting. A cross-hair cursor shows the origin of your sampling. If necessary, reestablish a clone source as you work by Alt/Option-clicking again.

Coloring the "background" layer with the Basic Round variant of the Tinting brush

3 Making a new layer and coloring the background. Create a new layer by clicking the New Layer button on the bottom of the Layers palette. So the paint will appear transparent, in the Layers palette, set the layer's Composite Method to Gel. Also, disable Preserve Transparency (so you can add pixels to the layer) and turn off Pick Up Underlying Color, so the Tinting brushes will not pick up gray from the Canvas as you paint. Choose a color in the Color picker and the Basic Round variant of the Tinting brush from the Brush Selector Bar. Begin to brush color onto your image. If the color looks too strong, reduce the opacity of the Basic Round variant using the Opacity slider in the Property Bar. For grainier brushstrokes, try the Soft Grainy Round variant.

4 Coloring elements on separate layers. It's often helpful to color areas of the image (such as the skin, clothing and background) on separate layers to make it easy to edit a specific element. Add more layers as needed by clicking the New Layer button on the Layers palette. Remember to set each new layer to Gel Composite Method before you start to paint. We added new layers for each of these elements: the skin and hair, clothing, and the foreground plants.

5 Emphasizing the area of interest. After you've painted color washes, look at the overall balance and color density of your image. Add more or brighter color to the areas that you want to emphasize and apply less saturated colors to make other areas appear to recede. For detail work, reduce the size of the Basic Round variant using the Size slider on the Property Bar. To remove color from oversaturated areas or to clean up edges, use the Soft Eraser variant of Tinting, adjusting its Opacity setting in the Property Bar as you work. The Blender and Softener variants are useful for making color or value transitions smoother.

   We used the Blender variant to smooth the brush work in the face and shirt, by softly brushing over the areas using a low-opacity version of the brush.

Saving the image. If your coloring extends for more than one work session, save your image in RIFF format to preserve the layers set to Gel Composite Method. If you'd like import your image into Adobe Photoshop, you'll want to flatten a copy of the image first, because Gel method is not available in Photoshop and the color on your tinted layers may change if you open the layered file in Photoshop. Choose File, Clone to quickly make a flattened copy, then save the image as a TIFF file.

Flat, transparent washes on the "clothing" and "skin and hair" layers

4b

The Layers palette showing the "clothing" layer selected

5a

Bringing out highlights on the shirt using the Soft Eraser variant of Tinting

5b

We used the Blender variant of Tinting to smooth areas in the face and shirt.

Blending a Photo

Overview *Open a photo and clone it; use the Just Add Water variant of Blenders to smear pixels in the image; restore a portion of the original with the Soft Cloner variant of Cloners.*

ANDREW HATHAWAY

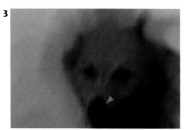

Hathaway's original photo of the dogs

Choosing the Just Add Water variant of the Blenders

Making loose strokes with the Just Add Water variant at 40% opacity

Partially restoring the dog's face using a low-opacity Soft Cloner variant of Cloners

TO CREATE THE EXPRESSIONISTIC *DOGS OF THE SURF*, Andrew Hathaway used Painter's Just Add Water brush to paint directly onto a clone of one of his photographs, transforming it into an intense, emotionally charged abstract painting. He gave the piece a touch of realism with a Cloners brush, using it to restore a hint of the original photo to the clone.

1 Choosing a subject and making a clone. Open your photo in Painter, then choose File, Clone to make a copy of your image to alter. Hathaway chose one of his own photos—an image of two dogs running toward him on the beach—then cloned it.

2 Blending with a Water brush. Hathaway used the Just Add Water variant of Blenders; since it uses the Soft Cover submethod and doesn't show paper texture, it's the smoothest of the blending brushes. For a more subtle smearing effect, you may want to reduce the Opacity in the Property Bar. To make more expressive strokes, with the brush size changing as you vary pressure on the stylus, open the Brush Creator (Ctrl/⌘-B) and in the Size panel of the Stroke Designer, move the Min Size slider to about 15%. Now, make some strokes on your clone. Hathaway painted energetic, angled, smeary strokes on the clone to emphasize the focal point and perspective in the foreground; then he smeared the background into more abstract shapes. He modified his brush as he worked, varying the Size between 10 and 30 pixels, and lowering the Opacity to 30–40% using the sliders in the Property Bar.

3 Partially restoring from the original. As a last step, Hathaway used the Soft Cloner variant of the Cloners brush with a very low opacity (5%) to subtly restore the foreground dog's face. Try this on your clone. Use the Soft Cloner brush to bring the original back into the blurred areas of your image. Experiment with the Opacity slider in the Property Bar until you find a setting that suits your drawing style and pressure.

Cloning a Portrait

Overview *Retouch a photo and soften background detail; clone the image with brushes; paint details by hand; add texture.*

1a

The original photograph

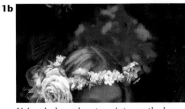

1b

Using darker colors to paint over the busy flowers in the background

2

Adding hand-painted details to the hair

3

Adding relief to the brushwork with Apply Surface Texture Using Image Luminance

LAUREL BECKER

PAINTERLY CLONING IS A GREAT WAY to add natural atmosphere to photos. To create *Flower Girl,* Laurel Becker began by retouching a photo. Then she enhanced a clone of the photo by painting expressive brushstrokes and adding texture. When cloning, after blocking in the image, add hand-painted details, highlights and shadows.

1 Scanning, adjusting and retouching. Becker scanned an 8 x 10-inch photo at 100% and 150 ppi. Then she bumped up the image contrast using Effects, Tonal Control, Brightness /Contrast. To focus attention on the girl, she selected the background and "played down" the busy foliage details. If your background is busy, consider making a selection and using Effects, Focus, Soften to blur details or paint over areas with darker colored brushstrokes, as Becker did. (For information about making selections, turn to Chapter 4.)

2 Cloning and painting. Next, Becker cloned the photo (File, Clone). For this portrait, she chose Basic Paper in the Paper Selector and the Captured Bristle variant of Acrylics from the Brush Selector Bar. Before beginning to paint, she checked the Clone Color box in the Color picker, to sample color from the original image. Then she painted over the entire clone. As she worked, she sized the brush using the Size slider on the Property Bar. She used a larger brush while painting loose strokes behind the girl and a tiny brush to paint the details on the face, dress and hair. She turned off Clone Color, then painted brighter highlights on the cheeks, nose, eyes, chin and lips, her brush following the contours of the forms.

3 Adding texture. After she was finished painting, Becker added relief and texture to her brushwork using two applications of Effects, Surface Control, Apply Surface Texture: The first, Using Image Luminance, Amount 20% and Shine 0%; the second, Using Paper, Amount 20% and Shine 0%. She left other settings at their defaults. 🖌

Creating a Photo-Painting

Overview *Open a retouched photo in Painter; paint a loose abstract background; clone and paint the image with brushes; add surface texture.*

MICHAEL CAMPBELL

The original photo shot by Campbell

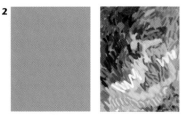

The clone filled with a tan color (left) and the loose brush work painted over the tan fill (right)

FOR *PORTRAIT OF PATRICE*, Michael Campbell combined photography with painting. Campbell is a professional photographer who specializes in portraits. He began the work by choosing a photo from a shoot and retouching it using Photoshop, then saving it as an RGB TIFF file. In Painter, he used cloning and paint applied with various brushes to combine the photograph with expressive brush work and texture.

1 Opening a photo and making a clone. To begin the image, Campbell opened his photo in Painter. The file was approximately 10 x 14 inches, at 150 pixels per inch. He made a clone of the image by choosing File, Clone. (Campbell left the original photo open so that he could sample color from it later using the Dropper, or clone from it later using the Cloners brushes.) He saved the cloned image, giving it the name "Step 1" to keep versions of his image organized.

2 Building a painted background. For a colored background that would provide a base for more tightly rendered brushstrokes,

Loosely cloning the photo into the painted background

Building the forms and colors

Using smaller brushes to refine the forms and background

Campbell used the Dropper tool to sample a light tan color from the original photo. Then he filled the clone canvas with the color by choosing Effects, Fill (Ctrl/⌘-F), choosing Current Color and clicking OK. Next, he applied loose brush work to this background using various Oils brushes (for instance, the Opaque Round variant of Oils), applying colors that he had sampled from the photo with the Dropper. At this point, he had not cloned imagery from the photo yet. He saved and named the painted background image "Step 2."

3 Beginning to clone in the photo. Next, Campbell added more loose brushstrokes to his image using a large cloning brush based on the Camel Oil Cloner variant of Cloners. (During this step in his process, he doesn't like to use Painter's Tracing Paper function much, because he feels that it hides the look and color of his brushstrokes).

4 Building form and color. As Campbell continued to paint the figure and basket, his brushstrokes followed the contours of the forms as they do when he uses conventional oil paints. While he worked, he often changed the Size of the brush using the Size slider popped out of the Property Bar. Sometimes he turned off the Clone Color button in the Color picker and painted freehand to retain a loose painterly feeling in the image. He saved this version of the image as "Step 3."

The final painted stage is shown in this detail.

5 Refining the painting. Campbell wanted to create a looser painted look in the clothing, flower basket and background, and more realistic detail in the model's face. To paint the dress, flowers and basket, he used a small version of the Camel Oil Cloner variant. He softly refined the detailed parts of the face, especially the eyes and mouth. In areas where he wanted even more realism, he switched to a small Soft Cloner variant of the Cloners and with the original photo as the clone source, he carefully restored the model's eyes, nose and lips. When Campbell was pleased with this stage, he saved it and named this version of the image "Step 4."

6a

The complete painted and cloned image before texture was added

6b

Detail of the face showing the Surface Texture applied to the paint

6c

Detail of the image showing the second Surface Texture application using the canvas texture

6 Applying two kinds of texture. Next, Campbell added three-dimensional highlights and shadows to his brushstrokes by choosing Effects, Surface Control, Apply Surface Texture, Using Image Luminance, with subtle Amount and Shine settings of approximately 30%, leaving other settings at their defaults. He named this textured image "Step 5."

He wanted to try a canvas-like texture, so he opened his "Step 4" image, and chose File, Clone again. With this image active, he chose Effects, Surface Control, Apply Surface Texture, this time Using Paper. He chose the Raw Silk texture from the Painter 7 texture library, loaded from the Painter 8 CD 2. He named the clone with the canvas texture "Step 6."

7 Cloning imagery from different versions. To hide the canvas in some areas as if it were thick paint covering up the canvas of a real painting, Campbell used various sizes of the Camel Oil Cloner variant to clone imagery from the "Step 5" clone into the "Step 6" clone. (To designate another image as a clone source, open it, then choose File, Clone Source and select its name in the menu.) After he was satisfied with the look of his image, he saved it as "Step 7," and as an RGB TIFF file for printing on a high-resolution inkjet printer using archival inks. The final image can be seen on page 230.

7

Detail of the final image showing areas of the first Apply Surface Texture application that accentuated the brushstrokes ("Step 5") cloned into the "Step 6" clone that included the Apply Surface Texture application Using Paper

Distressing a Photo

Overview *Open a photo; copy the image to a new layer; use Distress to make it black-and-white and texturize it; combine the layer and the canvas using a transparent Composite Method.*

CHER THREINEN-PENDARVIS

1a

CHER THREINEN-PENDARVIS

The original photo

1b

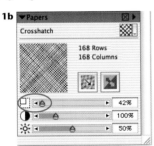

Scaling the Crosshatch paper texture

2

Applying the Distress effect

3

The image showing the layer set to Screen Composite Method before reducing Opacity

BY DEFAULT, THE DISTRESS FILTER IN PAINTER adds texture and changes a color image to black-and-white. In this example, we used custom settings to apply the filter to a layer, then set its Composite Method to Screen, so the effect would combine with the colored photo beneath it.

1 Choosing a photo and a texture. Open a photo with good contrast and color. A bold image with a strong focal point will respond best to this technique. Choose a high-contrast texture that will complement your photo. We opened the Papers palette (Window, Show Papers) and chose Crosshatch from the Painter 7 Textures library (loaded from the Paper Textures folder on the Painter 8 CD 2 CD-ROM). To achieve a finer texture in the final image we scaled the texture down to 42%.

2 Making a layer and applying the effect. The Distress process is easier to control when the filter is applied to a copy of the image on a layer, and then the filtered and original versions are combined. To put a duplicate of the image onto a layer in the Layers palette, choose Select all (Ctrl/⌘-A), then press the Alt/Option key and choose Select, Float.

With the layer active, access the Distress dialog box by choosing Effects, Surface Control, Distress. Experiment with the settings in the dialog box to suit your taste. We increased the Edge Size to 20.30 to bring out the highlights; lowered the Edge Amount to 36% to darken the shadows; reduced Smoothing to 1.00 so the filter would not "round" the edges, and reduced Threshold to 43% to lighten the image subtly. When you've achieved a texture with the amount of white you want, click OK.

3 Blending the treated layer with the original photo. In the Layers palette, to drop out the black areas of the layer to reveal the photo underneath, change the Composite method to Screen. For a more subtle effect, we also lowered the opacity of the layer to 75% using the Opacity slider in the Layers palette.

Making a Custom Solarization

Overview *Use Express Texture on positive and negative clones of an image; merge the images by filling with a Clone Source.*

The original image after equalizing (left), and the negative clone

Creating black-and-white positive (left) and negative versions of the clones using Express Texture

Merging the positive and negative images

Adjusting the image's brightness and contrast

IN THE DARKROOM, SOLARIZATION OCCURS when a negative or print is exposed to a flash of light during the development process, partially reversing the photo's tonal range. To achieve this effect digitally, we tested other image-processing programs and filters, and found that we got the most control and detail using Painter's Express Texture feature. This technique gives you a lot of control over the image's value contrast and it frequently creates a glowing edge-line effect where contrasting elements meet.

1 Making positive and negative clones. Open an image with good value contrast, then choose Effects, Tonal Control, Equalize (Ctrl/⌘-E) to increase its tonal range. Choose File, Clone twice. Make one of the clones into a color negative by selecting Effects, Tonal Control, Negative.

2 Making black-and-white separations. Use Painter's Express Texture feature to convert both clones to black-and-white: Choose Effects, Surface Control, Express Texture, and select Image Luminance from the pop-up menu. Experiment with the sliders and click OK. Repeat the process for the second clone. We set Gray Threshold to 72%, Grain to 72% and Contrast to 160%. These settings helped emphasize the gradient effect in the sky.

3 Merging the two exposures. Choose File, Clone Source and choose the positive clone. Now fill the negative image with a percentage of the positive (the "flash of light"): With the negative window active, choose Effects, Fill, Clone Source. Set the Opacity slider between 40% and 60%.

4 Pumping up the tonal range. To achieve a broader tonal range while maintaining a silvery solarized look, we selected Effects, Tonal Control, Brightness/Contrast. We increased the contrast (the top slider) and decreased the brightness slightly. 🖌

Solarizing Color

Overview *Use Correct Colors, Color Correction to make positive and negative tones; enhance the solarization by compositing a desaturated layer.*

LINNEA DAYTON / CHER PENDARVIS / PHOTO: CORBIS IMAGES

1

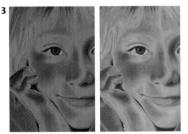

The color photograph from Corbis Images

2

Setting the curve for the solarization in the Color Correction dialog box

3

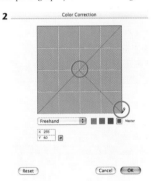

The color image on the Canvas (left) and the desaturated layer (right)

EARLY DARKROOM SOLARIZATIONS were black-and-white, but today they include color as well. Classic color solarizations have solid areas of color and glowing gradations with elements often separated by edge-line effects. To achieve the effect of a color solarization digitally, we used Painter's Color Correction, Freehand Curve function.

1 Choosing an image. For the best results, open an image with good value contrast and color.

2 Solarizing the image. Choose Tonal Control, Correct Colors. When the Color Correction dialog box appears, from the pulldown menu choose Freehand. As you'll notice in the Color Correction dialog box, the standard curve is a diagonal line from lower left to upper right. Making an inverted "V" shaped curve will create both positive and negative tones in an image. Press the Shift key and click in the center, then in the lower right corner to snap the line into an inverted "V." If you have trouble making the "V" shape, click the Reset button and begin again. To achieve a broader tonal range in the solarization, we selected Effects, Tonal Control, Brightness/Contrast and subtly increased the contrast (top slider).

3 Enhancing the solarization. We wanted to achieve more dramatic tone and color in our image, so we copied the solarized image to a layer that we could use to intensify the effect. Choose Select, All (Ctrl/⌘-A), press the Alt/Option key, then choose Select, Float. A layer will appear in the Layers palette.

Now, to make the image on the layer gray, while preserving its tonality, choose Effects, Tonal Control, Adjust Colors and move the Saturation slider all the way to the left. (Leave the Hue and Value sliders at 0.) To give the solarization richer colors and tones, we composited the gray layer with the colored image on the Canvas using the Luminosity Composite Method in the Layers palette. For different color effects, experiment with other Composite Methods such as Pseudocolor and Darken.

Creating a Woodcut from a Photo

Overview *Open a photo and clean up the background; copy the Canvas to make a new layer; create a color woodcut plate on the Canvas; create a black woodcut plate on the new layer; retouch the black plate; add clouds and texture.*

JOHN DERRY

The original digital photo of the pagoda

Setting the Tolerance for the Magic Wand in the Property Bar

WITH PAINTER'S WOODCUT FILTER you can start with a photo and achieve a look similar to a conventional wood block print. You can simply use the color arrived at by the Woodcut filter defaults, or you can enjoy complete control over choosing the colors.

The traditional wood block printing process involves simplification of detail in the lines and color areas. Inspired by Japanese wood block prints from the 1800s, John Derry created *Pagoda*, which is based on one of his own digital photos. Painter's Woodcut filter helped him to reduce the number of colors in the image and to fine-tune the colors for the final artwork.

1 Choosing a photo. Open a photo with good contrast and color. A bold image with a strong focal point will work best for this effect.

2 Cleaning up the sky. To focus more attention on the pagoda, Derry simplified the sky by selecting it and applying a blue fill. Choose the Magic Wand in the Toolbox and click in the sky. Adjust the Tolerance in the Property Bar until most of the sky is

2b

The Image viewed with the mask eye icon open (left), and the active selection with the blue fill applied (right)

3

The visibility of Layer 1 is turned off and the Canvas is selected.

4a

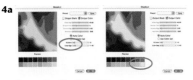

Increasing the Color Edge to make simpler, smoother shapes (left) and brightening the gold color (right)

4b

The color woodcut plate

selected; at this point, edges are most important, since you can clean up any small internal "debris" by painting on the mask later. Save the selection as a mask in the Channels palette by choosing Select, Save Selection. In the Channels palette, open the eye icon to the left of the mask's name. Choose *black* in the Color picker and paint on the mask where you need to *add* more mask; use *white* to *remove* areas of the mask (for instance, to remove debris). To use the mask to isolate the sky, choose Select, Load Selection. (See Chapter 4 to read more about working with masks and selections.) Next, fill the selection with blue by choosing Select, Fill, with Current Color.

3 Setting up layers. The Woodcut process is easier to control when the color elements are on a separate layer from the black elements. Derry started his layering by making a duplicate of the original image. To put a duplicate of the image canvas onto a layer, choose Select, All (Ctrl/⌘-A), press the Alt/Option key and choose Select, Float. In the Layers palette, turn the new layer's visibility off by toggling shut the eye icon to the left of its name.

4 Cutting the color "wood block." In the Layers section, click the canvas name to activate it for the colors. To access the Woodcut dialog box, choose Effects, Surface Control, Woodcut. When the dialog box appears, disable the Output Black checkbox. The options for Black Output will now be grayed out. In the lower portion of the window, accept the default number of colors (16), and smooth out the edges of the color blocks by adjusting the Color Edge slider to the right. (Derry set it at approximately 11.46.)

When the edges were as he liked them, Derry fine-tuned a few of the colors. For instance, he chose a tan color swatch (at the bottom of the dialog box) and made the color brighter. Click on a color square to select it; a red outline will appear around it. Now that it's selected, you can choose a new color in the Color picker and the swatch will change to the new color. To sample a color directly from the image Preview window, press the Ctrl/⌘ key and click on the Preview. To change the color, choose a new color in the Color picker.

To see other areas of your image in the Preview window, drag with the grabber hand cursor to move around the image

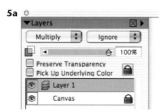

5a

Setting the Composite Method for Layer 1 to Multiply

5b

To achieve more detailed black edges, the Black Edge slider was adjusted to the left.

6a

The black plate (shown with the Canvas hidden) with black in the sky (left), and with the sky retouched (right)

6b

The in-progress woodcut with both color and black plates in place

preview. When you're satisfied with the colors, click OK to accept.

5 Cutting the black plate.

To begin making the black plate, target Layer 1 by clicking on its name in the Layers palette and open its eye icon. At the top of the Layers palette, set its Composite Method to Multiply so the white that will be generated on the layer by the Woodcut effect will disappear. Now, choose Effects, Surface Control, Woodcut and turn on Output Black and turn off Color Output in the dialog box. For more detailed edges, adjust the Black Edge slider to the left. (Derry set it to approximately 25.75.)

6 Cleaning up the black plate. The settings that worked well for the detail in the pagoda left too much black in the sky. Using the Scratchboard variant of Pens and white paint, Derry removed the black by painting white over the sky. He chose the Scratchboard Tool because it paints with a crisp edge. An Eraser variant would have produced a softer edge.

7 Adding clouds and texture. Next, Derry painted simple cloud shapes on a new layer using a large Scratchboard Tool and white paint. (To add a new layer, click the New Layer button near the bottom of the Layers palette.) Increase the size of the Scratchboard tool using the Size slider in the Property Bar (Derry adjusted his to about 25.4). Paint loose brushstrokes that complement your composition. Then he dragged the layer below the black plate layer in the Layers palette so the black would appear to be "printed" on top.

For added realism, Derry completed the woodcut by adding a subtle paper texture to the colored layer. To add texture, click on the colored layer in the Layers palette. Select Basic Paper in the Paper Selector, then choose Effects, Surface Control, Dye Concentration, Using Paper. In the dialog box, try moving the Maximum slider to the right until a subtle paper texture effect is visible. Adjust the settings to your taste and click OK.

7

The clouds and texture have been added.

Creating a Montage Using Masks and Layers

Overview *Create masks for the component photos in Photoshop or Painter; copy them into a single document; use a brush to edit the layer masks when compositing them; paint on the final image.*

1

The original photos

2

The cut-and-pasted comp ready to be scanned and used as a template

WHEN CONTINENTAL CABLEVISION asked John Dismukes of Capstone Studios to illustrate a direct-mail piece, he and his team turned to Painter. He combined photographs and splashy color with loose airbrush and chalk brushstrokes to illustrate the theme "Can Summer in California Get Any Better?"

1 Gathering illustration elements. Begin by collecting all of the individual elements that you'll need for your illustration. Dismukes and his associates photographed separate images of clouds, a pair of sunglasses, ocean foam, palm trees, and a television on the sand. The photo negatives were scanned in Kodak Photo CD format.

2 Making a template from laser prints. Dismukes's team created a traditional comp by printing the individual elements, then photocopying them at different scales and assembling them using scissors and adhesive. They turned the completed comp into a template by scanning it at 72 ppi, opening it in Painter and sizing it to the final image size of 4 x 5 inches at 762 ppi, using Canvas, Resize. The template would act as a guide for Dismukes to accurately scale and position the various elements. If you choose to include this step, don't be concerned about the "bitmapping" that occurs when scanning the comp at a low resolution; when the composition is finished, the template will be completely covered by the source images.

3

Three of Dismukes's Photoshop masks

4a

The glasses source file with active selection, ready to copy and paste or drag and drop into the background image

4b

Layers
Default | Ignore
100%
Preserve Transparency
Pick Up Underlying Color
trees
sunglasses
clouds
ocean waves
Canvas

Bringing the layers into the composite file

5

Layers
Default | Ignore
100%
Preserve Transparency
Pick Up Underlying Color
trees
sunglasses
clouds
ocean waves
Canvas

Channels
RGB
trees Layer Mask

Selecting the layer mask in the Layers palette and opening its eye icon in the Channels palette

6a

Using the Digital Airbrush variant and black paint to paint on the layer mask and hide the portion of the cloud layer that covers the TV

3 Masking unwanted portions of the source images.
Working in Photoshop, Dismukes used the Pen tool to cut masks for the sunglasses, ocean foam, palm trees and television on the beach. He converted each path to a selection, saved the selection as an Alpha Channel, then saved each image as an RGB TIFF file, including the alpha channel.

You can accomplish the same result in Painter. Open one of your source photos and use the Pen or Shape Design tool (Toolbox) to draw a shape around the desired portion of the image. When you're done, choose Shapes, Convert To Selection; then to save the selection as a mask, choose Select, Save Selection. View the selection as a mask by opening its eye icon in the Channels palette. You should see your image covered by a red overlay—the default color for the mask. To view only the mask in black-and-white, click the RGB eye icon shut in the Channels palette.

4 Compiling the source files. When you've finished masking the images, bring them into a single document. Open the template if you have one, or the photo that will become your background image. Choose the Layer Adjuster tool and if the Layers palette is not open, choose Window, Show Layers. Then open each of the source images and choose Select, Load Selection and Alt/Option-click on each selection to make a layer. Loading the selection and making a layer prepares Painter to export the item from the source image with its mask.

There are three ways to import source images into a composite file: Copying and pasting through the clipboard, performing a drag-and-drop, or using the File, Place command to bring the source image in as a reference layer. To paste using the clipboard, select the layer in the source image with the Layer Adjuster tool, choose Edit, Copy, then make the background image active and choose Edit, Paste. If your component images are approximately the right size, the easiest way is probably to drag-and-drop: Select the layer in the source image with the Layer Adjuster. Now use the Layer Adjuster to drag the masked item to the background image.

If you're working with large files, positioning and scaling can be accomplished much more quickly using reference layers. To import an image as a reference layer with a mask, save the source file in RIFF format (to preserve its mask), then choose File, Place, navigate to the source image and choose Open. In the Place dialog box check the Retain Alpha checkbox and click in the image to place the layer. (For more information about reference layers, see "Using Reference Layers" on page 182 in Chapter 5.)

6b

Compositing the clouds inside the glasses

6c

Revealing the cloud layer around the tree

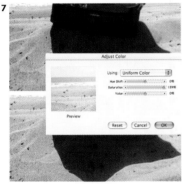

7

Using Adjust Colors to increase saturation in the image

8

Adding squiggles and lens glare (top) and smudges and blurs

5 Adding layer masks and putting them to work. To add a layer mask to a layer, select the layer in the Layers palette and click the Create Layer Mask button at the bottom of the Layers palette. To view the mask in black and white, open the layer mask's eye icon in the Channels palette. To switch back to color view so you can edit the layer mask while viewing the image on the layer, shut the layer mask's eye icon.

6 Positioning the layer and painting on its layer mask. First scale, rotate and position one layer on top of another and make sure that the top layer is selected in the Layers palette. Now, fit the top element inside the element below it by using a brush and black color to paint a portion of the top layer's mask, as follows: Begin by targeting the layer name in the Layers palette, then click on the layer mask's thumbnail to the right of the layer. (A dark outline will appear around the thumbnail when it is targeted.) Choose the Digital Airbrush variant of Airbrushes and choose black in the Color picker. Begin painting around the edge of the top layer to hide part of the layer imagery, making it appear "inside" of the layer beneath it. Paint with white to restore the layer.

When you've completed all compositing, turn off visibility for the template layer in your file by selecting its name in the Layers palette and shutting its eye icon. Then make a copy of your image with the layers merged with the background by choosing File, Clone. This step gives you a lot of flexibility—you have an "original" with layers intact, and a "working image" (the clone) on which you can paint and make other adjustments.

7 Shifting colors. To make the image "pop" a bit more, Dismukes increased the color saturation. Choose Effects, Tonal Control, Adjust Colors, and experiment with the Hue Shift, Saturation and Value sliders to modify the colors in your image.

8 Painting on the photo montage. To transform the television into a lively caricature in vivid color, Dismukes first used the Digital Airbrush variant to add details such as glare on the glasses. He switched to the Impressionist variant of the Artists brush to paint on the sand and water, and then painted spontaneous, textured squiggles around the TV and on the sand and water with the Artist Pastel Chalk variant of Pastels using the Big Canvas paper (loaded from the More Paper Textures library, in the Paper Textures folder on the Painter 8 CD 2 CD-ROM). As a final touch, Dismukes switched to the Grainy Water variant of Blenders. To smear while revealing texture, he changed the subcategory to Grainy Hard Cover in the General panel of the Stroke Designer (Brush Creator) and added the smudges and blurs on the sand and television.

Finishing the job. Using the same style, technique, tools and colors, Dismukes created similar illustrations on a smaller scale that were used throughout the brochure, as well as a border around the edge of the piece. 🐾

■ **Philip Howe** was commissioned by
Harry Hansen to create *Police,* a photo collage painting to promote positive aspects
of law enforcement. The final piece—
printed on canvas and enhanced with oil
paints—was part of a traveling show of
police art touring the United States. To
build the image, Howe began with two
source photos: a horizontal photo of a
brick wall with a cast shadow of a motor-
cycle rider, and a vertical photo of a
policeman standing against a brick wall.
Beginning in Photoshop, Howe copied the
rider image and pasted it into a copy of
the vertical wall image as a layer. He
worked back and forth between Photoshop and Painter as he retouched the
brick areas above the standing figure's

head to match the bricks of the top image.
When the retouching was complete, Howe
began the process of building relief on the
background wall image in Painter. He
applied Effects, Focus, Glass Distortion
Using Image Luminance and the Refraction
Map Type, using strong settings. Next, he
opened the original vertical brick wall
image and again applied Effects, Focus,
Glass Distortion, Using Image Luminance
and the Refraction Map type, this time
using subtle settings. Finally, he selected
the composite file and defined the subtly
distorted image as the clone source (File,
Clone Source). Using an Airbrush Cloner
variant, he cloned the subtle distortion
onto areas of the image canvas to softly
smooth out areas of the relief.

■ For *Capitola Encaustic,* a photo-illustration created with Liquid Ink, **John Derry** began by shooting a photograph of the colorful buildings in the town of Capitola, California with his Sony digital camera. He envisioned an image with bold colors and simple shapes. So before he began to paint on the photo, he reduced the number of colors by posterizing it using the Effects, Tonal Control, Posterize command, choosing eight Levels. Next, he put a copy of the Canvas on a layer by choosing Select, All, pressing the Alt/Option key and choosing Select, Float. He chose the Sparse Camel variant of the Liquid Ink brush, and reduced its size slightly in the Property

Bar. In the Layers palette, he enabled the Pick Up Underlying Color box so that when he painted new brushstrokes, color from the underlying layer would blend with the current color he was using. Derry sampled color from the photo using the Dropper tool as he worked. (To temporarily switch from the Brush tool to the Dropper, press the Alt/Option key.) He painted over the image using the Sparse Flat variant, changing the size of the brush as he worked. To achieve the look of thick paint, he double-clicked the Liquid Ink layer name in the Layers palette and slightly increased the Amount setting. Derry wanted to build up the look of thick paint with overlapping

strokes, so he created another new Liquid Ink layer (by clicking the right triangle on the right side of the Layers palette bar and choosing New Liquid Ink Layer). For a crosshatched, overlaid look, he built up Liquid Ink brushstrokes on the new layer, on top of the existing strokes on the layer below. (For more information about Liquid Ink, see "A Painter Liquid Ink Primer" on page 117 and "Encaustic Painting with Liquid Ink" on page 122.) To bring more detail from the photo back into the illustration, he placed another copy of the posterized photo on top of the Liquid Ink layer and reduced its opacity to 50% in the Layers palette.

■ For *Switches*, a collage made of several photos, **Aleksander Jensko** began by shooting his own photographs with a Nikon Coolpix digital camera. The rich textures in his collage were created by combining the layers when the collage was complete and then adding brushwork painted with Painter's Water Color brushes and the Coarse Spray variant of Airbrushes. To begin, Jensko opened all of the source photos: a black-and-white photo of a window curtain, an image of switches, a blurry photo of a woman, an image of a wooden crate with stenciled lettering and a photo with pronounced grain. He opened a new file, then copied and pasted each source image into the composite. Jensko used the Layer Adjuster tool to position the elements to his taste. To make areas of certain elements transparent (the Switches and the woman layers, for instance), he added

layer masks to the layers and painted on them with the Digital Airbrush variant of Airbrushes to hide portions of the layers. He created the edge effect on a new layer and set the layer's Composite Method to Overlay to make it translucent. For additional transparency effects, he used transparent Composite Methods and reduced opacity on some of the layers. When the composite was as he liked it, he dropped all of the layers to the Canvas by Shift-Selecting them and choosing Drop All from the menu on the right side of the Layers palette. He created the grainy texture behind the woman by spraying dark color using the Coarse Spray variant of Airbrushes. To complete the image, he added watercolor brushwork. To put the collage on a Water Color layer, he targeted the Canvas and chose Lift Canvas To Water Color Layer from the Lay-

ers palette menu. Once the image was on a Water Color layer, he could use various Water Color brushes, including the Dry Bristle and Wash Camel to paint subtle brushstrokes and soft washes.

■ *Dyrskap* by **Aleksander Jensko** began with a single photo of an abandoned road near Dyrskap in the mountains of Norway. (In Norwegian, Dyrskap means reindeer cap.) Jensko used an Olympus E-10 digital camera to capture the images.

Jensko imported the images into a layered file and blended them together using layer masks in Painter. He wanted the image to be spooky, so he quickly made a flattened copy by cloning it (File, Clone). Once the image was reduced to one layer, he darkened it (to add atmosphere) and made the colors more saturated and deeper using Effects, Surface Control, Dye Concentration. To bring even more mystery into the image, he added a glowing look to the window in the boat as follows: He selected the window with the Rectangular Selection tool, tilted the selection using the Selection Adjuster tool, then he feathered the selection by one pixel (Select, Feather) and saved the selection (Select, Save Selection). He added a new layer to color the window (by clicking the New Layer button at the bottom of the Layers palette), loaded the selection (Select, Load Selection) and filled the selected area on the layer with yellow, then he set the Composite Method of the colored layer to Multiply in the Layers palette. Next, Jensko adjusted the Opacity of the layer in the Layers palette to his taste. He gave the entire image a watercolor-like tex-ture, as follows: First, he flattened a copy of the image by Shift-selecting the layer names in the Layers palette and chose Drop All from the triangle pop-up menu near the top right corner of the palette. Then he chose Lift Canvas to Water Color Layer from the pop-up menu and finally, he chose Wet Entire Water Color Layer from the menu. To complete his image, he painted brushwork texture on some areas of the image using Water Color brushes. He added a new Water Color layer by clicking the New Water Color Layer button on the bottom of the Layers palette, and using the Dry Bristle and Wash Camel variants of Water Color, he painted brushstrokes on the cliffs, concrete, boat and pathway.

"My intent was to create a message of hope," says **John Derry** about *Imagine*, a collage which he created soon after the tragic events of September 11, 2001. When in New York City the previous July, Derry had shot many photos using his Sony digital still camera. *Imagine* incorporates three of these photos, an image of clouds (shot while in flight), a photo of the World Trade Center towers and a photo of the Strawberry Fields memorial to John Lennon in New York City's Central park. The memorial symbolizes the death of one man, and the towers the death of many; both are powerful symbols of dark days in American history. Through it all, the Imagine mosaic shines as a sunlike symbol, radiating hope. Derry opened the three source files, and

cut a "drop out" mask for the towers. Using the Pen tool from the Toolbox, he quickly drew a shape around the towers. He converted the shape to a selection by choosing Shape, Convert to Selection, then he saved the selection as a mask in the Channels palette by choosing Select, Save Selection. Derry saved the three source images and placed them into a new composite file by choosing File, Place. This command allowed him to bring each element into the collage file, with a mask (enable Retain Alpha). The names of the files also appeared as layer names in the Layers palette. Derry rotated the image of the towers to accommodate the Imagine mosaic using Effects, Orientation, Free Transform,

holding down the Ctrl/⌘-key and dragging a corner handle. Once the elements were in position, he clicked the Create Layer Mask button at the bottom of the Layers palette to add a layer mask to each layer and used the Digital Airbrush variant of Airbrushes to hide portions of the Imagine and cloud layers. He clicked on a layer, then on its layer mask in the Layers palette, then he used black paint to make soft transparencies in areas of the two layers. To enhance the "sun" effect, he added a new, empty layer, on which he airbrushed soft, white strokes radiating out from the edges of the Imagine mosaic tiles. To finish, he set the layer's Composite Method to Overlay in the Layers palette.

■ "Although the program is called Painter," says renowned photographer **Pedro Meyer**, "it's important not to exclude photography from its repertoire, given that the program can also be used effectively in that medium."

Meyer's keen photographic eye, and a Nikon digital camera, captured the initial photo for the image above in Glendale, California.

"One of the aspects that I do find intriguing with the tools that we have at hand today, is that we can explore after the image is taken, what works to our best advantage in making the image more effective," says Meyer.

Meyer had taken the photograph straight. To create an impression of dynamic motion, he tilted it slightly, then used focus and blur effects (for instance, Camera Motion Blur) to help the viewer concentrate on the most significant areas in the image. The stores in the background were not as important as the single figure, so Meyer turned them into more general texture elements.

Meyer says, "Before digital photography it was very hard to make credible images which had these traits (for instance, the special focus and blur effects which are used in *Glendale*). It was quite complicated and time-consuming. These days, almost all it takes is the imagination to use the tools in ways that are more about the ideas than about showing off the virtues of the tools themselves."

■ An internationally acclaimed studio portraitist, **Phillip Stewart Charris** has created elegant and timeless likenesses of celebrities, individuals and families for over three decades. Known for his life-size portraits, which are printed, and then mounted on canvas, Charris has drawn inspiration from artists such as John Singer Sargent, Raphael and Rembrandt. The portrait *Pretty Little Girl* was photographed in his studio in Southern California. Then a transparency was scanned, saved as an RGB TIFF file and opened in Painter. To protect the figure while he worked on the background, Charris made a mask. Then, using expressive brushwork, he painted over the image background with the Sable Chisel Tip Water variant of Brushes (loaded from the Painter 5.5 Brushes library from the Brushes folder on the Painter 8 CD 2 CD-ROM). To smooth some areas, he painted finer strokes with a low-opacity Just Add Water variant of Blenders. He used the brushes not to apply color, but to blend and smear pixels in the image in a painterly way. For the figure and clothing, Charris used smaller versions of the same two brushes. When brushing over the face and hair, he carefully painted with a small brush to preserve the important details. "The photographer must seek out the personality of the sitter, which lies beneath a veil that subtly alters the surface of the face. Piercing that veil to reveal the subject's character is something that, after the posing is taken care of, can only be done for a fraction of a second," says Charris.

■ An innovative professional photographer, **Michael Campbell** specializes in portraits and also excels in painting. When creating *Frances with Hat*, Campbell combined photography with painting using Painter brushes. He began the work by choosing a photo from his shoot and retouching it using Photoshop. In Painter, he used cloning and paint applied with various brushes to paint over the photograph, adding expressive brushwork and texture. He made a clone of the image (File, Clone) and painted a loose, expressive background with a modified version of the Camel Oil Cloner variant of Cloners. He saved the image and then began to gradually build up basic forms of the figure and clothing. He alternated between painting with Clone Color turned on and off in the Color picker. With Clone Color turned on, he could sample color from the original and with it turned off, he could paint with color he chose in the Color picker. He gradually built up details in the focal areas of the image (for instance, the model's face and hands), and he painted looser brushwork to suggest folds in the clothing. Finally, he used Effects, Surface Control, Apply Surface Texture to add three-dimensional highlights and shadows to the brushwork and canvas texture. Turn to "Creating a Photo-Painting" on page 230 to see Campbell's technique step by step.

7

EXPLORING
SPECIAL
EFFECTS

An innovative artist, Laurence Gartel combines digital photography with painting and special effects, as shown in this detail of Coney Island Baby. *He used Liquid Metal layers, Apply Surface Texture and transparent Composite Methods to add depth and excitement to the piece. To view the complete painting, turn to gallery at the end of this chapter.*

PAINTER'S SPECIAL EFFECTS ARE SO NUMEROUS and complex that an entire book could be written about them alone. Because they're so powerful, there's much less need for third-party filters than with Photoshop or other image processors. But with that power comes complexity; some of these effects have evolved into "programs within the program." This chapter focuses on five of Painter's most frequently used "mini-programs"—Apply Surface Texture, Apply Lighting, Patterns, Glass Distortion and Mosaics. It also covers several special-effects dynamic layers—including Bevel World, Burn, Tear and Liquid Metal—and a handful of other exciting effects.

ADDING EFFECTS WITH SURFACE TEXTURE

One of the most frequent "haunts" of Painter artists is the Effects, Surface Control, Apply Surface Texture dialog box. You'll find it used in a number of places throughout this book. The Apply Surface Texture dialog box contains intricate, powerful controls, allowing you to apply paper textures to images, build realistic highlights and shadows for masked elements, and more. First, the Softness slider (located under the Using pop-up menu) lets you create soft transitions, such as smoothing the edge of a mask or softening a texture application. Adding Softness can also increase the 3D effect produced when you apply Surface Texture Using Mask (when working with an image that contains a mask). And with the Reflection slider (bottom Appearance of Depth slider), you can create a reflection in your artwork based on another image or the current pattern.

Another very important Surface Texture control is the preview sphere, located below the image Preview. Think of the sphere displayed as a dome supporting lights above your image. Although the preview sphere seems to show a spotlight effect, any lights you set are applied evenly across the surface of your image.

Creating textured, dimensional brushstrokes with Apply Surface Texture Using Image Luminance

Creating the illusion of type under water (top), with Apply Surface Texture using Original Luminance and a reflection map. We applied the reflection using a clone source image of a cloudy sky (tinted red to match the color in the type by using Effects, Tonal Control, Adjust Color).

Experiment with adding more lights by clicking on the sphere. Adjust an individual light by selecting it and changing its color, and adjusting its Brightness and Conc (Concentration). Use the Exposure slider to control ambient light in the environment.

You can get some interesting effects by changing your color choices for the lights. For instance, if the area to be lit contains a lot of blue, you can add more color complexity by lighting with its complement, an orange-hued light.

Applying a reflection map. Reflections can add interest to shiny type and to other surfaces like glass or metal objects in your illustrations. The Reflection slider allows you to apply an image that you designate as a clone source to your illustration as a reflection. Open an image and make a selection or mask for the area where you'll apply the reflection. You can use a pattern as a source for a reflection map or you can open an image the same size as your working file (the current Pattern is applied automatically if you don't choose another image as clone source). (Turn to "Making an Environment Map" and "Applying an Environment Map," later in this chapter, to read about how Michelle Lill builds custommade reflection maps and applies them to her images. And for more inspiration, check out Michelle Lill's E-Maps folder on the *Painter 8 Wow! CD-ROM*, and the Pattern libraries in the Patterns folder on the Corel Painter 8 CD 2 CD-ROM.)

Creating 3D effects. You can use Apply Surface Texture to enhance the surface of your image and give dimension to your brushstrokes. Image Luminance, in the Using pop-up menu, adds depth to brushstrokes by making the light areas appear to recede or "deboss" slightly. If you want to bring the light areas forward, check the Invert box. Experiment with the sliders to get the effect you desire. You can get a stronger 3D effect by clicking to add a second light (a bounce or a fill light) to the preview sphere with a lower Brightness or a higher Concentration (Conc) setting.

RETURN TO DEFAULT SETTINGS

Painter remembers the last settings you choose in effects dialog boxes such as Effects, Surface Control, Apply Surface Texture and Color Overlay. This is helpful when designing scripts (see "Automating Movie Effects" in Chapter 10). To revert to Painter's default settings, save your image and quit Painter to clear the program's Temp file settings.

REFLECTING ANOTHER IMAGE

To use a separate image as a reflection map, bend it using Effects, Surface Control, Quick Warp to achieve a spherical or rippled look. (Quick Warp is applied to the entire image, not just to selections or to a single layer.) Open the reflection image and designate it as the clone source (File, Clone Source). Then (in the original image, not the map image) choose Effects, Surface Control, Apply Surface Texture Using Original Luminance to apply the effect to an entire image. To see the reflection, move the Reflection slider to the right, or distort the reflection effect by moving the Softness slider to the right. Experiment with the other settings.

In Still Life, *Chelsea Sammel created drama in her image using Effects, Surface Control, Apply Lighting. Then she painted over some areas with Brushes variants. She finished the image with an application of Apply Surface Texture Using Paper and a rough paper texture.*

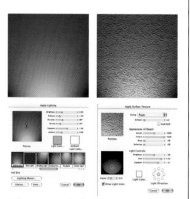

When you use Surface Texture together with Apply Lighting, you'll get more dramatic results if you choose similar lighting directions for both commands.

SOFT LIGHTING TRANSITIONS

If you're using Apply Lighting on a selection, you'll get a softer transition between lighted and unlighted areas if you use Select, Feather (with a high Feather setting) on your selections before you apply the light.

MOVING LIGHTS

To access the Lighting Mover in Painter, so you can copy lights from the Painter Settings file into a new custom library, press Ctrl/⌘-Shift-L. To load the new library, click the Library button in the Apply Lighting dialog box.

Combining Surface Texture with other effects. Apply Surface Texture works especially well when combined with other Painter tools. "Creating an Impressionist Look," on page 259 uses a Glass Distortion dynamic layer and Surface Texture to add paint-like texture to a photo; John Derry used a combination of Glass Distortion and Surface Texture to give the illusion of refracted water in "Creating a Tidepool," on page 270; "Draping a Weave," on page 272, uses a powerful Glass Distortion displacement in combination with Surface Texture to achieve the look of draped fabric. And Steve Campbell used Surface Texture and Apply Lighting together to add gradations to textured areas while creating the illustration "Art in Wartime" on page 278 in the gallery.

ADDING DIMENSION WITH LIGHTING

Painter's *User Guide* gives a good description of how to adjust the controls under Effects, Surface Control, Apply Lighting. Here are some tips and practical uses for the tool.

Applying Lighting to unify an image. Like most of the Surface Control effects, applying lighting across a composite image can help to unify the piece. (If the lighting effect is too dramatic, try using Edit, Fade immediately afterward to reduce it.)

Preventing hot spots. You can avoid "burnout" of lit areas by increasing the Elevation of the light, reducing the light's Exposure or Brightness, or giving the light a pastel or gray color.

Lighting within selections or layers. Add instant dimension to a selection or a layer by applying lighting within it.

Creating subtle gradient effects. To achieve colored gradient effects in an image, some artists prefer lighting with colored lights instead of filling with a gradient; they prefer the Apply Lighting command's smooth luminosity shifts over the more "mechanical" result usually achieved when using gradations.

Painting back into lit areas. For artists who want to achieve a more painterly effect, the Apply Lighting command can look a bit artificial. In creating *Still Life* (left), Chelsea Sammel used Apply Lighting and then she broke up the lit area with brushstrokes, sampling color from the image as she worked.

Creating softly lit backgrounds. On a white background, start with the Splashy Colors light effect. Increase the Brightness and Elevation and reduce the Distance on both colored lights until they form very soft-edged tinted circles on the background. Click in the Preview to add another light or two and change their colors. Move the lights around until the color, value and composition are working. Save and name your settings and click OK to apply the effect. Repeat this process two or three times, returning each time to your saved effect and making minor adjustments in light color, light position and other settings.

Painter's F-X brush variants are capable of creating many subtle or dramatic effects such as fire, glow, and shattered, to name a few.

For Caterpillar, *Matt Dineen used the Furry Brush variant of the F-X brush to paint the caterpillar's colorful hair. See the gallery at the end of this chapter for other examples.*

Grunion Run *is an illustration for a calendar designed and illustrated by Kathleen Blavatt. She used several special-effects brushes to paint the image. Beginning with a black-and-white pen drawing, she modeled the hills using the Pixel Dust variant of Pens (loaded from the Ver 5 Brushes library in the Painter 8 application folder). She added sparkling texture to the sky using the Fairy Dust variant of the F-X brush. Blavatt painted the water with the Piano Keys variant of the F-X brush. She added textured brushstrokes to the sun's head using the Grain Emboss variant of Impasto.*

EXPLORING PATTERNS

On the Patterns palette, there are commands that let you make seamless wrap-around pattern tiles. (To access the menu, click the right triangle on the Patterns palette.) Once a pattern has been defined and is in the Patterns section, it becomes the default Clone Source when no other clone source is designated. You can apply a pattern to an existing image, selection or layer with Cloning brushes, with the Paint Bucket tool (by choosing Fill With: Clone Source in the Property Bar), with any of the special effects features that use a clone source (such as Original Luminance or 3D Brushstrokes), or by choosing to fill with a pattern or clone source (Ctrl/⌘-F). (The Fill dialog box shows a Pattern button if no clone source image is designated; if a clone source *is* available, a Clone Source button appears.) Use the pattern feature to create screen design backgrounds, textile design, wallpaper—anywhere you need repeating images. (For step-by-step techniques, see "Creating a Seamless Pattern" and "Applying Patterns" later in this chapter.)

CANCELING A CLONE SOURCE

To turn off a clone source so you can fill an image with the current pattern (if the clone source is another image), close the clone source image. If you've cloned from one place to another in the *same* image, click on a pattern in the Patterns section of the Toolbox to clear the clone source.

Capturing a Pattern. To make and store a pattern image in the Patterns section, select an area of your document with the Rectangular Selection tool (or press Ctrl/⌘-A to select the entire image) and on the Patterns Palette, click the right triangle and choose Capture Pattern. To offset your pattern use the Horizontal and Vertical Shift options and the Bias slider to control the amount of the offset. Experiment with these settings to get nonaligned patterns—for example, to create a brick wall look, wallpaper or fabric.

Using Pattern wrap-around. Painter creates a wrap-around for the pattern tile you create. Here's a great way to see it work. Select a pattern in the Patterns palette. From the pop-up menu on the right side of the Patterns palette, choose Check Out Pattern; a pattern tile image will appear. Choose the Image Hose category in the Brush Selector Bar. Select an Image Hose nozzle from the Toolbox's Nozzles section. Begin spraying across your image and beyond its edge. Notice how the hose images "wrap around" the edges of the pattern tile (so that when the pattern is captured and an area is filled with these pattern tiles, the edges will match seamlessly).

Making a Fractal Pattern. Choosing Make Fractal Pattern from the Patterns palette menu automatically creates a pattern as a new file when you click OK in the Make Fractal Pattern dialog box. Some of the textures you can create with Make Fractal Pattern make very cool paper textures: Select the area of the fractal pattern

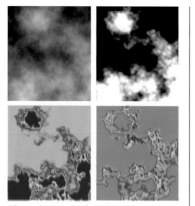

The evolution of a fractal pattern. The original pattern was made by choosing Make Fractal Pattern from the Patterns section menu (top left), then a hard edge was added with Effects, Surface Control, Express Texture Using Image Luminance (top right). We loaded the Earthen gradient from the Painter 6 Gradients library in the Gradients folder on the Corel Painter 8 CD 2 CD-ROM, and applied it via Express in Image—chosen by clicking the right triangle on the Gradients section bar (lower left). To change the color, we adjusted the Bias to 46% in the Express in Image dialog box (lower right).

After creating this topographic map using Make Fractal Pattern, we added clouds for more atmosphere by copying our original Fractal pattern file and pasting it into the map image as a layer. We changed the Composite Method in the Layers palette to Screen to apply only the light parts of the clouds to the topographic map image. Then we adjusted the Opacity slider for the clouds layer to 90%.

that you want for your texture (or choose Select, All) and on the Papers palette, click the right triangle and choose Capture Paper.

Enhancing Fractal Patterns. You can add any special effect to fractal (or regular) patterns and they still remain patterns. Here are two creative applications of fractal patterns.

To create a hard-edged fractal pattern with wild color, make a Fractal Pattern, setting Power to –150%, Feature Size to 75% (for a relatively coarse pattern), and Softness to 0. Click OK. Select Effects, Surface Control, Express Texture Using Image Luminance. Adjust the Gray Threshold and Grain sliders to about 80%, and set the Contrast slider at 200% for a contrasty effect. Click OK. Now color the pattern by choosing the Spectrum gradation from the Gradients palette and clicking the right triangle of the Gradients palette and choosing Express in Image. Experiment with shifting the distribution of color in the image by dragging the Bias slider. Choose Select, All and capture the pattern.

To make an abstract topographical map image with color and relief, create a new pattern using Fractal Pattern's default settings: Power, –150%; Feature Size, 100%; Softness, 0%; Angle, 0°; Thinness, 100%; and Channel, Height as Luminance, click OK. Give the image a "topographical" look by choosing Effects, Surface Control, Apply Surface Texture, Using Image Luminance (Amount, 200%; Picture, 100%; and Shine, 0% and Reflection, 0%). Tint the image with Express in Image and the Earthen gradation, loaded from the Painter 6 Gradients library, in the Gradients folder on the Corel Painter 8 CD 2 CD-ROM. Now, add a little relief by applying a second pass of Apply Surface Texture, Using Image Luminance (Amount, 100%; Picture, 100%; and Shine, 0%). To add a swirl to your "map" choose Effects, Surface Control,

CREATING REPEATING TEXTURES WITH MAKE PAPER

Using the Make Paper dialog box, accessed by clicking the right triangle on the Papers palette, you can make seamless repeating textures to apply to your images. For the image below, Corinne Okada created her own repeating texture that resembled a grid of pixels to represent the digital output process. She created the grid of beveled squares with Make Paper using the Square Pattern, then chose her new paper from the list on the Papers palette and applied the texture to the central portion of her image using Effects, Surface Control, Color Overlay.

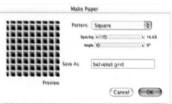

Left: Detail from a package design created by Corinne Okada for The Digital Pond. Above: Okada's settings for the grid of beveled squares.

Conventional diffuser screens attach to the camera lens, breaking up or softening the image as it refracts through the screen. Painter's Glass Distortion layer works the same way but with more variety. To make a Glass Distortion layer for your image, select Glass Distortion from the Dynamic Plug-ins menu at the bottom of the Layers palette. Choose Paper from the Using menu and experiment with refracting your image through different textures chosen in the Papers palette. On this photo, we used Diagonal 1 from the Paper Textures 2 library (in the Paper Textures folder on the Corel Painter 8 CD 2 CD-ROM).

Quick Warp and click the Swirl button. Experiment with different Angle Factor settings in the dialog box.

CREATING EFFECTS WITH GLASS DISTORTION

Try using another image as a "refractor" for your main image. With Painter's Glass Distortion features you can superimpose glass bas-relief effects (using a paper texture or another image). You can apply the procedure directly to your image by choosing Effects, Focus, Glass Distortion. Or you can use a Glass Distortion layer, which lets you preview the effects on a copy of your image without changing the original image; however, the Effects, Focus, Glass Distortion command features a dialog box with more controls. (To learn more about using Effects, Glass Distortion turn to "Diving into Distortion" and "Draping a Weave" later in this chapter. To read about using a Glass Distortion layer, turn to "Creating an Impressionist Look.")

WORKING WITH MOSAICS

Tile mosaics became a popular medium at about 200–300 BC in the Roman Empire, Greece, Africa and Asia; floors and walls of many buildings were decorated with mosaics made of small pieces of glass, stones or shells. They were most often built to celebrate a historic event or for religious purposes.

Inspiration for mosaics. You can build mosaics using Painter's Mosaic brush and dialog box in any of three ways: by drawing them from scratch, by basing them on a line drawing that you've scanned, or by creating a clone-based mosaic using an existing piece of art or a photo. Keep in mind that because of the nature of

---

TONAL CONTROL AND COLOR ENHANCEMENT

To change the hue of an image, use Effects, Tonal Control, Adjust Color, then drag the Hue Shift slider. Use Uniform Color to shift the hue of the entire image, or use Image Luminance to change color properties only in the lighter (but not white) areas.

Highpass (under Effects, Esoterica) acts like a color filter. It looks for smooth transitions in dark areas (as in a sky or shadowed background) and replaces them with abrupt edges or halo effects. Keep the Radius slider to the left for a more pronounced halo effect. To further enhance Highpass, try using Effects, Tonal Control, Equalize.

The initial, unaltered photograph

PHOTO: CHER THREINEN-PENDARVIS

Adjust Colors, Uniform Color: Hue Shift, –44%; Value, 25%

Adjust Colors, Image Luminance: Hue Shift, 20%; Value, 25%

Highpass: Amount, 26.05

To create Pencil and Brush, *artist John Derry built a mosaic in Painter beginning with white grout.*

A colored pen-and-ink sketch was used as reference for this mosaic. Top: The cloned sketch (with Tracing Paper turned on) shows the mosaic in progress with recently applied tiles. Bottom: The same stage with Tracing Paper turned off. Click Tracing Paper on and off without closing the Make Mosaic dialog box by using the checkbox.

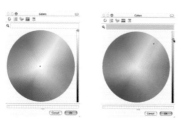

The default grout color is white, shown here (left) in the Colors dialog box. Dragging the Lightness slider to the bottom darkens the color of the grout. The Colors dialog is accessed by clicking on the Grout Color button in the Mosaic dialog box.

the Mosaic tool, your decorative design or photo reference should have a strong compositional focal point. If you want to use a photo that has a busy background, consider simplifying it first by desaturating or blurring. (For tips on neutralizing busy backgrounds, see the beginning of Chapter 6.)

Laying down tiles. Here's a way to try out Painter's Mosaics. Open a new blank file, or a reference on which to base your mosaic. Visualize the forms in your design before you begin laying down the tiles, and rotate your page by dragging with the Rotate Page tool (nested with the Grabber tool in the Toolbox) to accommodate your drawing style so you'll be able to make smooth, controlled strokes to describe the forms.

Open the Color picker, by choosing Window, Show Colors. (If the Color picker is *not* open, you cannot open it while the Mosaic dialog box is open). Then choose Canvas, Make Mosaic to open the Make Mosaic dialog box. Opening the dialog box will turn the background of the currently active image white, the default grout color. To change the grout color in the Colors dialog box, click in the Grout box, and choose a new color. Then choose a contrasting color in the Color picker to paint some tiles. Switch colors again and continue to make tiles. Once you have tiles in place, you can sample color from an existing tile by pressing the Alt/ Option key as you click on it. You can undo an action without closing the Mosaic dialog box by pressing Ctrl/⌘-Z. To erase a tile, click the Remove Tiles button and stroke with the Mosaic brush over the tile. While working on a mosaic, save it in RIFF format to preserve the resolution-independent nature of the mosaic. (Because mosaic tiles are mathematically described, a mosaic can be resized without loss of quality.) See the *Painter 8 User Guide* for an in-depth explanation of Painter's mosaic-building tools. And to read about using a photo-reference for a mosaic, turn to "Building a Clone-Based Mosaic," on page 268.

SPECIAL EFFECTS USING DYNAMIC LAYERS

Painter features seven kinds of dynamic layers (plug-ins) that allow you to create exciting special effects quickly. They are Glass Distortion, Kaleidoscope, Liquid Lens, Burn, Tear, Bevel World and Liquid Metal. In the paragraphs below, we focus on special-effects applications for several of these plug-ins. (To read more about working with plug-in layers turn to the introduction of Chapter 5; see Chapter 6 to see how dynamic layers apply to image correction and photography. Turn to "Creating an Impressionist Look" later in this chapter to read about using the Glass Distortion dynamic layer in combination with Apply Surface Texture. And the *Painter 8 User Guide* contains good descriptions of each of these dynamic layers.)

Painting with metal and water. Painter's versatile Liquid Metal dynamic layer allows you to paint with bas relief and give it the look of chrome, steel, ice, water and other materials. The Liquid

Hiroshi Yoshii painted Bird *with Painter's Liquid Metal. He used colored environment maps and multiple Liquid Metal layers to sculpt the bird's outline and body.*

©CDM-F.LLI MAGRO (ITALY)

Athos Boncompagni used the Liquid Metal Brush tool to draw trees and falling stars for this wrapping paper design.

We used the Kaleidoscope plug-in to make a seamless tile from a Corbis Images photo. To read a step-by-step description of the technique, turn to "Making a Seamless Tile" in Chapter 11, "Using Painter For Web Graphics."

Metal layer works in an existing file to make a layer on which you create the metal. To make a dynamic layer, open an image, click the Dynamic Plug-ins icon at the bottom of the Layers palette and choose Liquid Metal from the menu. To paint with chrome, select the Brush in the Liquid Metal dialog box and choose Chrome 1 or Chrome 2 from the Map menu. Drag in the image with the Brush. For thin lines, try a Size of 8.0 and a Volume of 25%. For thick lines, increase Size to 50 and set Volume over 100%.

If you'd like to paint with bubbles or water drops that reflect your image, begin by making a clone of the image (File, Clone). On the clone, make a Liquid Metal layer. From the Map menu choose Clone Source, choose the Circle or Brush and drag to paint on the layer. For fairly flat drops use an Amount of 0.5 to 1.5. For the look of 3D water drops on a camera lens, move the Amount slider to between 3.0 and 4.0. For bubbles use an Amount of 5.0.

You can color the objects on a Liquid Metal layer based on a clone source (as above) or on the current pattern. Begin by making a Liquid Metal layer. In the Liquid Metal dialog box, choose Clone Source from the Map menu. Select a pattern in the Patterns palette or open an image and define it as the clone source (File, Clone Source). Now use the Circle or Brush tool to apply metal to the layer.

Tearing, burning and beveling. The Tear, Burn and Bevel World layers require a selected "source image layer" to perform their effects. To **Tear** or **Burn** an image's edges, begin by opening a file. You can select a layer in the image and apply the plug-in to it or you can reduce the image canvas to accommodate the torn or burned edge to come: Choose Effects, Orientation, Scale—we scaled our image at 80%. The Scale command will automatically create a "source layer." With the layer still selected, click the Dynamic Plug-ins icon at the bottom of the Layers palette and choose the Tear or Burn plug-in from the menu. To change the color of the torn (or burned) edge, click in the Color box and choose a new color. **Bevel World** allows you to create complex bevels quickly. You can apply a bevel to a "source layer" in an image or make a unique beveled frame for an image. Open an image you'd like to frame, choose Select, All, and choose Bevel World from the Dynamic Plug-ins menu on the Layers section. Choose your settings and click OK. To read more about Bevel World, turn to "Creating Beveled Chrome," in Chapter 8 on page 292.

To design this striking beveled button Michelle Lill captured a custom-made environment map as a pattern, and applied it to the button graphic using the Reflection slider in the Bevel World dialog box. To learn more about reflection maps, turn to "Making an Environment Map" and "Applying an Environment Map," later in this chapter.

Diving into Distortion

Overview *Use Glass Distortion to displace an image using a clone source; then combine a dramatic distortion with a subtle one to create a water-stained effect.*

1a

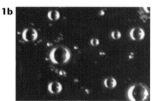

The original photograph

1b

The water image displacement map

2a

Settings for the subtle distortion

2b

The Extreme clone (left), and the Subtle clone (right)

3

Cloning in a dramatic water drop

PAINTER'S GLASS DISTORTION can move pixels in an image based on the luminosity of another image. We used it here to simulate water drops on a camera lens.

1 Choosing images and making clones. Choose an image for a displacement map (the water drops in this case) that has good contrast; both crisp and soft-focus images can give good results. Because you'll be applying the displacement map image to the original image as a clone source, you'll need to size the map image to the same pixel dimensions as the image you want to distort. (Our images were 883 x 589 pixels.) Make two clones of the image you want to distort by choosing File, Clone, twice. Save the clones, naming them Extreme and Subtle, then size and position them on your screen so that you can see both of them.

2 Applying the distortion. Open the displacement map image. Now, click on the Extreme clone, and designate the displacement image as the clone source (File, Clone Source). With the Extreme clone active, choose Effects, Focus, Glass Distortion, Using Original Luminance, and choose the Refraction Map model. (Refraction works well for glass effects; it creates an effect similar to an optical lens bending light.) Our settings were Softness, 2.3 (to smooth the distortion); Amount, 1.35; Variance, 6.00. We left Direction at 0, because it has no effect when using a Refraction map, and clicked OK. Click on the Subtle clone, and apply Glass Distortion with subtler settings. (Our settings were Softness 15.0; Amount, 0.07; and Variance, 1.00.) We wanted the diving board to curve, while preserving smoothness in the image.

3 Restoring from the Extreme clone. We added several dramatic water drops from the Extreme clone to enhance the composition of the Subtle image. Click on the Subtle clone to make it active and choose the Extreme clone as clone source. Use the Soft Cloner variant of the Cloners brush to clone dramatic effects from the Extreme clone into your Subtle image.

Creating an Impressionist Look

Overview *Combine Glass Distortion and Surface Texture special effects to transform a photo into a painting, creating brush-strokes and building up paint.*

The original photograph

Applying Glass Distortion to the photo

Adding highlights and shadows to the distorted image with Apply Surface Texture

BY COMBINING TWO POWERFUL EFFECTS, Glass Distortion and Apply Surface Texture, you can create an Impressionist look with textured highlights and shadows—turning a photo into a painting. This effect can be applied to an entire image, a selection or a layer, giving you much more flexibility than you would have in the darkroom working with diffuser screens and masks.

1 Choosing an image and making a selection. Choose an image with a strong focal point and good highlights and shadows. You can achieve good results with either crisp or soft-focus images. In preparation for generating a Glass Distortion plug-in dynamic layer for the image in the next step, choose Select, All.

2 Initiating strokes. Choose a coarse paper texture—woven textures with a broad tonal range help to emulate the look of paint on canvas. We chose Raw Silk from the Painter 7 Textures library on the Corel Painter 8 CD 2 CD-ROM, and scaled it down to 88% to complement our 883-pixel-wide image. To diffuse or break up the image into paint-like strokes on paper, apply the Glass Distortion dynamic layer: In the Layers palette, click the Dynamic Layers plug icon at the bottom of the palette and choose Glass Distortion from the pop-up menu. In the Using menu select Paper. Choose subtle settings—our settings were Amount, 0.71; Variance, 2.06; and Softness, 0. Click OK to apply your settings.

3 Adding texture and shadows. To add realistic relief, choose Effects, Surface Control, Apply Surface Texture. (If the Commit dialog box appears asking you if you'd like to convert the dynamic layer to an image layer, choose Commit.) In the Using menu choose Paper. Use subtle-to-moderate Surface Texture settings to avoid a harsh look and to preserve the original image. We used Amount, 90%; Picture, 100%; Shine, 10%; Softness, 0 and Reflection, 0; (to raise the highlights, we turned on Inverted). Choose a light direction that complements the light in your photograph, and click OK. 🖌

Creating a Seamless Pattern

Overview *Set up and capture a basic pattern layout; check this pattern out of the library; add more elements, shifting the pattern as needed; capture the final pattern; save it in a pattern library.*

ARENA REED

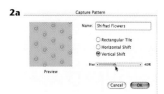

Reed's basic pattern layout image with peach fill and spiral "doodle"

2a

Setting up the Vertical Shift in the Capture Pattern dialog box

3a

Choosing Check Out Pattern from the Patterns palette

PAINTER'S AMAZING PATTERN-GENERATION tools make it easy to build even a complex pattern tile. You can capture a very basic layout for your tile into a Pattern library and then "check it out" of the library to add complex elements. The new elements will automatically wrap from one edge of the pattern to the opposite edge as you paint, to make a pattern that tiles seamlessly! *Shifted Flowers* is a pattern created by Arena Reed. See "Applying Patterns" on page 262 to see how Reed used this and other patterns.

1 Setting up your pattern layout. To start the pattern files, choose File, New, and in the New dialog box, set up a small image. Reed's image was 240 x 400 pixels. In the Color picker, choose the basic background color you want for your tile, then choose Effects, Fill, Fill With Current Color to fill the new image Canvas. To create the base color for her pattern tile, Reed filled the image with a light peach color.

To show how the process works, we'll create a test pattern with a quick doodle, which we can later use as a template. Then we'll describe the steps that Reed used in creating Shifted Flowers.

2 Capturing the pattern. With your basic pattern layout (solid-color background and stand-in pattern element) complete, capture the layout as a pattern tile: From the pop-up menu on the Patterns palette's bar, choose Capture Pattern. In the Capture Pattern dialog box, set up any Horizontal or Vertical Shift that you want for your pattern, and watch how your stand-in element repeats as you experiment with

3b

Pressing Shift-Spacebar and dragging in the image to shift the pattern

3c

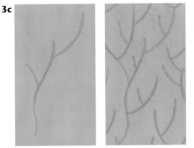

The painted background with the first branch (left) and the completed branches, leaves and flowers (right)

3d

The nearly completed seamless pattern with most of the flower buds and details in place

4

Saving the completed pattern using the Capture Pattern dialog box

5

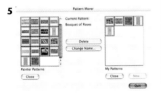

Dragging and dropping new patterns into the newly created "my patterns" library

the Bias slider. Reed chose a Vertical Shift and set the Bias slider to 40%. Name your pattern and click OK to accept. The working pattern will be saved to the current Patterns library.

3 Embellishing the tile. To access Painter's automatic seamless tiling feature for developing the pattern tile, make sure that your new pattern is selected in the Patterns library and choose Check Out Pattern from the pop-out menu on the right side of the Patterns palette bar. A new Painter window will open with the pattern tile in it.

By working in this "checked-out" pattern window, you'll be able to embellish your tile without having to do a lot of retouching at the edges. Notice that you can shift the pattern tile and view the repeating element: If you press the Spacebar and Shift keys, the cursor will change to a hand, and you can drag in the image window to shift the pattern so you can see the offset that you built into it in Step 2.

Now you can paint to embellish your basic layout, turning it into your final pattern tile. Reed used the Smeary Round variant of the Oils to paint a deep pink color over the background. Because of Painter's seamless wrap-around feature for checked-out patterns, her brushstrokes automatically wrapped around, and there were no obvious tile edges as the pattern repeated.

As you paint, shift the pattern continually (with the Shift key and Spacebar) to check the design and make sure it's balanced. Reed shifted the pattern as she used the Variable Colored Pencil variant of the Colored Pencils to draw the branches and their flowers, and to add the details.

4 Capturing the final pattern. When your pattern is complete, add the final tile image to the Patterns library: Choose Capture Pattern from the pop-out menu on the Patterns palette bar. In the Capture Pattern dialog box, leave the Shift and Bias settings as they are, give the pattern a new name (Reed named hers "Shifted Flowers") and click OK.

5 Saving your patterns in a library. Continue to make more patterns if you like, following the instructions in Steps 1 through 4. Then store your new pattern(s) in a library for safekeeping: Click the right triangle on the Patterns palette bar to open the pop-out menu and choose Pattern Mover. When the dialog box appears, the currently loaded pattern library, with the pattern(s) you created, will appear on the left of the mover. To create a new library, click the New button, then name and save the new empty pattern library. To copy an item from the current pattern library, click on the pattern thumbnail and drag and drop it into the new library. If you leave all of your custom patterns in the default Painter Patterns library, the library can become very large, taking up a lot of disk space. So after you've copied your new patterns to the new library, it's a good idea to delete the original(s) from the default library: For each one, click on the pattern swatch and then click the Delete button. 🖌

Applying Patterns

Overview *Make selections and fill them with patterns; add stitching on a new layer; give the stitching highlights and shadows; add clouds that have stitching and Surface Texture.*

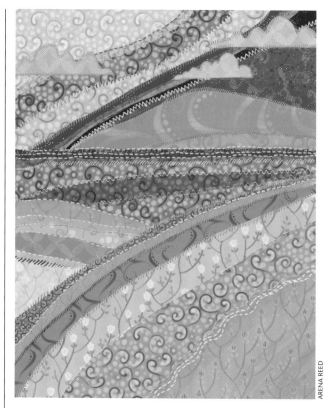

ARENA REED

1a

The Mixed Spirals pattern is chosen in Reed's pattern library.

1b

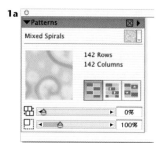

Reducing the opacity to 60% for a translucent fill

1c

Here the Mixed Spirals and Spirals in Blue patterns have been applied to the sky.

YOU CAN APPLY A PATTERN TO AN EXISTING IMAGE, selection or layer with Cloning brushes, with the Paint Bucket tool (by choosing Fill With: Clone Source in the Controls: Paint Bucket palette), with any of the special effects features that use a clone source (such as Original Luminance or 3D Brushstrokes), or by choosing Effects, Fill, Fill With Pattern (Ctrl/⌘-F).

Arena Reed built the colorful landscape image above, *Dreams in Distant Lands*, by filling selections with several illustrated patterns she created, then drawing stitching with pattern pens.

1 Setting up a new image, selecting and filling. Create a new image by choosing File, New. (Reed's image was 1200 x 1500 pixels.) For practice in using a pattern library, you can follow along with the process Reed used for the image above. Or you can create your own patterns and store them in a pattern library, then use them to create an image. (See "Creating a Seamless Pattern" on page 260 for more information.)

Reed's pattern library is located on the Painter 8 Wow! CD-ROM, in the Arena Reed's Patterns folder. Begin by copying the library from the Painter 8 Wow! CD-ROM to your Painter 8 application folder. Then, click on the right triangle on the Patterns palette bar, choose Open Library. Navigate to the Painter application folder, select Patterns_arenaReed and click the Open button.

For each area you want to fill with a pattern, make a selection

1d

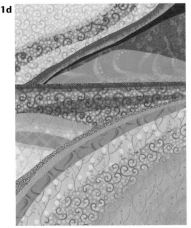

The quilt with basic fills completed

2

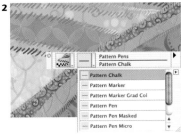

Reed created the stitching using the Pattern Chalk and custom patterns.

3

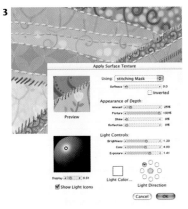

Apply Surface Texture was used to add highlights and shadows to the stitches.

4

The completed clouds with "embossed" stitching

(with the Lasso, for instance), then click in the Patterns palette to choose a pattern from the library and choose Effects, Fill, Fill With Pattern. As you fill, you can vary the scale of the pattern using the Scale slider on the Patterns palette. Reed made selections and filled them to create a landscape design, varying the scale and the opacity of her fills. The top of the sky was filled with her Mixed Spirals pattern at a reduced opacity of about 60% so the pattern would appear lighter in the sky than it would be in the foreground, where she planned to apply it at 100% opacity.

2 Making stitching on a new layer. Next, Reed created stitching on a separate layer using custom patterns that were applied with the Pattern Chalk variant of the Pattern Pens. To try out the Pattern Chalk, make a new layer on your image by choosing New Layer from the menu on the right side of the Layers palette bar. Click with the Magnifier tool to zoom in on your image. Choose a color in the Color picker and choose the Pattern Chalk variant of Pattern Pens in the Brush Selector. For wiggly-line style stitching, choose the stitching_luminance3 pattern in the Patterns section, and paint stitching along the edges of the filled areas. For smaller stitches, reduce the size of the Pattern Chalk using the Size slider in the Property Bar. Try out the other stitching patterns in Reed's library.

3 Adding highlights and shadows to the stitches. First select the stitching layer in the Layers palette. Then select Convert to Default Layer in the Layers palette. Go to Select/Load Selection and load the stitching layer's transparency mask. With this selection active, go back to Select and choose Save Selection, and name the mask. Next choose Effects, Surface Control, Apply Surface Texture and in the dialog box, set Using to the stitching layer's mask and use these approximate settings: Amount, 15%; Shine, 0; Softness, 2; and leave the other settings at their defaults.

4 Making clouds. Reed created a new layer for each cloud so they could be arranged and scaled independently. Add a new layer, draw a cloud shape with the Lasso tool and fill the selection with the Overlapping Circles pattern. After filling, adjust their color: Choose Effects, Tonal Control, Adjust Colors and in the dialog box, increase the Value and change the Hue to create contrast with the background. Use the Layer Adjuster tool to reposition the cloud layers. To scale them, choose Effects, Orientation, Free Transform, then choose Effects, Orientation, Commit Transform to accept. Choose one of the stitching patterns and stitch the edges of the clouds. After the clouds are as you like them, you can group them in order to make it easier to add dimension to the stitches. Shift-select their names in the Layers section and Group them (Ctrl/⌘-G). Then Collapse them by clicking the Layer Commands button on the bottom of the Layers section palette and choosing Collapse from the menu. Now, add highlights and shadows to the clouds by choosing Effects, Surface Control, Apply Surface Texture, using the same settings as in Step 4. 🖌

Making an Environment Map

Overview *Choose a file and resize it; make a selection; use Quick Warp to bend the image into an environment; capture it as a pattern.*

MICHELLE LILL

YOU CAN USE PAINTER'S QUICK WARP FEATURE to bend any image into a useful environment map, an image that shows an environment as if it were seen through a fish-eye lens or reflected in a shiny metal sphere. Multimedia designer Michelle Lill creates her own environment maps—like the one above on the left—and uses the maps to enhance images by applying them as she did in the image on the right.

1a

Michelle Lill's original photo

1b

Making a square selection on the image

2

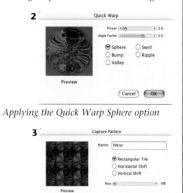

Applying the Quick Warp Sphere option

3

Naming the water map in the Capture Pattern dialog box

1 Opening an image and making a selection. Open the image that you want to use as the basis for your reflection map. To conserve disk space and optimize performance, Lill recommends that a reflection map image be a square that is 256 pixels or less. Using the Rectangle Selection tool, make a 256 pixel square selection (holding down the Shift key as you drag to constrain the selection to a square), as you check the Width in the Info palette. If you need to move or scale the selection, use the Selection Adjuster tool. (Turn to "Transforming Selections" in the beginning of Chapter 4 for more about manipulating selections.) Copy the selected area (Edit, Copy), and paste it into a new file by choosing Edit, Paste Into New Image.

2 Bending the image. To get the "fish-eye lens" effect that adds realism to the map (since most surfaces that reflect their environment are not flat), Lill chose Effects, Surface, Control, Quick Warp and selected the Sphere option. She used the default settings of Power 2.0 and Angle Factor 2.0. The effect was applied to the entire canvas.

3 Saving the image as a pattern. To save the map into the current Pattern library, capture it as a pattern: With the environment map image open, select all, click the right triangle on the Patterns palette bar and choose Capture Pattern from the menu. Name the map when prompted and click OK. The environment map is now a permanent member of the library. Now you can use the map to enhance special effects—as Lill did in her water illustration above. To read a step-by-step description of how Lill used a custom environment map to enhance an image, turn to "Applying an Environment Map," on the next page.

Applying an Environment Map

Overview *Open a file and set type shapes; convert the shapes into a layer; add an environment map, dimension and a soft drop shadow to the type; add a border to the image.*

1a

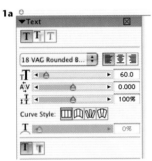

Choosing a font and size in the Text palette.

1b

The text set on a layer over the image

1c

The selected Text layer in the Layers palette.

2

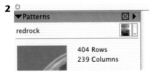

Choosing Lill's custom-made environment map in the Patterns palette.

MICHELLE LILL

TO CREATE THE TITLE DESIGN *RED ROCK*, multimedia designer Michelle Lill used a custom-made environment map in combination with one of Painter's most powerful and versatile tools, Apply Surface Texture.

1 Opening an image and setting the type. For this example, Lill began by setting 60-point VAG Rounded Bold text on top of a photo. Begin by opening a background image (Lill's image was 889 pixels wide). Select the Text tool and choose a font in the Property Bar. For the best results, choose a bold font with a broad stroke and rounded corners. Position the cursor in your image and type the text.

When you're finished setting the text, select the Layer Adjuster tool and drag to reposition the text layer to your taste. (To read more about using Painter's text features see Chapter 8, "Working with Type in Painter.")

2 Selecting the reflection map. Open the Patterns palette and choose the Reflection Map pattern from the list. Lill used her own pattern, made from the same Red Rock photo she used for the background. (To read about how to make your own environment map, check out Michelle Lill's method in "Making an Environment Map," on page 264.

PROPERTY BAR TEXT CONTROLS

You can format your type without opening the Text Palette. As soon as you select the Text tool, most of the controls you will need to format your text will be available in the Property Bar.

3a

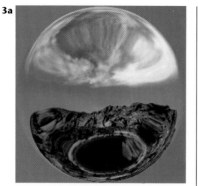

Michele Lill's Red Rock environment map

3b

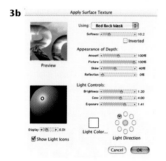

Settings for the second Apply Surface Texture application showing dimension on the type

4a

Setting up an automatic drop shadow

4b

The Red Rock image with the drop shadow applied to the text layer

3 Adding reflection and dimension to the type. To achieve a strong reflection in the type and a realistic 3D look, Lill used two applications of Apply Surface Texture. First select the text layer in the Layers palette to make it active. Then click on the right arrow of the Layers palette and select Convert to Default Layer from the menu. Next, choose Select, Load Selection and load the transparency mask for the text layer. Then choose Effects, Surface Control, Apply Surface Texture. To reflect the environment map onto your type, use these settings: In the Using menu choose the text mask to restrict the reflection to the type. Move the Reflection slider to 100% (so the environment map shows up) and move the Softness slider to the right (to scale the reflection map). Adjust the other settings to suit your image. The Apply Surface Texture dialog box is interactive, so you can scale your pattern while viewing the reflection map in the Preview window. When the reflection looks good, click OK in the Apply Surface Texture dialog box. Lill's Apply Surface Texture settings for the first application are as follows: Softness 40.0; Amount 200%; Picture 100%; Shine 40%; and Reflection 100%.

Now add a realistic 3D look to the text by choosing Apply Surface Texture a second time. This time, check the Inverted box (to add a second light source); decrease the Reflection slider to 0% by moving it all the way to the left; and decrease the Softness to about 10. Lill's second Surface Texture application settings are as follows: Softness 10.0, Amount 100%, Picture 100%, Shine 40% and Reflection 0%. Click OK. The image with Apply Surface Texture can be seen at the beginning of this story.

4 Adding a shadow and a soft black border. Next, Lill added a black drop shadow to her text, adding to the 3D look and giving her image more contrast. To generate the shadow, she chose Effects, Objects, Create Drop Shadow. In the dialog box, she specified settings for the X and Y coordinates to fit her image, and she increased the Opacity of the shadow to 80%, left the other settings at their defaults, and she checked the Collapse To One Layer box to combine the text and shadow.

Then, to finish the image with a more graphic look that would complement the shadow, Lill added a softly feathered black border to her image. To create her border effect, begin by choosing Select, All. Then from the Select menu choose Select, Modify, Contract. In the Contract Selection dialog box, type in 12 pixels. Now choose Select, Feather and set the feather to 24 pixels. Finally, Lill filled the selected, feathered edge with black. Begin by choosing black in the Color picker. Choose the Paint Bucket, and in the Property Bar make these choices: Click the Fill Image button, and from the Fill menu choose Current Color. Click inside the active selection with the Paint Bucket tool.

Building a Terrain Map

Overview Create a terrain map from elevation data; make a custom gradient; color the map; use Apply Surface Texture to give it realistic dimension.

Olympic National Park

MT. OLYMPUS   Mt. Mathias

West Peak   East Peak

Hoh Peak   Mt. Tom   Middle Peak

1

The grayscale image representing elevation

2a

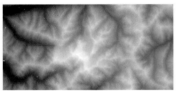

Edit Gradient

☑ Linear

Cancel   OK

Building a custom gradient for the map

2b

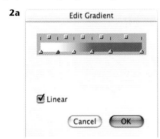

The map with the custom gradient applied using Express in Image

3

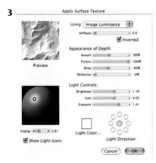

Apply Surface Texture

Using: Image Luminance

Preview

Gordon's settings in Apply Surface Texture, used to produce the terrain map

TO CREATE THIS REALISTIC MAP of Mount Olympus, Washington, Steven Gordon built a color terrain background from real data. As principal cartographer and owner of Cartagram, Gordon produces custom maps for electronic and print publication, specializing in tourism maps with relief renderings of the terrain.

1 Making a grayscale-to-height image. To begin the map, Gordon downloaded a digital elevation model (DEM) file from the USGS (www.usgs.gov). He processed it using a shareware DEM reader he found by searching for the keyword "DEM" in an Internet search engine. The resulting PICT image contained grayscale values mapped to elevation values, which Gordon could then use in building the image.

2 Coloring the image. Gordon opened the grayscale PICT file in Painter and built a custom gradient to color the map. To make your own gradation, open the Colors and the Gradients palettes; in the Gradients palette choose the Two-Point gradation. Now open the Edit Gradient dialog box by clicking the right triangle on the Gradients palette bar and choosing Edit Gradient. Using the dialog box, you can create a new gradation with color control points representing elevation zones (as Gordon did). Add control points to the center of the gradient by clicking in the Gradient bar. Click each control point and then click in the Colors section to choose a color for that point. Gordon's gradation progressed from dark blue-green valleys to white mountain crests. When the gradient looks good, click OK and then save it by choosing Save Gradient from the Gradients palette's menu. Apply the gradient to your image by choosing Express in Image from the Gradients section's menu.

3 Building Terrain. To add realistic relief to your map, choose Effects, Surface Control, Apply Surface Texture, Using Image Luminance. Click the Inverted box to make the light areas in the map "pop-up." To blur undesirable detail, move the Softness slider to the right. Adjust the Amount to build dimension and shadow. Gordon decreased the Amount to 85% to keep the shadows from being too dark and prominent. He used the default 11:00 light direction setting and left the Shine at the default 40%. 🖐

Building a Clone-Based Mosaic

Overview *Choose a photo reference and retouch it if needed; make a clone of the retouched photo; use the Make Mosaic dialog box to design and lay down colored tiles in the clone.*

The original photograph

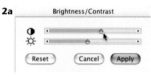

Increasing the contrast in the source image

Detail of the retouched source image

MOSAICS HAVE BEEN USED AS A NARRATIVE and decorative art form since Hellenistic and Roman times. Because of its graphic nature, the mosaic is a medium that can be used to express strong emotion. S. Swaminathan created the digital mosaic *Soul of Homelessness*, based on his photograph of a homeless man. His vision was to create an abstracted mosaic portrait of the man that would portray the dignity he projected.

1 Selecting a source image. Choose a photo with a strong focal point and meaningful content, so the mosaic technique does not overpower the image. The photo should also have a broad tonal range and good color detail to help build value and color complexity into the tiles. Swaminathan began with a 675 x 920-pixel photo.

2 Retouching and cloning. To separate the subject from the background, Swaminathan used a modified Digital Airbrush variant of Airbrushes to simplify the background of the photo, adding soft blue and white strokes. He also increased the contrast in the image using Effects, Tonal Control, Brightness/Contrast.

When he was satisfied with the retouching, he cloned the image. Choose File, Clone to make a clone of your source image. In preparation for laying down colored tiles in the clone based on the color of the clone source image, enable the Use Clone Color button (the rubber stamp) in the Color picker.

3a

Designing a horizontal tile to use on the face

3b

Using Tracing Paper to view the clone source while positioning tiles on the clone

4a

Erasing a course of tiles in the hair

4b

Adding new irregular tiles in the hair

3 Laying tiles. With the clone active, open the Make Mosaic dialog box (Canvas, Make Mosaic), and enable the Use Tracing Paper box so you can see the source image while laying down the tiles. To change the Grout from the default white to black, click the Grout square in the Colors dialog box and move the Lightness slider all the way to the bottom. To design a custom tile, begin by setting Dimensions for the tile; choose a Width, Length and Grout size. Make a stroke on your image to test the settings. Press Ctrl/⌘-Z to Undo a test stroke without closing the Make Mosaic dialog box. Experiment with the settings until you get just the look you want.

Swaminathan began with the face, which would become the focal point of the mosaic portrait. As he worked, he varied the size of the tiles, using larger tiles for the broader areas of the face (the forehead and cheeks), and smaller tiles to render detailed areas (the shadowed right side of the man's nose, eyes and eyebrows).

Generally, he worked from the center out, beginning with the face and hair and then rendering the shirt, shoes and background. To depict the long hair (and to contrast with the more uniform shapes of tiles on the subject's jacket) he designed narrow, irregularly shaped tiles. To vary the tile shapes and grout (as Swaminathan did), choose Randomness from the Settings pop-up menu to access the sliders. Begin by moving the Cut slider to the right to increase Randomness in the shape of the tile ends. To vary the spacing between tiles, move the Grout slider to the right. Experiment with each of the sliders individually until you arrive at the look you want.

4 Completing the image. To refine the tile design, Swaminathan sampled color from existing tiles and applied the color to new tiles. (Before sampling color from a tile, click the Clone Color button in the Color picker to toggle it off, then press the Alt/Option key and click on a tile.) To erase tiles, click the Remove Tiles icon and drag the cursor over the tiles that you want to remove. Click back on the Apply Tiles icon and drag to add new tiles.

Adding highlights and shadows. Finally, Swaminathan used Apply Surface Texture to add realistic highlights and shadows like those you would see on the slightly uneven surface of handmade tiles. Choose Effects, Surface Control, Apply Surface Texture Using Image Luminance. Try these subtle settings: Softness, 0; Amount, 20; Picture 100; Shine, 25; and Reflection, 0. Click OK.

Creating a Tidepool

Overview *Create a sandy background; spray plants onto the ocean floor using the Image Hose; light the scene; combine special effects to "ripple the water."*

JOHN DERRY

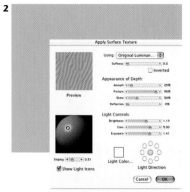

Wheat Stalks texture applied to the blank image (left), then Super Softened

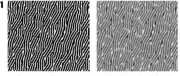

Applying Surface Texture with Original Luminance to the sand-colored clone

The Pressure Plant nozzle file with images from small to large size

Using short spiral strokes to Spray plants and pebbles onto the sandy ocean floor

THE ILLUSION OF LIGHT REFRACTING through water is essential to creating a realistic underwater scene. In *Tidepool*, after using a variety of Image Hose nozzles to paint undersea plant life, John Derry engineered the look of rippling water by applying Lighting, Glass Distortion and Surface Texture to the image.

1 Creating a soft sandy bottom. To begin as Derry did, open a new 1200-pixel-wide image with a white background. Select black in the Color picker, choose Wheat Stalks paper texture in the Papers palette (loaded from the Painter 7 Textures library located on the Corel Painter 8 CD 2 CD-ROM). Scale it to 400% using the Size slider. Apply the black texture to your file with Effects, Surface Control, Color Overlay, Using Paper and Hiding Power at 100% Opacity. Derry liked the Wheat Stalks texture but felt it needed softening to look like rippled sand. Soften the background by choosing Effects, Focus, Super Soften; enter 12 when the dialog box appears. Click OK.

2 Giving the rippled sand color and texture. To make the background look like sand, you can combine a sand-colored file with the gray rippled image. First, clone the gray image (File, Clone), choose a sand color and fill the clone with color (Ctrl/⌘-F, Current Color, 100% Opacity). Next, combine the sand-colored clone with the gray image. Go to Effects, Surface Control, Apply Surface Texture and choose Original Luminance. For a subtle effect use these settings: Amount, 25; Picture, 90; Shine, 30. Set the Light Direction at 11 o'clock, Brightness at 1.19, increase Concentration (Conc) to 5.00 (to decrease the spread of the light) and Exposure at 1.41.

3 Loading a nozzle and spraying images. Most of the Image Hose nozzles that Derry used in this piece can be found in the Tidepool Nozzles library on the *Painter 8 Wow!* CD-ROM, in the John Derry's Nozzles folder. To choose an Image Hose nozzle from the current library click on the Nozzles Selector on the bottom right of the Toolbox. To paint with a nozzle, select the Image Hose icon

4

Creating a soft, diffused custom light

5a

Applying Glass Distortion to initiate the ripple effect

5b

Adding Surface Texture to complete the illusion of rippling water

in the Brush Selector and begin painting. To make a nozzle spray in a specific way, change the hose variant in the Brush Selector or use the controls in the Property Bar.

Load the Tidepool library from the *Painter 8 Wow!* CD-ROM by clicking on the Nozzle Selector, clicking on the right arrow and choosing Open Library from menu. For the undersea image, choose the Pressure Plants nozzle, select

INDIVIDUAL NOZZLE FILES

To load an individual nozzle that isn't part of a library, press Ctrl/⌘-L while the Image Hose is chosen (or choose Load Nozzle from the menu accessed by clicking the right triangle on the Nozzles Selector on the Toolbox), open a folder containing nozzle files and open a nozzle. Once you've loaded a nozzle, you can choose to add it to the current library (Add to Library), or view it (Check Out Nozzle) from the menu on the Nozzles Selector bar.

the Image Hose icon and paint with short, spiral strokes in your image. Derry added strokes to the piece using a number of nozzles: Shadowed Coral, Pastel Coral, Shiny Coral, Pointed Plant, Nasturtium, Pressure Plants and Pebbles. See the *Painter 8 User Guide* to learn how to create your own Image Hose nozzle.

4 Applying Lighting. To create a diffused lighting effect with soft pockets of light and dark areas, Derry modified an existing light, copied it four times, then modified the individual lights. To create a look similar to the one he achieved, choose Effects, Surface Control, Apply Lighting, Slide Lighting. Reduce the Brightness, Distance and Spread settings, then click on two new locations in the Preview window to create two more lights with settings identical to the original. To reposition a light, drag on the large circle, and to aim the light in a new direction, drag on the small circle. Make further modifications to one of the three lights, then click in the Preview window two more times to create two more lights with those new settings, making a total of five lights. To create a softer effect on the whole scene, drag the Exposure slider to the left and the Ambient slider to the right. Store your custom light in the library by clicking the Save button, then click OK to apply the lighting to the image.

5 Creating a water ripple effect. Derry used a powerful but subtle combination of Glass Distortion and Apply Surface Texture to create a realistic water ripple effect. To ripple your image, in the Papers section choose the Seismic texture loaded from the Wild Textures library (on the Corel Painter 8 CD 2 CD-ROM) and scale it to 400%. Now select Effects, Focus, Glass Distortion using Paper and accept the default settings of Amount, 0 and Variance, 1.00, with the Refraction Map type. To add a subtle bump to the transparent water ripple, choose Effects, Surface Control, Apply Surface Texture using Paper: Amount, 22%; Picture, 100%; and Shine, 0%. Click the 11 o'clock Light Direction button to set a general light direction. *W*

Draping a Weave

Overview *Paint a grayscale file that will be your source image; fill a clone of that file with a weave; use a combination of Glass Distortion and Surface Texture to wrap the weave around the source image.*

1

The grayscale form file with strong values

YOU CAN USE PAINTER'S WEAVES, located in the Weaves palette, to fill any selection or document, using either the Fill command or the Paint Bucket tool. Weaves can be used in fashion design and they make good backgrounds for scenes, but their flat look can be a drawback. To create the appearance of fabric—to hang behind a still life, for instance—we added dimension to a weave by "draping" it over a painted form using a powerful Glass Distortion displacement effect along with Apply Surface Texture.

WEAVES IN THE TOOLBOX

You can access Weaves in the Weave Selector on the bottom right of the Toolbox. By clicking on the right arrow to open the menu, you can choose to open another library, edit a weave, or launch the Weaves palette from the menu.

1 Making the form file. Think of the form file as a kind of mold—or fashion designer's dress form—over which you'll drape your fabric. Create a grayscale form file that has strong value contrast and smooth dark-to-light transitions. As a reference for our 500-pixel-square form file, we draped fabric over a chair and sketched it in Painter, then cleaned up the sketch with the Digital Airbrush variant of Airbrushes. Since any hard edges in the form file would make a noticeable break in the weave's pattern, we softened the image with Effects, Focus, Super Soften. We used a 7-pixel Super Soften setting on our file.

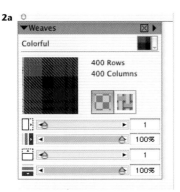

2a

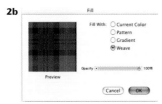

Choosing a weave in the Weaves section

2b

Filling the clone with the weave

3

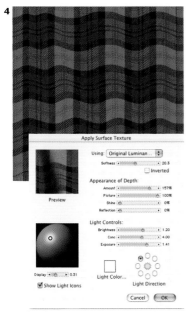

Applying Glass Distortion to the weave

4

Adding highlights and shadows to the distorted image using Surface Texture

If you don't want to paint the form file, here's a fast, but less "organic" way to create it. Open the Make Paper dialog box by clicking the right triangle on the Papers palette. Choose Line from the pop-up menu, use a high spacing setting and to make vertical lines, set Angle at 90°. In the Save As field, type a name for the new paper. Choose it in the Papers palette and choose black in the Color picker. Then select Effects, Surface Control, Color Overlay, Using Paper and Hiding Power at 100% Opacity. Use Super Soften as described above.

2 Making a clone and filling it with a weave. Choose File, Clone to make a duplicate of the form file with identical dimensions. Now choose a weave from the Weaves palette. Fill the clone file with your weave (Ctrl/⌘-F, Weave, 100%). We used the Baird 4 weave from the Scottish Tartans library (loaded from the Weaves folder on the Corel Painter 8 CD 2 CD-ROM).

3 Initiating the distortion. Here's where the movement begins. Choose Effects, Focus, Glass Distortion, Using Original Luminance. Now let Painter know the direction that you want the fabric to go when it overlies the form file. When a clone image is displaced by Glass Distortion using Original Luminance, the distance each pixel moves is based on the luminance of each pixel in the source file. We chose Vector Displacement to move pixels in a specific direction, and used the Amount slider to get a moderate "ripple" effect in the Preview (we chose 1.54), leaving Variance at 1.00. To establish the direction (and make the light areas move up and to the right, dark areas move down and to the left—based on the form file), we moved the Direction slider to 80°. We added a Softness of 15.2 to smooth any rough edges that might be caused by the distortion of the weave. Experiment with your settings; the Softness, Amount and Direction may change based on the size of your file.

4 Adding highlights and shadows. Using Apply Surface Texture adds to the illusion of folded fabric by contributing highlights and shadows based on the form file. Choose Effects, Surface Control, Apply Surface Texture, Using Original Luminance. Experiment with your settings—paying special attention to how the lighting controls affect the look—and click OK. We set Softness to 20.3 (to smooth the image and slightly increase the depth of the folds), Amount to 151%, Picture to 100% (to make the image lighter while maintaining weaving detail), and Shine to 0%, then chose the 9 o'clock Light Direction button. 🎨

■ **Hiroshi Yoshii** is known for his fantastic characters and animals and his unique illustration style. Yoshii created *Party* using Painter's Chalk and Blenders variants, which were applied over the Ribbed Pastel paper texture (loaded from Painter 6 Painter Textures on the Corel Painter 8 CD 2 CD-ROM). When working with the Chalk variants in Painter 8, Yoshii prefers to disable the Directional Grain button on the Papers palette, because he can achieve more control over the grain while modeling the forms of his characters. He began by drawing a tight black-and-white sketch of his composition using the Sharp Chalk variant. Then he used the Sharp Chalk and Large Chalk variants of Chalks to color the drawing. Yoshii carefully built up layers of chalky strokes so that the paper texture would be preserved. To softly blend areas, he used the Just Add Water variant of Blenders. He also added details and redefined edges using a tiny Sharp Chalk. Finally, to further enhance the grainy effect, he chose Effects, Surface Control, Apply Surface Texture Using Paper, with subtle settings.

■ **Chet Phillips** created *Mediterranean* for self-promotion. He began by drawing an expressive black-and-white illustration with the Scratchboard Tool variant of Pens. Then he cut the black-and-white drawing to a separate layer by choosing Select, All, then Select, Float. Next, he composited the layer using the Gel Composite Method, chosen from the Composite Method menu in the Layers palette. Next, he selected the Canvas in the Layers palette and chose Effects, Fill, using a sepia color. Then he painted with the Chalk and Pastels brushes in varying sizes to color the background. For richer

texture, he layered varied color onto the image using the Artist Pastel Chalk variant of Pastels. To achieve an interesting randomness to the texture, Phillips opened the Stroke Designer panel of the Brush Creator. In the Random section, he toggled the Random Brush Stroke Grain on and off as he worked. This technique is most noticeable in the sky and foreground. Then Phillips merged the layers by clicking on the black-and-white drawing layer name in the Layers palette and choosing Drop from the pop-out menu on the right side of the Layers palette. For the look of an antique woodcut print,

Phillips applied subtle paper textures to the image using special effects. He sampled a brown color from his image using the Dropper tool and chose Effects, Surface Control, Color Overlay, Using Paper and the Hiding Power option, with a very low opacity setting. He then applied several additional applications of Color Overlay with different textures using the dark brown. The built up Color Overlay applications simulated the texture that a wood block print receives when it rubs against the grain of the wood. To read more about his "woodcut" technique, turn to "Coloring a Woodcut" in Chapter 2.

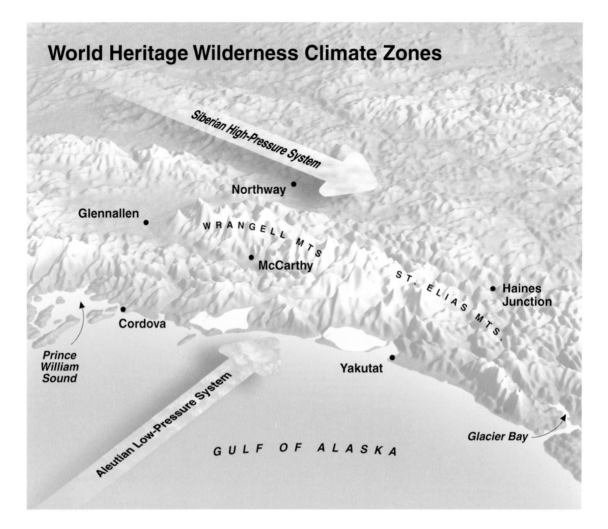

World Heritage Wilderness Climate Zones

Siberian High-Pressure System

Northway

Glennallen

WRANGELL MTS

McCarthy

ST. ELIAS MTS.

Haines Junction

Cordova

Prince William Sound

Yakutat

Aleutian Low-Pressure System

Glacier Bay

GULF OF ALASKA

■ Alaska Geographic commissioned **Steven Gordon** to create this weather map of south-central Alaska for their publication *World Heritage Wilderness*. Using the process described on page 267, Gordon created a grayscale PICT of the terrain and colored it with Painter's Express in Image command from the Gradients palette. In the 3D program Bryce, Gordon used a copy of the original grayscale terrain PICT to create the perspective landscape. He imported the color PICT he had made in Painter and wrapped the landscape with it. Back in Painter, Gordon imported the landscape and created a coastline vignette with the masking tools. To begin the three-dimensional arrows, Gordon drew shapes in Free-Hand, and saved the file as a PICT. He used Bryce to help visualize the three-dimensional arrows, as follows: He opened the file in Bryce, where the arrows became 3D objects and part of an overall scene. When he had positioned the arrows the way he wanted them and the scene's view and lighting were set, he saved the scene as a Photoshop file, and then opened it in Painter. Gordon wanted to use the Bryce file as a guide for tracing, so he cloned it (File, Clone), deleted the contents of the clone (Ctrl/⌘-A and Backspace/Delete), and turned on Tracing Paper (Ctrl/⌘-T). Then he used Painter's Pen tool to trace the two arrow shapes and he used the shapes to make selections (Shapes, Convert To Selection). For the clouds in the arrows, he dragged and dropped an image of clouds (taken with a digital camera on a warm spring morning) into the composite file. He used the arrow selections to capture the imagery from the cloud layer by activating the layer, loading the selection (Select, Load Selection), and Alt/Option clicking with the Layer Adjuster tool to copy the selected area of the clouds image to a new floating object. To make the floating object into a standard layer, he dragged it above the layer it was copied from in the Layers palette. To differentiate the two kinds of cloud masses represented by the arrows, he used the Effects, Tonal Control, Adjust Colors feature to make the moisture-laden Aleutian Low grayer, and the drier Siberian High bluer. To complete the illusion of depth, Gordon added drop shadows to the arrows using Painter's Effects, Objects, Create Drop Shadow command. Next, he used the Digital Airbrush variant of Airbrushes to spray the two white glacier fields with light blue color. To finish, he flattened the layers in his file by choosing Drop All from the Layers command menu (accessed by clicking the right arrow on the Layers palette bar). Gordon saved the Painter image as a TIFF file and placed it in FreeHand, where he added the rivers, the type and the leader arrows.

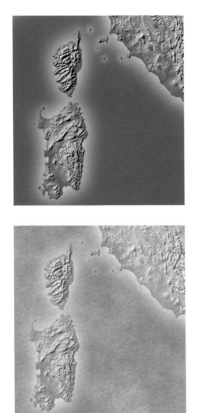

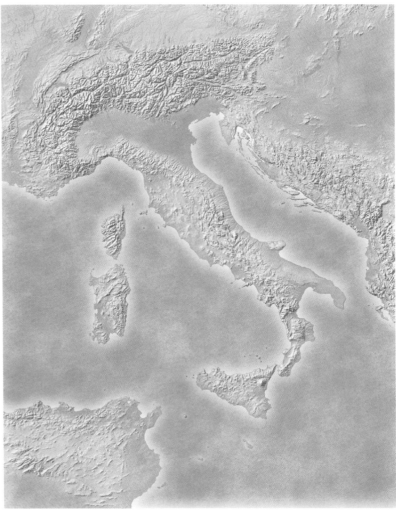

ILLUSTRATION: STEVEN GORDON / CREATED FOR ART SERVICE

■ This richly textured map of Italy was created by **Steven Gordon**, and commissioned by ArtService in Rome, Italy. The map is one of five maps the artist produced for the *Alitalia for you* section of Alitalia Airlines' in-flight magazine. To make the maps distinctive and different, Gordon turned to Painter's brushes and Auto Clone command to transform terrain images into faded watercolor landscapes.

Gordon began the maps by constructing color terrain images from elevation data in Digital Wisdom's MapRender3D. He used the same color-to-elevation scheme, so all five terrain images would result in a consistent color appearance. After exporting TIFF files from MapRender3D, Gordon opened each image in Photoshop where he cropped it and set its resolution to 300 pixels-per-inch. For the map of Italy, Gordon opened the Photoshop file in Painter. He cloned the image (File, Clone) and in the cloned file, chose Select, All and then hit the Backspace/Delete key to clear the clone

canvas. To begin auto-cloning the Italy map, Gordon selected the Impasto Soft Oil brush (loaded from the Painter 8 Wow! CD-ROM). He enabled the Clone Color button in the Color picker and in the Property Bar, he set Size to 100 and Opacity to 10%. (For all of the brushes, Gordon set Grain to 20.) Then he chose Effects, Esoterica, Auto Clone and let it run for one minute, which filled the image with light brush strokes based on the source image.

Next, Gordon selected Digital Water Color in the Brush Selector Bar, and the Soft Diffused Brush variant, then he enabled Clone Color in the Color picker. He set the brush Size to 40 and Opacity to 10% in the Property Bar. He chose Effects, Esoterica, Auto Clone again, and let it run for 12 seconds which began filling in gaps between the brush strokes laid down by the first Auto Clone and darkening the clone with more of the source image. He ran Auto Clone with the same brush for 12 seconds again, but

this time changing its Size to 5 to bring out more detail. To complete the Italy image, Gordon selected the Impasto, Soft Oil brush again, enabled Clone Color in the Color picker, set the Size to 5 and Opacity to 10% in the Property Bar. He chose Effects, Esoterica, Auto Clone again, time running the effect for 12 seconds. Some parts of the image appeared to be diffused or too light, so Gordon selected the Soft Cloning variant of Cloners, set its Size to 200 and Opacity to 3% in the Property Bar and manually stroked over light areas to make them darker and to bring them more into focus. When he had finished retouching, Gordon selected all of the image, copied it and then selected the source image and pasted the cloned image into it as a layer. He set the resulting layer at 65% Opacity and with a Normal blending mode in the Layers palette. This allowed the clone image to be combined with the original source image. Finally, he saved the image as a TIFF file.

■ *Art in Wartime* by **Steve Campbell**
began as a low-resolution sketch of a sax
player drawn during a trade show demo.
"Once I decided to work up the original
image at higher resolution, I knew I was
going to add a rain of bombs falling as
my hero plays his sax," says Campbell,
Before adding the bombs and other elements, he used the Studio Artist program
to render the image at the higher resolution of 300 pixels per inch and also to
create a rough, complex texture at the
new size. When the processing was complete, Campbell opened the new image
in Painter and isolated the figure and
background elements, by making selections using the Lasso tool and floating
the elements to layers. (Alt/Option-click

on an active selection with the Layer
Adjuster tool to cut it to a layer.)
Campbell painted the rainbow using
Oils variants. With a custom Image
Hose he painted the flora at the sax
player's feet. Using the File, Place command, he added the 3D bombs that
were created in Ray Dream Studio (a 3D
program), placing them as several layers. The city in the background was
drawn with Painter's Shape tools and its
layers were given partial transparency
(as were some of the bombs layers), by
adjusting their Opacity in the Layers
palette. Campbell painted and sketched
using several Oils variants and smudged
using the Just Add Water variant of
Blenders on the figure. Then he

adjusted the Composite Method for
some of the layers. He used the Digital
Airbrush variant of Airbrushes to paint
smoky clouds. When he was finished
working on the layers, he combined the
sky, bombs and city layers into one
layer by choosing Group from the Layer
Commands pop-up menu at the bottom of the Layers palette, then choosing Collapse from the same menu.
Next, he created a copy of the same
layer, by choosing Select, All, then Alt/
Option-clicking it with the Layer Adjuster tool. He used Effects, Surface
Control, Apply Lighting on this layer,
and then adjusted the strength of the
lighting effect on the image by reducing the Opacity of the "lighted" layer.

■ **Karen E. Reynolds** created the colorful illustration *New York Chicken* using Painter's brush and woodcut effects.

For this bird in the city, Reynolds began by opening a photo she had taken of the New York skyline. The photo included a window with diagonal panes. To create a background based on the photo that had a simplified, layered look, she added a woodcut effect to the photo by choosing Effects, Surface Control, Woodcut. In the Woodcut dialog box, she experimented with the Black Edge and Heaviness sliders to bring out the texture in the photo and the diagonal panes in the window. She also reduced the number of colors to create a more limited palette, then clicked OK to transform her photo into a woodcut. When the background was as she liked it, she began to sketch the chicken from memory, using expressive, scribbly strokes. She switched among the Oils, Pens, Erasers, Chalk and Pastels and other tools, using colors that complemented those used in the background.

■ *To the Rescue, Part 1* by **Donal Jolley**
is the first in a series of three paintings
featuring different World War II fighter
planes. Jolley began the image by taking
pictures of accurately scaled model
planes with a Nikon 5700 digital camera.
Then he carefully created the painting
using many brushes including the Chalk,
Pastels, Oils, Artists, Blenders and F-X.
After shooting the photos, Jolley built a
composite image in Painter that he could
use for reference during the painting process. He painted a silhouette mask for
each plane in the source files then used
the mask as a selection to copy and paste
each plane into a composite file, to its
own layer. He also incorporated an image
of clouds that he had shot for the background by copying and pasting it into

the working file. When the composition
was as he liked it, he saved the image in
PSD format so he could preserve the layers. Next, Jolley made a flattened duplicate of the reference image by choosing
File, Clone. He kept the original composite file open so he could import color
from it using cloning techniques. To create the look of vivid afternoon lighting,
Jolley painted saturated color on the
planes, using Pastels variants, then he
added highlights using a low-opacity
Square Chalk variant of Chalk. For the
details, Jolley switched to the Round
Camelhair and Smeary variants of the
Oils. The smeary brushes allowed him to
apply new color and blend it with the
existing pigment, just like wet traditional
paint. To soften some areas, he blended

with the Just Add Water variant of the
Blenders brush. For more drama in the
sky, Jolley used variants of the F-X brush.
He added a watercolor-like salt effect, by
sampling a color from one area of the
clouds and sprinkling it into nearby sections of the cloud using the Fairy Dust
variant of F-X; to blend and enhance
highlights in the edges of some of the
clouds he painted with the Fire variant.
When this brushwork was laid in, Jolley
used the Square Chalk variant of Chalk to
add texture. Then he used the Sargent
Brush variant of the Artists brush to paint
over areas to simulate the look of traditional blended oils. To sample color from
the original image in some areas, he
turned on Clone Color for the Sargent
Brush in the Color picker.

■ To create the surreal photo-collage *Coney Island Baby,* **Laurence Gartel** began by scanning each of the source photos into Photoshop, where he made selections to isolate the subjects from their backgrounds. He opened a large new blank file, copied each component image and pasted it onto its own layer in the composite. Next he opened the layered image in Painter and used the Layer Adjuster tool to position elements until the composition seemed balanced. To build a flashy surreal look, Gartel added several Liquid Metal layers by clicking the Dynamic Plugins button at the bottom of the Layers palette and choosing Liquid Metal from the menu. He used the Brush tool in the Liquid Metal dialog box to paint chrome brushstrokes of different thicknesses on the woman's face, neck and hair and to outline the ice cream cone. To reposition droplets of the chrome, he used the Liquid Metal Selection tool (arrow). He applied Standard Metal and Chrome using the pop-up Map menu in the dialog box. For some of the layers, he increased the Refraction setting to create the look of clear glass. The "live" nature of the Liquid Metal dynamic layers allowed Gartel to finesse the Liquid Metal on each layer until he was satisfied with the effect. When these elements were complete, he converted the dynamic layers into image layers by choosing Convert To Default Layer from the menu accessed by clicking the right triangle on the Layers palette bar. To create the granular texture in the lower right of the image, Gartel made a new layer by choosing New Layer from the same menu, and painted the area with dark gray. With a rough texture chosen in the Papers palette, he increased its size using the Scale slider. Then he chose Effects, Surface Control, Apply Surface Texture, Using Paper, with strong settings to apply the texture with highlights, shadows and shine. To complete the image, Gartel changed the Opacity and Composite Method in the Layers palette for a few of the layers (for instance, the purple Liquid Metal droplets in the middle area of the work).

■ *Trattoria* is an image from **Michela Del Degan's** *Storia 2000* series. Del Degan began the illustration by adding a new empty layer to her image by clicking the triangle on the right side of the Layers palette. On the new layer, she created a black-and-white sketch using the 2B Pencil variant of Pencils over Basic Paper texture. When the sketch was complete, she colored the image using several layers, often painting an object on its own layer. First, she laid in brown colors over the background using variants of the Chalk brush category. For the clock, she began by making oval selections, then filled them with blue and white using the Paint Bucket from the Toolbox, setting the fill color in the Property Bar. Using the Sharp Chalk variant of Chalks, she redefined the outlines on the

clock and drew wood grain and shadows. To add the glassy sheen to the clock face, she used the Digital Airbrush variant of Airbrushes and light gray paint. Next Del Degan colored the plants and other elements with the Smooth Ink Pen variant of Pens, adding highlights with the Digital Airbrush and refining the elements with the Sharp Chalk variant. To add 3D texture to the hat, she selected it with the Magic Wand and chose Effects, Surface Control, Apply Surface Texture Using Paper. Then she drew over it using the Sharp Chalk. She added a new layer, and drew the pasta-eating character using the Smooth Ink Pen and Digital Airbrush, as before. For his hair, she added another new layer, and painted the curls with the Opaque Bristle Spray variant of the Oil Brushes. She smoothed over

areas on the face using the Round Camelhair variant of Oils. The dish of spaghetti and the bread were also drawn with the Smooth Ink Pen. For the embossed effect on the bread, she used the Add Grain variant of the Photo brush over a fine, even-textured paper. Finally, she touched up the outlines of many objects in the illustration with the 2B Pencil variant of Pencils. To create the "Trattoria sign," she used the same brushes as before using white and red paint. For the highlights on the sign she used Effects, Surface Control, Apply Lighting and the Plain Light choice. Finally, she added a highlight on the character's face using the Dodge variant of the Photo brush. She also used the Dodge variant to paint diagonal strokes across the window to create the illusion of window glass.

■ *Musica* (above) and *Obsesión* (right) were created by **Eduardo Diaz**, also known as **Kaffa**. To paint *Musica*, Diaz began by using the Opaque Bristle Spray and Variable Flat variants of the Oils to block in the shapes of the instruments. To blend new color with existing color, he used the Smeary Bristle Spray variant. For crisper lines and edges, he switched to a Thick n Thin variant of Pens. Finally, to add three-dimensional highlights and shadows to the paint, he chose Effects, Surface Control, Apply Surface Texture, Using Image Luminance, with moderate settings.

For *Obsesión* Diaz began by blocking in areas of color using the Digital Airbrush variant of Airbrushes. Then, with the Rocky texture loaded from the Painter 7 Texture Library, he added textured brushstrokes by brushing lightly with the Gritty Charcoal variant of Charcoal. To draw the hair, eyebrows and lines around the eyes and mouth he used the Scratchboard Tool variant of Pens. For the look of thick, textured paint, he used Effects, Surface Control, Apply Surface Texture, Using Image Luminance with subtle settings. Then he used Apply Surface Texture again, this time Using Paper, with even subtler settings. To further enhance the textured effect on the floating eyes, he made a selection of the eyes with the Lasso tool, then pressed the Alt/Option key and chose Select, Float to put a copy on a new layer. Then he used Apply Surface Texture, Using Image Luminance on the layer.

WORKING WITH TYPE IN PAINTER

Diablo Publishing commissioned Susan LeVan to illustrate an article in Sutter Health *magazine about head injuries. LeVan used Painter's Text layers to build elements for her illustration.*

PAINTER IS A POWERFUL TOOL FOR DESIGNING creative display type and for special effects. With Painter you can set type and put an image inside it; add texture to type; rotate type, stretch it and paint on it; fill and stroke type for a neon look; add type with special effects to your illustration (for a book cover design, for example); and create three-dimensional chrome type for a logo. You can set text on a path, fill the type with a color, add a shadow and much more. This typography primer will help you get the most out Painter's type tools.

A TYPOGRAPHY PRIMER

Painter is not recommended for setting large amounts of text—it's a good idea to leave this task to your favorite page layout program, such as QuarkXPress, InDesign or PageMaker. Instead, we'll focus on type as a design element using display type, because this is where Painter's tools shine. Display type is generally set in sizes 14-point or larger; it's usually used for feature headlines in magazines, for book covers, for posters and billboards and for Web page headers, to name a few applications.

Fonts and font families. A *font* is a complete set of characters in one size and one typeface. The characters usually include uppercase and lowercase letters, numbers, punctuation and special characters. A *font family* is all of the sizes and style variations of a typeface (for instance, roman and italic styles in light, medium and bold weights).

Serif and sans serif. One way typefaces differ from one another is in the presence or absence of *serifs*, the small cross-strokes on the ends of the strokes that make up the letters. Serif faces were the first typefaces designed for printing. The serifs help our eyes to recognize the shape of a letter sooner and to track horizontally

The letter "E," showing the City font family, which includes upper-and lowercase City Light and City Light Italic, City Medium and City Medium Italic and City Bold and City Bold Italic

Serif fonts have small cross-strokes at the ends of the strokes. The letter "G" is shown here in a serif font, Goudy, (left) and a sans serif font, Stone Sans Semibold (right).

The letter "T," demonstrating examples of several type classes. From left to right, top row: Black Letter, Fette Fraktur; Roman, Century Old Style; Slab Serif, City Bold. Bottom row: Script, Reporter Two; Sans Serif, Stone Sans; and Novelty, Arnold Boecklin.

from one letter to the next across a page, which makes these faces typically easier to read than sans serif faces.

The term *sans serif* refers to type without serifs. Usually sans serif fonts have a consistent stroke weight. Because of this quality, they can be ideal for display type because they look good in larger sizes and are good candidates for graphic treatments such as beveling and edge texture application. A sans serif font with very broad strokes has plenty of weight to work with when you apply special effects!

Classes of fonts. Fonts can be further grouped into several classes: Black Letter, Roman, Slab Serif, Sans Serif, Script and Decorative. *Black Letter* type resembles the style of hand-lettering that was popular during the time of Gutenberg's first printing press in 1436; Fette Fraktur is an example. These faces are usually used for an old-fashioned, formal look. Many typefaces fall into the *Roman* classification, including Old Style (for instance, Caslon and Century Old Style), Transitionals (Times Roman), and Modern (Palatino). The Old Style fonts have angled serifs, while the Modern Roman faces have straight vertical or horizontal serifs. *Slab Serifs* are also known as Egyptians, and they are characterized by even stroke weights and square serifs (examples are City Bold and Stymie). *Sans Serif*, mentioned earlier, is also considered a classification of type. Examples are Helvetica, Franklin Gothic, Futura and Stone Sans.

Designs for *Script* type were originally inspired by penmanship. Script fonts with dramatic thick-and-thin strokes (such as Linoscript) are often not good candidates for special effects because many techniques

We set type using two script fonts, Linoscript (top) and Monoline Script. Our example shows the original typeset word above the type with textured edges. As you can see, the Monoline type kept its integrity of design through the special-effects application because of its thick, even stroke weight, while the thick-and-thin Linoscript did not.

Each typeface has its own aesthetic and emotional feel, as shown in this example. With Painter's text you can easily set type in different faces and colors. Shown here, from left to right are Fenice Ultra, Brush Script, Vag Rounded Black and City Medium. In this example, each letter was set on a separate layer so the different fonts could be applied.

John Dismukes employed Painter's airbrushes, selections and layers to hand-letter The 1800 Grand Margarita *logo, shown here in this detail. To view the entire image and more of Dismukes's exceptional work, turn to the gallery at the end of this chapter.*

For the storyboard for The Crossing Guard, *shown here in this detail, Geoff Hull used Painter. To see more of Hull's innovative typography work, turn to the gallery at the end of Chapter 10.*

involve blurring of the edges or beveling, which can destroy the thin strokes. If you'd like to try special effects and still preserve the script typeface, find a font with thick strokes, such as Kaufmann Bold, Monoline Script or Reporter Two.

Finally, the *Novelty* category is diverse and graphic. These faces are often used to communicate emotion in special projects like poster designs (Arnold Boecklin and Stencil are examples).

Legibility. Have you ever driven past two billboards and noticed that one was easy to read as you drove by, and the other was not? The easier-to-read one was more *legible* than the other. When it's easy to recognize the words so you can absorb their meaning quickly, the type is legible. Legibility was important when you drove by the billboard, or when you were able to efficiently scan the headlines on the front page of a newspaper this morning.

When you set type in Painter, choose fonts carefully if you intend to manipulate them with special effects. Are you

> **TWO COMBINED INTO ONE**
>
> Since Painter 7, the functionality of dynamic text and type shapes from earlier versions has been combined into one solution for text. If you like to use type shapes, it's easy to convert a text layer to shapes by choosing Convert Text to Shapes from the menu on the right side of the Layers palette.

using the typeface simply as an element in a collage, where the letters are employed for graphic purposes only and content is not as important? Or do you plan to set an important, legible headline and enhance it with beveling? If the latter is the case, make sure to choose a font with strong enough strokes to withstand the bevel effects, such as a bold sans serif face. Turn to "Creating Beveled Chrome" on page 292 for a step-by-step example of a three-dimensional chrome effect applied to sans serif type with Painter's Bevel World plug-in.

DESIGNING WITH PAINTER'S TYPE TOOLS

Each type element that you design has its own purpose: a Web page header, a food advertisement in a magazine, a billboard, the headline for a feature story in a magazine or a signage design. Know your client and research the style aesthetics needed for the design. This knowledge will help you choose the tools to use for the project.

Painter's Text is editable, which means you can easily change the size, color, font or content of the text, until you decide to convert the text layer into an image layer so you can paint on it or add special effects, or convert it to shapes so you can edit the outlines or do hand-kerning of the individual letters. Painter can display TrueType or Adobe Type 1 fonts if the printer font is installed. Painter can't display bitmap fonts because it needs the printer font's outline information to render the text. Each text layer can display a single font.

This Frutiger Black text was set using the Text tool from the Toolbox. It shows the bounding box around the selected type and the insertion point crosshair.

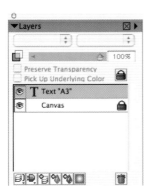

When the Text tool is clicked in the image window, a new Text layer represented by a "T" icon is generated in the Layers palette.

Setting text in your image. Begin by choosing the Text tool in the Toolbox. Using controls in the Property Bar, you can specify a font and the size, leading, tracking, and alignment. Click the cursor anywhere on the image and enter your text. The type will be displayed on a special new Text layer in your image. Using controls in the Text palette (Window, Show Text), you can also add a shadow and apply a curve style to the baseline of the type. Any changes that you make will be applied to the entire text layer.

In the Property Bar or Text palette: To specify the size, adjust the Point Size slider or click on the number to the right of the slider and enter a numerical value. Adjust the Tracking slider in the Text palette to globally change the spacing between the letters. To specify the alignment of the text, click the Align Left, Align Center or Align Right icon.

TEXT LAYER TO IMAGE LAYER

To convert a text layer to an image layer, choose Convert to Default Layer from the menu on the right side of the Layers palette. The text will be converted to a pixel-based layer so that you can paint on it or apply effects; the text layer's name will be preserved in the Layers palette.

If you'd like to set more than one line of text, press the Return key (without moving the cursor), and Painter will begin a new line of type. To remove the last letter you typed, leave the cursor where it is and press the Backspace/Delete key. To adjust the spacing between multiple baselines of the Text, adjust the Leading slider, or enter a numerical value.

Applying a new color. The current color chosen in the Color picker will automatically be applied to the text as you set it. If you'd like to change the color of the text, make sure that the Text Attributes button is chosen in the Text palette. Choose a new color in the Color picker and the text will update to display the new color.

Adding a shadow. When you'd like to add a shadow to your type, click the External Shadow or Inside Shadow icon on the left side of the Property Bar or in the Text palette. By default, a black shadow will be applied and the Shadow Attributes button will automatically be chosen. To adjust the opacity or the softness of a shadow, use the Opacity and Blur sliders. To blur the shadow

SPECIFYING TEXT ATTRIBUTES USING THE PROPERTY BAR

When the Text tool is chosen in the Toolbox, you can specify a font as well as the point size, alignment, color, opacity, shadow and a Composite Method in the Property Bar.

Choosing 200-point Minion Bold in the Property Bar

The Text palette contains controls for specifying the appearance of the type, including putting type on a curve and specifying an angled blur for a shadow.

This type was set along a path using the Curve Perpendicular style.

more on one edge than on the opposite edge, enable the Directional Blur checkbox and adjust the Angle slider. For a colored shadow, choose a new color in the Color picker.

Setting type on a curve. The Text controls in Painter include the capability to create a Bézier path for the type baseline right in the Text palette. (The Curve Style controls are in the Text palette underneath the sliders, as shown in the illustration on page 287.) To begin, enter your type on the image. To place the type on a curve, click on a non-straight Curve Style icon. The first icon is Curve Straight, which will not create a curve. The other three icons will generate a curved baseline and allow you to edit the baseline using Bézier curves: the Curve Ribbon style specifies that the vertical strokes of the type will be straight up, and Curve Perpendicular places each character perpendicular to the curve, without distorting the letters. The fourth option, Curve Stretch, distorts the shape of individual letters to fit the space created by the bend of a curve. Use the Centering slider on the Text palette to move the type along the baseline curve. See "Setting Text on a Curve" on page 290 for a step-by-step description of the process.

Converting Text to Shapes. After you set type with Painter's Text tool, you can convert each letter that you set to an individual vector object on its own layer by choosing Convert Text to Shapes from the triangle pop-up menu on the right side of the Layers palette. Shapes have certain advantages over type: They have editable Bézier curve outlines and unique transparency

SELECTING A WORD

To select an entire word on a text layer so you can edit it, begin by clicking on the Text layer's name in the Layers palette, then double-click on the word with the Text tool to select it.

Double-clicking with the Text tool

MOVING A SHADOW

After adding a shadow to type, if you'd like to move the shadow, click on the shadow with the Layer Adjuster tool and drag in the image.

We dragged the shadow slightly down and to the right.

SLANTING OR ROTATING TYPE

In Painter you can skew or rotate type easily. After you've completed setting the type, choose the Layer Adjuster tool in the Toolbox. To rotate it, press the Ctrl/⌘ key and drag on a corner handle. To slant the type, press the Ctrl/⌘ key and drag on the top or bottom handle.

This Futura Extra Bold type was slanted by pressing the Ctrl/⌘ key and dragging the bottom handle to the left.

The Curve Ribbon style chosen in the Text palette allowed us to rotate this text set in the Bauer Bodoni Italic font around a path. We set text and clicked the Curve Ribbon button to place the text on the curve. Then we used the Add Point tool to add an anchor point near the center of the path and used the Shape Selection tool to manipulate the path.

We created this clear, embossed look by setting text in the Machine Bold font, converting it to an image layer, then using Apply Surface Texture and Composite methods.

PHOTO: CORBIS IMAGES

To create this painted text, we began by setting type in the Sand font and converted it into an image layer by choosing Convert To Default layer from the menu on the right side of the Layers palette bar. The Opaque Round variant of Oils was used to add colored brushstrokes.

PHOTO: CORBIS IMAGES

To make the type break up into sharp ice shards, we set type on a Text layer using Futura Extra Bold, then painted on the type with the Shattered variant of the F-X brush, clicking the Commit button when the warning dialog box appeared.

capabilities. You can stroke and fill them, then change fill and stroke. As with type, you can rotate them without loss of quality. Because each letter is a separate element, it's easy to do custom kerning of the individual letterforms, which isn't possible with text.

Convert text to shapes when setting small amounts of type, when you want to pay special attention to spacing between individual letters, or when you want to edit the outline shape of the letters. Also, shapes are useful when you want to make a quick selection or mask from type (Shapes, Convert To Selection)—for instance, when you want to put an image inside of the type. (For more information about shapes, turn to "Working With Shapes," in the beginning of Chapter 5.)

When to convert text to pixels. If you'd like to paint on type, add special effects such as Apply Surface Texture or manipulate a layer mask on the type layer to erode the edges of the type, you'll need to convert the text layer to an image layer. To convert a text layer to an image layer, choose Convert To Default layer from the triangle pop-up menu on the right side of the Layers palette. If you attempt to paint on a text layer without converting it, a Commit dialog box will appear, asking if you would like to convert the text layer to an image layer. Click Commit to convert it. 🖌

This text was set in Meta Bold. The original text had "uneven" letterspacing (top), so it was converted to individual shapes and kerned to tighten the spacing and to make it more consistent (bottom).

Setting Text on a Curve

Overview *Set the text; choose a Curve Style; use the Shape Selection tool to finesse the length and shape of the path; adjust the text on the path.*

CHER THREINEN-PENDARVIS / PHOTO: CORBIS IMAGES

1a

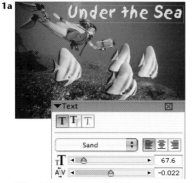

We set type using the Sand font and used the Tracking slider to tighten letterspacing.

1b

Choosing the Curve Stretch style

2a

Using the Shape Selection tool to pull an end point and lengthen the curve

2b

With two more points added, the curve is taking shape.

IT'S A SNAP TO SET TEXT ON A CURVE in Painter. The Text controls in Painter 8 allow you to create a Bézier path for the type baseline right in the image window. Here's a quick method, applied to a comp for an advertising layout.

1 Setting the type and applying it to a curve. For this technique you can begin with a new blank image, or start with a photo, as we did. Choose the Text tool in the Toolbox and open the Text palette by choosing Window, Show Text. Choose a font and size and set your type. We chose the typeface Sand, because its organic shape and playful feel would work well with the Curve Stretch curve style we planned to use.

Click on the Curve Stretch button in the Text palette (the button farthest to the right in Curve Styles), and you'll see the text curving around the baseline of a newly generated path in your image. The Curve Stretch curve style distorts the letters to fit the spaces in the curve. The slight distortion adds to the ripply underwater effect. To reposition the text layer on the image, use the Layer Adjuster tool.

2 Adjusting the path. To change the shape of the path, choose the Shape Selection tool in the Toolbox (it's the hollow arrow), select the text layer in the Layers palette and click on an end point. Pull on the end point to lengthen the path. To change the shape of the curve, drag a control handle in the direction that you want the curve to go. As you manipulate the path, aim for gentle curves so the type will flow smoothly.

To add more anchor points (for instance, to make a gentle wavy line, like we did), choose the Add Point tool (it's nested under the Shape Selection tool in the Toolbox) and click the baseline curve. To remove a point, choose the Delete Point tool (it's also nested under the Shape Selection tool in the Toolbox) and click the anchor point. Use the control handles on each anchor point to finesse the curve. To adjust the position of the text on the path, use the Centering slider in the Text palette. We set Centering at 2%.

A Spattery Graffiti Glow

Overview *Use the Text tool to set text over a background; convert the text to an image layer, then to selections; stroke the selections using the Draw Outside mode, to spatter the background outside the type.*

WITH THE HELP OF PAINTER'S TEXT LAYERS, selections and Draw modes you can stroke around the edges of type with an Airbrush to create this fast, fun title solution.

1 Choosing an image and setting type. Open an image to use as a background; our photo was 864 x 612 pixels. Choose the Text tool in the Toolbox, then select a font and size in the Property Bar. (We chose 200-point Berthold City Bold Italic.) Click in the image and begin typing. If the Layers palette is open, you'll see a text layer appear when you begin typing. To adjust the spacing between the letters, open the Text palette (Window, Show Text) and adjust the Tracking slider.

2 Converting the text to selections. To achieve the result at the top of this page, it's necessary to convert the text to an image layer, then to selections. Select the text layer in the Layers palette, click the right triangle on the Layers palette bar and choose Convert To Default Layer from the menu. Now reduce the opacity of the layer to 0% using the Opacity slider in the Layers palette and choose Drop and Select from the menu on the right side of the Layers palette bar. The layer will disappear from the list in the Layers palette and will reappear as animated marquees. To prepare the selection for stroking, choose Select, Transform Selection.

3 Stroking outside of the selection. With the help of Painter's nifty Draw icons in the bottom left of the image window, we used a brush to stroke around the edge of the selection. The Draw icons allow you to use a selection just as you would a traditional airbrush frisket, to paint inside or outside of the selection. From the pop-up in the bottom left corner of the image window, choose the Draw Outside (center) icon. In the Brush Selector Bar choose the Pixel Spray variant of the Airbrushes. (We increased the size of the brush to 60 pixels, using the Size slider on the Property bar.) Choose white in the Color picker, then choose Select, Stroke Selection and watch as Painter gives your type a fine grained, spattery glow. Try stroking your selection with other Airbrushes such as the Coarse Spray or the Variable Spatter variant. 🖌

The text set in City Bold Italic

The selection marquee created from the layer

Choosing the Pixel Spray variant of the Airbrushes in the Brush Selector Bar

Selecting the Draw Outside mode and stroking outside the active selection

Creating Beveled Chrome

Overview *Open a file and apply lighting to build a background; set text; convert the text to shapes and then to a layer; bevel the forms and apply a reflection; add a shadow.*

Creating a brighter soft diagonal spotlight based on Gradual Diagonal light

The softly lit background, ready for the type

The selected type shapes and the background with lighting before the spacing was adjusted between the individual letters

PAINTER'S BEVEL WORLD DYNAMIC LAYER allows you to try an endless variety of custom bevels on a selected layer quickly, without time-consuming masks and channels. To create this three-dimensional chrome title, we applied effects that included custom lighting, a rounded bevel with a reflection map and a shadow.

1 Creating a background with custom lighting. Begin by creating a new file with a deep blue-green background (our file was 800 x 500 pixels). To add depth to the background we applied soft diagonal lighting that would complement the bright, shiny chrome to come. To open the Lighting dialog box, choose Effects, Surface Control, Apply Lighting. When the dialog box appears, click on the Gradual Diagonal choice. To increase the Brightness of your light, move the Brightness slider to 1.50. To save your new light, click the Save button and name it when the Save Lighting dialog box appears.

2 Setting the type and converting it to shapes. Now that the backdrop is finished, you're ready to create the type. Choose a color (that contrasts with the background) in the Color picker to automatically fill the text with color as you type. The contrasting color will make it easier for you to see your type as you adjust the space between individual letters. Select the Text tool in the Toolbox and in the Property Bar, choose a font and size. Click in the image with the Text tool and enter the type. We set 320-point type using Vag Rounded Bold. (If you don't have the typeface we used, choose a bold font with broad strokes to accommodate the beveling effect to come.) So you can adjust the spacing of individual letters, convert the text to shapes by choosing Convert Text to Shapes from the triangle pop-out menu on the right side of the Layers palette. Painter will convert the text layer to letterform shapes and group them. To "hand-kern" the letters, in the Layers palette, open the eye icon to the left of the group of shapes. Click on a letter's name in the Layers palette and use the arrow keys on your keyboard to adjust the space between the letters. Make sure to leave room between the letters to allow for the bevel to be extended outside of each letter.

3a

The rough bevel generated by the Bevel World layer default settings.

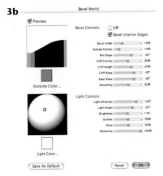

3b

Our settings in the Bevel World dialog box

4

We used "emap 4" from the "Wow! Patterns on the Painter 8 Wow! CD-ROM.

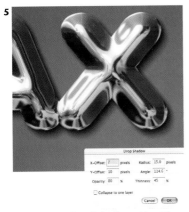

5

The Drop Shadow dialog box with settings for casting the shadow down and to the right of the chrome type

3 Beveling the type. In preparation for using the Bevel World dynamic layer, merge the shapes group to a single image layer by selecting the group in the Layers palette and choosing Shapes, Convert To Layer. With the layer still selected, click the Plug-ins button at the bottom of the Layers palette and choose Bevel World from the menu. To build a 3D effect with a smooth rounded shape that would show off the reflection map we planned to add, we used these settings: Bevel Width slider to 15% (for narrower sides and a broader top); Outside Portion, 14% (for a small bevel outside the original pixels on the layer); Rim Slope, 26° (for a rounder top); Cliff Portion, 50% (the vertical distance between the base and rim); Cliff Height, 29% (to reduce the height of the sides); Cliff Slope, 45° (the angle for the middle of the bevel); Base Slope, 45° (leaving the angle of the outermost portion at its default); Smoothing, 52% (to add roundness to the base, cliff and rim of the bevel and to make any ridges smoother). Ignore the outside color, because it will disappear when the reflection is applied. Leave the dialog box open.

4 Achieving the chrome effect. The secret to achieving this chrome effect is choosing a bright shiny environment map in the Patterns Selector, then going back to the Reflections slider in the lower part of the Bevel World dialog box. We chose an environment map that included shiny metal reflections and bright red colors. To apply the reflection map that we used, you'll need to load the "Wow emap" library. Locate it in the Wow! Patterns folder on the Painter 8 Wow! Book CD-ROM and copy it into the Painter 8 application folder. To load this library, click the Pattern Selector on the Toolbox and choose Load Library from the triangle menu. Navigate to the "Wow emap" library in the Painter application folder, select it and click Open. Back in the Pattern Selector, choose "emap 1" from the triangle menu. Now move the Reflection slider in the Bevel World dialog box to the far right (we used 99%). Your type will magically change to bright shiny chrome! Click OK to close the Bevel World dialog box.

5 Adding a shadow. To increase the depth of our image, we added a drop shadow using Painter's automatic drop shadow feature. To build your shadow, select the beveled layer and choose Effects, Objects, Create Drop Shadow. In the dialog box, we set X-Offset to 7 pixels, Y-Offset to 10 pixels and increased the Opacity to 80%. For a softer shadow, we set Radius to 15.0 pixels, and we left the Angle (114.6°, which would cast the shadow down and to the lower right of the object) and Thinness (45%) at their defaults. (A low Thinness setting creates a streaked look similar to a motion blur.)

Painting with Ice

Overview *Set Text to use as a template for "hand-lettering;" paint icy script on a Liquid Metal plug-in layer; composite a copy of the layer to enhance the design.*

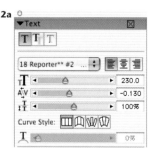

The original photograph

The Text palette with settings for our title, including the tighter Tracking

The image with the Text set and in position

YOU CAN CREATE TEXT EFFECTS QUICKLY with dynamic layers. To begin this cover comp for an online travel agency catalog, we set type on a Text layer. Using this text as a template, we "hand-painted" new 3D letters onto a Liquid Metal dynamic layer using a tablet and stylus. Then we applied special settings to give the liquid letters a clear, frozen look.

1 Choosing an image. We began by selecting a photo that measured 768 x 512 pixels. Although the final art used online would be smaller, we preferred to work at a larger size so we could zoom in and finesse the details, and then reduce the size later. We chose a photo with a Mediterranean theme and refreshing colors that would complement the "ice" or "glass" title.

2 Setting Dynamic Text. To make it easier for you to see the type over the image, choose a contrasting color in the Color picker to automatically fill the text with color as you type. Select the Text tool in the Toolbox. In the Property Bar, choose a font and size and set the type directly on the image. (We set our text using the Reporter Two font). Open the Text palette by choosing Window, Show Text, and adjust the spacing between the letters, using the Tracking slider in the Text palette. To interactively resize the type, use the Size slider in the Property Bar or Text palette. To use the Layer Adjuster tool to resize the type: Position it over a corner of the text, and when the arrow cursor appears, drag on the text. Drag the text with the Layer Adjuster to reposition it in your image. When you've finished making adjustments to your text, click OK.

3 Drawing with crystal-clear ice. Using the text as a template, we drew new letters using a Liquid Metal plug-in layer. Set up your Liquid Metal layer as follows: Open the Layers palette, click the Dynamic Plug-ins button at the bottom of the Layers palette and choose Liquid Metal. Painter will generate an empty,

3a

3a

Liquid Metal		
Amount		1.1
Smooth		90%
Size		16.3
Volume		97%
Spacing		0.331
Map:	Standard Metal	

☐ Display Handles ☑ Surface Tension

Refraction ◄ 90%

(Rain) (Clear) (Reset) (**OK**)

The settings in the Liquid Metal dialog box for the icy look

Beginning to hand-letter the Liquid Metal type using the dynamic text as a template

The underlying template layer is visible through the "ice."

The icy type with text layer removed

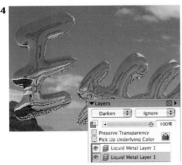

Detail of the icy type showing the underlying layer's Composite Method set to Darken

transparent Liquid Metal dynamic layer, and the Liquid Metal dialog box will appear. With the title as an underlay, we used a stylus to trace the text with the Liquid Metal brush tool. To begin, move the Refraction slider all the way to the right (so you can paint with crystal-clear ice). Choose the Brush tool in the Liquid Metal dialog box and carefully paint your title.

Adjust the Amount, Smooth, Size and Volume settings to your liking. To select all of the Liquid Metal so that you can apply new settings, choose the Liquid Metal Selector (arrow) and drag a marquee around what you've painted. Our settings were Amount, 1.1; Smooth, 90; Size, 16.3; Volume, 97; Spacing, .331; Map, Standard Metal, with Surface Tension checked. We reduced the Refraction setting to 90%, because it helped the type stand out from the photo.

After completing your letters, click OK to close the Liquid Metal dialog box. Then delete the Text layer you used as a template: Select its name in the Layers palette and click the Delete (Trash can) button.

A Liquid Metal dynamic layer is *live*, which means you can continue to finesse the dialog box settings. To keep a layer dynamic, do not "commit" the layer (change it into an image layer), and make sure to save the file in RIFF format. For more information about dynamic layers, turn to Chapter 5, "Using Layers."

4 Compositing a second layer. As you can see in your image, Painter's Liquid Metal dynamic layer "refracts" an underlying image. To give the ice more texture and make it look shinier, we set up another layer between our ice layer and the image beneath. To begin, make a copy of the Liquid Metal layer (Alt/Option-click with the Layer Adjuster tool). To enhance the copy of the Liquid Metal layer using tonal effects, choose Effects, Tonal Control, Brightness/Contrast and slightly increase the contrast. When the Commit dialog box appears, asking if you'd like to convert the dynamic layer to an image layer, click Commit. To add more texture and bring out the highlights in the icy type, we changed the underlying layer's Composite Method in the Layers palette to Darken.

So many options! When you have the underlying layer in place, experiment with changing the Composite Method in the Layers section to different settings. We experimented with Gel (left), and Pseudocolor (right). Control the effect with the layer's Opacity slider.

■ **Keith MacLelland** designed this colorful cover illustration for *Summertime Fun Bunch Comics*, a self-published zine that he creates with several other artists.

MacLelland started by creating a new file and filling it with a medium-toned brown for the background. Then he added colored squares to the background by making constrained rectangular fills with the Paint Bucket as follows: He chose the Paint Bucket tool and clicked and dragged with the Paint Bucket to "sketch" the area where the fill would be applied. He repeated this process until the background was covered with small squares of varying color. When he was happy with the background, he built the Tiki character using his typical working process, which includes sketching with the 2B Pencil variant of Pencils, making a back-and-white ink drawing using the Scratchboard Tool variant of Pens, and adding color by painting with the Airbrushes, Chalk, Pastels and Oils brushes.

To apply paper textures to areas in his image (for instance, the Tiki's head) he used the Square Chalk variant of Chalk. For the three-dimensional texture on the bathing suit, he made a selection of the bikini with the Lasso tool, then he loaded a custom floral texture in the Paper Selector and chose Effects, Surface Control, Apply Surface Texture, Using Paper, with subtle settings.

To draw the wood grain effect on the Tiki, he used the Scratchboard Tool. Working on a separate layer, he drew the wood grain, then he set the Composite Method for this layer to Gel, and made the layer partially transparent using the Opacity slider in the Layers palette.

MacLelland created all of the text in Painter. For the list of contributors, he chose a color and size in the Property Bar and set the text. To adjust the angle of the text to match the sign under it, he chose the Layer Adjuster tool, positioned it over a corner point on the Text layer and pressed the Ctrl/⌘ key to rotate the layer. For the title, he set the type, then duplicated it five times. He experimented with the color of each title layer (finally choosing yellow, orange, pink and magenta colors), and used the Layer Adjuster tool to finesse the position of each one to achieve the effect shown in the final illustration.

■ **Keith MacLelland** was chosen by *Philly-Tech* magazine to create the illustration *Seeds* for an article on job searching. The image was created using several layers for the sketch, ink drawing, coloring and text. Working on layers allowed him to keep elements separate, so he could reposition them and independently adjust the Opacity and the Composite Methods. MacLelland began by clicking the New Layer button on the Layers palette to add a new empty layer, where he drew a rough pencil sketch. He added a second layer and used the Scratchboard Tool variant of Pens to create an ink drawing with flowing black lines. After adding another new layer, he blocked in the basic color areas using the Chalk, Pas-

tel and Oil Pastels brushes, then MacLelland refined the color using his own custom variants of the Oils. Now that he had the line drawing and color as he liked them, MacLelland wanted to enhance the lines, so he selected each ink stroke by clicking on it with the Magic Wand and painted it using a custom brush based on the Smeary Round. He used the Square Chalk variant of Chalk to apply more texture around the elements on the basic color layer (for instance the shaking hands, gloves and laptop computer). MacLelland also painted textures onto areas of the bags, gloves and a few other elements using the Square Chalk. Then he used his custom Smeary Round brush to paint the water pouring from

the watering can (a wet paint smear effect) and to paint more soft reflections onto the laptop screen. MacLelland added the type using Painter's Text tool. So he could paint, erase and apply effects to some of the type elements, he converted them to image layers by selecting each Text layer in the Layers palette, clicking the triangle on the right side of the Layers palette and choosing Convert to Default Layer from the menu. Besides adding brushstrokes and texture to many of the converted Text layers, he also erased areas of some of them (such as the Seed House text in the lower right) where the text covered areas of the plant and the water pouring from the can.

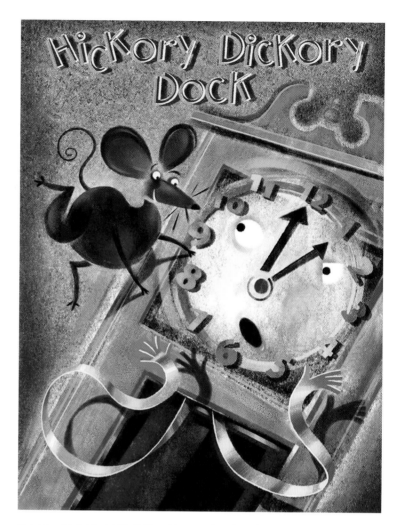

■ *Hickory Dickory* was created by **Mike Reed** as a promotion for his agent, HK Portfolio. To develop the illustration, Reed painted with the Chalk, Pastels and Oil Pastel variants on several layers and used the Text tool to set the type for the title and clock numerals. He sketched the composition in saturated colors using the Square Chalk variant of Chalk on Wood Shavings paper texture (from the Wow! Textures on the CD-ROM that comes with this book). So he could paint freely in some areas while protecting other areas of his composition, he made soft-edged selections by feathering each selection (Select, Feather), then saving it (Select, Save Selection) so he could use the selection later as a mask in the Channels palette. Reed created new layers for the background, the clock's body, the hands and the mouse. Working on each layer, he painted loose brushstrokes using the Square Chalk and varying colors. To refine areas, he used the Oil Pastel (Oil

Pastels) and Artist Pastel Chalk (Pastels) variants.

For the title and numerals, Reed set type in the Block font. He set the title on one text layer and the numerals on individual text layers so he could rotate them easily as follows: He chose the Layer Adjuster in the Toolbox, positioned the tool over a corner of a number, then pressed the Ctrl/⌘ key to make the cursor change into a circular rotation symbol, and then dragged to rotate the element. When the numerals were in place, Reed grouped all of the numeral layers and collapsed them into one layer, then he converted the layer to pixels by choosing Convert to Default Layer from the menu on the Layers palette bar.

For a soft look on the edge of the layer, he added texture to the edge of some of the layers by selecting a layer in the Layers palette, disabling the Preserve Transparency checkbox and brushing along

the edge of the layer using the Square Chalk and the Wood Shavings texture. Then he enabled Preserve Transparency in the Layers palette and painted over the numbers and title with the Square Chalk using various colors.

For the shadow on the title, he duplicated the title layer by Alt/Option-clicking on it using the Layer Adjuster. Then he dragged the copy below the title in the Layers palette. Using a darker color, he painted this shadow layer using the Square Chalk. Then he softened the edge of this shadow layer as he'd done before, by painting along the edge with the Square Chalk. He created the shadow for the letters and the hands of the clock in much the same way. When the shadow layers were complete, he set their Composite Method to Gel in the Layers palette. Finally, using the Oil Pastel and Sharp Chalk (Chalk), he added a few reddish details to the mouse and brighter highlights to the clock's hands.

■ **Susan LeVan** used several layers when she created *Going Global* for her agents, Bruck and Moss: She began by drawing the figures on separate layers with the Smooth Ink Pen variant of Pens and the Square Chalk (Chalk) and Oil Pastel variants, and added their drop shadows using Painter's Effects, Objects, Create Drop Shadow command. For the background behind the figures, LeVan used two patterns that she had made in separate source files. To build the "text" pattern, she used Futura, Bubble Dot and a few other fonts to set letters and symbols using the Text tool and sized them using the Size slider in the Property Bar. She positioned them with the Layer Adjuster tool. When the text elements were complete, she dropped the text layers to the Canvas by choosing Drop All from the triangle pop-up menu on the right side of the Layers palette. Then she captured the text design as a pattern in the Patterns palette by choosing Capture Pattern from the triangle pop-out menu on the right side of the Patterns palette. (See "Creating a Seamless Pattern" and "Applying Patterns" in Chapter 7.) Now working in the final image, she added new layers and filled each one with the type or globe pattern by selecting one of the custom patterns in the Patterns section and choosing Effects, Fill, Fill With Pattern. To make the white areas of the layers transparent, she set the Composite Method to Gel in the Layers palette. LeVan wanted to add more color and texture interest to the background, so she adjusted the size of each pattern using the Scale slider in the Patterns palette and filled two more new layers with them. She selected white areas on the new layers and deleted them. Next, she colored one of the layers gold and the other green by turning on Preserve Transparency in the Layers palette and filling the layers with new color. Finally, she set their Composite Method to Colorize and adjusted the Opacity of each layer.

■ **John Dismukes** of Capstone Studios is well known for his creative logo design and hand-drawn typography. He used similar processes to design and airbrush the three images on these pages. Dismukes begins each design by drawing many sketches, and when the direction is established, he draws a tight visualization of the typography on paper. The approved pencil sketch is then scanned and used as a template in FreeHand to create Post-Script outlines. He imports the outlines into Photoshop and builds elements on layers. Then he opens the file with layers in Painter for the airbrushing. In Painter, some of the layers are duplicated and used to make selections (via Drop and Select from the Layers palette bar menu), and they are then saved as masks. (Alternatively, outlines can be imported directly into Painter as shapes via File, Acquire,

Adobe Illustrator File and then converted to layers.) Dismukes uses selections to limit paint as he airbrushes using the Digital Airbrush variant of Airbrushes. For a step-by-step description of a similar technique using Painter, turn to "Selections and Airbrush," in Chapter 4.

The *Grand Margarita Metallic Cactus* illustration (top) was commissioned by Alcone Marketing Group and art-directed by Liliana Marchica. Dismukes began with a tight sketch, but he wanted a rough look for this logo, so he did not import outlines. He painted masks for the type, then converted them to selections he could use to limit the paint. Using the Digital Airbrush, Dismukes airbrushed the lettering. To add texture to the leaf, he cloned texture onto a layer from another file: He opened a texture file with the same dimensions as the logo file, defined it as

the clone source by choosing File, Clone Source and used a Cloning brush variant to softly brush the texture onto the layer.

For the packaging of an action game, art director (Mark Rein) and client (Epic Games, Inc.) wanted a logo with a progressive, "Gothic Tech" style. After scanning his tight sketch, Dismukes began *Unreal* (above), by importing the sketch and outlines into a new file. For an underpainting, he filled the type with brown. Using the imported outlines, he made masks for the letter faces and bevels. With selections loaded from the masks to constrain the spray, he carefully airbrushed the shadows and highlights, working from dark to light. To intensify the bronze color, he duplicated the finished layer and set its Composite method to Multiply, with 30% Opacity.

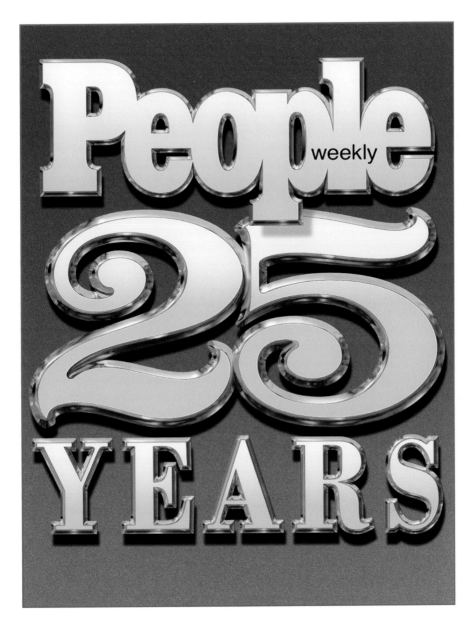

■ For *People's 25th Anniversary logo*, a cover illustration for Time Warner's *People Weekly* magazine, **John Dismukes** and **Jo-Anne Redwood** worked closely with their team at Capstone Studios and the art directors from *People* magazine, Phil Simone and Hilli Pitzer. Making hundreds of sketches, Dismukes and Redwood designed the type to complement the existing *People* magazine logo, make a strong statement, and be legible from a distance. After the design was approved, Dismukes took the time he needed to perfect the letterspacing, and then carefully rendered the realistic reflections. Like a traditional airbrush artist using friskets, Dismukes built a mask for the front face of the type and another for the bevels. After making a new layer, he filled the letters with light gray. Then he loaded the bevel selection and used the Digital Airbrush variant of Airbrushes to paint detailed reflections, highlights and shadows. Finally, he loaded a selection from the face mask again, and with a tiny airbrush, he painted the fine strokes that set off the flat front of the letters from their beveled sides. He finished by adding a drop shadow and background. "For high-quality work, you have to bring artistry to the computer," says Dismukes.

USING
PAINTER
WITH
PHOTOSHOP

When creating Quarry, Marc Brown used
Illustrator, Photoshop and Painter. To see
more of his work, turn to page 310.

turn to page 310.

MASK MAXIMUMS

A Painter file can contain up to 32
masks in the Channels palette, plus
one layer mask for each layer.
Photoshop's maximum is 24 channels in an RGB file, but three of the
channels are taken up by the Red,
Green and Blue color channels
(leaving room for 21 masks). If you
attempt to open a file with 32
masks in Photoshop, you will be
greeted by a polite dialog box asking if you would like to discard the
extra channels (numbers higher than
21 will be discarded).

IT'S EASY TO MOVE FILES back and forth between Painter 8 and Photoshop.
And what does Painter have to offer the Photoshop user? Fantastic
natural-media brushes that give your images warmth, a multitude of
textures and fabulous special effects! In addition to the work showcased
in this chapter, several of the other artists whose work appears in this
book have used both Painter and Photoshop in the development of
their images. If you're an avid Photoshop user and would like to see
more examples of how others have combined the use of the two programs, check out the work of these artists for inspiration: Jeff Burke,
John Dismukes, Donal Jolley and Pamela Wells. The index in the
back of the book lists page references for each of their names.

PAINTER TO PHOTOSHOP

Here are some pointers for importing Painter 8 files into Photoshop:

• To preserve image layers when moving an image from Painter 8
  into Photoshop, save a file in Photoshop format. Photoshop will
  open the file and translate the layers with their names and the
  layer hierarchy intact. (Photoshop rasterizes any dynamic layers
  such as Text, Liquid Metal, and Water Color, as well as Shape layers.)

• If a Painter file contains layers that extend beyond Painter's live
  image area, and that document is opened in Photoshop 4 and later
  versions, the areas outside of the live area are retained. (Photoshop
  3 clipped the layer information outside the live area.)

• Painter offers most of the Photoshop Blending modes; some exceptions are Color Dodge, Color Burn and Exclusion. And Painter has
  seven additional Compositing Methods of its own. Photoshop converts Magic Combine to Lighten mode, Gel to Darken mode, Colorize
  to Color mode, and Shadow Map to Multiply. When Photoshop
  encounters a Painter-native Composite Method it can't convert (such as

John Dismukes used FreeHand, Photoshop and Painter when building the Risk Game Board, *a detail of which is shown here, for the Parker Bros./Hasbro Games Group. See the entire image on page 311.*

See the entire image on page 311.

DYNAMIC LAYERS

When a Painter file that includes a Dynamic Layer such as Liquid Metal is opened in Photoshop, the layer is preserved but the dynamic capabilities are lost. To retain the dynamic properties for further editing in Painter, save a copy of your file with live dynamic layers in RIFF format.

A PATH TO PHOTOSHOP

You can store path information with a selection in Painter for import to Photoshop, and it will appear in the Photoshop Paths palette. When you make a selection with Painter's Lasso or Rectangular or Oval Selection tool, or set text and convert it to shapes and then to a selection in Painter (by choosing Convert Text to Shapes from the triangle pop-out menu on the Layers palette and then choosing Shapes, Convert to Selection), path information is automatically stored in the file. Then if you save the Painter file in Photoshop format, these kinds of outlines will appear in Photoshop's Paths palette. If you save a selection as a mask in the Channels palette you can build path information back into the file: Choose Select, Load Selection to create a selection based on the mask, then convert this mask-based selection to outline information using Select, Transform Selection. (Painter's Transform Selection command adds vector information to the selection border.)

Pseudocolor or Reverse-out), it converts that layer to Normal.

- To preserve the alpha channels (masks) in Painter's Channels palette and use them in Photoshop as channels, save a Painter file in Photoshop format. When you open the file in Photoshop, the named masks will automatically appear in the Channels palette.

PHOTOSHOP TO PAINTER

Here are some pointers for importing Photoshop files into Painter 8:

- If you prefer to begin your file in Photoshop, and the file contains layers, Painter can open Photoshop format files saved in RGB, CMYK and Grayscale modes.

- Although Painter 8 will open CMYK files in both Photoshop and TIFF formats, keeping files in RGB color mode when porting files from Photoshop to Painter will make the best color translation, because RGB is Painter's native color model.

- If you save your Photoshop image (version 4 or later) with layers in Photoshop format, Painter 8 will open it and translate the layers with their names intact. If you are using Photoshop 3, save the file in Photoshop 3 format.

- Photoshop type layers will be rasterized by Painter. However, shape layers, layer clipping paths and clipping groups will not translate.

- Photoshop layer masks translate consistently into Painter.

- A Photoshop document made up of transparent layers only—that is, without a Background layer—will open in Painter as layers over a white-filled background in the Canvas layer.

- Painter can recognize most of Photoshop's Blending modes when compositing the layers (some exceptions are Color Dodge, Color Burn, Vivid Light, Linear Light, Pin Light and Exclusion). Painter converts blending modes that it doesn't recognize to the Default Compositing method.

- Layer sets created in Photoshop will be recognized by Painter, and the layers within them will translate.

- A layer with a live layer style will disappear when the file is opened in Painter. You can try this work-around: Converting a "styled" layer to a series of rasterized layers (Layer, Layer Style, Create Layers) before attempting to open it in Painter. But this often doesn't work either, since the conversion often involves a clipping path group, and clipping groups don't translate to Painter.

- Photoshop Alpha Channel masks are recognized by Painter 8. The channels will appear in Painter's Channels palette.

- Photoshop layer masks will also convert to layer masks in Painter. (They will be listed in the Layers palette, as they are in Photoshop.) To view a layer mask in black and white, select the layer in the Layers palette, click the layer mask thumbnail and in the Channels palette, open its eye icon.

Compositing, Painting and Effects

Overview *Scan a drawing and a sheet of paper and composite the scans; add color and texture with brushes; add a colored lighting effect; open the image in Photoshop and convert it to CMYK.*

1a

The sheet of speckled Oatmeal paper

1b

The pencil-and-charcoal drawing on paper

2

Compositing the scans of the Oatmeal paper and the sketch

JOHN FRETZ COMBINED TRADITIONAL DRAWING materials and digital ones in Photoshop and Painter to build the composite illustration *AM Exercise* for an American Lung Association calendar.

1 Drawing and scanning. As a basis for his illustration, Fretz drew a black-and-white study using pencil and charcoal on a rough newsprint paper. Then he used a flatbed scanner to scan the drawing and a sheet of Oatmeal paper into Photoshop using RGB mode.

2 Compositing the scans. Fretz built the image in Photoshop because he was more familiar with Photoshop's compositing procedures. (His compositing process, which follows, can be accomplished almost identically in Painter.) Fretz copied the drawing and pasted it as a new layer on top of the Oatmeal paper background. To make the white background of the drawing transparent, he applied Multiply blending mode to the drawing layer using the triangle pop-up menu on the Layers palette.

For the soft, irregular edge on the background layer, Fretz first used the Lasso to draw a selection around the perimeter of the image. He reversed the selection by choosing Select, Inverse and feathered it 30 pixels (Select, Feather), then he filled the border area with 100% white. He saved the file in Photoshop format to preserve the layers for import into Painter.

3 Modifying brushes. At this point, Fretz opened the composite drawing in Painter, where he planned to add color and texture. Before beginning to paint, he made two custom Soft Charcoal brushes. The first, for adding soft values, used the Soft Cover subcategory; the second, for subtly darkening color, used the Grainy Soft Buildup subcategory and a low opacity. To make Fretz's

Building up color on the faces using the custom Soft Charcoal brushes

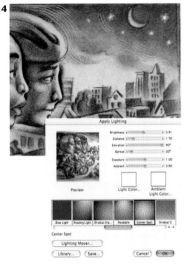

Creating a colored glow in the sky using Apply Lighting

Painting details on the foreground

"darkener," in the Brush Selector Bar, choose the Soft Charcoal variant of Charcoal. In the General section of the Stroke Designer (Brush Creator), change the method to Buildup and the subcategory to Grainy Soft Buildup. A lower opacity will give you more control when building up color, so in the Property Bar, change the Opacity to about 15%. Save your new variant by choosing Save Variant from the Brush Selector Bar's triangle menu. Name it and click OK.

Adding color and texture in Painter. Fretz chose Basic Paper texture in the Paper Selector. To enlarge the texture to complement the grain of the Oatmeal paper background, he used the Scale slider on the Papers palette (Window, Show Papers). He brushed color onto his drawing using two grain-sensitive brushes, the Large Chalk and Square Chalk variants of Chalk and used his custom Charcoals to deepen color saturation in some areas. Choose a Chalk brush and begin painting color onto your image background; switch to the custom Soft Charcoal variant using Grainy Soft Buildup to darken color. To change the brush size and the opacity while you work, use the Size and Opacity sliders in the Property Bar.

4 Emphasizing the sky with lighting. For a warm glow in the sky that faded across the people's faces, Fretz applied a colored lighting effect within a soft-edged selection. Begin by choosing the Lasso tool and making a loose freehand selection. Now give the selection a soft edge by applying a feather: Choose Select, Feather, type in a feather width, and click OK. Now apply the lighting effect to make the sky glow as Fretz did: Choose Effects, Surface Control, Apply Lighting. In the Lighting dialog box, choose the Center Spot light. To give the light a colored tint, click on the Light Color box to open the Select Light Color dialog box. Then choose a color by clicking on it in the Color picker. (If the circle is black, move the slider to the right.) Click OK. To move the spotlight to a new location in the Preview window, drag the large end of the light indicator. To save the custom light, click the Save button and name the light when prompted, then click OK to apply the light to your image, and deselect (Ctrl/⌘-D).

5 Painting final details. To make the layer and image canvas into one surface on which he could paint details, Fretz merged all the layers. (Click the right triangle on the Layers palette bar to open the menu and choose Drop All.) Then he chose the Scratchboard Rake variant of Pens, and modified it by reducing the number of bristles. To build a similar brush, open the Rake section of the Stroke Designer (Brush Creator). Reduce the number of Bristles to 5. Fretz added finishing strokes in various colors to several places in the foreground, the grass, and highlights on the cars. He also used a smaller brush and more subtle colors to add textured strokes to areas of the background.

Fretz saved a copy of the image as a TIFF file. He opened the file in Photoshop and converted it to CMYK for use in the calendar. 🖌

Collage Using Cloning and Layers

Overview *Scan photos into Photoshop and retouch; use Painter's brushes and textures to build a background image and add textured brushwork to source files; build the composite image in Photoshop; add blending and airbrushed highlights in Painter.*

ART DIRECTION AND IMAGES: BURKE / TRIOLO PRODUCTIONS / DESIGN: BOB MARRIOTT, MARRIOTT & ASSAY
CLIENT: ACAPULCO RESTAURANTS

1a

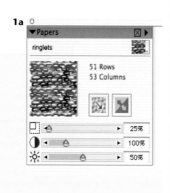

Burke's custom Ringlets texture was used for the background.

1b

The test file with tonal variations

WHEN JEFF BURKE AND LORRAINE TRIOLO—owners of Burke/Triolo Productions—were commissioned to create new menus for Acapulco Restaurants, they turned to Photoshop for image compositing and to Painter for a textured, painted look. The final composed menu pages are filled with unique, stylized graphics that reflect the texture and style of Old Mexico and suggest the qualities of handmade food and old-world service.

Burke began by exploring techniques in Painter, settling on a rough-edged, textural look with lively brushstrokes, which he presented to the client and the designer. After approval, he built the interior menu pages using several elements: a background paper texture image, textured food images and border graphics. The source files were all composed into a single image file in Photoshop and then opened again in Painter, where more texture and brushwork were added. Later, in QuarkXPress, the type and the dingbat illustrations were placed on top of the composed image as EPS files. The folded menu was composed of several panels, each built using the same process. The steps that follow use panel 3 as an example. Turn to page 309 in the gallery to see the front cover of this menu.

1 Building a textured background. The partners realized that a textured feel would contribute to the old-world atmosphere they wanted to achieve. To accomplish this, Burke created a new

The retouched food photograph

Using the Chalk Cloner variant of Cloners to paint a rough edge around the elements

Refining the texture around the edge of the plate and beverage

The food photograph with brushwork nearly complete

document in Painter that matched the page size of the menu, measuring 9 x 14.5 inches at 300 pixels per inch. He created a custom paper texture in Painter, called Ringlets. (To read about making a custom paper texture turn to "Applying Scanned Paper Textures" in Chapter 3, on page 104.) Then, using a warm-colored Oil Pastel variant of Oil Pastels, he brushed the texture over the surface of the page, using light pressure on the stylus. He saved this master texture image for use on each panel of the menu.

Burke converted the light, delicate paper texture to CMYK and created a test file with tonal variations. He sent the test file to his service bureau for a Fuji ColorArt film proof, and when the proof came back, the partners chose the darkest, yellowest variation.

2 Scanning and retouching the images. The team at Burke/ Triolo scanned the food images on a Scanview ScanMate 5000 drum scanner, then converted them to RGB. Burke used Photoshop's Rubber Stamp tool to lightly retouch scanning imperfections and to improve details, such as stray rice grains, sauce smears on the plates and dark areas in the food. To whiten most of the background, he made a loose selection completely outside of the elements and reversed it by choosing Select, Inverse. Then he pressed the Delete key.

3 Texturizing the source images. Burke opened each food image in Painter and created a clone by choosing File, Clone. He chose Big Grain Rough paper texture in the Paper Selector (loaded from the Painter 6 Textures library on the Painter 8 CD 2 CD-ROM). Using the Chalk Cloner variant of Cloners, with brush sizes varying between 20 and 100 pixels, he gently painted over the image in the clone file along the edges of the plates, the base of the glasses and the stone surface material, in varying densities. This produced a painterly quality in the images reminiscent of painting by hand. By constantly varying the size of the brush and by using a light touch on the stylus, he changed the amount of chalk texture applied. His goal was to add texture to the original without obscuring it completely. As specialists in food styling and photography, Burke and Triolo know that it's important to avoid obscuring the food products in an image.

To add subtly colored brushwork to the edges of the elements, Burke used an Oil Pastel variant (Oil Pastels). He sampled the color from the image (using the Alt/Option/⌘ key) and then painted diagonal strokes. He likes using the Oil Pastel when applying dark colors over a light background or light over dark, because the brush smears color slightly, making the strokes appear to bleed. He carefully applied the treatment consistently over the photo.

Wherever the image became too obscured with brushwork, Burke used the Soft Cloner variant of Cloners to gently bring back detail from the original, after designating the original retouched

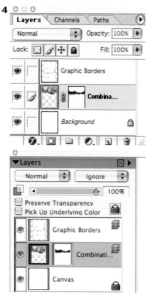

4

The named layers in the composite file, shown here in the Layers palette in Photoshop (above) and the Layers palette in Painter (below)

5

SOFT TACOS Y ENCHILADAS ESPECIALES

Burke painted with the Just Add Water variant to blend the border elements into the page.

6

COMBINACIONES

A detail of the final image with airbrush highlights added

photo as the Clone source by choosing File, Clone Source. After completing each individual food image, he saved it for later.

4 Compositing the menu elements. Because the layout also included border graphics created in Adobe Illustrator, these elements were rasterized (converted from CMYK PostScript elements to bitmapped RGB graphics) so they could be blended into the final page composition. To do this, the designer's QuarkXPress document was modified to remove all of the elements except certain borders (and some headline type, which was retained for position, but later removed). Burke saved the page individually as a separate EPS file from QuarkXPress.

Burke built each panel of the menu as a single image file in Photoshop. However, the elements could have been combined in Painter in almost exactly the same way. He opened the master paper-textured background and the treated food image in Photoshop and dragged and dropped the food image file on top of the background into the position specified in the designer's layout. To blend the images softly into the paper background, he added a layer mask to the food element layer.

Finally, Burke opened the QuarkXPress EPS file and dragged and dropped it into position. To create the illusion of plates and other objects overlapping the graphic elements, he added layer masks for the graphic elements where they appeared to go "behind" the food objects. He also removed the headline type at this point. Because he wanted to use Painter to add brushwork that would blend elements that were currently on separate layers, he merged the layers in the file. Then he saved the file as an RGB TIFF.

5 Adding final details in Painter. Burke opened the file in Painter and prepared to add texture and brushstrokes throughout the image. For editing flexibility he began by creating a clone of the image by choosing File, Clone. To enhance and blend the graphic borders into the image, he used the Oil Pastel 30 variant, and roughly filled in the hollow borders with a warm-white color. Then, to gently blur the colored border graphics into the background paper, he used the Just Add Water variant of Blenders. Again, if he overdid the effect, he switched to the Soft Cloner brush (with the original image designated as the Clone Source) and restored detail and clarity.

6 Airbrushing highlights. To complete the menu panel, Burke wanted to embellish the bright highlights on the plate, glass and food. For optimal flexibility, he added a new layer for the highlights by clicking the New Layer button on the Layers palette (making sure that Preserve Transparency was turned off in the Layers palette). Using the Digital Airbrush variant of Airbrushes and a bright, warm-white color, he softly painted strong, yet natural brushstrokes to "blow out" the highlights. 🖌

■ When partners **Jeff Burke** and **Lorraine Triolo** were commissioned to create the new *Acapulco Restaurants menu cover*, several people played important roles: Photography and imaging, Jeffrey Burke; food and prop styling, Lorraine Triolo; art direction, Jeff Burke and Bob Marriott; Design Firm, Marriott & Assay; and client, Acapulco Restaurants.

To begin the menu cover, Burke built a composite that included several images of food and live models, shot in the studio against a white cove background. To add to the atmosphere, he incorporated a sky image from a recent Caribbean vacation, as well as an outdoor fountain photographed with a point-and-shoot digital camera. He made masks for several of the images in Photoshop using the Lasso and Pen tools and dragged and dropped elements into a composite file. After several preliminary compositions and the client sign-off on a final arrangement, he flattened the file and saved it in TIFF format. (Burke could have brought the file into Painter with layers, but he wanted a flat document with all of the elements merged together so that he could use Painter's brushes to paint over the entire image, completely integrating the elements.)

Burke opened the file in Painter and used much the same process as described in "Collage Using Cloning and Layers" on page 306. He cloned the file and used the Big Grain Rough texture (loaded from the Painter 6 Textures library on the Painter 8 CD 2 CD-ROM) and a pressure-sensitive tablet and stylus. He smudged the edges of some of the elements and added colored brushwork to some areas using an Oil Pastel variant of Oil Pastels. By selectively blending areas in the image with the Just Add Water variant of Blenders, and leaving other edges in focus, Burke created a dynamic feeling of movement in the illustration. For instance, in the server's skirt and blouse, the leading and trailing edges are blurred with soft diagonal brushwork, but the sash and ruffle are sharper. To lead the eye to the food tray, Burke airbrushed a glow under the tray and along the sleeve of the blouse. Because the food was the focal point of the composition, Burke avoided adding brushwork here. To balance the design, he left the faces of the mariachis in clearer focus than most of the other elements. It was easy to restore the focus where it was needed by designating the original file as the clone source (File, Clone Source) and using the Soft Cloner.

Finally, Burke airbrushed highlight hints on the image on a separate layer (for editing flexibility), using the Digital Airbrush to "blow out" the highlights, while keeping the look natural.

■ Designer/illustrator **Marc Brown** was commissioned by Angie Lee, art director at Grindstone Graphics, to create *Museum Store* (above). He created *Iron Casters* (right) for Amanda Wilson, art director at The Evans Group Advertising. Brown employed similar techniques to create both illustrations. He started with a loose pencil drawing, then scanned the drawing and placed it into Adobe Illustrator as a template. In Illustrator he drew the elements on individual layers and filled them with flat color. To rasterize the image, he copied each Illustrator layer and pasted it into Photoshop as a layer. (This process can also be accomplished in Painter by drawing shapes and filling them with color, or by importing Illustrator art into Painter. See Chapters 4 and 5 for more information about using and importing shapes.) At this point, Brown opened the layered file in Painter. He used Airbrushes and Chalk variants to add colored details to the faces and clothing, blending color with Blenders variants. After he had completed the composite, he merged the layers by choosing Drop All from the menu on the right side of the Layers palette bar. To finish, he broke up some of the smooth edges by painting them with the Just Add Water variant of Blenders.

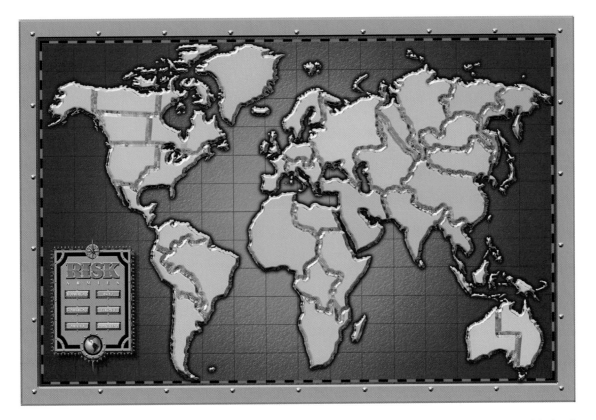

■ **John Dismukes** and **Jo-Anne Redwood,** principals of Capstone Studios, began the *Risk Game Board* for the Parker Bros./Hasbro Games Group, by creating many pencil sketches on paper. After settling on the look they wanted, they presented a tight visualization to the art director of the project, Steve Krupsky. After approval, the pencil sketch was scanned and used as a template in Macromedia FreeHand to create Post-Script outlines, which were saved in EPS format. Because he was more familiar with layers in Photoshop when he built the map, Dismukes imported the outlines into Photoshop, where he made layers for the water, each land region, the legend and the border. (Alternatively, the outlines could have been brought directly into Painter as shapes via File, Acquire, Adobe Illustrator File and converted to layers. For a step-by-step description of a

similar technique using Painter, turn to "Selections and Airbrush" on page 161.) To give each element a basic color, he turned on Preserve Transparency in the Layers palette and filled the areas with mid-tone colors. (He planned to add highlights and shadows in Painter with the Digital Airbrush later.) He saved the file in Photoshop format, so it could be opened in Painter with its layers and masks intact. Dismukes loves the responsiveness of Painter's Airbrushes and their performance with a pressure-sensitive tablet and stylus. When he opened the file in Painter, he turned on Preserve Transparency in the Layers palette and, using the Digital Airbrush variant of Airbrushes, he hand-painted the edge of each individual layer to create a "retro-style" bevel. For each bevel, he first sampled color from the region using the

Dropper tool, and then painted the bevels using light and dark variations of the color. As he worked, he changed the size and opacity of the Digital Airbrush, paying careful attention to detail and spending the time needed to hand-paint realistic highlights and shadows along the edges. He also used the Digital Airbrush to give the chrome studs in the map's border realistic dimension. For the luminous texture on the water, Dismukes selected a rough custom paper texture in the Papers Selector, then chose Effects, Focus, Glass Distortion, Using Paper, with Refraction. To strengthen the focal point of the composition, he applied a custom lighting effect to the water layer, by choosing Effects, Surface Control, Apply Lighting. (To see more work from Capstone Studios, turn to pages 300–301.)

■ Graphic designer and artist **Donal Jolley** created *Winter Morning* and *Independent Baptist Church*, two of twelve images for the *Turning Point 2002 Calendar*. To begin the calendar, Jolley worked with his client David Jeremiah to select reference photos. Beginning in Photoshop, Jolley opened the reference photos for *Winter Morning* (shot by Robert Hayes) and *Independent Baptist Church* (taken by Jolley). He removed unwanted elements from the foreground, trees and skies by cloning using the Rubber Stamp tool. To achieve the mood he wanted in each image, he intensified the yellows and oranges in *Winter Morning* and the background greens in *Independent Baptist Church* using Photoshop's Hue and Saturation controls. So that he would be able

to isolate areas of the images (for instance, the snow, sky and water in *Winter Morning* and the truck, wood buildings and sign in *Independent Baptist Church*), he made selections and saved them as alpha channels. Then he saved the image with its alpha channels in Photoshop format, so he could work on it in Painter. Jolley planned to use Painter's brushes for textured brushwork that would add painterly movement to the images and break up the smooth photographic look. Using several layers and paying careful attention to the volume of the forms, he painted with the Artist Pastel Chalk variant of Pastels and the Square Chalk variants of Chalk (with a rough paper texture chosen in the Paper

Selector). When he wanted to constrain paint to a particular area of a layer (such as the sky), he loaded a selection based on the alpha channel he had saved for that area by choosing Select, Load Selection and choosing it in the Load From menu. Then he painted within the area. When he wanted to sample color from the layers below, he enabled Pick Up Underlying Color in the Layers palette. To blend and pull color while adding texture in the sky, he used the Grainy Water variant of Blenders. To achieve a "salt" effect on the water reflections in *Winter Morning*, he used the Fairy Dust variant of the F-X brush. Then he added final colored details to the snow, church and water with a small Artist Pastel Chalk.

■ For *Independent Baptist Church,* **Donal Jolley** used Water Color brushes in addition to the Chalk, Pastel and Blenders variants. Jolley appreciates the flexibility of painting on layers. When he wants to make changes to an area, he often paints the changes on a new layer so he can control the strength of the effect using the Opacity slider in the Layers palette. After establishing the overall brushwork using the Square Chalk (Chalk) and Artist Pastel Chalk (Pastels) variants and then blending with the Grainy Water variant of Blenders, he painted transparent watercolor glazes onto the truck to create the look of shiny metal and glass. He also added light watercolor washes on top of

the pastel brushwork on the wood buildings and street, then painted subtle texture on the street and wood siding using a small Splatter Water variant of Water Color. When the brushwork on *Independent Baptist Church* was complete, Jolley added more texture as follows: First he saved a copy of each image using a different name and flattened the layers in the copies by choosing Drop All from the menu on the right side of the Layers palette bar. Next, he made two duplicates of each image by selecting all (Ctrl/⌘-A) and Alt/Option-clicking with the Layer Adjuster. On the top layer, he used Effects, Surface Control, Apply Surface Texture, Using Paper, also with subtle

settings, to add paper grain. On the next layer, he used Effects, Surface Control, Apply Surface Texture, Using Image Luminance, with subtle settings, to "emboss" the brushstrokes. Then he adjusted the Opacity of both layers to his liking, using the slider on the Layers palette. He saved a duplicate of each of the final layered files in TIFF format, flattening the images. Because Jolley was more familiar with color correction and conversion in Photoshop, he opened both final TIFF files in that program, made color adjustments and then converted the images to CMYK for printing in the calendar.

■ **Rhoda Grossman** was commissioned by *Emergency Medical Services* magazine to create this painterly collage illustration for an article titled "Create the Carnage and We Will Come," which discussed the tendency for rescue workers to plunge into dangerous situations without sufficient regard for their own safety. Grossman's image depicts an overenthusiastic rescue worker armed only with an oxygen tank and a hard hat (emblazoned with the "Star of Life" logo for emergency services). The menacing eye and smoking gun represent a variety of dangers that might be awaiting the rescue worker behind the door.

To begin the collage, Grossman opened source files for the menacing eye, the hand with gun, the oxygen tank, the hand with palm facing out, the helmet and various facial parts she could use to

assemble the head of the worker. She copied elements from the source files and pasted them into a composite file, where she arranged them using Painter's Layer Adjuster tool. When she had the elements where she wanted them, she chose File, Clone to quickly make a flattened copy. The Clone command dropped all layers in the clone, but the original was left with its layers intact. She saved the new flattened image under a unique name so that she would not overwrite the original layered file. Next, she used the Grainy Water variant of Blenders (over Basic Paper texture) to smear and blend the hard edges of the items into each other and into the background. She avoided smooth transitions, wanting her brushwork to show. She enhanced the smoke from the gun using the Distorto variant of Distortion. When she was happy with

this stage, she saved the image as a TIFF file, then opened it in Photoshop.

Working in Photoshop, she applied the Find Edges filter (Filter, Stylize, Find Edges), and then faded the effect to 35% (Edit, Fade). This reduced the saturation, lightened the image and enhanced the brushstrokes. She saved this stage of the file again using TIFF format and under a unique name.

Next, Grossman opened both the filtered image and the painted, flat image in Painter. She wanted to add more emphasis to the brushstrokes, so she created a new clone of the painted image (File, Clone), and with this clone active, she chose Effects, Surface Control, Apply Surface Texture, Using Image Luminance. Then she used the Soft Cloner variant of Cloners both to bring back the previous painted stage wherever the texture was too strong, and to add elements from the filtered image. She made each of the two files in turn the Clone Source by choosing File, Clone Source and choosing from the menu of file names. Finally, she saved the image as a TIFF file, then opened it in Photoshop again, where she converted it to CMYK for placement in the magazine's page layout.

The most recent works of artist **Pamela Wells,** which focus on feminine archetypes, are sold in commercial and fine-art markets. For *Magician,* Wells began by shooting photos to use as reference for her composition. She scanned the photos into Photoshop and made a collage in that program, then merged the layers and saved the file in TIFF format to use as a reference while working in Painter. Wells opened the flattened collage file in Painter and made a clone by choosing File, Clone. She wanted to use Tracing Paper so she could see her reference as she sketched, so she deleted the contents of the clone by choosing Select,

All and then pressing the Backspace/Delete key. To turn on Tracing Paper, she pressed Ctrl/⌘-T. Then she used a pressure-sensitive tablet and stylus to draw a detailed black-and-white line sketch with the 2B Pencil variant of the Pencils. Wells created solid lines that would completely enclose areas in the drawing because she wanted to use the Paint Bucket to fill the areas with flat color. She began the coloring process by applying color fills to the figure, clothing and other elements in her composition. Then, using the Soft Charcoal variant of Charcoal and a light pressure on the stylus, she carefully painted over the filled areas to model the forms.

Wells brushed subtly different colors over existing colors. To render the fabric, she painted the areas with a light cream color, then covered them with a darker gold and finished with deeper tones. To add texture to the trunks of the trees, she sampled color from the image using the Dropper tool, then adjusted the color in the Color picker to a darker value and then used a tiny Soft Charcoal variant to paint the bark texture. When the illustration was complete, Wells saved it as a TIFF file and opened the image in Photoshop, where she applied color and tonal adjustments.

■ For *Winter/Spring,* **Pamela Wells** was inspired to create a visual metaphor for the transitional time between seasons. She began the image by shooting photos of a model to use as reference for her composition. Later she would paint two characters from these photos, changing facial features so the characters looked different. Wells scanned the photos into Photoshop and made a rough collage in that program and used it as a reference while working in Painter, as described for *Magician* on page 315. She drew a tight line drawing using the 2B Pencil variant of Pencils and a dark neutral color.

Because she wanted to begin the coloring of the sketch by filling areas with flat color, she made sure to create solid lines to enclose the areas she wanted to fill. She could then apply color fills to the figures and clothing, for example, using the Paint Bucket from the Toolbox. To model the forms of the figures and their clothing, she carefully painted over the filled areas. Wells used the Soft Charcoal variant of Charcoal to apply layers of color using a light pressure on the stylus. To blend areas, she laid subtly different colors over existing ones. For instance, to render the skin, she brushed the areas

with a light tan color, then covered them with a darker orange and finally a peachy red. To add texture to the fabric and brighter colors to the flowers, she used more contrasting values and a tiny Soft Charcoal variant. When she had finished painting the illustration, Wells saved it as a TIFF file and opened it in Photoshop, where she applied a few minor color and brightness adjustments. To read about how Wells made a fine-art print of her image, turn to the beginning of Chapter 12, "Printing and Archival Concerns."

■ An innovative professional photographer, **Michael Campbell** specializes in digital photography and portraiture. When creating *Girl on the Beach*, Campbell began the work by shooting the model against a gray paper background. He also painted a sheet of rough paper with acrylic paints in pastel colors, then scanned both images into Adobe Photoshop. In the scanned photo file, he chose Select, All and placed the portrait on a layer by choosing Layer, New, Layer Via Cut. Then he used the program's Extract function to isolate the figure and drop out the background. After retouching the figure, Campbell adjusted its color and tones using Photoshop's Hue/Saturation and Levels features. Next, he copied and pasted the scan of the painted paper into the portrait file below the figure, then saved the composite image as a PSD file that he could import into Painter with the layers intact. In Painter, he used cloning and paint applied with various brushes to paint over the photograph, adding expressive brushwork and a canvas-like texture. He made a clone of the image (File, Clone), and roughed in a loose, ocean scene for the background using the Chalk Cloner variant of Cloners. He saved the image and then began to gradually build up basic forms of the figure and clothing using the Oil Brush Cloner. To gradually build up details in the focal areas of the image (for instance, the girl's face) he used a small Camel Oil Cloner, and he used a larger version of this brush to paint the looser brushwork on the clothing. Finally, he used Effects, Surface Control, Apply Surface Texture to add three-dimensional highlights and shadows to the brushwork and canvas texture. Turn to "Creating a Photo-Painting" on page 230 to see a similar step-by-step technique featuring Campbell's work.

MULTIMEDIA
AND FILM
WITH
PAINTER

Film artist Dewey Reid created this pre-production comprehensive for the Nike All Conditions Gear *TV commercial using scanned images and Painter's brushes, effects and Scripts; he worked back and forth between Painter and Adobe Premiere, using Premiere for timing and transitions.*

WHETHER YOU'RE AN ANIMATOR, film artist, designer, or 3D artist, Painter's multimedia capabilities offer you dozens of practical techniques. Multimedia artists appreciate the creative freedom offered by Painter's brushes, textures and effects. If you're producing an animation or making a movie, many of the techniques and effects shown in this book can be applied to frames in a Frame Stack, Painter's native animation format, or to an imported movie clip. Although it isn't a full-featured animation or film-compositing program, Painter is good for making comps so you can preview motion. And Painter gives 3D artists a wide variety of choices for creating natural, organic textures to be used for texture mapping. In addition, the ability to record painting scripts lets you make tutorials to show others how your painting was built and even lets you batch-process a series of images.

WORKING WITH SCRIPTS

Painter's versatile Script feature lets you record your work, then play the process back, either in Painter or as a QuickTime or AVI (video for Windows) movie. But if you use this feature a lot, you'll soon discover its limitations—for example, its inability to record some Painter operations can produce a different effect during playback.

There are two basic kinds of scripts—Painter's automatically recorded Current Script and scripts that are recorded by enabling the Record feature. Both kinds of scripts are visible in the Scripts palette when you install Painter: The white icon with a date represents the Current Script and the icons with pictures represent scripts that were manually recorded by artists while they worked, to demonstrate various

The Scripts palette with a current script chosen in its menu

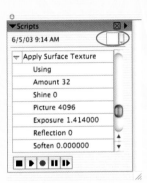

An open Current Script showing the instructions for an application of Apply Surface Texture. The white icon in the picker near the top right of the Scripts palette represents the Current Script.

You can use these buttons on the front of the Scripts palette to begin recording a single script (center red button) and to stop recording when you're finished (left square button).

Athos Boncompagni saved a series of scripts when creating La Luna e le Stelle, and played them back at higher resolution to build a larger image. For more information about using scripts in this way, see the tip "Increasing File Resolution With Scripts," on page 320.

kinds of images that can be created using Painter. If you record your own scripts they will also appear in the Scripts palette.

Understanding the Current Script. The Current Script starts when you launch Painter and closes when you quit the application. While you work, Painter transparently records your actions automatically, saving them as the Current Script in the Painter Script Data file in the Painter application folder. If you have launched and quit Painter several times during a 24-hour day, you'll notice several white icons in the Scripts menu list, with the dates and times for each work session listed in the pop-out resource list menu on the Scripts palette (for instance, "5/22/03 8:07 AM.")

Playing back a complete Current Script in which you created and saved more than one image can cause problems. For instance, if you opened a file, added brushstrokes and saved it, playing back the Current Script may result in Painter finding the first file, redrawing your strokes over the image and then resaving over the file. A more practical way to use an automatically recorded script is to open it and copy a specific series of commands from it (a lighting and texture effect, for instance) to paste into a new script, which can then be played back on other images.

Using a portion of a Current Script. To use a portion of a current script, copy specific commands from it and paste them into a new script, begin by opening the Scripts palette (Window, Show Scripts). Click the right triangle on the Scripts palette bar and from the menu select Open Script. In the dialog box that opens, choose Current Script from the Painter Script Data file list and click Open. The Current Script cannot be edited, but to use only a specific set of instructions from it, you *can* copy them to the clipboard and paste the instructions into a new script. Then you'll be able to use your new script to re-create just that series of actions. To do this, open the Current Script, Shift-select the instructions that you want to use (you may want to start at the bottom of the list, where the most recent instructions are found), choose Copy from the Scripts menu, choose Close Script and then choose New Script from the menu. Type a name for your new script in the Script Name dialog box, and click OK. Then choose Paste from the Scripts menu, and choose Close Script. To play your new script, choose Playback Script from the menu, then select the new script by name from the pop-out list in the Scripts palette and click the Playback button.

Recording a planned script. To record a series of deliberate actions into a script (instead of copying and pasting from the automatically recorded script), click the right triangle on the Scripts palette bar to open the menu and choose Record Script to begin recording, or click the Record button (the red dot) on the Scripts palette. When you've finished working on your image choose Stop Recording Script (or click the square Stop button). When you click OK, the dialog box will close and Painter will prompt you to name

To add lighting and a paper texture to this Mediacom video clip, we played a special effects script (using Effects, Surface Control, Apply Lighting and Apply Surface Texture) on each of the frames

your script. The new named script will appear in the pop-out list in the Scripts palette, available for later playback. To play the new script, select it from the list and click the Play (forward arrow) button.

Recording and saving a series of scripts. If you want to record the development of a complex painting (so you can use the script to demonstrate how you created the painting) but you don't want to finish the painting in one sitting, you can record a series of work scripts to be played back. First note the dimensions of your file by choosing Canvas, Resize, then click OK to close the dialog box. Click the right triangle on the Scripts palette bar, and choose Record Script. Include a number in the name of your script (such as "01") to help you remember the playback order. Then begin your painting. When you want to take a break, stop recording (Scripts palette bar, Stop Recording Script). When you're ready to continue, choose Record Script again and resume working on your image. Record and save as many scripts as you need, giving them the same basic name but numbering them so you can keep track of the order. To play them back, open a new file of the same dimensions as the original, then choose Playback Script from the menu on the Scripts palette bar. Choose the "01" script, and when it's done playing, choose the next script: It will play back on top of the image created by the first script. Continue playing back scripts in order until the image is completed. (You can also record a script so that it can be played back on a canvas of a different size; see the tip below.)

QUICKTIME CAN'T CONVERT

Scripts that contain Painter commands that QuickTime cannot convert can't be turned into QuickTime movies. It's not possible to use the Record Frames on Playback function with scripts that contain commands such as File, New, or File, Clone (an Illegal Command error message will appear).

INCREASING FILE RESOLUTION WITH SCRIPTS

You can use Painter's Scripts function to record your work at low resolution, then play it back at a higher resolution. This technique gives you a much crisper result than simply resizing the original image to a new resolution. Here's how to do it: Start by opening the Scripts palette (Window, Show Scripts). Click the right triangle on the Scripts palette bar to open the menu and choose Script Options. In the Script Options dialog box check the Record Initial State box, then click OK. Open a new file (File, New) and choose Select, All (Ctrl/⌘-A). From the Scripts palette menu, choose Record Script (or press the round red button on the Scripts palette) to begin recording. Then begin painting. When you're finished, from the menu on the Scripts palette bar, choose Stop Recording Script (or click the square black button on the Scripts palette). Open a new document two to four times as large as the original (this technique loses its effectiveness if your new file is much bigger than this). Again press Ctr/⌘-A to select the entire Canvas. Then choose Playback Script from the menu, or click the black triangle button (to the left of the red button) on the Scripts palette. Painter will replay the script in the larger image, automatically scaling brushes and papers to perfectly fit the new size. A word of caution—scripts can be quirky: Your higher-resolution image may not match the lower-resolution one if you use imported photos, complex selections, shapes or the Image Hose, for instance.

Choosing Script Options from the menu on the right side of the Scripts palette bar

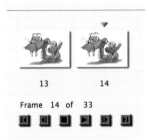

The Frame Stack palette for Donal Jolley's animation Rattlesnake *showing the movement in frames 13–14.*

FRAME STACK FILE SIZES

When you're turning a script into a frame stack by checking the Record Frames on Playback box (accessed by clicking the right triangle on the Scripts palette bar and choosing Script Options), a long script may result in a huge frame stack. There is currently no way to preview the number of frames that will be created when you enter an interval number in the dialog box, so you need to make sure you have plenty of hard disk space available.

118   119   120

Frame 120 of 120

To record the painting process of Mill Valley *(720 x 540 pixels, painted with Pastels and Blenders brushes), we made a movie using Save Frames on Playback and an interval of 10. The resulting movie was 110.6 MB with 120 frames.*

Automating a series of operations. Recording a series of actions can save you a lot of time when you need to apply the same effect to several images. Test a combination of operations (such as a series of choices from the Effects menu) until you get something you like. Choose Record Script from the menu on the Scripts palette bar (accessed by the right triangle), and repeat the series of choices that produces the effect you want. After you've stopped recording and have saved your script, you can apply the operations to a selection, a layer or a still image by selecting your script in the Scripts palette and clicking the forward arrow button on the front of the palette.

You can also apply your script to a Frame Stack. Turn to "Automating Movie Effects" later in this chapter for a detailed explanation of this technique.

Saving a script as a movie. This is a great option if you'd like to "play back" a painting for someone who does not have Painter. QuickTime movies can be played on Macintosh and PC/Windows computers with a freeware QuickTime projector such as Movie Player. First you'll record your work as a script, then you'll play it back on a new file, and then you'll save it as a QuickTime/AVI movie.

Begin by clicking the right triangle on the Scripts palette bar and choosing Script Options. In the Script Options dialog box, turn on Record Initial State (otherwise Painter will play back the first few commands or brushstrokes of your script using whatever colors, brushes and textures are active, instead of the ones you actually used during the recording of the script). Check Save Frames on Playback. You can leave the time interval Painter uses to grab frames from your script at 10, the default, but you may want to experiment with lower settings instead, to get a smoother playback result.

Next, open a new file of the dimensions you want for your eventual movie file. Click the right triangle on the Scripts palette bar, choose Record Script from the menu, and make your drawing. When you've finished, from the same menu, choose Stop Recording Script; name your script and click OK to save it. Now Painter will

SAVING FRAMES ON PLAYBACK

To save a script as a movie, check Save Frames on Playback in the Script Options dialog box (chosen by clicking the right triangle on the Scripts palette bar and choosing Script Options). Painter will grab a part of your script as a frame at the interval (tenths of a second) that you set. A lower setting in the interval box (such as 1 or 2) results in smoother playback than the default setting of 10, but file sizes for lower settings are larger because more frames are created. For instance, a short script with an interval setting of 1 resulted in a 4.2 MB Frame Stack; the same script recorded with an interval of 10 produced a 1.4 MB file.

Script Options

Every [1] 1/10ths of a second: ☑ Record Initial State
                                ☑ Save Frames on Playback

(Cancel) (OK)

A storyboard frame from the MGM movie Stargate. *Peter Mitchell Rubin used Painter to build digital storyboard illustrations for the movie, saving them as numbered PICT files and animating them with Adobe Premiere.*

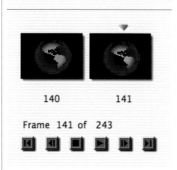

140   141

Frame 141 of 243

To change the continents from brown to green in this Cascom video clip, we recorded a script while performing the New From Color Range procedure and Color Overlay tinting process on one frame, then stopped recording and saved our script. After undoing the effects applied to the first frame, we chose Movie, Apply Script to Movie and took a break while Painter completed the masking and tinting process on all 243 frames. Above: The Frame Stack palette shows frame 140 with the operations applied, and frame 141 as yet untouched.

convert the script to a movie. First, watch your recorded script played back as a Painter Frame Stack by opening a new file (same dimensions) and choosing Playback Script from the menu, choosing your script from the list and clicking the Playback button. Painter will prompt you to enter a name for your new movie file. Name it, click Save and then specify the number of layers of Onion Skin and color depth by clicking on the appropriate buttons. (For most uses, select 2 layers of Onion Skin and 24-bit color with 8-bit alpha.) Click OK, and your script will unfold as a Frame Stack. When it's finished playing, save it in QuickTime/AVI movie format by choosing Save As, Save Movie as QuickTime. The Quick-Time/AVI file will be smaller than a Frame Stack (if you use a Compressor choice in the Compression Settings dialog box) and will play back more smoothly. (Because most compression degrades quality, compress only once—when you've completed the project. Film artist Dewey Reid suggests using Animation or None as the Compressor setting.) To read more about preserving image quality when working with movies, turn to "Importing and Exporting," on page 324.

Making movies using multiple scripts. You can save a series of successive scripts, then play back the scripts as frame stacks and save them as QuickTime movies without compression to preserve quality. Then you can open the movies in a program such as Adobe Premiere or Adobe After Effects and composite the movies into a single movie.

ANIMATING WITH FRAME STACKS

If you open a QuickTime or AVI movie in Painter, it will be converted to a Frame Stack, Painter's native movie format. Frame Stacks are based on the way conventional animators work: Each frame is analogous to an individual transparent acetate cel. You can navigate to any frame within a stack and paint on it or apply effects to it with any of Painter's tools (see "Animating an Illustration" on page 327).

Artists accustomed to specialized animation and video programs such as Adobe After Effects and Adobe Premiere will notice the limitations of the Frame Stack feature (there are no precise timing or compositing controls, for instance). If you use one of

A frame from an animation based on a video clip. We began by using Painter's Water Color brushes to illustrate the frames, which created a Water Color layer. Because a Water Color layer sits on top of the entire Frame Stack, we copied the layer to the clipboard, then dropped it to the Canvas when we had finished painting the frame. We advanced to the next frame and pasted in the copied watercolor and added new brushstrokes, repeating this copying, dropping, pasting and painting process until the frames were complete. As a final touch, we applied an effects script (with Apply Surface Texture Using Paper) to complete the piece.

these programs, you will probably want to work out timing and compositing in the specialized program, then import your document into Painter to give it an effects treatment.

When you open a QuickTime or AVI video clip in Painter or start a brand-new movie, you'll specify the number of frames and color bit depth to be used in the Frame Stack. You will be asked to name and save your movie. At this point the stack is saved to your hard disk. A Frame Stack will usually take up many more megabytes on your hard disk than it did as a movie (depending on the kind of movie compression used), so have plenty of space available. Each time you advance a frame in the stack, Painter automatically saves any changes you have made to the movie. When you choose Save As, Painter will ask you to name the movie again. This is not a redundant Save command, but an opportunity to convert the file to another format: Save Current Frame as Image, Save Movie as QuickTime or AVI format, or Save Movie as Numbered Files (to create a sequence of frames to edit in another program such as Adobe Premiere).

USING A VIDEO CLIP REFERENCE

Painter's cloning function allows you to link two movies—a video clip and a blank movie of the same pixel dimensions—and use the video as a reference on which to base an animation. Open a video clip that you want to use as a reference (File, Open), then make a blank movie (File, New Movie) of the same pixel dimensions as your video clip. (The second movie doesn't need to have the same number of frames). Under File, Clone Source, select the video clip. In the blank movie frame, turn on Tracing Paper (Ctrl/⌘-T). Using the clone source as a guide, choose a brush and paint on the frame. To use the Frame Stacks palette to advance one frame in the original, click the appropriate icon (circled in the palette shown below), or press Page Up on your keyboard. Do the same to advance the clone one frame. Use Movie, Go to Frame to move to a specific frame in either clone or original. You can also apply special effects such as Effects, Surface Control, Apply Surface Texture and Color Overlay, or Effects, Focus, Glass Distortion (all using Original Luminance), to your new movie using the clone source.

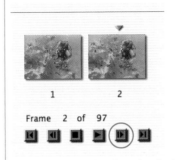

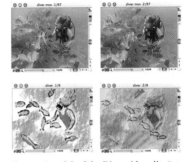

We opened a video clip (shown here in the Frame Stack palette) and a new Frame Stack, both using two layers of Onion Skin to show the position of the diver in both frames. Click on the circled button to advance one frame in the Frame Stacks palette.

Frames 1 and 2 of the Diver video clip (top row), and corresponding frames in the animation (bottom row), painted with the Sharp Chalk variant of Chalk. Tracing paper is active on the bottom right image.

Artist Dewey Reid advises using Effects, Surface Control, Apply Lighting to add cohesiveness and to smooth out transitions in a movie. For instance, using Apply Lighting with the same setting on all frames will smooth color transitions between clips and make elements from different sources blend together more successfully.

Reid used Apply Lighting and Apply Surface Texture (using Paper Grain) on the animated character Yuri the Yak for Sesame Street (produced by Children's Television Workshop).

When you record a drawing as a script, all of your actions are captured. Keep this in mind if you plan to play back your script as a movie. Plan to storyboard your movies so that you'll be able to execute the operations as smoothly as possible. If, in spite of your best efforts, you need to edit your movie, here's how to do it: After you Record Frames on Playback, look at the frame stack carefully and make changes to individual frames you want to edit. If you want to remove frames choose Movie, Delete Frames. Or you can save the Frame Stack as a Quick-Time/AVI movie and edit it in iMovie or Adobe Premiere.

Creating animated comps. Painter provides a good way to visualize a rough animation. An animatic (a comp of an animation, consisting of keyframe illustrations with movement applied) can be comprised of images drawn in Painter, scanned elements, or numbered PICT files created in Painter, Photoshop or even object-oriented programs that can export PICT files (such as Illustrator). (See "Making an Animated Comp" on page 330, featuring Dewey Reid's illustrations in a demonstration of an animatic technique.) You can also alter individual frames in a movie with Painter's effects or brushes. For a demonstration of frame-by-frame painting, see "Animating an Illustration" on page 327.

Rotoscoping movies. There are numerous ways to rotoscope (paint or apply special effects to movie frames) in Painter. Many of the techniques in this book can be used for rotoscoping—brushwork, masking, tonal adjustment or filters or Effects, Surface Control, Apply Lighting and Apply Surface Texture, or Effects, Focus, Glass Distortion, for example.

Basing an animation on a movie. You can use Painter's Tracing Paper to trace images from a source movie to a clone to create an animation. This feature lets you shoot video and use it as a reference on which to base a path of motion. This process is described in the tip "Using a Video Clip Reference" on page 323.

IMPORTING AND EXPORTING

With a little planning and understanding of file formats, still and animated files can easily be imported into Painter and exported out of Painter to other programs.

Preserving image quality. Because compression can degrade the quality of image files, when you obtain source files to bring into Painter, choose uncompressed animation and video clips. And because quality deteriorates each time you compress (the degree of degradation depends on the compression choice), save your working files without compression until your project is complete. If you plan to composite Painter movies in another application, such as Adobe Premiere, After Effects or Final Cut, save them without compression. For an in-depth explanation of compressors for QuickTime or for AVI, see the *Painter 8 User Guide*.

Importing multimedia files into Painter. Painter can accept QuickTime and AVI movies from any source, as well as still image PICT files and numbered PICT files exported from PostScript drawing programs, Photoshop and Premiere. To number your PICT files so that they're read in the correct order by Painter, you must use the same number of digits for all the files, and you must number them sequentially, such as "File 000," "File 001," "File 002" and so on. With all files in a single folder, choose File, Open and check the Open Numbered Files option. Select the first num-

Jon Lee of Fox Television used Painter's brushes and effects to progressively modify the logo for the comedy Martin, *creating numbered PICT files for an animated sequence. The modified files were animated on a Quantel HAL.*

bered file in your sequence and, when prompted, select the last file. Painter will assemble the files into a Frame Stack.

You can create a mask in a Painter movie and use it in your Frame Stack, or export it within a QuickTime movie to another program such as Premiere or After Effects. To make a movie with a mask, choose File, New, click the Movie button and enter the number of frames desired and click OK. In the New Frame Stack dialog box, choose one of the options with a mask: for instance, 24-bit color with 8-bit Alpha. (You can also make a Frame Stack from a sequence of numbered PICT files in which each file includes its own mask.) To export the movie from Painter as a QuickTime movie and include the mask, choose Save As and select the QuickTime movie option. When the Compression Settings dialog box appears, in the Compressor section, choose Animation or None from the top pop-up menu to make the mask option available, then choose Millions of Colors+ in the lower pop-up menu. Click OK.

Exporting Painter images to multimedia applications.

Since multimedia work is created to be viewed on monitors and the standard monitor resolution is 72 ppi, set up your Frame Stacks and still image files using that resolution. Most files used in multimedia have a 4 x 3 aspect ratio: 160 x 120, 240 x 180, 320 x 240 or 640 x 480 pixels. Television also has a 4 x 3 aspect ratio, but for digital television the pixels are slightly taller than they are wide. Artists and designers who create animation for broadcast usually prepare their files at "D-1 size," 720 x 486 pixels. Digital television uses a ".9" pixel (90 percent the width of standard square pixels). The narrower pixel causes circles and other objects to be stretched vertically. To create a file for D-1 maintaining the height-to-width ratio (to preserve circles), begin with a 720 x 540-pixel image. When the image is complete, scale it non-proportionally to 720 x 486. This will "crush" the image slightly as it appears on your computer screen, but when it's transferred to digital television it will be in the correct proportions.

QuickTime movie files can be exported from Painter and opened in multimedia programs such as Premiere, After Effects and Macromedia Director. If you're using one of these programs to create an 8-bit color production, you'll save processing time if you start with an 8-bit Frame Stack in Painter: Choose the 8-bit Color System Palette option in the New Frame Stack dialog box (after choosing File, New and naming your movie). If you don't set up your file as 8-bit in Painter, you should consider using Photoshop or Equilibrium Debabelizer—both offer excellent color-conversion control.

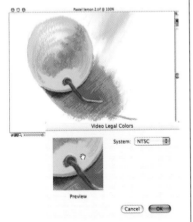

Highly saturated colors can smear when output to video. Choose Effects, Tonal Control, Video Legal Colors to make the colors in your file compatible with NTSC or PAL video color. In the Preview, press and release the grabber to toggle between the RGB and Video Legal Colors previews; click OK to convert the colors in your file.

We used a modified photo to create this repeating pattern. To generate seamless, tiled textures for 3D, use any of the commands in the menu of the Patterns palette. Turn to "Exploring Patterns" on page 253 in the beginning of Chapter 7 and to "Creating a Seamless Pattern" on page 260, for more about working with patterns.

Some experienced artists prefer to export their Painter images as PICT files rather than as movies because they can easily remove frames from the sequence if they choose. To export Painter still images to applications such as Premiere and After Effects, or to other platforms, save them as single PICT images or as a series of numbered PICT files. You can include a single mask in a Painter PICT file that can be used in compositing in Premiere or After Effects. See "Animating a Logo," on page 332, for a demonstration of exporting Painter images to another platform.

You can also import Painter-created QuickTime movies and still PICT images into Macromedia Director. A QuickTime movie comes in as a single linked Cast Member in the Cast Window, which means it will be stored outside the Director file, keeping file size manageable.

CREATING TEXTURE MAPS FOR 3D RENDERING

A *texture map*—a flat image applied to the surface of a 3D object—can greatly enhance the realism of rendering in 3D programs such as Bryce, Maya, LightWave 3D, 3ds Max and Strata Studio Pro. Many kinds of images can be used for mapping—scanned photographs, logo artwork or painted textures, for example. 3D artists especially like Painter's ability to imitate colorful, natural textures (such as painted wood grain or foliage). There are several kinds of texture maps: A *color texture map* is an image that's used to apply color to a 3D rendering of an object. Other types of mapping affect other qualities of the surface; for instance, a *bump map* (a two-dimensional representation of an uneven surface), a *transparency map* (used to define areas of an image that are transparent, such as glass panes in a window) and a *reflectance map* (used to define matte and shiny areas on an object's surface). If you're developing more than one of these texture maps to the same 3D object, you can keep them in register by using Save As or making clones of the same "master" Painter image to keep file dimensions the same. Remember to save your surface maps in PICT or TIFF format so the 3D program will be able to recognize them.

These floating globes were rendered by John Odam in Strata Studio Pro. He created a texture map in Painter using the Wriggle texture from the More Wild Textures library (in the Paper Textures folder on the Painter CD 2 CD-ROM) and applied the texture to the objects as follows: color map (A), bump map (B), reflectance map (C) and transparency map (D). The Studio Pro document size was 416 x 416 pixels; the texture map size was 256 x 256 pixels.

Animating an Illustration

Overview *Create an illustration; open a new movie document; paste the drawing into the movie and on to each frame as a layer; copy an area you want to animate; position it and drop it as a layer into a precise position; advance to a new frame and repeat the pasting, moving and copying process; use brushes to paint on individual frames.*

DONAL JOLLEY

Jolley's finished Painter illustration

Making a selection of the tail and rattle

The Layers palette showing the Tail layer selected

CREATING AN ANIMATION—whether you use Painter or draw on traditional acetate cels—is labor-intensive because of the sheer number of frames required to get smooth motion. But working digitally does have advantages. You can save a lot of time by copying and pasting a single illustration onto multiple frames. Corrections to digital art are easier to make than with conventional methods; and, thanks to the Frame Stacks player, you can see results immediately.

To begin *Rattle Envy*, Donal Jolley painted and animated a comical snake with Painter's brushes. Once the basic animation was complete, Jolley composited some extra layers at a reduced opacity to add the feeling of movement, further enhancing the effect with painted speed blurs.

1 Planning the animation and illustrating. Create an illustration in Painter, choosing a file size no more than a few inches square at 72 ppi (Jolley's illustration was 3 x 3 inches at 72 ppi.) Use Painter's brushes to paint just the essential image; you'll be adding the details to each individual frame later. To keep the animation process simple, choose a subject that you won't need to redraw in every frame, such as a character winking an eye. Jolley sketched a whimsical rattlesnake, and then copied the tail area, eyebrows and tongue elements to separate layers so that he could transform them later to create motion in the animation.

After sketching the snake using the Scratchboard Tool variant of Pens, Jolley added color and modeled forms using the Digital Airbrush variant of Airbrushes and the Square Chalk variant of Chalk. Then he added more linework and shadows using the Colored Pencil variant of Colored Pencils and blended color with the Grainy Water variant of Blenders.

He carefully selected each of the areas he planned to animate—three elements in the illustration—the tail area, the eyebrows, and the tongue—and pasted copies of them on separate layers as described below. In addition, he created a layer with a copy of only the stationery parts of the snake's body without the tail, eyebrows and tongue, so when he rocked the tail back and forth or moved the parts, the area underneath it would be white.

When you've finished your illustration, make a selection around an area that you want to animate (Jolley used the Lasso tool), press Alt/Option and choose Select, Float to place a copy of

2

New

Canvas Size: 183K

Width: 3.0 inches

Height: 3.0 inches

Resolution: 72.0 pixels per inch

Paper Color...

Picture Type:

○ Image
● Movie with 33 frames

Cancel OK

Beginning a new Frame Stack, 3 x 3 inches, 72 ppi, with 33 frames

3 snake test:1/33

Pasting the base illustration into the movie

4a

Frame 1 of 33

Clicking the Rewind button to return to frame 1

4b

Frame 3 with Tracing Paper/Onion Skin (three layers) turned on

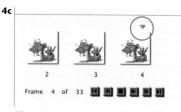

4c

2 3 4

Frame 4 of 33

The red marker shows that Frame 4 is active.

it on a new layer. Repeat for any other parts that you want to animate. Also prepare a layer that includes everything that will *not* be animated. Now, click on the non-animated layer's name in the Layers section and choose Select, All, and copy it to the clipboard (Ctrl/⌘-Shift-C). It's now ready to be pasted into a movie. Leave the original illustration file open so you can copy elements from it into your movie.

2 Starting a new Frame Stack. To open a new movie file, choose File, New. Choose a small size so Painter will play the movie quickly; then click the Movie Picture Type, and enter enough frames to give you a smooth animation. Jolley created a 3 x 3-inch movie at 72 ppi (that matched the dimensions and resolution of his illustration), with 33 frames to start, though he added more frames as he needed them using Movie, Add Frames, so that his finished animation was 38 frames. Click OK; name and save your movie, and in the New Frame Stack dialog box, choose Jolley's options: three layers of Onion Skin (so you can see three frames back into the stack) and full 24-bit color with an 8-bit mask.

> **MOVIE AUTO-SAVE**
>
> Painter saves your movie every time you advance a frame.

3 Pasting the illustration into the frame stack. Paste the non-animated part of your illustration from the clipboard into the movie file—it will come in as a layer—then use the Layer Adjuster tool to move it into position. Copy it in its new position, then drop it to the Canvas by choosing Drop from the triangle menu on the right side of the Layers palette. Because a layer sits on top of the entire frame stack, make sure that you've dropped it before you begin the next step. To advance the frame stack one frame, click the Step Forward icon on the Frame Stack palette (or press the

> **COPYING AND POWER-PASTING**
>
> You can greatly improve precision and productivity by copying an item then *power-pasting* it: To copy an item from a frame press Ctrl/⌘-C, then advance to the next frame and press Ctrl/⌘-Shift-V to paste it into the exact same position. You can also use this method to copy and paste between two single images that are exactly the same size.

Page Up key on your keyboard). Paste the copied base illustration into a new frame in the same position (press Ctrl/⌘-Shift-V) and drop, repeating the paste and drop sequence for each frame of the movie.

4 Creating movement by offsetting layers. Then, to return to the first frame in the stack, click the Rewind button. Back in your original illustration file, choose the Layer Adjuster tool and select the layer for a part that you want to animate by clicking on its layer name in the Layers palette, and choose Ctrl/⌘-C to copy

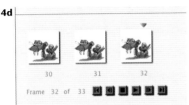

The frame stack palette, showing movement in frames 30–32

Frame 29 shows a copy of the tail layer pasted in, rotated and at 58% opacity

6a

Frame 32 showing the Gritty Charcoal smudges and a low-opacity layer

6b

Frame 30 showing a speed blur painted with the Grainy Water variant

it. Now activate your frame stack file and choose Ctrl/⌘-Shift-V to paste it into exact position.

So that he would have an unmanipulated copy that he could use later, Jolley made a copy of the pasted tail area layer by Alt/Option-clicking on it with the Layer Adjuster tool. Then he hid the copy by shutting the eye icon to the left of its name in the Layers palette.

With the original tail section layer selected, he chose Effects, Orientation, Free Transform and used the feature to rotate the tail. When you choose Free Transform, an eight-handled bounding box will appear. Now choose the Layer Adjuster tool, press the Ctrl/⌘ key and position the tool over a corner handle. Drag to rotate the layer to a position that you like. So you can bring the layer in its new position into the next frame, store a copy of the layer in the clipboard by pressing Ctrl/⌘-C. Then choose Drop from the triangle menu on the right side of the Layers palette to drop the layer onto the current frame, and go to the next frame by pressing Page Up on your keyboard. Paste the copied illustration again, and use the Layer Adjuster tool to reposition the element in the frame; then drop it.

As you work, look at the Frame Stacks palette to check your progress. You can view previous frames "ghosted" in your main image—much like an animator's light box—by choosing Canvas, Tracing Paper (Ctrl/⌘-T). The number of previous frames displayed is determined by the number of Onion Skin layers you chose when you opened the movie. To change the number of layers, close the file, reopen it, and choose a new number of layers. Use Ctrl/⌘-T to turn the Onion Skin view on and off as you work. Click the Play button to play the animation, and take note of the areas that need to be smoother.

5 Making the animation smoother. After playing the animation, Jolley wanted to make the transition between some of the frames smoother and slower. So he used the tail area layer copy that he had hidden in the Layers palette (in Step 4) as a basis to add several more low-opacity layers to a few of the frames. Then he replayed the animation again to check its smoothness. To blur a few of the edges, he used the Just Add Water variant of Blenders on some of the frames.

6 Adding more motion with brushstrokes. Now that he liked the way the animation played, Jolley added to the feeling of motion by painting more noticeable brushstrokes on the tail area. Using the Gritty Charcoal variant of Charcoal, he painted darker smudges on the tail—altering it slightly in each frame. He also added speed blurs by smearing the edges of the snake's tail and the rattle using the Grainy Water variant of Blenders. When the frame stack was completed, Jolley saved it as a QuickTime movie. (Turn to "Importing and Exporting" on page 324.)

Making an Animated Comp

Overview *Set up a layered illustration file; record the movement of a layer using scripts; play the script back into a movie.*

DEWEY REID

Reid's original street scene illustration

The topmost layer (with the Canvas hidden) showing the dropped-out area that will reveal the background scene underneath

The Dino character showing the painted mask (left), and with the background dropped out

TO VISUALIZE MOTION in the early stages of creating an animation, Dewey Reid often makes an animated comp (a conceptual illustration with a moving element). Adding motion is a great way to help a client visualize a concept, and it's more exciting than viewing a series of still images. Reid's storyboard, above, shows frames from a movie created by recording a script of a moving layer.

Using scripts and the Record Frames on Playback feature, you can record a layer's movement. When you play the script back, Painter will generate a Frame Stack with the appropriate number of frames, saving you the tedious work of pasting in and moving the character in each frame. After you've made your Frame Stack, convert it into a QuickTime movie (or AVI/VFW on the PC) for easier and faster playback using a freeware utility like Movie Player.

1 Beginning with an illustration. Begin with an image at the size you want your final movie to be. Reid started with a 300 x 173-pixel street scene illustration from his archives.

2 Setting up a layered file. Like conventional animation where characters are drawn on layers of acetate, this animation technique works best when all elements in the image are on separate layers. You may want to create masks for the various elements in separate documents, then copy and paste them into your main image. (For more about layers and masking, turn to Chapter 5.)

Reid envisioned three "layers" for this comp: a background image (the street scene) in the bottom layer, a copy of the street scene with a portion of the scene removed in the top layer, and a dinosaur positioned between the two street scenes that would move from left to right across the "opening" in the top layer. Reid made a duplicate layer from the Canvas by selecting all and Alt/Option-clicking on the image with the Layer Adjuster tool. To make it easier to see the top layer as you work, hide the Canvas layer by clicking its eye icon shut in the Layers palette. Select the top layer. To erase an area of the layer, choose a Pointed Eraser variant of the Erasers for most of the editing; for removing small

2c

The Dino layer, selected in the Layers palette and in starting position, ready to be moved by the arrow keys

3

Setting up the Script Options to Save Frames on Playback

4

Selecting the Dino script in the Scripts palette

5

Save Movie

Save options: ○ Save current frame as image
         ● Save movie as QuickTime
         ○ Save movie as numbered files
         ○ Save movie as GIF animation

Cancel   OK

Choosing the QuickTime button in the Save Movie dialog box

areas, you may want to try the 1-Pixel Eraser variant. To see the background layer again, click open the eye icon for the Canvas in the Layers palette. You'll see a complete background image, since the lower layer shows through the hole in the top layer.

In a separate file, Reid painted a mask to isolate Dino the dinosaur from the background and turned the mask into a selection by choosing Select, Load Selection. He copied Dino to the clipboard and pasted him into the street scene RIFF file. (An easy way to add a character is to drag an item from the Image Portfolio palette into your image—like the strawberry, the pumpkin or the lollipop, for example.) In the Layers palette, Reid dragged Dino down to a position between the two street scene layers. Using the Layer Adjuster and the arrow keys, Reid positioned the dinosaur so that only the red nose was visible behind the left front building, establishing Dino's starting position in the animation.

3 Recording the script. Click the right triangle on the Scripts palette to open the menu and choose Script Options; check Record Initial State, check Save Frames on Playback and enter a number for Every ¹⁄₁₀ths of a second (Reid chose 5), and click OK. Select the layer that will be moving by clicking on its name in the Layers palette (for Reid, the Dino Layer). Choose Record Script from the menu on the Scripts palette bar (or click the round red button on the front of the Scripts palette). Then hold down an arrow key to move the layer smoothly in the RIFF file. When you have completed the path of motion, choose Stop Recording Script from the Scripts palette menu (or click the Square button) and name the script. Return the character to its starting position by pressing Ctrl/⌘-Z.

4 Playing back the script into the movie. Click the right triangle on the Scripts palette bar to open the menu, choose Playback Script, choose your script from the list in the Apply Script to Movie dialog box and click Playback. When prompted, name your movie a different name than the RIFF file. Click the Save button and Painter will convert your RIFF image to a movie (leaving the original RIFF intact) and will add the movie frames needed. As the movie is generated, you will see the frames accumulating in the Frame Stack palette. When Painter finishes generating the Frame Stack, turn off visibility for the layers that are above the Canvas by clicking their eye icons in the Layers palette. (If you don't hide the layers, you won't be able to see your movie, which is recorded on the Canvas.) Finally, press the Play button on the Frame Stacks palette to play your movie!

5 Converting the Frame Stack to QuickTime or AVI. To play the movie without having Painter loaded, convert the Frame Stack to QuickTime or AVI format: Choose File, Save As, and when the dialog box appears, choose Save Movie as QT/AVI. Give your movie a new name (such as "Dino movie.qtime"), click Save and in the Compression Settings dialog box, choose from the top pop-up menu (Reid recommends Animation or None).

Animating a Logo

Overview *Make a clone of existing artwork and modify it with Painter's brushes and effects; save it, make another clone, and alter the new clone; continue to progressively make and alter clones, restoring the image when needed by pasting a copy of the original logo from the clipboard.*

ON LEE / FOX TELEVISION

1

Starting with the existing Martin logo

2a

Lee began manipulating the logo by selecting and scaling a portion of the cloned image (left). Then he selected and inverted a portion of the next clone in the sequence (right).

"IMPROVISATIONAL, FRESH, SPONTANEOUS, and very flexible!" says Jon Lee, Director of Art and Design for Fox Television, when describing his artistic experience with Painter. For the Fox TV program *Martin,* Lee built an animated title sequence like a painting, saving frames at different stages of development. He created a wild, hand-done, organic look to express the comedic street sensibility of the TV show.

Lee created a series of 35 keyframes in Painter (keyframes are the frames that establish essential positions in an animated sequence), eight of which are shown above. When he finished, he moved them from his Macintosh to a lightning-fast Quantel HAL system, where he added dissolves to blend one frame into the next. (Dissolves can also be achieved on the Macintosh desktop in Adobe After Effects or Adobe Premiere.)

1 Beginning with existing art. Lee began by opening the existing Martin logo in Painter. He copied and pasted it into a new file measuring 720 x 486 pixels (the aspect ratio of the Quantel HAL) with a black background, then merged the layers by clicking the right triangle on the Layers palette bar, and choosing Drop from the menu.

2b

Adding colored boxes to Frame 05 with the Rectangular Selection tool and the Fill command

2c

Using a variety of Liquid brushes to pull paint onto the background in Frame 07

2d

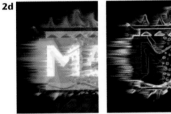

A motion blur effect applied in 14 (left), and then cloned and filtered in Frame 15

3a

Adding hand lettering and colored brush strokes to a clone of Frame 15 in Frame 16

3b

Restoring readability with a layer in Frame 17

Choose an image that you want to manipulate in your animated sequence and open it in Painter. Save your file in PICT format, naming it "01." In order for a numbered sequence of files to automatically play in numerical order, the files must be named using the same number of digits, such as 01, 02. . . 10, 11 and so on.

2 Manipulating progressive clones. After planning how many keyframes you'll need and how the artwork will progress through the frames, begin your manipulation. Clone the first document (File, Clone) and use Painter's tools and special effects on your clone. If you don't like the result of a brushstroke or applied effect, undo it and try something else. When you're satisfied with the result, save the file, name it "02," and make another clone from it. The new clone will become the next canvas for your experimentation. Working quickly and intuitively, Lee treated the logo with a wide variety of brushes, filters and effects from the Effects, Surface Control menu, saving progressive versions in a numbered sequence.

3 Restoring the logo. After a few progressively altered clones, your image may become unrecognizable. To restore the original to some degree, go to your original file, select all and copy, then paste it into your current clone. Adjust the Opacity using the slider in the Layers palette and Drop the layer by choosing Drop from the triangle menu on the right side of the Layers palette bar. Lee used this technique to periodically restore the readability of the type, working the original logo back into the progressive image.

Outputting the Painter files. When Lee was finished with the series of PICT frames, he used Electric Image Projector (a subprogram within Electric Image) to automatically shuttle the files over to the Quantel HAL platform for compositing and output to Beta videotape for broadcast. The workstation is set up with the Quantel HAL and Mac systems side-by-side; they're connected with an Intelligent Resources card that helps convert the digital imagery from one platform to another. Part of the translation process involved converting RGB color to the NTSC video color system for television.

On the HAL, Lee "stretched" the 35 original frames to 90 frames; the HAL added the appropriate number of frames to achieve the dissolves between each pair of keyframes, keeping the animation even and smooth. To create a 10-second title sequence at 30 frames per second, Lee needed 300 frames total. He made a loop of the 90-frame sequence and let it cycle until it filled the necessary frame count. ◆

Automating Movie Effects

Overview *Open a video clip; test a series of effects on a single frame; undo the effects; repeat the effects while recording a script; apply the script to the entire clip.*

1

Frame 1 of the original video clip

2

The Apply Surface Texture and Apply Lighting settings chosen for the movie

3

Choosing Movie, Set Grain Position to create a "live" texture on the movie

4a

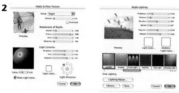

The Stop button (left) and the Record button (center)

4b

Detail of effects on Frames 35 and 50

WITH PAINTER'S SCRIPTS FEATURE, you can automate any series of recorded effects and apply them to each frame of an entire movie.

1 Starting with a video clip. Tests will be processed faster if you begin with a small video clip like the one we used—320 x 240 pixels with 67 frames. When you open a video clip (a QuickTime or AVI movie), Painter converts it to a Frame Stack. (When you save the Stack, give it a new name so the original clip isn't replaced.)

2 Testing a series of effects on a frame. Before you test a sequence of effects on a single frame, set up multiple Undos so you can return the clip to its original state: Choose Edit, Preferences, Undo, and enter a number that exceeds the number of effects you plan to use. Choose a rough paper texture (we chose Thick Paint from the Painted Effects 3 library on the Painter 8 Wow! CD-ROM) and apply it to Frame 1 in your movie with Effects, Surface Control, Apply Surface Texture, Using Paper (we settled on Amount 22%, Picture 90% and Shine 12%). Next, we added a look of cloud-filtered sunlight by choosing Effects, Surface Control, Apply Lighting. We customized the Slide Lighting, named it "sunlight," and saved it. (See Chapter 7 for more about lighting techniques.) When you've finished testing, undo the effects you applied to Frame 1. (Painter will remember the last settings you used in the dialog boxes.)

> ### HI-RES MOVIE EFFECTS
>
> If you want to apply effects to a broadcast-quality (640 x 480 pixels) video, use an editing program (such as Premiere) to create a low-resolution version on which to test a combination of effects. Because it takes a higher setting to get a result in a larger file, you may want to adjust the settings before treating the larger file.

3 Moving paper grain in the movie. To add subtle interest to your movie, you can change paper grain position on a frame-by-frame basis by choosing Movie, Set Grain Position. We chose the Grain Moves Linearly button and a 2-pixel horizontal movement.

4 Recording and playing back the session on the movie. Begin recording the effects by clicking the Record button in the Scripts palette; then repeat your sequence of effects. When you're finished, click the Stop button. Give your script a descriptive name, and undo your effects again. To apply your script to the movie, choose Movie, Apply Script to Movie. When the dialog box appears, find your new Script in the list, click the Playback button, and watch as Painter applies the recorded series of effects to each frame. 🔊

■ When creating the image on this page, **Athos Boncompagni** used scripts saved during several work sessions to record the development of the images so that he could play them back, one on top of the other, to demonstrate how the images were created. (For more information about how to use a series of scripts, turn to "Recording and Saving a Series of Scripts" on page 320.) He also used Painter's ability to playback the images at a higher resolution. (See the tip "Increasing File Resolution with Scripts" on page 320.)

Testalibro is a proposal for a book cover. Boncompagni started with a blank 6 x 9-inch canvas. In the Script Options dialog box, accessed by clicking the right triangle on the Scripts palette bar, he disabled Record Initial State. (This would enable him to have Painter redraw the image using a different size Pen and color, later.) Next, so he could play the script back at a different resolution later (as described on the opposite page), he chose Select, All (Ctrl/⌘-A); this would store the file dimensions as part of the script information. Then he clicked the Record button. He drew the line drawing and added crosshatching with the Scratchboard Tool variant of Pens and black ink, then clicked the Stop Recording button on the Scripts section. Next, he reduced the size and opacity of the Scratchboard Tool (using the sliders in Property Bar), chose a brown color in the Colors picker, then played the pen-and-ink script back on his image using brown ink to paint finer brown lines over the black. To add more color to the illustration, he began recording a new script, chose Select, All and used Water Color brushes to add transparent washes. Then he clicked the Stop button on the Scripts palette and saved the script.

Dewey Reid of Reid Creative, illustrated the 30-second animation *Yuri the Yak* for Sesame Street, a production of Children's Television Workshop. In the story segment, Yuri travels the countryside eating yellow yams and yogurt, and teaching the letter "Y." Reid stresses the importance of preproduction planning in animation. He created the *Yuri the Yak* animation with a total of only 35 drawings (it could have taken hundreds). His background in conventional animation helped him determine which drawings to make, and which to generate by tweening in an animation program, saving time and a lot of work. Reid used Painter to create individual parts of the Yak, such as the head, body and arms. He opened the illustrations in Photoshop and created a mask for each image, then saved the illustrations as PICT files in a numbered sequence. (He prefers using PICT files rather than QuickTime movies, since PICT files allow higher quality. Also, a sequence of PICT files allows for more flexibility—it's easier to remove a frame or two, if necessary.) He imported the masked files into Adobe After Effects, created animation cycles for each of the Yak parts, then joined animation cycles together. A virtuoso with effects, Reid completed his artistic vision by adding subtle lighting and texture. He opened the animation in Painter as a Frame Stack. After recording a script of Effects, Surface Control, Apply Lighting and Apply Surface Texture, he chose Movie, Apply Script to Movie to add the effects to the frames.

Snuffy 1 and 2 are two compositional layout illustrations by **Cindy Reid** of Reid Creative for a proposed Sesame Street production of Children's Television Workshop. The animation was conceived to accompany the children's song "I Wish I Were Small." In frame 1, Snuffy (who is normally mammoth-size) becomes small enough to fit into a bird's nest; in frame 2, small enough to fit in a buttercup. To create both frames Reid shot photos of a bird's nest, a bee, the sky and clouds, foliage and buttercup flowers for "scrap." She scanned the photos into Photoshop and pasted the images onto layers to build two composite files. When the elements were in place, she opened the layered composite file in Painter, where she added painterly brushwork to each layer using the Grainy Water variant of Liquid. She added details using a small Sharp Chalk variant (Chalk). When the brushwork was complete, she flattened the image by choosing Drop All from the Layers palette bar menu.

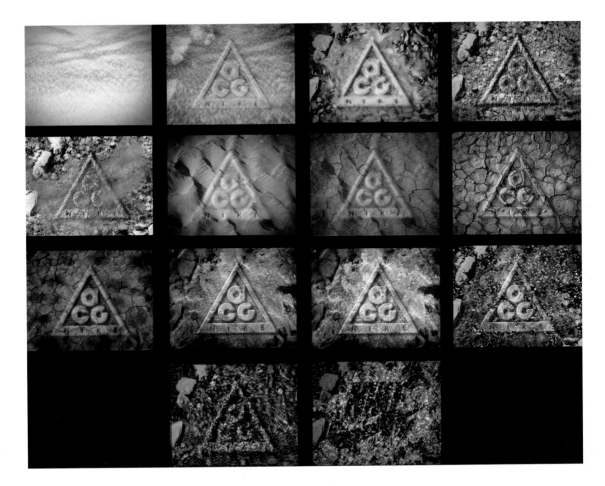

■ Creative director and film artist **Dewey Reid,** working with Colossal Pictures, engineered the preproduction for the *Nike All Conditions Gear* TV commercial. To begin the preproduction visualization, Reid scanned a variety of images. Then he used Painter to create keyframes to establish the essential positions in the animated sequence. He imported the Nike logo (by copying it from Illustrator and pasting it into the Painter file as shapes while both applications were running), converted the logo shapes to selections (Shapes, Convert To Selection) and applied a feather to the selections. He embossed the artwork in stages, with Effects, Surface Control, Apply Surface Texture (Using Mask), creating the illusion that the logo pushes up through the scanned images. Reid saved the keyframes as numbered PICT files, then used Adobe Premiere to create transitions (such as Cross Dissolves) between the keyframes. He manipulated a few of the masks in Adobe After Effects. Back in Painter, Reid painted clouds of dust with the Digital Airbrush variant of Airbrushes and used Effects, Surface Control, Image Warp to subtly change the shape of the clouds. He imported the dust image into Premiere and moved the dust across one series of frames. After working out the timing in Premiere, Reid used Painter to add special effects to the entire movie to increase the 3D look. A whiz with scripts, he opened the movie as a Frame Stack and treated it with an effects script that included Effects, Surface Control, Apply Lighting and Apply Surface Texture, Using Image Luminance.

■ **Jean-Luc Touillon's** passion for drawing shows in *Endormie*, a page for an animated sketchbook that was created in Painter and Adobe After Effects. The animation shows the process of the drawing and then the addition of layers of color being added to the completed black-and-white drawing. Touillon prefers to draw with his pressure-sensitive tablet and stylus, watching the drawing develop on-screen, without the use of photographs. After opening a new file with a white background, he used various Liquid Ink brushes to draw a series of Liquid Ink drawings, the woman, pen, bath, teapot and the movie camera. Liquid Ink is resolution-independent, so Touillon could sketch quickly and expressively using a tiny file size, then increase the file size using Canvas, Resize. (For more information about Liquid Ink, turn to "A Painter Liquid Ink Primer" on page 117.) After all the black-and-white sketches were complete, he colored them using separate layers for each color. Then he converted each black-and-white drawing and its colored areas to shapes as follows: Touillon targeted each Liquid Ink layer and con-verted it to a default layer by clicking the right triangle on the Layers palette and choosing Convert to Default Layer from the pop-up menu. Next, he made a selection for each drawing and its colored elements by choosing Select, Auto Select, Image Luminance, and converted each selection to shapes by choosing Select, Convert to Shape. Finally, he exported the shapes from Painter by choosing File, Export, Adobe Illustrator File. He used the Adobe Illustrator-format vector files to create an animation in After Effects.

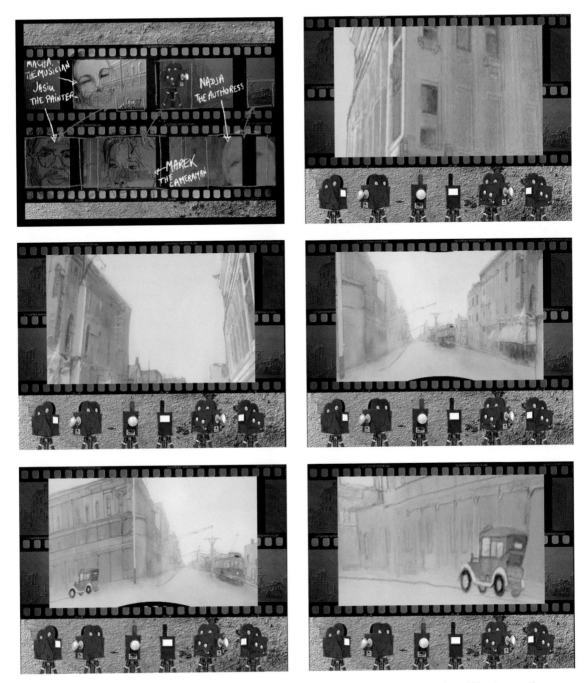

■ **Jean-Luc Touillon** also known as "**Jasiu**" created the illustrations for *L'histoire digitale évolutive d'une ville imaginaire,* an interactive mystery story on CD-ROM, while working with the team at LA F@KTORY in Paris. Touillon built the frames for the story entirely within Painter. QuickTime VR was used to produce the panoramic environment.

With QuickTime VR, the viewer can manipulate the camera by zooming in and out and scrolling 360° to the left and right as they tour the imaginary city. To begin, Touillon created a new frame stack and painted on the individual frames using the Artist Pastel Chalk (Pastels) and the Basic Crayon variant of Crayons. To blend the paint, he used the Grainy

Water variant of Blenders, creating a dream-like atmosphere. When the images were complete, he saved them as a series of PICT files. Touillon later assembled the frames using Metropolis and Macromedia Director software. For information about using QuickTime VR, see http://www.apple.com/quicktime/qtvr and http://www.iqtvr.org

■ An innovative storyboard artist, **Peter Mitchell Rubin** used
a variety of Painter's brushes
and compositing controls to
create the storyboards for the
MGM movie *Stargate.* The Giza,
Egypt, sequence is shown here.
Rubin outputs his illustrations
from Painter as numbered PICT
files, then animates them in
Adobe Premiere. Rubin's love of
drawing shows in his storyboards. He works very quickly,
in gray, at 72 ppi. His document
size depends on the amount of
detail needed, but is usually
under 600 pixels wide. The
aspect ratio depends upon how
the film will be shot. Rubin
organizes the thousands of
drawings that he creates for a
film in folders according to
scene. He sets up QuicKeys
macros to automate actions
wherever possible, automating
the processing of all the files in
a folder. When Rubin adds other
elements to an image, he pastes
the element, drops it, then
paints into it to merge it seamlessly into the composition. He
also uses Painter's Cloners
brushes. For example, he created the texture in Frame 15
(left column, third frame down
from top) by photographing the
actual set sculpture used in the
movie, scanning it and cloning
the scan into his drawing.

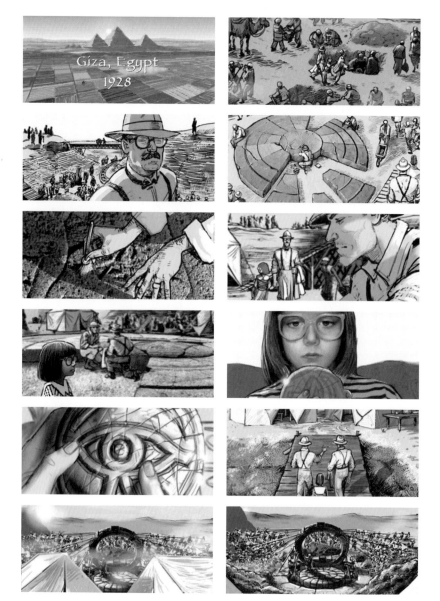

■ As both a broadcast designer for Fox Television and a freelance graphic designer, **Geoff Hull** employs a spontaneous, progressive approach when designing with type.

Hull began the *Fox Logo Pattern* with a black background. He imported a file with both solid and outline versions of the Fox logo (using File, Acquire, Adobe Illustrator file—which creates a new file). He copied the shapes from the new file and pasted them into the larger background file, then converted the two logo shape groups into two layers. Working quickly and intuitively, he painted on the logo layers with Oils brushes and saturated color. To build a layered look, Hull made additional copies of the layers and added more brushstrokes. In busier areas, he erased portions of layers by painting the layer masks with white paint.

To create the animated title sequence for the TV show *Wild Oats*, Hull envisioned a hand-done, calligraphic look. He began the image with a white background and set type in Painter using the font Earthquake, a typeface from the T26 foundry. After setting black text, he made a clone (File, Clone) and erased its contents. He chose Canvas, Tracing Paper and expressively traced the letterforms. For the frames of the animation Hull made a series of progressive clones, switching clone sources (File, Clone Source) among the original and several later versions of the title sequence.

Hull created *The Crossing Guard* storyboard for a Miramax Films movie title and trailer. He began with a black background and set individual letterform shapes in Painter using Mason from the Emigré font library. After converting the shapes to layers, he filled them with color and erased portions of the letters by painting the layer masks with white paint. He also used Effects, Orientation, Scale on the layers to vary the size of the elements.

■ Artist and multimedia designer **Ted Larson** created the images on these pages as part of an educational CD-ROM about the book of Revelation in the Holy Bible. These pictures were designed as both large-format digital prints and PowerPoint-ready digital slides for seminary and church presentation aids.

Larson used similar techniques to create both of the illustrations on these pages. He began by sketching in Painter to establish a composition. He started in Formz (a 3D modeling program), building the doorway for the *Door to Heaven* (above) and the throne set (for *Throne of God* (page 343). Using Cinema 4DXL (a 3D animation program), he could move around the sets with virtual cameras like a photographer looking for effective posi-

tions and angles. Using a frame from the Cinema 4DXL file for reference, Larson built a gray-toned composite image that included the clouds and lightning, his own photos of the models, and stock photos of animals (from a Corel stock-photo CD-ROM). Larson dressed his models in costumes and created the hair and beards with theatrical wigs and crepe hair, then photographed them. He built the creatures' wings from two eagle photos from a Corel CD-ROM. When he was satisfied with the composition, he merged the layers and used various brushes in Painter to color the images.

For *Door to Heaven,* Larson wanted to show the grand scale of the door by contrasting it with a human figure. So he shot photos of a friend posing as the

apostle John. Inside the doorway he used sunshine and clouds to give the feeling one was leaving the known universe and stepping into another dimension. He began the work by assembling a black-and-white composite image, which included the decorated door. Next, he made an empty new layer for the coloring, and to make the layer like a transparent color overlay on top of the gray image, he set the Composite Method of the layer to Color. Then, using warm colors, he painted over the clouds, and he colored the figure and the door using low-opacity Airbrushes variants. He also used Water Color brushes to paint transparent details. Finally, he brightened the edge of the door and areas of the clouds using the Fire and Glow variants of the F-X brush.

■ **Ted Larson** began *Throne of God* by drawing a color sketch in Painter. Using the Sharp Chalk (Chalk) and Charcoal variants, he roughed out the positions of the figures and other elements in the scene. Using a frame from the Cinema 4DXL file he had created for reference, Larson photographed friends dressed in costume as well as other elements, such as the Menorah. Then he scanned the photos and opened all of the elements in Painter, where he pasted them as layers into a composite file.

The artwork was still black-and-white at this point. This helped Larson see just tones, which helped him to blend everything together. To give the finished black-and-white composition a sepia-tone, he tinted it with a custom gradient

(by clicking the right triangle on the Gradients palette bar and choosing Express in Image from the menu). Then he painted transparent glazes over the image using various brushes. Larson adopted this technique from Renaissance painters who often added color over a monochromatic painting. "This is where my traditional art skills are very handy," says Larson. Some of Larson's favorite painters who used a similar glazing technique are Leonardo, Holbein, Vermeer, Rembrandt and Titian.

Larson used several layers during the coloring of his image. He added a new layer and painted subtle color onto the clouds in the sky and on the water reflections. Then, on another layer, he added deeper color and tone using the Airbrushes and F-X brushes. To add more detail to the

figures and clothing, Larson painted transparent washes using Water Color brushes. For additional color and texture in some areas, he used the Variable Splatter and Digital Airbrush variants of Airbrushes with low opacity settings. Larson gave the figures' hands a metallic look by applying a custom bronze gradient using the Express in Image command (located in the triangle pop-up menu on the Gradients palette). Finally, to achieve the look of a colorful children's book, Larson enhanced the colors using the Effects, Tonal Control, Adjust Colors command. For more information about Larson's large-format prints and the educational CD-ROM see his Web site at http://home.earthlink.net/~theoneson/index.html

11

USING
PAINTER FOR
WEB
GRAPHICS

Ben Barbante created Efolio, *an illustration for his Web site's index page. To see the entire image, turn to the gallery at the end of this chapter.*

WHAT DOES PAINTER OFFER AN ARTIST who designs graphics for the World Wide Web? In addition to its powerful natural media brushes, compositing tools, mosaics and other effects, Painter can help you prepare images for Web pages. For example, you can set type for titles with the Text tool, use shapes to draw polygons, convert the shapes to layers and define the polygons as clickable regions for use on your Web page. Use the Image Slicer to segment an image into smaller parts so the viewer can see pieces of the image as they load, then export some of the slices with JavaScript rollovers. You can open source video in Painter as a frame stack and grab stills to use as graphics or as references for your Web illustrations, or export the frame stack directly from Painter as a GIF animation. (If you need help with the painting techniques or compositing methods referred to in this chapter, you can find more information in Chapters 3, 4 and 5. Turn to Chapter 10 for information on scripts and frame stack animations. And see Appendix E for recommended books relating to Web design.)

CREATING GRAPHICS FOR THE WEB

Painter has tools that make it easy to adapt graphics for the Web. For instance, you can save in GIF and JPEG (the two most popular image formats used on the Web). And you can tell Painter to do some of the coding to help you set up image maps or linked graphics. Here are some tips for creating Web graphics in Painter.

First, there are two basic uses for images on a Web page. One is an in-line graphic or "static" image embedded in a page without a link to another location—for example, an embedded background graphic. The second use for graphics is as "hot spots," or "buttons." A hot spot is a clickable region on your artwork that will allow the user to hyperlink (or travel) to another location on the Web, either within the same Web site or at another site. There are two general types of hot

Susan LeVan created images for "Off" and "On" button states, for the Nichole Shoes Web site. To see the entire set of buttons, turn to the gallery at the end of this chapter.

TO QUANTIZE OR TO DITHER?

Painter offers two methods for reducing the number of colors in the Save as GIF dialog box: Quantize to Nearest Color and Dither Colors. Quantize to Nearest Color uses areas of solid color, picking the colors in the current palette that are the closest match to the color you're trying to convert. Dither Colors converts colors using a random pattern in the same color range (giving a less banded result or a better visual color match), but it generates a file that can't be compressed as small as one with solid colors.

spots. The simpler one is a *button* that links to one location (URL, or Uniform Resource Locator) such as www.peachpit.com. The second is an *image map*—an image that has been divided into regions, each of which lets you link to a different URL.

Making an image map. You can choose any kind of graphic as an image map: title type, a photograph or an illustration you've painted. Define an image map by selecting all or part of an image (by dragging around it with a selection tool and copying it to make a layer). Then double-click on the new layer's name in the Layers Palette to access the Layer Attributes dialog box. Use the checkbox to make it a WWW Map Clickable Region. In the Save As GIF Options and JPEG Encoding Quality dialog boxes, you can choose to export a client-side image map (directions for the image map are included in the HTML for the page) or server-side image map (directions for the map are stored on the server) by telling Painter to create an image map definition file with dimensions for the hot spots. Client-side image maps are more efficient to use when designing for newer browsers, but if you want your image map to work with older browsers as well, consider including both client-side and server-side directions in the HTML for the image map. For more information, see "Building an Image Map for a Web Page" on page 353.

Using Web-friendly file formats. The JPEG and transparent GIF formats that Painter supports are two of the most popular file formats used in Web page design. Transparent GIF files make use of the mask you've saved with the file, allowing a graphic to be placed on the page with an irregular edge or with holes cut into it to reveal the background underneath. You can make a transparent GIF by choosing File, Save As, GIF, and then using the Output Transparency checkbox In the Save As GIF Options dialog box. You can pan around the Preview area to preview the transparency. We suggest using GIF format to save simple line art and flat-color graphics without gradations and soft edges. Save photos and painted artwork in 24-bit JPEG format.

Building small files that load fast. Web-savvy designers recommend making graphics files small, between 20 and 30K, because most Web visitors will not wait for images that take a long time to load. Typical modem speed is 56,600 bps and graphics of 20–30K will download within 1–3 seconds. To make GIF images small, use Painter's Save As GIF Options dialog box to compress the number of colors from millions to 256 (8-bit) or fewer. Save as GIF in the exact pixel dimensions needed for the page design. When you use JPEG format to preserve the 24-bit color of an image, experiment with the JPEG Encoding Quality settings to determine how much compression an image can withstand. JPEG is a lossy compression (it removes information, which can't be restored), so make sure to use File, Save As to create the new

Arthur Steuer and Even Steven Levee, principals of i~potato production company, commissioned artist/animator Sharon Steuer to create the i-potato logo for the cover of their pop music CD and Web site. Steuer used Painter's Water Color Brushes variants, Oils variants and Airbrushes variants to paint the image. Steuer created an animation of the eye blinking for the launching of the Web site (www.i-potato.net). She created the cels for the eye-blink in Painter, using a separate layer to draw each stage of the animation. So the animation would load quickly, her client chose to use only two of the three stages. (See a QuickTime movie with music that includes all three stages in Steuer's folder on the Wow! CD-ROM.) To read about creating a GIF animation step by step, turn to "Making a Slide Show Animation" on page 356.

JPEG file with a different name, preserving your master file.

Creating a subdued background. Painter has tools for creating exciting backgrounds, but a busy, contrasty background can take attention away from the subject of the screen and overwhelm your audience. Here are two suggestions that will help you make a background more subtle: Turn down the contrast using Effects, Tonal Control, Brightness/Contrast, or desaturate the background (using Effects, Tonal Control, Adjust Colors) to call attention to brighter-colored content. To desaturate, move the Saturation slider to the left. Click OK when you see the look you want in the Preview window.

Adding movie stills and video to your page. You can open a movie in Painter and capture frames to use as static images or hot spots. And you can save a QuickTime or AVI movie using effective compression such as Cinepak, so it can be played within a Netscape or Internet Explorer browser.

Exporting a movie as a GIF animation. Painter makes it easy to add movement to your Web pages with GIF animations. You can open a QuickTime/AVI movie as a frame stack (or create your own animation in Painter) and export it directly from Painter as a GIF animation. Here are some tips to help you make a GIF animation that loads quickly and plays smoothly on your Web page: Make movies with a small frame size (such as 160 x 120). (Painter doesn't permit movies to be resized. So if you plan to import video into Painter, reduce the frame size in a video editor such as Adobe Premiere before opening it in Painter.) Use as few frames as possible. (You can use the Movie, Delete Frames dialog box to remove any unnecessary frames.) Reduce the number of colors—using black-and-white or just a few colors, for instance, will help to make a smaller animation file.

To save a completed frame stack as a GIF animation, choose File, Save As, Save Movie as GIF Animation. In the Save As GIF Options box, make the choices you need. To read about making a GIF animation step-by-step, turn to "Making a Slide Show Animation" on page 356.

WEB-FRIENDLY COLOR

Painter ships with several color sets built for Web graphics. To load a Web-friendly color set, open the Color Set palette, click the right arrow and from the menu, choose Open Color Set. Navigate to the Painter 8 application folder and open the Color Sets folder. Select one of the seven choices in the Hexadecimal folder, the Netscape 216, the Macintosh default 256 or the Windows Default 256 Color Set and click Open.

SHRINKING A COPY

If you're doing detailed painting or retouching to be displayed on the Web at 72 ppi, you may want to create your art at a higher resolution so you can zoom in and paint the details. Then use Canvas, Resize to shrink a copy of your image down to 72 ppi. Sharpen areas that become soft (Effects, Focus, Sharpen).

Reducing Color Using Apply Screen

Overview Choose an image; reduce color using Apply Screen; edit the color to make it Web-safe; export the image.

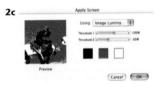

The original photograph with selection active and background sky made lighter

To choose a Web-safe HTML color in the Select Screen dialog box on a Mac, first click on the icon for Color palettes.

Scroll down the list to select a Web-safe HTML color or type in the hexadecimal number of the color desired.

The Apply Screen dialog box with preview showing the new color choices

REDUCING THE NUMBER OF COLORS is a frequently used method for making small files for faster downloading of Web graphics. To create this three-color image, we used Apply Screen—one of Painter's most efficient "color reduction" tools. It allows you to create images composed of only three colors without the anti-aliasing that creates many intermediate colors when it smooths edges.

1 Choosing a photo and making adjustments. Open an image that you want to convert to a three-color composition. In our first attempt to modify color using the Apply Screen function, the skiers merged with the background sky because the sky's value did not contrast enough with the skiers. We undid the Apply Screen, and before trying again, we isolated the sky by making a selection, and then lightened the sky. To make a selection of an area like the sky based on color, click on the area with the Magic Wand. To add areas of noncontiguous color to the selection, turn off the Contiguous checkbox in the Property Bar; expand or shrink the range of colors by adjusting the Tolerance. (To read more about the Magic Wand, turn to page 147–148 in Chapter 4.) Then we increased the value within the selected sky using Brightness/Contrast (choose Effects, Tonal Control, Brightness/Contrast). After adjusting the Brightness, we chose Select, None.

2 Reducing color. To apply the color effect to your entire image choose Effects, Surface Control, Apply Screen, Using Image Luminance and choose a color by clicking the middle of the three color squares. In the Color picker that opened, we settled on an aqua color, in addition to the black and white. In the Colors picker, click on the icon for Color Palettes, on the top row of the window. Click on the drop-down list and select Web Safe Colors, and choose a color. If your computer does not have the HTML color option, choose a color to serve as a preview of the final effect. It doesn't have to be a Web-safe color. In Step 3 you can

3a

The image showing active selection made with the Dropper and the Auto Select, Using Current Color dialog box

3b

Close-up of the image with selection. The original aqua color shows dithering when viewed on a monitor with only 256 colors.

4a

The Netscape Navigator 216 Color Set, showing the new aqua we used for the fill.

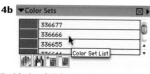

4b

The Hexidecimal Color Set, shown as a list.

4c

Filling with the Web-safe color

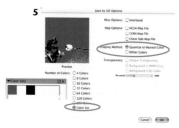

5

Our settings in the GIF Options dialog box and the Color Set with three Web-safe colors

replace it. We adjusted the Threshold sliders to bring out important details in the skiers' faces. The Threshold 1 slider controls the relationship between aqua (the middle color) and white (the color on the right); the Threshold 2 slider controls the amount of black (the left color).

3 Making a selection. In Windows, Painter's Apply Screen dialog box does not let you directly apply color from a Web-safe color set (unless you have the option described in Step 2). To replace our color with a Web-safe color when using our Windows machine, we first made a hard-edged mask. To make a hard-edged selection based on color, choose the Dropper and click on the colored area you want to mask. From the Select menu choose Auto Select, Using Current Color. Click OK; you'll see a selection marquee appear on your image.

4 Filling the selection with a Web-safe color. Now load the Web-safe Netscape Navigator 216 Color Set as follows: On the Colors Set palette, click the right triangle to open the menu and choose Open Color Set. Navigate to the Netscape Navigator 216 Color Set. This set can be found in the Color Sets folder, in the Painter 8 application folder. Next, click on a Web-safe color that complements your design (we chose a bright aqua). Choose Effects, Fill With Current Color, and click OK.

5 Making a color set and exporting a GIF file. To preserve the Web-safe colors that you used in your illustration, export a GIF that uses a custom color set that contains the three Web-safe colors in your image. (This process is similar to setting up an Indexed Color palette in Photoshop.) Before you make the Color Set, open the Color Variability palette, choose "In HSV" from the pop-up menu and set the ± H, ± S and ± V sliders to 0. Now choose the Dropper tool and click on one of the three colors in your image. The Color picker will display the color. In the Color Sets palette, click on the right arrow and select New Empty Color Set from the pop-up menu. The Color Sets palette window will now be empty. Click on the Add Color to Color Set button to add the selected color to the Color Set. Sample and add the two remaining colors by using the Dropper and the Add Color to Color Set button. To save your colors, click on the right arrow in the Color Sets palette and select Save Color Set, name the set and Save. (For more information about making color sets, turn to "Capturing a Color Set" on page 38, in Chapter 2.)

To export a GIF from Painter to use on your Web page, choose File, Save As, GIF. When the Save As GIF Options dialog box appears, under Imaging method, turn on Quantize to Nearest Color and choose the Color Set button.

Posterizing with Web-Safe Colors

Overview *Open an image; load the Netscape Navigator 216 Color Set; posterize the image using the Color Set; retouch it using flat color fills and Painter's Web-safe brushes; export the file.*

The original photo

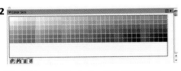

The Netscape Navigator 216 Color Set

POSTERIZING CAN ADD AN INTERESTING GRAPHIC LOOK to a photo, and at the same time simplify color for faster downloading. We posterized the image above using Painter's Netscape Navigator 216 Web-safe color set so the color would not dither on most monitors. Then we exported our GIF file with color constrained by the color set.

1 Choosing a photo. We opened a 512-pixel-wide photo. Select a photo or an illustration with a simple background, such as this snowboarder image.

2 Posterizing using a Color Set. Begin by loading the Netscape Navigator 216 Color Set. On the Color Sets palette, click the right triangle to open the menu and choose Open Color Set. Navigate to the Netscape Navigator 216 Color Set. This set can be found in the Painter 8 application folder, in the Color Sets folder. Now choose Effects, Tonal Control, Posterize Using Color Set. The command doesn't allow you to have complete control over how color reduction is performed, but it does automatically constrain all of the colors in the image to the Netscape 216-color palette and can be a real time-saver.

3

Making a selection with the Magic Wand

4

Painting with a Web-safe brush

5a

To constrain our GIF to Web-safe colors, we turned on the Quantize to Nearest Color and Color Set buttons in GIF Options.

5b

Detail of our final GIF shows no dithering when viewed using 256 colors.

3 Cleaning up the background. Posterizing with the Netscape Navigator 216 Color Set provided a close match for the important colors in our image (such as flesh tones), but it produced some distracting debris in the sky. We used the Magic Wand to select these areas. Click with the Magic Wand on the color you want to select. To select noncontiguous color, turn off the Contiguous checkbox in the Property Bar. If needed, adjust the Tolerance slider in the Property Bar. To read more about the Magic Wand, turn to page 147–148 in Chapter 4, "Selections, Shapes and Masks." After making the selection, we filled the area with blue sampled from the sky. To sample color in your image and fill as we did, choose the Dropper tool and click in your image. Then choose Effects, Fill, Fill With Current Color.

4 Touching up with a Web-safe brush. There was still some debris left after we applied the fill, so we painted the area using a "Web-safe" brush. To access the WebMedia Brushes, copy them from the Painter 8 CD 2 CD-ROM to your Painter 8 application folder as follows: Begin by opening the Painter 8 Application folder then open the Brushes folder: Now, insert the CD-ROM and open its Brushes folder. Select the WebMedia Brushes folder, and drag and drop it into the Brushes folder within the Painter 8 application folder. Now load Painter's WebMedia Brushes library by first opening the Brush Creator window. In the Menu Bar under Brush, select import brush library. Click on Import, then click Open.

> **WEB-SAFE BRUSHES**
>
> Painter ships with a WebMedia brush library. The WebMedia Brushes use Grainy Edge Flat Cover and Grainy Flat Cover (two subcategories that incorporate aliased edges). The brushes are ideal for painting when you want to avoid the in-between colors that are generated during anti-aliasing.

Once the library was loaded, we chose the Calligraphic Winner brush variant of the W Thick-n-Thin brush. Then we used the blue, sampled from the sky, to paint over the remaining purple speckles. The sky was now a solid blue.

5 Exporting the image. You can export a GIF from Painter, while retaining Web-safe colors from the Netscape Navigator 216 Color Set chosen in Step 2, as follows: Choose File, Save As, GIF, and when the Save As GIF Options dialog box appears, under Imaging method, turn on Quantize to Nearest Color, and under Number of Colors, choose Color Set.

This function works similarly to the indexed color palettes supported by Equilibrium DeBabelizer, Macromedia Fireworks and Adobe ImageReady that allow Web-safe colors to be preserved. Our final image is at the top of the previous page.

Making a Seamless Tile

Overview *Select an image; use the Kaleidoscope plug-in to make a tile; edit its color; test the tile; save the tile in JPEG format.*

PAINTER HAS SEAMLESS-TILE-CREATION TOOLS that are unequaled by other programs. To make this background for a Web site's welcome screen, we began by using the Kaleidoscope dynamic layer to create a symmetrical design based on a photo of palm trees. After making the seamless tile and testing it in Painter, we saved the finished image as a JPEG file for import into a Web page editor.

The original photograph of palm trees

1 Choosing an image. For this nostalgic background design, we chose and opened a 768 x 512-pixel image with gold-to-brown colors.

The image with Kaleidoscope dynamic layer

2 Using Kaleidoscope as a lens. As you move it over your image, a Kaleidoscope dynamic layer distorts the underlying imagery into symmetrical designs that are ideal for perfect seamless tiles or fabric design. To make a Kaleidoscope layer, open the Layers palette (Window, Show Layers). Click the Plugins button at the bottom of the Layers palette and choose the Kaleidoscope plug-in from the pop-up menu. When the dialog box appears, it will reflect the default size of 100 x 100 pixels. We typed 200 into the field to make a larger "lens." Use the Layer Adjuster tool to move the Kaleidoscope layer around your image until you find a "tile" effect you like. (To read more about dynamic layers, turn to Chapter 5, "Using Layers.")

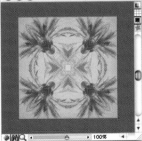

The new tile image

3 Making a tile image. Building a background by importing a single repeating tile into a Web page editor is much more efficient than importing an entire background image. That's because the smaller tile image downloads faster, and it can be repeated very quickly by the browser. Here's the quickest way to prepare your tile: With the Layers palette opened, choose the Layer Adjuster tool and select the Kaleidoscope dynamic layer by clicking the Dynamic Plug-Ins drop-down menu, on the bottom of the Layers palette. To capture the Kaleidoscope imagery, convert the dynamic layer into an image layer by clicking the right triangle on the Layers palette bar to open the pull-down menu and choosing Convert To Default

4

Lightening the color for a subdued look

5

Naming the pattern in the Capture Pattern dialog box

6

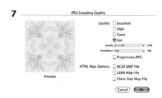

The Painter image filled with the Golden Palms pattern. The pattern can be found in the Palm Patterns library on the Painter 8 CD-ROM in the Wow! Items folder.

7

Saving the tile as a JPEG with Fair quality and a Smoothness setting of 5%

SOFTEN WITH SMOOTHNESS

When low-quality JPEG settings are used, square artifacts can appear in an image. The Smoothness setting in the JPEG dialog box can help to soften artifacts. Use Smoothness with care, however, because a setting that's too high can blur the image. A bonus: Smoothness can further reduce the size of the file.

---

layer. Copy the layer (Edit, Copy), and then choose Edit, Paste into New Image.

4 Lightening the tile image. We lightened the new image to make a background that would not compete with text and other elements on the page by choosing Effects, Tonal Control, Adjust Colors. To lighten, move the Value slider to the right. Our setting was 120%.

5 Making a pattern. Select the entire tile image by choosing Select, All. Now you can capture the tile as a pattern and test its tiling in Painter. On the Pattern palette, click the right triangle to open the menu and choose Capture Pattern. When the dialog box appears, name your pattern. For a Rectangular tile with no Horizontal or Vertical Shift (like ours), leave the other settings at their defaults and click OK. (See Chapter 7 for more information about working with patterns.)

6 Testing the tile. To see the overall effect of your pattern in Painter, create a new 800 x 800-pixel document. Now choose Effects, Fill, and in the dialog box, click the Pattern button. Click OK to fill the new document with the pattern.

7 Exporting the seamless tile. At this point we saved our 200 x 200 pixel full-color file (File, Save). Always remember to keep your original file in a format that preserves its image quality, such as TIFF, RIFF or Photoshop. Because the audience for this site would be viewing its images using millions of colors, we didn't want to limit the colors. So we saved a copy of the tile in JPEG format, to preserve the 24-bit color depth. If you have Photoshop, Photoshop Elements or Fireworks, consider using one of these programs to save your file as a JPEG since they all allow you to see the file size as well as the quality. In Painter, you can save a copy of your file as a JPEG. Choose File, Save As, JPEG, and remember to add the proper file extension (.jpg) to its name. To make the image small, we chose the Fair setting, and we applied a Smoothness of 5% in the JPEG dialog box to soften the JPEG artifacts. Our final background (viewed in Explorer) is shown at the top of page 357. 🖌

BRACKETING TO COMPARE JPEG IMAGE QUALITY

Most designers export continuous-tone images for the Web using JPEG format. Often, a low JPEG setting will provide adequate quality and a tiny file size. To know for sure in Painter, test the file by "bracketing," or saving it using several different quality settings. Begin by opening the image you want to compress. To duplicate the image, choose File, Clone, and save it using the lowest quality setting (Fair). Name the file so you can compare results later. Select your original file, choose File, Clone again and save the second image using Good quality. Repeat the process twice more using High and Excellent quality settings. Close the images, and reopen to compare the results. (JPEG compression artifacts are not visible until an image is closed and reopened.)

JPEG settings: Excellent (top left), High (top right), Good (bottom left), and Fair (bottom right).

Building an Image Map for a Web Page

Overview Choose photos and other elements; fill with a patterned background; create layers and designate an image map in Painter; finish the HTML.

CHER THREINEN-PENDARVIS

1a

Setting up the file in the New dialog box

Selecting the blue palm pattern

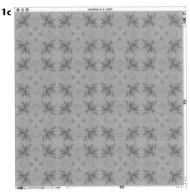

The new file showing the pattern text

TO BUILD A PROTOTYPE WEB SITE for *Surf Nostalgia,* an ocean-related art and collectibles gallery, we used Painter to create a background pattern, graphics, and image map buttons for the index page (including some of the HTML code for the image map). We designed the site to be viewed with any browser and used our own site, http://www.pendarvis-studios.com, to develop the prototype.

1 Setting up the page. This step sets up the home page for the Web site. There are no absolute size restrictions on Web pages. They can be any length, because the viewer can scroll. We set up an 800 x 800-pixel file that would easily accommodate viewers' screens with resolutions of 1074 x 768 pixels and larger.

To test how the background pattern would look on the image, we filled it with a blue version of the golden palms pattern which was created step-by-step in "Making a Seamless Tile" on pages 351–352. (To load a blue version of the palm pattern, copy the Palm Patterns library from the Wow! Items folder on the Painter 8 Wow! CD-ROM to your Painter 8 application folder. Then choose Open Library from the right arrow from the drop-down menu on the Patterns palette.)

For your prototype Web page design, create a new file. To see how your pattern will look as a background, fill the image by

2a

The Text settings in the Text palette

2b

The centered white text set on top of the filled background

2c

The settings in the Property Bar and Text palette for the hard-edged shadow

2d

The shadow shows the color sampled from a dark area of the background.

choosing Effects, Fill, Fill With Pattern. The pattern will be removed from the file before the final export is done and a single pattern tile will be exported as a JPEG file to be repeated by the browser's tiling function for the finished page.

2 Creating a logotype and graphics. Using the Text tool with white as the current color, set large bold letters for a logotype. We typed "Surf Nostalgia" using the Reporter Two font and pressing the Enter/Return key after typing "Surf," to set the "Nostalgia" type on a second line. In the Property Bar, we clicked the center button to center the type, then clicked the External Drop Shadow button to apply a solid, hard-edged shadow. The default color of the shadow is black. To change the shadow color, click on the color square and select one of the colors from the current Color Set. To load a new Color Set, hold down the Right Arrow and select Load Color Set. To adjust other shadow settings, open the Text palette.

3 Completing the layout. Now that the title type is complete, choose the Layer Adjuster and drag the type into position. Open the other element files that you'd like to add to your page, including those that you want to use as button graphics. Then copy and paste them into the file with the background and type. Use the Layer Adjuster to position them. Painter's Rulers and Guides are helpful with positioning. To use the Rulers and Guides, choose Canvas, Rulers, Show Rulers (Ctrl/⌘-R). When the Rulers appear, click on a ruler to create a guide; you can drag an endpoint to reposition the guide. The Effects, Objects, Align command is also useful when positioning a series of images or text blocks. To read more about these useful tools, turn to Chapter 1, "Getting to Know Painter." (After the three images were pasted in, we set small text in the dark color used for the shadow under each image.)

4 Making the image map. Painter allows you to define an image file as an *image map* (a document that's divided into non-overlapping clickable regions, each of which lets you link to a different URL, or location on the Web). In the finished layout, target one of the button picture layers that will become a clickable region. (Our file included three layers that would each be designated as a clickable region.)

Now it's time to tell Painter what to include in the image map definition file (ours included the picture buttons, but omitted the tiled background layer; it would instead be tiled in the browser). For each layer you want to include in the image map, double-click the layer name in the Layers palette to open the Layer Attributes dialog box. In the Name field, enter the name you want the layer to have on export. Use the checkbox to select WWW Clickable Map Region (the Region button will default to Rectangle Bounding Box), and type into the URL field the URL you want to link to. Repeat for the other buttons.

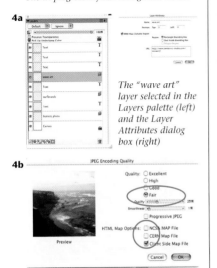

3

The in-progress layout with guides visible

The "wave art" layer selected in the Layers palette (left) and the Layer Attributes dialog box (right)

4a

4b

Setting the Quality and Smoothness, then checking the Client Side Map File box to generate the map definition file for the client-side version of the image map

Painter can create image map definition files for both server-side and client-side image maps. We chose to create a client-side image map, which would be more efficient when viewed using newer browsers because the instructions for client-side image maps are included in the HTML for the page. To export a map definition file for a client-side version of the image map, click the Client Side Map File box in the JPEG Encoding dialog box. (We chose the JPEG file format because of the art and photos present on the page and because most people in the site's viewing audience use 24-bit color systems.)

5 Finishing the HTML. Painter will make the map definition file for you—which lists the name of each region, defines its position using *x* and *y* coordinates and lists the URL it links to. Instructions for client-side image maps are downloaded with the file when it is viewed in newer browsers. For server-side maps, which are important for much older browsers, ask your service provider where the CGI script for image maps is stored and how to use it (CGI is an acronym for Common Gateway Interface, and CGI script is the external programming script used by the Web server). Check out these URLs on the World Wide Web to learn how to set up programming for client-side and server-side image maps: http://www.ihip.com/cside.html and http://www.ihip.com. You'll also need additional HTML programming to make the links work. A Painter-generated image map definition file text can be copied and then pasted into the html for the Web page. 🖌

Highlighting the file extension, in preparation for deleting it for the export

5

```
<map name="SurfNostalgiaMain">
<areas shape="rect" href="http://pendarvis-studios.com/waveart/html" coords= "295,500,
517, 722">
```

| URL that hot spot links to | name of the hot spot | coordinates of upper left and lower right corners of the rectangle |

The anatomy of one of the clickable regions in the client-side map definition file that Painter automatically generates

Making a Slide Show Animation

Overview *Choose images and resize them; create a new frame stack; paste each image into a frame; export the movie as a GIF animation.*

CHER THREINEN-PENDARVIS

IT'S EASY TO ADD MOVEMENT to your Web pages using a slide show created as a GIF animation in Painter.

1 Preparing the images. Open several images that you want to include in your slide show. Resize your images to 72 ppi (choose Canvas, Resize, disabling the Constrain File Size box and entering a new size), then sharpen them (Effects, Focus, Sharpen). Save your resized and sharpened images under a unique name so that you don't accidentally destroy your originals. Keep the images open.

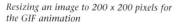

Resizing an image to 200 x 200 pixels for the GIF animation

2 Making a new frame stack. To open a new frame stack, choose File, New and click the Movie button. Enter the dimensions and the number of frames you want to use. It's a good idea to make the movie a small size so that it will load and play quickly on your Web page. (We set up a 200 x 200-pixel frame stack with 3 frames and chose the 24-bit Color with 8-bit Alpha Storage Type.)

Setting up a new frame stack with three frames and 24-bit color

3 Pasting images into the frames. Activate the image you want in your first frame, choose Select, All (Ctrl/⌘-A), then copy it to the clipboard (Ctrl/⌘-C). In the new frame stack, the first frame should already be selected. Paste the image into the first frame (Ctrl/⌘-V), then drop it to the Canvas by pressing Ctrl/⌘-Shift-D. Because a layer sits on top of the entire frame stack, make sure that you've dropped it before advancing to the next frame. To advance the frame stack one frame, click the step forward icon on the Frame Stack palette (or press the Page Up key on your keyboard). Repeat the copy-paste-drop process to get the other images into the frame stack. (See Chapter 10 for more about working with frame stacks.)

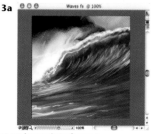

Pasting an image into frame 1

4 Exporting the animation. To save the completed frame stack as a GIF animation, choose File, Save As, Save Movie as GIF Animation. Make sure to save your GIF animation under a new name

The Step Forward icon is circled here.

Saving the frame stack as a GIF animation

Our settings in the Save As GIF Options dialog box

so you don't accidentally replace your frame stack. (Painter will not open a GIF animation as a frame stack.) In the Save As GIF Options box, make the choices you need. (We chose 64 colors and Quantize to Nearest Color for the Imaging Method. Under Animation Options we chose a Frame Delay of 500 ms, Default Disposal Method and entered 3 times for the Loop.)

■ Art director **Ben Barbante** designed and illustrated *Efolio* for his Home page using a combination of Painter, Illustrator and Photoshop. He used Painter's Image Slicer to separate the picture into both GIF and JPEG files for optimal file compression, then he exported HTML code (including navigational buttons with JavaScript rollovers) and a GIF animation from Painter for the final page.

To begin the slicing and export process, Barbante opened the completed layered illustration, which included the efolio case with a light bulb (for the "off" state). He made a new layer and created a black screen on top of the light bulb as a placeholder, for the rollover "on" state. (Later, the "on" state graphic would be replaced by a GIF animation.) Then he hid the layer that would show the Mouse "on" state (the efolio with the black screen) by turning its eye icon off in the Layers palette. He targeted the image canvas and chose the Image Slicer from the Dynamic Plugins menu on the Layers palette. In the Image Slicer, Barbante used the Horizontal and Vertical tools to divide the image, and used the Select tool to group some of the slices. Then, using the Slice menu and the File Name field in the Image Slicer box, he named each slice that he planned to export and chose a compression method (File Type), choosing GIF format to save slices with

flat areas of color in the gray border outside the illustration, and JPEG format to save the slices within the illustration, which included airbrushed color gradations.

For most slices in the image, Barbante selected a slice that would not be exported and under HTML and JavaScript, he set the Rollover State to No Rollover. Next, he selected the efolio case slice that would be the Mouse "off" state, set the Rollover State to Mouse over-out and clicked the Export settings for Current Image State button. When the Export Settings dialog box appeared, he chose the Mouse out button, turned on Include JavaScript and clicked Export. He clicked OK in the Image Slicer, temporarily leaving the dialog box so he could turn on the hidden layer that would be the Mouse "on" state (when the cursor is over the button). He reopened the Image Slicer, selected the slice he wanted to export for the mouse "on" state and repeated the process he had used for the "off" state, but this time, he chose the Mouse over button in the Export Settings box. Painter saved the images and generated the JavaScript and the HTML.

For the final Home page, Barbante substituted a GIF animation for the "on" state image (the black screen). After slicing the image and creating the JavaScript rollover, he noted the exact pixel dimensions of the mouse-over slice in the Image Slicer. He made a frame stack in Painter with five

frames (featuring his illustration portfolio) using the exact dimensions of the efolio screen with the light bulb. He exported a copy of the frame stack as a GIF animation and gave it the exact name of the "on" image so the HTML would replace it in the Home page. The rollover displays the animated GIF when the cursor is placed over it. (For more information about using the Image Slicer tools in Painter 8, refer to the Painter 8 User Guide.)

■ When **Karen Dodds** was looking for something lively and hip for the launch of a Web site Dodds Design had developed for *Nicole's Shoes*, she commissioned **Susan LeVan** of LeVan/Barbee Studio to create a series of colorful on-off buttons.

LeVan began by choosing a saturated color palette from Painter's default color set, including warm oranges and yellows, accented by blues and greens. (Painter's default color set is composed of Web-safe colors.) LeVan applied colorful textures to the backgrounds using a variety of favorite textures from earlier versions of Painter (such as the Simple Textures library from the Painter 7, CD_2 CD-ROM). She applied the textures with Effects, Surface Control, Color Overlay, Using Paper and Hiding Power. LeVan drew the shoes, flower and face with the Scratchboard Tool variant of Pens. For the abstract elements, she drew shapes using the Pen tool (Toolbox) and filled the shapes with color. When she was satisfied with the arrangement of colored shapes, she merged the layers by selecting their names in the Layers palette and Grouping them, by clicking the Layer Commands button at the bottom of the palette, choosing Group from the menu and then choosing Collapse. To finish, she set the layer's Composite method to Gel.

■ Designer and artist **Debi Lee Mandel** created *DT-Car* and *DT-Space* (top), two proposed animated banners for the DigitalThink Web site (left), and two screens for the DuraFlame Web site, entitled *Campsite* (bottom).

Mandel began the banner animations by drawing the elements (the cars and buildings in *DT-Car* and the rocketship and planets in *DT-Space)* using the Pens variants, custom variants from the Oils category and Painter's frame stacks, finally adding the type with the Text tool.

For *Campsite*, she began by sketching in Painter with a custom "indigo-color crayon" (based on the Waxy Crayon variant) on a black background. Mandel began by painting elements for the animations (the comet and fire) using Painter's frame stacks. When she was pleased with the progression, she saved each frame stack as a GIF animation. After completing the crayon drawing, Mandel painted crisp-edged brushstrokes using flat color. To build up deep color saturation, she used custom variants from the Oils category with oval-shaped tips for a calligraphic feel.

■ While working as the consulting Content Architect and Creative Director for the *TechView Consulting, Inc.* Web site, **Mario Henri Chakkour, AIA** used Painter to transform the original company logo into an image that looked like it had been drawn on a chalkboard.

He began the illustration by making a pencil drawing based on the already-existing company logo, using conventional pencil and paper. Then he scanned the drawing and opened the scan in Painter. Using the Effects, Tonal Control, Correct Colors, Curve dialog box, he adjusted the tonal range to bring out the texture of the pencil on paper and to "reverse" the values. After clicking OK to accept, he painted on the image. For

instance, to "stain" the illustration with color, he used the Felt Marker variant of Felt Pens, with which he could apply transparent color that would darken down to black. He also used the Eraser and Darkener variants of the Erasers to manipulate the values. Then, he added brushstrokes drawn with the Sharp Chalk variant of Chalks.

To create the animated glows, Chakkour selected and copied tiny pieces from the image and noted the coordinates of each piece, using the width and height measurements in the Info palette when he made each selection. Then he pasted the selection contents into a new file, by choosing Edit, Paste Into New Image and saved the images as numbered PICT files.

He opened them in Adobe After Effects, where he applied a Lens Flare filter over the Timeline. Then he saved a copy of the animation, as a series of numbered PICT files, again in After Effects.

When the main image was complete, Chakkour saved it in Painter as a TIFF file, which he opened in Adobe Image Ready. In that program, he saved it as a JPEG file for export into a Web page editor. He also opened the PICT files for the animation in Image Ready and pasted each PICT into a frame, optimized the timing and color, and then saved it as a GIF animation. When all of the graphic elements were complete, he assembled the page in Macromedia Dreamweaver.

■ **Judy Miller** developed the interface for the Flash-based Web site *ForGET REALity Multimedia* using Painter. After the interface was built, she exported the files to Macromedia Fireworks to optimize them, then to Flash and Dreamweaver, where she assembled the site.

Miller imported the pillar shapes (which she had drawn in Adobe Illustrator) into Painter by choosing File, Acquire, Adobe Illustrator File. She converted all of the shapes into masks because she knew that she would need to load them numerous times as selections while she was painting the pillars. To convert each shape, she chose it in the Layers palette and chose Shapes, Convert to Selection. Then she saved the selection as a new mask by choosing Select, Save Selection. (See Chapter 4 "Selections, Shapes and Masks" for more about working with masks.)

The pillars were built using several layers. After adding a new layer (click the right triangle on the Layers palette and choose New Layer from the menu), she loaded a selection for the pillars (Select, Load Selection) and filled the active selection with a custom stone pattern (Effects, Fill, Fill With Pattern). Then she blocked in the base colors with the Fine Wheel

Airbrush variant of Airbrushes using rich browns and black. So that she could efficiently paint inside and outside of the selections as she worked, she used the Draw Outside and Draw Inside buttons on the lower left of the Painter window. To paint the very fine details, she sized the Airbrush to a tiny size using the Size slider on the Property Bar, continually adjusting the size of the Airbrush as she worked.

Miller wanted to create a richer layering of color, so she added another new layer and airbrushed varied colors including rose and moss green. She set the Composite Method of this layer to Gel in the Layers palette. Then using the Opacity slider on the Layers palette, she reduced its Opacity to 35%. Finally, Miller added yet another layer on top and using a pale blue, she carefully painted reflected light along the left sides of both pillars.

The central "backdrop" began as a photo of clouds taken by Miller with a digital camera from an airplane window. To add it to her design, she opened the source file, and copied and pasted the cloud image onto a layer in the interface composite file. Then she clicked on the new cloud layer and dragged it under the pillars layers in the Layers palette list, and

carefully positioned it using the Layer Adjuster. Next, she added a new layer directly above the clouds layer and using the Digital Airbrush and black color, she painted a dark shadow along the top of the clouds image and along the inside of the left-hand pillar to help the clouds recede into the design. She also added a very slight white highlight along the inside of the right pillar. She saved the image as a RIFF file in her Painter archive in case she needed to make changes later. Then she saved a copy as a Photoshop file for import into Fireworks.

In Fireworks, Miller added the company's logo graphics and type and used the program's slicing tools to segment the interface and to optimize the graphics. The final sliced file was saved as a PNG for import into Flash, where the logo was animated. Then the Flash movie was brought into Dreamweaver, where a new page was created with a frame set in order to house the Flash movie in the center of the page, regardless of screen resolution. This was used as an alternative to having the entire Flash movie open in a pop-up window the dimensions of the Flash movie.

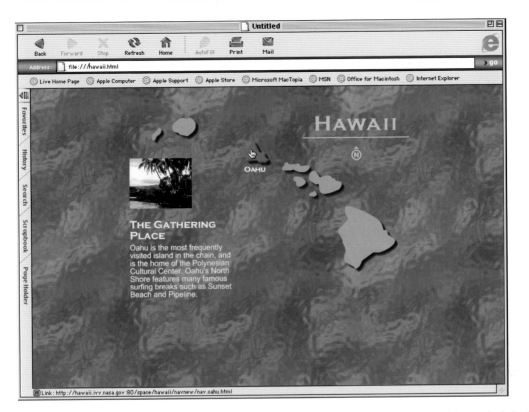

Link: http://hawaii.ivv.nasa.gov:80/space/hawaii/navnew/nav.oahu.html

■ **Shawn Grunberger** created this interactive map of *Hawaii* using Painter's Natural Media tools and effects. He used Painter's Image Slicer plug-in to divide the image into pieces that he could export from Painter with JavaScript rollovers. Because the irregularly shaped islands would be shown over a tiling background, he created two masks to achieve the transparency for each state. Grunberger opened the Painter RIFF file that contained the map elements. When making the file, he had saved two versions of the island images as two layer groups—"Islands On" and "Islands Off." The island name text labels were also organized in a layer group. Other elements were on separate layers. (For information about layer groups, turn to "Using Groups" in the beginning of Chapter 5.)

Before creating any slices, Grunberger set the File Type menu in the Image Slicer dialog box to "No export." Since all new slices inherit the settings of the first slice, this meant that all slices in the image would be set to "No Export" by default. He planned to export only the slices of the image that contained the islands and thus would have two different versions. Since most of the slices were open areas of the ocean, they wouldn't be exported, so using the "No Export" setting saved some time later. (Instead, the open ocean would be filled with a tiled background that would be tiled in the browser, which would make the total size of the page and graphics smaller.) While Grunberger was setting up

the image slices, he also adjusted the position of the text captions, which had to fit within the slice boundaries.

To make a slice for the area with the four small closely associated islands, Grunberger selected and grouped them to create a single slice. (Grouping makes a single larger slice from multiple smaller slices in the grid.) To group the slices for the small islands, he chose the Select tool in the Image Slicer dialog box, clicked on the top left slice in the area he wanted to group and dragged the tool to the right and down to create a rectangular shape around the cels he wanted to combine. Later, he would make a separate image map for this area so it could include a hot spot for each island. He also grouped the large areas of the ocean that did not contain islands since they would not be exported at all.

When all of the slices were in place, he tested the HTML export of the sliced image table. In the Image Slicer dialog box, Grunberger set Rollover State to No Rollover for this test, because he wanted to check the image slice table in a browser before adding the complexity of rollover effects to the HTML code. Once he had exported the slices, Grunberger opened the HTML page in a browser. Now that the slices were ready, back in Painter, Grunberger set the final Image Slicer export. He set each of the island slices to GIF file type with 32 colors, as he had for the test, but this time with transparency. In the GIF Options dialog box he panned the

Preview window to check the GIF Output Preview; the Preview revealed that the transparency worked correctly. He also set each of the island slices to a two-state rollover (Mouse over-out), and gave each island a URL pointing to the island's page on a NASA Web site. To export the images and code for two-state JavaScript rollovers, Grunberger did two separate export operations, one for each rollover state. (For more about exporting, see page 361.) When the settings were complete, he clicked OK and loaded the new HTML page into a browser to test, again. The map test was successful, but as exported from Painter, the map page didn't have a designated background color or background image. To add these instructions, Grunberger opened the HTML file in a text editor and modified the <body> tag to incorporate a tile (oceantile.jpg) he had designed and stored in the HTML folder. The process of applying a single tile using the browser's tiling function offers flexibility (the browser window can be resized to fill a large screen, with the ocean tiles covering the entire area). To complete this phase of the map production, Grunberger wrapped the HTML table in a <center> tag. This HTML tag ensured the map would always appear in the horizontal center of the page, regardless of the browser window size. The finished interactive map of Hawaii can be seen on the Web (http://www.peachpit.com/ wow/painter/map/part3.1/hawaii.html).

PRINTING
AND
ARCHIVAL
CONCERNS

Wise Woman is a part of the series
Journey of the Spirit *by Dorothy Simpson
Krause. The image was printed on the
Roland HiFi Jet on Concord paper using
the Roland six-color pigmented ink set. The
35 x 28-inch print was printed in an edition of 20, coated with encaustic (beeswax)
and rubbed with pearlescent pigment.*

PAINTER AND CMYK TIFFS

Painter can open CMYK TIFF files,
but in doing so, it converts them to
RGB, Painter's native color space.
You can also save a CMYK TIFF
from Painter by choosing File, Save
As, selecting TIFF from the Format
menu and then clicking the CMYK
button in the Export Options box.

HOW WILL YOU PRESENT YOUR PAINTER ARTWORK to the world? Will it
be as a limited-edition digital painting, printed on archival paper by a
print studio or service bureau, then matted, framed, and hung on a
gallery wall? Or as an illustration in a magazine, where it's part of a
page layout that's output direct-to-plate, to be printed on an offset
press? Or as a desktop color print? Or as part of a slide show? For each
of these and other output options, there are things you can do to prepare your Painter file so the output process runs smoothly. We hope
the tips that follow will help you as you plan your own project.

COLOR FOR COMMERCIAL PRINTING

Most types of printing involve the use of four-color process, or CMYK
(cyan, magenta, yellow, black) inks and dyes. Painter's native color
mode is RGB (red, green, blue), which has a larger color *gamut*
(range of colors) than the CMYK color model. (An illustration that
compares RGB and CMYK color gamuts is on page 8 in Chapter 1.)
Although Painter doesn't let you specify CMYK color mixes as
Adobe Photoshop and some other programs do, it does allow you
to work in Output Preview mode, using only those colors within
the RGB gamut that are realizable in CMYK. You can also output
CMYK TIFF and EPS files for color separation directly from Painter.

Using Color Management. Before you turn a file over for output in a form that will be used for CMYK printing, consider using
Color Management with Output Preview. With this system you
can set up a monitor-to-printer calibration loop that will allow
you to see an on-screen approximation of how your printed image
will look. (A word of caution: There are many variables besides the
RGB-to-CMYK conversion that will affect how a color print will
look—for instance, the color cast of your particular monitor and

Many illustrators prefer to have control over the prepress process by ordering their own four-color film of their illustration files that will be printed on a four-color press. Rather than an electronic file, they deliver the film separations and a laminated proof to the client. When ordering the film, check with the operator who will be doing the *output*, to find out the correct setup for the equipment that will output your job.

Click the Color Correction icon to toggle between RGB and the Output Preview.

Settings for Color Management to soft proof an image from our system. Internal RGB: Adobe RGB 1998, output profile: US Sheetfed Coated, monitor profile: Apple Cinema Display.

When you're preparing files to be printed on an offset press, ask what line screen will be used for printing so you can begin your file with a high enough resolution (ppi) to accommodate it. A factor of 1.5 to 2 times the line screen is typical. For example, to accommodate a 150-line screen, set up your file with the dimensions you need at a resolution of 225 to 300 ppi.

the color of your paper. Output Preview doesn't account for these factors.) Begin by choosing Canvas, Color Management to open the Color Management dialog box. In the dialog box, choose an Internal RGB color space, a Monitor Profile and an Output Profile depending on whether you'll be outputting to separations or to a composite printer in your studio such as an Epson 2200. When you perform a Painter Easy Installation, the program automatically installs a selection of Color Profiles into the Painter 8 application folder. You'll find more profiles in the Color Profiles folder on the Painter 8 CD 2 CD-ROM. (If you don't see your monitor or printer profile in the list, it can often be obtained from the manufacturer.) To add profiles to your system, copy them from the Painter 8 CD 2 CD-ROM to the following location: Macintosh OS X/Applications/Corel Painter 8/Color Profiles, and change the suffix from .icc to .cc. Windows users should copy profiles into the Windows\Color folder.

To toggle between the broader-gamut RGB image and the Output Preview, click the Color Correction icon above the right scroll bar. Remember to change the Color Management settings if you plan to print to another device. For more information about Painter's color management tools see "Making an Archival Desktop Print" late in this chapter and "Color Management," in the *Painter 8 User Guide*.

Making CMYK conversions in another program. Some Painter artists prefer to work in the broader RGB color gamut and convert their finished images to CMYK in another imaging program such as Photoshop or Equilibrium DeBabelizer, because these programs allow more control of how the conversion is made. There are several good resources that give detailed explanations of color conversion using Photoshop, including the *Adobe Photoshop User Guide* and *The Photoshop 7 Wow! Book* and *Photoshop in 4 Colors* (these last two are from Peachpit Press). Some printing studios—for example, Cone Editions—prefer to receive RGB files from artists and make the conversion themselves using custom color tables they create in Photoshop especially for that image. (See "Making a Fine Art Master Print" on page 376 for an explanation of Cone Editions' process.) Check with your printer to work out a conversion method.

Using Color Management provides a preview only, and makes no permanent changes to the file. To include an embedded ICC profile in a saved file (so the file will look the same when viewed in another programs), choose Canvas, Color Management and in the Color Management dialog box, click the Import/Export icon (the page), and choose a profile in the Advanced Import/Export dialog box.

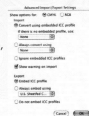

The Advanced Import/Export Settings dialog box with a profile chosen for export

Detail of Winter/Spring, *by Pamela Wells. When making the fine art print of her image, Wells calibrated her computer system to the profile of the Iris inkjet printer at the service bureau she planned to send it to. Turn to page 316 in Chapter 9 to view the entire image.*

Bonny Lhotka created the digital file for Day Job *in Painter, by painting with brushes and using layers to composite several source files. Before printing the digital image, Lhotka prepared a one-of-a-kind surface using gold-and-ochre-colored acrylics. She painted an abstract design on a nonporous surface to create a monotype that she could transfer to a piece of rag paper using a large roller. After drying and coating the surface of the monoprint with inkjet receiver to help it absorb the ink, she printed the image on top of it using an Encad NovaJet 3. A photograph of the final print is shown above.*

FINE ART PRINTING AT A SERVICE BUREAU

Many artists prefer to choose a service bureau or master printer who specializes in output for fine art printmaking. Rather than attempt to print an edition in their studio, they rely on fine art service bureaus for high-quality equipment—for instance, an Iris inkjet printer is not affordable for most artists. (Iris prints are accepted by many galleries and museums; they are no longer thought of as "experimental prints.") The expertise needed for a fine art print studio differs greatly from that of a commercial service bureau accustomed to making film and proofs for offset printing. Choose a printer who has experience working with artists and who understands archival and editioning issues. (See Appendix C for a list of service bureaus that specialize in working with artists.)

Printing digital watercolors with the Iris. Iris printers are special inkjet machines capable of producing images with luminous color and no visible dot, making the output desirable for fine art printmaking. The Iris sprays water-based CMYK dyes or pigment-based inks (similar to watercolors) through four extremely narrow nozzles. The paper or other substrate is taped to a rotating drum in the machine and sprayed with millions of droplets per second. Many fine art printers modify the Iris 3047 (the largest of the Iris printer line) so it can handle thicker substrates. Cone Editions and Nash Editions were among the first printers to pioneer this technique; they moved back the printing heads, allowing 400-lb. watercolor paper, canvas or metal to be taped onto the drum.

More large-format inkjet printers. Many more excellent choices are available for the artist who wants to order high-quality archival large-format prints of their work from bureaus. Some service bureaus offer prints from the Hewlett-Packard DesignJet 5500 CP series using the CP UV six-color archival ink set. These 1200 x 600 dpi printers can accept rolled watercolor paper and canvas and the largest model can print up to 60 inches wide. With these printers, sometimes images with very light, graduated tones can produce areas with tiny dots in a dither or scatter pattern. Printing on canvas can help hide these dots. Wilhelm Imaging Research Inc. reports that the HP DesignJet CP ink systems' UV inks will hold true color for 150+ years.

High-quality prints from large-format Epson printers are also available from some service bureaus. The Epson 7600 (24 inches wide) and the 9600 and 10600 (both 44 inches wide) are 1440 dpi inkjet printers that use six-color archival inks. They're capable of producing prints on a wide variety of media, including paper, canvas and posterboard with a thickness of up to 1.5 mm.

Large, high-quality prints from Roland printers are also available at service bureaus. The Roland HiFi or Pro V8 has a resolution of 1440 dpi and uses an eight-color archival ink set. The largest model can accommodate media widths to 64 inches.

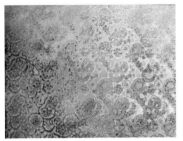

Robert Manning of Supersample Corporation / Lilika Productions designed this scarf using Painter's brushes, special effects and pattern features. Then the image was printed on cotton twill fabric with a twelve-color Colorspan inkjet printer using Fiber Reactive dyes.

Colorspan offers several large-format printers, even a model specifically designed to print fabric. There are three models that can be used for fine art printing that accommodate media up to 72 inches wide and up to 3mm thick. The printers use either a set of eight-color or twelve-color light-fast dye inks.

Outputting to a digital positive. Major advances have been made in the area of direct digital photographic prints. In general, the three printing methods discussed below use a laser to image the digital file onto a photographic substrate.

Prints made from the Fujix Pictrography 5000 (up to 12 x 18 inches) offer better registration and permanency and more natural color than a dye-sublimation print such as the Kodak XL7700 or 3M Rainbow. The Fujix uses a laser to image the digital file onto a "donor" sheet, which is then printed onto photographic paper using a single-pass, silver-halide printing process. The appearance and permanency (about 20 years) of the Fujix are similar to those of a photographic Cibachrome (C-print). Prints can be laminated with a coating that includes an ultraviolet inhibitor, extending their life further. Additionally, the Noritsu 2701 produces high-quality Cibachrome-like prints up to 12 x 18 inches.

The Cymbolic Sciences Lightjet 5000 also uses a laser, imaging the digital file to large-format archival photo paper and creating a continuous-tone print without visible dots, as large as 48 x 96 inches. Because the Lightjet 5000 uses 36-bit RGB color, the broad color gamut in these prints is comparable to that in photographic "R" prints. To prepare Painter files for the LightJet 5000, set up your file at its final output size, using a resolution of 150–200 ppi and save it as an uncompressed RGB TIFF file. The LightJet's software incorporates an interpolation algorithm that makes it possible to increase the resolution of the image while retaining its sharpness. Artist and photographer Phillip Charris often outputs his Painter-enhanced photographs using a Lightjet 5000, then carefully strips the print from its backing paper and mounts it on canvas.

To check color and detail before printing on a Hewlett-Packard 2500CP with archival UV inks, Cher Threinen-Pendarvis proofed Forked Path *as an 8 x 10-inch Fujix Pictrography print. (Fujix Pictrography prints are described in "Outputting to a Digital Positive" on this page.) The final print was made at 15 x 17 inches on Arches cold-pressed watercolor paper and framed with UV-protective glass.*

Another recommended photo-slick, archival printmaking method is the Durst Lamda system. (Using a laser, it images to archival photo media, such as paper, color negative media or color reversal media.) It's also a 36-bit RGB system. The Durst Lamda 76 can print seamless 32-inch-wide images up to 164 feet long. Durst Lamda prints are reported to be lightfast for a minimum of 50 years. Some artists strip the prints, mount them on canvas, then finish them with glazes of UV-protectant varnish (such as Golden Varnish, described on page 367) to protect the print from humidity and to add a hand-finished look.

PHOTOGRAPHIC IMAGING OPTIONS

Many new technologies are available for Painter output at graphic arts service bureaus and photo labs that use digital equipment.

John Derry printed Capitola, *shown here as a detail, on an Epson 1270 six-color printer using Epson's archival ink set.*

Imaging to transparencies using a film recorder. Small- and large-format film recorders are used to image digital files such as Painter artwork to transparencies ranging from 35mm to 16 x 20 inches. For output via a film recorder, images should be in landscape orientation (horizontal) to take advantage of the width of the film.

To avoid *pixelation* (a jaggy, stair-step look caused by lack of sufficient resolution) on transparencies generated by a service bureau's film recorder, here are some guidelines from Chrome Digital and Photodyne (San Diego) for creating or sizing your files. Most professional-quality 35mm film recorders (such as the Solitaire 16 series) use a minimum resolution of 4,000 lines; for this resolution, your image should be 4,096 x 2,732 pixels (about 32 MB). The minimum resolution for 4 x 5-inch transparencies is 8,000 lines, requiring an 8,192 x 5,464-pixel (approximately 165 MB) file. For even more crispness, devices such as the Solitaire 16XPS will image at a resolution of 16,000 lines (a 16,384 x 10,928-pixel file, of approximately 512 MB). Two powerful film recorders used to create 4 x 5-inch, 8 x 10-inch and larger-format transparencies are the LVT (from Light Valve Technology, a subsidiary of Kodak) and the Lightjet 2080 (from Cymbolic Sciences, Inc.) Plan to create huge images (up to 15,000 x 18,000 pixels and approximately 800 MB) to take full advantage of the resolution capabilities of these machines.

Printing your images as Fujichrome. For fine art images, Fujichrome prints made from transparencies offer excellent detail and saturated color, and can be ordered with a high gloss. Prints can be made from 35mm slides or 4 x 5-inch transparencies. To print to the maximum size of 20 x 24 inches, a 4 x 5 transparency is recommended. The permanency of the Fuji print is 40–50 years, and this can be extended by adding a lamination with an ultraviolet inhibitor. Diane Fenster, a noted fine artist and photographer, produces much of her digital work as large-format Fujichrome prints.

FINE ART PRINTING IN THE STUDIO

Today, many exciting alternatives are available for artists who want to proof their images, or make fine art prints in their own studio using archival ink sets and papers.

Printing digital images with desktop printers. Desktop inkjet printers can deliver beautiful color prints if they are set up properly. The affordable HP printers (such as the 1220c) and the Epson Stylus series (the 1280, for instance) are great printers not only for pulling test prints before sending images to an Iris, but also for experimental fine art prints. Most inkjet inks are water-soluble, so you can try painting into a print with a wet brush. There are a few exceptions, and the Epson 2200 is one. It ships with a seven-color ultrachrome pigmented inkset and it produces water resistant prints, especially when used with Epson's Enhanced Matte or Velvet Fine Art paper. These prints will accept

Detail of Indigo, *an experimental Fresco print by Bonny Lhotka. To view the entire image, turn to page 383 in the gallery.*

PAPER-AND-INK COMBOS

The correct paper-and-ink combination can contribute to the greater longevity of your prints. Check out Henry Wilhelm's Web site, www.wilhelm-research.com, for suggested paper-and-ink combinations.

Sometimes Philip Howe uses his digital paintings as templates for oil painting, as he did here for Profile. *Howe printed the digital painting onto canvas using an HP 2500 CP printer and archival inks. Then he painted over the entire image with oil paint. To see another of Howe's paintings using this technique, turn to the gallery on page 379.*

acrylic paint without smearing or running. Most desktop printers work best with slick paper, but archival-quality cotton papers produce excellent results on some machines. For example, the Epson 1520 and 3000 print on thicker acid-free papers, either the new enhanced art papers or traditional drawing or printmaking papers, if you feed the paper manually.

New inks and substrates for desktop art prints. With the increased interest in desktop art-making, new inks and papers keep coming out. Henry Wilhelm has done important research regarding the longevity of different ink and substrate combinations. A comparison of color gamut and longevity with the different inks is available through Wilhelm Imaging Research, Inc., on the Web at www.wilhelm-research.com.

New inks with better longevity and waterproof characteristics are becoming available for many inkjet printers. For information about products for use with the Hewlett-Packard printers, check out www.hp.com; for information about Epson products, visit its company Web site at www.epson.com. Also, InkJet Mall (a sister company of Cone Editions) is another good resource for information and you can buy sets of archival inks (such as Generation Enhanced Micro Bright Pigmented Inks) for several desktop printers; it's found on the Web at www.inkjetmall.com. Several other companies offer new archival inks sets for desktop printers. One is Media Street, offering Generations Inks, among many other products, found on the Web at www.mediastreet.com. Another source is MIS ink, which manufactures and sell its own archival pigmented inks, as well as its own set of ultra chrome pigmented inks for many of the Epson printers, on the Web at www.inksupply.com.

Several traditional art papers are now manufactured for digital printmaking—for instance, Somerset Enhanced, Concorde Rag, Hahnemuehle's German Etching 310 and Orwell, all available from Cone Editions' Ink Jet Mall. And there are many canvases available for use with inkjet printers. For instance, check out the artist-grade canvases available from Sentinel Imaging, located on the Web at www.inkjet.com, and the pure-white artist-grade canvas from Dr. Graphix Inc. at www.drgraphix.com.

Inkjet receivers and protective coatings. To seal custom substrates (like handmade papers), so the ink will hold better, paint thin rabbit skin glue on to the substrate with a brush and dry it thoroughly. Then make your print.

You can treat prints yourself so the color will last much longer. Several protective coatings are available at your local art supply store, from Daniel Smith via mail order, or from Media Street on the Web at www.mediastreet.com. One of our favorites is Golden MSA Varnish with UVLS (soluble with mineral spirits). Use a protective respirator and gloves for the process because the fumes from this coating are *very* toxic. To minimize contact with dangerous

Flint, *by Dorothy Simpson Krause, includes elements collected during a journey to Tibet. After the collage was complete, Krause prepared the surface of the substrate (dimensionally stable spunbond polyester) for printing by painting it with Golden Molding Paste. When the surface was dry, she added a coat of gel medium mixed with pearlescent pigment. To provide a receiver for the inks, she painted the substrate with rabbit skin glue, dried it, then compressed it by running it though a Coda laminator. The final print was made on a Roland HiFi using the Roland pigmented six-color inks.*

airborne particles, dilute the varnish and apply it with a brush. Golden Varnish is also available in a spray can, as is Krylon UV Protectant spray. Make sure to use a protective respirator when using the spray varnishes.

Caring for prints. After a UV-protective coating has been applied, treat your print as you would a watercolor and avoid displaying it in direct sunlight. Frame it using UV-resistant glazing (glass or Plexiglas) and preserve air space between the surface of the print and the glazing.

EXPERIMENTAL PRINTMAKING

In today's world of experimental printmaking, anything goes if it works with your vision of the image you're printing. For instance, many different substrates can be used successfully with inkjet printers; among the favorites are archival-quality papers with a high cotton content. Browse your local art store for Saunders handmade watercolor paper, Arches hot-press and cold-press watercolor paper, Rives BFK printmaking papers, and Canson drawing and charcoal papers. You can hand-feed these papers into a studio desktop printer, or request that a fine art print studio create an Iris print with paper that you supply. Fine art print studios often keep special papers in stock—Cone Editions, for instance, has hundreds of fine art papers on hand. Some print studios also print on canvas, film or metal.

Mixing media. Prints from an Iris or another inkjet printer can be modified with traditional tools and fine art printing processes, such as embossing, intaglio and silkscreen. (Turn to page 370 to read about Carol Benioff's technique of overprinting a copperplate etching on top of an Iris print.) If you plan to hand-work an inkjet print with media such as pastels, pencils or oil paint, make the print on rag paper with enough body to hold together when you apply the traditional media to the print. Arches 140-pound watercolor paper and Rives heavyweight printmaking paper are good choices.

DIFFERENTIAL AGING

If you plan to add another medium (such as acrylic or pastel) to a digital print, keep in mind that different pigments and dyes can age at different rates. So the strokes you carefully hand-work into the print may begin to stand out over time.

Making Translite transfers. The Translite transfer technique was pioneered by Jon Cone. First, a digital image is printed onto Translite film using an Iris printer. Then a piece of archival-quality paper (such as Rives BFK) is soaked in water, and when it is partially dry, the image is transferred from the Translite "plate" onto the dampened printmaking paper using an embossing press—producing a monoprint with softly graduated color.

Bonny Lhotka creates a flexible waterproof decal using artist gloss acrylic medium and inkAID™ White Matte Precoat which will be removed from a polypropylene carrier sheet printed on the Encad 880 with GO pigment inks. Other printers like the Epson 7500, 7600, 9500, and 9600, 10600, Roland and Mutoh, can be used for this process if the polypropylene plate is thin enough. The decal can be glued to canvas, paper or wood using acrylic gel medium. The surface can be sealed with acrylic medium.

Overprinting a digital file onto a monotype. To create a surface that she would later use for printing *Day Job* (shown on page 364), Bonny Lhotka created a one-of-a-kind monotype "plate" by applying acrylic paint onto prepared acetate. She laid a piece of rag paper onto the "plate" and used a custom-made 40-lb. roller to transfer the painted image onto the paper. After transferring, she lifted the paper off the "plate" and allowed it to dry. Then she used a Novajet inkjet printer to overprint the digital file on top of the monoprint. She believes that the overprinting process produces a broader range of color than is possible if the entire image is composed and printed digitally. The result is a print with more depth.

FINE ART EDITIONS FROM DIGITAL FILES

Some artists scan finished, traditionally created artwork and then print it on an Iris or another high-quality printer (such as an Epson 7600 or a Roland HiFi). This process is actually *replicating* an original piece of work. However, when artwork *originates* as a digital file—using a program such as Painter—and is then output to a high-quality printer using an archival ink set, that print itself becomes an original. (Think of your Painter image as a kind of "digital printing plate" stored in your computer.)

Advantages of digital editions. Printing a digital edition has advantages over traditional, limited-run printing methods. Any number of multiple originals can be made from a digital file without loss of quality: The "digital plate" won't deteriorate. Also, the setup charge for the digital process is usually much less than when an edition is printed conventionally. And while an edition printed with traditional methods needs to be printed all at once, with digital editions, an artist may request prints from the fine art service bureau as needed.

CERTIFICATE OF AUTHEN
Title **Swimmers 2**
Image Size **12 x 18"**   Edition # **2/50**
Edition Size **50**   Artist Proofs **5**
Date Created **July 1, 1995**   Date Purchased **July 14,**
Art Media **Iris print on Rives BFK**
Uniqueness of this Print **This print is hand-worked with pe**
Artist
The above information contains all the information pertaining to this Edition. As... or watercolor, do not display this artwork in direct sunlight. Frame it under UF3 pla...

Detail of a sample certificate of authenticity. You'll find a PageMaker 6.5 file and a PDF of this sample certificate on the Painter 8 Wow! CD-ROM.

Planning an edition. An edition should be carefully tracked and controlled, just as it would be if printed with traditional methods. It's wise to make a contract between the master printer and artist, stating the type of edition, the number of prints in the edition and that no more prints will be made. When an original is sold, the artist should give the buyer a certificate of authenticity that contains the name of the artist and the print, the date sold, the edition size, the print number, the number of artist proofs, the substrate, and any details of hand-working done on the print. Once the edition is complete, the artist should destroy the digital file, just as the screen would be destroyed after a silkscreen edition. (See "Making a Fine Art Master Print" on page 374.) 🦉

Combining Digital and Intaglio Printmaking

Overview *Make a print using a traditional printmaking method; scan the print; use the scan as a guide to create a colored image in Painter; output the digital file to an Iris printer; overprint the traditional print on top of the Iris print in register.*

CAROL BENIOFF

1a

Photograph of the etched copperplate. The composition is created in reverse.

1b

Grayscale scan of the black-and-white intaglio print

CAROL BENIOFF'S INNOVATIVE PRINTMAKING method combines classic intaglio techniques with digital printing. An award-winning fine artist and illustrator, she has illustrated for magazines such as *Atlantic Monthly* and *Parenting*, and her work appears in the *CA Illustration Annual*. Currently she works at Kala Art Institute, a traditional and digital printmaking studio and gallery in Berkeley, California that has been in existence for over thirty years. To create *The Game*, a portfolio piece, Benioff overprinted a copperplate etching on top of an Iris inkjet print made on Hahnemuhle Copperplate printmaking paper.

1 Making an intaglio print. Benioff planned the 6 x 7-inch copperplate knowing that she would be adding color and depth with imagery created in Painter. Using primarily a hard ground etching technique, she etched fine lines with a fine-point carbide tipped stylus. When making a classic hard ground etching, an artist scribes lines into an acid-resistant coating, exposing the metal underneath. Then the plate is soaked in a acid bath to etch the drawing deeper into the plate. The acid-etched lines hold the ink, yielding warm, velvety black lines when printed.

Benioff rolled black ink onto the plate, working it into the lines with a cardboard dauber, then rubbed off excess ink with tarlatan (starched open-weave muslin). Next, she chose a piece of archival

2

The two images: A painted landscape (left), and a watercolor tint image to match the etching (right)

3

Photograph of the Iris print composite

4a

Inking the plate (left) and making registration marks on a clear acetate sheet to help align the copperplate to the Iris print (right)

4b

After lifting the press felts on the intaglio press, Benioff carefully pulled the finished print off the copperplate.

printmaking paper and soaked it, so it would absorb the ink better. After blotting the paper till it was partially dry, she made a print using an etching press.

When the print was dry, she scanned it and saved the scan to use as a guide to help develop two color images (described in Step 2). Benioff's grayscale scan measured 2400 x 2800 pixels.

2 Creating color images and compositing. Open your scan, make a clone (File, Clone), and delete the contents of the clone (Select, All, and press the Backspace/Delete key). Now, turn on Tracing Paper (Ctrl/⌘-T). Using the scan as a guide, paint a colorful image that will complement your traditional print.

Benioff created two images: a painted landscape and a loose watercolor version of the etched composition. The landscape was designed to add dynamic tension to the composition. To begin the landscape, she sketched larger shapes with the variants of the Digital Water Color brushes, then added details with the Pastels and Oils variants. When the image was complete, she saved it for use later in the process.

To paint a second image, which would add colored tints to elements in the etching, she made a second clone of the scan, again deleting the contents. Using the scan as a guide, she painted a loose color composition with the Wash Camel variant of the Water Color brush.

Benioff merged the two color images in Painter. She opened both images and made the second image active, then she selected the entire image, copied it and pasted it into the first image. In the Layers palette, she chose the Composite Method Multiply, so the color from the two layers mixed with each other.

3 Choosing paper for the print. To achieve a good ink impression of the copperplate, paper should be softened by dampening so that it will press into the grooves of the etched plate. This poses a problem when printing over an Iris print, because Iris prints bleed when wet. To resolve this problem, Benioff experimented extensively with different papers. She found that some very soft papers will soak through—even when you spritz the back of the paper to dampen it slightly—destroying the water-based Iris image. The paper she chose to print *The Game* (Hahnemuhle Copperplate printmaking paper) is fibrous enough to soften and swell when slightly moistened but thick enough that the dampness did not soak through to the inks on the front.

4 Overprinting the etching. After preparing the copperplate with ink, Benioff made an acetate template to register the image on the paper and plate. The elements in the Iris print needed to align perfectly with the copperplate, so she carefully traced the position of the figures and table onto the acetate. She aligned the template, the plate and the paper (Iris print) on the press bed and pulled the print.

Constructing a Lenticular Work

Overview *Build textured elements and layer them into a collage; set up multiple versions of the file for the lenticular; print the images on an inkjet printer; glaze the wood mat and embellish its surface.*

BONNY LHOTKA

The handmade paper, the letterpress type block with the radio tower image and the tray filled with "lava"

The lava and paper elements with the Apply Surface Texture emboss added

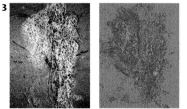

An impression of the photo of sand and foam was embossed into the working image.

"A LENTICULAR IMAGE SUSPENDS TIME, space and movement. It adds a level of ambiguity that engages the viewer's attention," says artist Bonny Lhotka. (A lenticular image is actually several images sliced into strips and alternated. A plastic sheet with a series of parallel lens strips, or lenticules, embossed into one surface is applied over the assemblage, so the different images are seen one at a time, as a viewer moves past the artwork.) To create *Ancient Echo*, Lhotka scanned elements, applied textural effects, then composited the source files into a collage. To build the lenticular, she created eleven variations of the file. As a viewer walks past *Ancient Echo*, the central portion of the image turns to black. At the same time, the background rotates through a rainbow of color shifts and the lower portion appears to recede. You may want to loosely follow Lhotka's process and also experiment with your own effects.

1 Preparing the source images. Lhotka chose squares of painted handmade paper from an earlier project, and a letterpress type block with a radio tower image. For one of the background layers, she built a surface using modeling paste and painted it with acrylics to look like lava. Lhotka scanned and touched up the source images. She created the rings in Painter and colored them with a gradient. To give the rings wire-like dimension, she used Glass Distortion.

2 Adding texture to elements. Lhotka likes to emulate the look of handmade paper, using Painter's Apply Surface Texture feature. For this work, she embossed several elements (including the lava and paper elements) with Apply Surface Texture Using Image Luminance and subtle settings.

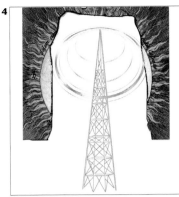

The composite in progress

Printing the images

6a

Preparing the transfer board

6b

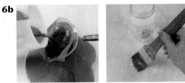

Mixing the gel and applying it to the board

7

Preparing to transfer the mat print

8

Burning the mat surface to crackle the glaze

3 Giving the colored fields texture. She wanted to add texture to more colored areas in the image. So she opened an original photo of beach sand and used Apply Surface Texture, Using Original Luminance to emboss the pattern of the foam and sand into her image. To ensure that the emboss effect will apply to your entire image, choose as your clone source an image with the same pixel dimensions as your working file. Make the image that you want to emboss active, target a layer you want to emboss and designate the clone source by choosing File, Clone Source. Choose Effects, Surface Control, Apply Surface Texture, Using Original Luminance.

4 Assembling the composite. After all of the elements were embossed with Apply Surface Texture, Lhotka copied and pasted the elements into Photoshop, where she completed the composite. After the image was finished, she created eleven different color variations of the central portion of the file, which would become the lenticular.

5 Processing and printing the lenticular. For the next step, Lhotka used SuperFlip software. Using a sophisticated mathematical formula, the software sliced the images into linear strips and reassembled them according to the specifications for the lenticular that Lhotka had chosen. When the assemblage was complete, Lhotka printed it on a Roland HiFi. The six-color printer uses a CMYKOG archival pigment set with saturated colors. After the interlaced image was printed, it was aligned with the lens.

6 Setting up a gel transfer for the glaze. When building the fine art mat for the lenticular, Lhotka chose Baltic birch. As she planned to pour liquid onto the wood, to prevent the wood from bowing, she temporarily attached a one-by-three-foot board to the back of the birch mat. To hold the liquid, she placed duct tape around the sides to make a tray. Then she made a gel: She dissolved rabbit skin glue in water, warmed it, and allowed it to return to room temperature, then added powdered pearlescent pigment to it. She used a strainer to remove undissolved colorant and large bubbles, then poured the mixture onto the wood.

7 Printing the image for the mat. Lhotka printed the image for the mat on Rexam white film. After printing, she transferred it to the gel on the wood. Placing the printed film on the gel caused the image to transfer immediately without pressure. When the gel dried, the image was permanently bonded into the wood.

8 Embellishing the surface of the mat. To give the glaze a crackled effect, Lhotka used a torch to burn the surface of the mat after it was dry. This caused the glue to bubble, creating a crackled glaze surface. The completed presentation of *Ancient Echo* measures 34 x 28 inches; the 28 x 22-inch center of the image with the 3D animated lenticular sits inside a one-half inch recession on the glazed mat board.

Making a Fine Art Master Print

Overview *Make a custom color conversion of a Painter image; choose a textured, handmade paper that will enhance the image; after a first, light printing, paint an iridescent polymer onto some areas of the print; print the image a second time; apply a UV-protective coating to the print; document the edition.*

CHER THREINEN-PENDARVIS / PRINTED BY JON CONE, CONE EDITIONS PRESS

1a

Cone at the Mac that's connected to the Iris system

1b

One of Cone's custom ink settings

JON CONE OF CONE EDITIONS PRESS has been making prints and editions for artists since 1980. In 1985, Cone Editions began using computers in printmaking, pioneering techniques such as digital gravure, digital silkscreen and various digital monotype techniques. The firm has made Iris inkjet prints since 1992 and has become a leader in printing technology, sharing methods, materials and techniques with other fine art service bureaus.

When he makes a fine art master print, Cone interprets the artist's image in a collaborative manner. Often the selection of a paper, a special color transformation or perhaps even an experimental printing method can enhance an image. Cone used all three of these to realize the Painter image above.

1 Resizing and converting the color mode. An image may need to be resized to take advantage of the Iris printer's resolution (300 dpi) and replication capabilities. The Iris achieves the look of a much higher resolution because of the way the ink sprays onto the paper. Although the optimal resolution for files that will be printed on the Iris is 300 ppi, the printer can interpolate resolutions of 150 ppi or 100 ppi to produce high-quality prints.

Cone prefers to use Adobe Photoshop for a monitor-to-output calibration loop. He has written a proprietary color transformation engine for Photoshop that he uses to convert images from RGB to CMYK. This interface also helps him calibrate the Iris, allowing the monitor to show a close approximation of the printed image. After converting this image, Cone used Photoshop's Image, Adjust, Curves

IRIS FACTS

The Iris printer's drum spins at 110 inches per second; up to 1 million droplets of ink per second are sprayed at 90 mph through each of its four nozzles. Using only cyan, magenta, yellow and black inks, it can simulate millions of colors.

Positioning the paper on the Iris drum

Carefully painting the iridescent polymer coating on the print

Drying the iridescent solution

Stopping the printer to show how the cyan, magenta, yellow and black inks are printed in sequence on the substrate

Using a silkscreen process to add a protective archival coating

dialog box to compensate for out-of-gamut blues that had been lost. (Since RGB has a broader color gamut than CMYK, out-of-gamut colors are dulled when an image is converted to CMYK.) The black plate was adjusted separately to bring out detail in the darkest areas of the image. Finally, a proprietary plug-in Iris format RIP (raster image processor) was used to save the image in a form that the Iris can use for printing.

2 Choosing a paper and setting up the Iris. Cone selected a sheet of heavy, handmade paper with a very soft, large surface grain and an exaggerated deckled edge that would complement the vivid color and lively brushstrokes in the image. He taped the paper to the drum of the Iris.

3 Printing, painting and drying. Cone used the Iris to print this particular image twice. For the first pass, he adjusted the ink tables in the Iris's RIP to print a faint version of the image. With the print still taped to the drum, Cone brushed an experimental iridescent solution (composed of titanium dioxide-coated mica and hydroscopic polymer) onto the lily only. Then he dried the hand-painted coating with a hair dryer.

4 Printing the image a second time. Cone loaded a new set of rich-printing color ink tables into the Iris's RIP and made a second printing pass. The transparent Iris inks adhered to the polymer coating on the lily as easily as they did to the uncoated paper; the iridescent polymer provided a subtle reflection, adding luminance to the lily.

5 Applying a protective coating to the print. Michael Pelletier, Systems and Production Manager for Cone Editions, applied a silkscreen coating of hindered amine light stabilizers (HALS) and ultraviolet absorbers (UVA) to the finished print. This solvent-based coating developed by Cone carries the protective additives deep into the printed image where they fully encapsulate the dyes, helping to produce what Cone Editions says is "the longest-lasting archival Iris print available today."

Documenting the edition. The artist now signs the finished print to make it the "right-to-print proof" against which future prints in the edition will be compared. After the artist has signed approval, an edition can be printed on demand while the image file is stored safely on CD-ROM at Cone Editions. A documentation sheet signed by both master printer and artist details the size of the edition, number of proofs printed, methods used and dimensions. Most importantly, it specifies that no other proofs or prints can or will be made. (After completing an edition, Cone destroys all copies of the image file.) Each print will bear a unique print identification number and will be signed and numbered in pencil by the artist.

Making an Archival Desktop Print

Overview *Create a painting using a custom color set; use color management tools for consistent viewing between Painter and Photoshop; create an ICC profile for printing with archival inks on enhanced artist paper.*

CAROL BENIOFF

1

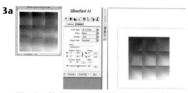

One of Benioff's custom Color Sets which she created from an image

2a

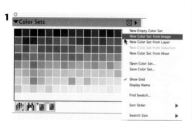

Selecting the type of calibration sensor and mode of calibration in OptiCal, a monitor calibration software made by ColorVision

2b

Selecting the monitor, curve and white point settings in OptiCal

3a

The ProfilerPlus target file as it appears on screen (left), scanning the printed Profiler Plus target file (right)

CAROL BENIOFF COMBINED AN ETCHING AND A PAINTING created in Painter with watercolor and pastel to create the powerful image *Age of the Disturbed*. She printed the final image on an Epson inkjet printer using archival inks and enhanced archival paper.

1 Painting with printable colors. To begin, Benioff loaded one of her custom color sets. (She has a variety of colors sets made from images that have printed well using a commercial offset method or on her Epson 3000.) To create your own custom color set from an image, first open the image in Painter, go to the Color Sets palette, click on the right triangle and select New Color Set from Image. A new Color Set will appear in the palette. Then click on the triangle again and choose Save Color Set, name your set and save it to the Painter 8 application folder, or wherever you like.

2 Managing color. So her monitors would display colors accurately, Benioff calibrated them using OptiCal, which includes both software and a sensor. (The calibration sets the white point, the black point, the color temperature and the dynamic range or gamma of each monitor, and then generates an ICC profile based on the calibration.) To set this up in Photoshop: Under the Photoshop menu choose Color Settings, Workspace, and select

COLOR MANAGEMENT

Color Management is part science and part art; some factors can be measured, some are subjective. CMM or Color Management Modules (ColorSync on the Macintosh, ICM on Windows) perform the calculations between the color profiles (the numerical description of the color) of your devices, such as your monitor and printer. For more information check out *Real World Color Management* by Bruce Fraser, Chris Murphy, and Fred Bunting, published by Peachpit Press.

Build Profile dialog box from ProfilerPro (left) and Save profile dialogue (right)

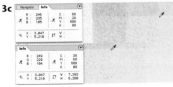

A color sample measured in Photoshop from the printed target file right after printing (top) and 24 hours later (bottom)

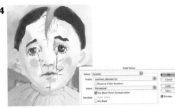

Soft-proofing the image in Photoshop using the new printing ICC profile

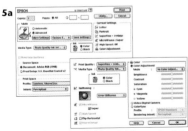

Photoshop print (left) and Advanced print (right) dialog boxes for the Epson 3000

Scan of the final print. Benioff then overprinted the etching and applied watercolor and pastel.

Adobe RGB. In Painter, (with an image open), from the Canvas menu choose Color Management and select Adobe RGB 98 under the RGB circles icon. (Adobe RGB 98 is the recommended standard internal color space.)

3 Making color profiles. For a cost-effective way to generate custom ICC printing profiles for her many combinations of ink and paper, Benioff uses ColorVision's Profiler Plus, which is a plug-in for Photoshop. To generate the ICC profile, she opened the Profiler Plus target file, and printed it using Luminos Silver Archival inks on Crane Museo enhanced paper, with the same printer driver settings she planned to use to print the final image. After letting the print dry for 24 hours, she scanned the printed target file at 300 pixels per inch, at 100% magnification and with no color correction or filters applied during the scanning. With the scanned target file open, she opened ProfilerPlus in Photoshop and selected Build Profile. The ProfilerPlus program asks you to name the ICC file and choose the destination library.

4 Making a soft proof. In Photoshop, Benioff chose Proof from the View menu, Setup and Custom, then selected her new printing profile. For Intent she picked Perceptual (use this same Intent when printing; each of the four choices have a pronounced effect on the final results), and checked Use Black Point Compensation. (This is more critical when converting from RGB color space to a CMYK.) Next, she chose Proof Colors from the View menu to view the results. The "soft" (onscreen) proof is only an approximation. Benioff recommends keeping in mind these critical factors: the effects of your lighting, ambient light, and angle of viewing on your perception of the color.

5 Printing from the desktop. Next, Benioff opened her final image in Photoshop and chose her correct page setup in the Print dialog box and these settings: For the Source Space, she selected her internal RGB space, which was Adobe RGB 98; for Print Space she selected her ICC profile for the Luminos Silver inks and Museo paper keeping the Intent as Perceptual. She selected Photo Quality Ink as her Media. Since each Media setting lays down different amounts of ink, she made test prints with different Media settings to find the one she liked best. In the Advanced Print dialog box, she selected the same settings as when she printed the profile target file, including No Color Adjustment. (If you were to enable ColorSync at the printer driver level there would be two layers of color management, distorting the final outcome.) 🖌

Here's how to set up Color Management for printing from Painter 8: With the image open choose Canvas, Color Management. Select the same internal RGB space with which you have been working. Click on the arrows from the internal RGB space to the Printer and to the Monitor icons. Select your printer and monitor ICC profiles. Click on the Plus button if you wish to save these settings. Choose your page setup, and in the print dialog, select the media type, resolution or print style. Open the dialog box where color management is enabled in your printer driver, and make sure that it is turned off.

■ Artist **Judi Moncrieff** created *Traditions* (above) and *Generations* (right), two works in her series called *First Nation*, for a New York art exhibition. She began by taking photos of the people, artifacts and landscape surroundings at Spirit Days in Anchorage, Alaska. Spirit Days is a celebration of Native Americans from southeast Alaska to central and northern Alaska, and she had been invited to photograph people at the event. After the shoot, she used both Photoshop and Painter to create composite images from bits and pieces of many photographs, then added textures, more color and brushwork in Painter. "Nothing you see is real and, yet, *it is real*," says Moncrieff.

For the exhibition at the A.I.R. Gallery in SoHo, she created the main series as "one of a kind" (instead of members in an edition) because the images were presented using a complex printing, transfer and installation process that allowed Moncrieff to achieve a unique multidimensional look. To begin, the images were printed onto heat transfer paper on a Hewlett-Packard 2500CP with HP's pigment-based light-fast ink set. Then the resulting images on the heat transfer paper were applied to leather using heat and pressure. For the exhibition, the works were hung on the wall behind free-standing Plexiglas pieces on pedestals that were prepared with a black-and-clear image (printed onto a clear cling by the HP 2500 CP). Placing the Plexiglas elements one-half-inch away from the leather created a multidimensional effect.

■ *Heart of the Tree* is the second work in **Philip Howe's** series of angel paintings. It suggests that there is a life energy in everything and the ancient angel senses the old tree's history. Howe began the image by roughing out the concept in Painter—sketching and assembling finished drawings and photos from his archives into a composition. He turned the assemblage into an underpainting, using sepia-toned color, which he printed out on canvas to use as a base for working with oil paints. Then he printed the underpainting using a Hewlett-Packard DesignJet 2500CP printer, with Hewlett-Packard's archival ink set. To seal the canvas before painting on it, Howe used Liquin, which he had purchased from the Daniel Smith art store. The Liquin brought out rich values in the darker areas of the image and provided a good surface to paint over. When the sealer was thoroughly dry, he tacked the canvas up on the wall and applied oil paints over its entire surface. The tight, accurate underpainting allowed him to paint more loosely and concentrate on final effects. Howe used mostly wet-into-wet oil techniques, although he did let the image dry a few times, and painted translucent glazes over some areas of the canvas.

■ When artist **John Derry** created *A Slice of Ward Parkway,* his intent was to create a photo-illustration from an illustrator's viewpoint, rather than a photo-realistic look. Derry shot twelve digital photos with his Sony DSC-707 digital camera of a series of homes on Ward Parkway that exemplify the architectural style of early Kansas City developer N.W. Dible. Derry was inspired by the artist Ed Ruscha, who had created amazingly long panorama images, one of which is called "Every Building on Sunset Strip."

To begin the panorama, Derry shot photos of the colorful, quaint homes. Back at the studio, he assembled the photos into a wide panoramic montage. To create a planar panorama of the street, he repositioned the tripod to be directly in front of each house and driveway for each shot. If trees obscured important architectural details, Derry took additional photos to provide him with enough source imagery so that he could piece together a complete view of the home. "It is critical that each photo have some overlap with the previous shot, says Derry. "The repetitious data becomes important later when "stitching" the image pieces together." Derry imported each of the source files into a composite file in Painter. Keeping the images on separate layers allowed him to reposition elements easily. To align the images precisely, he lightened their opacity and moved them into place. When they were aligned, he blended the images into one another at their edges using layer masks, which he painted using the Digital Airbrush variant of Airbrushes. Derry also used Cloners brushes to retouch a few artifacts. The final composite shows each house and driveway interleaved with the next, as if they are each viewed head on. When the composition was complete, Derry flattened a copy of the image and saved it as a TIFF file, which he opened in Photoshop for printing. He printed the image on his six-color Epson 1270 using Epson's archival ink set on 13 x 19-inch sheets of Epson Radiant White Watercolor paper.

■ In preparation for painting *Paths to Water 4*, **Cher Threinen-Pendarvis** made several loose color studies on location. She observed how light and atmosphere affect the color in highlights and shadows on the seascape.

Pendarvis's *Paths* series (of which *Path to Water 4* is a member) is inspired by favorite paths that lead to breathtaking coastal views and surf spots in California. For this painting, Pendarvis began by making pastel sketches of the hillside, plant life and seascape, using Canson paper and pastels that she'd carried in her backpack. Later, back at the studio, she created a new file in Painter and set her on-site sketch beside the computer as a reference. Using the Square Chalk variant of Chalk and a Round Soft Pastel variant of Pastels over the Char-

coal Paper texture, she loosely sketched the composition, first blocking in larger areas of color. Then she gradually focused on areas that she wanted to define with crisper details. To build up layers of color interest on the hillside and water, she dabbed small strokes of subtle color on top using a small Soft Oil Pastel variant of Oil Pastels. Then she blended distant areas of the hillside and trees using the Grainy Water variant of Blenders. To move and pull paint in the sky, she used a Subtle Palette Knife variant of Palette Knives. Pendarvis added lighter areas to the water using the Square Chalk, then smoothed and blended color using the Grainy Water. To add textured color to the path and tonal interest to the hills, she lightly scumbled using a Square Chalk and a Round Hard Pastel. To enhance the ser-

pentine path, which was the focal point of the composition, she added brighter color using a Soft Oil Pastel. Then, to bring the foreground closer, she reworked the nearest foliage with the Round Camelhair variant of Oils using dynamic, curved strokes. She also added a few strokes of brighter color to the shadows on the path using a small Round Camelhair brush. Finally, Pendarvis used expressive, quick strokes to paint the foreground grasses using the small Round Camelhair brush and the Soft Oil Pastel. She wanted to print the mixed media work on even-textured paper with light fast inks, so she chose 13 x 19-inch Epson Archival Matte paper and printed the final image on an Epson 2000P printer using Epson's six-color pigmented archival ink set.

Within the image:
SUNRISE
MOONRISE
SUNSET
MOONSET

+29 WINTER MOON HIGH
+24 SUMMER SUN
+19 WINTER MOON LOW
−19 SUMMER MOON HIGH
−24 WINTER SUN
−29 SUMMER MOON LOW

CENTER

0 10 20 30 40 50

■ Fine artist **Dorothy Simpson Krause** created the collage *Primordial Fear* as the subject for a 35 x 28-inch lenticular. Krause assembled the image from six scanned objects and set each one up on its own layer: a photograph by Viola Kaumlen of a dramatic sky, a diagram of Babbage's computing engine, an early transistor, a photograph by Jan Doucette of the model Linda Serafin, a drawing of celestial alignments at Stonehenge and a compass.

Krause created several versions of the image, with elements in different positions, that would "animate" in the lenticular. To make objects recede in space, Krause moved elements in small increments to the left. To make an object come forward in space, she moved it in small increments to the right. Greater increments and a larger number of steps created more depth. Krause saved eight "frames" as TIFF files. Then she used the Flip program to interlace the eight frames into vertical strips. She printed the interlaced image using a Roland HiFi Jet onto Roland PETG white film with Roland's six-

color archival inks. Then she used a CODA laminator to apply the print to a plastic lenticular lens.

As a viewers moves past the completed image, they see one "frame" at a time and the image changes with each frame, creating the illusion of depth and movement. For instance, the transistor rises and sets (like a sun or moon) behind the woman, who is frozen with fear and does not move, the compass covering her face becomes a mask, and the lines of the azimuth and one circle from the Babbage diagram come forward in the picture plane.

■ *Indigo* is a 28 x 35-inch fresco transfer, and a member of **Bonny Lhotka's** *Heartland* series. The artist found inspiration for the work while visiting her hometown in Illinois in a unique store that had items left over from garage sales, the discarded possessions of everyday life. This mosaic of commonality inspired Lhotka, and she took many photographs while at the store. To create the image, she used the photos and also made scans of actual elements. For instance, she captured the position of a fragment of cheesecloth and her hand holding the marigolds. For another source image, she dyed the integra branches purple, and when they were dry, she laid them on a large-format Epson scanner and covered them with cheesecloth. When the collage was complete, she printed it onto clear film with an Encad printer using the GO pigment ink set. Then she transferred the clear film print to a plaster fresco surface. (In her search for ways to apply her images to walls, Lhotka researched old masters' ways of creating gesso grounds and frescos. She made a fresco-like surface by applying a strained mixture of rabbit skin glue and calcium carbonate to a board.) When the fresco was nearly complete, she wanted to add a darker, metallic and iridescent look to the image's center (using a portion of the image she had printed earlier). So she coated a piece of translucent silver fabric with diluted rabbit skin glue (as an inkjet pre-coat), and when it was dry, printed the fabric on an Epson 3000 using Lysonic archival dye-based inks. Then she attached the print to the center of the fresco.

■ *Siberian Summer Tales* was created by artist **Cynthia Beth Rubin** based on her own photographs taken while visiting Novosibirsk in Siberia, Russia. "I am interested in how we can connect with the world beyond our own individuality, how we can connect with the past, and with each other living in the present," says Rubin. In *Siberian Summer Tales*, Rubin wanted to re-create the feeling of the homes of people who resisted moving into high-rise Soviet-era housing.

Although most of the compositing was done in Photoshop, Rubin used Painter extensively to bring out textures in the image and to enhance the color and lighting. She used the versatile Apply Surface Texture feature to add highlights and shadows to the foliage and the wood planks on the homes, making them look more three dimensional. When the image was complete, she saved a copy of the image as a TIFF file and opened it in Photoshop for printing. She printed *Siberian Summer Tales* in two sizes, one large (about 22 x 36 inches) and the other small (on 13 x 19-inch paper). The large print was done on a Roland HiFi Jet printer with pigmented inks in the Faculty Research Lab at the Rhode Island

School of Design. For the Roland print, Rubin set up the image with an Adobe RGB color profile embedded in Photoshop on a Macintosh, and then ported it over to the ripping PC for the Roland. The Roland color choice software does the final color conversion from RGB to CMYK. After running a few tests at 20% size, she subtly color corrected the image. For the smaller print, Rubin used her studio Epson 1280 printer, using Jon Cone's system (inkjetmall.com). She bought paper, inks and color profiles from him, and followed his instructions. Again, she printed out of Photoshop.

■ Artist **Steve Rys** began *Crazy Horse* by making conventional sketches using pencils and paper. While sketching, he referred to source photographs. When he was happy with the sketch, he opened a new empty file in Painter and used brushes and a pressure-sensitive tablet and stylus to develop a color study. To build the large masses of color, he used the Round Camelhair variant of Oils, continually varying the size of the brush to achieve an expressive feeling with dynamic movement. He began with the lightest colors and then gradually built up darker tones as he developed the forms in the portrait. To blend areas, he used the Just Add Water variant of Blend-ers, also varying the size of the brush, adding more color with Round Camelhair when needed, for the look of wet paint.

The final image was saved as a 240 ppi RGB file in TIFF format and was printed using two methods—as a large inkjet print from a Roland printer, and as a series of unique monoprints. The inkjet print was printed on a Roland Hi-Fi Jet inkjet using an archival eight-color ink set on Concord Rag Bright White watercolor paper (which was manufactured with an inkjet receptive coating). Rys sealed the Roland print with a Krylon overcoat spray to protect the inks and paper from moisture and to increase the light-fastness of the print. For a second series of prints, Rys created a series of monoprints using a hand transfer process that allowed him to create one-of-a-kind images. After making several 5 x 5-inch inkjet prints using water-soluble inks on paper, he used a burnishing tool to transfer each image onto a sheet of bristol board that had been dampened with Golden flow retarder solution. By varying the pressure and direction and the amount of damp-ness on the paper, and by burnishing onto inkjet prints that had been ghosted by previous burnishing sources, Rys created a variety of images. He ganged and matted these images in the order shown above.

■ **James Faire Walker** created *Global Coffee* (a member of his Color and Motion series) by collaging bits and pieces of his own digital photos, then painting brushstrokes and adding special effects. Walker loves the immediacy with which he can create an image—taking digital photos, opening them in Painter, pasting them into a collage, manipulating the pieces of photos on their own layers and then painting on the image with brushes. To color some of the photo pieces, he used Painter's Tonal Control effects, such as the Posterize feature. Then he added brushwork, which was painted on transparent layers above the photo elements. He added the new transparent layers for the brush work by clicking the New Layer button on the Layers palette. Then he painted using the Opaque Round variant and other Oils variants to create colorful, loose strokes over and around the imagery of the coffee cups. To give the image depth and make the brushwork layers stand out from the background, he applied soft drop shadows using the Create Drop Shadow command. As he developed the image, he proofed it in his studio on an Epson 3000 inkjet printer. The final 17 x 22-inch prints for the Global Coffee edition of 20 were printed on Somerset Radiant Velvet White paper on an Iris printer using the Pinnacle Gold archival ink set.

■ For *Interiors* (above) and *In Transition* (left), **Helen Golden** began by shooting several digital photos of weathered historic buildings. For Golden, the Northern California site felt very mysterious, as she looked through and beyond the walls into the unknown. In building the images, she worked to convey that feeling of mystery and unreality.

As Golden shot photo "sketches," she was fascinated by the site's crumbling surfaces and was moved by the feeling that she was actually witnessing the decay of the place. Back at the studio, she used LucisArt software to extract hidden details and information. Then she used Photoshop to combine pieces from the photos into interesting compositions. For *Interiors*, Golden created improbable angles and shapes in the image using the Distort command in Photoshop. Then, using different blending modes including Overlay, Multiply, Soft Light and Luminosity, she created the rich transparency effects. (The use of the Luminosity blending mode can be seen in the lower part of *In Transition* where the colors change to rich, textured grays.) Because she was striving for emphasis and enhancement of the textural elements, she brought the layered images into Painter and used Effects, Surface Control, Apply Surface Texture Using Image Luminance.

Golden printed both images as Variant Editions, so in the future she could make changes to the size, the media and the printer used. She printed *In Transition* on Hahnemuhle's Photo Rag Paper with a Hewlett-Packard DesignJet 5000 using the archival Hewlett Packard UV Ink set; she printed *Interiors* on Hahnemuhle's Albrecht Durer Paper, using the same printer and UV ink set.

John Derry was contacted by Corel Art Director Adrian Garcia about creating the *Painter 8 packaging "hero" image*. As in many AD/Artist relationships, they communicated ideas using sketches and roughs throughout the process.

Garcia initially sent Derry a basic pencil sketch of the can containing several art tools. Derry was asked to do a quick "blended" study of the image, progressing from a rough pencil sketch to a painted final. This early concept piece was designed to visualize the range of media used, as well as the sketch-to-final-image transition. In order to eliminate a lot of guesswork, Derry chose to set up a photographic equivalent of Garcia's sketch for use as a master reference. So he photographed the can at several slightly different angles and sent the thumbnails to Garcia for selection. When the can angle was approved, Derry proceeded to photograph each of the individual art tools that would appear within the can. Keeping each element separate,

would afford him the maximum flexibility in fine-tuning the placement of each according to Garcia's art direction. "We used the term 'bouquet' to describe the arrangement of the art tools in the can," says Derry. "It was to look almost like a flower arrangement." Once the photographic composite was approved, he could translate the source imagery into a drawn and painted rendition. The approved photographic master made the final image much quicker to create. For the rough sketch version (that appears on the left side of the final illustration), Derry created a new layer over the reference photo and drew a loose sketch-like version of the underlying photo. As he continued to blend from one medium to the next, he created a new layer for each medium. He intentionally created the "band" of imagery wider than he needed so that he could adjust the transitions later using layer masks. Once the initial composite was complete, Derry sent it to Garcia for comments. Garcia liked the image but wanted the can itself to

appear almost chrome-like. Derry had photographed an older Painter can that was gold, so he photographed a generic silver can to get a sense of the coloration and highlighting. He shot the new can outside in natural light to get the correct reflections and highlights. Then he used these new photos as a reference to airbrush the new surface of the can on a separate layer. Derry added final touches—paint drips and a splat that would later be used on the packaging. In order to provide Garcia maximum latitude in tweaking the image for production, Derry submitted his final image with these elements on separate layers. The final 54 x 57 pica image had a resolution of 300 ppi. Derry opened a copy of the final layered file in Photoshop, and saved it as a CMYK TIFF file. Later, Garcia changed the blue color (to Corel corporate blue) using Photo-Paint, then he imported the final flattened file into CorelDraw 11, where he set up the die-lines for the box. The final layout file was printed on a commercial offset press.

■ **Chet Phillips** created these larger-than-life-size vehicle graphics (top and middle left) for *Dallas Photo Imaging*, using the Scratchboard technique described on page 211. To make sure the three images would fit the truck exactly, he used a full-size template of the Suburban's shape (provided by the service bureau) to plan each panel. He created individual panels for the driver's side, passenger's side and the truck's back. Phillips built the original files at a resolution of 65 ppi; each file was over 100 MB. When the illustrations were complete, they were output on Dallas Photo Imaging's Idanit inkjet printer onto Avery fleet graphic vinyl with adhesive backing, then attached to the truck.

■ As the principal and creative director for Cinco de Mayo Design Studio, **Mauricio Alanis** conceived and built the *Shouting Bucket* vehicle graphics (bottom left) for Abigarrados, a service bureau in Monterrey, Mexico, which specializes in large-format printing. Using Painter, he created a layered image that included the paint can photo, the circular shapes around the can image and the exploding paint. To give the paint more realistic dimension, he added a semi-transparent layer of Liquid Metal brushstrokes. To add to the relief, he used Apply Surface Texture with Image Luminance. The final 65 ppi image was output onto adhesive-backed vinyl media using a large-format inkjet printer, and mounted on the Abigarrados van.

Appendix A
Images on the *Wow!* CD-ROM

These vendors provided photos or video clips from their collections for the Wow! CD-ROM *in the back of this book.*

Artbeats
Volumes of backgrounds and textures, including Wood and Paper and Leather and Fabric; sizes to 16.5 MB; Reel Textures, a collection of 40 animated backgrounds

Corbis Images
Extensive collection of royalty-free images, available on CD-ROM or online. Business, lifestyle, nature, backgrounds and more; sizes to 32MB.

Fabulous Fonts
Volumes 31–36 (e.g. Friz Quadrata Book, Corroded Rust and Vidigris; Shelley Volante, Gold and Platinum); picture fonts in sizes to 2.6 MB, designed by John Dismukes and Jo-Anne Redwood of Capstone Studios

Digital Wisdom
Body Shots: One volume of photographs shot with twelve models in various business situations against a white background; sizes to 4 MB

Image Farm
Volumes including Arizona Desert, Berlin Walls, Cottage and Country, Real Rock, Streets of London, and Industrial Backgrounds and Objects; high quality photographic textures and backgrounds; sizes to 18 MB.

Mediacom
Adclips: One volume (2 CDs) of video clips including Recreation, Corporate, Historical, Lifestyles, Wildlife; sizes to 320 x 240 pixels

Getty Images / PhotoDisc
85,000 images downloadable from the Web; over 190 thematic CD-ROM discs; including Signature Series; Object Series (with clipping paths); Fine Art series and Background Series discs; sizes to 28.5 MB

PhotoSpin
Premiere Series and Photo Objects (images with masks); sizes to 25 MB; 50–100 images per disc

Visual Concept Entertainment
*Pyromania 1, 2 and Pyromania! Pro:
3 volumes of digitized video of explosions,
fireworks, smoke, and other incendiary
displays; sizes to 640 x 480 pixels*

Appendix B Vendor Information

IMAGE COLLECTIONS

Artbeats, Inc.
1405 N. Myrtle Road, Ste. 5
Myrtle Creek, OR 97457
541-863-4429   541-863-4547 fax
www.artbeats.com

Corbis Images
15395 S.E. 30th Place, Ste. 300
Bellevue, WA 98007
800-260-0444   425-641-4505 fax
www.corbis.com

Digital Wisdom, Inc.
Box 2070
Tappahannock, VA 22560
800-800-8560   804-443-9000
804-443-3632 fax
www.digiwis.com

Fabulous Fonts
c/o PhotoSpin
4030 Palos Verdes Drive North, Ste. 200
Rolling Hills Estates, CA 90274
310-265-1313   888-246-1313
310-265-1314 fax
www.photospin.com

Image Farm, Inc.
490 Adelaide Street West, Suite 301
Toronto, ON
Canada M5V 1T2
800-438-3276   416-504-4163 fax
www.imagefarm.com

Mediacom
9210 Arboretum Pkwy. Ste. 150
Richmond, VA 23236
804-560-9200   804-560-4370 fax

Getty Images / PhotoDisc
701 North 34th Street, Suite 400
Seattle, WA 98103
800-528-3472   877-547-4686 fax
www.gettyimages.com
www.photodisc.com

PhotoSpin
4030 Palos Verdes Drive North, Ste. 200
Rolling Hills Estates, CA 90274
310-265-1313   888-246-1313
310-265-1314 fax
www.photospin.com

Visual Concept Entertainment
P.O. Box 921226
Sylmar, CA 91392
818-367-9187   818-362-3490 fax
http://www.vce.com

HARDWARE

Apple Computer, Inc.
800-767-2775

Color Vision / *Color Management*
5 Princess Road
Lawrenceville, NJ 08648
609-895-7430   609-895-7447 fax
800-554-8688
www.colorvision.com

Epson America / *Desktop color printers*
P.O. Box 2854
Torrance, CA 90509
800-289-3776   800-873-7766
www.epson.com

Encad, Inc. / *Desktop color printers*
6059 Cornerstone Court West
San Diego, CA 92121
800-453-6223
www.encad.com

Hewlett-Packard / *Desktop color printers*
16399 West Bernardo Drive
San Diego, CA 92127
858-655-4100
www.hp.com

Wacom Technology Corporation
Drawing tablets
1311 SE Cardinal Court
Vancouver, WA 98683
800-922-6613
sales@wacom.com

INKS AND SUBSTRATES

Charrette Corporation / *Substrates
and Inks*
800-367-3729
www.inkjet.com

Digital Art Supplies / *Substrates and Inks*
877-534-4278
858-273-2576 fax
www.digitalartsupplies.com

Dr. Graphix Inc. / *Substrates*
www.drgraphix.com

Epson / *Substrates and Inks*
www.epson.com

Hewlett-Packard / *Substrates and Inks*
www.hp.com

ilab Corporation, Inc. / *Inks for Epson,
Iris and Novaget*
P.O. Box 1030
Atkinson, NH 03811
603-362-4190
603-362-4191 fax
www.ilabcorp.com

InkjetMall / *Substrates and Inks*
P.O. Box 335
148 Main Street
Bradford, VT 05033
802-222-4415
802-222-3334 fax
Contact: Sarah Lyons

Luminos Photo Corporation / *Inks for
Epson and other printers*
P.O. Box 158
Yonkers, NY 10705
800-586-4667   914-965-0367 fax

Media Street / *Substrates and Inks*
888-633-4295
888-329-5991 fax
www.mediastreet.com

MIS Associates, Inc / *Substrates and Inks*
248-391-2163
248-391-2527 fax
www.inksupply.com

TSS Photo / *Substrates and Inks*
801-363-9700
801-363-9707 fax
www.inkjetart.com
www.tssphoto.com/sp/dg/

Wilhelm Imaging Research, Inc. / *Ink
and paper longevity information*
P.O. Box 775
Grinnell, IA 50112-0775
515-236-4222 fax
www.wilhelm-research.com

SOFTWARE

Adobe Systems / *After Effects, Dimensions, GoLive, Illustrator, PageMaker, Photoshop, Premiere*
345 Park Avenue
San Jose, CA 95110
800-833-6687

Auto F/X / *Photographic Edges*
511 Highland Park Circle
Birmingham, AL 35242
205-980-0056
205-9801121
www.autofx.com

Corel / *Corel Painter, CorelDraw, WordPerfect, KPT, Bryce*
1600 Carling Avenue
Ottawa, ON
Canada K1Z 8R7
800-772-6735
www.corel.com

Macromedia / *Director, Dreamweaver, FreeHand, Fireworks, Flash*
600 Townsend Street, Suite 310-W
San Francisco, CA 94103
800-989-3762
415-252-2000

Appendix C
Fine Art
Output
Suppliers

These bureaus specialize in making large-format prints for fine artists. More are listed on the Wow! *CD-ROM.*

Cone Editions Press / *Fine Art Prints*
P.O. Box 51
17 Powder Spring Road
East Topsham, VT 05076
802-439-5751
802-439-6501 fax
Contact: Sara Larkin

Chrome Digital / *Fujix Pictrography prints; film recorder output*
858-452-1588

Color Reflections / *Durst Lamda and Fujix Pictrography prints; film recorder output*
www.colorreflections.com

Dallas Photo Imaging *LightJet 5000 prints; vehicle graphics*
3942 Irving Boulevard
Dallas, TX 75247
800-852-6929
214-630-4351
www.dpitexas.com

Digicolor / *Fine art prints*
Seattle, WA
206-284-2198

Digicolorado / *Fine art prints*
610 South Lipan Street
Denver, CO 80223
303-777-6720

Digital Output Corp. / *Fine art prints*
2121 5th Avenue
San Diego, CA 92101
619-685-5800
619-685-5804 fax
www.digitaloutput.com

Durst Dice America / *Lenticular prints*
16 Sterling Road
Tuxedo, NY 10987
914-351-2677

Electric Paintbrush / *Fine art prints*
Hopkinton, MA
508-435-7726

Foto 1 Imaging / *LightJet 5000; Fujix Pictrography prints*
800-761-3686
www.foto1.com

High Resolution / *Fine art prints*
Camden, ME
207-236-3777

Imagestation / *Fine art prints*
Kihei, HI
808-536-1718

Lenticular Products / *Lenticular prints*
www.lenticulardevelopement.com

Nash Editions / *Iris fine art prints*
Manhattan Beach, CA
310-545-4352

Paris Photo Lab / *Fine art prints*
Los Angeles, CA
310-204-0500

Photodyne / *Hewlett-Packard DesignJet CP prints; Durst Lamda prints; film recorder output*
7012 Convoy Court
San Diego, CA 92011
858-292-0140

Photoworks / *Noritzu prints; Cibachrome*
858-755-0772

River City Silver / *LightJet 5000 prints*
800-938-2788

Salon Iris / *Iris fine art prints*
Vienna, Austria

Trillium Press / *Fine art prints; monotypes; silk screen*
91 Park Lane
Brisbane, CA 94005
415-468-8166
415-468-0721 fax

Urban Digital Color / *Fine art prints*
San Francisco, CA
415-626-8403

Appendix D
Contributing Artists

Mauricio Alanis
c/o Cinco de Mayo
5 de Mayo Pte., Monterrey, N.L.
Mexico, 64000
malanis@mail.cmact.com

Ben Barbante
1176 Key Avenue
San Francisco, CA 94124
415-657-9844

Laurel Becker

Carol Benioff
2226 11th Avenue #4
Oakland, CA 94606
510-533-9987
www.carolbenioff.com
carol@carolbenioff.com

Richard Biever
117 N. Frederick
Evansville, IN 47711
812-437-9308

Kathleen Blavatt
4261 Montalvo Street
San Diego, CA 92107
619-222-0057

Ray Blavatt
4261 Montalvo Street
San Diego, CA 92107
619-222-0057

Athos Boncompagni
Viale Michelangelo Buonarroti, 8
52100 Arezzo, Italy
+39 02-700433445
web: http://go.to/athos
http://utenti.lycos.it/athos
e-mail: athos@libero.it

Marc Brown
2786 South Monroe
Denver, CO 80210
303-758-9411

Jeff Burke
8755 Washington Boulevard
Culver City, CA 90232
310-837-9900

Michael Campbell
9974 Scripps Ranch Blvd., #141
San Diego, CA 92131
858-578-8252
mccphoto@san.rr.com
www.michaelcampbell.com

Steve Campbell
1880 Fulton #5
San Francisco, CA 94117
415-668-5826
campbell12.home.mindspring.com
campbell12@mindspring.com

Karen Carr
www.karencarr.com

Mario Henri Chakkour, AIA
703-317-1923
www.chakkour.com
mario@chakkour.com

Phillip Charris
27184 Ortega Highway
San Juan Capistrano, CA 92675
949-496-3330

Gary Clark
823 Lightstreet Road
Bloomsburg, PA 17815
717-387-1689

Stephen Crooks
scrooks@earthlink.net

James D'Avanzo
(11/2/73–5/28/96)
Family of James D'Avanzo
1446 Jennings Road
Fairfield, CT 06430
203-255-6822

Linda Davick
4805 Hilldale Drive
Knoxville, TN 37914
615-546-1020

Michela Del Degan
Via Podgora 36
40131 Bologna, Italy
+31-339-58-99-741
+31-02-700-41-40-90 fax
mdegan@infinito.it
www.micheladeldegan.com

John Derry
Overland Park, KS
derry@pixlart.com

Eduardo Diaz Juliano
kaffa@retemail.es

Matt Dineen
1465 Dougmar Road
Santa Cruz, CA 95062

John Dismukes
949-888-9911
www.dismukes.com

Mary Envall
1536 Promontory Ridge Way
Vista, CA 92083
760-727-8995

Grace Ferguson
2226 11th Avenue
Oakland, CA 94606

John Fretz
707 S. Snoqualmie Street, #5D
Seattle, WA 98108
206-623-1931

Laurence Gartel
P.O. Box 971251
Boca Raton, FL 33487
561-477-1100

Helen Golden
460 El Capitan Place
Palo Alto, CA 94306
650-494-3461
hsgolden@aol.com

Steven Gordon
Cartagram, LLC
136 Mill Creek Crossing
Madison, AL 35758
256-772-0022
StevenGordon@cartagram.com

Rhoda Grossman
rhoda@dnai.com

Shawn Grunberger
415-552-0367
shawn@deepstorm.com

Kathy Hammon
bouchedoree@wanadoo.fr

Andrew Hathaway
805 Page Street
San Francisco, CA 94117
415-621-0671

Fiona Hawthorne
47 Barlby Road
London W10 6AW, UK
+44 (0)20-8968-8889
fionahawthorne@beeb.net
fionahawthorne@dsl.pipex.net
www.portfolio.com/fionahawthorne

Brent Houston
brenthouston@earthlink.net

Philip Howe
12425 68th Avenue SE
Snohomish, WA 98296
425-385-8426
dooder1@aol.com

Geoff Hull
4054 Cartwright Avenue
Studio City, CA 91604
818-761-6019

Aleksander Jensko
www.aljen.de
www.kreaftwerk.com
madmac@aljen.de

Donal Jolley
c/o Studio 3
1506 Black Spruce Court
Lilburn, GA 30047
770-279-7753
www.studio3o.com

Ron Kempke
217-278-7441

Rick Kirkman
11809 N. 56th Drive
Glendale, AZ 85304
623-334-9199

Dorothy Simpson Krause
P.O. Box 421
Marshfield Hills, MA 02051
781-837-1682
www.dotkrause.com

Ted Larson
7718 Corliss Avenue North
Seattle, WA 98103
206-524-7640
theoneson@earthlink.net

John Lee
2293 El Contento Drive
Los Angeles, CA 90068
213-467-9317

LeVan/Barbee
LeVan/Barbee studio
P.O. Box 182
Indianola, WA 98342
www.bruckandmoss.com
lvbwa@earthlink.com

Bonny Lhotka
Bonny@Lhotka.com
www.Lhotka.com
www.inkAID.com

Michele Lill
2503 Kieffer Court
Valparaiso, IN 46383
219-531-4728
lill@netnitco.net

Keith MacLelland
617-734-2428
617-953-9550 cell
www.yourillustrator.com
keith@yourillustrator.com

Debi Lee Mandel
530-886-8910
www.catsprite.com

Robert Manning
Supersample Corporation
Lilika Productions
212-414-1680
212-414-1681 fax
meglartin@aol.com
www.supersample.com

Janet Martini
4857 Biona Drive
San Diego, CA 9211
619-283-7895

Craig McClain
9587 Tropico Drive
La Mesa, CA 91941
619-469-9599

Pedro Meyer
Ortega #20
Coyoacan 04000
Mexico D.F., Mexico
011-525-55-54-39-96
011-525-55-54-37-30
pedro@zonezero.com
www.zonezero.com

Judy Miller
31 Martin Drive
Fall River, NS
B2T 1E7 Canada
902-861-1193
judy@creativeartist.com

Judi Moncrieff
(10/25/41–4/06/01)
Family of Judi Moncrieff
122 North 83rd Street
Seattle, WA 98103

Brian Moose
P.O. Box 927
Capitola, CA 95010
831-425-1672

Wendy Morris
wendydraw@aol.com

Richard Noble
899 Forest Lane
Alamo, CA 94507
510-838-5524

Louis Ocepek
1761 Pomona Drive
Las Cruces, NM 88011
505-522-0427
505-646-7550

John Odam
2163 Cordero Road
Del Mar, CA 92014
858-259-8230

Corinne Okada

Dennis Orlando
116 West Norton Drive
Churchville, PA 18966
215-355-1613
215-355-6924 fax
dennisorlando@comcast.net
www.dennisorlando.com

Cris Palomino
1457 Bellevue Avenue
Los Angeles, CA 90026
elektralusion@elektralusion.com
http://www.elektralusion.com

Chet Phillips
6527 Del Norte
Dallas, TX 75225
214-987-4344
www.chetart.com
chet@chetart.com

David Purnell
c/o New York West
8145-100th Street W
Lonsdale, MN 55046
507-744-5408

Arena Reed
617-945-2754
arena@visualarena.com
www.visualarena.com

Mike Reed
1314 Summit Avenue
Minneapolis, MN 55403
612-374-3164
mikelr@winternet.com

Cindy Reid
cindy@reidcreative.com

Dewey Reid
dewey@reidcreative.com

Cecil Rice
5784 Salem Terrace
Acworth, GA 30102
770-974-0684

Lew Robinson
Photography and Digital Imaging
310-837-7009

Cynthia Beth Rubin
85 Willow Street #9
New Haven, CT 06511
http://CBRubin.net
info@cbrubin.net

Peter Mitchell Rubin
c/o Production Arts Limited
310-915-5610

Steve Rys
12051 256th Avenue
Trevor, WI 53179
262-862-7090
www.rysdesign.com
steve@rysdesign.com

Chelsea Sammel
P.O. Box 30132
Oakland, CA 94604-6332
510-628-8474

Don Seegmiller
www.seegmillerart.com
donseeg@xmission.com

Nancy Stahl
www.nancystahl.com
nancy@nancystahl.com

Sharon Steuer
205 Valley Road
Bethany, CT 06524
www.ssteuer.com

Don Stewart
336-854-2769
www.donstewart.com

Jeremy Sutton
415-626-3871
jeremy@portrayals.com
www.portrayals.com

S. Swaminathan
P.O. Box 1547
Capitola, CA
408-722-3301

Jean-Luc Touillon
jean-luc.touillon@wanadoo.fr
jasiu@lafactory.fr

Lorraine Triolo
8755 Washington Boulevard
Culver City, CA 90232
310-837-9900

Stanley Vealé
zetar@yahoo.com

Pamela Wells
136 Verdi Avenue
Cardiff, CA 92007
760-632-8495
www.artmagic.com
artmagic1@cox.net

James Faure Walker
88 Greenwood Road
London E8 1NE, UK
jamesfaurewalker@compuserve.com

Hiroshi Yoshii
1-2-13-304, Tamagawadai, Setagaya-ku
Tokyo 1580096, Japan
tel/fax 81-3-5491-5337
hiroshi@yoshii.com

Appendix E
Reference
Materials

Here's a sampling of recommended references for both traditional and digital art forms.

ART BOOKS

Art Through the Ages
Fifth Edition
Revised by Horst de la Croix and Richard G. Tansey
Harcourt, Brace and World, Inc.
New York, Chicago, San Francisco, and Atlanta

The Art of Color
Johannes Itten
Van Nostrand Reinhold
New York

**Drawing Lessons
from the Great Masters**
Robert Beverly Hale
Watson-Guptill Publications
New York

Mainstreams of Modern Art
John Canaday
Holt, Reinhart and Winston
New York

Printmaking
Gabor Peterdi
The Macmillan Company
New York
Collier-Macmillan Ltd.
London

The Natural Way to Draw
Kimon Nicolaïdes
Houghton Mifflin Company
Boston

The Photographer's Handbook
John Hedgecoe
Alfred A. Knopf
New York

TypeWise
*Kit Hinrichs
with Delphine Hirasura*
North Light Books
Cincinnati, Ohio

COMPUTER IMAGERY BOOKS

Creating Killer Web Sites
Second Edition
David Siegel
Hayden Books
201 West 103 Street
Indianapolis, IN 46290

Elements of Web Design
Second Edition
Darcy DiNucci with Maria Giudice and Lynne Stiles
Peachpit Press
Berkeley, CA

Deconstructing Web Graphics
Second Edition
Lynda Weinman and Jon Warren Lentz
New Riders Publishing
Indianapolis, IN

Designing Web Graphics
How to Prepare Images and Media for the Web
Lynda Weinman
New Riders Publishing
Indianapolis, IN

Digital Character Design and Painting
Don Seegmiller
Charles River Media
Hingham, MA

Non-Designers Web Book
Robin Williams and John Tollett
Peachpit Press
Berkeley, CA

The Illustrator 10 Wow! Book
Sharon Steuer
Peachpit Press
Berkeley, CA

The Photoshop 6 Wow! Book
Linnea Dayton and Jack Davis
Peachpit Press
Berkeley, CA

The Photoshop 7 Wow! Book
Jack Davis
Peachpit Press
Berkeley, CA

Real World Color Management
Bruce Fraser, Fred Bunting and Chris Murphy
Peachpit Press
Berkeley, CA

PUBLICATIONS

Communication Arts
110 Constitution Drive
Menlo Park, CA 94025
www.commarts.com

Design Graphics
Design Editorial Pty. Ltd.
11 School Road
Ferny Creek
Victoria 3786 Australia
www.designgraphics.com/au

EFX Art and Design
Roslagsgatan 11
S-113 55 Stockholm, Sweden
+46-8-15 55 48
+46-8-15 55 49 fax
www.macartdesign.matchbox.se

Graphis
307 Fifth Avenue, 10th Floor
New York, NY 10016
www.graphis.com

How
Design Ideas at Work
104 Fifth Avenue
New York, NY 10011
www.howdesign.com

Print
104 Fifth Avenue
New York, NY 10011
www.printmag.com

STEP Inside Design
P.O. Box 9940
Collingswood, NJ 99470
888-698-8543
www.dgusa.com

SBS Digital Design
P.O. Box 10826
Collingswood, NJ 99470
888-698-8544
www.dgusa.com

Index

J

JavaScript rollovers, 344, 357, 361
Jensko, Aleksander, 244, 245
Jitter settings, 110
Jolley, Donal, 132, 133, 280, 312, 313, 321, 327–329
JPEG format, 8–9
  for web graphics, 344, 345, 352

K

Kaffa, 283
Kaleidoscope dynamic layer, 4, 257, 351–352
Kempe, Ron, 191–192
kerning, 286–287, 289
keyframes, 332–333, 337
Kirkman, Rick, 8, 172, 183, 188, 196–198
Kodak Color Management System (KCMS), 28
Kodak Photo CD format, 239
Krause, Dorothy Simpson, 362, 368, 382

L

Larson, Ted, 342, 343
Lasso tool, 37, 144, 165, 168
Layer Adjuster tool, 11, 14, 146, 147, 151, 164, 178, 180, 202, 296, 328, 329
layer masks. *See* visibility masks
layers, 4, 178
  adding, 56
  aligning, 14
  for animation, 330–331
  applying special effects to, 180
  auto selecting, 188
  converting shapes to, 184, 196, 197

copying, 179
creating, 179, 180
deselecting, 180
distorting, 181
duplicating, 6
Equalize, 215
erasing from, 180–181, 189, 330
exporting to Photoshop, 302
flipping, 181
floating objects and, 179, 181–182, 233
frame stacks and, 328
grouping, 188, 204, 276
for image maps, 353–354
importing from Photoshop, 303
lighting for, 252
Liquid Ink, 50, 119, 122, 123, 187, 338
locking, 188
making from active selection, 180
media, 179, 187
merging, 178, 195, 211, 275
merging select, 188
merging several, 182
merging with canvas, 181
moving, 181
opacity of, 181, 222
organizing, 188–189
painting on, 56, 180, 191–192, 194, 197, 203, 204, 205, 206, 207, 208, 209, 210, 211, 212, 213, 313
for photo compositing, 215
preserving, 7–8, 178–179
reference, 7, 178, 179, 182–183, 191–192, 240
renaming, 124
rotating, 181
scaling, 181
selecting, 180
stacking of, 4, 178
transformations to, 181, 182
transparent, 56
types of, 179
ungrouping, 188

using Composite Method with, 178, 189–190
using selections to make, 201–202
using selections with, 142, 225
woodcut effect using, 237
See also dynamic layers; image layers; Water Color layer
Layers palette, 12, 143, 178, 179, 188
  Create Layer Mask button, 180, 221, 241
  Layer Commands button, 181, 188, 204, 205
  Dynamic Plugins button, 186, 224
Lee, Jon, 325, 332–333
legibility, of type, 286
lenticular images, 366, 372–373, 382
letter spacing, 286–287, 289
LeVan, Susan, 28, 149, 169–170, 175, 284, 299, 345, 358
Lhotka, Bonny, 364, 367, 369 372–373, 383
libraries, 17–19
Lift Canvas to Water Color Layer, 80–81, 245
Light Valve Technology, 366
lighting, for Impasto, 55
  See also Apply Lighting
Lighting Mover, 252
LightWave 3D, 326
Lill, Michelle, 264, 265–266
line art
  adding color to, 30–31, 32–35, 36–37
  scanning, 32
line screen, for offset printing, 363
line screen effects, 218, 219
Liquid Ink, 117–121, 122–124
  Coarse Bristle variant, 120
  Coarse Bristle resist variant, 121
  dab types for, 118
  encaustic painting with, 122–124
  erasing, 123

Posterize command, 243, 386
PostScript files, importing, 145, 163, 300
PowerPoint, 342
power-pasting, 328
preferences, setting, 16–17, 25
prepress process, 362–363, 365
Preserve Transparency, 188, 187, 204, 210, 227, 298
presets, saving, 238
pressure, stylus, 25, 228, 316
pressure-sensitive stylus, 5
pressure-sensitive tablet, 5, 47, 52, 130, 311, 315, 338, 385
 with Liquid Ink brushes, 119
preview sphere, of Surface Texture control, 250–251
Preview window, 14
primary colors, 21
printing
 fine art, 364–369, 374–375, 386
 four-color, 362–363
printmaking, archival, 365–367, 374–375, 376–377, 380, 381, 384, 385, 387
 experimental, 368–369, 383
 intaglio, 370–371
prints, digital, 365–366
ProfilerPlus, 376, 377
Projected dab type, 59
Property Bar, 46, 47, 70, 91, 161
PSD format, 280, 317
Purnell, David, 181, 188, 212, 213

exporting, 325
with masks, 325
QuickTime VR, 339

R

rainbow effect, 29
Rake stroke type, 60–61
RAM, Painter's need for, 4–5
Record Script, 319–320, 321
rectangular selection tool, 143
rectangular shape tool, 143
Redwood, Jo-Anne, 301, 311
Reed, Arena, 260–261, 262–263
Reed, Mike, 176, 177, 298
reference layers 6, 178, 179, 182–183, 191–192, 240–241
reflection maps, 251, 264, 265, 326
Reflection slider, 250, 251
Refraction Map, 258
Reid, Cindy, 336
Reid, Dewey, 318, 322, 324, 330–331, 336, 337
rendered dab brushes, 48
Rendered dabs, 59
rendering, 326
Replace Mask, 154
Reselect, 143
resists, 50, 121
resist-type brushes, 118, 119, 121
Resize dialog box, 7
resizing, 6
 of brushes, 49
 of files, 6
 of selections, 146
 of type, 284
resolution, 7
 brush size and, 50
 for movie editing, 325
 for offset printing, 363
 for transparencies, 366
retouching, of photos, 214–205, 226, 268

RGB mode, 7, 20, 21, 302, 303
 converting to CMYK, 10, 362–363, 374–375
RGB Variability, 25
Rice, Cecil, 171
RIFF files, 7–8, 178, 185, 227, 203, 331
ripple effect, 271
Roland printers, 364, 369, 373, 382, 384
Roman type, 283
Rotate Page tool, 256
rotating
 of layers, 181, 296
 of page, 13
 of reference layers, 182
 of selections, 146–147
 of shapes, 183
rotoscoping, 324
Rubin, Cynthia Beth, 384
Rubin, Peter Mitchell, 322, 340
Ruler and Guides, 15, 354
Runny brushes, 75, 78
runny washes, 75, 78, 200
Rys, Steve, 385

S

Salgado, David, 368
Sammel, Chelsea, 53, 102–103, 114–116, 252
sans serif type, 284–285
saturation, 21, 22, 217
Scale command, 257
scaling
 of layers, 181
 of reference layers, 182
 of selections, 146
 of shapes, 183
scanning
 of paper textures, 104
 of pencil sketches, 108–109
Scissors tool, 147
scratch disk, 5
scratchboard, emulating, 50

Q

Quantel HAL system, 332–333
Quantize to Nearest Color, 345, 350
QuarkXPress, 308
Quick Curve (Shape Design) tool, 143, 144–145
Quick Warp, 251, 254
QuickTime movies, 10, 320, 321–322, 323, 324, 330, 331

U

undos, multiple, 16–17
ungrouping, 164, 188
Uniform Color, 255
unsharp mask, 217

V

UV-protective varnish, 365, 366, 368
value (color), 22
variable strokes, 46
varnish, protective, 366, 368
Vealé, Stanley, 112–113
video clips, 321–322, 323
  importing, 334
  for Web pages, 346
Video Legal Colors, 28, 325
vignettes, 150
  with texture, 216
vinyl media, 389
Virtual Memory, 4–5
visibility (layer) masks, 171, 180, 181, 189
  dropping and saving, 189
  editing, 189, 197
  exchanging, 189
  Liquid Ink layers and, 188
  painting on, 201–202, 221
  for photos, 221, 222, 223

W

Wacom tablets, 5, 48, 52, 130, 174
Walker, James Faire, 386
wash effect, 65

washes, emulating, 101, 343
Water Color brushes, 244
  Camel variants, 51, 74, 82, 175, 200
  Diffuse Bristle variant, 81
  Diffuse Flat variant, 74
  Diffuse Grainy Camel variant, 24, 82
  Dry Bristle variant, 244, 245
  Eraser Dry variant, 51, 55, 79
  Eraser Salt variant, 51, 75, 79
  Fine variants, 77, 79
  Runny variants, 75, 78, 200
  Runny Wet Bristle variant, 78
  Runny Wet variants, 75, 78
  Splatter Water variant, 75
  Wash Bristle variant, 24, 51, 74, 83, 199
  Wash Camel variant, 74, 101, 175, 244
  Wash Pointed Flat variant, 74
  Wet Bristle variant, 74
Water Color dab types, 59–60, 73
Water Color layers, 51, 72–75, 77, 78–79, 80–83, 109, 187, 199–200, 244
  adding, 81, 199
  dropping, 128, 129
  editing, 79
  lifting canvas to, 82–83
  masks for, 187, 200
  selections for, 200
water drop effect, 257, 258
water drop icon, 72
Weaves palette, 272, 273
Weave Selector, 11, 272, 273
Web graphics
  designing, 344–361
  file formats for, 345–346
  file size for, 345, 347–348, 352
Web pages
  backgrounds for, 351–352
  banners for, 358
  designing, 353–353
  slide show for, 356

Webmedia brushes, 350
Web-safe color, 347–348, 349–350
Wells, Pamela, 315, 316, 364
Wet Entire Water Color Layer, 83, 245
wet-into-wet watercolor, 76–79, 80, 82, 199
Wetness setting, 73
white, leaving areas of, 77
Whole Shape Selection tool, 183
Wilhelm, Henry, 367
Wilhelm Imaging Research, 367
Windows
  file formats for, 9
  memory allocation, for 5
  Painter's requirements for, 4
  shortcut, making, 19
woodcut effect, 36–37
Woodcut filter, 8, 9, 236–238, 279
workspace, customizing, 16–17
World Wide Web
  file formats for, 8, 9
  graphics for 344–361
WWW Map Clickable Region, 345

Y

Yoshii, Hiroshi, 257, 274

Z

Zoom Blur, 223
Zoom to Fit Screen, 13
zooming in and out, 13
Zoom, variable, 14

Notes

Notes

Notes

Notes

Notes

Notes